The Law of Evidence

D1354945

To Alan, and Mum and Dad

The Law of Evidence in Ireland

Third Edition

by

Caroline Fennell

BCL (NUI), LLM (Osgoode), PhD (Wales), BL
Professor of Law, University College Cork

Bloomsbury Professional

Published by
Bloomsbury Professional
Maxwelton House
41–43 Boltro Road
Haywards Heath
West Sussex
RH16 1BJ

Bloomsbury Professional
The Fitzwilliam Business Centre
26 Upper Pembroke Street
Dublin 2

ISBN 978 1 84766 063 3
© Bloomsbury Professional

British Library Cataloguing-in-Publication Data
A catalogue record for this book is available from the British Library

Typeset by Marlex Editorial Services Ltd., Dublin, Ireland
Printed and bound in Great Britain by
CPI Antony Rowe, Chippenham, Wiltshire

Preface

This volume, although a third edition, is rather more representative of the latest in a series of conversations about a topic, focusing as it does on the emerging influences and ongoing events which shape the law of evidence in Ireland. I am grateful as ever to the students of evidence in UCC for their insight into how popular culture and its changing dynamic may influence the application of those rules.

Although the text focuses in the main on the jurisprudence of the appeal courts, it attempts not to neglect the fact that the application of law is very often in its shadow: increasingly so with the extension of powers of detention after arrest, which may never culminate in a charge; and the proliferation of the use of the civil process and regulation in place of traditional criminal process. The danger that the loss of the traditional promise of the criminal process and trial might be overlooked is a very real and prevalent one, and it is perhaps timely to have regard to the view of an Australian judge in a case concerning a Commissioner appointed to inquire into the activities of a trade union to see if it had been engaged in activities contrary to the law:

> The authority given to the Commissioner to exercise such an important ingredient of judicial power as finding a person guilty of ordinary crimes, is in itself an undermining of the separation of powers. It is a fine point to answer that the finding is not binding and does not of itself make the person liable to punitive consequences. It is by fine points such as this that human freedom is whittled away...The trial and finding of guilt of political opponents and dissenters in such a way is a valuable instrument in the hands of governments who have little regard for human rights. Experience in many countries shows that persons may be effectively destroyed by this process. The fact that punishment by fine or imprisonment does not automatically follow may be of no importance; indeed a government can demonstrate its magnanimity by not proceeding to prosecute in the ordinary way If a government chooses not to prosecute, the fact that the finding is not binding on any court is of little comfort to the person found guilty; there is no legal proceeding which he can institute to establish his innocence. If he is prosecuted, the investigation and findings may have created ineradicable prejudice. This latter possibility is not abstract or remote from the case. We were informed that the public conduct of these proceedings was intended to have a 'cleansing effect'.[1]

---

[1] Murphy J (dissenting) in *Victoria v Australia Building Construction Employees' and Builders Labourers'* Federation (1982) 152 CLR 25 quoted by Hederman J in *Goodman International v Hamilton* [1992] 2 IR 567 at 599–560.

The ongoing and continuing relevance of that statement to events in Irish life and media, where despite no lessening in the number of criminal offences the invocation of the (full) criminal trial is less than characteristic, should cause pause.

Inevitably, a text is always selective in terms of what it chooses to focus upon – what cases it selects, what narrative it tells. A law story is like any other and influenced by the teller of the tale and the particular stories they choose. Burrell likens this to the parenting of children or the tactics of advertisers:

> Children love stories; parents carefully choose which ones to read to them, knowing the power stories have to shape our lives. Advertisers know this as well, designing episodes calculated to let our fantasies spin out the rest. And like the advertisements, many stories have the goal of persuading us to see the world in a certain way, or even to become this kind of person....Sensing the power of rhetoric, we need to protect ourselves from its blandishments so that we can "make up our own mind", as we put it, about the situation at hand.[2]

However in adjudicating between the various narratives Burrell cautions against '... our culture's lazy injunction simply to *choose*... In matters of import, choosing won't do; we need to understand. Yet as Socrates reminded us, the only reliable path to understanding matters of human worth must wend its way through competing narratives.'[3]

That provides a useful justification for a text that is selective in its focus, attempts to offer at times competing narratives or change perspective, and always tries to remember the context – factual and political alike. It is done towards the aim of understanding.

I am grateful to colleagues in the Law Faculty UCC, particularly the Centre for Criminal Justice and Human Rights for insight into the intersection of human rights and criminal justice. Thanks are also due to the staff of Bloomsbury – particularly Amy Hayes – for patience with the long gestation. All faults are the author's own.

Finally, and most especially, my thanks to Alan who has been a constant source of encouragement and support, and to our canine companions Pingin & Max who proved a welcome source of company in the office and occasional distraction.

CF

Kinsale, 22 November 2009

---

[2] David B Burrell 'Narratives Competing for our Souls' in *Terrorism & International Justice* (ed James P Sterba Oxford University Press NY Oxford 2003), 88 .

[3] *Ibid.*

Contents

Preface v
Contents vii
Table of Cases xiii
Table of Legislation xxxi

Introduction 1

The importance of facts 3
The importance of evidence 5
The hypothetical 7

Part 1: General

Chapter 1   Rules of Evidence: Fact-Finding, Determinations and Application

The role of popular culture 13
The trial 14
The role of the jury 15
The role of the police 17
Reconstructing the law story 18
Media 20
Changing societal needs 24
Conclusion 26

Chapter 2   The Constitutionalism of the Irish Criminal Process

Crime and justice 29
    Constitutional constraints 34
    Judicial concept of 'fair' procedure................................... 37
    Normalisation: the beginnings... 44
    Arrest 45
    Extraordinary arrest... 48
Crisis discourse and decision-making in the Irish criminal process 52
    Terrorism 54
    Drugs 58
    The Bail Amendment to the Constitution............................ 62
    Further and continuing extension of exceptional provision 69
Future perspectives, new rights 74
    (Absolute) rights in face of countervailing (public) interests:
      Recent US/UK decisions a false dawn?............................ 90
    Concluding remarks... 97

Part 2: The Rules of Evidence

Chapter 3   Basic Concepts of the Law of Evidence

Terminology 104
Categories of evidence 104
    Direct evidence 104
    Real evidence 105
    Documentary evidence 105
Functions of judge and jury: arbiter of fact and law 105
Receivability of evidence 105
    Distinctions: relevance/admissibility 106
    Trial judge's discretion to exclude relevant evidence 108
Determination of the ultimate issue 108
Burden of proof 110
    Shifting the burden of proof 110
    Evidential burden of proof 111
    Who bears the burden of proof? 112
    Res ipsa loquitur 112
Criminal cases: the 'golden thread' 115
    Exceptions to the rule in Woolmington 118
Reverse onus provisions and the right to silence 119
    Criminal Justice Act 2007 128
Imposition of a legal burden on the accused – compatibility
    with the ECHR 131
Peculiar knowledge principle 132
Standard of proof 135
    Tribunals; other contexts 137

Chapter 4   Illegally-Obtained Evidence

Introduction 147
Historical perspective: the criminal trial 149
Search and seizure 151
Search warrants 153
    Warrants – recent changes 154
Provisions regarding issuance of search warrants 155
    Search warrants in relation to arrestable offences 155
    Search warrants for entry for the purpose of arrest 156
    Warrants for the Criminal Assets Bureau in relation to the proceeds
        of crime 157
    Warrants for the purposes of drug trafficking 158
    Warrants for the purpose of surveillance 160
Judicial approach – historical and comparative 163
    Approach of the English courts 164
    Approach of the United States courts 164
    Approach of the Irish courts 165

Causation 182
'Fruit of the poisoned tree' 183
Conclusion 183

Chapter 5   Witness System: Competence and Compellability

Competence and compellability 191
Process of elicitation of testimony 192
Hostile witnesses 194
Calling of witnesses 195
Elicitation of testimony 195
Competence of witnesses 195
Physical disability 195
Mental disability 195
Children's evidence 196
Reform 201
Children 201
Other vulnerable witnesses 203
Inappropriate questions on cross-examination 203
Criminal Justice Act 2006 204
Defendant's spouse as a witness 206
The accused as a prosecution witness 207
Diplomats and prosecution witnesses 207

Chapter 6   Witness System: Corroboration

Corroborative Evidence 209
Doctrine of recent complaint 212
Corroboration required as a matter of law 215
Corroboration required as a matter of practice 215
Accomplices 216
Evidence of witnesses in Witness Protection Programme 224
Corroboration requirement in relation to confession evidence 240
Visual identification evidence 241
Rationale 241
The requirement 242
Discretion to give warning 250
Sexual offences 250
Children's evidence 251
They haven't gone away, you know 252
Constructions of 'fairness' 254
The context of sexual offences 254
Historic sex abuse cases 256
The 're-claiming' of corroboration 260
Impact of Strasbourg jurisprudence on fair trial 274

Chapter 7   Opinion Evidence

Introduction 279
Expert evidence 280
   Qualification 280
The Ultimate Issue Rule 284
   The common knowledge rule 288
   Expert and non-expert opinion evidence of fact 288
   Defence access to evidence and the duty to preserve evidence 290
   Belief evidence 291
Intoxication 293
The rule in Hollington v Hewthorn 298
   Expert evidence: personal injuries actions 299
Expert opinion: controversy 300
DNA evidence 301
   The Castro case 303
   Criminal Justice (Forensic Evidence) Act 1990....................... 307
Practical pointers in relation to the examination of the expert witness 314
   Examination-in-chief.. 314
   Cross-examination... 315
   Reform.. 315
   Junk science... 317

Chapter 8   Privilege

Introduction 319
Private privilege 319
   Legal professional privilege 320
   Is legal professional privilege merely a rule of evidence? 336
   'Without prejudice' statements 337
Marital privilege 340
The privilege against self-incrimination 341
Sacerdotal privilege 343
Marriage counsellors 346
Journalistic privilege 349
Police privilege 354
Private privilege: conclusion 359
Public privilege 360
   Origins of public privilege 362
   Irish case law on public privilege.. 363
   Tromso Sparebank v Beirne (No 2) 370
   Bula Ltd v Tara Mines.. 372
   Ambiorix Ltd v Minister for Environment................................ 374
   Breathnach v Ireland (No 3)... 375
   Irish case law on tribunals 378

Chapter 9   The Rule Against Hearsay

Introduction 385
The distinction between original evidence and hearsay evidence 388
Implied assertions 388
Exceptions to the rule against hearsay 390
    Admissions 390
    Confessions.. 391
    Provisions regarding the treatment of persons in custody.......................... 417
    Detention under the Criminal Justice (Drug Trafficking) Act 1996 425
    Confrontation between the police and the citizen 426
The doctrine of res gestae 437
    Declarations against proprietary/pecuniary interests............................... 441
    Declarations by deceased persons in the course of duty 442
    Declarations as to pedigree matters... 442
    Declarations as to public rights 442
    Post-testamentary declarations by testators as to the contents
      of their wills 442
    Dying declarations of the deceased on a charge of homicide 443
Special provisions – exceptions to the Hearsay Rule 444
    Admission of documentary evidence 444
    Copies of documents 445
    Wardship proceedings 451
    Bail proceedings 452
    Civil proceedings – children.. 452
    Reluctant witnesses 454
    Proceeds of crime and Criminal Assets Bureau 458
    Offences against the State 458
    Organised crime... 458
    Reform.. 458
Further exceptional provisions – incremental reform 460

Chapter 10   Similar Fact Evidence

Introduction 461
Rationale for admission 464
    The categories.. 466
The distinct nature of sexual cases 470
Relevance in other cases 473
Burden and standard of proof 474
Irish case law 474
Judicial discretion/reform 481
Other jurisdictions 484

Chapter 11   Cross-Examination of the Accused

Introduction 489
Loss of the shield: section 1(f) 493
    Credibility/guilt distinction: judicial discretion with regard
       to divisibility of character 508
    Reform 510
Conclusion 516

Index 519

Table of Cases

Please note that for ease of reference in cases tried on indictment, the cases are arranged by reference to the second-named party: eg *DPP v X* will be listed as *X, DPP v*; *Attorney General v X* as *X, Attorney Gerneral v* and *R v X* as *X, R v*

A

A & BC Chewing Gum Ltd, DPP v [1968] 1 QB 159 .... 3.18, 7.20
A v Secretary of State for Home Department [2005] UKHL 71 .... 2.130, 4.47
A, R v (2002) 1 AC 45, HL 6.174
A, R v UKHL 25 .... 6.129
Agar, R v [1990] 2 All ER 442 .... 8.92
Air Canada v Secretary of State for Trade (No 2) [1983] 2 AC 394 .... 8.107
Allen, DPP v [2003] 4 IR 295 .... 7.79
Alterton, R v [1912] 2 KB 251 .... 8.60
Ambiorix Ltd v Minister for Environment [1992] 1 IR 277 .... 8.146, 8.154
America Coy v Iowa (1987) 487 US 1012 .... 5.23
Amos v Hughes 1835 1 Mood & R 464 .... 3.28
Anderson & Neville, R v [1971] 3 All ER 1152 .... 7.21
Andrews, R v [1987] 1 All ER 513 .... 9.148
Armstrong, R v [1922] 2 KB 555 .... 10.16
Arthurs v Attorney General for Northern Ireland (1971) 55 Cr App R 161 .... 6.94
Ashburton v Pape [1913] 2 Ch 469 .... 8.37, 8.39
Ataou, R v [1988] 2 All ER 321 .... 8.21

B

B v DPP [1997] 3 IR 140, [1977] 2 ILRM 118 .... 6.134–6.137, 10.65
Bagley, R v [1980] Cram LR 572, CA 6.49
Bagshaw, R v [1984] 1 WLR 477 .... 6.109
Bailey, R v [1924] All ER 466 .... 10.11
Baldry, R v (1852) 2 Den 430 .... 9.27–9.29
Balfe, DPP v [1998] 4 IR 50 .... 4.72
Ball, R v [1911] AC 47 .... 10.10
Ball, Re (1890) 25 LR 556 .... 9.155
Barr, DPP v (2 March 1992, unreported), CCA 5.04
Barrington, R v [1981] 1 All ER 1132 .... 10.30
Barsoum [1994] Crim LR 194 .... 11.55
Barton, R v [1972] 2 All ER 1192 .... 8.20
Baskerville, R v [1916] 2 KB 658 .... 6.01–6.06, 9.18
Beddingfield, R v (1879) 14 Cox CC 341 .... 9.144
Binead and Donoghue, DPP v [2006] IECCA 147 .... 3.71
Binead, DPP v [2007] 1 IR 374 .... 8.99

Bishop, DPP v [2005] IECCA 2 .... 9.147
Bishop, R v [1975] QB 274 .... 11.31
BK, DPP v [2000] 2 IR 199 .... 10.09, 10.58, 10.66–10.71
Blanchfield v Harnett [2001] 1 ILRM 193 .... 3.13
Blastland, R v [1985] 2 All ER 1095 .... 9.148
Boardman v DPP [1974] 3 All ER 887, [1975] AC 421 ...... 10.26–10.34, 10.81, 10.85
Bond, Attorney General v [1966] IR 214 .... 11.26
Bond, R v [1906] 2 KB 389 .... 10.14, 10.28
Bord na gCon v Murphy [1970] IR 301 .... 8.10
Boumediene v Bush 128 SCt 2229 (2008), 171 L Ed 2d 41,
    2008 US Lexis 4887 .... 2.129
Bowes, DPP v (25 February 2002), CCA 4.60
Boyce, DPP v [2005] IECCA 143 .... 4.100, 7.107
Boyd v US (1866) 116 US 616 .... 4.48
Boyes, R v (1861)1 B & S 311 .... 8.59
Boyle, R v [1987] Crim LR 111 .... 9.148
Braddish v DPP [2002] 1 ILRM151, [2001] IR 127 .... 7.33
Bratty v Attorney General for Northern Ireland [1963] AC 386 .... 3.43
Breathnach v Ireland (No 3) [1993] 2 IR 458 .... 8.43, 8.152–8.153
Breathnach, DPP v [1982] IR 64 .... 9.39, 9.111
Briamore Manufacturing Ltd (in liq), Re [1986] 3 All ER 132 ...... 8.36, 8.39
Bridgett v Dowd [1961] IR 313 .... 3.85
British Steel Corporation v Granada TV Ltd [1981] 1 All ER 417,
    [1981] AC 1096 .... 8.62, 8.78
Brogan v United Kingdom (1989) 11 EHRR 117 .... 2.65, 9.66, 9.116
Brophy, DPP v [1992] ILRM 709 .... 6.11–6.13
Brown v Stott [2001] 2 All ER 97, [2003] 1 AC 681,
    [2001] 2 WLR 817 .... 1.39, 2.103, 2.117, 6.176
Buchanan, Re [1964–1965] NSWR 1379 .... 8.81
Buckley v Bough (2 July 2001), HC 8.18
Buckley v Incorporated Law Society [1994] 2 IR 44 .... 8.17
Buckley, DPP v [2007] IEHC 150 .... 7.29
Buckley, R v (1873) 13 Cox CC 293 .... 9.147
Bula Ltd v Crowley (19 December, 1989) HC, [1990] ILRM 756,
    [1991] 1 IR 220 .... 8.40
Bula Ltd v Crowley [1990] ILRM 756, [1991] 1 IR 220 .... 8.29, 8.140
Bula Ltd v Tara Mines Ltd (No 4) [1991] 1 IR 217 .... 8.143
Burke, Attorney General v [1955] IR30 .... 2.37
Burmah Oil Co Ltd v The Bank of England [1980] AC 1090 .... 8.154
Butler v Board of Trade [1970] 3 All ER 593, [1971] Ch 680 ...... 8.12, 8.35
Buttes Gas & Oil Co v Hammer (No 3) [1981] QB 223 .... 8.138
Byrne v Grey [1988] IR 31 .... 4.34
Byrne, Attorney General v [1974] IR 1 .... 3.36
Byrne, DPP v (7 June 2000), CCA 9.07
Byrne, DPP v [1974] IR 1 .... 3.39, 3.92

Byrne, DPP v [1989] ILRM 613 .... 4.74, 9.86
Byrne, DPP v [1994] 2 IR 236 .... 6.130
Byrne, DPP v [2002] 2 ILRM 97, [2003] 4 IR 423 .... 2.108, 3.46, 4.33

C

C v DPP (31 July 2001, unreported), CCA 9.67
C, DPP v [2001] 3 IR 345 .... 3.40, 6.120
Calcraft v Guest [1898] 1 QB 759 .... 8.35–8.37, 8.41
Carney, Attorney General v [1955] IR 324 .... 6.35
Carrigan Ltd v Norwich Union Fire Society Ltd [1987] IR 618 .... 8.28
Casey (No 2), DPP v [1963] IR 33 .... 6.93, 6.97–6.108
Casey, DPP v [2004] IECCA 49 .... 9.142–9.142
Cash, DPP v [2007] IEHC 108 .... 2.24, 4.94–4.104
Chance, R v [1988] QB 932 .... 6.109
Chandler v Church [1987] 127 NLJ 451 .... 8.38
Chandor, R v [1959] 1 QB 545 .... 10.42
Chard, R v (1972) 57 Cr App R 268 .... 7.18
Ching, R v (1976) 63 Cr App R 7 .... 3.95
Christie v Leachinsky [1947] AC 573 .... 9.71
Christie, R v [1914] AC 557 .... 6.03
Cleary, Attorney General v (1938) 72 ILTR 84 .... 9.29
Cleary, R v (1963) 48 Cr App R 116 .... 9.51
Coffey, DPP v (6 March 1981, unreported) 9.121
Coleman, Attorney General v [1945] IR 237 .... 8.12, 11.25
Collins, DPP v (22 April, 2002), CCA 6.06
Connaughton, DPP v (5 April 2001), CCA 6.21
Connell, DPP v [1995] 1 IR 245 .... 2.02, 2.56
Connolly, DPP v [2003] 2 IR 1 .... 9.17–9.19, 9.133, 9.138
Connors, DPP v (10 May 1990, unreported), HC 3.115
Conroy, DPP v [1986] IR 460 .... 9.109, 9.126
Constantine (Joseph) Steamship Line Ltd v Imperial Smelting Corp Ltd
    [1942] AC 154 .... 3.28
Conway v Rimmer [1968] AC 910 .... 8.113–8.114, 8.132
Cook v Carroll [1945] IR 515 .... 8.66–8.68, 8.72–8.75, 8.80–8.83, 8.155
Cooney, DPP v [1997] 3 IR 205 .... 6.115
Costigan, DPP v [2006] IECCA 57 .... 4.56
Cox & Railton, R v (1884) 14 QBD 153 .... 8.12
Cox v Ireland [1992] 2 IR 503 .... 3.56
Cramp, R v (1880) 5 QB 307 .... 6.37
Crompton (Alfred) Amusement Machines v Commissioners of Customs
    & Excise [1973] 2 All ER 1169 .... 8.24
Crown Court ex p Baines & Baines, R v [1987] 3 All ER 1025 .... 8.11
Crown v Crumley [1984, unreported) 6.58
Crown v Mooney (1851) 5 Cox CC 318 .... 9.156
Cullen v Clarke [1963] IR 368 .... 9.02

Cullen, DPP v (7 February 2001), HC 9.96
Cummins, Attorney General v [1972] IR 312 .... 9.90, 9.114
Cummins, DPP v (19 December 2003, unreported), CCA 3.64
Curtin v Dáil Éireann [2006] 2 IR 556 .... 4.93, 8.65
Curtin, DPP v (23 April 2004, unreported), CCC 4.77–4.78
Customs and Excise (Commissioners of) v Harz
    [1967] 1 AC 760 .... 9.22, 9.28–9.31
Cutts v Head [1984] 1 Ch 290 .... 8.55

D

D v National Society for Prevention of Cruelty to Children
    [1978] AC 171 .... 8.111, 8.130, 8.155
Darcy, DPP v (29 July 1997, unreported), HC 9.99, 9.142
Daubert v Merrell Dow Pharmaceuticals (1993) 509 US 579 .... 7.14, 7.113
Davie v Edinburgh Magistrates (1953) SC 34 .... 7.13
Davies v DPP [1954] AC 378 .... 6.24–6.25
Davies v Fortior [1952] 1 All ER 1355 .... 9.147
Davies, R v [1962] 3 All ER 97 .... 7.45
Davis v St Michael's House (25 November 1993, unreported), HC 8.27
Davis, DPP v [1993] 2 IR 1 .... 2.25
DC v DPP & O'Leary (31 October 1997, unreported), HC 6.138
Deen, R v (1994) The Times, 10 January 7.100
Delaney, DPP v (27 January 2003, unreported), HC 4.67
Delaney, DPP v [1997] 3 IR 453 .... 4.83
Dempsey, DPP v [1961] IR 288 .... 10.22
Dental Board v O'Callaghan [1969] IR 181 .... 6.28, 6.78
Deokinian v R [1961] 1 AC 20 .... 9.48
Derby Magistates Court ex p B, R v [1996] 1 AC 487 .... 8.46
Descoteaux v Mierzwinksi [1982] 1 SCR 860 .... 8.47
Devlin, DPP v (2 September [1998, unreported), HC 9.96
Dillon v O'Brien & Davis (1897) 20 LR Ir 300 .... 4.16
Dillon, DPP v [2002] 4 IR 501 .... 4.99
Director of Consumer Affairs v Sugar Distributors Ltd [1991] 1 IR 225 .... 8.153
Diver, DPP v [2005] IESC 57 .... 2.24, 9.133–9.135
DO v DPP [2006] IESC 12 .... 2.108, 10.07, 10.83–10.84, 11.17, 11.20
DO, DPP v [2006] IESC 12 .... 11.61
Doheny [1997] 1 Cr App R 396, CA 7.76
Doherty v Liddane [1940] Ir Jur Rep 58 .... 9.78
Donnelly v Ireland [1998] 1 IR 321 .... 5.19–5.28
Donoghue, DPP v [2008] 2 ICLMD 20, CCA 8.101
Doorson v Netherlands (1996) 22 EHRR 330 .... 2.114, 8.100
DOT, DPP v [2003] 4 IR 286 .... 2.109, 3.41
Douglas, R v (1989) 89 Crim App R 264 .... 11.13
Dowie v Edinburgh Corporation [1953] SLT 54 .... 7.31
DR, DPP v [1998] 2 IR 106 .... 5.35

Duff, DPP v [1995] 3 IR 296 .... 6.115
Duffy, Attorney General v [1931] IR 144 .... 10.62
Duncan v Cammell Laird & Co Ltd [1942] AC 624 .... 8.106, 8.112, 8.117
Duncan v Govenor of Mountjoy Prison [1997] 1 IR 558 .... 8.46
Dunne v Clinton [1930] IR 366 .... 2.37, 9.70, 9.77
Dunne v DPP (25 April 2002, unreported), SC 7.34–7.35
Dunne, DPP v [1994] 2 IR 537 .... 4.71
DW v DPP [2003] IESC 54 .... 7.108

E

Early, DPP v (2 December 1997, unreported), HC 9.116
Eastern Health Board v MK & MK [1999] 2 IR 99 .... 9.167
Edwards, R v (1872) 12 Cox CC 230 .... 9.147
Edwards, R v [1975] QB 27 .... 3.78, 3.88
Egan, DPP v [1990] ILRM 780 .... 2.19, 7.24–7.27
Ellis, R v (1826) 6 B & C 145 .... 10.17
English and American Insurance Co Ltd v Herbert Smith & Co
    [1988] FSR 232 .... 8.37, 8.39
ER v JR [1981] ILRM 125 .... 8.72, 8.75
Esso Australia Resources Ltd v Sir Daryl Dawson [1999] FCA 363 .... 8.47

F

F v L (Orse F) [1990] 1 IR 348 .... 7.109
Fagan, Attorney General v (1974) 1 Frewen 375 .... 6.99–6.102, 6.108
Fagan, DPP v [1993] 2 IR 95 .... 4.15
Farrell, DPP v [1978] IR 13 .... 2.48
Fauerheerd v London General Omnibus Co Ltd [1918] 2 KB 1565 .... 8.33
Ferris, DPP v [2008] 1 IR 1, CCA 11.14–11.16, 11.61, 11.67
Finnerty, DPP v [1999] 4 IR 364 .... 2.109, 3.62, 6.123–6.124
Fitzpatrick v DPP (5 December 1997, unreported), HC 6.138
Fitzpatrick, R v (1912) 46 ILTR 173 .... 9.157
Flack [1969] 2 All ER 784 .... 10.42
Fleming, Attorney General v [1934] IR 166 .... 10.47
Flood v Lawlor [2000] IESC 76 .... 8.158
Flood v Russell (1891) 29 LR Ir 91 .... 9.151
Flynn, Attorney General v [1963] IR 255 .... 9.33, 9.37
Flynn, R v [1972] Crim LR 428 .... 9.113
Folens v The Minister for Education [1981] ILRM 21 .... 8.123
Fontaine v British Columbia (Official Administrator) [1998] 1 SC 424 ...... 3.35
Forbes, DPP v [1994] 2 IR 542 .... 4.66
Forbes, R v (2001) AC 473 .... 1.39
Forristal v Forristal & O'Connor (1966) 100 ILTR 182 .... 8.68
Fox, DPP v (23 January 2002, unreported), SCC 7.30–7.31
Freeman v DPP [1996] 3 IR 565 .... 4.28–4.29, 4.84, 4.88
Fressoz & Roire v France (1999) 31 EHRR 28 .... 8.87

Friedl v Austria Applic 15225/89 (26 January [1995]) 4.40
Frye v US 54 App DC 46, 293 F 1013 .... 7.14
Fulton v Andrews (1875) LR 7 HL 3.99

G

G v Coltart [1967] 1 QB 432 .... 10.04
G v DPP [1994] 1 IR 374 .... 6.15, 6.132, 6.135
Gaffney, DPP v [1987] IR 173, [1988] ILRM 39 .... 4.64
Gavin, DPP v [2000] 4 IR 557 .... 6.16
Gay, R v (1909) 2 CR App R3 27 .... 6.38
Gentlemen, DPP v (25 February 2002, unreported), CCA 6.151
Geraghty v Minister for Local Government [1975] IR 300 .... 8.119–8.123, 8.144
German, R v [1947] 4 DLR 68 .... 7.02
Giant's Causeway Co Ltd, Attorney General v (1905) 5 Ir Jur Rep 301 .... 9.154
Gilligan v CAB [1998] 3 IR 185 .... 2.63, 9.175
Gilligan, DPP v (15 March 2001, unreported), SCC, [2006] 1 IR 107 (SC) . 6.53, 6.68
Gilligan, DPP v [2006] 1 IR 107 .... 6.01, 6.07, 6.73–6.85, 6.116
Glasgow Corporation v Central Land Board (1956) SC 1 .... 8.116
Glick v Campion (1795) 2 Wils 275 .... 4.19
Glynn (William) (decd):Glynn v Glynn (defendant) [1990] 2 IR 326 .... 7.07
Goddard v Nationwide Building Society [1987] QB 670 .... 8.37, 8.39
Goodman International v Hamilton (No 1) [1992] IR 542 .... 2.28
Goodman International v Hamilton (No 3) [1993] 3 IR 320 .... 8.155
Goodwin v United Kingdom (1996) EHRR 123 .... 8.87
Gormley v Ireland [1993] 2 IR 75 .... 8.134
Gray, R v [1974] 58 Cr App R 177 .... 3.93
Great Atlantic Insurance Co v Home Insurance Co [1981] 2 All ER 485,
    [1981] 1 WLR 529 .... 8.32
Greenwood v Fitts (1961) 29 DLR 260 .... 8.50
Gregg, R v (1934) 24 Cr App R 13 .... 6.02
Guinness Peat Properties Ltd v Fitzroy Robinson Partnership
    [1987] 2 All ER 716, [1987] 2 WLR 1027 .... 8.28, 8.39

H

H, R v [1995] 2 All ER 865 .... 10.38
Hall, R v [1952] 1 KB 302 .... 10.26
Hamdan v Rumsfeld, Secretary of Defense (2006) 548 US 557 .... 2.127
Hamdi v Rumsfeld, Secretary of Defense (2004) 542 US 507 .... 2.127–2.128
Hamilton v Nott (1873) LR 16 .... 8.30
Hanahoe v Hussey [1998] 3 IR 69 .... 4.81, 4.93, 8.48
Hannigan v Clifford [1990] ILRM 65 .... 9.79, 9.107
Hannigan v DPP [2001] 1 IR 378 .... 8.109
Hannigan, Attorney General v [1941] IR 252 .... 5.09
Hanrahan v Merck Sharp & Dohme (Ireland) Ltd [1988] ILRM 629 .... 3.30
Hanson, R v [2005] EWCA Crim 824 .... 11.62

Hardy v Ireland [1994] 2 IR 550 .... 3.45
Harris v DPP [1952] All ER 1044, [1952] AC 694 .... 10.10–10.14, 10.42, 10.51
Harris v Lambert HC [1932] IR 504 .... 9.152
Haughey, Re [1971] IR 217 .... 5.21, 8.161, 9.181
Healy, DPP v [1990] ILRM 313 ....2.23, 9.46, 9.74, 9.106
Heaney & McGuinness v Ireland [1994] 3 IR 593 (HC), [1996] 1 IR 580 (SC),
    (2001) 33 EHRR 12, 21 December 2000 ....2.60, 2.98, 2.107, 3.49–3.55
Heaney v Ireland (2001) 33 EHRR 264 .... 3.60
Hehir v Metropolitan Police Commissioner [1982] 2 All ER 235 .... 8.133
Hernon, DPP v (3 December 2001, unreported), CCA 6.159
Herron v Haughton (19May 2000), SC 5.11
Herron, DPP v (27 October 1981, unreported), HC 2.40, 9.121
Hester, DPP v [1973] AC 297 .... 6.38
Hirabayashi v United States 320 US 81 .... 2.124
Hoey, DPP v (16 December 1987, unreported), SC 9.42
Hogan v President of Circuit Court [1994] 2 IR 513 .... 6.133
Hogan, DPP v (21 January 1994, unreported), CCA 6.31, 6.51
Holland, DPP v (15 June 1998, unreported), CCA 1.31, 2.64, 6.53, 6.71, 6.122
Hollington v Hewthorn [1943] 1 KB 587 .... 7.52
Holly, DPP v [1984] ILRM 149 .... 8.153
Holmes v Newman [1931] 2 Ch 112 .... 9.143
Horwath v Queen [1979] 3 WCB 181 .... 9.112
Howe, DPP v (2003) The Irish Times, 15 October, CCC 7.78
Howley, DPP v [1989] ILRM 629, [1988] IECCA 2 .... 9.102–9.104
Howlin v Mr Justice Morris [2006] 2 IR 321 .... 8.157
Hudson, R v [1912] 2 KB 464 .... 11.27, 11.73

I

Ibrahim v R [1914] AC 599 .... 9.23, 9.111
Incorporated Law Society of Ireland v Minister for Justice
    [1987] ILRM 42 .... 8.124
Inland Revenue, Board of, ex p Codibert, R v [1988] 3 WLR 522 .... 8.138

J

Jalloh v Germany [2006] ECHR 721 ....2.98, 2.121
Jeffrey v Black [1978] 1 All ER 555 .... 4.17
JEM, DPP v [2001] 4 IR 385 ....6.119–6.119
Jenkins v The Queen [2004] HCA 57 .... 6.07
Jennings v Quinn [1968] IR 30 .... 4.16
Jethi, DPP v (7 February 2000, ex tempore), CCA 6.17
JL v DPP [2000] 3 IR 122 .... 6.150
Johannsen (1977) 65 Cr App R 101 .... 10.36
John Lewis and Co Ltd v Timms [1952] AC 676 ....2.37, 9.78
Johnston v Church of Scientology Mission of Dublin Ltd
    [2001] 1 IR 682 ....8.74, 8.165

Jones v DPP [1962] AC 635 .... 11.04–11.08
Joy v Phillip Mills & Co Ltd [1916]1 KB 849 .... 3.02
Joyce and Walsh, Attorney General v [1929] IR 526 .... 10.46
JPD v MG [1991] ILRM 212 .... 7.63
JWH v GW and DK v TH (25 February 1998, unreported), HC 7.110

K

Kahn v UK (2000) 31 EHRR 1016 .... 2.116
Kavanagh v Government of Ireland, DPP, Attorney General
    [1996] 1 IR 321 .... 2.04, 2.50
Kearley, R v [1992] 2 AC 228 .... 9.14
Kehoe, DPP v [1992] ILRM 481 .... 2.20, 7.22
Kelly v Ireland [1986] ILRM 318 .... 7.52
Kelly, DPP v (26 November 2004), SCC 9.138, 9.142
Kelly, DPP v [1983] ILRM 271 .... 2.45, 9.119–9.122
Kelly, DPP v [2006] 3 IR 115 .... 2.112, 7.37, 8.97, 8.100
Kemp v R (1951) 83 CLR 341 .... 10.04
Kempster, R v [2003] EWCA Crim 3555 .... 7.113
Kenneally, DPP v [19851 ILRM 8.58
Kenny, Attorney General v (1960) 94 ILTR 185 .... 7.41
Kenny, DPP v [1990] ILRM 569, [1990] IR 110 .... 2.22–2.23, 2.67
    .... 4.68, 4.71, 7.45–7.47, 7.87, 9.47
Keogh, DPP v [1992] ILRM 481 .... 7.27
Kerry County Council v Liverpool Salvage Association (1903) 38 ILTR 7 .... 8.23
Khan v UK (2000) Crim LR 684 .... 4.47
Kiely v Minister for Social Welfare [1971] IR 21 .... 9.03
Kiely v Minister for Social Welfare [1977] IR 267 .... 9.181
Kiely, DPP v (21 March 2001), CCC 3.39, 3.96
Kilbourne, DPP v [1973] AC 728 .... 6.39
King, R v (1914) 10 Cr App R 117 .... 6.26
King, R v [1967] 2 QB 388 .... 10.32
Kirkpatrick, R v [1998] Crim LR 63 .... 11.45
Kirwan, Attorney General v [1943] IR 279 .... 10.48, 10.56
Klass v Germany A28 (1978) 2 EHRR 214 .... 4.41
Kopp v Switzerland [1998] ECt HR 18 .... 4.40
Korematsu v United States (1944) 323 US 214 .... 2.105, 2.124
Kostovski v Netherlands [1989] 12 EHRR 434 .... 2.114, 7.38, 8.100
Kumho Tire Co Ltd v Carmichael (1999) 119 SC 1167 .... 7.15
Kuruma, Son of Kaniu v R [1955] AC [197 .... 8.42
Kuzmack, R v (1955) 111 CCC 1, 20 CR 377, [1955] SCR 293 .... 7.05

L

Lalor v Lalor (1879) 4 LR 678 .... 9.150
Lambert, R v [2002] 2 AC 545 .... 3.75

Lavery v Member in Charge, Carrickmacross Garda Station
    [1999] 2 IR 390 ....2.50, 2.111, 3.58, 9.62
Lawless v Ireland (1961) 1 EHRR 15 ....2.76–2.76, 2.116
Lawless, DPP v (28 November 1985, unreported), CCA 4.59, 4.96
Leach v Money (1765) 19 St Jr 1001 ....4.19
Leahy v Corboy [1969] IR 148 ....3.99, 3.105
Leatham, R v (1861) 8 Cox CC 498 ....4.46
Lee, R v [1976] 1 All ER 570 ....11.12
Leon (1983) 468 US 897 ....4.68
Levinson, Attorney General v [1932] IR 158 ....6.07
Lewes Justices ex p SS Home Dept, R v [1973] AC 388 ....8.131
LG, DPP v [2003] 2 IR 517 ....6.154–6.158
Liberty v UK (2009) 48 EHRR 1 ....4.43
Lillyman, R v [1896] 2 QB167 ....6.12
Lindsay v Western Health Board [1993] 2 IR 147 ....3.35
Linehan, Attorney General v [1929] IR 19 ....6.29, 6.36
Liu Meilin v R [1989] 1 All ER 359 ....11.43
Lloyd v Powell Duffryn Steam Coal Co Ltd [1914] AC 733 ....9.11
Lowery v R [1974] AC 85 ....3.16, 7.20
LPB (1990/1) Criminal Appeal Reps 6.133
Lupien, R v [1970] SCR 263 ....3.17
Lynch, DPP v (7 November 1990, unreported), HC 7.50
Lynch, DPP v [1982] IR 64, [1981] ILRM 389 ....2.02, 2.35–2.40
    ....4.52–4.54, 6.90, 9.109, 9.120
Lyons v Lyons [1950] NI 181 ....3.110

M

M v D [1998] 3 IR 175 ....9.175
MA, DPP v [2002] 2 IR 601 ....6.18
MacEoin, DPP v [1978] IR 27 ....7.23
MacMahon, DPP v [1984] ILRM 461 ....10.56
Madden, DPP v [1977] IR 336 ....2.23–2.25, 2.42–2.47, 4.54, 7.86, 9.119
Maguire v Ardagh [2002] 1 IR 385 ....9.181
Maher, Attorney General v [1973] IR 140 ....3.15
Mahon Tribunal v Keena [2009] IESC 64 ....8.85, 8.87
Makanjoula, R v [1995] 3 All ER 730 ....6.119
Makin v Attorney General for New South Wales
    [1894] AC 57 ....10.02, 10.13, 10.20, 10.51
Manley, R v (1962) 126 JP 316 ....11.31
Mansfield, R v [1978] 1 WLR 1102 ....10.40
Mapp v Gilhooley [1991] 2 IR 253, [1991] ILRM 695 ....2.17, 5.31
Mapp v Ohio (1961) 367 US 643 ....4.48
Marks v Beyfus (1890) 25 QBD 494 ....8.131, 8.153, 8.164
Martin v Quinn [1980] IR 244 ....7.104
Martin, DPP v [1956] IR 22 (CCA) 6.103

Maryland v Craig (1989) 497 US 836 .... 5.23
Mason, R v [1988] 1 WLR 139 .... 4.47
Mathews, DPP v [2006] ECCA 103 .... 2.112
Maxwell v DPP [1935] AC 309 .... 11.10
McCabe, Attorney General v [1927] IR 129 .... 9.20, 10.45
McCann, DPP v [1998] 4 IR 397 .... 2.50, 4.89, 9.53
McCarrick v Leavy [1964] IR 225 .... 9.117
McCormack v Judge Circuit Court & DPP [2008] 1 ILRM 49,
    [2007] IEHC 23 .... 9.139–9.141
McCormack, DPP v [1999] 4 IR 158 .... 9.72
McCreesh, DPP v [1992] 2 IR 239 .... 4.65
McDonald v RTÉ [2001] 1 IR 355 .... 8.108
McFadden, DPP v [2003] 2 IR 105 .... 4.18
McGinley, DPP v [1998] 2 IR 408 .... 9.168, 9.179
McGowan v Carville [1960] IR 330 .... 3.82–3.84
McGrail, DPP v [1990] 2 IR 38 .... 2.17, 2.107, 11.16, 11.21, 11.34, 11.73
McGranaghan [1995] 1 Cr App R 559 .... 10.43
McKenna (Patricia) v An Taoiseach [1995] 2 IR 10 .... 2.81
McLeod [1994] 1 WLR 1500 .... 11.56
McLintock, R v [1962] Grim LR 549 .... 9.49
McMahon, McMeeland Wright, DPP v [1987] ILRM 86 .... 4.63
McNaghten, R v (1843) 10 Cl & F 200 .... 3.43
McNally, DPP v [1981] 2 Frewen 43 .... 9.111
McNee v Kay (1953) VLR 520 .... 6.27
Meehan, DPP v (29 July 1999, unreported), SCC 2.64, 6.07, 6.32
    .... 6.53, 6.68, 6.115
Meehan, DPP v [2006] 3 IR 468 .... 6.07, 6.72, 9.08
Meleady & Grogan, DPP v [1995] 2 IR 517, (4 March 1997), SC 2.02, 2.56
Meleady (No 3), DPP v [2001] 4 IR 16 .... 3.12
Melling v Ó Mathgamhna [1962] IR 1 .... 2.20
Miles, R v (1943) 44 SR WSW 198 .... 10.04
Miley v Flood [2001] ILRM 489, [2001] 2 IR 51 .... 8.16, 8.46
Mill, DPP v [1957] IR 106 .... 6.100
Miller v Minister for Pensions [1947] 2 All ER 372 .... 3.91
Minahane (1921) 16 Cr App R 38 v R 8.58
Minister for Industry and Commerce v Steele [1952] IR 301 .... 3.80
Minter v Priest [1930] AC 588, [1929] 1 KB 655 .... 8.08, 8.14
Miranda v Arizona (1966) 384 US 436 .... 2.23, 9.26
Mitchell v DPP [2000] 2 ILRM 396 .... 7.33
Molloy, DPP v (28July 1995), CCA 6.119
Moore, DPP v [1964] Ir Jur 6 .... 3.10
Morgan, DPP v [1976] AC 182 .... 3.20
Muff v R (2 November 1979, unreported) CA 6.49
Mulholland, Attorney General v [1963] 2 QB 477 .... 8.78
Mullen v Quinnsworth Ltd [1990] 1 IR 59 .... 3.31

Mulligan, DPP v (17 May 2004, unreported), CCA 7.37
Mulligan, DPP v (1982) Frewen16 .... 2.19
Muragh, DPP v [1990] 1 IR 339 .... 6.30
Murdoch v Taylor [1965] AC 574 .... 11.42–11.43
Murphy v DPP [1989] ILRM 71 .... 7.25, 7.32
Murphy v Dublin Corporation [1972] IR 215 .... 8.14, 8.90, 8.116
.... 8.122, 8.146–8.151
Murphy v Green [1990] 2 IR 566 .... 3.111–3.113
Murphy v Queen (1988–89) 167 CLR 94 .... 7.25
Murphy, DPP v (3 November 1997, unreported), CCA 6.08
Murphy, DPP v [1947] IR 236 .... 9.51
Murphy, DPP v [2005] 1 ECCA 1 .... 1.33
Murphy, DPP v [2005] 2 IR 125 .... 6.07, 9.136, 11.46–11.48
Murray v Miller (14 November 2001), CC 3.34
Murray v United Kingdom (1996) 22 EHRR 29 .... 1.39, 3.57, 6.176
Myers v DPP [1965] AC 1001 .... 9.02–9.06

N

National Irish Bank and the Companies Act 1990, Re [1999] 3 IR 145 .... 3.73
NC v DPP [2001] IESC 54 .... 6.149, 7.102, 7.112
Neilson v Laugharne [1981] 1 All ER 829 .... 8.133
Nevin, DPP v (13 December 2001, unreported), CCA 8.166
New York v Neysmith (1987) Lander, p 50 .... 7.74
Nicholas, R v (1846) 2 Car & Kir 246 .... 9.147
Noakes, R v (1832) 5 C&P 326 .... 6.38
Northern Banking Company v Carpenter [1931] IR 268 .... 9.08
Novak, R v (1976) 65 Cr App R 107 .... 10.35, 10.74
Nye & Loan, R v (1978) 66 Cr App R 252 .... 9.148

O

Ó Laighleis, Re [1960] IR 93 .... 9.71
O'Brien v DJ Ruane and Attorney General [1989] ILRM 732 .... 5.06
O'Brien, DPP v [1965] IR 142 .... 2.25, 2.38–2.39, 2.107, 2.131
.... 4.50, 4.54, 4.71, 4.93, 6.82
O'C(J) v DPP [2000] 3 IR 478 .... 6.146–6.148, 7.102
O'C(P) v DPP [2000] 3 IR 87 .... 1.15, 1.36, 6.125, 6.175
O'Callaghan v Ireland [1994] 1 IR 555 .... 2.76, 4.14
O'Callaghan v Mahon [2006] 2 IR 32 .... 5.05, 8.158–8.160
O'Callaghan, Attorney General v [1966] IR 501 .... 2.73, 2.78
O'Callaghan, DPP v (30 July 1990, unreported), CCA 6.111
O'Callaghan, DPP v [1966] IR 501 .... 2.54
O'Connell, DPP v [1995] 1 IR 244 .... 9.98
O'Connor, DPP v [1985] ILRM 333 .... 7.51
O'Connor, R v [1995] 4 SCR 411 .... 6.129
O'Donnell, DPP v [1995] 3 IR 551 .... 4.18, 4.92

O'Donoghue, DPP v (15 February 1979,unreported), HC 7.103
O'Dowd v North Western Health Board [1983] ILRM 186 .... 3.111–3.113
O'Driscoll, DPP v (1972) 1 Frewen 351 .... 6.105
O'Flanagan v Ray-Ger Ltd (28 April [1983, unreported), HC 8.50
O'Flynn v DJ Clifford [1990] ILRM 65 .... 9.79
O'Halloran & Francis v UK [2007] ECHR 545 .... 2.120
O'Kelly (Kevin), Re (1974) 108 ILTR 97 .... 8.77–8.83
O'Leary v Attorney General [1991] 2 ILRM 454 .... 2.26, 3.44
O'Leary, Attorney General v [1993] 1 IR 102,
      [1995] 1 IR 254 .... 2.27, 2.107–2.109, 3.48
O'Leary, R v (1946) 73 CLR 566 .... 10.18
O'Loughlin, DPP v [1979] IR 85, CCA 2.40, 7.86, 9.118
O'Neill, Attorney General v [1964] Ir Jur Rep 1 .... 3.09–3.12
O'Neill, DPP v (28 January 2002, unreported), CCA 9.18–9.18
O'R(D) v DPP [1997] 2 IR 273 .... 6.137, 6.138
O'R(E) v DPP (21 December 1995, unreported), HC 6.133–6.135
O'Reardon v O'Reardon (February 1975, unreported), HC 3.110
O'Reilly v Lavelle [1990] 2 IR 372 .... 3.32–3.34
O'Reilly, DPP v [1990] 2 IR 415 .... 6.101–6.116
O'Reilly, DPP v [1991] 1 IR 77 .... 3.25
O'S(D), DPP v [2004] IECCA 12 .... 10.08–10.09, 10.70–10.73
O'Shea, Attorney General v [1931] IR 713 .... 11.24
O'Shea, DPP v [1965] IR 142 [1982] IR 384 .... 2.21
O'Shea, R v (27 July [1986, unreported) 9.148
O'Sullivan v Hamill [1999] 3 IR 9 .... 5.15
O'Toole, DPP v (25 March 2003), CCA 4.55
OC(P), DPP v [2000] 3 IR 119 .... 8.160
Osborne, R v [1905] 1KB 551 .... 6.13
Owens, DPP v (16 February 1999, unreported), SC 4.73

P

P, DPP v [1991] 2 AC 447 .... 10.37, 10.63
P, R v [1991] 3 All ER 337 .... 10.38
Pais v Puis [1970] WLR 830 .... 8.72
Palermo, The (1883) 9 PD 6 .... 8.137
Palmer v Palmer (1885) 18 LR Ir 192 .... 9.153
Parker v Felgate (1883) 8 PD 171 .... 3.107
Payne v Shovlin [2006] IESC 5 .... 7.56
PC v DPP [1999] 2 IR 25 .... 6.137–6.145, 7.102
PC, DPP v [1999] 2 IR 25 .... 1.36
PD v DPP (19 March 1997, unreported), HC 6.138
Perera v Perera [1901] AC 304 .... 3.107
Perry v United Kingdom (2004) 39 EHRR 76 .... 4.40
Pfennig v R (No 2) (1995) 69 ALJR 147 .... 10.76
Phillion, R v [1978] 1 SCR 18 .... 7.108

Piche v R (1970) 11 DLR 9.22
Ping Lin, DPP v [1976] AC 574 .... 9.25, 9.50
Pitchfork, R v (1998) The Guardian, 23 January 7.64
Pitre v R (1933) SCR 69 .... 7.06
PJ, DPP v [2003] 3 IR 550 .... 6.160–6.163
Powell v Superior Court 283 Col Rptr 777 .... 1.08
Powell, R v [1988] 1 All ER 193 .... 11.53
Poynton v Poynton (1903) 37 ILTR 54 .... 7.07
Prager, R v [1972] 1 All ER 1114 .... 9.111
Prager, R v [1972] 1 All ER 1114, (1972) 56 Cr App Rep 151 .... 9.39
Preston-Jones v Preston-Jones [1951] AC 391 .... 3.108
Priestly, R v (1965) 50 Cr App R 183 .... 9.39, 9.111
Pringle, DPP v (22 May 1981, unreported), CCA 2.56, 9.34–9.40
Pringle, DPP v [1995] 2 IR 547, (No 2) [1997] IR 225 .... 2.02, 2.56
PW v DPP (27 November 1997, unreported), HC 6.138

Q

Quilligan, DPP v [1986] IR 495, [1987] ILRM 606 .... 2.04, 2.57, 9.88
.... 9.101–9.106, 9.138
Quinn v Ireland (2001) 33 EHRR 27 .... 3.60

R

R Ltd, Re [1989] IR 176 .... 3.113
R v O'Connor [1995] 4 SCR 411 .... 6.129
R, DPP v ex p Kebilene (28 October 1999) (2001) 2 AC 326 .... 1.39, 6.176
Ramachchandran, DPP v [2000] 2 IR 307 .... 10.69
Rance (1975) 62 Cr App R 118 .... 10.41
Rasul v Bush (2004) 542 US 1 .... 2.129
Ratten v R [1971] 3 All ER 801, [1972] AC 378 .... 9.13, 9.143–9.146
RB, DPP v (12 February 2003, unreported), CCA 6.163–6.163
Reddan, DPP v [1995] 3 IR 560 .... 8.164, 9.98
Redpath, R v (1962) 46 Cr App R 319 .... 6.04
Regina v A UKHL 25 .... 6.129
Reid, DPP v [1993] 2 IR 186 .... 6.08, 6.160
Renda, R v [2005] EWCA Crim 2826 .... 11.63–11.63
Richards, R v [1967] 1 All ER 829 .... 9.29
Richardson v London County Council [1957] 1 WLR 751 .... 3.111
Riley, R v (1887) 18 QBD 481 .... 10.04
Robinson v R [2005] EWCA Crim 3233 .... 11.65
Rock v Ireland [1998] 2 ILRM 35 .... 2.60, 3.66
Rogers v Secretary of State for the Home Department
    [1973] AC 388 .... 8.107–8.113
Rooney, DPP v [1992] 2 IR 7 .... 4.18
Rothman v The Queen (1981)121 DLR (3d) 578 .... 9.52
Rothwell v Motor Insurers Bureau of Ireland (6 July 2001), HC 3.35

Rouse, R v [1904] 1 KB 185 .... 11.30
Rowe & Davis v UK (2000) 30 EHRR 1 .... 8.161
RT v VP [1990] 1 IR 545 .... 3.110, 7.109
RTZ Corporation v Westinghouse Electric Corporation [1978] AC 547 .... 8.61
Rush & Tomkins Ltd v Greater London Council [1988] 3 All ER 737 .... 8.51
Rushbrooke v O'Sullivan [1926] IR 500 .... 8.23
Ryan v (People) DPP [1989] IR 399 .... 2.73–2.76
Ryan v Connolly & Connolly [2001] 1 IR 627 .... 8.55
Ryan, Attorney General v [1975] IR 367 .... 7.40

S

S v S (1 July 1976, unreported), SC 3.110
S(J) v S(C) [1997] 2 IR 506 .... 7.28
Saadi v Italy [2008] ECHR 179 .... 2.122
Saunders (1997) 23 EHRR 313 ....2.98, 2.103, 2.131, 3.60, 6.176
Schmerber v California (1966) 384 US 757 .... 8.65
Schneider v Leigh [1955] 2 All ER 173 .... 8.09
Science Research Council v Nasse [1980] AC 1028 .... 8.133
Scott v London and St Katherine's Docks Co (1865) 3 H & C 596 .... 3.29
Scott v R [1989] 2 All ER 305 .... 6.97
Scott, R v [1983] IR 165 .... 6.109
Secretary of State for Defence v Guardian Newspapers Ltd
    [1984] 3 All ER 601 .... 8.127
Selvey v DPP [1970] AC 304 .... 11.12, 11.27
Shaw, DPP v [1982] IR 1 .... 2.34, 2.37, 4.52, 9.58, 9.78, 9.107
Shea v Anhold and Horse Holiday Farm Ltd (23 October 1996), SC 3.34
Sherrard v Jacob [1975] NI 151 .... 7.46
Shorten, Attorney General v [1961] IR 304 .... 3.83
Silver Hill Duckling Ltd v Minister for Agriculture [1987] ILRM 516,
    [1987] IR 289 .... 8.27–8.29
Silverlock, R v [1894] 2 QB 766 .... 7.04
Simple v Revenue Commissioners [2000] 2 IR 243 .... 4.90
Simpson (No 2), Attorney General v [1959] IR 105 .... 8.89, 8.115
Sims, R v [1946] 1 KB 531 .... 10.26, 10.33
Skeffington v Rooney [1997] 1 IR 22 .... 8.164
Slater v HM Advocate [1928] JC 94 .... 11.70
Smith v Cavan County Council (1927) 58 ILTR 107 .... 9.158
Smith, DPP v (5 November 1990, unreported), CC 7.16
Smith, R v [1914–15] All ER 262 (CA) 10.15
Smith, R v [1959] 2 QB 35 .... 9.29–9.31, 9.49
Smith-Bird v Blower [1939] 2 All ER 406 .... 8.13
Smurfit Paribas Bank Ltd v CAB Export Finance Ltd (No 1) [1990] ILRM 588,
    [1990] 1 IR 469 ....8.13–8.16, 8.44
Solosky v Canada (1980) 105 DLR (3d) 745 .... 8.47
South Shropshire District Council v Amos [1987] 1 All ER 340 .... 8.54

Southern Health Board v CH [1996] 1 IR 219 .... 7.111, 9.167
Special Criminal Court, DPP v [1999] 1 IR 60 ....2.90, 3.13, 8.96, 8.164
Spencer, R v [1985] 1 All ER 673 .... 6.109
Spratt, DPP v [1995] 1 IR 585, [1995] 2 ILRM 117 .... 9.95, 9.99
State (Brennan) v DJ Conlon [1986] ILRM 635 .... 9.79
State (Burke) v Lennon [1940] IR 136 .... 2.76
State (Comerford) v Governor Mountjoy Prison [1981] ILRM 86 .... 8.91
State (Hanley) v Holley [1984] ILRM 149 .... 8.90–8.94, 8.122
State (Healy) v Donoghue [1976] IR 325 ....2.18, 2.46–2.49, 5.20–5.21
 .... 6.130, 9.73, 9.138
State (Magee) v O'Rourke [1971] IR 205 .... 8.59
State (O'Connell) v Fawsitt [1986] IR 362 .... 9.79–9.81
State (Quinn) v Ryan [1965] IR 70 .... 4.54, 8.89
State v Caldwell (No 88–9–2938) (SC, Cobb County, Ga) (1989) 7.74
Steenson, R v [1986] 17 NIBJ 36 .... 6.58
Stirland v DPP [1944] AC 315 .... 11.12
Stockwell, R v [1993] 97 Cr App 260) 7.113
Straffen, R v [1952] 2 QB 911 .... 10.21
Strafford, DPP v [1983] IR 165 .... 6.97
Subramaniam v DPP [1956] 1 WLR 965 PC 9.09
Succession Act 1965, s 117, Re and IAC decd, Re C and F v WC & TC
 [1989] ILRM 815 .... 3.101
Sullivan v Robinson [1954] IR 161 .... 7.48
Swaine v DPP (26 April 2002, unreported), SC 7.35
Synott, DPP v (29 May 1992, unreported), CCA 6.15

T

T, DPP v 3 Frewen 141 ....2.16, 5.30, 5.43
Talbot (Lord) de Malahide v Cusack (1864) 17 ICLR 213 .... 9.08
Tallant, DPP v (19 March 2003, unreported), CCA 4.76
Taylor, Attorney General v [1974] IR 97 .... 5.09
Teixeira de Castro v Portugal (1998) 28 EHRR 101 .... 2.131
Teper v R [1952] 2 All ER 447 .... 9.12
Thompson v R [1918] AC 221 .... 10.10, 10.24, 10.31, 10.74
Thompson, R v (1892) 2 QB 12 ....9.25–9.29
Tomlin v Standard Telephones and Cables Ltd [1969] 3 All ER 201 .... 8.50
Tompkins (1977) 67 Cr App R 18B v R 8.35
Toner, R v (1991) 93 Cr App R 382 .... 7.26
Travers v Ryan [1985] ILRM 163 .... 9.92
Trayers, Attorney General v [1956] IR 110 .... 6.02
Trimbole v Governor of Mountjoy Prison [1985] ILRM 465 .... 4.53, 9.124
Tromso Sparebank v Beirne (No 2) [1989] ILRM 257 .... 8.29, 8.137
Turnbull, R v [1977] QB 224 ....6.95–6.97
Turner, R v [1944] KB 463 .... 11.29
Turner, R v (1975) 61 Cr App R 67 .... 6.46

Turner, R v [1975] 1 All ER 70, [1975] QB 834 ....3.16, 7.18, 7.24–7.25
Two Sicilies (King of) v Willcox (1851)1 Sim NS 301 .... 8.60

U

Unilever plc v Proctor & Gamble 2001] 1 All ER 783 .... 8.56
US v Leon (1983) 468 US 897 .... 2.23, 4.49
US v McRae (1868) IR 3 Cr App 79 .... 8.60

V

Valenzuela Contreras v Spain [1999] 28 EHRR 483 .... 4.40
Varley [1982] 2 All ER 519 .... 11.44
Velveski, R v [2002] 76 ALJR 402 .... 7.10
Vetrovec, R v [1982] 1SCR 811 .... 6.07
Victoria v Australian Building Construction Employees and
    Builders' Labourers Federation (1982) 152 CLR 25 .... 2.30
Vincent, R v (1840) 9 C & P 275 .... 9.147
Voisin, R v [1918] 1 KB 531 .... 9.90

W

Wainright, R v (1875) 13 Cox CC 171 .... 9.147
Wallace, DPP v (22 November 1982, unreported), CCA,
    2 Frewen 1982 ....6.98, 10.49–10.52
Wallace, Re: Solicitor for the Duchy of Cornwall and Batten
    [1952] 2 TLR 925 .... 3.107
Walsh v Ó Buachalla [1991] 1 IR 56 .... 4.91
Walsh, DPP v (25 July 1986) SC 9.104
Walsh, DPP v [1980] IR 294 .... 7.86, 9.71
Walsh, DPP v [1985] ILRM 243 .... 3.116
Ward v Her Majesty, Queen [1979] 2 SCR 30 .... 9.112
Ward, DPP v (22 March 2002, unreported), CCA 6.53, 6.62
    ....6.66–6.68, 7.53–7.53
Ward, DPP v (23 October 1998, unreported), HC 6.54
Ward, DPP v [1998] IEHC 154 ....1.28, 1.33, 2.64, 6.53
    ....6.59–6.62, 9.128–9.130
Ward, R v 96 Cr App R 1 .... 7.26
Warickshall, R v (1783) 1 Leach 263 .... 9.24
Watson v Cammell Laird & Co Ltd [1959] 2 All ER 757 .... 8.137
Watts, R v [1983] 3 All ER 101 .... 11.50, 11.72
Waugh v British Railways Board [1980] AC 521 .... 8.25
Weber & Savaria v Germany (2008) 46 EHRR 515 .... 4.42
Weeks v US (1914) 332 US 383 .... 4.48
Weightman, R v [1978] 1 NZLR 79 .... 6.42
Weit, R v [2005] EWCA Crim 2866 .... 11.64
Wheeler v Le Marchant (1881) 17 Ch D 675 .... 8.06
White v Ireland [1995] 2 IR 268 .... 5.19–5.22

Williams v R; Smith, R v [1995] 1 Cr App R 74 .... 7.54
Williams, Attorney General v [1940] IR 195 .... 6.02
Windle v Nye [1959] 1 WLR 284 .... 3.100
Wolfe v Colorado (1949) 338 US 25 .... 4.48, 4.80
Woolmington v DPP [1935] AC 462 ....2.108, 3.36, 3.43, 3.78, 3.88

X

X Ltd v Morgan-Grampian Ltd [1990] 2 All ER 1 .... 8.132

Y

Yamanoha, DPP v [1994] 1 IR 565 .... 2.67, 4.70
Yasuf Ali Abdi, DPP v [2004] IECCA 47 .... 7.27
Youman v The Commonwealth of Kentucky 189 Ky 152 .... 2.25

Z

Z v DPP [1994] 2 IR 476 .... 6.77, 9.141
Z, R v [2000] 2 AC 483 .... 10.05
Zaveckas, R v [1970] 1 All ER 413 .... 9.51
Zielinski, R v ([1950) 34 Cr App R 193 .... 6.04

Table of Legislation

Primary Legislation

Animals Act 1985
  2 .... 3.34
    (1) 3.32
Bail Act 1997 .... 2.72, 2.85, 9.168
Bankers' Books Evidence Act 1879 .... 3.13
Central Bank Act 1989
  16 .... 8.79
Child Trafficking and Pornography Act 1998
  7 .... 4.77
    (2) 4.77
Children Act 1997 .... 5.27–5.29, 9.169
  21 .... 5.31
  22 .... 5.31
  23 .... 5.31, 9.170
  24 .... 9.171
  25 .... 9.172
  28 .... 5.31
Companies Act 1990
  10 .... 3.73
  Pt 2 .... 3.73
Company Law Enforcement Act 2001
  100(2) 3.77
Competition Act 2002
  9 .... 7.39
Contempt of Court Act 1981
  10 .... 8.84
Courts and Court Officers Act 1995
  45 .... 7.55
Courts of Justice Act 1928
  5(1)(a) 9.178
Criminal Assets Bureau Act 1996
  14 .... 2.63, 2.67, 4.30

Criminal Evidence Act 1992 .... 2.01, 2.51, 2.70, 5.28–5.31
.... 5.36, 6.51, 6.122, 6.128, 9.07, 9.160–9.166, 9.179
  1 .... 9.160
  2 .... 9.166
  4 .... 9.166
  5 .... 9.160–9.166
  6 .... 9.07, 9.160, 9.166
  7 .... 9.160, 9.166
  8 .... 9.166
    (1) 9.160
    (2) 9.162
    (3) 9.163
  9 .... 9.163, 9.166
  10 .... 9.166
  11 .... 9.166
  12 .... 5.19, 5.24
  13 .... 5.18, 5.24
  14 .... 5.18
    (2) 2.01
  15 .... 5.18
  16 .... 5.18
    (2)(a) 2.01
     (b) 5.18
  17 .... 6.114
  21 .... 5.27, 5.42
  22 .... 5.27, 5.42
  23 .... 5.44
    (1) 5.27
  24 .... 5.44
  25 .... 5.44
  26 .... 8.57
  27 .... 5.16, 6.125
    (3) 5.15
  28 .... 5.27, 6.121
  30 .... 9.164
  39 (1) 5.28
  Pt II 9.160
  Pt III 5.18
  Pt IV 5.42
  Pt V 8.57
Criminal Justice (Evidence) Act 1924 .... 11.02, 11.16, 11.23, 11.37, 11.67
  1 (1) 11.28
    (e) 11.02–11.08
    (f) 11.02–11.11, 11.16, 11.46–11.47, 11.68
     (ii) 11.10–11.15, 11.23–11.24, 11.35, 11.39, 11.50, 11.69
     (iii) 11.41–11.43

Criminal Justice Act 1951
15 .... 2.37, 9.77
Criminal Justice Act 1984 .... 2.57, 2.61, 2.87, 2.91, 2.111
.... 3.62, 3.65, 7.83, 9.89–9.94
4 .... 2.32, 2.56, 2.57, 2.62, 2.89, 2.95
.... 3.62, 3.65, 4.73, 4.85, 7.30, 7.82
.... 9.63–9.66, 9.70, 9.89, 9.133
7 (3) 9.94
18 .... 2.60, 3.65–3.69, 8.63
19 .... 3.65–3.70, 8.63
19A 3.70
10 .... 2.74
27 .... 9.97
Criminal Justice (Forensic Evidence) Act 1990 .... 7.82–7.86, 8.63
2 .... 7.86
(5)(a) 7.92
(8) 7.93
3 .... 7.94
4 .... 7.95
(5) 7.95
(b) 7.88
38 .... 7.85
(1) 7.85
39 .... 7.85
43 .... 7.85
Criminal Justice Act 1993 .... 2.02, 2.21, 5.28
Criminal Justice Act 1994 .... 2.61, 4.81
6 .... 4.94
63 .... 4.81
64 (1) 4.81
Criminal Justice (Public Order) Act 1994
32 (1) 6.50, 6.119, 6.124
Criminal Justice (Drug Trafficking) Act 1996 .... 2.61, 2.91, 3.70, 9.84
2 .... 2.93, 9.66, 9.116
(1) 9.115
(2)(g)(i) 9.115
4 .... 9.116
7 .... 2.53, 2.60–2.66, 2.86, 2.111, 3.67–3.70
8 .... 4.32
(2) 4.33–4.34
(3) 2.108
Criminal Justice (Miscellaneous Provisions) Act 1997 .... 4.26
10 .... 2.88, 4.27

Criminal Justice Act 1999 .... 2.51, 2.69
    25 .... 7.30
    39 .... 5.19, 5.28, 5.34
       (2) 5.28
    Pt 2 .... 2.69
    Pt 6 .... 2.70
Criminal Justice (Theft and Fraud) Offences Act 2001
    57 .... 7.11
Criminal Justice Act 2003 .... 10.06, 11.58, 11.71
    98 .... 11.59
    98–108 .... 11.60
    99 .... 11.60
    101 .... 11.60–11.64
       (3) 11.71
    105 .... 11.68
    112 (1) 11.63
    114 .... 9.181
    115 .... 9.14
    Pt 11 .... 9.181, 11.59
Criminal Justice Act 2006 .... 4.36, 4.107, 5.36, 8.64
    4–8A 7.89
    8A 7.89
    6 .... 4.26
    9 .... 2.89, 9.66, 9.89
    14 .... 7.89
    15 .... 9.173
    16 .... 5.37, 9.173
       (2)(b) 5.37
       (3) 5.38
       (4) 5.39, 9.174
    17 .... 9.173
    18 .... 9.173
    19 .... 5.40, 9.173
    20 .... 9.173
    21 .... 4.107
    190 .... 4.30
    74B 4.36
    Pt 3 .... 5.37, 9.173
Criminal Justice Act 2007 .... 2.50, 2.89, 2.91, 2.101, 2.107, 2.111, 2.139
    7 .... 7.39, 9.168
    28 .... 2.111, 3.69
    29 .... 2.111, 3.70
    30 .... 2.111, 3.70
    31 .... 3.71

Criminal Justice Act 2007 (contd)
32 .... 3.72
50 .... 2.94, 9.66
52 .... 2.112
Pt 4 .... 2.60, 3.68
Criminal Justice Act 2009
22 (4) 2.65
Criminal Justice (Amendment) Act 2009 .... 1.34, 2.08, 2.14, 2.53
.... 2.91, 4.44, 6.87, 9.142
1 .... 4.40
3 .... 9.66
8 .... 2.90
13 .... 4.36, 4.105
21 (1) 2.91, 2.92, 9.177
22 .... 2.93–2.93
23 .... 2.94
24 .... 2.95
Criminal Justice (Surveillance) Act 2009 .... 4.35, 4.105
5 .... 4.35
6 .... 4.35
7 .... 4.35
8 .... 4.36
14 .... 4.36–4.38
Criminal Law (Amendment) Act 1935
1 (1) 6.06
Criminal Law Act 1976
2 .... 8.97–8.99
3 (2) 8.99
Criminal Law (Jurisdiction) Act 1976
7 (1) 7.84
Criminal Law (Rape) (Amendment) Act 1990 .... 6.51, 6.117
7 .... 6.119, 6.125, 6.151
Criminal Law (Sexual Offences) Act 1993
10 (2) 4.20
Criminal Law Act 1997
6 .... 4.28, 4.88
Criminal Procedure Act 1967
34 .... 4.107
Criminal Procedure Act 1993 .... 2.02, 9.17
3(1)(a) 4.33
10 .... 2.56–2.56, 6.88, 9.17–9.19, 9.132

Diplomatic Relations and Immunities (Amendment) Act 1976
  1 .... 5.46
Disclosure of Information for Taxation and Other Purposes Act 1994 .... 2.68
Disclosure of Information for Taxation and Other Purposes Act 1996 .... 2.63–2.63
Domestic Violence Act 1996
  3 (4) (b) 7.39
Emergency Powers Act 1976 .... 2.33
  3 .... 2.33
Explosive Substances Act 1883
  2 .... 9.53
  4 (1) 3.45
Extradition Act 1965
  27 .... 4.53
  Pt II 4.53, 9.124
Family Law (Divorce) Act 1996 .... 8.73
Gaming and Lotteries Act 1956 .... 4.63
Greyhound Industry Act 1958 .... 8.10
Human Rights Act 1998 .... 6.171
Interpretation Act 1937
  11 (h) 4.77
Judicial Separation and Family Law Reform Act 1989
  7 .... 8.73
Larceny Act 1916
  41 .... 4.84–4.85
  42(1) 4.72
Local Government (Planning and Development) Act 1963 .... 8.119
Medical Practitioners Act 1978 .... 8.18
Mental Treatment Act 1945 .... 3.112
  260 .... 3.111–3.112
Misuse of Drugs Act 1971
  5 .... 3.75
Misuse of Drugs Act 1977 .... 4.02, 4.32–4.33, 4.59
  23 .... 4.14
  26 .... 2.66, 4.24, 4.32, 4.70–4.76
    (1) 4.68
    (2) 4.19
Misuse of Drugs Act 1984
  12 .... 4.14
  13 .... 4.70

Non-Fatal Offences Against the Person Act 1997
10 .... 10.69
15 .... 9.66

Offences Against the Person Act 1861
23 .... 8.45
62 .... 11.14

Offences Against the State Act 1939 .... 2.11–2.14, 2.43–2.48
.... 2.53, 2.86, 2.111, 2.140, 3.58, 3.65
12 .... 2.26
21 .... 2.26, 8.95–8.99
24 .... 2.26–2.27, 3.44
29 .... 2.86
30 .... 2.04, 2.32–2.33, 2.45–2.50, 2.53–2.57
.... 2.62, 2.87, 2.91, 2.140, 3.50, 3.53, 3.58, 4.53
.... , 4.74, 4.92, 6.56, 7.84, 9.35, 9.53–9.58
.... 9.63–9.66, 9.79–9.85, 9.92, 9.102–9.106
.... 9.119–9.128, 9.136–9.138
   (3) 2.41
   (4) 9.62
30A 2.91
52 .... 2.60, 3.53, 3.60, 9.119
   (1) 3.50
   (2) 3.50
Pt V 2.04, 2.11, 2.57

Offences Against the State (Amendment) Act 1940 .... 2.76, 8.135

Offences Against the State (Amendment) Act 1972
3 (2) 7.36, 8.95

Offences Against the State (Amendment) Act 1998 .... 2.53, 2.58–2.60
.... 2.88, 2.111, 3.58, 9.138, 9.176
2 .... 2.60, 3.58, 3.67–3.71, 9.138
2–5 .... 9.176
5 .... 3.58, 3.67–3.70
6 .... 2.58
7 .... 2.58
8 .... 2.58
9 .... 2.60
10 .... 2.53, 9.62
12 .... 2.58
18 (3) 2.59
30 .... 2.58

Prevention of Terrorism Act 2005 .... 2.134

Proceeds of Crime Act 1996 .... 2.63
    1 .... 2.68
    2 .... 2.68
    3 .... 2.68, 9.175
    8 .... 7.39, 9.175
Protection of Persons Reporting Child Abuse Act 1998 .... 8.102
Residential Institutions Redress Act 2002
    7 .... 3.98
Road Traffic Act 1961 .... 6.21, 7.40
    39 (2) 4.67
    49 .... 7.41
        (1)(4)(a) 7.47
        (2) 9.72
        (6) 7.47, 7.51
        (8) 4.67, 9.72
    50 (8) 3.46, 3.77
    105 .... 6.20
        (a) 6.20
Road Traffic (Amendment) Act 1964
    10 .... 3.46
Road Traffic Act 1968 .... 3.15
    44 .... 3.15
Road Traffic (Amendment) Act 1978 .... 7.51
    13 .... 7.50
        (3) 7.103
    16 (5) 3.116
    21 .... 3.116, 5.06, 5.07
        (4) 3.116
    22 .... 3.116
        (3) 3.115
    23 (2) 3.116
Road Traffic Act 1988
    172 .... 2.120
        (2)(a) 2.103
Road Traffic Act 1994
    2 .... 4.65
    10 .... 4.65, 9.72
    11 .... 4.65
    23 .... 4.65
    39 .... 4.65
    44 .... 6.20
    106 (3) (a) 4.65

Safety, Health and Welfare at Work Act 2005
    81 .... 3.77
Sexual Offenders Act 2001 .... 2.51
    34 .... 6.128
Status of Children Act 1987 .... 7.82
    37 .... 7.84
    38 .... 7.63
    Pt VII 7.84
Statute of Limitations 1957 .... 8.55–8.56
Succession Act 1965
    77 .... 3.102
    117 .... 3.101
Treason Act 1939
    14 .... 6.19
    22 .... 6.19
Tribunals of Inquiry (Evidence) Act 1921 .... 8.156
Violence Against Women Act 1994 .... 10.78

Bunreacht na hÉireann

Art   15 .... 2.76
       15.10 .... 8.157
       34 .... 2.18, 3.113
       34.3.3° 2.76
       38 .... 2.09, 2.27–2.29, 2.113, 3.44–3.48, 3.54, 3.74, 8.97–8.101
       38.1 .... 2.09, 2.25–2.27, 2.60, 3.50–3.53, 5.19, 6.77
       38.3 .... 2.10
       38.4 .... 2.09
       38.5 .... 2.25, 5.19
       40 .... 3.53
       40.1 .... 3.53, 5.19
       40.3 .... 2.29, 5.19, 5.43
       40.5 .... 4.64–4.68, 4.85
       40.3.1° 4.69
       40.4.1° 2.33, 2.72, 9.70
       41 .... 5.43
       15.2 .... 2.117
       38.5 .... 2.09

United Kingdom

Anti-Terrorism Crime and Security Act 2001 .... 2.100
Children Act 1908
   30 .... 6.121
Civil Evidence Act 1968
   11–13 .... 7.52
Contempt of Court Act 1981
   10 .... 8.78, 8.127–8.129
Criminal Evidence Act 1898 .... 11.02
Criminal Evidence Act 1965 .... 9.05
Criminal Justice Act 1988
   34 (2) 6.50
Criminal Justice Act 1991
   55 .... 5.30
Criminal Justice and Public Order Act 1994
   32 (1) 6.40
Criminal Justice Procedure Act 1866
   6 .... 5.03
Diplomatic Relations Immunity Act 1962 .... 5.46
Evidence (Scotland) Act 1853 .... 8.57
   3 .... 8.57
Human Rights Act 1998 .... 2.103, 4.47, 6.129
   Sch 3.76
Misuse of Drugs Act 1971
   28 (3)(b)(i) 3.75
Police and Criminal Evidence Act 1984
   .... 7.95
   62 (2) 7.93
   65 .... 7.91
   74 .... 7.52
   75 .... 7.52
   78 .... 4.46
   62–63 .... 7.91
Prevention of Terrorism Act 2000 .... 2.65, 2.100
Public Nuisance Act 1887 .... 5.45
Youth Justice and Criminal Evidence Act 1999 .... 6.128–6.129
   41 .... 6.129
   53 .... 5.29

Conventions and Treaties

European Convention for the Protection of Human Rights and
   Fundamental Freedoms 2.65, 3.75, 9.66
    2 .... 2.117, 8.101
    3 .... 2.117, 2.121–2.122, 4.47
    4 .... 2.117
    5 .... 2.76, 2.117, 9.138
    6 .... 1.39, 2.113, 2.117, 2.120, 3.60, 3.72–3.76
    .... 4.47, 6.129, 6.171, 6.176, 7.38, 8.48, 8.99–8.101
        (1) 3.60
        (2) 3.48, 3.60
    7 .... 2.117
    8 .... 2.117, 4.40
    8–11 .... 6.171
    10 .... 8.85–8.87
Geneva Convention 5.46
UN Convention on the Rights of the Child
    12 .... 5.29–5.29

Statutory Instruments

Bail Act 1997 (Commencement) Order 2000 (SI 118/2000) 2.72

Criminal Justice Act 1984 (Electronic Recording of Interviews)
   Regulations 1997 (SI 74/1997) 2.89

Criminal Justice Act 1984 (Treatment of Persons in Garda Custody)
   Regulations 1987 (SI 119/1987) 2.56, 9.56, 9.64, 9.94–9.96

Emergency Powers (Pork Sausages and Sausage Meat) (Maximum Prices)
   Order 1943 (SR & O 192/1943) 3.80

Regulations as to the Measuring and Photographing of Prisoners
   (S1 114/1955) 7.83

Rules of the Superior Courts (Bail Applications) 2004 (SI 811/2004) 2.72

Rules of the Superior Courts (No 6) (Disclosure of Reports and Statements) 1998
   (SI 391/1998) 7.56

Rules of the Superior Courts (SI 15/1986)
   Ord 81 r 15(1) 2.72

E Other Jurisdictions

Domestic Security Enhancement Act of 2003 (US) 2.100

Fight Against Crime Act 1994 (Ger) 4.42

G10 Act (Ger) 4.42

Patriot Act 2001 (US)... 2.100

Introduction

No one can say

That the trial was not fair. The trial was fair,

Painfully fair by every rule of law,

And that it was made not the slightest difference.

The law's our yardstick and it measures well

Or well enough when there are yards to measure.

Measure a wave with it, measure a fire,

Cut up sorrow in inches, weigh content.

You can weigh John Brown's body well enough,

But how and in what balance can you weigh John Brown?

Benêt, *John Brown's Body* (1928).

There was a moment when I didn't have the answer, and then there was a moment when I did. I can't say I did anything to make this happen. I didn't work anything out. I kept picking up pieces of the puzzle, I kept turning them this way and that, and all of a sudden I had the whole puzzle, with one piece after another locking effortlessly and infallibly into place. They were so obvious I felt as though I were discovering something I had known all along.

Block, *When the Sacred Ginmill Closes* (1986).

A book about evidence is predicated on making choices: what to cover, what perspective to take and who to target as an audience. One can either decide to delineate *all* the rules in their current particularity, or focus on what might unite them in orientation and delineate those rules, relevant case law and legislation whose report might best illustrate the power and potential of this area of the law and indicate how it might in future develop.

If there is a commonality underlying the rules of evidence it is that they are concerned with fact-finding and determinations – often, indeed always, in a context of partial knowledge of what might have transpired. To that extent they are very closely linked to issues of perception and interpretation in a manner that at times might be under-appreciated. This relates not just to the perceptions, understandings and interpretations of witnesses, judges and jurors but also of those who frame and make the law and those who are now reading about it. Hence, at the very beginning it is useful to examine – or at least be aware of – our own frame of reference, of which we may well betimes be unaware. This is difficult to do – not least for those immersed already in the system that is law,

1

whether as students or practitioners. William Boyd in *Restless*[1] makes the comment 'Sometimes, if you don't know a place, you can see things the locals miss.' My mother tells the story of a class of primary school children in a rural school who she asked one day to describe what they saw out the window. It was a particularly cold clear winter day and the surrounding hills were beautifully capped in snow. They described everything except the hills which were so familiar a part of their backdrop of reference that they did not even see or mention them. It is that frame of reference or lens we should avoid or take off in facing this area of the law, as it is all about what we see and do not, or what we hear and remain deaf to.

If perception is at the heart of what we see and know, evidence and fact finding in our courts, and in their shadow, is predicated in part on that which we perceive and in part on how we interpret that finding. Seeing listening/hearing and belief are all a part of that process.

Hence, this study of evidence focuses on the rules which deal with those issues – particularly those relating to testimonial evidence and witnesses.

Some sense of value or norm also imbues any legal process and at the heart of the evidentiary process which our system adheres to, is a claim to be fair: found constitutionally espoused but also adhered to in the many statements from judiciary and legislature as to the aspiration to be fair. There can, therefore, be said to be two underlying themes to evidence in this jurisdiction which form the basis for the choices made in this text as to its focus:

- one normative-adherence to fairness and fair play in our criminal process in particular

- one based on the factual reality of our own limitations and that of the inability to ever know in any real sense '*what really happened*'.

The text is therefore fashioned around these two principles which also at times overlap in various areas:

- fairness and the rules which relate more immediately to a construction of same through the manner of the obtenance of evidence, in particular by agents of the state

- the implications of adherence to a testimonial system of evidence which focuses on the manner in which such evidence is received and how we value (hear) certain categories of witnesses.

Hence those rules which are more directly related to procedural issues connected directly with certain aspects of litigation (Discovery and Estoppel in particular) are on this occasion left to be dealt with more fully elsewhere.

---

[1] William Boyd *Restless* (Bloomsbury London, 2006) at p 322.

The importance of facts

It is useful to remind ourselves of the arena in which the rules of evidence operate – for these are not rules with a very obvious need for a context in which to operate. An extract from William Twining's *Rethinking Evidence: Exploratory Essays*[2] serves to remind us of the context in which the rules of evidence are usually studied and the limitations of legal education in relation to fact-finding. Although all readers of this book may not be law students or lawyers, it is important to realise the limitations of a particular perspective (eg the policing function) and how that may affect or structure our approach to the finding of facts, even if it is one of our main concerns.

Twining opens his text thus with a tale:

> Once upon a time, on the eastern seaboard of Xanadu, a brand new law school was established. An innovative, forward-looking, dynamic young dean was appointed, and he quickly recruited a team of innovative, forward-looking dynamic young colleagues in his own image. At the first faculty meeting – there were as yet no students to complicate matters – the only item on the agenda was, naturally, curriculum. The dean opened the proceedings: 'Persons,' he said, 'there is only one question facing us today: What can we do that is new, creative, innovative, path-breaking …?' His colleague nodded assent; being young and forward-looking they had not yet learned that even in legal education there is nothing new under the sun. Suggestions followed quickly: law and the social sciences, a clinical programme, psycho-legal studies, eco-law, computer-based instruction, law and development, and many of the fads, fashions, follies, and frolics of the 1970s and 1960s, and even some from the 1950s (for how far back does the history of legal education stretch?) were all quickly rejected as old hat. They were, in Brainerd Currie's phrase, 'trite symbols of frustration'. For our subject is governed by a paradox: In general education there is no reported example of an experiment that has ended in failure; in academic law no movement or programme has ever achieved success.

> Eventually the Oldest Member spoke up. He had actually looked backward into past numbers of the Journal of Legal Education and other forgotten sources:

> 'It was once suggested that 90 per cent of lawyers spent 90 per cent of their time handling facts and that this ought to be reflected in their training. If 81 per cent of lawyer time is spent on one thing, it follows that 81 per cent of legal education ought to be devoted to it. There have been some isolated courses on fact-finding and the like, but no institution has had a whole programme in which the main emphasis was on facts. I propose that we base our curriculum on this principle and that we call our degree a Bachelor of Facts.'

> Opposition to this proposal was immediate and predictable.

---

[2] Twining, *Rethinking Evidence: Exploratory Essays* (Basil Blackwell, 1990), pp 12–15.

'We do it already.'

'Illiberal!'

'It's only common sense. Therefore it is unteachable.'

'Fact-finding can only be learned by experience.'

'None of us is competent to teach it.'

'There are no books.'

'You cannot study facts in isolation from law.'

'Law schools should only teach law.'

'The students would not find it interesting or easy.'

'The concept of a fact is a crude positivist fiction.'

'Who would want to go through life labelled a BF?'

The Oldest Member was an experienced academic politician; he had studied not only the *Journal of Legal Education* but also Cornford's *Microcosmographia Academica* which, as you know, is our special supplement to Machiavelli's *The Prince*. Adapting the tactic of the Irrelevant Rebuttal, he seized on the objection to the title of the degree and made a crucial concession: 'It need not be a bachelor's degree,' he said; 'there are good American precedents for calling the undergraduate law degree a doctorate. To call our graduates Doctors of Facts will not only attract students and attention, it will also signal that we are well aware that reality is a social construction and not something out there waiting to be found.'

The opposition having been routed, a curriculum committee was set up to work out the details. To their surprise they learned that the range of potential courses was virtually limitless and, what is more, that there already existed an enormous, if scattered, literature. They submitted a detailed plan for the curriculum, including a full range of options, and added a recommendation that the length of the degree should be increased to five years.

Twining therefore uses this story of a new law school and dean in search of new ideas to illustrate that the study of evidence is potentially a very broad subject and yet one that has been relatively neglected in legal education, in the sense that '... Evidence, Proof and Fact-finding ... does not seem to be generally accepted as an integral and central part of the core curriculum nor of legal discourse generally.'[3] While the curricular debate should be of interest perhaps only to those whose focus is on academia and education generally, the issue of neglect or relegation of the study of facts should be one of concern for all who engage in the law and, most particularly, in the practice of same.

---

[3]   Twining at p 14.

The importance of evidence

Karl Llewellyn in *The Bramble Bush: On Our Law and Its Study*[4] makes a related point, this time as to the import of the rules themselves. He focuses on the classification of the rules as 'adjectival' and makes the point that this does not in any way diminish their power.

[N]o division is more vital, or more necessary for your immediate understanding, than that between so-called substantive law and so-called adjective law. The idea behind that division is something like this: That certain bodies of law, which we call substantive – the substance of the law – deal with what ought to be, with whether contracts ought to be enforced at law, and when; with what formalities are necessary to make a last will stick; with how to form a corporation and how to issue its stock, and how to keep investors from having any say in it; with what words are necessary to make an effective lease or deed of land; and so on. The idea, so far as I get it, is that these are matters which can be thrashed out without immediate reference to the courts; that these are matters which can be determined and are determined in terms of what ought to happen, and that rules can be laid down by legislatures or by courts, and are, making clear what ought to happen in such cases.

Adjective law, on the other hand, is supposed to be the mere regulation of the work of the courts. The business procedure, if you please, by which they go about doing what they ought to do and go about solving disputes to ends already indicated by the substance of the law. That some procedure is necessary should be fairly obvious. There may once have been a society so simple that all one had to do when there was a dispute was to go up to Uncle Obediah, pull him away from his plough for ten minutes, talk the matter over, and listen to what he had to say. But when there are enough disputes to take up all the time of ten or a thousand Uncle Obediahs, an *order* of business becomes necessary. We cannot all run in on the same judge at once, or none of us will get our business done. We cannot even all run in upon the particular judge who has been assigned to our case, or most of us will sit around for three weeks waiting for the others to have their cases heard. Moreover, there are defendants who will not be willing to come to court with us when we have a dispute against them, and there must be some regular procedure for getting them there and some regular means for letting them know what the row is about. Indeed, there is some importance in getting the disputes fairly well stated in advance so that the judge, too, will know what the row is about. And so it goes. To economize the time of judges and parties, to make the issues clear in advance, to give due notice and due chance for a hearing to defendants, and again due notice and chance for a hearing to plaintiffs in regard to what defendants claim by way of a defence, to make the trial itself orderly; again, to economize time and make regular and fair the presentation of the case to an upper court when one side claims that the lower court has not acted

4   Llewellyn, *The Bramble Bush: On our Law and its Study* (Oceana Publications, 1981), pp 7–9.

according to the proper rule; finally, to have a record of just what dispute was litigated, so as to prevent its being brought up a second time – these things make up procedure. And from one angle it is perfectly clear that this procedure has nothing whatever to do with the subject matter, the substance, of the dispute, nor with the desirable way of deciding it. From one angle, I say, it is clear that procedure has nothing whatever to do with substantive law. For these reasons it is worthwhile to take a distinction between the two. It is worthwhile to make off a course in procedure, a course in trial practice, a course in evidence, and set them apart as technical studies which run free of any particular substantive subject matter. From this angle these procedure courses appear as the technical tools of the trade and nothing more; as books of etiquette through which one learns to use the legal oyster fork for legal oysters and to avoid the knife when picking bones from legal fish.

But from the other angle this distinction tends to disappear. For if you whistle your soup you may be looked at queerly, you may be laughed at; you may even fail to be invited out again, another time. But if you slip in your legal etiquette it is not a question of queer looks or laughter or of what may happen later; it is likely to cost you your case right here and now; your case, and your client's case. The lawyer's slip in etiquette is the client's ruin. From this angle I say procedural regulations are the door, and the only door, to make real what is laid down by substantive law. Procedural regulations enter into and condition all substantive law's becoming actual when there is a dispute. Again this is no reason for not marking off procedure and evidence and trial practice as fields for special and peculiar study apart from substantive law. They should be marked off. They should be marked off for the most intensive study. But they should be so marked off not to be kept apart and distinct, but solely in order that they may be more firmly learned, more firmly ingrained into the student *as conditioning the existence of any substantive law at all*. Everything that you know of procedure you must carry into *every* substantive course. You must read each substantive course, so to speak, through the spectacles of the procedure. For what substantive law says should be means nothing except in terms of what procedure says that you can make real.

You will have observed that I do not take too much stock in this demarcation of substantive law from adjective, as *meaning* much. I see the distinction as offering simply a certain convenience in one's thinking. Substantive law presents the problem of where officials *would like* to get with a problem, and of where they say that they *are going* to get – either because they want to, or because tradition forces them. But discussions of substantive law become so easily misleading; one falls so easily into thinking that because he would like to get somewhere, he has arrived. *If wishes were horses, then beggars would ride*. If rules were results, there would be little need of lawyers.

The hypothetical

To sharpen the focus on the importance of facts and their vulnerability to context, an example of a hypothesis – in the fashion of those put forward by Anderson, Schum and Twining[5] – is useful:

Consider the tale of *A Murder Mystery* with the following *dramatis personae*:

Crime

The victim's death is due to knife wounds totalling 40, some piercing vital organs.

Locus in quo: Eastern Star public house – known to be frequented by animal lovers.

The victim was found in the lavatory.

Victim

Pete, aged 50, single, lived with mother, reputed to be money lender.

Suspects

Maeve – Murphy's drinker, regular in pub.

Mark – publican's son.

Steve – the publican.

Frank – local wino.

Consider the construction of an argument that either:

- it was Maeve who murdered the victim, or
- it was not Maeve who murdered the victim.

You now have the following additional data:

(1) Maeve is unemployed and was on the premises at the time the victim was killed. She is believed to have an extensive collection of knives in her home, which were collected on a series of trips to the Middle East;

(2) Mark is 9 years of age and was on the premises at the time of the murder;

(3) Publican Steve was on the premises at the time of the murder. He is a member of an animal rights activist group. He was recently jilted by the victim;

(4) Frank was not on the premises at the time of the murder but presents himself at the police station and confesses. He has a previous conviction for stabbing.

---

[5]   Anderson, Schum and Twining, *Analysis of Evidence* (Little Brown, 1991), p 41 *et seq.*

Using (1) to (4), construct an argument that:

- it was X (choose X – your suspect – from the list above) who murdered the victim.

You now have the following information:

(5) Witness 2 says he saw the publican running out of the pub shortly before the body was found.

(6) Witness 2 says the publican was in a great state of agitation.

(7) Witness 3 says he heard the publican say openly to the victim, 'I shall not forget this'.

Taking (1) to (7) into account, consider your current state of mind:

Is it *possible / more likely than not / beyond reasonable doubt* that the publican Steve murdered the victim?

Now reflect on how and whether your view might be different if you were a police officer with a promotion riding on obtaining a successful conviction. How does that enable you to change your lens or framework of perception?

This text is divided into two: a general part and a specific part. The general part forms a foundation for subsequent review of the individual rules which comprise, in the main, the rules of evidence operating in Ireland. The purpose of the general part is twofold: to elevate the rules of evidence from a rather dry, limited enunciation of their precepts into a context which illustrates their strength and power; and to imbue in the reader a sense of their history and possible future. More than any other area of law, that of adjectival law – in cutting across and through the substantive areas of law and in structuring fact-finding and adjudications therein – tells us much about, and is itself much informed by, human nature. Fact-finding, decision-making and distillation of assumption, are what lie at the heart of the rules of evidence. Their development, growth and application is inevitably influenced by our views of others and of ourselves. They are therefore culturally and traditionally contingent in a manner that is somewhat underappreciated.

The law of evidence also has the power to influence our values – in the intersection of human and individual rights, for instance – and facilitate our response to crisis events. Very often it fails us only if we do not appreciate how it is comprised of parts of a whole and that some of its parts cannot be tinkered with in isolation, as it is a product of, and reflective of, the type of society – and justice – we offer now and in the future. Part 1 of this book attempts to remind us of that context in reviewing the whole of the system, not simply its constituent parts. Adherence to *fairness* and what that might comprise is assessed to some extent in this part and indeed reappears as a theme emergent in the more detailed consideration of some of the rules in part 2. It may indeed be seen to form a unifying and possible influential value in considering the rules overall. Part 2 attempts to focus on issues of contemporary concern, thereby covering the main topics in evidence law but preferring issues of controversy over a comprehensive treatment of relevant doctrinal principle, and preferring to focus on those rules which relate in greater measure to the themes identified above: fairness and testimony. The focus is thus unapologetically one preferring reflection and at times critical analysis of judicial reasoning and legislative action, thereby attempting to engage the student with the rules as well as equip them for future developments, and to provide insights and arguments for the practitioner and reformer.

Part One
General

Chapter 1

Rules of Evidence: Fact-Finding, Determinations and Application

The role of popular culture

[1.01] Cultural nuances dictate how we assess the information before us. Courts have always been sensitive to that fact. The rules of evidence contain many examples of this and indeed in the past have been characterised as rooted in the need identified by Weinstein[1] to control 'a group of ignorant illiterates', to wit the jury. Of course, cultural nuances change over time and if they are fossilised in law, certain rules relating to fact determination or credibility can be found to contain the vestiges of another age, ill-suited to the current climate.

[1.02] Corroboration rules provide a good example of this. In several jurisdictions these have been subject to change both as to the need for a warning at all (Canada in the case of accomplices) and its required application in certain cases (Ireland in relation to sexual offence victims and children). Wigmore's suggestion that every sexual offence complainant should be subjected to psychiatric examination before being allowed to testify seems extraordinary today, as do those general assumptions regarding the veracity of women in rape cases or the supposed hierarchy of trustworthiness between different types of sex offence victims.[2] Nonetheless, a continuing theme is the distillation of assumptions regarding veracity into law, and these then being brought to bear on assessments of credibility and fact-finding, either on the basis of preventing dangerous assumptions by jurors, or in order to mitigate societal or cultural norms regarding certain offences or victims. Once solidified, they become part of legal culture, and can be correspondingly difficult to uproot, even in the face of legislative reform.

[1.03] One avenue of pursuit is whether any particular bias or thread is to be found throughout these rules, or whether indeed such a theme varies over time to introduce newer rules and eliminate others? A single or deeper pattern to the ways in which such evidentiary rules develop would have very different

---

1   Weinstein, 'Some Difficulties in Devising Rules for Determining Truth in Judicial Trials' (1966) 66 Col LR 223, at 225.
2   See further: Fennell, 'Differential Treatment of Sexual Complaints by the Law of Evidence: A Case for Reform?' [1987] V51 XXII Ir Jur 228.

implications for inquiry than if the rules were the product of the vagaries of popular, and hence legislative and judicial, sentiment, at the time (or a reaction to them).

[1.04] It is appropriate to locate the rules of evidence in the context of their application: the adjudicative process. As Jonakait[3] reminds us:

> Evidence law is only a small part of the much larger fact-determination system ... We need to be scholars of the fact-determination, not just of evidence. The accurate determination of facts is crucial to justice, and we need to explore all the possibilities that can affect that accuracy.

Even more profoundly, Nicolson[4] states:

> Adjudicative decisions are not, however, only about 'what happened'. They do not only rule on factual truth; they actually purvey truth. In a banal sense every decision is itself a truth in the sense that its outcome creates a truth for the parties: guilty/not guilty, responsible/not responsible, etc. Decisions and trials may also communicate a number of truths of a more overtly moral and political nature.

It is that communication between trial and culture or society – and a corresponding one from society back to trial – that lies at the heart of an exploration of evidentiary rules.

The trial

[1.05] The adjuncative process which is the trial involves the roles of judges, jurors, and investigators (police) in (re)constructing the 'law story'. Hence legal adjudication within the criminal process carries within it the elements of individual or situational bias, inequity of bargaining power and inevitable error due to human fallibility and forensic inaccuracy, set against what is evidently the most powerfully symbolic procedure or event that is most symptomatic of the hegemony of the state. The system is demonstrably vulnerable to prevailing shifts in public opinion as to what factors or features of that system are the most valuable, or essential, to the manner in which we do justice.

[1.06] Language is, of course, a major consideration here, not only in terms of setting the tenor or context for change, but also more centrally and continually in the criminal process itself. Goodrich comments that:

> ... irrespective of the aura of rationality and of specialism that surrounds legal hearings, they are best depicted not in terms of the law's own image, that of

---

3   Jonakait, 'Making the Law of Factual Determinations Matter More' [1992] 25 Loyola LR 673.
4   Nicolson and Donald, 'Truth, Reason and Justice: Epistemology and Politics in Evidence Discourse' [1994] MLR 726.

impartiality and the inexorable necessity of the application of pre-existent rules of statute and precedent, but rather in terms of the uneven exchange that characterises the flawed dialogue or 'distorted communication' of the most contemporary bureaucratic discourses. What underpins and prolongs the unilateral monologue of most legal auditoria is not the exquisite precision of scientific expression but simple *political expedience and the linguistic manifestation of the vested interest of economically and sexually dominant social groups.*[5] [Emphasis added.]

In this context, the jury is of course the most obvious conduit for the transference of popular nuance.

The role of the jury

[1.07]

It is commonly suggested that lawyers use stories to organise evidence, but the actual presentation of evidence in trials does not conform easily to a coherent normative structure. Juries too will construct stories from the evidence and will test the plausibility of such stories by reference to common sense generalisations.[6]

Two interesting factors identified by Jackson and Doran are, first, that the prevalent view among counsel is that sexual cases are particularly difficult to defend before juries and, second, that one of the reasons for having juries is their ability to channel 'community values' into the decision-making process.[7] Arguing for the necessity of both judge and jury in fact-finding, they conclude:

In the absence of any perfect line of communication to 'how it happened', triers of fact must play a part in bringing their own experiences, their own 'evidence', to bear on the case.[8]

The use of a jury has, of course, been a major factor in the development of the rules of evidence. Garcia[9] advises closer scrutiny of the jury:

The rules of evidence are a child of the jury system, yet we seldom focus on the issues of jury composition and jury selection in evidence courses. We should. We can. Selection strategies depend heavily on the particulars of a specific case, such

---

5   Goodrich, *Languages of Law – From Logics of Memory to Nomadic Masks* (Weidenfeld & Nicolson, 1990), pp 185–186.

6   Jackson and Doran, 'Judge and Jury: Towards a New Division of Labour in Criminal Trials' [1997] MLR 759 at 763.

7   Jackson and Doran, 'Judge and Jury: Towards a New Division of Labour in Criminal Trials' [1997] MLR 759 at 764–766.

8   Jackson and Doran, 'Judge and Jury: Towards a New Division of Labour in Criminal Trials' [1997] MLR 759 at 766.

9   Garcia, 'Rape, Lies and Videotape' [1992] 25 Loyola LR 711 at 736.

as the nature of the charge, what the evidence shows, who the witnesses are, who the defendant is, who the lawyers are, and who else is in the jury pool. It is not enough to read about empirical studies in the abstract. We should think about these issues in the context of a particular case.

[1.08] The Rodney King trial[10] in the United States threw up the issue of jury selection – the locale of the trial being a central concern, particularly with regard to race. A commentary in the Harvard Law Review argues for race to be made a consideration in the judge's determination of alternative venues. Although change of venue is a relative rarity, such a decision, it is suggested, would have an important symbolic value:

> Our society does not perfectly reflect the idea of a melting pot, and today more closely resembles a 'salad bowl'. Different geographical areas can produce widely different jury pools, with different experiences, different cultural knowledge, different sympathies and different beliefs. [It is important] ... to recognise that a change of venue can sometimes lead to a trial being held in a locale that differs markedly from the original community, and that such an outcome effects a deviation from principled notions at the heart of community involvement in the criminal process. The question, then, is not if we should explicitly recognise race in choosing a new venue. For if we are to remain true to the goals of impartial juries and community participation, the question is really how can we ignore it?[11]

Jury composition issues in our own jurisdiction might include those situations where travellers may be tried by an all-settled jury.

[1.09] Jackson and Doran[12] invoke the Diplock Court system to make the case that the roles of the judge and jury in the criminal justice system are not as simplistic or obvious as one might think. Moreover on the demerit side, both can suffer from a lack of diversity and a facility for prejudice. The Runciman Commission in England looked at the jury by means of a jury questionnaire.[13] What is remarkable is the extent to which jurors declared themselves satisfied with their ability to comprehend the material presented and the points of law. Such confidence in the ability of the jury is not, by contrast, found among those interviewed by The Observer,[14] amongst them leading barristers and criminologists who doubted the jury's ability and representativeness, which

---

[10] *Powell v Superior Court* 283 Cal Rptr 777.

[11] 'Out of the Frying Pan or into the Fire? Race and Choice of Venue After Rodney King'. (1993) Vol 106 Harv LR 705 at 722.

[12] Jackson and Doran, 'Judge and Jury: Towards a New Division of Labour in Criminal Trials' (1997) 60 MLR 759.

[13] Zander and Henderson, *The Royal Commission on Criminal Justice Crown Court Study Research Study No 19* (HMSO, 1993).

[14] (1994) *Observer*, 20 October.

ensured that, certainly in fraud trials, defendants were not tried by their peers. Jackson and Doran do make the suggestion that just as jurors may be skilled on credibility issues (what might be called 'gut instinct'), judges may have the edge in emotionally charged cases (eg sexual offences), where the legal scales on the eyes of lawyers help stop the high beam of political and media discourses. Defence lawyers in these cases might well like the option of a non-jury trial.

[1.10] The non-representativeness of juries is not a unique example of lack of diversity in law. The technique of storytelling has been invoked by some to challenge orthodoxy and exclusion in law. The power of the law story is examined by Green *et al*:[15]

> A power of the law story is that it can translate other stories, including the stories of experts in other fields like psychiatry, paediatrics, criminology. The 'law story' may therefore carry more weight than many other stories, not because it is intrinsically more valuable but rather because it has a special power, traditionally seen as the power to command backed by the supreme force of the state. Minow amongst others points out: 'When judges interpret text somebody loses his freedom, his property, his children, even his life.' However, law is not just a power to command. It can also be seen as the power to exclude, for the law sets its own boundaries, establishes what is to lie at the core and what beyond its margins.

Later they comment:

> Thus law restricts, confines and places into hierarchy those who may speak the discourse, the texts of the discourse and the settings where legal discourse takes place. This power of exclusion may indirectly render invisible individuals and even whole communities, for the law places at its liberal centre the equal, disembodied individual and thereby robs human beings of much of themselves – sex, colour, religion, class, age ...[16]

The role of the police

[1.11] The police themselves in the pre-trial process have had an impact upon what is presented to (and further (mis)interpreted by) the courts, sometimes leading to miscarriage of justice. Zuckerman[17] comments:

> It is widely believed that the case presented by the police to the prosecutor and, through him to the court, consists purely of facts. Nothing could be further from the truth. The police case does not contain just raw objective facts. The police

---

[15] Green, Lim and Roche, 'The Indeterminate Province: Storytelling in Legal Theory and Legal Education' (1994) 28 *Law Teacher* 138 at 148.

[16] Green, Lim and Roche, 'The Indeterminate Province: Storytelling in Legal Theory and Legal Education', (1994) 28 *Law Teacher* 138 at 142.

[17] Zuckerman, 'Reducing Miscarriage of Justice' [1993] 44 NILQ 3 at 4.

construct and present an entire picture of reality which is interlaced with evaluative conclusions (such as the description of the conduct to fit a particular legal definition), with evidence created by the police in their interaction with the suspect (the confession), and is shaped by numerous decisions, mostly unrecorded and sometimes even unconscious, to pursue certain leads or hypotheses and drop others, to ask certain questions rather than others, and to look in some places but not in others.

Reconstructing the law story

[1.12] Particular contexts can also influence the way in which decision making within the criminal legal process evolves and is undertaken. An interesting commentary in this regard is made by Patton, in so far as the implications of earlier decision making in child abuse scenarios can affect the later determinations in a way which remains unappreciated by the judiciary at the earlier stage. Patton notes the various ways in which the decision-making process has been altered to attend to the micro-concerns in different contexts, and compares that unfavourably with the composite whole:

> Compare this series of separately rational evidentiary and procedural rulings to individual body parts waiting to be transplanted. Independently each appears normal, but when combined they create a horrible Frankensteinian creature. The resulting body of law does not at all resemble anything remotely similar to traditional notions of fairness.[18]

[1.13] Patton's thesis is that we must pay attention to the multiplicity of hearings now emerging from any core issue, and consider the extent to which the variety of decision-making processes we now create therein merge:

> Since the number of fact patterns triggering multiple hearings in different courts is increasing, we must begin to develop new procedures and evidentiary theories to assure cumulative accuracy and fairness in all proceedings ... [E]vidence law still must play a vital role because a court's rulings can dramatically affect the strategy and results of subsequent jury trials based upon the identical facts.

[1.14] This is particularly important given the recent tendency to legislate for particular issues, to accommodate certain concerns, without an eye on the composite whole.

[1.15] This is not without direct relevance to the application, for example, in the Irish jurisdiction of the presumption of innocence in the context of applications for prohibition on the basis of pre-trial publicity or delay. In *P O'C v DPP*[19]

---

[18] Patton, 'Evolution in Child Abuse Litigation: The Theoretical Void Where Evidentiary and Procedural Worlds Collide' [1992] 25 Loy LAL Rev 1009 at 1023.

[19] *P O'C v DPP* [2000] 3 IR 87. See Ch 6 on corroboration.

there were differences between Supreme Court Justices Murray and Denham regarding same. Denham J would not apply the presumption of innocence, whereas Murray J was of the view that it was a fundamental right of the citizen.

[1.16] It is also important to appreciate the limitations of the effects of change when introduced – the notion that law can act, for example, as a vigorous feminist instrument. Althouse[20] debunks the rape shield rules, making the point that at the level of interpretation and application a rule's purpose can be skewed:

> One cannot simply rely on the promise of the rule because a judge or jury that does not share the goals and beliefs embodied in the rule can drastically undercut its effect.[21]

Generous interpretation of exceptions to the rape shield rules, particularly when coupled with expansive definitions of constitutional rights, Althouse contends, can substantially influence the impact of the rule:

> Thus if the judge thinks the evidence of past sexual behaviour has strong probative value, it becomes more likely that the right to confront the witness or the process right to present evidence will require its admission.[22]

Althouse continues:

> Rape shield rules cannot simply outlaw this kind of decision-making. Nevertheless, they convey a strong message to judges that many persons who have considered the relevance of past sexual behaviour have reached the conclusion embodied in the rape shield rule. Knowing this, a judge may become more likely to agree and assign the evidence low probative value and consequently reject the constitutional claim. On the other hand, a judge could still maintain independent doubt about that conclusion, particularly if he or she sees the statute as a mere political move, dismissive of the rights of the criminally accused and intended to appease a powerful group or to make a show of crime control. If so, the judge can interpret either the rule's exceptions or the defendant's constitutional rights to minimize the effect of its general ban on the use of evidence of sexual behaviour.[23]

The point that is made by Althouse is of general significance: 'The way people think about the evidence they hear is more important than any rule.'[24]

---

[20] Althouse, 'Thelma and Louise and the Law: Do Rape Shield Rules Matter?' [1992] 25 Loyola LR 757.

[21] [1992] 25 Loyola LR 757 at 764.

[22] [1992] 25 Loyola LR 757 at 765.

[23] [1992] 25 Loyola LR 757, 765, 766.

[24] [1992] 25 Loyola LR 757 at 768.

[1.17] Althouse finally poses the question as to whether the rape shield matters. She sees its importance as lying in its value as a 'cultural phenomenon'. It matters in her view as a film or a famous rape case might:

> It is a cultural phenomenon that shapes the minds of the judges and juries who decide the outcomes of trials. The rule represents an attempt to control the information a jury will hear and to rein in their tendencies to decide rape cases by judging the victim, but it cannot in one grand gesture change those tendencies. Judges who resist the conclusions that underlie the rule can find their way out from underneath even its strictly worded prescriptions. Juries who do not share the mindset of the rule's legislators can, even when the rule is used to bar evidence, find whatever way they can to judge the victim and not the defendant.[25]

Althouse places faith, however, in the power of such a rule to influence judges and juries because of the weight of expertise and political opinion behind it. This process she acknowledges is '... disconcertingly slow and uncertain, particularly compared with the impressive (but deceptive) speed and clarity of a new rule.' However, she concludes that: '[i]f their minds genuinely undergo this change, then the rule will finally have its intended effect.'

Media

[1.18] Much has been made of the interpretive role of judge or jury, or indeed legislator, yet the subtext of the crime debate is often ignored. Those who are involved in decision-making in the criminal process, most particularly the jury, are interpreting the tales told to them in accordance with a background and criteria imbued with popular images and the interpretations of the media. In this sense adjudication by one's peers is influenced by popular wisdom as to the nature and gravity of particular types of harm, as well as the credibility of particular victims, accused and witnesses. There is the symbiotic relation of fact, faction, fiction and the interconnectedness of media tales of real life, crime fiction and the audience response in home or trial. We quite literally hear and see, interpret and believe through the prism of interpretation provided by how the media fills our lives and leisure.

[1.19] Sparks, writing on television and the drama of crime, comments:[26]

> The fictional narration of thematics of crime and law enforcement stands in a more oblique relation to the immediacy of current concerns than do news, documentary and polemic. This does not mean that they are any the less fundamental, however, only that the effort of translation between their manifest appearance and the underlying principles of their operation is more complicated

---

25 [1992] 25 Loyola LR 757 at 772.
26 Sparks, *Television and the Drama of Crime* (Open University, 1992).

and less clear-cut, and that it is unwise to foreclose the range of meanings which they may be taken to carry ... It may thus be that the expectation of narrative resolution in fiction frames the expectations which are brought to the reporting of real events. Equally, it may be that the audience turns to crime fiction precisely in consolation for the messy inconclusiveness of their process of justice in the world and its obdurate failure to conform to morally or aesthetically satisfying patterns.

[1.20] In the Irish context, O'Mahony[27] points to the role of the media in distorting the discourse about crime in Ireland, given that the role of programmes such as 'Crimeline' is doubly powerful in such a small and media-saturated country. Kerrigan and Shaw in an article on crime and the media suggested that:

> The real problem of crime, the real evidence of its origins and causes and of measures which have a chance of relieving the problem, are all buried and distorted by vested interests for whom crime is a useful phenomenon.[28]

[1.21] Box[29] takes a cynical, if not sinister, view of the role of the public fear of crime, much touted by media and politicians:

> It appears that public opinion is the last refuge for the politically bankrupt. Justifications which use an imaginary public opinion to support them usually have something to hide. At this instance it is not too hard to discover. In both the USA and the UK the recession has produced a growing number of economically marginalised people amongst whom ethnic minorities are over represented. While it would be impossible for a government to justify 'law and order' policies as attempts to defuse the threat posed by these 'problem populations', it is easier to announce that public opinion demands that something be done now about the growing crime problem. The media can be safely left to fill in the script and provide the characters. In this unfolding drama, equations are easily made between unemployment, black and crime, thus justifying increased policing against the unemployed and the blacks as well as the imposition of stiffer sentences and the building of more prisons. But in making this response, government spokespersons hammer home the 'crime' part of the equation and leave other state officials quietly to get on dealing with the other parts – the unemployed and the blacks.[30]

[1.22] Chomsky is equally cynical and critical of the role of the media in contemporary politics:[31]

---

[27] O'Mahony, *Crime and Punishment in Ireland* (Round Hall Press, 1993).
[28] Kerrigan and Shaw, 'Crime Hysteria' (1985) *Magill*, 18 April.
[29] Box, *Recession Crime and Punishment* (Macmillan, 1987).
[30] Box, *Recession Crime and Punishment* (Macmillan, 1987), p 124.
[31] Chomsky, *Media Control, Open Fire Anthology* (1993), p 270.

The compelling moral principle is that the mass of the public are just too stupid to understand things. If they try to participate in managing their own affairs, they're just going to cause trouble. Therefore it would be immoral and improper to permit them to do this ... So we need something to tame the bewildered herd, and that something in this new revolution in the art of democracy: the manufacture of consent. The political class and decision makers have to provide some tolerable sense of reality, although they also have to instill the proper beliefs.

Chomsky later comments:[32] 'Propaganda is to a democracy what the bludgeon is to a totalitarian state.' In the Irish context (coinciding with the reportage on the 'drugs crisis') Farrel Corcoran, writing in *The Irish Times*, drew some broad concerns for the Irish situation from looking at the Italian media. Making the point that all media are about the making of public meanings, Corcoran comments:[33]

The media intimately affect our thoughts and actions because they have the power to decide what is important in the public sphere, to set the agenda, to light up certain events and keep others in darkness. They have the power to define the world in a particular way, to establish a partial (maybe even a bespoke) point of view as universal common sense, not to be questioned.

They may not tell us what to think but they control the crucial information with which we make up our minds about the world, influencing what we think about and what we think with.

This is not to say that people are in any simple way manipulated by the dominant voices structured into media texts. People do negotiate meaning and use for their own purposes the cultural materials made available to them by the media.

But it would be as mistaken to believe that reader interpretations are entirely random as it would be to believe that cultural texts are never used for manipulative purposes, just because the mechanisms and effects of ideological power are not immediately available to experience.

The notion of power is therefore crucial to any analysis of the press.

[1.23] A useful analogy can be found in the realm of feminist critique of law. Susan Edwards[34] draws on Lacan to make the point that, at least in part, pornography precedes sexual relations and so communicates, largely to men, a particular meaning for sexual relations underpinned by the conflation of sex and violence and pleasure.

---

[32] Chomsky, *Media Control, Open Fire Anthology* (1993), p 272.
[33] Corcoran, (1995) *The Irish Times*, 26 July.
[34] Edwards, *Sex and Gender in the Legal Process* (Blackstone Press, 1996).

[1.24] By similar means the media in its presentation of a criminal event or identity of a perpetrator of a particular crime fashions for its audience a particular identity for criminals and a knee-jerk response to that class. Hence priests (eg Fr Brendan Smyth), nuns (eg Sr Xavier, Goldenbridge; Nora Wall) and rape victims (eg Lavinia Kerwick) bear a particular hallmark and evoke a ready response. Such news is literally 'worthy' to the papers – it sells, is plentiful, is cheap and creates a prurience amongst the public which can be readily satiated by vast column inches of great detail on the latest trial with salacious overtones. Victims are freed to go public (eg Kerwick) and we the public justify our intimate knowledge of their lives by reference to our horror. The Lavinia Kerwick incident arose out of her dissatisfaction with a suspended sentence handed down to William Conry (her former boyfriend) on 15 July 1992 on his pleading guilty to having raped her. Lavinia Kerwick became the first Irish rape victim to go public on the issue, thereby waiving her anonymity. The ensuing public debate centred on matters related to the trial and sentencing of sexual offenders generally.[35] The cycle is complete and intractable: the story is horrific so we publicise and justify reading it and in turn are horrified. The 'public interest' then is largely constructed by the media who lend further legitimacy to the subject (whether it be crime or pornography); its growing ubiquity thus bringing crime/pornography into mainstream popular culture. Since the public define crime or harm, that has consequences then for the framing of legislation.

[1.25] Edwards[36] points out that in the 1990s a new approach opened up to constructing violence and abuse. Her claim is that in the wake of sexual liberalism, the comments made by the courts indicates that what otherwise would have been in the domain of the violent is now considered part of the sexual. Criminal issues are arguably similarly circumscribed.

[1.26] The problem lies in media influences and the 'schooling' of the public response. Consider the difficulty of establishing a case for the defence that has cultural meaning or significance in relation to battered women who kill, where, as Edwards remarks,[37] 'the nagging husband does not have the same cultural meaning', yet 'when building up the case for the defence the scene constructed must be one capable of convincing a jury of the congruence between social and legal accounts.'[38]

---

[35] See further Shanahan, *Crimes Worse than Death* (Attic Press, 1992).

[36] Edwards, *Sex and Gender in the Legal Process* (Blackstone Press, 1996), ch 8.

[37] Edwards, *Sex and Gender in the Legal Process* (1996), pp 398–399.

[38] Edwards, *Sex and Gender in the Legal Process* (1996), p 400.

Changing societal needs

[1.27] Just as the upswing in the number of sexual abuse/offence cases leads to a greater likelihood that witnesses will be believed, which increases the number of successful prosecutions, the upsurge in organised crime leads to the use of devices such as the witness protection programme (WPP) and greater reliance on accomplice evidence. Miscarriages of justice can also lead to a change in attitude to confessions and an apparent greater concern for justice.

[1.28] In *The People v Ward*,[39] for example, rejection and disbelief of the police and confession at trial combined with belief of the accomplice, and refusal to 'upgrade' that doubt regarding accomplices in the case of WPP participants – thus strengthening the credibility of 'ordinary' accomplices.

[1.29] Similar difficulties surely now exist for the defence of certain accuseds – the innocent person accused of being a paedophile priest, or the innocent person accused of being a stranger rapist? Ramsey's maxim[40] claims that:

> ... where there is a prolonged and persistent dispute ..., it is often the case that the disputants ... are really in agreement about an assumption, hypothesis, premise, fundamental to their argument, which is false. They share a common but false premise ... the truth lies not in one of the two disputed views but in some third possibility which has not yet been thought of, which we can only discover by rejecting something assumed as obvious by both the disputants. Both the disputed theories make an important assumption which to my mind, has only to be questioned to be doubted.[41]

Both parties in a criminal trial currently assume an operative principle in the presumption of innocence and the burden of proof resting on the state. What if, at least in certain cases, that was a false premise?

[1.30] Foucault's discourse analysis allows us to identify and recognise the power of language and certain voices to distort a discussion:

> Truth is not outside power or lacking in power ... Each society has its regime of truth, its 'general politics' of truth: that is the types of discourse which it accepts and makes function as true; the mechanisms and instances which enable one to distinguish true and false statements, the means by which each is sanctioned; the

---

[39] In *The People v Ward* (27 November 1998, unreported), SCC (Barr J).

[40] Invoked by Russel Christopher in the context of the Dadson principle in self-defence. 'Unknowing justification and the logical Necessity of the Dadson Principle in Self Defence' (1995) *Oxford Journal of Legal Studies*, Vol 15, No 2.

[41] Ramsey, *The Foundations of Mathematics & Other Logical Essays* (RB Braithwaite ed) New York Harcourt, Brace & Company; London Kegan Paul, Trench Trubner & Co Ltd. 1931, pp 115–116.

techniques and procedures accorded value in the acquisition of truth; the status of those who are charged with saying what counts as true.[42]

[1.31] An extreme example of loss of meaning between reportage and what is actually happening is provided by the 'Dutchy' Holland trial.[43] Patrick 'Dutchy' Holland was convicted before the Special Criminal Court of possession for purposes of supply of a controlled drug (cannabis). He was convicted and appealed, succeeding only in having his sentence reduced from 20 to 12 years. In this case, an ostensible drugs trial for cannabis possession was reported and interpreted in the context of the Veronica Guerin murder and, although commented on as 'unfortunate' on appeal, at trial virtually no one found that strange. It is interesting to reflect on the meaning of that event for the status of truth within Irish society. White's comments[44] are apposite:

> It is not in general surprising for any of us to miss the reality and force of language, for as we lead our ordinary lives we normally look right through our languages and our habits of thought. They are in fact what we see with.[45]

He later comments that "what is said does matter, and it matters in the law. The law is in fact a complex texture of things said, of relations established with and through language".[46] White makes the point that language matters as much as conduct:

> Such horrors as lynching are part of power, of course; but power is most complete when resort to physical violence is unnecessary. And even power that seems physical in form is dependent upon power of a consensual and linguistic kind: I can call out the police to fire bullets at you only if the police agree to be called out by me, and for these purposes. This power is created through persuasion, it is textual, not physical, in nature.[47]

Law needs then to take account of the kind of community that language creates. As explained by White:

> A discipline based on these assumptions ... [that language is a machine/that texts can depict the real world etc] ... erases the whole world of people talking to each other in the hope of being understood, the whole dimension of meaning that is created whenever we speak, which I have called constitutive: who we are and become in our talking with each other. This is not only a central question for literature: it is a central concern of the law as well, for the law is not simply an

---

[42] Foucault, *Power/Knowledge; Selected Interviews and Other Writings 1922–1977*, translated by Gordon *et al* (Pantheon Books, New York, 1980), p 131.

[43] *The People v Holland* (15 June 2002, unreported), CCA (Barrington J).

[44] White, Book Review of *Posner's Law and Literature* [1989] Harv LR 2014.

[45] [1989] Harv LR 2014 at 2036.

[46] [1989] Harv LR 2014 at 2044.

[47] [1989] Harv LR 2014, at 2045.

instrument for achieving a certain distribution of items in the world, but a way of creating and sustaining a political and ethical community.[48]

[1.32] Undoubtedly we face uncomfortable challenges here. Sherwin[49] provides a sharp insight into our reason for collusion or blindness here, as well as a mark to its import:

> ... [L]aw's demand for truth and justice can clash with the modern mind's demand for closure and certainty. When truth defies certainty and becomes complex, justice requires difficult decisions on the basis of that doubt.[50]

Conclusion

[1.33] Within the Irish context, the existence of the non-jury Special Criminal Court is pivotal to the application of the rules of evidence in certain cases and to general perspectives on their value. It exemplifies the artificiality of fact-finding as being divisible from legal application – what Zuckerman calls the cosmetic application of rules of evidence. The trial of Paul Ward[51] provides a good example of judicial self-warning of the dangers of accomplice evidence – and reliance on same – as well as scepticism regarding confession evidence and on that occasion its (symbolic) rejection. The *DPP v Colm Murphy*[52] illustrates similar difficulty in the context of the Special Criminal Court having regard to inadmissible evidence of previous misconduct.

[1.34] In *Ward*, prosecutorial bias is evident in the rejection of the confession, yet securing of conviction, alongside criticism of police behaviour. Who knows the effect the excluded confession had on the judges as triers of fact and law? Certainly refusal to countenance the WPP witnesses as anything 'more' than mere accomplices secured the double effect of strengthening accomplice evidence generally and of sanctioning the WPP. The conclusion of the court on appeal in *Ward* that the trial court was 'confused' does not augur well for professional, as opposed to lay, fact-finders. The Hederman Committee[53] Report's majority recommendation on review of that court that the non-jury court be retained, which has been strengthened by the recent extension of the Special Criminal Court remit, in the context of organised crime, by the Criminal Justice (Amendment) Act 2009 providing that such cases will automatically go

---

[48] [1989] Harv LR 2014 at 2047.

[49] Sherwin, 'Law Frames: Historical Truth and Narrative Necessity in a Criminal Case' [1994] 47 Stan LR 39.

[50] [1994] 47 Stan LR 39 at 41.

[51] *People v Ward* (27 November 1998, unreported) SCC, Barr J.

[52] *People (DPP) v Murphy* [2005] 1 ECCA 1 (Kearns J).

[53] The Committee to Review the Offences Against the State Acts 1939–1998 & Related Matters (Chairman Mr Justice Hederman) *Final Report* Government Publications May, 2002.

to that court, will undoubtedly be a factor having major implications for the Irish criminal justice system.

[1.35] Another crucial issue is whether there is any continuing justification for corroboration-type rules – do they alert fact-finders to hidden prejudice which may skew their findings or merely reinforce outmoded beliefs and so result in judgments not just out of synch with 'reality' but dangerous and duplicitous in what they represent?

[1.36] Is Hardiman J right to counsel caution in the face of historic sex abuse claims and is McGuinness J correct in the identification of a parallel response equally reprehensible to that previously applicable to sex abuse victims, now affecting the accused?[54] Has the construction of fairness in sexual offences resulted in the accused's presumption of innocence being usurped by a presumption of guilt?

[1.37] In truth is it better to rely on the unexpressed biases and prejudices in all fact-finders to cancel each other's effect rather than try to counterbalance them with legislative attempts at collective wisdom representing only the distillation of another bias, inevitably to fall prey to an equal (and equally misinformed) counterreaction as society will inevitably have moved on? Is fact-finding so central to our system of justice and so obtuse that we have to constrain it on occasion? If so, should those occasions be greater, or do we remain confined within the boundaries identified by their '*bête noir*': sex offenders, children and accomplices?

The refusal to address this may leave others subject to judicial discretion on an individual basis, or community feeling, manifest through the jury on occasion when they feel so moved: most likely by non-identification with the victim or accused – prostitute, drug dealer, paedophile or rapist – those currently furthest from us and so 'other'. Is it right that our criminal process should be nakedly vulnerable to current emotion or, on the contrary, victim to the grip of an earlier age?

[1.38] Taking the current culture into account, can one argue for a pro-accused approach in dealing with that which the 'story' of a criminal trial is written against? Any crime that is currently the subject of a perceived 'crisis' or 'witch-hunt', whose perpetrators are thus distanced from all fact-finders – jury, judge, legislator and public – requires an adjustment in terms of credibility as we cannot recognise their 'story'. It literally makes no sense or does not ring true to us, in as equal measure as the opposing tale does. It is here that we need to be

---

54   Hardiman J in *PO'C v DPP* [2000] 3 IR 87 at 120–121; McGuiness J in *PC v DPP* [1999] 2 IR 25 at 43.

very afraid if we do not hinder their accusers. This may undoubtedly be uncomfortable for us as a society collectively and individually, as we do not like these people and are not 'like' them, yet to use the criminal process to draw that distinction is not just wrong, it is a travesty and a perversion of justice. It is to those whom we regard as perverse that we owe most or we pervert not only the course of justice, but by definition, ourselves. In the long term we also benefit by guarding against the inevitable backlash – the 'Oleanna' effect:

> The symbolic trial is viewed as a signifier within the dominant legal culture: it is a forum that projects authoritative messages through language and legal form about identity and social relationships in a struggle between the antagonistic world views of the defence and the prosecution.[55]

[1.39] In adjudging whether European precedents are purely symbolic, and whether art 6 of the European Convention on Human Rights guarantee of fair trial offers any more protection than its domestic incarnations for those who are seen as abhorrent – the victims of current witch-hunts and collective wisdom – one must consider precedents such as *Forbes,*[56] *Brown v Stott*[57] and *Kebilene*[58] where *Murray*[59] (which sanctioned inference from silence provisions) is consistently preferred to *Saunders* (which vindicated the right not to incriminate oneself).[60] Occasional rights vindications do appear, but they are either drowned in the rush of certainty and belief or, worse, invoked merely to reassure as to the prevailing and overarching nature of justice. It is human nature to want to be on the side of the angels but there must be a recognition amongst those of us concerned with criminal law that that is a moveable feast and that for criminal lawyers, it is with the devils we ride.

[1.40] The rules of evidence are very often criticised as being the product of another climate or age. Perhaps, however, it is *precisely* when they reflect another climate and not the certainties or tenor of our own culture and values that they are of most worth and, indeed, are necessary to effect a counterbalance to our prejudices as fact-finders and law-makers. Currently, that may be to operate in favour of tilting the balance for the accused if that is to remain or be sustained as our criminal justice system's bias.

---

[55] Bumiller, 'Fallen Angels: The Representation of Violence Against Women in Legal Culture' [1990] 18 *International Journal of the Sociology of Law* 125 at 126.

[56] *R v Forbes* (2001) AC 473.

[57] *Brown v Stott* [2001] 2 All ER 97, [2003] IA C 681.

[58] *R v DPP ex p Kebilene* (28 October 1999) (2001) 2 AC 326.

[59] *Murray* (1996) 22 EHRR 29.

[60] *Saunders* (1997) 23 EHRR 313.

Chapter 2

The Constitutionalism of the Irish Criminal Process

Poets, philosophers and other creative thinkers are not, however, the only representatives of the Irish mind. The characteristics of this mind have also found negative expression. For example, the logic of ambivalence, the ability to have 'two thinks at a time' can equally manifest itself in our own particular brand of 'double-think', our peculiar relish for moral equivocation and evasiveness, for having it both ways: Tadgh an dá thaobh. No culture, Irish or otherwise, is above critical approach ... the need to discriminate between positive and negative, authentic and inauthentic, expressions of mind.

Kearney (ed), *The Irish Mind: Exploring Intellectual Traditions* (1985), p 14.

Crime and justice

[2.01] 'Crime' and 'justice' are traditional concepts. This begs many questions and may cloak an assumed and unwarranted familiarity with their meaning and purpose. Previously, debate centred on what was criminal.[1] A more critical or central question nowadays is, perhaps, what is justice or, more specifically, criminal justice in the Irish criminal system? As seen in Chapter 1, Dahl[2] would suggest, for instance, that a 'fair trial' would be one that A would choose in the knowledge that he was to be tried. The traditional concept of justice or fairness that has grown up in Ireland has a constitutional basis. Recently, the Irish criminal justice system has undergone much change in procedure.[3] Lip service at least is paid to concepts such as 'interests of justice' or 'fairness to accused' in the context of change, but the question is whether their traditional meanings persist in light of these changes.

---

[1] For example, should drugs be decriminalised or certain victimless crimes removed from the criminal code? Resonances of that debate continue in Ireland in the context of the legalisation of cannabis. See Murphy, *Rethinking the War on Drugs in Ireland* (Cork University Press, 1996).

[2] Dahl, *Democracy and its Critics* (Yale University Press, 1989).

[3] The Criminal Evidence Act 1992, for example, allowed testimony to be given by certain witnesses by live television link, and questions to be put to those witnesses through an intermediary, provided such is required by 'the interests of justice' (s 14(2)). A video recording can similarly be admitted as evidence in chief, provided it is 'in the interests of justice' (s 16(2)(a)), and the court is specifically directed in considering this to have regard to any risk of 'unfairness to the accused'.

[2.02] The victim's role has come more to the fore in the Irish criminal justice system as a result of some of these recent changes.[4] Other changes such as the bail amendment to the Constitution or the detention provision for seven days focus on the accused, and might be said to constitute a 'narrowing' of his rights. Of course a focus on victims' rights need not necessarily result in a narrowing of the accused's rights. There are other avenues such as a victims' charter to improve services for and treatment of victims.[5] The current concept of the 'victim' is, moreover, circumscribed in its definition. It is not taken to include the families of those accused,[6] nor those accused who find themselves victims of miscarriages of justice.[7] While acknowledging that no system may be accurate, it is important to remember that we do a double disservice to the community if we fail to adhere to the standard of convicting the guilty and not convicting the innocent.

[2.03] The centrality of certain principles to our criminal justice system may change and other principles replace them. What is important is that these principles of 'political morality'[8] either get replaced or renewed, not just sidelined and forgotten. If the latter happens, there is a risk of change occurring in a vacuum, where it is considered legitimate merely because of the *process* that brought it about. For example, a Discussion Paper issued by the Irish Department of Justice entitled *Tackling Crime*[9] comes uncomfortably close to endorsing such a limited concept of 'legitimacy' without any reference to principle, when, regarding the mood for reducing rights, it comments: 'It is perfectly understandable that the mood should be thus and perfectly *legitimate*

---

4   The Criminal Justice Act 1993 made provision for victim impact statements to be introduced at sentencing, and empowered the court to award compensation to the victim.

5   See, eg, publication by the Department of Justice, Equality and Law Reform, *Victim's Charter and Guide to the Criminal Justice System* (1999).

6   Rynn, 'Working with Perpetrators: What are the Issues?' in *Safety for Women Conference* (Government of Ireland, 1993), p 49 at 52.

7   Irish miscarriage of justice cases include such as the Tallaght Two (*People v Meleady & Grogan* [1995] 2 IR 517, (4 March 1997), SC); *O'Connell* (*People v Connell* [1995] 1 IR 245, (16 October 1997), SC) and *Pringle* (*People v Pringle* [1995] 2 IR 547, (4 March 1997), SC). The Martin Committee Report (*Report of Committee to Enquire Into Certain Aspects of Criminal Procedure* (1990)) and the subsequent Criminal Procedure Act 1993, which introduced a process for review of such miscarriages, can be said to identify two injustices: in the conviction of an innocent person and the non-conviction of a guilty one. In *DPP v Lynch* [1982] IR 64, for example, there were two victims – both Vera Cullen, the homicide victim, and Lynch, the victim of the miscarriage of justice.

8   Zuckerman, *Principles of Criminal Evidence* (Clarendon Press, 1989).

9   Discussion Paper, Department of Justice, May 1997, *Tackling Crime* (Government of Ireland, 1997), ch 8, p 57.

that the balance should be constantly reviewed' [emphasis added].[10] The report offers a qualification that the changes in the balance of legal rights 'proceed with caution and following public debate in which the case for change has been demonstrated, and not on the basis of hastily devised responses to events',[11] yet surely the important issue here is the quality of that debate and the very necessary reference to principle. Legislative debates on recent criminal procedural changes in Ireland have evidenced an absence of any such acknowledgement or reassessment of principle.[12]

[2.04] By contrast with the legislative field, the Irish courts seem to at least struggle with principle in the context of criminal cases. Judicial statements evidence a relative prioritising of interests, principles, and rights, and carve out a notion of exceptions to general principle where appropriate. There is no evidence of this happening in legislative or policy terms. More worrying, however, is evidence that in some areas judicial imprimatur of change is itself contributing to the 'normalisation' process. In other words, 'extraordinary' changes to our criminal process become over time, and with judicial sanction, sanitised and acceptable within the 'ordinary' regime. Instances of this include the Irish Supreme Court decisions in *DPP v Quilligan*,[13] sanctioning the use of emergency powers of detention under the Offences Against the State Act 1939 (the 1939 Act), s 30, in relation to 'ordinary' offences, and in *DPP v Kavanagh*, approving the use of the non-jury Special Criminal Court (established under Part V of the 1939 Act) in relation to 'non-subversive' related crimes.[14]

[2.05] The establishment of the Irish National Crime Forum in February 1998[15] may have been seen as recognition that a system of criminal justice needs constant reassessment and change. The brief of the Forum was to canvass

---

[10] Discussion Paper, Department of Justice May 1997, *Tackling Crime* (Government of Ireland, 1997), para 8.38.

[11] Discussion Paper, Department of Justice May 1997, *Tackling Crime* (Government of Ireland, 1997).

[12] A failure to address the issue of subversive crime in *Tackling Crime* is even more significant. In that discussion paper the existence of particular provision with regard to subversive crime and the significance of the resource implications are acknowledged, but neither is engaged with (paras 5.23–5.25). This both ignores and obscures the very heavy influence 'terrorist legislation' has had in criminal procedure reform methodology in the Irish jurisdiction.

[13] *People (DPP) v Quilligan* [1986] IR 495, [1987] ILRM 600.

[14] *Kavanagh v Government of Ireland, DPP, AG* [1996] 1 IR 321.

[15] *Report of the National Crime Forum* (Government of Ireland, 1998). There was a strong case for a fulsome discussion — comfortable or not — cognisant and encompassing of all the issues relating to crime and conscious of the visibility and significance of the criminal law in our society. Such a discussion had indeed been anticipated by the earlier *Tackling Crime* document, which had also promised the establishment of a Crime Council.

comment, assessments and suggestions on crime and crime-related issues from the general public, and from national and international experts. In the Chairman's Foreword to the *Crime Forum Report* there is an acknowledgment of change to the context in which the Irish criminal justice system operates:

> Old values are challenged. Individualism has caused traditional restraints to be weakened. We are witnessing the emergence of a drug culture and the growth of organised crime.[16]

Recognising that outrages such as the Omagh bombing and the killing of Veronica Guerin require a response, the Chairman referred to the restraints on government:

> The constitutional constraints are ever present and even though the State must be in a position to defend itself in such situations, legislative reactions must always be measured, proportionate and constitutionally permitted.[17]

Those limitations are then instanced:

> Ireland can be classified as a liberal democracy with a written constitution. It is in the tradition of a liberal democracy that its criminal justice system is to be defined …The presumption of innocence, the right to silence and the right to a jury trial, to mention but a few, are some of the features inherited from this [common law] tradition … Bunreacht na hÉireann … provides the defining context within which our criminal legal system must operate.[18]

[2.06] Interestingly, the Chairman identified the fundamental provisions of the Constitution as providing a check on legislative attempts to regulate or suppress certain activities. The reinforcement of those principles by international measures guaranteeing human rights was also noted. Moreover, reference was made to the presence of 'a natural tension between governments which promote "law and order" politics … and the judiciary who, by and large, champion the individual's liberty, and who seem in these matters to prefer a policy of minimum intrusion'.[19]

[2.07] The second defining feature of the Irish criminal justice system, identified by the Chairman, was the political unrest as a result of the situation in Northern Ireland. The existence of two systems of criminal justice was remarked upon, as was the inherent danger of normalisation whereby, '[i]f exceptional measures are required, they should clearly be seen to be unusual and irregular

---

[16] *Report of the National Crime Forum* (Government of Ireland, 1998), Chairman Professor Bryan ME McMahon, p 9.

[17] *Report of the National Crime Forum* (Government of Ireland, 1998), p 11.

[18] *Report of the National Crime Forum* (Government of Ireland, 1998), pp 11–12. Bunreacht na hÉireann is the Constitution of Ireland (1937).

[19] *Report of the National Crime Forum* (Government of Ireland, 1998), p 14.

and they should not be allowed to stretch out beyond their intended sphere of application, or translate into permanent status when the temporary crisis is past'.[20]

[2.08] Significantly these were the Chairman's comments, separate from the body of the *Crime Forum Report* itself, and contained in a Foreword specified as personal.[21] While the Forum process was undoubtedly useful, a quintessentially democratic exercise, and one which served to debunk some myths regarding the public mood, ultimately it was not normative in nature or effect.[22] Neither were the Chairman's views, while reflective of the liberal democratic paradigm to which our system *should* belong, necessarily constitutive of it. Mere reference to and endorsement of such values does not ensure their currency and relevance. In a similar vein, the more recent *Balance in the Criminal Law Review Group Final Report*[23] took the view:

> that the fundamental principles of our criminal justice system are sound, including the adversarial nature of the trials, the general rule of trial with a jury, the requirement that the burden must rest with the prosecution and the requirement that guilt be proved beyond a reasonable doubt. The Review Group considers that these traditional fundamental features of the system are necessary and appropriate and would not wish to see these elements changed.

The question remains as to our continuing alliance to such an ideal in light of recent (and some not so recent) legislative events, the latest of which constitutes

---

20 *Report of the National Crime Forum* (Government of Ireland, 1998), p 18.

21 *Report of the National Crime Forum* (Government of Ireland, 1998), p 10. The Chairman categorised the Forum Report as 'a series of reflections', presenting the citizens' views on crime and crime-related matters (at p 18). The most surprising result of this, as he noted, was the absence of any significant demands from the public for dramatic reactions to crime from the authorities (at p 10).

22 In the context of the Runciman Commission (*Royal Commission on Criminal Justice Report* Cm 2263), Walker has commented that the 'absence of principled argument was a wasted opportunity for civic education'. Furthermore he noted that 'the publication of the Report coincided with the advent of a period of attempted populist repression by the Home Office which found the Report to be suitably malleable for its purposes to achieve its own agenda without having to snub the Commission.' (Walker, 'The Commodity of Justice in States of Emergency' (1999) 50 NILQ 164.)
    Despite the considerable civic involvement in the work of the Crime Forum in Ireland, which received oral and written submissions from individuals and community groups, that Report may prove equally ineffectual in terms of influence, given the subsequent contrast between public demands and government legislative response. The public quietude with regard to harsher crime control measures, and the Chairman's invocation of value and principle, may not prove any more impervious to subsequent government interpretative measures.

23 *Balance in the Criminal Law Review Group Final Report* (Dept of Justice, Equality and Law Reform, 15 March 2007), p 9.

the extension by the recently passed Criminal Justice (Amendment) Act 2009 of the Special Criminal Court's jurisdiction in relation to organised crime. Viewed from an angle where the exceptions become the rule, our position may have become quite different.

Constitutional constraints

[2.09] Since concepts of fairness and justice in Ireland have been identified as having a constitutional base, it is perhaps appropriate to introduce the outlines of traditional criminal justice in Ireland in terms of these parameters. On paper, the backdrop to the criminal trial is a Constitution with an explicit guarantee that 'no person shall be tried on any criminal charge save in due course of law'.[24] This has been variously interpreted to include: in accordance with fair procedures in the pre-trial process, expeditiously, with access to a lawyer, in the absence of oppression in interrogation, with fundamental fairness in the execution of search warrants; and at trial: the presumption of innocence, the right to counsel, the opportunity to cross-examine and the opportunity to have access to information. Some constitutional rights are, of course, qualified. There is, for example, an explicit Constitutional guarantee under Art 38 of the 1937 Constitution of the right to trial by jury on any criminal charge[25] with provision for exception in three circumstances:

1. minor offences which may be tried by a court of summary jurisdiction;

2. military offences alleged to have been committed by persons while subject to military law, which may be tried by military tribunals; and

3. where special courts may be established.

[2.10] With regard to the establishment of special courts, Art 38.3 states:

> (1) Special courts may be established by law for the trial of offences in cases where it may be determined in accordance with such law that the ordinary courts are inadequate to secure the effective administration of justice and the preservation of public peace and order.

> (2) The constitution, powers, jurisdiction and procedure of such special courts shall be prescribed by law.

[2.11] The Irish State can declare a state of emergency to the effect that the ordinary courts are inadequate to secure the effective administration of justice, and the preservation of public peace and order, thereby invoking the 1939 Act, Part V, and so operate the non-jury Special Criminal Court. A resolution of

---

24 Article 38.1, Bunreacht na hÉireann (Constitution of Ireland).

25 Article 38.5 'Save in the case of the trial of offences under s 2, s 3 or s 4 of this Article no person shall be tried on any criminal charge without a jury.'

national emergency was passed by the Oireachtas on 3 September 1939, and was terminated on 1 September 1976 and replaced by a similar declaration based on the strife in Northern Ireland.[26]

[2.12] Writing in 1974 on the rationale for the provision of special courts, Mary Robinson[27] commented:

> It is a precondition to the establishment of special courts that the ordinary courts are found to be inadequate. In other words, their establishment testifies to the existence of extraordinary circumstances in the State during a particular period. It is vital to maintain a strict scrutiny of such circumstances – which justify departing from the norm – to analyse the way in which special courts can be introduced to cope with such circumstances, and to keep under constant review the day to day functioning of these special courts.

[2.13] Given the difficulty in estimating exactly how much of our criminal business goes to the Special Criminal Court, it is hard to substantiate but – given its high profile in Irish criminal cases – easy to make the argument that it compromises the strength of our right to trial by jury. Gearty and Kimble in the context of the Northern Irish non-jury Diplock Courts make the point that:

> [t]he integrity of the criminal justice system that has developed in England and Wales depends to a large degree on the combination of judge and jury. Removing either one from the other seriously affects the balance and integrity of the system.[28]

[2.14] Undoubtedly the access of the state to a non-jury court in relation to drugs and organised crime in the aftermath of the resolution of the Northern Ireland conflict ensures it has a future. The Hederman Committee Review of the Offences Against the State Acts and related matters conducted by virtue of the

---

[26] See further Hogan and Whyte, *JM Kelly: The Irish Constitution* (4th edn, Tottel Publishing 2003).

[27] Robinson, *The Special Criminal Court* (Dublin University Press Ltd, 1974), p 5.

[28] Gearty and Kimble, *Terrorism and the Rule of Law: A Report into the Laws Relating to Political Violence in Great Britain and Northern Ireland* (London: Civil Liberties Research Unit, School of Law, King's College, 1995), pp 53–54. Gearty and Kimble identify the principal reason for assigning to a jury the determination of guilt as the need to secure public confidence in the criminal process. This is precisely because there is no external check for the accuracy of verdicts. The three features of jury participation which engender confidence are: '... first through the jury twelve citizens have a direct effect on how a law operates in a particular set of circumstances. Secondly it is through the jury that contemporary standards of justice and morality are imported into the system. Thirdly apparently 'perverse verdicts' can provide a direct impetus to change 'unjust' laws or alternatively they can act as a way through which ordinary people are empowered to condemn oppressive behaviour generally. The latter point highlights the fact that producing results that satisfy prosecuting authorities or the police or government ministers is not a feature of the jury system.' (At p 55).

government's commitment under the Good Friday Agreement, in its terms of reference, specifically referred to *inter alia* 'the threat posed by international terrorism and organised crime.'[29] The Minister for Justice Dermot Ahern has taken up that latter element by extending the remit of the Special Criminal Court under the recently passed Criminal Justice (Amendment) Act 2009 by providing under that Act that organised crime cases shall all be heard in that court unless the DPP certifies otherwise. This was presented by the Minister as a necessary response to the threat of gangland crime.[30]

[2.15] In the Irish context, the existence of an 'emergency' or extraordinary regime outside constitutional parameters in the context of the Special Criminal Court has been facilitated by the folk devil of terrorism, now joined by gangland crime. This emergency measure has facilitated the existence of differential, exceptional or 'non-constitutional' treatment for certain offenders. Moreover, as Cohen[31] would suggest, the phenomenon would appear to be ongoing as the demonisation of drugs and organised crime may ensure a future currency for this exceptional provision, and its persistence even in light of elimination or resolution of its originating raison d'être. This dissonance at the heart of the

---

[29] The Committee to Review the Offences Against the State Acts 1939–1998 and Related Matters under the Chairmanship of Hederman J was established to review the Offences Against the State Acts and mandated by the 'Good Friday Agreement' of 10 April 1998, which required that the Irish government initiate a wide ranging review with a view to both reform and dispensing with those elements no longer required as circumstances permit. It had the following terms of reference:

The Committee is requested to examine all aspects of the Offences Against the State Acts 1939–98, taking into account:

(a) the view of the participants to the Multi-Party negotiations that the development of a peaceful environment on the basis of the Agreement they reached on 10 April 1998, can and should mean a normalisation of security arrangements and practices;

(b) the threat posed by international terrorism and organised crime, and

(c) Ireland's obligations under international law;

And to report to the Minister for Justice, Equality and Law Reform as soon as practicable with recommendations for reform. (1999) *The Irish Times*, 23 July.

The Committee produced an interim and final report: Interim Report, *The Special Criminal Court* (June 2001); Final Report: *Report of the Committee to Review the Offences Against the State Act 1939–1998 and Related Matters* (Government Publications, May 2002).

[30] See Dáil Éireann Criminal Justice (Amendment) Bill 2009 Second Stage speech – 3 July 2009. Mr Dermot Ahern Minister for Justice Equality and Law Reform stated: "In recent years the activities of organised crime gangs have intensified and have been marked by an increasing ruthlessness … we cannot stand by and let our criminal justice system be undermined" http://www.justice.ie/en/JELR/pages (Dáil).

[31] Cohen, *Folk Devils & Moral Panics The Creation of Mods & Rockers* (2nd edn, Martin Robertson Oxford, 1980).

Irish criminal justice system in terms of departure from overt constitutional values is not insignificant in assessing its adherence to principle.

Judicial concept of 'fair' procedure

[2.16] Judicial commentary in Ireland with regard to constitutional constraint and fair procedure might indicate that the Irish judiciary have a strong sense of fair procedure. They have not been reluctant to invoke an over-arching and constitutionally grounded concept of fairness or justice in order to avoid or amend the strictures of rules of procedure or evidence. In the decision of the Court of Criminal Appeal in *DPP v T*,[32] for example, which secured the competence of a spouse to testify in the context of charges of sexual abuse by a father of his child, Walsh J declared that the common law rule impeding such testimony was contrary to and negated by the Constitution as 'the administration of justice itself requires the public has a right to every man's evidence'.[33]

[2.17] In *Mapp v Gilhooley*,[34] a decision concerned with the necessity of swearing in a child in a civil case, Finlay CJ stated that it was a fundamental principle of common law in criminal or civil trials that *viva voce* [oral] evidence must be given on oath or affirmation. In a similar vein, Hederman J, in *McGrail*[35] abandoned the previous common law rule inhibiting accused persons from attacking prosecution witnesses stating that 'the principles of fair procedure must apply. A procedure which inhibits the accused from challenging the veracity of the evidence against him at the risk of having his own previous character put in evidence is not a fair procedure'.

[2.18] O'Higgins CJ in *State (Healy) v Donoghue*[36] stated that:

> ... the concept of justice, which is specifically referred to in the preamble [to the Constitution] in relation to the freedom and dignity of the individual, appears again in the provision of Article 34 which deals with the Courts. It is justice

---

[32] *DPP v T* (27 July 1988, unreported), CCA, judgment of court delivered by Walsh J (Record No 106/86).

[33] *DPP v T* (27 July 1988, unreported), CCA, p 42. He also declared: 'The exercise of the judicial power carried with it the power to compel the attendance of witnesses, the production of evidence and, *a fortiori*, the answering of questions by the witnesses. This is the ultimate safeguard of justice in the State, whether it be in pursuit of the guilty or vindication of the innocent.' (At p 43.) In relation to the common law rule that one spouse may not give evidence against the other in a criminal prosecution, he stated: 'Insofar as that may be based upon the view that it would tend to rupture family relationships it must be set against the public interest in the vindication of the innocent who have been subjected to injustice.' (At p 43.)

[34] *Mapp v Gilhooley* [1991] 2 IR 253.

[35] *DPP v McGrail* [1990] 2 IR 38 at 51.

[36] *State (Healy) v Donoghue* [1976] IR 325 at 348.

which ... must import not only fairness, and fair procedures, but also regard to the dignity of the individual.

[2.19] In contrast to the aforementioned co-existence of a non-jury court in Ireland with a constitutional guarantee of jury trial, is the attitude of courts to the jury. The fact-finding role of a jury at trial, in terms of its centrality to the process, is endorsed by the view that appellate courts should be slow to interfere, as that finding is made on the basis of physically seeing and hearing witnesses, and not simply receiving their testimony in documentary form. McCarthy J, for example, in *DPP v Egan*[37] pointed out that:

> [i]n reading the record of the evidence, the appellate Court cannot assess the credibility of witnesses nor the cogency of evidence of primary facts, or of inference of fact which are dependent upon the credibility of a witness or witnesses.

[2.20] *DPP v Kehoe*[38] was concerned with the role of the jury, and their potential overshadowing by an expert. In this case the expert had testified that the accused, who was mounting a defence of provocation, did not have the intent to kill and was telling the truth. O'Flaherty J, delivering the judgment of the court, stated:

> These are clearly matters four square within the jury's function and a witness no more than the trial judge or anyone else is not entitled to trespass on what is the jury's function.[39]

Ó Dálaigh J, in a similar vein, commented in the case of *Melling v Ó Mathgamhna and AG*: 'The safeguard of trial by jury is against an improbable

---

[37] *DPP v Egan* (30 May 1990, unreported), SC (McCarthy J), p 9, [1990] ILRM 780 *per* McCarthy J quoting Griffin J delivering judgment of Criminal Court of Appeal in *People (DPP) v Mulligan* (1982) Frewen 16 at 20–23.

[38] *DPP v Kehoe* (6 November 1991, ex temp), CCA (O'Flaherty J).

[39] A later comment is interesting for its endorsement — and faith — in jurors' roles, rather than that of the trial judge. O'Flaherty J may be said to be placing a brake on the judicial role in this area: 'Increasingly, it is the experience in this jurisdiction as in other jurisdictions that a trial judge abstains from offering any view of the evidence, good bad or indifferent. That is not to say that trial judges are not entitled to offer a view but more and more trial judges consider that *juries are best left to see evidence through a glass clearly rather than to have it either magnified or diminished by the judge's intervention.*' [emphasis added] at p 20.
This is particularly significant in a jurisdiction where judicial charges to the jury on matters of law are largely unbridled and a matter of judicial discretion. This latter can be exercised very powerfully, without ever overstepping the mark, and matters of inflection, tone of voice and intonation, cannot be derived from transcripts. In the United States, by contrast, instruction by the trial judge to the jury is taken from a composite code mandating in a very pragmatic way the central role of the jury, and the limited input from the bench.

but not-to-be-overlooked future; and it is for this reason the Constitution enshrines it.'[40]

[2.21] In *DPP v O'Shea*,[41] O'Higgins CJ said of a criminal trial that:

> ... the outstanding and truly distinguishing feature of such a trial, and the one that puts it apart from any other form of judicial investigation, is that the guilt or innocence of the accused and the determination of relevant facts are exclusively functions of the jury and not of the judge.

Henchy J in *DPP v O'Shea* expressed the view that the prosecution had no right of appeal from an acquittal by a jury for reasons which he describes as being 'part of the price that has to be paid for the independent verdicts of lay people sitting as jurors and applying community standards.'[42]

In a defence of the perverse verdict, Henchy J continued:

> Both judges and legislators have accepted that while a jury properly instructed by the trial judge have no right to bring in a verdict for the accused which is against the evidence, yet they have a power to do so; and that the risks inherent in any efforts at controlling the exercise of that power would not be warranted. The use of the power to err in favour of the accused is left to the consciences of the jurors. In any event, what may seem to judges to be a perverse verdict of acquittal may represent the layman's rejection of a particular law as being unacceptable. So it is that such verdicts have often led to reform of the criminal law.[43]

[2.22] One of the strongest statements to date on the overall philosophy behind constitutional 'due process' in the Irish criminal justice system, and the role of procedure, remains that of the Supreme Court in *Kenny*.[44] In a pragmatic sense the effect was considerable, as it led to the jettisoning of 'real' evidence in the form of drugs found on the accused's premises, and invalidated a procedure for the obtaining of warrants used by the gardaí for over thirty years on the basis of which thousands of warrants had been issued, and searches carried out.

[2.23] The Irish Supreme Court also specifically referred to the American Supreme Court decision of *US v Leon*,[45] which introduced the 'good faith' exception to the *Miranda* ruling and, in the view of some, mortally wounded the American exclusionary rule, in its sanitising of any police (mis)behaviour carried out in 'good faith'. While a previous line of decisions by the Irish courts

---

[40] *Melling v O'Mathgamhna* [1962] IR 1 at 39.
[41] *DPP v O'Shea* [1982] IR 384 at 402.
[42] *DPP v O'Shea* [1982] IR 384 at 438. This is interesting in light of the provision for prosecution appeal against leniency of sentence in the Criminal Justice Act 1993.
[43] *DPP v O'Shea* [1982] IR 384 at 438.
[44] *DPP v Kenny* [1990] ILRM 569, [1990] IR 110.
[45] *US v Leon* (1983) 468 US 897.

had similarly seemed to allow for a good faith or 'green Garda' exception to the exclusionary rule (particularly in confession cases[46]), these were now subsumed by the Supreme Court decision in *Kenny*, where a firm protectionist stance was taken. Finlay CJ, delivering the majority judgment, noted the precedent adopted by him and McCarthy J in *Healy*,[47] the 'absolute protection test' for evidence obtained by reason of breach of a detained person's constitutional right of access to a lawyer. As between two alternate rules or principles governing the exclusion of evidence obtained as a result of the invasion of personal rights of citizens, the court had, according to Finlay CJ, an obligation to choose the principle which was likely to provide stronger and more effective defence and vindication of that right. That leads to the absolute protection rule of exclusion, which he acknowledged placed a limitation on the capacity of courts to arrive at the truth and so administer justice. Nonetheless the position of Finlay CJ, and ultimately of the Supreme Court in *Kenny*, was that:

> [t]he detection of crime and the conviction of guilty persons, no matter how important they may be in relation to the ordering of society, cannot ... outweigh the unambiguously expressed constitutional obligation 'as far as practicable to defend and vindicate the personal rights of the citizen.[48]

[2.24] It will be seen however below that recent judicial pronouncements, most notably in *DPP v Cash*[49] by Charleton J, take issue with that rights-based stance. Indeed Charleton J in that case reviews *Kenny* in light of a progression of cases which could be seen to minimise its impact. This perspective, when coupled with legislative moves increasing Garda powers, might be seen as evidence of a more crime-focused than rights-focused approach (at least in relation to the rights of the accused). This is despite occasional warnings from the Bench regarding judicial scrutiny of extended Garda powers (see Hardiman J in *Connelly*[50] and *Diver*[51]). This different perspective is best given expression by Charleton J in *Cash* where he states:

> Any system of the exclusion of improperly obtained evidence must be implemented on the basis of a balancing of interests. The two most fundamental competing interests, in that regard, are those of society and the accused. I would also place the rights of the victim in the balance.[52]

---

[46] See *DPP v Madden* [1977] IR 336.
[47] *DPP v Healy* [1990] ILRM 313.
[48] *DPP v Kenny* [1990] IR 110 at 134, Finlay CJ.
[49] *DPP v Cash* [2007] IEHC 108.
[50] *DPP v Connelly* [2008] 2 IR 1.
[51] *DPP v Diver* [2005] IESC 57.
[52] *DPP v Cash* [2007] IEHC 108, para 66.

[2.25] A further statement as to the bias of the Irish criminal justice system is found in the endorsement by the Supreme Court in *Davis*[53] of the statement of Carroll CJ in *Youman v The Commonwealth of Kentucky:*[54]

> It is much better that a guilty individual should escape punishment than that a court of justice should put aside a vital fundamental principle of the law in order to secure his conviction. In the exercise of their great powers, courts have no higher duty to perform than those involving the protection of the citizen in the civil rights guaranteed to him by the Constitution, and if at any time the protection of those rights should delay, or even defeat, the ends of justice in the particular case, it is better for the public good that this should happen than that a great constitutional mandate should be nullified.

[2.26] Challenges to that protectionist stance have emerged, not least in the context of terrorism. *O'Leary v AG*[55] concerned the conviction of O'Leary, in the Special Criminal Court, for membership of an unlawful organisation contrary to s 21 of the 1939 Act (as amended), and possession of incriminating documents contrary to s 12 of that Act. Section 24 of the 1939 Act provides that proof of possession of incriminating documents shall, without more, unless the contrary is proven, be evidence that such person was a member of the organisation at the time of the charge. O'Leary claimed this infringed the constitutional right to a trial in due course of law and, in particular, the presumption of innocence by placing on the accused the burden of disproving his guilt.

[2.27] In the High Court, Costello J found the presumption of innocence, part of the common law prior to 1937, to have been for so long a postulate of every criminal trial, that a criminal trial held otherwise was *prima facie* not held in due course of law. Costello J confirmed that the Constitution conferred on every accused in every criminal trial a constitutionally protected right to the presumption of innocence, but went on to state that in certain circumstances the Oireachtas could restrict the exercise of such a right, which is not absolute. The Supreme Court confirmed his decision on appeal. O'Flaherty J declared that:

---

53 *DPP v Davis* [1993] 2 IR 1 at 15 (Finlay CJ), previously cited with approval in *People v O'Brien* [1965] IR 142 and *People v Madden* [1977] IR 336). In *DPP v Davis* the Supreme Court also considered both the guarantee in Art 38.1 of the Constitution that 'no person shall be tried on any criminal charge save in due course of law' and by virtue of Art 38.5 that 'no person shall be tried on any criminal charge without a jury'. In this case, where the trial judge had unduly interfered with the jury's function by instructing them to bring in a verdict of murder, the Supreme Court allowed the appeal emphasising a series of decisions underscoring the importance of the role of the jury and judgment of one's peers.

54 *Youman v The Commonwealth of Kentucky* 189 Ky 152.

55 *O'Leary v AG* [1991] ILRM 454, Costello J.

...the presumption of innocence in a criminal trial is implicit in the requirement of Article 38.1 of the Constitution that no person shall be tried on any criminal charge save in due course of law...[56]

With regard to s 24 of the 1939 Act, O'Flaherty J stated that the opinion of the court was that it permitted no more than that:

> ... if an incriminating document is proved to be in the possession of a person ... that shall, without more, be evidence until the contrary is proved that such possession is to amount to evidence only; it is not to be taken as proof and so, the probative value ... might be shaken in many ways ... there is no mention about the burden of proof changing, much less that the presumption of innocence is to be set to one side at any stage.[57]

He later stated his view that it was the evidentiary burden of proof which has shifted. (The latter belies the fact that the evidentiary burden had always been regarded as of tactical or pragmatic effect. By contrast here, the accused has to 'shake' the evidence, or face conviction.) Despite trenchant acknowledgement at both High and Supreme Court levels that the presumption of innocence is inherent in Art 38, the section was 'saved'. Such an apparent 'strong rights' stance in the face of accommodation of exceptional provision represents a Janus-like approach, prescient of decisions to come.

[2.28] Recent adjustment to procedure in Ireland in response to perceived crisis 'events' includes the invocation of the civil process in the context of organised crime to secure forfeiture of the 'proceeds of crime', absent a trial or conviction. In this regard it is worth remembering the response of the Irish judiciary to a challenge to the fairness of proceedings in the context of the Beef Tribunal, which latter was enquiring into the sales of beef from Ireland into the European Community.[58] A challenge was made to Tribunal procedures by Goodman (one of the factory owners engaged in selling beef), whereby it was contended that the proceedings were unconstitutional in not according due process or fair procedure by adhering to all of the rules of evidence in its proceedings. The challenge was ultimately unsuccessful but the Supreme Court acknowledged that the constitutional right to fair procedure did require adherence to many of the rules of evidence, and incorporated notions like cross-examination, the right to confront etc. McCarthy J stated that common law rights were subsumed by the Constitutional guarantee of fundamental rights:

---

[56] *O'Leary v AG* [1995] 1 IR 254 at 263, O'Flaherty J.

[57] *O'Leary v AG* [1995] 1 IR 254 at 265.

[58] In brief, the allegation was that Goodman International engaged in questionable practices in the processing of beef in Ireland, thus defrauding both the government and the EC. It was a tribunal of inquiry, not a court, though it was headed by the President of the High Court with the power to call witnesses.

The prescripts of natural justice – to hear the other side and not to be a judge in one's own cause, have, themselves, been subsumed by the constitutional right to fair procedures.[59]

[2.29] Finlay CJ rejected the submission made, but accepted the proposition that a guarantee of fair procedure is a part of Art 40.3 and made some interesting comments about criminal trials and Art 38:

The essential ingredient of a trial of a criminal offence in our law, which is indivisible from any other ingredient, is that it is heard before a court or judge which has got the power to punish in the event of a verdict of guilty. It is of the essence of a trial on a criminal charge or a trial on a criminal offence that the proceedings are accusatorial, involving a prosecutor and an accused, and that the sole purpose and object of the verdict, be it one of acquittal or conviction, is to form the basis for either a discharge of the accused from the jeopardy in which he stood, in the case of an acquittal, or for his punishment for the crime which he has committed, in the case of a conviction.[60]

[2.30] Hederman J also took the opportunity to address the suitability of the process here (a tribunal hearing), quoting from a dissenting judgment of Murphy J in the High Court of Australia, as follows:

The trial and finding of guilt of political opponents and dissenters in such a way is a valuable instrument in the hands of governments who have little regard for human rights. Experience in many countries shows that persons may be effectively destroyed by this process. The fact that punishment by fine or imprisonment does not automatically follow may be of no importance; indeed a government can demonstrate its magnanimity by not proceeding to prosecute in the ordinary way. If a government chooses not to prosecute, the fact that the finding is not binding on any court is of little comfort to the person found guilty; there is no legal proceeding which he can institute to establish his innocence. If he is prosecuted, the investigation and findings may have created ineradicable prejudice. This latter possibility is not abstract or remote from the case. We were informed that the public conduct of these proceedings was intended to have a 'cleansing effect'.[61]

Hederman J's comments are prescient with regard to the use of the civil process in order to avoid the strictures of the criminal regime, in particular procedural

---

[59] *Goodman International v Hamilton* [1992] 2 IR 542 at 609, McCarthy J.

[60] *Goodman International v Hamilton* [1992] 2 IR 542 at 588, Finlay CJ.

[61] *Goodman International v Hamilton* [1992] 2 IR 542 at 599–600, Hederman J referring to the dissent of Murphy J in the High Court in Australia in *Victoria v Australian Building Construction Employees and Builders' Labourers Federation* (1982) 152 CLR 25. That case involved the appointment of a Royal Commissioner to inquire into the activities of a trade union. The organisation challenged the validity of the appointment claiming the Commission would be in contempt of court and interfere with the course of justice.

rights of the accused, to the detriment of the individual, and consequent advantage to the state of the appearance of action.

[2.31] If then there is evident a consciousness of principle on the part of the Irish judiciary, seen to have been elucidated in terms of the criminal process and constitutional parameters, the question arises as to how that is affected by the co-existence and tolerance of an emergency regime. If the latter does not conform to prior judicial assertion of standard, that may render the extraordinary regime constitutionally invalid. Alternatively if the constitutional structure is capable of accommodation of such exception, does that render the Constitution a façade, in the manner suggested by Nicolson:

> It is possible that the cathedral of legal process is fronted by a façade of contested cases in the higher courts, in which, at least from a distance, the values of liberal justice are seen to operate. However behind this façade stretches the vast majority of cases in which these values are significantly absent. Nevertheless, because these liberal claims are seen to be fulfilled with sufficient (but by no means universal) frequency, and because the liberal façade is so overwhelmingly visible in legal discourse and contemporary culture, the system somehow coheres, despite the gaps between liberal rhetoric and sociological 'reality'. This greater visibility – through textbooks, academic journals, the media, films etc – detracts attention from day to day business of the courts and creates the impression of a legal system which impartially seeks truth, protects the weak, gives ordinary citizen his or her day in court and even allows for an element of democracy through the jury system. As in many areas of modern Western law, we thus see a highly visible ideology of justice and rights grafted onto an older more authoritarian system of power and control.[62]

Exploration of this tension through the medium of case law concerning judicial consideration of compatibility and constitutionality of the extraordinary regime may indicate the true nature of the system.

Normalisation: the beginnings

[2.32] To gain a perspective on the Irish judiciary's approach to matters of fair procedure in the criminal process, it is useful to focus on the conceptual confusion that arose in relation to arrest and detention, an area of the criminal process to experience change directly as a result of special provision for the arrest of 'terrorists' under s 30 of the 1939 Act. In considering its treatment in the courts, one may gain an insight into the manner in which change was introduced in a particular context, and accommodated by the Irish courts in terms of principle and constitutional parameters. It is worthwhile, therefore, to

---

[62] Nicolson, 'Trust, Reason and Justice: Epistemology and Politics in Evidence Discourse' [1994] 57 MLR 726 at 743.

examine the case law surrounding 'ordinary' arrest, arrest under s 30 of the 1939 Act, and arrest leading up to the introduction of s 4 of the Criminal Justice Act 1984, which may be seen to represent the commencement of normalisation with the introduction of an emergency-type measure into the ordinary or normal criminal justice system.

[2.33] Section 30 of the 1939 Act provides for a period of detention consequent on arrest of 24 hours, with a further possible 24-hour period being authorised by a garda officer of a certain rank.[63] Section 4 of the Criminal Justice Act 1984 as initially introduced provided for a period of detention subsequent to arrest of six hours with a further possible extension of six hours. The relevant constitutional provision, Art 40.4.1° of Bunreacht na hÉireann, guarantees that: 'No citizen shall be deprived of his personal liberty save in accordance with law.'

Arrest

[2.34] At common law the arrest process is the only means whereby Irish law envisages a legitimate deprivation of liberty. Its function is to ensure the presence of an accused at trial. Strict rules were traditionally laid down with regard to powers of arrest: who could exercise them and on what grounds.[64] Further, arrest as a process was seen as being part of the pre-trial process whereby an accused was put on a path leading irrevocably to judicial scrutiny. An arrest originally, indeed, was seen as indicative of the culmination of the investigative process. When a person was arrested, it was a signal that the State's case against him had been established to their satisfaction and now merely awaited airing in a court of law. Over the years, however, the concept of arrest has become more nebulous. Courts have distinguished between 'lawful' and 'unlawful' arrests and between the former concepts and that of 'detention'. In addition, the function of arrest had been metamorphosed somewhat, in that arrest became viewed by many as forming not part of the process by which an accused is brought to trial, but rather as part of the investigative process of which, heretofore, arrest was the end result. Because of this conceptual confusion, the function of an arrest became uncertain, and within this uncertainty, grew away from its original raison d'être. Instances of this confusion can be seen in the statement of Griffin J in *The People v Shaw*[65] that 'I do not think it is correct to state without qualification that no person may be

---

[63] In 1976 the passage of the Emergency Powers Act created a temporary substitution for s 30 of the 1939 Act, a power to detain for up to seven days (s 3). This Act, which was implemented as part of a response to the assassination in Dublin of the British Ambassador Sir Christopher Ewart-Biggs, went out of operation after one year and the declaration of emergency, which lent it constitutional validity, has now been revoked.

[64] See Ryan and Magee, *The Irish Criminal Process* (Mercier, 1980), pp 95–99.

[65] *People v Shaw* [1982] IR 1 at 55.

arrested with or without a warrant for the purpose of interrogation or securing evidence from that person', which contrasts with Walsh J's view in that case that arrest was 'simply a process of ensuring the attendance at Court of the person so arrested'.[66]

[2.35] The judiciary initially might be seen to have aimed to vindicate the rights of the individual in the face of state infringement on liberty. This led to judgments such as that of *People v Christopher Lynch*[67] where the Supreme Court effectively abolished the police tactic of 'inviting someone to the police station to help them with their inquiries' thereby taking advantage of the latter's misconception of his obligation to comply with their request and so remain and answer their questions. The police, in turn, developed a hostile attitude to what they regarded as the 'over-watchfulness' of the judiciary. They began to resent judgments such as *People v Lynch* which outmanoeuvred their efforts to take advantage of the 'grey areas' in the arrest process. At the time Garda Commissioner McLaughlin commented:

> ... for a while we surmounted this problem of being unable to detain a suspect by inviting him to come voluntarily to the Garda station to be interviewed. For many years suspects who had in this fashion come voluntarily to Garda stations were interviewed, unless they expressed a desire to leave the station. [68]

[2.36] Far from regarding the arrest process as the culmination of the investigative function, it seemed that the Gardaí regarded it as the very vehicle by which they could solve crimes. This view is supported by the finding of the O Briain Committee[69] that '80% of serious crimes, in respect of which convictions are obtained, are solved by confessions ie as the end product of questioning sessions.'[70]

[2.37] A contrasting judicial view of the role and function of the process of arrest was given emphatically by Hanna J, in *Dunne v Clinton*:[71]

> In law there can be no half-way house between the liberty of the subject, unfettered by restraint, and an arrest ... But the practice has grown up of 'detention' as distinct from arrest. It is, in effect, keeping a suspect in custody ... without making any definite charge against him and with the intimation in some form of words or gesture that he is under restraint and will not be allowed to

---

[66] *People v Shaw* [1982] IR 1 at 29.

[67] *People v Lynch* [1981] ILRM 389.

[68] McLaughlin, 'Legal Constraints in Criminal Investigation' (1981) XVI Ir Jur (ns) 217 at 210–211.

[69] Committee to Recommend Certain Safeguards for Persons in Custody and for Members of An Garda Síochána, Report (1978) Prl 7158 (Chairman: The Hon Mr J Barra O'Briain).

[70] O Briain Committee Report (1978) Prl 7158 at para 38.

[71] *Dunne v Clinton* [1930] IR 366 at 372.

leave. As in my opinion, there could be no such thing as notional liberty, this so called detention amounts to arrest, and the suspect has in law been arrested and in custody during the period of his detention.[72]

[2.38] In decisions in the context of 'ordinary' powers of arrest, the individual's right to liberty seemed to be trenchantly defended. Protection in relation to the initial stages was provided by the courts on the occasion of trial of the charge, if they felt the arrest to have been unlawful, the detention to have been insufficiently justified, or the rights of the accused insufficiently protected. The tactic of excluding evidence against an accused, if obtained in breach of his constitutional rights (leading to automatic exclusion in all but 'extraordinary excusing circumstances'), or otherwise illegally obtained (leading to a discretion to exclude), was developed by the judiciary in the hallmark cases of *People v O'Brien, People v Shaw* and *People v Lynch*.[73]

[2.39] The court in *People v O'Brien*[74] provided the basic format for safeguarding the individual right to liberty (although the case itself dealt with an issue of search and seizure concerning a defective warrant), namely, illegality gives the trial judge the discretion to exclude the evidence obtained as a result of same, while evidence obtained as the result of a deliberate and conscious breach of an individual's constitutional rights must be excluded. In *People v Shaw*[75] the

---

[72] The requirement to bring a person under arrest before a court within a reasonable time, if someone was arrested on a warrant, existed by virtue of s 15 of the Criminal Justice Act 1951. In *AG v Burke* [1955] IR 30 Davitt J said that in the case of an arrest without a warrant the common law rules applied; ie, the person arrested must be brought before a court within a reasonable time. The question arises, of course, as to what constitutes a 'reasonable time' in the view of the Irish judiciary. In *Dunne v Clinton* [1930] IR 366 at 374–375, it was stated, 'No hard and fast rule can be laid down to cover every case. It must depend on many circumstances, such as the time and place of the arrest, the number of the accused, whether a Peace Commissioner is easily available, and such other matters as may be relevant.' In *The People v Shaw* [1980] IR 1 Costello J accepted the propositions set forth by the English Court in *John Lewis & Co Ltd v Timm* [1952] AC 676 at 691, where Lord Porter stated:

> The question throughout should be: has the arrestor brought the arrested person to a place where his alleged offence can be dealt with as speedily as is reasonably possible? But all the circumstances in the case must be taken into consideration in deciding whether this requirement is complied with. A direct route and rapid progress are no doubt matters for consideration, but they are not the only matters.

> Those who arrest must be persuaded of the guilt of the accused, they cannot bolster up their assurances or the strength of their case by seeking further evidence and detaining the arrested man meanwhile or taking him to some spot where they may or may not find further evidence … Whether there is evidence that the steps taken were unreasonable or the delay too great is a matter for the Judge.

[73] *People v O'Brien* [1965] IR 142; *People v Shaw* [1982] IR 1; *People v Lynch* [1982] IR 64.

[74] *People v O'Brien* [1965] IR 142.

[75] *People v Shaw* [1982] IR 1. Mr Shaw was arrested at 11:30 pm on 26 September 1976 at Salthill. He was not given any reason for the arrest, ergo it was unlawful. (contd/)

Supreme Court counterbalanced the constitutional right to liberty of the accused – a right that *prima facie* would seem to have been infringed – with the girl's constitutional right to life, which right also had been infringed. The court in *Shaw* acknowledged the deliberate violation of constitutional rights by the Gardaí, yet excused it because of the existence of 'extraordinary excusing circumstances'. In this case, breach of the individual's constitutionally guaranteed right to liberty was deemed sanctioned, albeit the said breach being deliberate and conscious, by the prevailing right to life of the accused's suspected victim.[76]

[2.40] In *People v Lynch*,[77] where the accused was held for questioning without any lawful arrest having been made and 'grilled' for 22 hours, Walsh J stated:

> If a person is asked to come to a Garda station and he goes voluntarily … [w]hen he is subjected to interrogation of a nature which would suggest he may well be a suspect in the case or questioned or interrogated in circumstances which reasonably would give rise to that inference, he should be informed that he is free to leave at any time unless and until he is arrested.[78]

It can be seen, therefore, that the situation of an accused in the aftermath of an arrest and prior to the fulfilment of the obligation to bring him before a court was somewhat uncertain, but characterised by judicial pronouncements on the importance of vindicating the accused's rights in that trial process.

Extraordinary arrest

[2.41] The measure of discretion given to the police, and as such the dilution of the protection of the individual, was greater, however, in the case of the

---

[75] (\contd) At 12:10 am the 'unlawfulness' was 'cured' when Shaw was told of the correct reason for the effecting of his arrest. In the normal course of events he would then have been brought before Galway District Court on the morning of 27 September 1976. Yet, in fact, he was detained throughout 27 September and 28 September. The Supreme Court held that, *prima facie*, the detention of Shaw after 10:30 am on 27 September was unlawful. However, the Gardaí pointed out that the reason for so detaining Shaw was the fact that he and another man were charged with the abduction of two girls, and there remained the possibility that one or other or both of the girls might still be alive.

[76] Though Griffin J in *Shaw* attempted to restrict the *O'Brien* rationale to instances of real evidence only, such a suggestion was later castigated by O'Higgins CJ in *People v Lynch*, where the *O'Brien* criteria were confirmed to justify the exclusion of confessions made by the accused while detained in breach of his constitutional rights.

[77] *People v Lynch* [1982] IR 64.

[78] *People v Lynch* [1982] IR 64 at 85 (followed in *People v Coffey* (6 March 1981, unreported), HC and *DPP v Herron* (27 October 1981, unreported), HC). Similarly, in *People v O'Loughlin* [1979] IR 312 where an investigating garda stated in court that, although O'Loughlin was not arrested while in the barracks if he had attempted to leave, he would have been arrested, the court determined the deprivation of liberty to have been unlawful.

individual dealt with under extraordinary legislation introduced in relation to terrorism. Section 30(3) of the 1939 Act provided for a possible 48-hour period of detention consequent on arrest. After said period of detention, of course, the normal rule comes into operation, and the individual must be charged before a court (though the court is the Special Criminal Court), and offered the right to bail etc. It is interesting to assess the performance of the Irish judiciary in relation to the vindication of rights in the context of such extraordinary powers.

[2.42] In the *People v Madden*,[79] a case where the arrestee (Madden) was indeed held under s 30(3) of the 1939 Act, a question arose as to the requirement of bringing the arrestee before the court within the time allotted. Madden had been detained longer than is allowed under s 30(3), allegedly for the purpose of giving a statement, which he commenced within the time period allowed yet finished after the said period had elapsed. It was held by the Court of Criminal Appeal that his statement was inadmissible in evidence as it had been obtained when the accused was unlawfully in custody. O'Higgins CJ stated:

> This lack of regard for and failure to vindicate, the defendant's constitutional right to liberty may not have induced or brought about the making of this statement, but it was the dominating circumstance surrounding its making. In the view of this Court this fact cannot be ignored ...[80]

[2.43] In the judgment of O'Higgins CJ in *People v Madden*, the loyalty of the judiciary to their constitutional mandate and to the fundamental adversarial nature of the criminal justice seems readily apparent. The judgment, it might be thought, would reassure all civil libertarians, who might quail at the thought of emergency powers being introduced into the realm of the ordinary criminal law. If the judiciary will protect the rights of the subversive, it would seem certain that the ordinary accused will have his rights safeguarded. An alternative interpretation could, however, be that while such a regime as that prevailing under the 1939 Act, in regard to extensive powers of detention, exists *outside* the rationale of our normal criminal justice system, its use may well be carefully monitored, and abuses seen as a temporary aberration in our criminal justice system, and not symptomatic of a basically illegitimate system of justice.

[2.44] Very grave dangers may arise, however, when such powers are no longer 'extraordinary', but have been integrated into the normal criminal process. They may cease to receive special consideration and monitoring. That integration may take many forms: the sanctioning of the use of extraordinary powers in ordinary situations; the introduction of similar provisions in the ordinary regime; or the

---

[79] *People v Madden* [1977] IR 336.
[80] *People v Madden* [1977] IR 336 at 347–8.

desensitisation of legislature, judiciary and people to such powers, implicit, and indeed essential, to any such move.

[2.45] *DPP v Kelly*[81] was a case concerning the appeal of the accused against a conviction based solely on the evidence of a number of verbal statements and one comprehensive written statement made while in police custody. The appellant had been arrested pursuant to s 30 of the 1939 Act and thereafter moved to several garda stations in succession. It was held by the Supreme Court that as long as the duration of the detention was within the permitted period and for the purpose of removal to or in a place complying with the subsection, it was permitted, and plurality of such places or of removals thereto did not contravene the subsection.[82]

[2.46] A certain retrenchment can perhaps be observed in the attitude of the judiciary in this case. In regard to the right to counsel, this phenomenon may be more evident. At the time of trial, an accused has a recognised right to legal counsel free of charge (if indigent) and a consequent right to be informed of that right. In *State (Healy) v Donoghue*[83] the right to legal representation at trial had been recognised as inherent in an accused person caught in the Irish criminal process, with, of necessity, a corresponding right to be informed of it.

[2.47] In the *People v Madden*[84] it was held, however, that in the pre-trial period an accused's right to counsel is not infringed by the failure to inform him of it.[85] It could be said that the court in *Madden* retreated from the very strong position taken in *State (Healy) v Donoghue* in regard to the right to counsel in the case of an accused before a court, to a correspondingly much weakened guarantee in the pre-trial scenario.

[2.48] *Madden* and a subsequent decision, *Farrell*,[86] were cases in which a retrenchment from the general right to counsel of an accused, particularly in relation to individuals caught in the pre-trial process, was effected. It may be significant that they also involved the use of the extraordinary pre-trial holding powers under the Offences Against the State Act. Such extraordinary powers are not traditionally part of the ordinary common law and so it may well be questioned why, in regard to an ordinary accused (who is or should be placed under arrest only for the purpose of bringing him before a court of trial), a right to counsel should only be recognised as inherent in the accused at the trial. To

---

[81] *DPP v Kelly* [1983] ILRM 271.
[82] *DPP v Kelly* [1983] ILRM 271 at 275.
[83] *State (Healy) v Donoghue* [1976] IR 325.
[84] *People v Madden* [1977] IR 336.
[85] *People v Madden* [1977] IR 336 at 355–356, O'Higgins CJ.
[86] *DPP v Farrell* [1978] IR 13 at 20.

distinguish between such an accused's position before and after appearance at trial seems incongruous as, unlike an individual caught in the throes of extraordinary powers, his or her position will not materially have changed (or should not) in the intervening period.

[2.49] *State (Healy) v Donoghue*[87] did not involve the exercise of an extraordinary pre-trial detention power and so presented the court with an ideal opportunity to vindicate the rights of an accused, by ensuring him of the right to legal counsel at the trial and, equally importantly, of his right to be informed of such right. Why the courts saw fit to retreat from this position in the case of the pre-trial process is difficult to understand. The court in *Madden* did not deny the right of such an accused to legal representation but it effectively emasculated such a right by not imposing any obligation on the police officers in charge of the case to inform the individual of such right. Perhaps the courts were motivated by considerations related to extraordinary offenders; yet this was not clearly enunciated. Arguably, it is the extraordinary accused who needs greater protection at this pre-trial stage. Behind the rationale of the extraordinary powers, invoked for his detention, lies the philosophy that his arrest is not just 'a step in the criminal process', but is rather a vital and rather large part of the investigative process, if not the entirety, as a large number of cases do not reach a court of trial at all.[88]

Whether or not one accepts the latter suggestion, it would seem that a legal system which tolerates two co-existent regimes for 'terrorist' and 'non-terrorist' offenders, with very different (indeed even contradictory) legitimising philosophies underlying both, risks the distinction between the two being obliterated to the disadvantage of both. In essence, this is what may have happened in *State (Healy) v Donoghue, Madden* and *Farrell*.

[2.50] It may be that the Irish judiciary, sanguine in the face of exceptional powers, or desensitised to the necessity for vigilance in the maintenance of strict borders around their operation, is one careless of its constitutional mandate, or at least vulnerable to complicity in the accommodation of those powers within the 'normal' regime. It will be interesting to reflect on the origins and development of this tendency, when the judiciary are later faced directly with questions concerning the use of s 30 of the 1939 Act and the Special Criminal Court with the 'extraordinary' regime, as well as those validating the constitutionality of 'emergency' powers in the ordinary criminal process. Moreover, subsequent

---

[87] *State (Healy) v Donoghue* [1976] IR 325.
[88] O'Mahony, *Criminal Chaos: Seven Crises in Criminal Justice* (Round Hall, 1996), p 33 notes that: '[b]etween 1975 and 1985, 14,000 people were arrested under section 30, but only 500 of these were charged and less than 300 were eventually convicted under the Act.'

decisions such as *Lavery*[89] demonstrate the weakness of the countervailing right to a lawyer as well as the extent to which the lawyer's presence can be said to 'sanitise' the process (see below *McCann*[90] paras **[9.68]** *et seq*), something the legislature later used to good effect in the Criminal Justice Act 2007 to facilitate the widespread application of inference provisions.

Crisis discourse and decision-making in the Irish criminal process

[2.51] A recurrent theme in the Irish criminal justice system might be the sustained and ever renewable 'politics of the last atrocity' in the State, which until recently, has been seen to be single focused, short-lived and only dangerous in terms of 'leakage' or 'normalisation' in the criminal process. A more sophisticated analysis has to take account of ongoing 'crises' within the state, addressed through the medium of the criminal justice system, which go beyond the direct threat to the State's existence posed by the 'terrorist' or political offender. That analysis would focus also on threats posed more immediately personally to individual citizens. The occasions of these 'crises', together with their implications for the nature of the State and more particularly, its criminal justice system, include the immediately obvious one of 'terrorism' or direct violence related to the overthrow of the State, but also the abuse of drugs and more recently gangland or organised crime.[91] The international and financial aspects of the drugs underworld gives a dimension to that problem which is of national and international concern, and posit an occasion for consensus and change in a virtually unparalleled unanimity regarding 'good' and evil.

[2.52] In the aftermath of happenings in Britain such as Dunblane and the Bulger and Philip Lawrence murders, Downes and Morgan[92] documented the change from a broadly bipartisan to a sharply contested politics of law and order,

---

[89] *Lavery v Member in Charge Carrickmacross Garda Station* [1999] 2 IR 390.

[90] *People (DPP) v McCann* [1998] 4 IR 397.

[91] This can also be said of sexual abuse, which is disruptive of gender roles, identity and family, each of which is of great import to the state. In relation to sexual offences, the changes in criminal procedure include facilitation of live television link and video testimony by witnesses, under the Criminal Evidence Act 1992, extended to intimidated or vulnerable witnesses by the Criminal Justice Act 1999. The Sexual Offenders Act 2001 also provided for limited separate legal representation for rape victims. With regard to due process and counter terrorism interplay in Ireland see further Vaughan and Kilcommins, *Terrorism, Rights and the Rule of Law* (Wilan Publishing, Devon, 2008).

[92] Downes and Morgan, 'Dumping the "Hostages to Fortune?" The Politics of Law and Order in Post-War Britain' in Maguire, Morgan and Reiner (eds), *The Oxford Handbook of Criminology* (2nd edn, OUP, 1997), p 87.

noting there was little parliamentary scrutiny or debate of change,[93] while the 'politics of law and order in the post-war period have been shaped by the nature of responses to the continuous rise in rates of recorded crime and to the unforeseen explosion of politically inspired terrorism and illicit drug trafficking.'[94]

[2.53] That comment could with equal measure be made of Ireland. A plethora of legislative moves has greeted each of the designated crises. The 1939 Act was invoked in the 1970s in response to Northern Ireland related subversive activity. The Criminal Justice (Drug Trafficking) Act 1996, the Constitutional Bail Amendment and the establishment of the Criminal Assets Bureau were in response to the perceived prevalence of drug trafficking in the 1990s. The Omagh bombing[95] led to the introduction of further extended powers of detention relating to terrorism under the Offences Against the State (Amendment) Act 1998.[96] More recent events such as the collapse of the Kieran Keane trial in Limerick and the killing of several civilians caught up in Limerick's feuding gangs have led to the Criminal Justice Acts 2006 and 2007, as well as Criminal Justice (Amendment) Act 2009 passed in July 2009.

[2.54] The issue of the availability of bail provides a useful insight into the pressure for law reform and its impact. Prior to the change in the law relating to bail, under the Supreme Court decision in *O'Callaghan,*[97] bail could only be refused on limited grounds. It would subsequently seem as though the change was indeed symbolic, as the urgency in relation to the introduction of extended grounds for refusal could not be said to be reflected in the delay with regard to their eventual enactment and implementation. Of course, the point may well be

---

93 Downes and Morgan 'Dumping the "Hostages to fortune?" The Politics of Law and Order in Post-War Britain' in Maguire, Morgan and Reiner (eds), *The Oxford Handbook of Criminology* (2nd edn, OUP, 1997), p 120.

94 Downes and Morgan 'Dumping the "Hostages to fortune?" The Politics of Law and Order in Post-War Britain' in Maguire, Morgan and Reiner (eds), *The Oxford Handbook of Criminology* (2nd edn, OUP, 1997), p 128.

95 The bombing of Omagh town on 15 August 1998. Twenty-eight people were killed and the incident was interpreted as a direct attack on the peace process, which had been endorsed through the ballot box, North and South. Two weeks later the Offences Against the State (Amendment) Bill 1998 was introduced, providing for inferences from silence (s 2), and the amendment of s 30 of the Offences Against the State Act 1939 allowed for further detention of 24 hours.

96 Offences Against the State (Amendment) Act 1998, s 10, authorises an officer not below the rank of superintendent to apply to a District Court for a warrant authorising the detention of a person detained under s 30 for a further period not exceeding 24 hours if he or she has reasonable grounds for believing that such further detention is necessary for the proper investigation of the offence concerned.

97 *DPP v O'Callaghan* [1966] IR 501.

that the appearance is what is important, not the effect. Alldridge makes this point in the context of the field of sexual tourism, and exceptions to the territoriality provisions, where the explanation as to why no prosecution had been brought might be 'that the legislation ... was not enacted for any effect it might have, but ... is purely symbolic'.[98] This notion of legislation being implemented as part of a political public relations exercise may be seen to be pervasive. Celia Wells has identified the core of assumptions and beliefs underlying the debate on criminal law in the context of stalking as 'that "violence" is on the increase; that "something must be done"; and that law, as a vehicle of social change, is the neutral instrument with which to achieve results.'[99]

[2.55] It is important to examine the cumulative effect of the changes to the Irish criminal justice system. Each of the recent changes in its particular context merits some attention in order to ascertain the implications for the entirety of criminal justice. An examination of the impetus and background to the introduction of each of these measures, and their subsequent judicial reception, or judicial vindication of rights in those targeted areas, should facilitate an understanding not just of their import for criminal justice and the accused's rights, but also for the sustainability of a judicial mandate to uphold rights in the criminal justice system. In the context of a regime with an historic and ongoing toleration of differential treatment of certain accused, it may be especially important to gauge the effect of differential treatment(s) and the impact of such exceptions on the overall system.

Terrorism

[2.56] Section 30 of the 1939 Act provided for 48-hour detention after arrest in the context of a regime where the ordinary criminal process did not conceive of an arrest as anything other than a mechanism for bringing the accused before a court. The difficulty with this piece of legislation, however, was that it had been introduced for, and was presumed to be, confined to 'terrorist' offences. Hence its use in relation to ordinary crime was perceived as problematic. Indeed, this was the origin of the demand for s 4 of the Criminal Justice Act 1984.

Section 4 of the Criminal Justice Act 1984 was introduced as part of a package to combat a contemporary crisis of 'joy riding' in Dublin and other inner-city areas in the country. There was, at the time, widespread concern with regard to civil liberty implications regarding the proposed powers of detention and, as a result, certain safeguards were put in place by the then Minister for Justice. These comprised a provision in the Act itself, s 1(2), that certain of its

---

98 Allridge, 'Sex Offenders Act 1997 – Territoriality Provisions' [1997] Crim LR 655 at 658.
99 Wells, 'Stalking: The Criminal Law Response' [1997] Crim LR 463 at 464.

provisions, notably those relating to powers of detention, would not come into operation until such time as regulations regarding the treatment of persons in Garda custody were introduced and a Garda Complaints Board was established. The 'Regulations regarding the treatment of persons in Garda custody' were introduced[100] and comprised, in the main, provisions relating to the appointment of a custody officer (not the person instigating the arrest), the keeping of a custody record of the individual's detention, limitations on powers of interrogation and the number of persons present during same etc. Under the 1984 Act's regime there was then at least the appearance of a modicum of protection for the accused. Prior to 1984 there had been decisions like *Pringle* and *Lynch*[101] where s 30 of the 1939 Act powers were used. Pringle involved the interrogation of Pringle, arrested under s 30, for lengthy periods over 43 hours, and the involvement of his girlfriend by the Gardaí bringing her to the station and interrogating her while he was in custody. Nonetheless, he was convicted solely on the basis of a confession. Due to the subsequent discovery of non-disclosure of forensic evidence to the defence, Pringle was later processed as a miscarriage of justice case.[102]

People (DPP) v Lynch is perhaps the least well-known of the miscarriage of justice cases, as the individual did not pursue any such claim. Here a conviction was based on a confession obtained under interrogation of 22 hours' duration, and was later revealed in the Supreme Court to be contrary to factual evidence which supported Lynch's account.

Subsequent to 1984, despite the safeguards introduced to allay civil liberties concerns, in decisions like *People (DPP) v Connell*,[103] interrogation was revealed to be conducted in breach of all directions regarding length and conduct of investigations. Connell had been arrested under s 30 of the 1939 Act, interrogated in breach of the 1987 Custody Regulations and denied access to his solicitor. His conviction of murder on the basis of an inculpatory statement was quashed. In *People (DPP) v Meleady & Grogan*,[104] relating to the conviction of two young men from Tallaght (to be known as the 'Tallaght Two' case) on the basis, primarily, of the visual identification evidence of the car owner who clung to the hood as they escaped, it later emerged as a result of a TV investigation that forensic evidence of a fingerprint which would have substantiated the boys' account was not revealed by the prosecution.

---

[100] SI 119/1987.

[101] *People (DPP) v Pringle* (22 May 1981, unreported), CCA, O'Higgins CJ; *People (DPP) v Lynch* [1982] IR 64.

[102] *People (DPP) v Pringle* [1995] 2 IR 547.

[103] *People (DPP) v Connell* [1995] 2 IR 244.

[104] *People (DPP) v Meleady & Grogan* [1995] 2 IR 517.

It was in recognition, perhaps, of these miscarriages of justice, as much as their more highly publicised counterparts in England, that the provision found in the Criminal Procedure Act 1993, s 10 requiring corroboration of confession evidence, was introduced, which provides 'where at the trial of a person evidence is given of a confession made by that person and that evidence is not corroborated, the Judge shall advise the jury to have due regard to the absence of corroboration.' (See Chapter 9 below).

[2.57] It is somewhat ironic that following the introduction of the Criminal Justice Act 1984 and its powers of detention in relation to 'ordinary' crime under s 4, the Irish Supreme Court in *DPP v Quilligan*[105] confirmed the lawfulness of the use of s 30 of the 1939 Act in relation to non-subversive crime. Nevertheless, the 1984 Act continued to be the main vehicle for powers of detention after arrest in the case of ordinary, 'non-subversive' related activities.[106]

[2.58] The change in relation to the function of arrest and the general facilitation of interrogation subsequent to arrest, can be identified as the beginning of the process of normalisation in Ireland. The focus of this work is not on the manner of that particular accommodation – other than to note its occurrence – so much as the ongoing effects of the existence of an 'extraordinary' regime within the jurisdiction, and in particular the more recent manifestations of exception. In other words, exceptional situations have proliferated and the concept of emergency or crisis has broadened beyond terrorism itself. Nonetheless, the purchase of terrorism is still effective and its usefulness to the State is not spent. This is evidenced by the augmentation of the powers of detention under s 30 by the Offences Against the State (Amendment) Act 1998, which allows for an additional 24-hour period of detention (72 hours in total) introduced in direct response to the Omagh bombing.[107] The Minister was reported as describing the provisions as 'draconian'. The Government statement in its response to Omagh, left open the option of internment, and in relation to measures which were introduced, stated '(t)he primary consideration in considering any case for amendment of the criminal law is to maximise its efficiency in tackling the

---

[105] *DPP v Quilligan* [1987] ILRM 600.

[106] In similar vein, the use of the Special Criminal Court, established under Part V of the 1939 Act and operating as a non-jury court despite the explicit guarantee to trial by jury under the Constitution, was accommodated out with the terrorist context, and in relation to non-subversive cases by the Supreme Court in *Kavanagh*.

[107] The Offences Against the State Act 1998 also introduced new offences of directing an unlawful organisation (s 6), possession of articles for purposes connected with certain offences (explosives, firearms) (s 7), unlawful collection of information (s 8) and training persons in the making or use of firearms (s 12).

activities of criminals.'[108] Several cabinet members, it was reported, were in fact in favour of the use of internment.[109] It was argued at the time (although not a generally held view) that such re-introduction of internment would be more honest than:

> ... further attempts to undermine the fundamental principles of our criminal justice system with the attendant risks of police brutality, forced confessions, miscarriages of justice, unacceptably long detention periods, abolition of the right to silence, the perversion of the rules of evidence and ultimately the discrediting of the legal system itself.[110]

[2.59] This legislation was due to lapse on 30 June 2000. Significantly, on the occasion of its renewal for a further year, the Minister reported to the Dáil that not a single prosecution had been brought under the Act and that the only provisions used were those relating to the extension of detention. This was used in 29 instances, none leading to a charge. Despite reference in the debates to the view of the Garda Commissioner that those responsible for Omagh were unlikely now to be discovered, the continuance of the legislation was approved for a further year.[111] There could hardly be greater evidence of the symbolic nature of such legislation in terms of effectiveness or of the state's appetite for continuance and extension beyond its remit.

[2.60] Under the Offences Against the State Act regime, an infringement on the right to silence existed by virtue of s 52 of the 1939 Act. The right to silence was nonetheless found to be constitutionally guaranteed under Art 38.1 in *Heaney v McGuinness*[112] by Costello J, who classified s 52 as a proportional infringement of that right of the accused. Such provision with regard to inferences from silence is now mirrored by ss 18 and 19 of the Criminal Justice Act 1984 (the constitutionality of which was upheld in *Rock v Ireland*[113]), and s 7 of the Criminal Justice (Drug Trafficking) Act 1996. The right to silence has been further eroded by the 1998 Act, ss 2 and 5, which allow inferences to be drawn from the failure of an accused to mention facts later relied on in his defence, while s 9 of the 1998 Act makes it an offence for a person to stay silent without a reasonable excuse, when he has information he knows or believes may be of

---

[108] (1998) *The Irish Times*, 20 August.

[109] (1998) *The Sunday Business Post*, 23 August, p 1.

[110] Hogan, 'Internment Preferable to Laws that Fail the Tests' (1998) *The Irish Times*, 19 August, p 14.

[111] The Minister expressly referred to garda advice as to the necessity for continuance of the legislation, and the desire to maintain the existing regime pending the Hederman review which would address the overall Offences against the State Acts regime, Dáil Debates Official Report 20-06-00. In accordance with the requirements of the 1998 Act, s 18(3), the Minister has to lay a report before the Dáil on the use of the legislation.

[112] *Heaney & McGuinness v Ireland & AG* [1994] 3 IR 593.

[113] *Rock v Ireland* [1998] 2 ILRM 35.

assistance to the gardaí. More recently, the Criminal Justice Act 2007 facilitated the widespread applicaton of inference from silence provisions.[114]

Drugs

[2.61] The legacy of the 'terrorist regime' was evident when the Minister for Justice, Nora Owen TD, pledged in 1995 in relation to 'major initiatives' (termed the 'New Government Measures to Combat Drugs') that the government would 'wage an all out fight against the drugs scourge', which she described as 'a threat to the very fabric of our society'. [115] The Minister stated that these were tough measures but described drug trafficking as 'a form of modern day terrorism' which attacks the very core of our society.[116] The press statement issued declared that the measures proposed an enhancement of Garda powers, though this must be proportionate at all times. The Minister concluded by stating:

> We must be prepared to wage the fight on the educational, health and law enforcement sides for as long as it takes. We are confronted by ruthless people who are destroying whole *communities* all over the world. We must face them down. [Emphasis added.][117]

---

[114] Criminal Justice Act 2007, Part 4.

[115] Nora Owen TD, in the press statement issued by Government Information Services on 19 July 1995. It is instructive to note that initially the locus of change here was the criminal justice system generally, and not the drugs problem simpliciter. The Criminal Justice Bill 1994, which might be seen as the precursor of what is now the Criminal Justice (Drug Trafficking) Act 1996, was introduced as a Private Members' Bill by Progressive Democrat TDs Liz O'Donnell and Michael McDowell. It proposed to increase existing infringements on an accused's right to silence (thus building on initial incursions introduced by the Criminal Justice Act 1984), amend the law in relation to bail and bring about a radical shift in emphasis from traditional criminal procedure in so far as the accused could be called upon to testify by the prosecution and might be interrogated in the District Court. Although this was a measure emanating from a small political party with a perceived right-wing orientation, it is illustrative of the level of cross-party support and indeed pressure for a 'law and order' approach.

[116] The use of 'war-like' terminology in this area continues as a theme: *The First Annual Report of the Department of Justice, Equality and Law Reform* (1997), p 7, comments that the state agencies are 'in the battle against crime'; and the press release issued by the Department of Justice, Equality and Law Reform on the launch of the *First Report of the Expert Group on Probation and Welfare Services* by the Minister for Justice John O'Donoghue, states: 'We are winning the war against crime, crime levels are down.' http://www.irgov.ie/justice/ Press%20releases/Press.htm.

[117] *First Report of the Expert Group on Probation and Welfare Services*. At that stage, the key measures to combat drugs were to include: interagency co-operation, and increased powers to include the amendment of the Criminal Justice Act 1984 so as to allow the Gardaí, on the certification of a Chief Superintendent, to detain a person suspected of drug trafficking for a period of 24 hours initially and, if necessary, for a further period up to a maximum of an additional 72 hours if satisfied that this is necessary and, upon further request, may permit a final extension to the detention period for up to a maximum of a further 48 hours, if satisfied that this is necessary. (contd/)

[2.62] The Criminal Justice Act 1984 was to be the vehicle for the introduction of these extended powers of detention subsequent to arrest. This was not a novel function for that particular piece of legislation, which, as seen in 1984, introduced the first power of detention after arrest in relation to 'ordinary' crime. Although the Criminal Justice (Drug Trafficking) Bill 1996, when ultimately introduced, contained a power of arrest and detention in its own right, and not an amendment of s 4 of the 1984 Act, the initial connection is interesting, not least for the historical connection with the 'terrorist' power under s 30, which might be said to have honed police powers of investigation by interrogation in Ireland, but also because of the particular crisis or context in which the 1984 Act was itself introduced.

[2.63] The process of change and normalisation can be seen to culminate in the drugs context with the introduction of further and extensive powers of detention, search and confiscation of assets, by virtue of the so-called 'crime-package'.[118] The measures introduced included the following: increased powers of detention – up to seven days – together with garda power to issue search warrants in certain circumstances provided for under the Criminal Justice Drug Trafficking Act 1996; broad powers of search under the Criminal Assets Bureau Act 1996 (s 14), which established the Bureau and allowed for the issuance of search warrants by certain of its officers; and provision for the issuance of production orders, and increased powers relating to the proceeds of crime, enabling confiscation of proceeds of crime independent of conviction introduced under the Proceeds of Crime Act 1996 (this was to lead to constitutional challenge – see *Gilligan v Criminal Assets Bureau*[119]). The Disclosure of Information for Taxation and Other Purposes Act 1996 also amended and extended an earlier

---

[117] (\contd) There was also to be extension of responsibility for the issue of search warrants in drug-trafficking cases to a Garda Superintendent, new structures and demand reduction/ education measures.

It is an indication of the overall tenor of the response and its perception that on 22 November 1995 the *The Irish Times*, in a report in relation to the new Drugs Bill, mentioned simply the tough measures which were to be introduced to combat drug trafficking and which were said to have been given priority by the government. The measures mentioned were the increased powers of detention for gardaí, which would mean that suspects could be detained for up to seven days, a judge having to authorise detention after 48 hours. There was also mention of the Garda Superintendent's power to issue search warrants under the Bill, and that the Naval Officers were also to be given new powers of search and seizure and arrest under orders made under the Criminal Justice Act 1994. There was no mention of the alternative measures to combat the drugs problem, simply the law enforcement ones.

[118] The legislation in relation to drugs and organised crime, referred to as the 'Crime Package', was introduced in the aftermath of the Veronica Guerin murder and guillotined through on a recall of the Dáil. It met with a stultifying cross-party consensus.

[119] *Gilligan v Criminal Assets Bureau* [1998] 3 IR 185.

Disclosure of Information for Taxation and Other Purposes Act 1996 to allow for wider use of information obtained under money-laundering provisions of that Act.

[2.64] The drugs scenario also saw the birth of the state's first Witness Protection Programme. The Witness Protection Programme was established by the government in November 1997[120] to be administered entirely by An Garda Síochána. Announcing the scheme, the Minister for Justice, Mr O'Donoghue, said, 'the new breed of ruthless and well-organised criminals, particularly in drugs and money-laundering showed the need for new measures'. Issues surrounding criminal convictions on the ground of the uncorroborated evidence of accomplices have subsequently arisen in the cases of *Holland*, *Ward* and *Meehan*.[121] It is also true to say that the spectre of the supergrass phenomenon, in the context of terrorism in Northern Ireland, hangs over these cases and is reinforced by the fact that these cases take place in the non-jury Special Criminal Court. The legal issues arising are central to the heart of pre-trial and trial justice and include those of access to a lawyer, recording of interviews, treatment during detention, admissibility of statements and accomplice evidence.[122] The manner of their resolution raises the question of the relationship between legislative change and judicial monitoring of criminal justice principles, together with the ongoing implications of exceptional provisions and their ring-fencing. The accommodation of exceptional provision and its implication for overall principle can be usefully pursued through the language of these judgments and their conclusions.

[2.65] Section 2 of the Criminal Justice (Drug Trafficking) Act 1996 provides for powers of detention of the order of 6 hours followed by a further period (directed by a garda not below the rank of Chief Superintendent) of 18 hours if he has reasonable grounds for believing that such further detention is necessary for the proper investigation of the offence concerned. He can then further sanction a period of 24 hours on the same basis. At this point, application can be made by an officer, not below the rank of Chief Superintendent, to a Circuit Court or District Court judge for a warrant authorising detention of the person

---

[120] See (1997) *The Irish Times*, 7 November.

[121] *DPP v Holland* (15 June 1998, unreported), CCA Barrington J; *DPP v Ward* (27 November 1998, unreported), SCC (Barr J); (22 March 2002, unreported), CCA (Murphy J; *DPP v Brian Meehan* (29 July 1999, unreported), SCC.

[122] In terms of consistency or coherence in the non-jury court, it is interesting to note that in *DPP v Brian Meehan* (29 July 1999, unreported), SCC Charles Bowden, one of several state Witness Protection Programme witnesses whose testimony formed the state's case against Meehan, and whose testimony alone had been the basis of Ward's earlier conviction, was found to be entirely incredible.

detained for a further period of 72 hours if he has reasonable grounds for believing that such further investigation is necessary for the proper investigation of the offence concerned. This may be authorised if the judge is satisfied that such further detention is necessary and that the investigation is being conducted diligently and expeditiously. A further period of 48 hours can again be authorised on application to a judge if the officer has reasonable grounds for believing such is necessary for the proper investigation of the offence concerned and the investigation is being conducted diligently and expeditiously. In total, a person can be detained for a maximum period of 168 hours (one week) under the terms of the Act. The reason for the judicial intervention after 48 hours is to ensure compliance with the European Convention of Human Rights, found to mandate same in the context of the *Brogan* case relating to the Prevention of Terrorism Act in the United Kingdom. The detention provisions under the drug trafficking legislation were to be renewed every two years by resolution of the Houses of the Oireachtas. The Criminal Justice Act 2009, s 22(4), however, removed that need ensuring these provisions would now operate indefinitely. Their application is similarly broadened by the inclusion of their application to serious offences and organised crime offences.

[2.66] Section 8 of the Drug Trafficking Act 1996 provides for the issuance of search warrants by a member of An Garda Síochána, not below the rank of Superintendent, under s 26 of the 1977 Act, where he is satisfied:

    (a)   that the warrant is necessary for the proper investigation of the suspected drug trafficking offence, and

    (b)   that circumstances of urgency giving rise to the need for the immediate issue of the search warrant would render it impracticable to apply to a District Court judge or Peace Commissioner.

[2.67] The Criminal Assets Bureau was given similarly broad powers to issue search warrants (under s 14 of the Criminal Assets Bureau Act 1996) and was equipped with powers to seize assets suspected of being the proceeds of crime. The powers to issue warrants without judicial intervention is unusual, with precedent only in the Offences Against the State context, and in stark contrast to a series of higher Irish court decisions underscoring the importance of the judicial role in the issuance of search warrants and their invalidity in the case of rubberstamping police suspicions (*DPP v Kenny* and *DPP v Yamanoha*[123]).

[2.68] The Proceeds of Crime Act 1996, ss 2 and 3, permit the High Court to make orders preventing someone from dealing with specified property worth not less than £10,000 (€12,697.38). It must be shown that the property represents the proceeds of crime (the civil standard applying). When the order is made, the

---

[123] *DPP v Kenny* [1990] ILRM 569; *DPP v Yamanoha* [1994] 1 IR 565.

respondent bears the onus of proof to establish the property is not the 'proceeds of crime' in order to have the court discharge or vary the order. Once an order has been in place for seven years, the High Court can make a disposal order transferring all rights in the property to the Minister for Finance. The concept of 'proceeds of crime' is defined very broadly in s 1 of the 1996 Act as 'any property obtained or received at any time (before or after the passing of the Act) by or as a result of or in connection with, the commission of an offence'. This Act had a precursor in the Disclosure of Information for Taxation and Other Purposes Act 1996, but augments previous powers included in the 1994 piece of legislation in so far as a conviction is not now required as the basis for forfeiture, and a burden of disclosure is placed on a greater number of professionals.

[2.69] The Criminal Justice Act 1999, signed into law on 26 May 1999, contained further provisions particularly targeted at the area of drugs. Part 2 of the 1999 Act, which came immediately into effect, created a new offence of possession of drugs with intent to supply with a value of £10,000 (€12,697.38) or more, with a minimum mandatory 10-year sentence, which signified, according to Minister O'Donoghue, that 'there is no room for complacency, the Act is further evidence of the Government's zero tolerance approach to crime'.[124]

[2.70] Part 6 of the 1999 Act also came into operation immediately and contained provisions dealing with the intimidation of witnesses. The provisions (similar to those in operation for victims of sexual offences under the Criminal Evidence Act 1992) allow intimidated or vulnerable witnesses to give evidence by video-link and provide further evidence of the facility for expansion of exceptional provisions. A new statutory offence of intimidation of witnesses, jurors etc, with a penalty of up to ten years, was created, as well as a new offence, with a penalty of up to five years, of attempting to track down witnesses who have been relocated under the Witness Protection Scheme.

The Bail Amendment to the Constitution

[2.71] The background to the Constitutional amendment on bail was the announcement in September 1995 of an increase in crime rates in Dublin of 8%. The immediate response of the Fianna Fáil spokesperson on justice, John O'Donoghue, was to urge Nora Owen, the then Minister for Justice, to urgently bring forward what she had already proposed: a referendum which would allow refusal of bail if the gardaí and the judge in question thought the individual was likely to commit crime while on bail.[125]

---

[124] (1999) *The Irish Times*, 27 May 'Ten year mandatory drug term from today' Jim Cusack, p 9.

[125] See editorial, 'Bail Reform: Expediency Before Principle' (1995) 13 (10) ILT 223. In the event, the killing of Veronica Guerin also had an input, as that journalist was on record as wanting a change in the bail laws.

[2.72] Article 40.4.1° of the Constitution provides that no one shall be deprived of liberty save in accordance with law. Under Irish law, prior to the Sixteenth Amendment to the Constitution,[126] there were only two grounds on which a person could be refused bail:

(a)   the likelihood that the accused will not turn up for trial; and

(b)   the likelihood that he will interfere with witnesses or evidence.

[2.73] That these were the only grounds on which bail could be refused was stated by the Supreme Court in *O'Callaghan*[127] and confirmed by the Supreme Court in *Ryan v DPP*.[128] The Sixteenth Amendment would widen the grounds for refusal considerably. It would provide that someone charged with a serious offence could be refused bail where it was reasonably considered necessary to prevent the commission of a serious offence – serious offences included those meriting five years of imprisonment or more, thereby including most criminal offences. The criteria or matters to be taken into account by the court in deciding whether to grant bail to an accused charged with one of these offences are the following:

(i)   the nature and degree of seriousness of the offence charged and the potential penalty;

(ii)   the nature and degree of seriousness of the offence apprehended and the potential penalty;

(iii)   the conviction of the accused in respect of an offence committed while on bail on a previous occasion;

(iv)   any previous conviction of the accused;

(vi)   any other offence in respect of which the accused is charged and awaiting trial;

(vii)   the nature and strength of the evidence in support of the charge; and

(viii)   whether the accused has a substance addiction.

---

[126] The Sixteenth Amendment stated: 'Provision may be made by law for the refusal of bail by a court to a person charged with a serious offence where it is reasonably considered necessary to prevent the commission of a serious offence by that person.' This was an 'enabling' provision in the Constitution to be followed by a separate Bill indicating the terms on which bail could be refused. The amendment was passed and the implementing legislation, the Bail Act 1997, enacted in May 1997. The 1997 Act came into full effect by way of the Bail Act 1997 (Commencement) Order 2000 (SI 118/2000). The Rules of the Superior Courts (Bail Applications) 2004 (SI 811/2004) amended the Rules of the Superior Courts, Ord 81, rule 15(1) to provide for the basis on which application shall be made to the High Court regarding bail applications.

[127] *People (AG) v O'Callaghan* [1966] IR 501.

[128] *Ryan v DPP* [1989] IR 399.

Should an accused be refused bail, and where the trial has not commenced within four months, the court could order his release if satisfied that the 'interests of justice' required it. Once again it was left to the judiciary to finesse that equation.

[2.74] Finlay CJ in *Ryan* had stated the proper methods of preventing crime were the long-established combination of police surveillance, speedy trial and deterrent sentences. As an example of the latter he instanced s 11 of the Criminal Justice Act 1984, which provides for consecutive sentences for offences committed while on bail. Since its introduction, the latter had been somewhat stymied as the courts had taken the opportunity to suspend that sentence, by looking at the proportionality of the totality of the sentence in relation to the crime. The Law Reform Commission[129] had earlier been asked by the government to examine the law on bail (but not make recommendations) and had put forward alternative strategies such as an offence of breaching bail conditions, attaching a good behaviour condition to bail, estreatment of bail if the accused commits a further offence, as well as reduction of delay and the implementation of s 11.

[2.75] With regard to the argument that under current conditions, criminals on bail could re-offend with impunity and be unlikely to receive greater sentences, the Commission had commented that:

> ... this argument ... prescribes stronger medicine than is warranted by the disease. If Judges do not punish offenders adequately for bail offences, it may be argued that the appropriate solution is that they should so punish them, not that offenders be preventatively detained to prevent these offences.[130]

[2.76] The Constitutional Review Group in its report[131] had pointed out that art 5 of the European Convention on Human Rights provides for an exhaustive enumeration of the categories of deprivation of liberty. It noted that these correspond broadly with the categories of detention authorised by Irish law except in two respects: Irish legislation provides for internment and, in some cases, the Convention permits preventive detention.[132] The Constitutional

---

[129] *Report on an Examination of the Law on Bail* (LRC 50-1995). The Commission was asked in February 1994 to undertake examination of, and conduct research in relation to, the law on bail but was not asked to formulate and submit proposals for reform.

[130] *Report on an Examination of the Law on Bail* (LRC 50-1995), p 166.

[131] *Report of the Constitution Review Group* (Government of Ireland, 1996).

[132] The power of internment they note is conferred by the Offences Against the State (Amendment) Act 1940, which came into law following reference to the Supreme Court by the President as to its constitutionality (an almost identical provision had been struck down by Gavan Duffy J in *State (Burke) v Lennon* [1940] IR 136 the year before). (contd/)

Review Group noted that pre-trial preventive detention expressly contemplated by art 5(1) had been held to be inconsistent with the provisions of the Constitution in *O'Callaghan* and *Ryan*.[133] It noted that a switch to an art 5(1)(c) type provision 'would result in a lessening of the general protection of the right to individual liberty in the circumstances'[134] and recommended no change.

[2.77] Prior to the amendment campaign, therefore, neither the Constitutional Review Group nor the Law Reform Commission (albeit that the latter had not been asked for a recommendation) evidenced a need for a change in the law. Pre-amendment judicial statements with regard to bail gave an insight into judicial views on its position within our system, and so helped assess the effect of the proposed change.

[2.78] In *O'Callaghan*[135] Ó Dálaigh CJ stated in response to the argument that there should be such further grounds for refusal of bail:

> The reasoning underlying this submission, is in my opinion, a denial of the whole basis of our system of law. It transcends respect for the requirement that a man shall be considered innocent until he is found guilty and seeks to punish him in respect of offences neither completed nor attempted. I say 'punish' for deprivation of liberty must be considered a punishment unless it can be required to ensure that an accused person will stand his trial when called upon.[136]

[2.79] Walsh J also emphasised that the sole purpose of bail was to secure the attendance of the accused at his trial, as '[t]he presumption of innocence is a very real thing and is not simply a procedural rule taking effect only at the trial.'[137] Walsh J emphatically rejected the likelihood of committing further offences as a reason for refusing bail, which he saw as 'a form of preventative justice which has no place in our legal system'.

[2.80] In *Ryan v DPP*,[138] upholding the decision in *O'Callaghan*, Finlay CJ (Walsh, Griffin and Hederman JJ agreeing) stated that an intention to commit a

---

[132] (\contd) It was deemed constitutional and, on one view, remains unassailable by virtue of the provisions of Art 34.3.3° of the Constitution. Some doubt is expressed in the Constitutional Review Group's Report as to the decision, as it is a decision of the old Supreme Court (see further Report, p 282). However, an Art 15 derogation could 'save' such internment, as happened when Ireland reintroduced internment in 1957, which event was reviewed by the Court of Human Rights in the *Lawless* case. (*Lawless v Ireland* (1961) 1 EHRR 15.)

[133] *People (AG) v O'Callaghan* [1966] IR 501; *Ryan v DPP* [1989] IR 399.

[134] *Lawless v Ireland* (1961) 1 EHRR 15 at 283.

[135] *The People (AG) v O'Callaghan* [1966] IR 501.

[136] *The People (AG) v O'Callaghan* [1966] IR 501 at 508–509.

[137] *The People (AG) v O'Callaghan* [1966] IR 501 at 513.

[138] *Ryan v DPP* [1989] IR 399.

crime is not itself a crime unless furthered by overt acts or converted by agreement with others into a conspiracy:

> The criminalising of mere intention has been usually a badge of an oppressive or unjust system. The proper methods of preventing crime are the long-established combination of police surveillance, speedy trial and deterrent sentences. Section 11 ... constitutes a good example of such a deterrent.[139]

McCarthy J stated that if a person were to be denied his liberty because of a well-founded suspicion, there was:

> '... no logical reason why any other citizen, not so charged, might not be detained upon a similar contention supported by similarly impressive evidence. The pointing finger of accusation, not of crime done, but of crime feared, would become the test. Such appears to me to be far from a balancing of constitutional rights; it is a recalibration of the scales of justice.[140]

It would seem that the judiciary firmly espoused the cause of individual rights, seeing the limited grounds for restriction of bail as fundamental to the Irish system of criminal justice.

[2.81] By contrast, in terms of the construction of the 'public voice' on the matter of the bail amendment, government speech and lobbyist voices in the run up to the referendum placed the option before the people of whether they chose protection of the accused's rights in the face of, or as opposed to, the community's need to prevent crime.[141] As a result of the Supreme Court judgment in *McKenna*[142] in November 1995, it was unconstitutional for the

---

[139] *Ryan v DPP* [1989] IR 399 at 407.

[140] *Ryan v DPP* [1989] IR 399 at 410.

[141] One representative of the victims' association stated the case thus: 'Victims of crime will see the introduction of the bail amendment as an acknowledgement of their plight. It will also represent a hopeful sign that after years of marginalisation, the rights of crime victims are moving towards the centre-stage. (Keaveney, 'Victims of Crime also have Right to Justice' (1996) *The Irish Times*, 20 November.) The *The Irish Times* in its editorial of 14 October 1996 recognised the 'right to bail' had been one of the fundamental freedoms of this jurisdiction over the last 30 years, but stated that concerns about same must be 'set against public unease about crime and criminality'. By contrast, the Irish Commission for Justice and Peace (a commission of the Irish Catholic Bishops Conference) calling for a 'no' vote, tailored their argument to try to persuade victims by making reference to the lack of prison spaces available. ('The Bail Referendum: Adequacy and Costs of Proposed Additional Prison Accommodation' statement issued on 26 November 1996). In a similar vein the Irish Council for Civil Liberties' *Position Paper on the Forthcoming Bail Referendum* (1996) pointed out that the Law Reform Commission had found that, despite the powers of the English courts to remove from circulation persons who might re-offend on bail, the percentage of offences committed by persons on bail for both 1992 and 1993 was at 9%, lower than its English equivalent.

[142] *In the matter of Bunreacht na hÉireann: Patricia McKenna v An Taoiseach and Others* [1995] 2 IR 10.

government to spend public moneys in a referendum advocating a particular result. An ad hoc Commission on Referendum Information was therefore established for the purposes of informing the public and took out advertisements in national newspapers, advocating the cases for and against the amendment.[143]

[2.82] In favour of the amendment, under the heading 'The Amendment will give Greater Protection to the Public', it was stated: 'There is ... a public demand for changes in criminal law and procedure and the Amendment will help to restore the balance between the rights of victims and the rights of those charged with crime.' The opposition of accused and victim is neatly effected. A later statement that '[t]he proposal is a carefully balanced and reasonable measure under which it will be necessary for the court to be satisfied of the risk to society posed by an accused person before bail is refused' made the further opposition between society and the accused clear.[144]

[2.83] The statement of the case against the Amendment commenced with the heading: 'The Amendment will Breach a Fundamental Principle of Justice.' This was followed by the statement: 'Every person is presumed innocent until, after a valid trial, such person is found guilty. This simple statement, so well known to everybody, is a fundamental principle of justice both constitutional and natural.' The right is clearly stated here as an individual right, which is not related directly to the public as important in their terms.

Under the next heading, 'The Crucial Importance of Bail', the section commenced: 'Fundamental principles of liberty are involved in the law of bail. The right to bail is that right which every accused has to personal liberty until his/her trial.' Once again, the right is that of the accused, not related to the public or society. The remainder of the argument set out the consequences if the

---

[143] *Referendum on a Proposal to Amend the Constitution in Relation to Bail* published in the Provincial papers 18–22 November 1996; national daily and evening papers on 21 November 1996; *Foinse* (in Irish only), *Sunday Independent*, *The Sunday Business Post*, *The Sunday Tribune* and *Sunday World* on 24 November 1996. The Minister for the Environment, Mr Brendan Howlin TD, requested the Chairman of the Bar Council to nominate two Senior Counsel, one of whom, Mr Sean Ryan, prepared the statement of the case in favour of the proposed constitutional amendment and the other, Mr Edward Comyn, the case against.

[144] It is then declared that: 'The Amendment complies with international Standards and makes Common Sense' and the statement concludes: 'The question is not an ideological one but is basically a matter of common sense. The proposal does not dictate that bail will be refused in any particular case. It just gives the court the capacity to refuse it if the accused is likely to commit serious crime while awaiting trial. The State has an obligation to protect people against individuals who persistently re-offend while on bail.' Once again the identification is made between state and people, and their opposition with the individual underscored. The appeal to common sense and denial of ideology would seem both duplicitous and worrisome.

amendment was passed – solely in terms of repercussions for the accused and prison places – and stated the amendment to be unnecessary. No public or community dimension to the (individual) right was acknowledged. Moreover, quiescent in the case made in favour of the Amendment, is the assumption that the current charges were validly laid – hence as Kieselbach points out, '[p]redicating detention on the basis of this assumed validity is inconsistent with the presumption of innocence ... charges [are] turned into evidence that the accused [is] guilty or would soon be guilty of something else.'[145]

[2.84] It would seem to be clear from the enunciation of the case for and against the Amendment in relation to bail, that the construction of a division between the individual (accused) and society (victim) in this context completely overwhelms and dominates the arguments, such that the public, on reading same, perceive its interests as on one side rather than the other. This implicit sacrifice of individual rights for the greater good involves, according to Von Hirsh:

> ... cost-benefit thinking [which] is wholly inappropriate here. If a system of preventative incarceration is known systematically to generate mistaken confinements, then it is unacceptable in absolute terms because it violates the obligation of society to do individual justice. Such a system cannot be justified by arguing that its aggregate social benefits exceed the aggregate amount of injustice done to mistakenly confined individuals.[146]

[2.85] It was not all that surprising that the Amendment passed on 28 November 28 1996. Given the urgency with which the amendment was presented, it is insightful, however, that the implementing legislation, the Bail Act 1997, was not enacted until May 1997, and the provisions were not brought fully into effect until May 2000.[147] Despite that fact, the first reported use of the Bail Act 1997 was in October 1999, when it was reported as having been invoked to refuse bail in the case of individuals caught at a 'Real IRA' training camp where gardaí had

---

[145] Kieselbach, 'Pre-trial Criminal Procedure and Preventative Detention and the Presumption of Innocence' (1989) 31 Crim LQ 168.

[146] Von Hirsh, 'Prediction of Criminal Conduct and Preventive Confinement of Convicted Persons' (1972) 21 Buffalo LR 717 at 740.

[147] At the Fianna Fáil Ard Fheis on 3 March 2000, the Minister announced that the Act would be brought into effect in its entirety on 15 May 2000. The Minister's speech made the point that the 'Government's unprecedented prison building programme where over 1,200 additional prison spaces have to date been provided' made it possible for him to bring this 'key anti-crime measure' into force. 'O'Donoghue Announces Bail Act to Come into Force on 15 May next' (2000) Press Release, 3 March. The Minister for Justice signed the commencement order to implement the Bail Referendum on 4 May 2000. See Cleary, 'Minister Warned over Bail Law' (2000) *The Sunday Tribune*, 2 July, p 4.

discovered guns and ammunition.[148] O'Higgins J, presiding in the Special Criminal Court, was reported to have refused bail on the grounds that the accused would not have turned up for their trial and that he believed they would commit further offences if granted bail. The former is in fact the original pre-amendment basis for refusal of bail which was effective here solely, as the Amendment could not have been invoked, not having been brought into law. Yet the interpretation of what had occurred in the public context – and indeed judicially referenced – was the essence of what had been passed through the Amendment, even though the latter was merely of appearance and not of substantive effect. There could hardly be better manifestation of the symbolic role of the Amendment or legislation. In terms of the ostensible use of the new power, the case was moreover a 'terrorist' one connected with a recent atrocity, always suitable for invocation of extraordinary measures.

Further and continuing extension of exceptional provision

[2.86] On the occasion of each of these legislative changes, whether introduced in the context of drugs or terrorism, the language of the media, politicians and protagonist representatives is similar. The unanimity can be chilling. The suggestion that exceptional provision, once introduced, will find a host of new justifications for its continued presence – outside its originating rationale – is further supported by the expansion of the ambit of many of these provisions, envisaged by the *Report of the Expert Group on Criminal Law*.[149] The Expert Group was established arising out of the recommendations in the Report of the Steering Group on the Effectiveness of the Garda Síochána (the Garda SMI Report) to consider the changes in the criminal law recommended therein with particular reference to the Constitutional and European Convention on Human Rights implications.[150] One such recommendation endorsed by the Expert Group was that in all circumstances of immediate urgency, a garda, not below the rank of Superintendent, be able to issue a search warrant (which would expire after 24 hours). This mirrors previous provision under the Offences Against the State Act

---

[148] 'Bail for Seven Men on Meath arms charges is Refused Under 1977 (sic) Act' (1999) *The Irish Times*, 28 October. Detective Chief Superintendent Walsh said the seven were members of the 'Real IRA', which was responsible for the Omagh bombing and dedicated to bringing down the peace process in Northern Ireland. Chief Superintendent Walsh was reported as having invoked the provisions in the Bail Act to refuse bail where the gardaí believe an accused might commit further offences if granted bail.

[149] *Report of the Expert Group on Criminal Law Appointed to consider changes in the Criminal Law which were recommended in the Garda SMI Report Department of Justice* 25 November 1998.

[150] The Garda SMI Report Department of Justice November 1997 – Section 4 Legal Framework contained the recommended changes to the criminal law to enhance Garda efficiency and effectiveness.

1939,[151] subsequently followed in the Criminal Justice (Drug Trafficking) Act 1996.

[2.87] The Expert Group also concluded that the 12-hour period of detention consequent on arrest under the Criminal Justice Act 1984 is 'inadequate for the proper investigation of murder, rape or other serious offences', and recommended a provision similar to s 30 of the Offences Against the State Act 1939 for specified serious offences to include murder, manslaughter, kidnapping, false imprisonment and rape.

[2.88] With regard to the right to silence, the Expert Group's recommendation was that the provisions of the Criminal Justice (Drug Trafficking) Act 1996, relating to the right to silence, be extended to all serious offences. (It noted that this had already been done in relation to a number of offences in the Offences Against the State (Amendment) Act 1998.) Where a defendant relied on a fact in his defence which he could reasonably have been expected to mention on being questioned, such adverse inferences as may appear proper may be drawn from a failure to mention it (this could corroborate other evidence but not suffice for a conviction).[152]

[2.89] The Expert Group in considering each of the Steering Group's recommendations stated that in accordance with its terms of reference it was conscious of the need to balance additional powers with appropriate safeguards, and considered each recommendation having regard

> "to the implications for it of the Constitution and the European Convention on Human Rights and to the effect it would have on the balance between the rights of the individual and the common good."[153]

---

[151] Offences Against the State Act 1939, s 29, permits a member of An Garda Síochána not below the rank of Superintendent to issue a 'search order' to search any place if there is reasonable ground for supposing an offence under that Act has been, or is about to be, committed.

[152] Although not particularly related to a given exceptional provision under consideration here as related to emergency provisions, but rather part of the generalised trend towards 'law and order' powers, it is interesting to note with regard to search warrants the Group recommended that the Criminal Justice (Miscellaneous Provisions) Act 1997, s 10 — which provides for the issuance of a warrant by a District Court Judge authorising a garda to search a place for evidence of certain offences, and which currently applies only to a limited number of serious offences (indictable offences involving death or serious injury, false imprisonment, rape and certain other sexual offences) — be extended to all criminal offences punishable by five years' imprisonment or more. Other recommendations of the group relate to seizure of evidence, power to arrest, crime scene preservation (ie parades, fingerprinting and forensic evidence) and station bail.

[153] *Report of the Expert Group on Criminal Law Appointed to consider changes in the Criminal Law which were recommended in the Garda SMI Report Department of Justice* 25 November 1998 at p 1.

In this regard it recommended video-taping of interviews in garda custody or the right of a suspect to have a solicitor present during questioning.[154] These proposals have been implemented in the Criminal Justice Act 2006, Pt 2, s 9 of which amends s 4 of the Criminal Justice Act 1984 by the addition of a further 12 hours' additional detention on a Chief Superintendent's sanction. This brings the 'normal' regime into line with the 'extraordinary'. The 2006 Act also provides for the seizure and retention of evidence and for the admissibility of certain prior witness statements (Part 3). In Part 7 it creates new offences in relation to the concept of 'organised crime'. The Criminal Justice Act 2007 extends inference provisions to all crimes, with the caveat of safeguard provisions requiring video surveillance of interrogation and access to a lawyer, thereby copper fastening the facilitative role of lawyers in securing extensive garda powers.

[2.90] With regard to the operation of non-jury trial in Ireland – which as noted has implications in particular for the effective operation of rules of evidence predicated on the division of friction between arbiter of fact (jury) and law (judge) – the future of the Special Criminal Court would seem secure. The Hederman Committee,[155] in reviewing the continued operation of the non-jury court, sanctioned the centralising of the non-jury court in the criminal justice system proper. The majority of that Committee found justification for its

---

[154] On 4 August 1999 the Minister announced government approval to introduce a nationwide scheme of electronic recording of garda questioning of detained persons. This followed the recommendations of a Committee chaired by Esmond Smyth J which had been monitoring and evaluating a pilot scheme of both audio and audio/video recording of garda questioning of detainees in selected garda stations for a number of years. The Smyth Committee recommended only one exception to recording: where it is considered absolutely necessary by An Garda Síochána to obtain confidential information in life-threatening situations. The scheme was to be introduced over 12–18 months and operate in accordance with existing regulations, ie the Criminal Justice Act 1984 (Electronic Recording of Interviews) Regulations 1997. The time lag indicated by the year of the Act was significant, as was the very different context into which the regulations now become operative. The 'Third Report of the Steering Committee on Audio and Audio/Video Recording of Garda Questioning of Detained Persons' (Sept 2004) notes that although there are in excess of 700 Garda Stations countrywide only 167 have detention facilities and are used to interview and detain people. Therefore it was never the intention that all stations be equipped. (para 2.21) The report points out (at para 2.2.3) that at that time 229 interview rooms in 132 Grada stations are so equipped and in use which the Committee was assured was sufficient to ensure all interviews as specified in the Regulations are recorded. (www.justice.ie/en/AudioVidoReport.pdf/files/AudioVideoReport.pdf).

[155] See Reports of the Committee to Review the Offences Against the State Acts 1939-1998 and related matters chaired by Mr Justice Hederman: Interim Report – The Special Criminal Court June 2001; Report of the Committee to Review the Offences Against the State Acts 1939–1998 and related matters May 2002.

continued maintenance, even in the absence of a 'terrorist' threat.[156] Despite assurances that the then Minister for Justice, Michael McDowell, was on record as wanting to maintain jury trial as much as possible, and specifically not introducing non-jury trial in fraud cases, it would seem the Irish Special Criminal Court is not so 'special', despite the disappearance of its originating rationale.[157] The recent Criminal Justice (Amendment) Act 2009 (s 8) extending its remit to all gangland/organised crime secures this notion.

[2.91] The Criminal Justice (Amendment) Act 2009 makes certain changes to detention provisions generally which are of interest here.

With regard to powers of detention:

Part 4 of that Act makes amendments to the following pieces of legislation and their respective detention provisions:

---

[156] See Interim Report – The Special Criminal Court June 2001 para 7.9 *et seq*. The Committee's final report Report of the Committee to Review the Offences Against the State Acts 1939-1998 and related matters May 2002 endorses that view (with the minority of Professors Walsh, Binchy and Judge Hederman dissenting). Regarding the issue as to whether the ordinary courts are capable of dealing with organised crime, according to the Committee's Interim Report: 'Recent experience has shown that juries have been made to feel distinctly uncomfortable in dealing with certain cases involving organised crime'. Hederman, para 7.4. They refer to *DPP v Special Criminal Court* [1999] 1 IR 60, where Carney J alluded to their ability to maintain a 'wall of silence' by resort to any means, including murder. There is also reference to 'instances' (not specified) where 'attempts have been made to tamper with juries in high-profile criminal trials in ordinary courts.' Hederman, para 7.7. Referencing in the reasoning process by the majority to Carney J in *Ward*; and Charleton & McDermott, 'Constitutional Aspects of Non-Jury Courts' (2000) 6 Bar Rev 106 (Part 1), 142 (Part II) (at para 7.5), facilitates a decision-making process here which reflects a consensus regarding the challenge posed to the ordinary courts by organised crime.

[157] Coulter, 'Minister with a Mission to Push Through Reform of the System' (2002) *The Irish Times*, July 13, p 8. Minister McDowell was also quoted as stating in a radio interview on RTÉ radio on 30 June 2002 that he did not believe in deviating from jury trial 'except where it is absolutely necessary' and that the protection for juries should be strengthened where necessary. He went on to state that the non-jury Special Criminal Court should 'remain for the time being because there is a very significant subversive threat still in existence in this state, and anybody who thinks that they have gone away, you know, is very mistaken.' Haughey, 'McDowell Disturbed that Tribunal is Needed to Investigate Donegal Gardaí' (2002) *The Irish Times*, 1 July, p 6. This interview occurred in the aftermath of statements by a retiring judge, Barr J, who had presided over the Special Criminal Court for 15 years. On retirement he made the point that he was not asked for his opinion by the Committee and argued that the government should consult the judiciary before making a decision. He pointed to the US where even Mafia leaders are convicted by juries who can be anonymous or located in a different place. He also raised the possibility of non-jury trials in particular cases, for the benefit of the accused, instancing the hypothetical case of a person charged with a vicious sexual assault of a child that ends in murder where a huge public outcry ensues. A jury may, because of the passions surrounding the case, decide to ignore any element of doubt. Breslin, 'Court Awaits Committee's Judgment' (2002) *The Irish Examiner*, 1 July, p 17.

(i)   The Offences Against the State Act 1939 (which provides for a 48 hour period of detention with Garda authorisation); is now to have a further 24 hours subject to judicial authorisation;

(ii)   The Criminal Justice (Drug Trafficking) Act 1996 (which provides for 48 hours with Garda authorisation, with a further 120 hours on judicial authorisation); now allows a Superintendent (not Chief Superintendent) to authorise beyond 6 up to 48 hours;

(iii)   The Criminal Justice Act 2007 (which provides for 48 hours with Garda authorisation; a further 120 hours on judicial authorisation in related to certain serious offences); now allows detention in relation to organised crime offences under that Act; and

(iv)   The Criminal Justice Act 1984 (which provides for up to 24 hour detention with Garda authorisation) will not count as part of that detention any periods connected with making a habeas corpus application or to attend hospital;

(v)   Section 21(1)(a) of the 2009 Act also amends s 30 and s 30A of the 1939 Act by inserting a new sub-s 3A to provide that a person detained under s 30 may continue to be detained for an offence other than the offence to which the detention originally related. (The other provisions such as the Criminal Justice (Drug Trafficking Act) 1996 and the 2007 Criminal Justice Act already had that provision).

[2.92] The Criminal Justice (Amendment) Act 2009 also makes a number of changes to the procedure for applying for an extension to detention. These apply to all the detention provisions above but will be examined in the context of the changes for the section 30 detention. The application can be heard other than in public at judicial discretion, with attendance limited to persons directly concerned with the application and officers of the court and bona fide representatives of the press; and certain information can be disclosed in the absence of the suspect and legal representative where this is under s 21(1)(b)(ii) "in the public interest". Prohibitions can be imposed on publication and broadcasting breach of which will constitute a criminal offence. Moreover the lawfulness of the detention cannot be raised at such hearing but has to be brought by way of habeas corpus to the High Court. Hearsay evidence can also be given by the applicant officer in support of such applications for extension under s 21(1)(f)(4BC), though the judge hearing the application can 'in the interests of justice' direct that the other member who has knowledge of such matters attend and give oral evidence.

[2.93] Section 22 of the 2009 Act provides that the same changes to procedure be made to applications for time extension under s 2 of the Criminal Justice

(Drug Trafficking) Act 1996. Section 22(4) repeals s 11 of that Act the effect of which is to make ss 2, 3, 4, 5 and 6 permanent eliminating the need for those sections to be renewed every 2 years by resolution of the Houses of the Oireachtas. Further provision is made in the case of all detention provisions that the detention period does not expire while the person is at the venue for the hearing. Regarding authorising a re-arrest it is also provided that a court can do so not only in the situation where information has come to the gardai since his arrest, but also where the gardaí had such knowledge prior to release but questioning would not have been in the interests of proper investigation.

[2.94] Section 23 of the 2009 Act amends s 50 of the Criminal Justice Act 2007 in order to extend the list of offences to which that section applies to include offences under Part 7 of the Criminal Justice Act 2007 (organised crime offences). Henceforth those offences together with the original offences of murder involving the use of a firearm or explosive, capital murder, possession of a firearm with intent to endanger life or the offence of false imprisonment involving the use of a firearm may allow suspects to be detained for seven days.

[2.95] Section 24 of the 2009 Act amends s 4 of the Criminal Justice Act 1984 so as to provide that when a person is intoxicated the period during which they are intoxicated and so unfit to be questioned does not constitute part of the period of detention allowable. (There was already provision that a period of hospitalisation be excluded).

Future perspectives, new rights

[2.96] To utilise the foregoing account of how changes have been accommodated in the past in various contexts to assess future perspectives for rights, one has to focus on the context in which rights are delineated: the language used, the concepts evoked to read rights, the notions invoked from other contexts – essence, proportionality, balance – and what the judiciary do with them. That is not to accept any of these words or indeed the centrality of the role of the judiciary, but we are where we are, with many words spilled and much judicial angst engaged over rights construction in our modern world. It is also difficult not to be acutely conscious of the timing of such constructions and of the fallibility of asserted assumptions such as that the 'ordinary' continues elsewhere while 'extraordinary' is now.

When one talks about rights, one always has to be a little cynical (or realistic): they may not always deliver what they pretend. That is not quite to say that they are 'nonsense on stilts' as Bentham[158] would have it but that their nature is to promise, and delivery is quite another task.

---

[158] Principles of the Civil Code, Part 1 [Bowring ed] Works 326.

[2.97] There are of course different kinds of rights, and there is acknowledgment in our charters and constitutions that some are stronger or more absolute than others. The interpretation of their meaning and their relevance in a given factual context may not always be appreciated or apparent. A changed understanding of rights or a changed appreciation of their import has characterised the development of our 'personal' rights under the Constitution in this jurisdiction in the second half of the twentieth century, and a change in the meaning of those same rights might be said to characterise the later and earlier stages of that and the twenty-first century.

[2.98] The notion of 'perspectives', which is hugely significant in the context of rights and criminal justice brings us to the land of interpretation, just as the recent notion of the 'essence' of rights emergent in European Court of Human Rights case law brings us to the question of whether they are 'new' when redrawn. This point emerges from decisions such as *Saunders*[159] and *Heaney & McGuiness v Ireland*[160] where the Court found "…that the security and public order concerns of the Government cannot justify a provision which extinguishes the very essence of the applicant's rights to silence…". [161] At the same time, behind the concept of these rights and underlying the language of their interpretation, there is an idea, a value. Judge Zupancic makes that important point in *Jalloh*[162] where he concludes in his concurring opinion:

> … human rights are not only matters of pedantic legal reasoning. They are also a subject matter of a value judgment. True only when this value judgment is converted into a verbally articulate legal standard can it sustain the rule of law. It is a mistake, however, to forget that at bottom – at the origin of the very legal standard to be applied-lays a moral resolution of those who not only have opinions or even convictions but also the courage of those convictions.

It is appropriate perhaps to explore the articulation of rights of late, to assess the role of the courts and lawyers and assess what that means for the fate of human rights in the criminal process into the future.

[2.99] We must explore ideas related to nuance in language and translation and also question the aperture through which we reflect on and analyse criminal process values and normative structures. At its simplest it may be assessing the normalisation of the exceptional – in itself unexceptional, except in so far as it is to place that exceptional central stage. 'Terrorism' proves a useful label for that

---

[159] *Saunders v United Kingdom* (1996) 23 EHRR 313.

[160] *Heaney & McGuiness v Ireland* (2000) 33 EHRR 246 at para 58.

[161] See further A, Ashworth 'Security, Terrorism and the Value of Human Rights' c 9 in Ben Goold & Liora Lazarus, *Security and Human Rights* (Hart Oxford, 2007), 203.

[162] *Jalloh* [2006] 44 EHRR 667.

which is dissident/abhorrent/monstrous. That nature affects the construction of 'fairness' in cases and what that might comprise. Contemporary artist Barbara Kruger in her book *Remote Control* makes the point as follows: 'the difference is not always in the story but the telling, not in the moment but It's representations and how these representations coalesce into an official history.' In exploring rights and fairness, very often it is the exception which proves the rule:

> [C]ommunities tend to constitute themselves by excluding difference, but … the task of a philosophical politics is to conceptualize new forms of association which let the different appear in their midst.[163]

Constructions of fairness in the criminal process, in times of crises, look to the exception to prove the rule, both of law and of our liberal credentials. They reveal the reality of our human rights commitment. In Ireland, the co-existence of constitutional rights and crisis or state of emergency has existed since the foundation of the state.

[2.100] The template used for threats, here as elsewhere, is not itself new. States in the past have left the boundaries of their values to meet threats to 'national security' – witness the conduct of the United States during World War II in relation to those of Japanese descent (*Korematsu*), or the conduct of the Canadian government during the FLQ crisis in the 1970s.[164] *But* whether it is now because the threats are graver, or the felt contradictions in the past too great, our need to reinvent ourselves seems greater. At least one element demands this – the transnational nature of crime and its necessary response. Certainly crime was international before, and states that were alike bound together in the face of perceived threat (extradition), or a similar nature and origin (political offence defence), but the dictating and significant boundaries were still national, as in the doctrine '*aut dedere aut judicate*'. Now national boundaries do not contain the threat. Transnational alliances best meet a threat like al Qaeda, which is not itself national in origin, but stateless and amorphous. Hence ideological blocks increasingly divide the world along lines which readily translate into 'good' and 'evil'. Recognising friends across boundaries means we are likely to see them as like 'us', and others as different and so 'foes'. Hence the childlike equation of good and evil translates readily into 'us' and 'them' across nation state lines in the global community. This is not just a simplistic mantra, but literally

---

[163] Benhabib, *Democracy & Difference: Reflections on Rationality, Democracy & Postmodernism* (1994), p 30 quoted by Lacey, *Unspeakable Subjects: Feminist Essays in Legal and Social Theory* (Hart, 1998), p 125.

[164] In the 1970s during a period of unrest in Quebec in Canada precipitated by the kidnapping of a senior British Trade Commissioner in Montreal by the Front de Liberation de Quebec (FLQ), the Canadian Government invoked and utilised the War Measure Act, a war-time piece of legislation with broad powers of arrest and detention.

transforms our view of ourselves, as well as the values we hold dear. What we now are as a people, or society, internationally and nationally (though that latter designate is increasingly less important), is a measure of what we deem we are *not*; our identity literally constructed by those we identify as apart, for it is by the nature and effect of that exclusion that we are defined. What we purport to guarantee is merely a front. When actually tested, what we deliver to the other side of our bipolar equation of good and evil is the test of what, *in extremis*, we are. Transnationally, this presents a clearer progression, as we commence co-operation at the sharper end, against common foes, whether drug traffickers, traffickers in human beings or terrorists. Revealing this same process nationally involves looking at national survival in the face of threat. What is revealed is that the designation 'criminal' is now not even felt as excluded from that category are many of those others: unlawful combatant, alien. Provisions relating to terrorism are continually broadened in scope (eco-, narco- etc) and rendered 'ordinary' by what now follows in its wake: further and better *special* provision. This can be seen in the earlier account of Irish legislation and is reflected in the sequence in the UK for example, whereby the Terrorism Act 2000 moved beyond the Prevention of Terrorism Acts by internationalising and nationalising the threat, was still deemed insufficient for recent events, and so replaced by the Anti-Terrorism Crime and Security Act 2001.[165] Each heralded a broader remit, greater sphere of application and stronger powers (beyond the targeted community). Similarly in the USA, in the aftermath of 9/11, the Patriot Act 2001 expanded the ability of law enforcement to conduct secret searches, phone and Internet surveillance, and access personal records with minimal judicial oversight. The proposed augmentation and extension of those powers in the draft Patriot II, demonstrates how the 'axis of evil' referred to by President Bush, may not be just a framework for initiating war, but a tool guiding everyday constructions of justice.[166]This escalation in both perceived threat and response indicates the extremes of which we are capable.

How can such action be taken in the face of rights declared to be valued in all our charters and constitutional documents? Why does crisis always trump human rights, or does it? How do courts (judges and lawyers) measure up when security and rights are put into play? History might suggest that the concerns

---

[165] Under the PTAs, the threat was confined to Northern Ireland. Regarding the role of law in relation to oppressive security policies see further: Walsh, *Bloody Sunday and the Rule of Law in Northern Ireland* (Gill and MacMillan, Dublin, 2000).

[166] Patriot Act – The Uniting and Strengthening America by Providing Appropriate Tools Required to Intercept and Obstruct Terrorism Act of 2001 (Pub L No 107 56 115 Stat 272 October 2001). Patriot II – Justice Department's draft Domestic Security Enhancement Act of 2003, 9 January 2003. http://www.aclu.org.

regarding security always hold sway. Does this mean our rights are set at naught? Or is it just some rights or the rights of some?

[2.101] What is interesting to consider is whether rights operate 'as illusion', facilitating, that is, the maintenance of belief in a vision of ourselves where nothing has altered fundamentally; whatever has occurred, is in part possible, by virtue of *rights*. To state that rights are not an unqualified good, has for a long time not been viewed as heretical. Rights can be construed as a managerial mechanism of the state – a controlling device – with differentiations facilitating their grant to certain (like) individuals, and not to others, or indeed to different socially or culturally constructed effect. This applies to the labelled 'terrorist', outsider or alien/unlawful combatant. What use to them is the 'right to a fair trial' if they are outside a trial (in a military tribunal or special court for example)? The case might be made that they are in fact controlled by those very rights which are granted: interference with the right to silence effected and sanctioned by the very right of access to a lawyer;[167] the extended detention sanitised by access to legal advice.[168] The right is literally turned on its head, as access to a lawyer aids not the individual, but the State, sanctioning the use of its extended powers. (The Criminal Justice Act 2007 in Ireland is just such a case in point.) The reality of life for those caught in exceptional punitive regimes mirrors *all* lives lived in the margins. Centralising that experience further by identifying the terrorist/paedophile/al Qaeda as *core* to criminal justice – nationally and internationally – as the cost for what human rights brings to a society may be precisely what is necessary to effect justice. For when, if not *in extremis* or crisis, do rights matter? Crisis situations and emergency response, if taken as the measure of (not the exception to) justice, construct a different edifice. To use this revelation and invoke such historic precedent(s) as there might be, to restore or reconstruct a set of principles or values, moves beyond mere intellectual thrashing of rights, towards their restoration.

[2.102] Brennan J identified as that 'crucible of danger' the situation wherein civil liberties and human rights are forged in the turbulence of war or crisis.[169] The United States of America, since 9/11, presents one of these. Israel has been

---

[167] *Murray v United Kingdom* (1994) A 300, 19 EHRR 193.

[168] *Lavery v The Member in Charge Carrickmacross Garda Station* [1999] 2 IR 390.

[169] Brennan J, Supreme Court judge, in a paper delivered in Jerusalem on 22 December 1987, 'The Quest to Develop a Jurisprudence of Civil Liberties in Times of Crisis': 'It may well be Israel ... that provides the best hope for building a jurisprudence that can protect civil liberties against the demands of national security, for it is Israel that has been facing real and serious threats to its security for the last forty years ... [I]n this crucible of danger lies the opportunity to forge a worldwide jurisprudence of civil liberties that can withstand the turbulences of war and crisis.' Quoted in Dershowitz, *Why Terrorism Works* (Yale University Press, 2002) at 141–142.

frequently so nominated, but there are many other states that face this dilemma of rights vindication under conditions of threat. Examples include the United Kingdom, Ireland and the fledgling federation that is the EU, which last reminds us that the increasingly global, or at least regional, basis on which threat is being met, in parallel with developing transnational rights consensus (through initiatives such as the European Convention on Human Rights; the International Criminal Tribunal for the Former Yugoslavia, the International Criminal Tribunal for Rwanda and the International Criminal Court) replicates the same conflict. As the liberal credentials of those societies, or fledgling federations, come under pressure in their response to threat, danger gives birth to new rights constructions. The question of whether they can in turn be accommodated in the older liberal sacks leads to some duplicitous assumptions at the heart of liberal democracies. States face the dilemma of accommodating dogma to action in a situation when only age-old restraint and ingrained manners prevent action – or at least render it slow or more uncertain. When faced with emergencies as a people, how far we go (in rights terms) in reacting may determine whether we abandon our (liberal) dogma or devalue our (human rights) creed or perhaps simply re-invent them as new rights.

[2.103] In the quieter waters of rights adjudication, this issue is manifest whenever the compromise of rights – most often on 'public interest' grounds – is mooted. It was considered, for example, in light of the Human Rights Act and ECHR guarantees in *Brown v Stott*.[170] A visibly drunken woman, who had told police that a nearby car was hers, was required by them under s 172(2)(a) of the Road Traffic Act 1988 to say who had just been driving it. On the basis of her answer: 'It was me', she was prosecuted for drunken driving. While the Sheriff felt that evidence to be admissible, the High Court of Judiciary relying on the European Court of Human Rights decision in *Saunders*[171] felt it was not. The Privy Council, however, felt the section was a proportionate and legitimate response to a major social problem and admitted her statement, holding that 'its [the privilege against self-incrimination] legitimate use is a question of proportionality of means to ends, not of rigid rules'.[172] Smedley[173] sees this as invoking the concept of a deal offered by society to individuals who choose to

---

[170] *Brown v Stott* [2001] 2 WLR 817.

[171] *Saunders v United Kingdom* (1997) 23 EHRR 313.

[172] Smedley, Vol 52 No 2 NILQ 107 at 124.

[173] Vol 52 No 2 NILQ 107. Lord Justice Smedley addresses this question at the micro level of the right, or what he would term the *privilege,* against self-incrimination. Smedley's focus is on reconciling that privilege/right, with provisions requiring information to be given, and the subsequent use of that information – admissibility – in criminal proceedings. Hence the focus is trial-based.

engage in certain activities (eg driving / financial dealing), whereby this is a regulated activity which, if undertaken, must be answerable to the authorities.[174]

[2.104] Gearty[175] points out that the constitutionalization of civil liberties has proved less secure than might have been imagined. Because of the 'ever more unwieldy basket of human rights', civil liberties have become just a few freedoms among the many; a lack of an international democratic culture; and the capacity for override found in human rights charters whereby the state can suspend or ignore such rights in 'emergency' situations. The latter in particular comes in for some consideration as Gearty notes when reviewing such legitimisation:

> a restriction of civil liberties that takes place within the framework of a human rights document (either a 'necessary' exception to free speech, for example, or an action to counter a 'public emergency') can be presented as not an attack at all, but rather as an action *mandated* by the state's *commitment* to human rights. Far from infringing human rights, the repression is (fully) compatible with them. This legitimization of what might have been considered by the naïve to be an attack on civil liberties then draws added strength from the (almost inevitable) judicial decision upholding the emergency action as valid, that is in accordance with human rights standards ... The repressive state can deepen its reactionary engagement with domestic dissent while all the time asserting confidently and (in legal terms) correctly that it is *respecting* human rights standards.[176]

He adds the perhaps prescient comment that 'it is not impossible to imagine that torture, called by another name of course and surrounded by judicial safeguards (at least initially), could fit itself neatly into this human rights paradigm.'[177]

Walker is of a similar view that 'the application of human rights discourse has been a two edged sword, with failed challenges to derogation notices resulting in entrenchment and legitimation and the insertion of human rights safeguards encouraging the grant of more stringent powers.'[178]

[2.105] The dilemma that faces human rights advocates and civil libertarians in the aftermath of 11 September 2001 is precisely that of engaging in a debate, the very basis of which may be problematic from a rights point of view. It invokes shades of previous complicity on the part of the judiciary, of which Justice Jackson warned in *Korematsu*[179] (whereby the Constitution would be

---

[174] Smedley, Vol 52 No 2 NILQ 107 at 126.

[175] Gearty, 'Reflections on Civil Liberties in an Age of Counterterrorism' [2003] 41 Osgoode Hall LJ 185 at 202.

[176] Gearty [2003] 41 Osgoode Hall LJ 185 at 205.

[177] Gearty [2003] 41 Osgoode Hall LJ 185 at 205–206.

[178] Walker, 'Terrorism and Criminal Justice: Past, Present and Future.' [2004] Crim LR 55 at 70.

[179] *Korematsu v United States* 323 US 214 (1944).

compromised by the acceptance and sanctioning of detention in war). The very process of inclusion of the civil libertarians in that debate is what is suspect. That civil liberties were hard won, and literally constructed in the face of state opposition should serve to underscore the importance of their now not being invoked in favour of that state. It is after all at the level of generality –national security, public interest, good of the community – that they are most easily compromised and lost. So often in rights construction, it is the case that the unquantifiable (or unrecognisable) individual is set up against the ill-defined public interest or good, to lose. That loss occurs all the more readily when the individual is already designated as *outside* the relevant community. Re-commencing at the level of the individual or human requires: (1) identification with the accused – in his or her worst manifestation as other – as us; and (2) a reconsideration of what is the presumed norm, to reveal its perhaps contradictory and extraordinary core.

[2.106] Let's review these issues in the following two contexts, looking at the role of courts and lawyers:

(i)   that of the status of the right to silence in Ireland, case law and recent developments; and

(ii)   that of the ECt HR jurisprudence constructing rights in context.

We can then try to draw some conclusions regarding the role of courts in wartime (*extremis*) and hence always – for 'always' constitutes both wartime and normality.

The status of the right to silence in Ireland, case law and recent developments

[2.107] The normalisation of emergency powers in Ireland has been persistent and progressively clearer and more evident: the most recent examples being found in the extension of inference provisions and further admissibility of garda opinion evidence under the Criminal Justice Act 2007. That is certainly a characteristic of the past as decisions such as *Quilligan* (transforming arrest and detention), *O'Leary*[180] (the rights to silence) and *Heaney and McGuinness*[181] (facilitating inference provisions) make clear.

By contrast, on other occasions, the ordinary criminal process has evidenced adherence to high moral principles with constitutrional grounding: fair trial issues concerning cross-examination of the accused in *McGrail* [182] for example, and rules regarding the admissibility of illegally obtained evidence in *O'Brien*.[183]

---

[180] *O'Leary v AG* [1993] 1 IR 102, [1995] 1 IR 254.
[181] *Heaney & McGuinness v Ireland & AG* [1994] 3 IR 593.
[182] *People (DPP) v McGrail* [1990] 1 IR 38.
[183] *People v O'Brien* [1965] IR 142.

[2.108] Recent flashes of criminal justice fairness issues resulting from the adherence to procedure can be found in the emphasis on the emergency nature of the power to issue warrants conferred on gardaí under s 8(2) of the Criminal Justice (Drug Trafficking) Act 1996 in *People (AG) v Byrne*.[184] Furthermore, vindication of character evidence rules is evident in the Supreme Court decision in *DPP v DO*,[185] to reject cross-examination which was used to portray the accused as one who 'fitted the bill' as a paedophile. The Supreme Court rejected this as constituting the use of evidence relating to previous misconduct or character, something which had been regarded as inadmissible for centuries.

The burden of proof, presumption of innocence and right to silence are part of that 'golden thread'[186] of principles underlying our criminal justice system (*Woolmington*[187]) – what Zuckerman called the principles of political morality. Even in a world where justice is an evolving concept, the fundamental nature of the notion that the state has to prove the case against an accused would seem to hold firm in judicial statements and its connection to the presumption of innocence, the right to silence and the fairness of the proceedings has often been made clear.

[2.109] This has been acknowledged by Costello J in *O'Leary v Attorney General*:[188]

> It seems to me that it has been for so long a fundamental postulate of every criminal trial in this country that the accused was presumed to be innocent of the offence with which he was charged that a criminal trial held otherwise than in accordance with this presumption ... would be one which was not held in due course of law.

O'Flaherty J in the Supreme Court[189] in that case stated that 'the presumption of innocence in a criminal trial is implicit in the requirement of Art 38.1 of the Constitution that no person shall be tried on a any criminal charge save in due course of law.

According to Keane J in *People v Finnerty*:[190]

> Our criminal law ... historically reflected a tension between two competing principles. The first was the right and duty of the police to investigate crime ... The second was the right of a suspect ... to refuse to answer any questions ...

---

[184] *People (AG) v Byrne* [2003] 4 IR 423.
[185] *DPP v DO* [2006] IESC 12.
[186] See para **3.36** *et seq*.
[187] *Woolmington v DPP* [1935] AC 462.
[188] *O'Leary v AG* [1993] 1 IR 102 at 107.
[189] *O'Leary v AG* [1995] 1 IR 254 at 263.
[190] *People v Finnerty* [1999] 4 IR 364 at 376–7.

Hardiman J in *People (DPP) v DO'T* stated that, '[t]he presumption of innocence ... is not only a right in itself: it is the basis of other aspects of a trial in due course of law at common law.'[191]

[2.110] A case study of the exact dimensions and reality of the accused's right to silence, however, from *O'Leary* (Costello J in the High Court) to *Finnerty* (Keane J) to *Heaney and McGuinness* (in our own context and the context of the ECt HR) to *Jalloh* (the ECt HR only) might be said rather to compromise its nature and ambit while accommodating state action and need. If the effect of these decisions is to do so, while at the same time paying lip service to the continuing fundamental nature of that right, can one only square the circle by concluding that the right itself has changed radically to become new?

[2.111] The legislative byplay that accompanies Irish case law development stems from the Offences Against the State Act 1939 through to the Criminal Justice Act 1984, the Criminal Justice (Drug Trafficking) Act 1996 and Offences Against the State (Amendment) Act 1998 to the recent Criminal Justice Act 2007.[192] The 'legalisation' of the restrictions on that right, or the (re) articulation of the right itself in the courts, reveals something also about the role of the lawyers who act as a counterpoint to the rights interference – clearly manifest in Part 4 of the Criminal Justice 2007 after the decision in *Lavery v Member in Charge Carrickmacross Garda Station*[193] had ensured the placebo effect of the right to counsel.

In other words, in the aftermath of the *Lavery* decision it was obvious that neither blanket access to a lawyer during interrogation, nor the presence of a lawyer at that interrogation was necessary for the fruits of that interrogation to be valid.

[2.112] Another interesting dimension to the case law is the language and logic used in the reasoning. Costello J starts the process in *O'Leary* by invoking the ECHR is asserting that the Constitution should not be construed as absolutely prohibiting the Oireachtas from restricting the exercise of the right to the presumption of innocence. The proportionality test is similarly invoked by Costello J in *Heaney and McGuinness* to save the restrictions imposed on silence by s 52.

The influence of the reasoning of the ECt HR is even more evident over time as *proportionality* as a concept is invoked to facilitate accommodating change

---

[191] *People (DPP) v DO'T* [2003] 4 IR 286 at 290.

[192] Criminal Justice Act 2007, ss 28, 29, 30 (right to silence inferences) make provision for explanation in ordinary language, reasonable access to a solicitor and electronic recording.

[193] *Lavery v Member in Charge Carrickmacross Garda Station* [1999] 2 IR 390.

within fairness construction. The decisions *People (DPP) v Mathews*[194] and *People (DPP) v Kelly*[195] are cases in point.

Both dealt with the issue of the admissibility of opinion evidence on the part of a Garda as to membership of an unlawful organisation.

[2.113] Mathews challenged the admissibility of belief evidence of a Chief Superintendent, in respect of which a claim of privilege was made. He argued that at the same time when a court is asked to draw conclusions adverse to an accused from that very evidence, this interferes with the lawful rights and ability of an accused to challenge that belief and so impedes fair trial under the constitution (Art 38) and the European Convention (art 6).

Macken J delivering the judgment of the CCA, declared the Court:

> ...satisfied that a restriction on the ability to cross examine the garda witness in question arising from his claim to privilege in respect of the underlying sources of information upon which his belief was based, does not...on the case law...constitute a failure to comply with Article 6 of the Convention of Human Rights.

Macken J goes on to state that it was specifically *counterbalanced* so as to ensure a fair trial by the fact that it is not the practice of the Special Criminal court to convict solely on the basis of this evidence, nor of the DPP to prosecute. There was also evidence of facts involving the applicant's prior association with persons who were established members, and inference from his own failure to respond to material questions.

[2.114] *Mathews* relied on *Kelly*, where Fennelly J gave considerable attention to whether the accused there had been deprived of a fair trail by limitations on cross-examination in similar circumstances. He reviews ECt HR case law and in particular points to *Kostovski v Netherlands*[196] where the use of anonymous witnesses in the context of 'the fight against organised crime' who were not available for cross-examination was held to be a violation of art 6. He also refers to *Doorson v Netherlands*[197] where he states the ECt HR backtracked and stated:

> principles of fair trial also require that in appropriate cases the interests of the defence are balanced against those witnesses or victims called upon to testify.

Fennelly J continues in *Kelly* (at para 78) to address this issue of whether the change in question can be accommodated within fairness. His reasoning is interesting:

---

[194] *People (DPP) v Mathews* [2006] IECCA 103.
[195] *People (DPP) v Kelly* [2006] 3 IR 115.
[196] *Kostovski v Netherlands* (1990) 12 EHRR 434.
[197] *Doorson v Netherlands* (1996) 22 EHRR 330.

The essential question to be answered in this case is whether the undisputed restriction on the right of the accused to cross-examine his accusers and to have access to the materials relied on by the prosecution has been unduly restricted so as to render his trial unfair and his conviction unsafe. I believe that all of the authorities cited from all relevant jurisdictions demonstrate that there is an inescapable obligation on the courts to guarantee the overall fairness of a trial. I also believe that, in our legal system, the right to cross examine one's accusers is an essential element in a fair trail. This is not to say that restrictions may not be imposed in the interests of overall *balance* and the *efficiency* of the criminal justice system. While there may be derogations for overriding reasons of public interests from normal procedural rights of the defence, these must not go beyond what is strictly necessary and must in no circumstances to use the language of Lord Bingham, 'imperil the overall fairness of the trial'. (emphasis added)

He then accepts that the infringement on the normal right of the accused here has the potential for unfairness but 'on the other hand' (this is balancing in operation) points to a number of compelling circumstances put forward by the prosecution as justification for its introduction.

[2.115] These are:

The exceptional resort to the opinion of the Chief Superintendent only in the case of organisations which represent a threat to the State:

> *One might suggest that is where the courts must review*

> The high rank of the said member

> *Unsure how this is compelling?*

> The procedure only applies where there is a Declaration in force 'that the ordinary courts are inadequate to secure the administration of justice'

> *Again precisely where one might say review must occur*

> The offence is a scheduled one and will be heard only by the Special Criminal Court now compose of judges presumed to apply the highest standard of fairness

> *This in a sense begs the question or just sends it back down to the trial court*

[2.116] The decision is replete with the language of balance – not to say compromise and overall fairness (in itself a European concept). ECt HR case law is replete with examples of 'overall fairness' being acceptable to the Court; manifest also in their not looking to the rules of evidence[198] and deference to state need in derogation 'margin of appreciation'.[199]

---

[198] *Kahn v UK* (2000) 31 EHRR 1016.
[199] *Lawless v Ireland* (1961) 1 EHRR 15.

The decisions do not give undue confidence in the Irish judiciary as a means of combating executive and legislative over reaction through legislation in moving outside criminal law paradigm and norms. The invocation of the European Court of Human Rights concepts to aid interpretation and accommodation however deserves further comment.

European Court of Human Rights – constructing rights in context.

[2.117] Andrew Ashworth[200] examines what he terms the balanced response thesis which takes the view that terrorist threat leads to an unavoidable dilemma between protecting the freedom of citizens from attacks and upholding human rights values in the Convention and so attempts to strike a balance. With regard to the meaning of balance Ashworth[201] comments as follows:

> ...as the very conceptualisation of this approach, in particular the use of the imagery of 'balance' is dubious. By adopting this imagery the thesis trades on a cluster of associated terms-such as proportionality, reasonableness and fairness-that appear almost incontrovertible. Thus the term 'balance' tends to disarm opponents because it has no tenable antithesis: nobody that is would stand up & argue for imbalance or indeed disproportionality, unreasonableness or unfairness.

Ashworth points out that four ECHR rights are non-derogable: art 2 right to life, art 3 right not to be subjected to torture; art 4 right not to be held in slavery; art 7 right not to be subject to retrospective criminal laws. In relation to assessing the position of arts 5 and 6 (right to liberty and security of the person and right to fair trial) he makes the point that although not in art 15.2 (with the four rights from which states cannot derogate) the Convention does not declare them to be qualified rights and there is no paragraph allowing member states interfere with them if necessary in a democratic society. Ashworth concludes:[202]

> This means that the concept of proportionality which plays such a significant role in setting the boundaries for interferences with the rights declared by Articles 8, 9, 10, 11 is not relevant in the same sense to Articles 5 and 6. Neither the Convention nor the Strasbourg jurisprudence suggests that the rights enumerated in those Articles can simply be pushed aside for public policy or other consequentialist reasons, on the grounds that such curtailments are proportionate.

---

[200] Ashworth, 'Security, terrorism and the value of human rights' in Gould & Lazurus (eds), *Security & Human Rights* (Hart, 2007), p 203.

[201] Ashworth, 'Security, terrorism and the value of human rights' in Gould & Lazurus (eds), *Security & Human Rights* (Hart, 2007), p 203 at p 208.

[202] Ashworth, 'Security, terrorism and the value of human rights' in Gould & Lazurus (eds), *Security & Human Rights* (Hart, 2007), at p 215.

Ashworth criticises Lord Bingham's judgment in *Brown v Stott*[203] where he held that a particular curtailment of the privilege against self incrimination implied into art 6 right to fair trial was not a disproportionate response to the problem of maintaining road safety. Lord Bingham balanced the general interest of the community against the interests of the individual. Ashworth holds this wrong on two fronts:

Article 6 provides for no such balancing; and if per contra some proportionality judgment were permissible, one would expect the conditions to be tougher than those set out in para 2 of art 8.

Ashworth terms this a heresy which does not represent European human rights law.[204]

[2.118] The European reasoning which the Irish courts have invoked to sanction and thereby sanitise Government action therefore has a dubious pedigree. It has had a fundamental effect however in so far as the high water mark of the acceptability of state action which curtails rights has becomes increasingly blurred. As Gearty puts it:[205]

The problem is at one level about an explicit conflict between counter terrorism law and human rights. But it is also about something more ominous altogether: a supposed lack of conflict between the two, flowing from a redefinition of human rights the effect of which is to excuse repression as necessary to prevent the destruction of human rights values.

[2.119] The Irish tale then is one that illustrates that one cannot rely on courts (Judges) to breath life into the human rights of a society. What we may have by contrast is a legitimation of repressive action by the executive; a domestic debilitation (possibly as a result of an overreliance or assumption of the legalisation of human rights); the 'hollowing out' of human rights (Ashworth) by reference to constructions of proportionality and public interest; and perhaps our non-appreciation of the effects of terrorist legislation, as legal strategies alone cannot measure same. In the context of the presumption of innocence this returns us to the reality of a situation where the increase in the powers of detention in the hands of the state is now weighted against the citizen accused whose rights have been redrawn.

---

[203] *Brown v Stott* [2001] 2 All ER 97.

[204] Ashworth, 'Security, terrorism and the value of human rights' in Gould & Lazurus (eds), *Security & Human Rights* (Hart, 2007), at p 215.

[205] Gearty, *Can Human Rights Survive* [The Hamlyn lectures] Cambridge University Press 2006 at 107–108.

European Court of Human Rights jurisprudence constructing rights in context

[2.120] The jurisprudence of the European Court of Human Rights and their constructing of rights in context is particularly insightful at this point. In this regard it is useful to now focus on two decisions at European level which Ashworth has recently characterized as examples of 'the hollowing out of rights'.[206]

In *O'Halloran & Francis v UK*[207] the issue which arose was whether the coercion of a person who is the subject of a charge of speeding under s 172 of the Road Traffic Act 1988 to make statements which incriminate him or might lead to his incrimination is compatible with art 6.

It was held that there was no violation of art 6.1 the Court holding:[208]

> While the right to a fair trial under Article 6 is an unqualified right, what constitutes a fair trial cannot be the subject of a single unvarying rule but must depend on the circumstances of the particular case. This was confirmed in the specific context of the right to remain silent in *Heaney and McGuinness* ...

The Court continued:[209]

> ... in order to determine whether the essence of the applicants' right to remain silent and the privilege against self incrimination was infringed, the Court will focus on the nature and degree of compulsion used to obtain the evidence, the existence of any relevant safeguards in the procedure, and the use to which any material so obtained was put.

[2.121] *Jalloh v Germany*[210] concerned the use of evidence in the form of drugs swallowed by the applicant which had been obtained by forcible administration of emetics. It was argued that the use of this illegally obtained evidence was contrary to art 6.

The Court found that the action was in violation of art 3 in so far as the 'impugned measure attained the minimum level of severity required'.[211] Regarding the claim under art 6 the Court pointed out[212] that its role is to consider whether the proceedings as a whole are fair.

---

[206] *Per* Ashworth, 'The Pernicious Side of Proportionality: Two Studies in the Hollowing out of Human Rights' Paper delivered to Centre for Criminal Justice and Human Rights, UCC, 24 January 2008.

[207] *O'Halloran & Francis v UK* [2007] ECHR 545.

[208] *O'Halloran & Francis v UK* [2007] ECHR 545 at para 53.

[209] *O'Halloran & Francis v UK* [2007] ECHR 545 at para 55.

[210] *Jalloh v Germany* [2006] ECHR 721.

[211] *Jalloh v Germany* [2006] ECHR 721 at para 82.

[212] *Jalloh v Germany* [2006] ECHR 721 at para 95.

The Court then goes on to comment:[213]

> The general requirements of fairness contained in Article 6 apply to all criminal proceedings, irrespective of the type of offence at issue. Nevertheless, when determining whether the proceedings as a whole have been fair the weight of the public interest in the investigation and punishment of the particular offence at issue may be taken into consideration and be weighed against the individual interest that the evidence against him be gathered lawfully. However, public interest concerns cannot justify measures which extinguish the very essence of an applicant's defence rights, including the privilege against self incrimination guaranteed by Article 6.

In order to determine if the right not to be incriminated was violated, the Court stated it will have regard to the nature and degree of compulsion used to obtain the evidence, the weight of the public interest in the investigation and punishment of the offence and the use to which the material so obtained is put.

Regarding the weight of the public interest, the Court observed here that it was a street dealer and a small amount of drugs so that in the circumstances did not justify recourse to such grave interference.

[2.122] Article 3 itself is under pressure though as the Court leaves open here the question as to whether the use of evidence obtained by an act qualified as inhuman and degrading treatment automatically renders a trial unfair![214] But having regard to the fact that it was a street dealer selling on a small scale decides …[215] 'the public interest in securing the applicant's conviction cannot be considered to have been of such weight as to warrant allowing that evidence to be used at the trial' Hence the Court finds the use of the drugs obtained by forcible means here rendered his trial as a whole unfair.[216]

Further evidence that even those absolute rights such as art 3 can come under pressure is provided by the decision in *Saadi v Italy*[217] which concerned a challenge to a decision to deport to Tunisia along the lines of Chahal ie that it would expose him to the risk of being subjected to treatment contrary to art 3.[218]

> The court notes first of all that states face immense difficulties in modern times in protecting their communities from terrorist violence ... It cannot therefore underestimate the scale of the danger of terrorism today and the threat it presents to the community. That must not however call into question the absolute nature of Article 3.

So far so good – on the rhetoric.

---

[213] *Jalloh v Germany* [2006] ECHR 721 at para 97.
[214] *Jalloh v Germany* [2006] ECHR 721 at para 107.
[215] *Jalloh v Germany* [2006] ECHR 721 at para 107.
[216] *Jalloh v Germany* [2006] ECHR 721 at para 108.
[217] *Saadi v Italy* [2008] ECHR 179.
[218] *Saadi v Italy* [2008] ECHR 179 at para 137.

[2.123] The Court continues[219] that it considers that the argument based on the balancing of the risk of harm if the person is sent back against the dangerousness he or she represents to the community if not sent back is misconceived, and found there was a real danger would be subjected to treatment contrary to art 3 if deported.

The concurring opinion delivered by Judge Zupancic is interesting regarding that suggestion made to the Court (and backed by the UK intervention in the case) that there be a balancing of the risk of harm if the person is sent back against the dangerousness he represents to the community if not which was rejected by the court:

He comments:[220]

> The spirit of the ECHR is precisely the opposite ie the Convention is conceived to block such short circuit logic and protect the individual from the unbridled 'interest' of the executive branch or sometimes of the legislative branch of the state.

> It is thus extremely important to read paragraph 139 of the judgment as a categorical imperative protecting the rights of the individual. The only way out of this logical necessity would be to maintain that such individuals do not deserve human rights – the third party intervenes is unconsciously implying that to a lesser degree – because they are less human.

(Absolute) rights in face of countervailing (public) interests: Recent US/UK decisions a false dawn?

[2.124] A critical issue here is that of the nature of these rights and the fact that those with which we are in the main concerned are not absolute, and so amenable to practices such as balancing or proportionality. The latter are invoked as tools in the context of state reaction to perceived threat: war on drugs/ war on terrorism etc.

Some scholars would argue that the minimalist role of the courts in wartime is concerned to just ensure that rights infringing measures are supported by the legislature.[221] More charitably (to the Judges) one could take the view that a decision on the merits is more damaging to the legal system.[222] This latter was certainly the view taken by Jackson J (dissenting) in *Korematsu v US*.[223] At issue in *Korematsu v United States* was an exclusion order which during a state of war with Japan and as a protection against espionage and sabotage, directed the

---

[219] *Saadi v Italy* [2008] ECHR 179 at para 139.
[220] *Saadi v Italy* [2008] ECHR 179 at para 139.
[221] See for example Cass R Sunstein, *Laws of Fear Beyond the Precautionary Principle* (New York Cambridge University Press, 2005).
[222] Martinez, 'Process & Substance in the War on Terror' [2008] 108 CLR 1013 at 1072.
[223] *Korematsu v United States* (1944) 323 US 214.

exclusion after 9 May 1942 from a described West Coast military area of all persons of Japanese ancestry. The petitioner, an American citizen of Japanese descent whose home was in the described area, claimed that it was unconstitutional. The validity of a curfew order had earlier been considered and upheld in *Hirabayashi v US*.[224] The majority view in *Korematsu* was to accommodate the measure; thereby sanctioning what normally would breach constitutional rights and values in that society. A dissent from Mr. Justice Jackson however, posits the question as to whether such accommodation is in fact capitulation, and suggests that principle would demand that the military policy stand outwith the constitutional order. Provision outside the constitution provided an answer, as Jackson J saw it, to the maintenance of the integrity of the constitutional order.

[2.125] It is the implication for the Constitution of the accommodation of such action that for Jackson J is crucial.

The majority view in *Korematsu* was to accommodate the measure; thereby sanctioning what normally would breach constitutional rights and values in that society. A dissent from Jackson J however, posits the question as to whether such accommodation is in fact capitulation, and suggests that principle would demand that the military policy stand outwith the constitutional order. Provision outside the constitution provided an answer, as Justice Jackson saw it, to the maintenance of the integrity of the constitutional order. Jackson J draws a distinction between military procedures or expedients and constitutional law:

> ... if we cannot confine military expedients by the Constitution, neither would I distort the Constitution to approve all that the military may deem expedient ... But even if they were permissible military procedures, I deny that it follows that they are constitutional.[225]

It is the implication for the Constitution of the accommodation of such action that for Jackson J is crucial:

> Much is said of the danger to liberty from the Army program for deporting and detaining these citizens of Japanese extraction. But a judicial construction of the due process clause that will sustain this order is a far more subtle blow to liberty than the promulgation of the order itself. A military order, however unconstitutional, is not apt to last longer than the military emergency. Even during that period, a succeeding commander may revoke it all. But once a judicial opinion rationalizes such an order to show that it conforms to the Constitution, or rather rationalizes the Constitution to show that the Constitution sanctions such an order, the Court for all time has validated the principle of racial discrimination in criminal procedure and of transplanting American citizens. The principle then

---

[224] *Hirabayashi v United States* 320 US 81.
[225] (1944) 323 US 214 at 244–245 *per* Jackson J.

lies about like a loaded weapon ready for the hands of any authority that can bring forward a plausible claim of an urgent need. Every repetition imbeds that principle more deeply in our law and thinking and expands it to new purposes. All who observe the work of courts are familiar with what Judge Cardozo described as 'the tendency of a principle to expand itself to the limit of its logic'. A military commander may overstep the bounds of constitutionality, and it is an incident. But if we review and approve, that passing incident becomes the doctrine of the Constitution. There it has a generative power of its own and all that it creates will be in its own image. Nothing better illustrates this danger than does the Court's opinion in this case.[226]

[2.126] The question is whether the delineation of rights in such a heightened context (such as the war on terror) is a momentary good thing but an ultimately bad one, as it engages with the redefinition of rights with long term implications and spillage in to the 'ordinary criminal justice regime.

Recent case law from the US and UK meets the very issue at stake: delivery of fairness or assessment of legislative change in a context of heightened state sensitivity, here the 'war on terror'. This assessment should indicate the effectiveness of human rights intervention and scrutiny in these contexts – useful for other 'wars' on drugs, organised crime etc – and will also aid assessment of the price to be paid long term by such use.

The very parties involved illustrate many of the issues here: marginal, even nameless, against the manifestation of state security authority. The crisis also has the merit of being a big one: the global war on terror – so the stakes are high for all.

[2.127] If we look briefly at decisions emanating in the context of the war on terror from the courts of those two major players the US and UK similar issues arise.

The majority decisions in the US cases of *Hamdi v Rumsfeld, Secretary of Defence*[227] and *Hamdan v Rumsfeld, Secretary of Defence*[228] illustrate the danger perhaps of engaging with emergency measures through rights (re)definition. In the dissents in those cases Scalia J in *Hamdi* in particular echoing fears expressed in an earlier dissent by Jackson J in *Korematsu* points to the fact that there is a price to be paid for judicial construction of rights 'inside the tent' so to speak, when the state has openly moved outside what is traditionally accepted in the criminal process-perhaps leaving it altogether in a state of war or

---

[226] (1944) 323 US 214 at 245–246 *per* Jackson J.
[227] *Hamdi v Rumsfeld, Secretary of Defense* (2004) 542 US 507.
[228] *Hamdan v Rumsfeld, Secetary of Defense* (2006) 548 US 557.

insurrection. What can be gained by attempting to tame that particular monster may be a limited gain in the long distance future. As Scalia J states in *Hamdi*:[229]

> If civil rights are to be curtailed during war time, it must be done openly and democratically, as the constitution requires, rather than by silent erosion through an opinion of this court.

[2.128] The other side of that argument is expressed by Stephens J for the majority in *Hamdan*:[230]

> We have assumed as we must, that the allegations made in the government's charge against Hamdan are true...that Hamdan is a dangerous individual whose beliefs if acted upon would cause great harm and even death to innocent civilians ... But in undertaking to try Hamdan and subject him to criminal punishment, the Executive is bound to comply with the *rule of law* that prevails in this jurisdiction. (emphasis added).

Connor J[231] in similar vein in *Hamdi* states:

> ... although Congress authorized the detention of combatants ... *due process* demands that a citizen held in the United States as an enemy combatant be given a meaningful opportunity to contest the factual basis for that detention before a neutral decisionmaker. (emphasis added)

Scalia J[232] finds these efforts of the majority in *Hamdi* unacceptable:

> '... the plurality...proceeds under the guise of the Due Process clause to proscribe what procedural protections it thinks appropriate. It 'weigh[s] the private interest...against the governments asserted interest' and – just as though writing a new constitution-comes up with an unheard – of system in which the system rather than the government bears the burden of proof, testimony is by hearsay rather than live witnesses and the presiding officer may well be a 'neutral' military officer rather than a judge and jury ... The problem with this approach is that not only that it steps out of the courts' modest and limited role in a democratic society; but that by repeatedly doing what it thinks the political branches ought to do it encourages their lassitude and saps the vitality of government by the people.

[2.129] Decisions of the US Supreme court in *Rasul*[233] endorsing habeas corpus jurisdiction (which Scalia J dissenting termed judicial adventurism) and more recently *Boumediene v Bush*[234] holding that the petitioner aliens held at

---

[229] *Hamdi v Rumsfeld, Secretary of Defense* (2004) 542 US 507 at 578.
[230] *Hamdan v Rumsfeld, Secetary of Defense* (2006) 548 US 557 at 635.
[231] *Hamdi v Rumsfeld, Secretary of Defense* (2004) 542 US 507 at 509.
[232] *Hamdi v Rumsfeld, Secretary of Defense* (2004) 542 US 507 at 575–579.
[233] *Rasul v Bush* (2004) 542 US 1.
[234] *Boumediene v Bush* 128 SCt 2229 (2008), 171 L Ed 2d 41, (2008) US Lexis 4887.

Guantanamo bay had the constitutional privilege of habeas corpus, underscore the willingness of the courts to 'get their hands' occasionally dirty in reviewing the actions of the executive. But the latent dangers in some sense identified by Scalia J's comment 'the nation will live to regret what the court has done today' remain. There is acknowledgment of the legitimate interest of the state in protecting sources and methods of intelligence gathering[235] and in delivering the opinion of the court Kennedy J[236] states that:

> In considering both the procedural and substantive standards used to impose detention to prevent acts of terrorism, proper deference must be accorded to the political branches...The law must accord the Executive substantial authority to apprehend and detain those who pose a real danger to our security.

Although lip service is then paid to fidelity to freedom's first principles and freedom from arbitrary restraint, the acknowledgment of the acceptability of executive resort to detention is disquieting. The opinion concludes[237] that 'The laws and Constitution are designed to survive, and remain in force in extraordinary times. Liberty and security can be reconciled; and in our system they are reconciled within the framework of the law'.

However it is that reconciliation and the price of survival (capitulation & change perhaps?) that is the story of our times.

[2.130] Is there room for hope in the UK which might indicate how a renewal of confidence might change the tide in this direction, and give the Irish judiciary the courage of their convictions, or is it simply a false dawn? In a decision rooted in the murky waters involving the use of evidence obtained by torture, the House of Lords in *A (FC) & ors(FC) v Secretary of State for Home Department; A & others v Secretary of State for Home Department*[238] all agreed that the use was unacceptable (although majority and minority disagreed on the burden of proof).

[2.131] Lord Bingham alludes to *O'Brien* where the Irish Supreme Court held that 'to countenance the use of evidence extracted or discovered by gross personal violence would ... involve the state in moral defilement.'[239]

Bingham finds support for European scrutiny of evidential rules and confirmation of that Courts view 'that the way in which evidence has been obtained or used may be such as to render the proceedings unfair'[240] in *Saunders*

---

[235] *Boumediene v Bush* (2008) 553 US Lexis 4887 at 135.
[236] *Boumediene v Bush* (2008) 553 US Lexis 4887 at 134.
[237] *Boumediene v Bush* (2008) US Lexis 4887 at 136 *per* Kennedy J.
[238] *A v Secretary of State for Home Department* [2005] UKHL 71.
[239] *People v O'Brien* [1965] IR 142
[240] *A v Secretary of State for Home Department* [2005] UKHL 71 at para 25.

v UK[241] a case of compulsory questioning, and *Teixeira de Castro v Portugal,*[242] a case of entrapment. He concludes thereby echoing the views of all the members on this:[243]

> The principles of the common law, standing alone, in my opinion compel the exclusion of third party torture evidence as unreliable, unfair, offensive to ordinary standards of humanity and decency and incompatible with the principles which should animate a tribunal seeking to administer justice. But the principles of the common law do not stand alone. Effect must be given to the European Convention, which itself takes account of the all but universal consensus embodied in the torture conventions. The answer to the central question posed at the outset of this opinion is to be found not in a governmental policy, which may change, but in law.

[2.132] So there we have it – the new dawn – European Convention underpinning common law fairness. But before we get all heady in our belief as to what is attainable here, Adam Tompkins[244] reminds us of what that decision *did not* achieve:

> First and most obvious it did not secure the release of the detainees, most of whom remain incarcerated. Secondly it triggered a response from the Government that is likely to increase not decrease the scope and scale of the state's repressive counter terrorist measures. In the statement to the House of Commons in which the Home Secretary announced what these measure will be, he stated that 'prosecution is and will remain, our preferred way forward when dealing with terrorists'. If only this were true. The statistics reveal that it is not. We must always remember that the UK has in the Terrorism Act 200, one of the world's most comprehensive anti-terrorism statues, which contains dozens of criminal offences specifically designed top facilitate the states prosecution of terrorist offences. Yet between September 2001 and January 2004, the 544 arrests made in Britain under the 2000 Act resulted in only 98 offences being charged and it has been reported in only six convictions. *It is the splintering of terrorism from ordinary criminal justice that results in human rights abuses such as those perpetrated under the 2001 Act.* (emphasis added)

[2.133] Ewing[245] gives us the longer perspective or historical view, pointing out that:

> [t]he present situation is simply part of a historical process of continuing legal restraints on civil liberties and clampdown on political protest and dissent which has presented in a number of cycles which the judges have ridden rather than

---

[241] *Saunders v UK* (1996) 23 EHRR 313, para 25.
[242] *Teixeira de Castro v Portugal* (1998) 28 EHRR 101.
[243] *A v Secretary of State for Home Department* [2005] UKHL 71 at para 52.
[244] Tomkins, Adam 'Readings of A v Sec of State for Home Dept' (2005) *Public Law* 259 at 265.
[245] Ewing, 'The futility of the Human Rights Act' (2004) *Public Law* 829 at 851.

opposed. The process begins in modern times with the first world war, moving to the international war against communism in the 1920s and 1930s, the second world war in 1939, the cold war in the 1940s and 1950s and the war against Irish republicanism in the 1970s. Now the war against international terrorism and its attendant war on civil liberties provides the occasion for greater powers. It is in effect the sixth cycle of restraint and the sixth occasion for the introduction of emergency powers, many of which will be permanent and which will remain long after the emergency which produced them. And – as we have seen – all the while as the judges themselves now acknowledge the courts have provided inadequate scrutiny of or control over executive powers.

Ewing then gives a foot note to these observations specifically addressing the *A* decision which he terms 'the most important decision since *Entick and Carrington (1765)*, not only for the fact that the House of Lords stood up so convincingly to the Executive but also for the manner of doing so.

[2.134] Nonetheless Ewing points to the aftermath: the Prevention of Terrorism Act 2005 and 'control orders' to be placed on individuals (infringing their rights to privacy, freedom of expression, assembly association and movement), and notes that although when the Bill was introduced the Home Secretary was to be responsible for issuing control orders, political pressure incorporated the judiciary into this extraordinary process as the permission of the High Court must be granted before the orders come into force. The result of this is a situation which causes Ewing to further comment:

> It is one of the most remarkable features of this whole affair that the judges have become instruments for the violation of human rights.[246]

He concludes that '... rather than regard the Lords decision [in *A*] as a challenge to the futility thesis, it in fact opens up a new dimension of futility, a third front. This is the rebound, in the sense that an apparently progressive decision may contain the seeds of further restriction.'[247]

That latter point has been the one encapsulating most clearly the fate of the rights examined in face of state approach towards the aim of combating some 'greater evil'.

[2.135] The logic of progression then seems one of risk apprehension (on the part of the state), through to uncertainty with regard to constitutionality of action taken, through to a creeping dissonance between charter or constitutional declaration and legislative action finessed by judicial acceptance, resulting in

---

[246] Ewing, 'The futility of the Human Rights Act: A Long footnote' 2005 *Bracton Law Journal* 41 at 46.

[247] Ewing, 'The futility of the Human Rights Act: A Long footnote' 2005 *Bracton Law Journal* 41 at 47.

the fracture of meaning of both the right (now 'new' in the sense that it is newly constructed or interpreted and no longer the old one) and the regime (purportedly one which deals with infractions through a rights infused criminal process or justice model-in fact dealing with dissent through a security regime.

Concluding remarks

[2.136] So is there any hope for the future? The review undertaken of the gradual but incremental and sustained normalisation of emergency powers in Ireland, coupled with consideration of where human rights are and might be gives an insight into the future for all rights – new and traditional – which does not augur well. This perspective is not an entirely pessimistic one, but if there is a emerging wisdom it is that the future of human rights should no longer – or can no longer exclusively – rest with the lawyers.

There is value yet to be had in the language of human rights. Gearty[248] in his Hamlyn lecture eloquently puts forward that view:

> In this current age of doubt, with cruelty abundant in the gaps left in our culture by the abandonment of all our truths, and with the retreat of our soldiers of certainty swelling into a panicked stampede, we have reached the point where we should now admit that human kind simply cannot cope with too much unreality. We need truths – especially if they are true but also even if we have to make them up. It is not enough to leave everything to sentiment – our better selves need more help than a few recommended readings, a movie or two, and a deft capacity to dodge unpleasant conversations. Our culture is simply not up to jettisoning so much of the past while holding out such intangible and unsupported hope for the future. And if the good guys give up on the language of human rights, the others-less principled, differently motivated-will fill the words with a bleaker kind of meaning ...The term 'human rights' is the phrase we use when we are trying to describe decency in our post-philosophical world. It provides a link with the better part of our past while guiding us towards the finer features of our future.

Yet the vulnerability demonstrated raises questions about a new approach. What has been revealed is both a perverse use of rights talk and the inevitable susceptibility of a rights culture that has fallen victim to over-reliance on lawyers; or at least in the context of individual litigation which inevitable using the paradigm of securing individual rights neglects the community dimension of public interest in establishing same.

[2.137] Sandra Fredman[249] moves to transform human rights by acknowledging that latter dimension:

---

[248] Gearty *Can Human Rights Survive* [The Hamlyn lectures] Cambridge University Press 2006 at 56–57.

[249] Fredman, *Human Rights Transformed: positive rights and positive duties* (Oxford, 2008) at viii.

Nor is it correct to view human rights as simply protecting the individual, separate from society. Basic human rights values are essentially communal...Transforming human rights therefore entails the recognition that the power of the state needs to be harnessed to securing the genuine exercise of human rights.

She strives towards recognition of:[250]

...the fact that the community as a whole benefits when all are able to enjoy these rights.

Cheong Tham & Ewing[251] also suggest also that what is needed is a 'culture of controversy':

Because questions of human rights are necessarily contextual and subject to disagreement amongst citizens, an effective rights regime is one that enlivens a 'culture of controversy' on questions of human rights.

This requires citizens to be participants in the process:[252]

A culture of controversy' regarding human rights requires equal political participation. It may also be the case that equal political participation in human rights debates clearly depends upon their ability to articulate arguments based on human rights principles. This in turn will probably be sustained on a widespread basis if there are diverse conceptions of human rights.

[2.138] To some extent here also, we need an understanding or sensitivity to language, in the sense that not all actors or participants are equally well placed to secure access to the language of human rights currently. Fredman herself notes a difficulty with the assumption of participation on an equal basis. Pointing to the nature of the communication process itself she states:

While Habermas assumes that language is an unambiguous medium of communication, Young shows that this conceals a particular view of rationality, which privilege speech that is formal and general, and values assertive and definitive approaches rather than that which is tentative or exploratory. This in turn can operate as a form of power, silencing or devaluing the speech of those who do not engage on those terms. As Black concludes:

We have to recognise the possibility of forms of communication that do not correspond to the ideal of communication that Habermas posits, in which there may not be orientation to mutual understanding, to public reason, and a commitment to take on obligations arising from the interaction...We

---

[250] Fredman, *Human Rights Transformed: positive rights and positive duties* (Oxford, 2008) at ix.
[251] Cheong Tham and Ewing, 'Limitations of a Charter of Rights in the age of Counter-Terrorism' 2007 31 Melb ULR 462 at 497.
[252] Cheong Tham and Ewing, 'Limitations of a Charter of Rights in the age of Counter-Terrorism' 2007 31 Melb ULR 462 at 498.

have to allow for manipulation by communicants, for insincerity, for lack of trust and belief in the others' motives, or quite simply for the fact that people may not be interested in communicating at all.[253]

[2.139] A culture of controversy and participation in deliberative democracy may yet be the ingredients in pointing the way forward: Towards a revolution in our thinking which moves lawyers out of situations of manipulation by the state in rights diminution;[254] and abandon an approach to the delivery of rights' favouring the centrality of interpretation in the courts. The aspiration has to be framework for securing traditional (and still important rights) as well as new emergent ones, which involves citizens and lets them take back the construction of their (the public) interests with respect for human rights at its core. Ashworth and Zedner[255] certainly see the Human Rights Act as not having been adequate to the task of vindicating individual rights in face of recent challenges to the traditional concept of the criminal trial, and identify the future challenge in part at least as being one of how far evidence and procedure rules can accommodate change.

[2.140] In Ireland, as has been seen, the progression is readily apparent whereby provision tailored exceptionally for a particular context gradually extends its ambit to include others. The prototype was provision under the 1939 Act, particularly s 30 targeted against terrorism, but the precedent has expanded to incorporate other forms of exceptional provision with distinct rationales for their introduction. Having regard to the fragility of judicial resilience in face of normalisation of such provision in the context of powers of arrest and detention, it may later prove useful to scrutinise their pronouncement in relation to direct questions as to the accommodation of such 'emergency' provisions within the constitutional process and their approach to 'newer' manifestations of difference. This particular issue, moreover, is likely to characterise and to be influential in very many of the judgments in the context of the individual rules of evidence to consideration of which we now turn.

---

[253] Fredman, *Human Rights Transformed: positive rights and positive duties* (Oxford, 2008) at 156.

[254] Criminal Justice Act 2007.

[255] Ashwoth & Zedner, 'Defending the Criminal Law: Reflections on the changing character of crime procedure and sanctions' (2008) *Crim Law & Philos* 2: 21–51 at p 48.

Part Two
The Rules of Evidence

Chapter 3

Basic Concepts of the Law of Evidence

> Beauty is truth, truth is beauty, – that is all ye know on earth, and all ye need to know.
>
> Keats, *Ode on a Grecian Urn*

[3.01] The following is an extract from Roberts and Zuckerman[1] on criminal evidence:

> Fact-finding and the application of rules of evidence in criminal proceedings do not proceed in the abstract. Criminal adjudication takes place in particular procedural environments comprised of rules, institutions, processes, routine working practices and professional cultures all of which, in combination, stamp their influence on the unique character of fact-finding in English criminal trials and mould the nature and significance of the evidentiary rules and doctrines applied in court. Stripped of this procedural context, the rules of evidence might seem like an abstruse and highly stylized legal parlour game, complete with an excess of fiendishly complicated rules. But the law of evidence is neither mental chewing gum for idle legal minds nor a special kind of aptitude test for law students but a practical, living, body of rules and doctrines, part designed and part evolved, to facilitate forensic fact-finding and serve the ends of criminal justice.

This extract comes from a volume which looks at criminal evidence, making the point that very often when we are talking about evidence, it is in the criminal context because that is where the rules receive strictest attention as the stakes are higher. When you are talking about the rules of evidence, you are also very often talking in the context of the adversarial criminal trial and the adversarial criminal jury trials on indictment. This is what we will be looking at mostly, though not exclusively because some time will be spent looking at the Special Criminal Court or non-jury trials. However, those trials are on indictment, in other words, they constitute the more serious criminal cases.

Zuckerman and Roberts[2] continue:

> Evidence law moulds the conduct of criminal investigation by regulating for example the procedures by which confessions and identification evidence must be procured in order to be admissible at trial. Rules of evidence influence

---

[1]   Roberts and Zuckerman, *Criminal Evidence* (OUP, 2004), p 38.
[2]   Roberts and Zuckerman, *Criminal Evidence* (OUP, 2004), p 41.

prosecutors' decisions to prosecute or discontinue a case and prompt decisions of an accused to plead guilty or go to trial. And beyond these more tangible impacts, evidentiary rules exert further diffuse and subtle influences on the progress of criminal proceedings and on the quality of justice dispensed in them, because the content of the rules and the example set by their enforcement or non-enforcement, symbolizes the values and objectives to which the justice system subscribes. The law of evidence is already a standing advert, good or bad, for the quality of justice dispensed in British courts before any particular evidentiary rule is invoked, or for that matter ignored, in individual cases.

This makes the point that the rules of evidence are very often wedded to certain kinds of objectives in order to ensure quality of justice and/or fairness in the proceedings.

Terminology

[3.02] A brief account of the terminology used in relation to the categorisation of evidence produced at trial is as follows: The *factum probandum* or *fact in issue* or *principal fact* refers to questions such as: Did A knock B down? Did X rape Y? The *factum probans* or *evidentiary fact* or *fact relevant to the issue* is that from which the jury may infer the existence of the *factum probandum*. This is sometimes referred to as 'circumstantial evidence' and could include, for example, the statement of a witness at the trial for the murder of X that he saw X carrying a blood-stained knife at the door of the house where X's friend was mortally wounded. It could also comprise evidence of habit or habitual behaviour as, for example, in the facts of *Joy v Phillip Mills & Co Ltd*[3] where, in the context of the death of a stable boy from the kick of a horse giving rise to a workman's compensation claim, evidence was allowed as to the boy's habit of teasing the horse.

Evidence is classified or categorised in a number of ways, aside from its relation with the question at issue in the proceedings. Such categories include the following.

Categories of evidence

Direct evidence

[3.03] Direct evidence is the statement, by a witness, of facts that the witness has perceived through his own senses. For example, if he sees a car hitting X, that constitutes direct evidence of the *factum probandum*. If he sees X at the side of the road in the aftermath of such an incident, that is direct evidence of the *factum probans*.

---

[3]   *Joy v Phillip Mills & Co Ltd* [1916] 1 KB 849.

Real evidence

[3.04] Real evidence can take a variety of forms. It can prove the fact in issue or a relevant fact by, for example, the presentation of a gun, the alleged murder weapon. It can comprise evidence of the view of the site of the incident giving rise to the case. It can amount to evidence of a physical characteristic: for example, a rupture may imply a man is not guilty of a charge of rape. Real evidence may also constitute simply the demeanour of a witness.

Documentary evidence

[3.05] Documentary evidence can form circumstantial evidence – for example, to prove motive – or could constitute testimonial evidence, ie say something about the fact in issue through, for example, a confession. Documentary evidence itself may be a piece of real evidence, as, for example, where the issue is one as to the existence of a physical document.

Functions of judge and jury: arbiter of fact and law

[3.06] All questions of law are for the judge to decide. The trial judge is the sole arbiter of questions of law. Arguments on points of law are always heard in the absence of the jury (where relevant). The judge determines the issue of law, and the jury accepts the judge's evaluation of law. The jury in turn, is then the arbiter of fact. Where there is not a jury, the judge has both distinct functions: arbiter of fact and arbiter of law.

Receivability of evidence

[3.07] The question as to what evidence – to use Montrose's[4] term – is 'receivable' in a court of law, should at this juncture be addressed, as it is related to the running of the trial. In the first place only relevant evidence is receivable, ie evidence relevant to the *factum probandum or factum probans*. Secondly, the evidence must be admissible in accordance with the rules of evidence. This leads us to the situation where evidence (like a confession, for example) could be very relevant yet not admissible. It is this factor which draws the fundamental distinction between scientific and legal investigation. There is also, however, the added refinement of the concept of relevance known as '*materiality*'. This is not the question of whether the evidence is adequately related to the facts sought to be established (relevance), but whether those facts are adequately related to the case made by the party. An example may serve to illustrate the point: X is accused of murdering Y. Witness A saw X running from Y's house brandishing a knife. Witness B knew Y was of a religious persuasion forbidding violence in

---

4   Montrose, 'Basic Concepts of the Law of Evidence' (1954) 70 LQR 689.

all circumstances. At the trial X pleads self-defence. The only issue at trial becomes self-defence. Hence the material evidence is only that of witness B.

[3.08] This introduces a further concept into this already terminologically overcrowded area of the law – that is, evidence that is 'receivable'. Receivable evidence is that which is relevant, admissible and material. It is important to keep clear the borderline between these concepts (something, as will be seen, the judiciary do not always achieve). Thayer[5] puts it thus: 'No evidence is receivable unless it is relevant' (the negative averment) and 'all evidence that is relevant is receivable unless excluded by a rule of admissibility' (the positive). In other words, only the concept of admissibility was ignored and all relevant evidence deemed receivable. Stephens[6] gives a very good definition of relevance:

> The word 'relevant' means that any two facts are so related to each other that according to the common course of events one, either taken by itself or in connection with other facts proves or renders probable the past, present or future existence or non-existence of the other.

This concept of relevance, then, is one of fact; that of admissibility, one of law.

Distinctions: relevance/admissibility

[3.09] The extent to which these distinctions are blurred or mistaken is illustrated by a comparison of two decisions of the Irish Court of Criminal Appeal. The first is that of *People (AG) v O'Neill*,[7] which involved a charge of manslaughter resulting from a motor car accident. The facts presented were as follows: the defendant had spent about an hour in the pub on the evening of the accident, and there consumed a shandy and two glasses of ale. There was evidence that he was sober when he left at around 8:50 pm. The accident occurred at 9:50 pm. The trial judge admitted the evidence as to the consumption of alcohol by the accused, but charged the jury to the effect that the prosecution disclaimed any suggestion that the accused was adversely affected by drink, and that the evidence was given for the purpose of tracing the accused's movements. The accused was found guilty and sentenced to 12 months' imprisonment. The accused appealed to the Court of Criminal Appeal. There it was held that the evidence as to the alcoholic drink taken by the accused prior to the accident should have been excluded on the ground that such evidence was irrelevant to the issues at trial. Kenny J[8] commented as follows:

---

5   Thayer, *Preliminary Treatise on Evidence and the Common Law* (1898), pp 264–6.
6   Stephens, *A Digest of the Law of Evidence* (12th edn, MacMillan and Co, 1936).
7   *People (AG) v O'Neill* [1964] Ir Jur 1.
8   *People (AG) v O'Neill* [1964] Ir Jur 1 at 4.

As the prosecution were not making the case that the accused's driving was affected by alcoholic drink, this evidence was wholly irrelevant to any of the issues in the trial. The argument that it was admissible because it was given for the purpose of tracing the movements of the accused before the accident assumes the very matter which the argument attempts to establish, that is, the relevance of those movements to any of the issues in the trial. As the evidence was not relevant it should not have been given.

[3.10] A similar factual situation led to consideration of the same issue in *People v Moore*.[9] In that case, a youth of 16 years was charged with dangerous driving causing death, contrary to the road traffic legislation. Unsworn statements by him made reference to visits to public houses and the consumption of three pints of stout. These were admitted in evidence, notwithstanding counsel's objections. In his charge to the jury, the trial judge read the statements without comment. After submission by the accused's counsel, the jury were recalled and told by the trial judge that the prosecution had not suggested that drink had anything to do with the case and there was no question of the accused being drunk. They should leave the matter of drink out of consideration. The accused was convicted. On application for leave to appeal to the Court of Criminal Appeal, Davitt P reasoned that:

> Where a person has during a period of time which is material, consumed a significant quantity of alcoholic drink it will therefore tend to render his driving unsafe. The evidence that he has consumed such a quantity during such a period is therefore in our opinion of probative value on a charge of dangerous driving and therefore relevant and admissible in law. To this end we venture respectfully to differ from the principles enunciated in *O'Neill's* case.[10]

He continued:

> We agree ... that he (the trial judge) should exercise his discretion to exclude evidence as to drink taken by a driver where he is satisfied that its probative value is outweighed by its prejudicial effect, that is, in our opinion, where the amount of drink is insignificant either as to the amount or time of consumption.

[3.11] The importance of clarity of concepts is evident. There are two stages: first the determination of relevance, then that of admissibility (one criteria of adjudication of the latter being that of balancing prejudicial effect against probative value). As can be seen from a comparison of the above case law, the delineation of same is not without consequence in substance.

---

[9] *People v Moore* [1964] Ir Jur 6.
[10] *People v Moore* [1964] Ir Jur 6 at 12.

Trial judge's discretion to exclude relevant evidence

[3.12] In *People (AG) v O'Neill*,[11] Kenny J had confirmed what has long been recognised as a general principle: that of a trial judge's discretion to exclude relevant evidence when its probable value is small but its prejudicial effect considerable. Although this principle has been overshadowed in this jurisdiction by constitutional parameters regarding fair trial (see Chapter 4 on Illegally Obtained Evidence), it is important to remember this particular judicial discretion to exclude relevant evidence which is core to the jury's function in any criminal trial. It was reaffirmed by Geoghegan J in *People (DPP) v Meleady (No 3)*:[12]

> It is well established that, although there is no authority to permit a criminal court to admit, as a matter of discretion, evidence which is inadmissible under an exclusionary rule of law, the converse is not the case. A judge, as part of his inherent power, has an overriding duty in every case to ensure that the accused receives a fair trial and always has a discretion to exclude otherwise admissible prosecution evidence if, in his opinion, its prejudicial effect on the minds of the jury outweighs its true probative value.

[3.13] A vindication of the role of the trial judge in determining all issues of admissibility is found in *Blanchfield v Harnett*.[13] Here, proceedings had been brought by the applicant by way of judicial review seeking *certiorari* to quash the respondent District Judge's order under the Bankers Books Evidence Act 1879. The respondent argued that the purpose of the application was to render the evidence obtained under the orders inadmissible at the criminal trial. It was held that whether the evidence could be admitted is a determination solely for the discretion of the trial judge. All questions relevant to the determination of such items were held to rest with the trial judge as, otherwise, trials would be suspended for lengthy periods while such issues were litigated in other courts. The desirability of such continuity had also been referred to by O'Flaherty J in *DPP v Special Criminal Court*.[14]

Determination of the ultimate issue

[3.14] One issue that merits attention at this stage, although it will arise and be dealt with more fully later (in the context of opinion evidence – see para **7.16**), is the extent to which evidence presented can come close to determining the fact in issue, which is more properly the prerogative of the jury, or indeed questions of

---

11 *People (AG) v O'Neill* [1964] Ir Jur 1.
12 *People (DPP) v Meleady (No 3)* [2001] 4 IR 16 at 31, Geoghegan J.
13 *Blanchfield v Harnett* [2001] 1 ILRM 193.
14 *DPP v Special Criminal Court* [1999] 1 IR 60.

law, which is the province of the trial judge. Particularly with increasingly specialised knowledge in the scientific arena, this can pose some considerable difficulty.

[3.15] An early instance of this is provided by the decision in *Maher v AG*.[15] This case examined the Road Traffic Act 1968, which stated that 'conclusive evidence' of intoxication would be given in the form of blood alcohol concentration where a certificate was tendered in the prescribed fashion. In the Supreme Court, Fitzgerald CJ commented that the Constitution, which allocates the administration of justice to the courts and judges, necessarily reserves to them the determination of all essential ingredients of any offence charged against the accused person. Such a statutory provision, as here encapsulated in this case, would purport to remove such determination and so constitute an invalid infringement of judicial power. Further instances of the tolerance of expert testimony coming close to determining the facts in issue were provided by a number of earlier English decisions, where the courts were faced with the phenomenon of the increased use of specialists. The courts' approach led to a legal culture tolerant (if not sanguine) in the face of same, and the development of a burgeoning industry of 'expert' advisers without which lawyers dared not present a case, and within which realm they were frequently peculiarly ill-equipped to challenge evidence prejudicial to their client.

[3.16] In *Lowery v R*,[16] the evidence of a psychologist was tendered on behalf of one of the two accused to establish that one of the accused's version of the facts was more probable than that put forward by the other accused. The Privy Council sanctioned the admissibility of same. By contrast, in *R v Turner*,[17] Lawton LJ made reference to the decision in *Lowery* and stated that:

> We do not consider that it [*Lowery*] is authority for the proposition that in all cases psychologists and psychiatrists can be called to prove the probability of the accused's veracity. If any such rule was applied in our courts, trial by psychiatrists would be likely to take the place of trial by jury and magistrates.

[3.17] In another jurisdiction faced with a similar issue, the Supreme Court of Canada stated in *R v Lupien*[18] that although expert psychiatric testimony was not admissible to show the absence of requisite intent on the part of an accused to commit the crime charged, it would be admissible to show his lack of capacity to form that intent.

---

[15] *Maher v AG* [1973] IR 140. The section in question was s 44 of the Road Traffic Act 1968.
[16] *Lowery v R* [1974] AC 85.
[17] *R v Turner* [1975] QB 834.
[18] *R v Lupien* [1970] SCR 263.

[3.18] The decision in *DPP v A & BC Chewing Gum Ltd*[19] came close to the position of usurping the function of the jury as determinants of the fact in issue. In the context of a charge of obscenity against the defendants in relation to a series of graphically violent 'war cards' issued with their product, the expert testimony of a child psychiatrist was admitted to show the likely effect of these allegedly obscene articles upon children. The expert testified as to whether they were likely to 'corrupt or deprave', the latter constituting the legal test for obscenity.

[3.19] Before exploring further the issue as to the relative functions of judge and jury and the pivotal nature of the role of the witness (not particularly the expert witness), it is timely to consider both the issue as to the onus of proof and its location, together with the extent of that obligation. These notions are referred to respectively as the 'burden of proof' and the 'standard of proof'.

Burden of proof

[3.20] The phrase 'burden of proof' is traditionally regarded as having two distinct aspects or meanings:

  (i)   the legal burden of proof; and

  (ii)   the evidential burden of proof.

The first of these, the legal burden of proof, is more typically what we regard as being the burden of proof proper, ie the obligation to persuade. It is what Wigmore termed 'the risk of non-persuasion' and the House of Lords in *DPP v Morgan*[20] called 'the probative burden'.

[3.21] The legal burden of proof may be differently placed in respect of different issues arising in the same case. If a person bears the legal burden of proof in respect of a particular issue or disputed question of fact (fact in issue), an adequate preponderance of probative materials in favour of that issue being decided in favour of that party must be adduced. Otherwise, the issue must, as a matter of law, be decided against him. In plainer terms, if the requisite standard of proof is not reached by the party bearing the legal burden, s/he loses.

Shifting the burden of proof

[3.22] A legal burden, once placed, cannot be shifted by the mere production of evidence by the other party to the proceedings. On the other hand, as the initial placement of the burden of proof is determined by a rule of law, so it may shift

---

[19] *DPP v A & BC Chewing Gum Ltd* [1968] 1 QB 159.
[20] *DPP v Morgan* [1976] AC 182.

as a result of the coming into operation of some other legal rule such as a compelling, although rebuttable, presumption of law.

[3.23] On a more pragmatic level, there may come a point in the course of a trial when the legal burden upon an issue seems, in the light of the evidence so far adduced, to have been satisfied. In such circumstances there is a real sense in which considerations of prudence or good tactics – but not of law – impose an obligation upon the opponent. He is then sometimes said to bear a tactical burden of proof or, as it is sometimes put, the legal burden of proof has tactically shifted to him.

Evidential burden of proof

[3.24] The evidential burden of proof is an obligation to raise an issue, or to make out a *prima facie* case and so get the issue past the trial judge and before the trier of fact. To describe the evidential burden as a burden of proof, therefore, is something of a misnomer. Similarly to the legal burden, the evidential burden relates to a particular issue and may therefore be differently placed in respect of the different issues which may arise in a case.

[3.25] The evidential burden is discharged by evidence sufficient to warrant, but not necessarily to require, an affirmative finding by a reasonable jury. If the evidence is sufficient, the issue must be put before the jury. Whereas it is for the jury or trier of fact to determine whether a legal burden has been satisfied, the discharge of an evidential burden is the exclusive concern of the judge. *DPP v O'Reilly*[21] is illustrative of a situation where a direction was given by the trial judge (though, as it transpired, incorrectly). The defendant was charged with aggravated burglary. The District Justice found *inter alia* that the only incriminating evidence against the defendant was contained in a cautioned statement. No evidence was tendered to show or suggest that the defendant was at or near the post office in question at any material time or to show or suggest that he had used a firearm at any material time.

[3.26] The learned District Justice, of the opinion that the State must prove the accused's physical presence on the premises, in the absence of evidence that the defendant had entered the premises, dismissed the case at the close of prosecution evidence. In the High Court on a case stated, Egan J asserted, however, that the District Justice was wrong in holding it was an essential ingredient of the charge that there should be proof the defendant was physically present at or about the premises where the offence was committed. However, although incorrectly applied here, as the District Judge was wrong in law, this case does demonstrate the power of the burden of proof.

---

[21] *DPP v O'Reilly* [1991] 1 IR 77.

Who bears the burden of proof?

[3.27] Case law precedent, or the construction of a statute, determines on which party to the proceedings the burden of proof lies. It is sometimes said that the legal burden rests upon he who affirms rather than he who denies, yet this is an uncertain guide. Carter[22] contends that the legal and evidential burdens often reflect the way in which a relevant rule of substantive law is formulated – for example, proof of what is described as a defence will often rest upon the defendant and, especially in civil cases, may project the policies underlying that particular rule. Criminal cases certainly, as Carter acknowledges, call for more general considerations. For instance, whereas at common law the evidential burden in respect of a defence in a criminal trial may lie upon the accused, the legal burden in respect of all issues except insanity lies upon the prosecution. Allowance must be made, however, for the instance where statutes may, by means of a 'reverse onus clause', expressly place the legal burden in respect of a particular issue upon the accused.

[3.28] Civil cases do not allow for such general statements. The nineteenth century case of *Amos v Hughes*[23] held that the burden of proof of the issue was upon the party who would be unsuccessful in the case if no evidence at all were given, and such party had the right to begin. In *Joseph Constantine Steamship Line Ltd v Imperial Smelting Corp Ltd*,[24] the House of Lords held that the burden of proof lay upon the party who affirmed and not upon the party who denied. This rule applies to a plaintiff who asserts an exception to the defence pleaded.

Res ipsa loquitur

[3.29] The doctrine of *res ipsa loquitur* merits a mention, as it may be considered to bear upon the incidence of the legal or evidential burden of proof in civil cases. The doctrine of *res ipsa loquitur* was given expression by Erle CJ in *Scott v London and St Katherine's Docks Co*,[25] namely:

> [W]here the thing is shown to be under the management of the defendant or his servants, and the accident is such as in the ordinary course of things does not happen if those who have the management use proper care, it affords reasonable evidence, in the absence of explanation by the defendants, that the accident arose from want of care.

Mostly, the doctrine is regarded as affecting the burden by the operation of a presumption.

---

[22] Carter, *Cases and Statutes on Evidence* (Sweet & Maxwell, 1981).
[23] *Amos v Hughes* (1835) 1 Mood & R 464.
[24] *Joseph Constantine Steamship Line Lid v Imperial Smelting Corp Ltd* [1942] AC 154.
[25] *Scott v London and St Katherine's Docks Co* (1865) 3 H & C 596 at 601.

[3.30] In *Hanrahan v Merck, Sharp & Dohme (Ireland) Ltd*,[26] where it was alleged that the escape of noxious gases caused damage to the plaintiff farmer's dairy herd, it was held that the plaintiff had failed to adduce *prima facie* evidence that the escape of malodorous fumes from the defendant's premises was the cause of deterioration in the condition of the plaintiff's herd and pastures. It was also held that the cause of the alleged damage was not a matter peculiarly within the knowledge of the defendant so as to transfer to the defendant the onus of proving that the damage had not been caused by the defendant's activities.[27] Henchy J's somewhat controversial restatement of the doctrine in the Supreme Court involves the notion that the defendant's superior knowledge of how the tort was caused would render it 'palpably unfair' to require the plaintiff to prove something 'peculiarly within the range of the defendant's capacity of proof'.

[3.31] Other cases involving application of the said doctrine of *res ipsa loquitur* include the 'supermarket negligence' actions. In *Mullen v Quinnsworth*,[28] the Supreme Court found *inter alia* that the maxim *res ipsa loquitur* applies to a claim of negligence asserted by the plaintiff in the context of a spillage of oil on the defendant's supermarket floor, which caused her to fall and sustain damage. This doctrine had the effect of shifting the onus of proof onto the defendants to show that they had taken all reasonable care.

[3.32] Similarly in *O'Reilly v Lavelle*,[29] the doctrine of *res ipsa loquitur* was applied in the context of liability for animals. Section 2(1) of the Animals Act 1985 provides that those rules of the common law relating to liability for negligence which exclude or restrict liability in respect of an animal straying on the highway are abolished. The plaintiff was driving on the highway after dark, when his car came into collision with a Friesian calf. The plaintiff sought to rely on the doctrine of *res ipsa loquitur*, which he had not specifically pleaded. The action was dismissed by the Circuit Court, as the plaintiff had not sufficiently discharged the burden of proof. On appeal to the High Court, Johnson J[30] referred to the statements of the law by Griffin J in *Mullen v Quinnsworth Ltd*,[31] where he adopted the principle of Erle CJ in *Scott v London and St Katherine's Docks Co* (at **3.29** above).

---

[26] *Hanrahan v Merck, Sharp & Dohme (Ireland) Ltd* [1988] ILRM 629.
[27] See 'Peculiar knowledge principle' at para **3.73** *et seq.*
[28] *Mullen v Quinnsworth Ltd* [1990] 1 IR 59.
[29] *O'Reilly v Lavelle* [1990] 2 IR 372.
[30] *O'Reilly v Lavelle* [1990] 2 IR 372 at 373.
[31] *Mullen v Quinnsworth Ltd* [1990] 1 IR 59 at 62.

[3.33] Griffin J also commented that the doctrine does not have to be pleaded before a plaintiff can rely on it. If the facts pleaded and the facts proved show that the doctrine is applicable to the case, this is sufficient. On application of the facts before him, Johnson J concluded that cattle properly managed should not wander on the road, and therefore the burden of proof in this case shifted to the defendant to show that he took reasonable care of his animals. 'I believe that there is no matter more appropriate for the application of the doctrine of *res ipsa loquitur* than cattle wandering on the highway'. On the balance of probabilities, he found the defendant failed to discharge the onus of proof.

[3.34] In *Murray v Miller*,[32] Judge McMahon imposed liability on the basis of s 2 of the Animals Act 1985 in a situation where a traffic accident occurred when the defendant's cow jumped out in front of the plaintiff's car. The judge provided a useful summary of the case law in this area:

> [T]he effect of this statutory provision is that reasonable care must now be taken to ensure that animals do not stray onto the highway and cause damage thereon. This normally translates into an obligation to ensure that the land is stock proofed and that the fencing is sufficient to prevent animals from breaking out. Moreover, in relation to proof, the case law indicates that the onus of proof, that the land was properly fenced, is now on the landowner or the owner of the animal who seeks to evade liability. In *O'Reilly v Lavelle* [1990] 2 IR 372 and again in *O'Shea v Anhold and Horse Holiday Farm Ltd* (Supreme Court, 23 October 1996) the courts in this jurisdiction have clearly accepted that the principle of *res ipsa loquitur* applies to these situations. Accordingly, in cases such as the present, to escape liability, the first and second defendants must provide the evidence to show that they took reasonable care in the management of the land to ensure that the fencing was secure. [T]he first and second defendants ... tendered no significant evidence in this regard, and on this ground, I have little hesitation in holding them liable for the damage which their straying animal caused to the plaintiff.

[3.35] Although the majority of *res ipsa loquitur* cases proceed on the basis of the 'classic formulation' in *Scott v London & St Katherine's Docks Company*,[33] *Hanrahan*'s grounding of the doctrine in 'unfairness' still has influence, as can be seen from the decision of *Rothwell v Motor Insurers Bureau of Ireland*.[34] Here, the plaintiff's vehicle had skidded on a patch of oil on the road, left by an unknown driver of a truck or lorry on which the fuel tank was ill-fitting. The plaintiff argued it was a case where *res ipsa loquitur* applied. McCracken J did

---

[32] *Murray v Miller* (14 November 2001), CC, Roscommon, 2001, Judge McMahon.

[33] See *Lindsay v Western Health Board* [1993] 2 IR 147; and *Merriman v Greenhills Foods Ltd* [1997] ILRM 46.

[34] *Rothwell v Motor Insurers Bureau of Ireland* (6 July 2001, unreported), HC, McCracken J at para 20.

not agree because there might be circumstances in which a spillage occurred without any fault on the part of the driver. Although McCracken J preferred the reasoning of *Hanrahan*, he disagreed on the facts:

> It appears to me that the judgment in *Hanrahan* requires not merely that a matter in respect of which the onus is to shift is within the exclusive knowledge of the defendant, but also that it is 'peculiarly within the range of the defendant's capacity of proof.' That is not the position here ... neither party could go further: the matter was not within the knowledge, exclusive or otherwise, of either of them.

However, he did find for the plaintiff without recourse to the doctrine, on the basis it would be contrary to the purpose of the Motor Insurers Bureau of Ireland agreement that a plaintiff would have a burden of proof (that the driver could have no defence) he would not have had if the identity of the driver were known.

Despite developments in other jurisdictions (eg Canada)[35] regarding the doctrine as no more than circumstantial evidence establishing a sufficient case to go to the jury, the Irish courts do seem to take the view that once the doctrine applies, the question then arises as to what the defendant must do to avoid liability.[36]

Criminal cases: the 'golden thread'

[3.36] The 'golden thread' running through our law is that enunciated in *Woolmington v DPP*[37] by the House of Lords and specifically approved and adopted in Ireland in *People (AG) v Byrne*,[38] to the effect that as a general rule in a criminal case, it is always the duty of the prosecution to prove the guilt of the accused beyond a reasonable doubt.

[3.37] In *Woolmington*, having fully considered the authorities to date, Viscount Sankey stated as follows:

> If at any period of a trial it was permissible for the judge to rule that the prosecution had established its case and that the onus was shifted on the prisoner to prove that he was not guilty and that unless he discharged that onus the prosecution was entitled to succeed, it would be enabling the judge in such a case to say that the jury must in law find the prisoner guilty and so make the judge decide the case and not the jury, which is not the common law.[39]

---

[35] *Fontaine v British Columbia (Official Administrator)* [1998] 1 SC 424.

[36] See further McMahon and Binchy, *Law of Torts* (3rd edn, Tottel Publishing, 2000), para 9.11 et seq.

[37] *Woolmington v DPP* [1935] AC 462 at 467 *per* Avory J and at 475 *per* Sankey LC.

[38] *People (AG) v Byrne* [1974] IR 1 at 5 *per* Kenny J.

[39] *Woolmington v DPP* [1935] AC 462 at 480.

[3.38] He then enunciated the rule which is reiterated to this day:

> Throughout the web of the English Criminal Law one golden thread is always to be seen, that is the duty of the prosecution to prove the prisoner's guilt, subject to what I have already said as to the defence of insanity and subject also to any statutory exception. If, at the end of and on the whole of the case, there is a reasonable doubt, created by the evidence given by either the prosecution or the prisoner, as to whether the prisoner killed the deceased with a malicious intention, the prosecution has not made out the case and the prisoner is entitled to an acquittal. No matter what the charge or where the trial the principle that the prosecution must prove the guilt of the prisoner is part of the common law of England and no attempt to whittle it down can be entertained.[40]

[3.39] In *People (DPP) v Kiely*,[41] one of the grounds of appeal was that the trial judge, in his charge to the jury, had not specifically stated that there were two versions of events and the jury should adopt the accused's version unless the prosecution version had been proven beyond reasonable doubt. Reliance was placed on *People v Byrne*,[42] where Kenny J had stated that 'the jury should be told ... that when two views ... are possible on the evidence, they should adopt that which is favourable to the accused.' McGuinness J held that it was the trial judge's charge as a whole that was important. Hence, although it would have been preferable if he had included an explanation of the benefit of the doubt as *per* Kenny J's judgment in *Byrne*, what was important was that he had emphasised the concept of the presumption of innocence and proof beyond a reasonable doubt and she was satisfied the jury had been properly instructed as to the burden and standard of proof here.

[3.40] In *People (DPP) v C*,[43] the applicant appealed on the basis that the trial judge failed to charge the jury correctly in relation to the conflict between the evidence given by the Complainant-in-Chief and her evidence under cross-examination. Murray J held that the trial judge had not erred in failing to direct the jury to accept the version more favourable to the applicant. He was of the view that to direct the jury to rely on one version rather than another was to usurp its function, and here the jury had been properly directed, that where a conflict arose, they should accept the version most favourable to the accused, when the other version had been proved beyond a reasonable doubt.

[3.41] In *People (DPP) v DO'T*,[44] the defendant had been convicted of rape. The case deals essentially with the issue of charging the jury on the burden of proof and the connection between that and the underlying principle of presumption of

---

[40] *Woolmington v DPP* [1935] AC 462 at 481 *per* Viscount Sankey.
[41] *People (DPP) v Kiely* (21 March 2001), CCA, McGuinness J.
[42] *People v Byrne* [1974] IR 1 at 9.
[43] *People (DPP) v C* [2001] 3 IR 345.
[44] *People (DPP) v DO'T* [2003] 4 IR 286.

innocence. The trial judge in this case had not referred to the presumption of innocence in his original charge to the jury, nor in his recharge. The relevant portion of the trial transcript reads:

> Now both sides have fairly spoken to you about the general onus of proof. As you surely know by now the onus of proof is with the prosecution. That onus of proof is not just in relation to whether or not the accused is guilty or not guilty as charged. In anything you are deciding in the case on any fact, you have to remember that the onus of establishing that fact is with the prosecution. The onus of proof is that each matter must be proved beyond a reasonable doubt. As [counsel for the accused] pointed out, there are a lot of different ways of explaining reasonable doubt and no one has yet found the perfect way of doing so. It does not mean beyond any doubt at all, but it means beyond the doubt that is reasonable. This can be expressed in a lot of ways. The doubt must be genuine. It must not be airy-fairy or whimsical, and you are not looking for any mathematical certainty in the matter. You are the jury, it is for you to decide if there is a doubt, if that doubt is a reasonable doubt. [45]

[3.42] Although the jury was called back in to recharge them, there had again been no reference to the presumption of innocence. An appeal followed on the basis that the trial judge had failed to direct the jury correctly. An appeal on the basis of this failure was considered by the Court of Criminal Appeal and upheld. Hardiman J gave the judgment of the court in which he emphasised the importance of the presumption of innocence and its link to the onus of proof:[46]

> The presumption of innocence, thus so securely entrenched nationally and internationally, is not only a right in itself, it is the basis of other aspects of a trial in due course of law at common law. The rule that, generally speaking, the prosecution bears the burden of proving all the elements of the offence necessary to establish guilt is a corollary of the presumption. To state the incidence of the burden of proof without indicating its basis in the presumption is to risk understating its importance and perhaps relegating it to the status of a mere technical rule. The presumption is the basis of the rule as to the burden of proof and not merely an alternative way of stating it. The presumption also exists, and has effect, in ways other than simply dictating the incidence of the burden of proof at the trial … [I]t is, for example, the basis of the right to bail.

Hardiman J's final statement points out that it is essential that the judge should ensure that the jury should understand this connection:[47]

> Due to the fundamental importance of the presumption of innocence, these shortcomings are a serious matter for the integrity of the trial. It is of course essential that the jury should understand that the onus of proof is on the

---

[45] *People (DPP) v DO'T* [2003] 4 IR 286 at 288–289.
[46] *People (DPP) v DO'T* [2003] 4 IR 286 at 290–291.
[47] *People (DPP) v DO'T* [2003] 4 IR 286 at 293.

prosecution and that they should understand the standard of proof. These things should be presented, not as arbitrary rules, but as the corollary of the basic principle of the presumption of innocence, which is a constitutional and universally recognised human right. The trial process, including the jury's role in it, has to be presented as one grounded in principle, and that principle is one of high constitutional significance.

Exceptions to the rule in Woolmington

[3.43] There are, of course, exceptions to that general principle laid down in *Woolmington*. As enunciated in the case itself, there may well be specific statutory exceptions – occasions when the burden of proof is placed on an accused person in relation to a given issue by virtue of an express provision in the relevant statute. There is also the well-established exception at common law: the defence of insanity. As confirmed in *McNaghten*[48] by the House of Lords, the legal burden of establishing the common law defence of insanity rests upon the accused. The relevant standard of proof in this, as on any occasion, indeed, when the burden of proof rests on the accused in a criminal case, is proof on the balance of probabilities. It is important to distinguish these occasions from situations in which the accused may bear only the evidential burden of proof – as in the case of the defence of 'sane-automatism', where the accused bears an obligation to adduce some evidence in relation to same, sufficient to raise that defence, or get the issue placed before the jury (*Bratty v AG for Northern Ireland*).[49]

[3.44] The validity of statutory exceptions to the golden rule was questioned in the Irish context in the case of *O'Leary v AG*,[50] discussed at **2.26** *et seq*. This case centred on s 24 of the Offences against the State Act 1939, which provides that proof of possession of incriminating documents shall, without more, unless the contrary is proven, be evidence that such person was a member of the organisation at the time of the charge, which O'Leary claimed infringed the constitutional right to a trial in due course of law and, in particular, the presumption of innocence by placing on the accused the burden of disproving his guilt. Despite acknowledgement at both High and Supreme Court levels that the presumption of innocence is inherent in Art 38, the section was 'saved'.

[3.45] Support for the notion that the burden of proof when placed on the accused will be considered by the Irish courts to be an evidential burden is found in *Hardy v Ireland*,[51] where it was held that the effect of s 4(1) of the Explosive

---

[48] *R v McNaghten* (1843) 10 Cl & F 200.

[49] *Bratty v AG for Northern Ireland* [1963] AC 386.

[50] *O'Leary v AG* [1991] 2 ILRM 454 at 459 *per* Costello J. Also [1993] 1 IR 102 at 107.

[51] *Hardy v Ireland* [1994] 2 IR 550.

Substances Act 1883 was to shift a persuasive burden of proof onto the accused requiring him only to raise a doubt of substance in relation to the prosecution case.

[3.46] Similarly, in *DPP v Byrne*,[52] in the context of the presumption of intention to drive in s 50(8) of the Road Traffic Act 1961, as inserted by s 11 of the Road Traffic Act 1964, the court did not take the view that that section placed a legal burden on the defendant to prove he did not have the intention to drive. Rather, the assumption appeared to be that the defendant bore an evidential burden to raise a reasonable doubt in the jury's mind.

Reverse onus provisions and the right to silence

[3.47] This exception to the golden rule concerns those occasions when through statutory provision the legislature has decided for whatever reason to place the burden of proof on the accused. It is important to link the placement of the burden of proof with the presumption of innocence. The burden is placed there as a fundamental principle of fairness in criminal law and its justification is rooted in the social and legal consequences of being convicted of a crime. It represents a recognition of the huge disparity that exists between the state and all its resources and the individual accused.

[3.48] The Law Reform Commission of Canada, when reviewing the Canadian criminal justice system, said quite clearly that criminal law always lies on the cutting edge of the abuse of power. The presumption of innocence provides a counterweight to that. The connection between the presumption of innocence and ensuring fairness in a criminal trial is clear in our constitutional mandate under Art 38. It is also found in art 6(2) of the European Convention on Human Rights (ECHR).

The reasoning of the Supreme Court in *O'Leary*,[53] which saves the reverse onus provision, is not persuasive but it is very clear in both courts that they are anxious to save this particular provision and do it by finding that s 24 does not actually shift legal burden of proof at all, a questionable judgement. See *O'Leary* case sets up a situation where the presumption of innocence and the placement of the burden of proof is no longer absolute, in the sense that Costello J discussed,[54] so that countervailing considerations and arguments can come into play to justify situations where the burden of proof (evidentiary or legal) can move onto the accused. This decision sets the scene that allows a plethora of such legislative provisions thereafter. It is to that legislation and its consideration by the courts that we now turn.

---

[52] *DPP v Byrne* [2002] 2 ILRM 97.

[53] *O'Leary v AG* [1995] 1 IR 254.

[54] See para **3.43** above.

[3.49] *Heaney and McGuinness v Ireland*[55] dealt with a statutory provision interfering with the presumption of innocence and the right to silence. It considered a provision under the 1939 Act, which is within the realms of extraordinary legislation. The Supreme Court once again saved the constitutionality of the provision but when it reached the European Court of Human Rights (ECt HR), the latter reached a different conclusion.

[3.50] The 1939 Act, s 52(1) was the provision in question. It allowed members of An Garda Síochána to demand of anyone they arrested a full account of their movements and actions and any information with regard to the commission of offences. Section 52(2) provided that failure to give information would be an offence resulting in six months' imprisonment. Heaney and McGuinness were arrested under s 30 on suspicion of having been involved in a bomb attack in Northern Ireland that killed six people and while in custody, they failed to answer questions under s 52. They began proceedings challenging the constitutionality of s 52 on the basis that it infringed the right to silence and a right to trial based on adversarial principles and the presumption of innocence. In terms of the test of constitutionality, Costello J in the High Court looked at the provision and identified the controversy as being as to the nature and scope of the right to silence and the plaintiff's reliance in that regard on Art 38.1 of the Constitution:

> This Article provides that 'No person shall be tried on any criminal charge save in due courts of law', an Article which, as the courts have shown, implies a great deal more than a simple assertion that trials have to be heard in accordance with laws enacted by parliament. It is an Article couched in peremptory language and has been construed as a constitutional guarantee that criminal trials will be conducted in accordance with basic concepts of justice. Those basic principles may be of ancient origin and part of the long-established principles of the common law, or they may be of more recent origin and widely accepted in other jurisdictions and recognized in international conventions as a basic requirement of a fair trial. Thus, the principles that an accused is entitled to the presumption of innocence, that an accused cannot be tried for an offence unknown to the law, or charged a second time with the same offence, the principle that an accused must know the case he has to meet, and that evidence illegally obtained will generally be inadmissible at trial, are all principles that are so basic to the concept of fair trials that they obtain constitutional protection from this Article. Furthermore, the Irish courts have developed a concept that there are basic rules of procedure which must be followed in order to ensure that an accused is accorded a fair trial and these basic rules must be followed if constitutional invalidity is to be avoided.[56]

---

[55] *Heaney and McGuinness v Ireland* [1994] 3 I R 593 (HC), [1996] 1 I R 580 (SC).
[56] *Heaney and McGuinness v Ireland* [1994] 3 IR 593 at 605, *per* Costello J.

This is a particularly strong elucidation of what is implicit or flows from Art 38.1 and the constitutional concept of a fair trial and its implications for rules of evidence and procedure. Quite apart from the end result of the case at hand, Costello J's reasoning is useful to remember in terms of future legislative moves on the burden of proof and silence. It also perhaps signals the beginnings of a departure emerging between principle elucidation and the practical accommodation of legislative provision at odds with same.

[3.51] Costello J went on, however, to have regard to restrictions on the right to silence. This reasoning was in many ways foreshadowed by the decision in *O'Leary*. In the immediate aftermath of concluding that the right to remain silent and not to incriminate himself (sic) 'is such a long standing one and so widely accepted as basic to the rules under which criminal trials are conducted that it should properly be regarded as one of those which comes within the terms of the guarantee of a fair trial contained in Art 38.1',[57] he went on to point out that this is not determinative of the matter:

> But this conclusion does not end the case. Once it is established that an asserted right is a constitutionally protected right, the courts must then go on to examine the validity of the restrictions imposed on its exercise by the enactment impugned in the case.[58]

The assumption quiescent here of course is that restrictions are potentially at least valid bringing us back to the issue of the strength of such constitutional guarantees.[59]

[3.52] Here Costello J invoked the test of proportionality, noting that the courts here and elsewhere 'have found it helpful to apply the test of proportionality, a test which contains the notion of minimal restraint on the exercise of protected rights, and of the exigencies of the common good in a democratic society.'[60] He stated:

> In applying the test of proportionality, the court is required to assess the detriment to the right-holder of which the restriction on the exercises of the right will impose. In relation to the right to silence, it will be recalled that the reason why the law protects the suspect in custody against self-incrimination is to minimise the risk that he may wrongfully confess to having committed a crime. Undoubtedly a law which requires a suspect to give information under pain of punishment if he refuses to do so will increase this risk, but in assessing the

---

[57] *Heaney and McGuinness v Ireland* [1994] 3 IR 593 at 606.
[58] *Heaney and McGuinness v Ireland* [1994] 3 IR 593 at 606.
[59] *Cf* Ashworth re the hollowing out of ECHR rights 'The Pernicious Side of Proportionality: Two Studies of 'Hollowing out' Human Rights' Paper delivered to the Centre for Criminal Justice and Human Rights, UCC, 24 January 2008.
[60] *Heaney and McGuinness v Ireland* [1994] 3 IR 593 at 607.

consequences of the law, it is both helpful and relevant to consider what other protection the law affords to minimise it and provide safeguards against the possible abuse of the statutory power.[61]

[3.53] Costello J then reviewed the protections afforded to those in custody under s 30 and, placing the issue in context, concluded:

> Recalling that the object which s 52 has been enacted to achieve, namely the investigation and punishment of serious subversive crime, and having regard to the legal protections which exist which will minimise the risk involved in the operation of the Section as outlined above ... it seems to me that the restriction on the right to silence imposed by the Section cannot be regarded as excessive and that it is proportionate to the objective which it is designed to achieve.[62]

Hence he determined that s 52 did not infringe Art 38.1 and was constitutionally valid. There was a further argument made on the basis of Art 40 to which he referred and which is equally important in terms of later developments. It was pleaded that the provision breached Art 40.1 in that it treated persons accused of crimes referred to in the section differently from those accused of other crimes, thereby impugning the equality guarantee. Costello J commented:

> There are perfectly rational and valid reasons why parliament should legislate in respect of the serious crimes referred to in the Act of 1939 in a manner different to that in which it legislates for other types of crimes ...[63]

In similar manner to how the *O'Leary* judgment was prescient and enabled the decision in *Heaney*, this last comment was prescient of future legislative trends and enabled their judicial accommodation.

[3.54] An appeal issued to the Supreme Court[64] and the judgment was given by O'Flaherty J. Until this point, in decisions such as *O'Leary* and *Heaney* in the High Court, the judiciary had connected the issue of the burden of proof, presumption of innocence, right to silence etc with Art 38. Flaherty J stated, however, that, while they agreed with the conclusion of the High Court judge, the Supreme Court preferred to rest its judgment on the proposition that the right to silence is but a corollary to freedom of expression as conferred in Art 40 of the Constitution. Each person has the right to join an association and to dissociate. This different classification is interesting, because where Art 38 is seen as a fairly strong fundamental constitutional right, the freedom of expression would not be viewed as quite as strong. Hence, locating the right to silence as part of freedom of expression, which is questionable in itself,

---

[61] *Heaney and McGuinness v Ireland* [1994] 3 IR 593 at 609.
[62] *Heaney and McGuinness v Ireland* [1994] 3 IR 593 at 610.
[63] *Heaney and McGuinness v Ireland* [1994] 3 IR 593 at 611.
[64] *Heaney and McGuinness v Ireland* [1994] 3 IR 593 (HC), [1996] 1 IR 580 (SC).

certainly lowers its place in the hierarchy of rights. This is immediately evident from the statement that: 'Just as the freedom of expression clause in the Constitution is itself qualified, so must the entitlement to remain silent be qualified.'[65]

With regard to self-incrimination, a revealing comment was subsequently made by O'Flaherty J, as follows:[66]

> There is a dichotomy to be noticed. It is between the absolute entitlement to silence as against the entitlement to remain silent when to answer would give rise to self-incrimination. Where a person is totally innocent of any wrongdoing as regards his movements, it would require a strong attachment to one's apparent constitutional rights not to give such an account when asked pursuant to statutory requirement. So the Court holds that the matter in debate here can more properly be approached as an encroachment against the right not to have to say anything that might afford evidence that is self-incriminating.

[3.55] A later comment reveals the basis for this approach – again a contextual one:

> Two observations have to be made about the old expressions of support for the immunity. They relate to a time when, as far as criminal trials were concerned, an accused was not competent to give evidence in his or her own defence and, in any event, a statutory provision must always prevail over the common law. A statutory provision is subject only to the Constitution.[67]

Once again here the court focuses on whether the power given to the gardaí is proportionate to the objects to be achieved by the legislation. In that regard the court reasons:

> The right to freedom of expression necessarily implies the right to remain silent … However it is clear that the right to freedom of expression is not absolute. It is expressly stated in the Constitution to be subject to public order and morality. The same must hold true of its correlative right – the right to silence.[68]

O'Flaherty J makes reference to the long title of the 1939 Act and points to the proclamation that the ordinary courts are inadequate to secure the administration of justice which brings Part V into operation and which proclamation was still in force since being made on 26 May 1972. He goes on to reason:

> It is in this context [*ie the exceptional nature of the* Offences Against the State Act] that the problem which arises in the present case falls to be resolved. On the one hand, constitutional rights must be construed in such a way as to give life and

---

[65] *Heaney and McGuinness v Ireland* [1996] 1 I R 580 at 585 *per* O'Flaherty J.
[66] *Heaney and McGuinness v Ireland* [1996] 1 I R 580 at 586.
[67] *Heaney and McGuinness v Ireland* [1996] 1 I R 580 at 589 *per* O'Flaherty J.
[68] *Heaney and McGuinness v Ireland* [1996] 1 I R 580 at 589.

reality to what is being guaranteed. On the other hand, the interests of the State in maintaining public order must be respected and protected. We must therefore ask ourselves whether the restriction which s 52 places on the right to silence is any greater than is necessary having regard to the disorder against which the State is attempting to protect the public.[69]

[3.56] Adopting and adapting the language of an earlier case regarding penalties and forfeitures arising from conviction in the Special Criminal Court,[70] the Supreme Court concluded:

[T]he State is entitled to encroach on the right of the citizen to remain silent in pursuit of its entitlement to maintain public peace and order. Of course, in this pursuit the constitutional rights of the citizen must be affected as little as possible. As already stated, the innocent person has nothing to fear from giving an account of his or her movements, even though on grounds of principle or on the assertion of constitutional rights, such a person may wish to take a stand.[71]

[3.57] In *Heaney and McGuinness* then, the Irish Supreme Court 'saves' a provision which criminalises silence. While *Heaney and McGuinness* were waiting to take their case to Strasbourg, the Murray case arose, which allowed inferences to be made from silence under the ECt HR. The Strasbourg Court in *Murray v United Kingdom*[72] held that the right to silence may be restricted in certain circumstances – there to allow inference provisions in anti-terrorist legislation.

[3.58] The case of *Lavery v Member in Charge Carrickmacross Garda Station*[73] is another Offences Against the State Act case, on this occasion involving the Offences Against the State (Amendment) Act 1998, which was introduced in the aftermath of the Omagh bombing and strengthened provisions regarding inference from silence. Sections 2 and 5 allowed inferences to be drawn from the failure of an accused to answer a question put to him by a guard. Lavery had been arrested under s 30 and could be kept for 48 hours plus an additional 24 under the amended legislation. Because of the additional provisions, his solicitor had asked for complete notes of the interview so he could have the information to advise his client.

[3.59] At the hearing to extend his period of detention, the solicitor again requested the notes and was not given them. An application was then made to the High Court and subsequently the Supreme Court challenging the detention

---

[69] *Heaney and McGuinness v Ireland* [1996] 1 I R 580 at 589–590.
[70] *Cox v Ireland* [1992] 2 IR 503.
[71] *Heaney and McGuinness v Ireland* [1996] 1 I R 580 at 590 *per* Flaherty J.
[72] *Murray v United Kingdom* (1996) 23 EHRR 29.
[73] *Lavery v Member in Charge Carrickmacross Garda Station* [1999] 2 IR 390.

and claiming it to be unlawful. McGuinness J in the High Court looked at the 1998 Act and the extended inference provisions and reasoned that these changes were so significant as to have merited allowing the solicitor access to the notes. McGuinness J then ordered Lavery's release. On further appeal to the Supreme Court (O'Flaherty J) however, it was held that a suspect had the right to 'reasonable' access to a lawyer. The Supreme Court essentially decided that there was no right to have a solicitor present throughout the interview; just reasonable access was required.

[3.60] A further judgment issued in *Heaney and McGuinness v Ireland*[74] when the case was heard on appeal in Strasbourg. The ECt HR looked at the submission in terms of arts 6.1 and 6.2 of the Convention and they reviewed some of their own judgments, including *Murray* (which had held that the art 6.1 right to silence was not an absolute right and that you could have inference provisions). The Strasbourg Court went on to look at s 52 in this context and made an interesting reference to the *Saunders* case,[75] which found the UK government had gone too far by forcing Saunders to give an account of his actions. Despite the UK government's argument that corporate fraud was so complex it needed certain powers to force people to talk, the ECt HR said that those provisions went too far. In *Saunders*, despite the public interest argument, the UK was found to have breached art 6. Essentially in *Heaney and McGuinness* the ECt HR looked at what the Irish government had said about combating terrorism, but again found the government's argument unconvincing and held that the applicants' right to silence in not wanting to incriminate themselves had been infringed.

[3.61] In the cases *O'Leary* and *Heaney and McGuinness*, there was an acceptance that you can have interference with the presumption of innocence, ie that there can be some degree of onus on the accused, or at least there can be provision for negative repercussions for the accused if they do not do something (a form of inferences from silences). These cases were set in the context of difficult and challenging situations for the state – eg terrorism, offences against the state, corporate complex fraud, insider trading etc. The State in each situation made the argument that, although there was a right, the countervailing interests and public interest were so great that that right had to be adjusted or curtailed. Each piece of legislation impugned in these cases was set in the context of an Act to deal with the scenario of a specific threat. The 1939 Act (targeting Northern Ireland activity) and prevention of terrorism or insider trading legislation are all specific pieces of legislation introducing these provisions interfering with the burden of proof/silence only in that context. In

---

[74] Final judgment, Dec 2000, ECt HR, 671. *Heaney v Ireland* (2001) 33 EHRR 264; *Quinn v Ireland* (2001) 33 EHRR 27.

[75] *Saunders v UK* (1996) 23 EHRR 313.

other words, these provisions are not general in their effect – at least not initially or individually. However, collectively and incrementally they combine and influence the general system beyond their originating remit.

[3.62] To give an indication of how influential such exceptional provisions can be on the judicial psyche, let us examine the case of *DPP v Finnerty*.[76] Joseph Finnerty was accused and convicted of the rape of a student in Letterkenny. He had been arrested under s 4 of the Criminal Justice Act 1984, which was the normal, standard power of arrest followed by detention. He availed of his right to a solicitor but he said absolutely nothing whilst in custody. He was subsequently charged and tried on two counts of rape and pleaded not guilty in the Central Criminal Court. The victim gave her evidence, then he gave his and he agreed with everything she said except he said that sex had been consensual. The prosecution commented on the fact that he had said nothing in the garda station. The judge made no comment on this. An appeal went to Court of Criminal Appeal on the basis that the trial judge had erred in allowing the prosecutor present evidence to the effect that Finnerty had said nothing during detention. Keane J delivered the judgment of the court:

> This case is solely concerned with the claimed right of a person detained under s 4 of the Act of 1984, to refuse to answer questions put to him by the gardai during the course of his detention, and the corollary of that right, ie the need to ensure no inferences adverse to him are drawn at any subsequent trial, from the exercise of that right.
>
> The history of the law prior to the enactment of the Criminal Justice Act 1984 is relevant. Our criminal law, deriving ultimately from the Anglo-American system, historically reflected a tension between two competing principles. The first was the right and duty of the police to investigate crimes of every sort in the interests of the community as a whole and the corresponding obligation on citizens to assist them in that task. The second was the right of a suspect at a defined stage in the investigation to refuse to answer any questions and the obligation on the police to inform him of that right in the almost universally-known formula of the traditional police caution.[77]

[3.63] Having set the context into which the 1984 Act emerged, Keane J then clarified what that Act did not do:

> The Act of 1984 … did not modify in any way the right of a person whom the Gardaí suspect of having committed a crime to refuse to answer questions put to him by the Gardaí and his entitlement under the Judges' Rules to be reminded of that right before questioning begins. That right would, of course, be significantly eroded if, at the subsequent trial of the person concerned, the jury could be

---

[76] *DPP v Finnerty* [1999] 4 IR 364.
[77] *DPP v Finnerty* [1999] 4 IR 364 at 376–377 *per* Keane J.

invited to draw inferences adverse to him from his failure to reply to those questions and, specifically, to his failure to give the questioning Gardaí an account similar to that subsequently given by him in evidence. It would also render virtually meaningless the caution required to be given to him under the Judges' Rules.

It must also be borne in mind that it is a usual practice for solicitors to advise their clients while they are in custody not to answer any questions put to them by gardaí, if they consider it would not be in their interests to do so. However, if the jury could be invited to draw inferences from the failure to reply to such questions, the result would be that the person in custody would have to be advised by solicitors that, notwithstanding the terms of the caution, it might be inimical to their client's interest not to make a full statement to gardaí, thereby eroding further the right to silence recognized at common law.

Had the Oireachtas intended to abridge the right to silence in this manner, it would have expressly so legislated ... this leads to the inevitable conclusion no such general abridgement to the right of silence was intended to be effected where a person declined to answer questions put to him by the gardaí during the course of a detention.[78]

[3.64] Finnerty had every right to remain silent in detention and his silence should not have been used as commentary against him afterwards. What is significant about this case is that it shows how, if you have in the system generally exceptional provisions which allow for comment on silence and allow for inferences to be drawn from silence, this can affect the culture or mindset of the judiciary such that they literally forget that this is an ordinary case and the normal position still applies. This is what happened at trial in *Finnerty*. Basically the Central Criminal Court allowed the prosecution to lead evidence to the jury that Finnerty had remained silent in detention. Negative inferences were then allowed to be drawn. On the basis that they should not have been, Finnerty's appeal was successful. Finnerty was followed in *People (DPP) v Cummins*.[79] where it was held by the Court of Criminal Appeal following *Finnerty* that the accused's privilege against self-incrimination was breached by the trial judge's charge to the jury where he lay particular emphasis on the failure of the accused to account for his movements when asked to do so by gardaí.

[3.65] If one reviews what the legislature has been doing in this area, the progression is revelatory. The starting position with regard to inferences from silence was that the system we had did not allow such inferences, unless you had specific and exceptional statutory provisions. Under in the Offences Against the State Act 1939, considered in *O'Leary* and then *Heaney and McGuinness*, some

---

[78] *DPP v Finnerty* [1999] 4 IR 364 at 379 *per* Keane J.
[79] *People (DPP) v Cummins* (19 December 2003, unreported), CCA, McGuinness J.

such provision was sanctioned but that was only in the context of exceptional situations of challenge to the state. The ECt HR showed in its response in *Heaney* and *McGuinness* that such provision was not always sanctioned. However, under the Criminal Justice Act 1984, two things happened to effect a subtle change in approach:

1. under s 4 for the first time ever in the criminal justice system not dealing with an extraordinary event, a power of detention after arrest was introduced; and

2. under ss 18 and 19 of that Act, for the first time again, there was provision for inferences from a failure to account for objects or marks (s 18) or a failure to account for presence in a particular place (s19) again in the context of the 'ordinary' criminal justice system.

[3.66] These inference provisions could not suffice to establish a conviction in isolation, or in the absence of other evidence, but they could help build a case against an accused. That was considered remarkable at the time since it applied to all criminal offences. Sections 18 and 19 nonetheless, while controversial, were not used very much. Their constitutionality was challenged, unsuccessfully, in *Rock v Ireland*.[80] Similar provisions were found to be compatible with the ECt HR view in *Murray* so that inference provisions were sanctioned in a manner that the criminalisation of silence in *Heaney* and *McGuinness* had not been.

[3.67] This legislative trend of incremental increase in such provisions continued with the Criminal Justice (Drug Trafficking) Act 1996, s 7, which provides for inferences from the failure of the accused to mention particular facts. In addition, the Offences Against the State (Amendment) Act 1998, ss 2 and 5, provided for inferences to be drawn from a failure to mention particular facts. There was a gradual increase in the number of pieces of legislation under which if the accused stayed silent, that silence would aid the development of the case against him or her.

[3.68] The culmination of this process has resulted in most of these sections now becoming moot because of Pt 4 of the Criminal Justice Act 2007, which goes further in relation to inference provision.

Criminal Justice Act 2007

[3.69] Part 4 of the Criminal Justice Act 2007 (the 2007 Act) provides for '[i]nferences to be drawn in certain circumstances'. These came into effect on 1 July 2007. According to the explanatory memorandum, Part 4 expands the circumstances in which inferences may be drawn in proceedings from a failure

---

80 *Rock v Ireland* [1998] 2 ILRM 35.

to mention particular facts and it provides a range of safeguards. Section 18 of the Criminal Justice Act 1984 (inferences from failure to account for objects, marks etc) is amended by s 28 of the 2007 Act in so far as the question may be put to the suspect by any garda, not just the arresting garda, and it introduces the safeguard that it will not be possible to convict on an inference alone without corroboration or to draw an inference unless the accused was cautioned in clear language and afforded a reasonable opportunity to consult a solicitor before such failure or refusal. Furthermore, the provision will not apply to questioning unless the interview is recorded or the person consents in writing to it not being recorded.

[3.70] The same amendments are made to s 19, which deals with inferences from the failure to account for the accused's presence at a particular place, by s 29 of the Act. The accused:

1. must be told in ordinary language what the effect is of the failure or refusal to account for a matter within that subsection; and

2. must be given reasonable opportunity to consult a solicitor before such a failure or refusal occurs.

Together with these changes, a new general provision was introduced under s 30 of the 2007 Act, which introduced a new s 19A in the Criminal Justice Act 1984 providing for the circumstances in which inferences may be drawn in any subsequent proceedings from failure by the accused to mention particular facts when questioned by gardaí or when being charged with an arrestable offence. The safeguards in ss 18 and 19 also apply here. Finnerty would have been caught by this section. This changes things for everybody, not just those arrested under the Criminal Justice (Drug Trafficking) Act 1996 or the Offences Against the State Act regime. It is in that sense a major change of general application whereby, if you say nothing now and rely on it later, inferences from silence can be drawn. Given that this new section deals with all arrestable offences, s 5 of the Offences Against the State (Amendment) Act 1998 and s 7 of the Criminal Justice (Drug Trafficking) Act 1996 are repealed. Hence this is a very clear demonstration of a particularised change moving to the general application.

[3.71] In the recent trial in the Cork Circuit Criminal Court involving a major cocaine haul in West Cork[81] during May/June 2008, the accused had been arrested and questioned but remained silent. Much of the case against them hinged on the use of this 2007 Act inference provision. It represented the first occasion on which gardaí were operating this new provision and explaining it to the accused. The inference-drawing provision under s 2 of the Offences Against

---

[81] 'Three Plead Not Guilty in Landmark Drug Trial' (2008) *The Irish Examiner*, 22 May. Judge Sean O'Donnobháin. Sentencing took place in Cork Circuit Court on 23 July 2008.

the State (Amendment) Act 1998 is amended by s 31 of the 2007 Act to add in to that particular provision, which still exists, the safeguards of ordinary language, reasonable access and electronic recording. That provision under the 1998 Act allows the drawing of inferences in prosecutions for membership of an unlawful organization from the accused's failure to answer any question 'material' to the investigation of the offence. A conviction involving such an inference and the Chief Superintendent's opinion that the accused were members of the IRA was upheld in *DPP v Binead and Donoghue.*[82]

[3.72] Section 32 of the 2007 Act provides for the Minister to make regulations as to cautions to be given to those to whom these inference provisions apply.

A fair concern is the extent to which these provisions will meet with scrutiny as to the courts' interpretation of what is a 'fact', and if the failure to mention a fact is relied upon, whether a sufficient opportunity was given to an individual to volunteer such information, as well as the possible emergence of the argument that legal advice was the basis for the accused's silence. McGillicuddy[83] comments:

> As a general starting point, it is submitted that a delicate balancing act will be required for this area. On the one hand, the courts may not want to allow defendants to avoid s 19A altogether by merely stating that they were relying on legal advice to stay silent during an interview so that no inference can be drawn. To permit otherwise will allow legal advice to circumvent the entire workings of the section by becoming a shield against inferences being drawn in all circumstances.

Outside the criminal law field, the UK government tried to introduce particular provisions in the realm of company law that could compel the provision of information which could then subsequently be used in a prosecution. The European Court in the *Saunders* case recognized the right to silence, although not specifically mentioned as part of the ECHR art 6 notion of fair procedure, and was intolerant of the use of information obtained by such compulsion in a subsequent trial.

[3.73] In Ireland, *National Irish Bank and the matter of the Companies Act 1990*[84] deals with a similar issue. Under Pt 2 of the Companies Act 1990 there was a provision for inspection of companies by inspectors who had powers to compel answers and compel production of documents. An application was made to the High Court for guidance as to whether those being questioned could

---

[82] *DPP v Binead and Donoghue* [2006] IECCA147.

[83] See further McGillicuddy, 'Restrictions on the Rights to Silence under the Criminal Justice Act 2007 – Part 1 (2008) 18 (3) ICLJ 77 at p 85.

[84] *National Irish Bank and the matter of the Companies Act 1990* [1999] 3 IR 145.

refuse to speak for fear of self-incrimination. The High Court held that the right to silence could be abrogated by statute, that a proportionality test would determine whether the restriction was greater than was necessary. They looked at s 10 and held that it was constitutional in so far as they said it was no greater than necessary in order to enable the state to carry out its obligations.

[3.74] The powers given to inspectors were no greater than the public interest required. What was objectionable under Art 38 of the Constitution was compelling a person to confess and then convicting someone on the basis of that confession. The Court pointed out that any such confession obtained by the inspectors would not be admissible in a criminal trial unless it was voluntary. They therefore saved s 10 and held that in certain circumstances a specific provision can be made interfering with the right to silence.

Imposition of a legal burden on the accused – compatibility with the ECHR

[3.75] In *Regina v Lambert*,[85] the House of Lords had the opportunity to address issues regarding the compatibility of reverse onus provision with the ECHR, hence indicating the possible future for such provisions which have become increasingly common in Ireland. The appellant here was convicted of possession of a controlled drug, cocaine, contrary to s 5 of the Misuse of Drugs Act 1971. He relied on s 28(3)(b)(i) of the 1971 Act, that he did not believe or suspect or have reason to suspect that the bag contained such a controlled drug. The judge directed the jury that the prosecution only had to prove he had possession, and that the bag had a controlled drug. He had to prove on the balance of probabilities that he did not know the bag contained a controlled drug. Hence he bore the legal burden of proof with regard to that.

[3.76] The appellant contended, on appeal to the House of Lords, that this latter violated art 6 of the ECHR, as set out in the Schedule to the Human Rights Act 1998. The majority of the House of Lords proceeded on the basis that it was possible to read that section as imposing an evidential, not a legal, burden on the appellant, and so ensured its compatibility with the ECHR. With regard to the general issue of placing a legal burden on the accused, the House of Lords did comment that the section if imposing a legal burden would be 'a disproportionate reaction to perceived difficulties facing the prosecution in drugs cases'.[86]

---

85 *Regina v Lambert* UKHL 37 [2002] 2 AC 545.
86 *Per* Lord Steyn at para 41.

[3.77] Nonetheless, increasingly, there are more provisions that are reverse onus provisions which attempt to put the legal burden of proof on the accused. For example:

> Road Traffic Act 1961, s 50(8), as amended, provides that in a prosecution for an offence under that section, there is a presumption that the defendant attempted to drive unless he shows to the contrary;
>
> Section 100(2) of the Company Law Enforcement Act 2001 reverses the burden of proof in relation to the prosecution of company officers; and
>
> Section 81 of the Safety, Health and Welfare at Work Act 2005 provides, in relation to offences under that Act, that it is for the accused to prove that it was not reasonably practicable to do more than was done.

Peculiar knowledge principle

[3.78] Quite apart from the case of insanity and statutory provisions, the existence of a third exception to the *Woolmington* principle has been a matter of some controversy. The English Court of Appeal in *R v Edwards*[87] held that if on its true construction an enactment prohibits the doing of an act, save in specified circumstances, the defendant must (by way of exception to the fundamental rules of the criminal law that the Crown must establish every element of the offence charged) prove the existence of the specified circumstances. This rule, moreover, the court in *Edwards* emphasised, does not depend upon his possession of peculiar knowledge, enabling him to prove the positive of a negative averment.

[3.79] The reason for this latter statement on the part of the Court of Appeal may have been related to the attempt to establish an exception to the general rule under the rubric and within the confines of 'peculiar knowledge'. Irish case law, certainly, had proven itself amenable to such a development and it is worth examining some earlier Irish decisions in that regard.

[3.80] In *Minister for Industry and Commerce v Steele*,[88] the defendant was prosecuted under the Emergency Powers (Pork Sausages and Sausage Meat) (Maximum Prices) Order 1943, which established certain requirements as to the meat content of sausages. Evidence was given at the hearing which showed that it was not possible to prove by analysis or any other scientific method what percentage of the meat content of the sausages was pork. On appeal against

---

[87] *R v Edwards* [1975] QB 27.
[88] *Minister for Industry and Commerce v Steele* [1952] IR 301.

conviction in the Circuit Court, it was contended on the appellant's behalf that no evidence had been adduced that what he had offered for sale were 'pork sausages' within the meaning of the Act. Hence the onus of proof, which lay on the prosecution, had not been discharged.

[3.81] A case was stated to the Supreme Court, where O'Byrne J held that an exception to the general rule as to the onus of proof existed where the subject matter of the allegation lies peculiarly within the knowledge of one of the parties and that the party must prove it, whether it be of an affirmative or a negative character, and even though there be a presumption of law in his favour. It was held that as the matter here was clearly peculiarly within the knowledge of the defendant, the burden of proof lay on him.

[3.82] Contrasting with this is the decision of the Supreme Court in *McGowan v Carville*,[89] where on a charge of driving a motor van without a licence, the onus of proving that the defendant had no licence was held to rest on the prosecutor, the possession or the contrary of such a licence not being a matter peculiarly within the knowledge of the defendant. In the High Court, Murnaghan J took the view that in order for peculiar knowledge to bring about a shift in the legal burden of proof, the prosecution would at the very least have to establish a prima facie case. The Supreme Court affirmed this view, pointing out that if on the facts the defendant had been stopped and asked to produce a driving licence by the garda, but failed to do so then or at a reasonable period thereafter, given the knowledge possessed by the parties, the burden of proof would shift to the defendant to show he had a licence. Since no evidence had been here produced by the complainant as to whether the defendant did in fact subsequently produce his licence, the onus of proof had not shifted and so remained with him.

[3.83] In *Attorney General v Shorten*,[90] the defendant had made a declaration on 6 May 1958 that his motor car had not been used by him or with his consent since 31 December 1957. He was charged with making such a statement, knowing it to be false and misleading. The prosecution gave evidence that the car was seen on the road, but the driver had not been identified. The District Justice stated that as the use of the car had been proved by the prosecution, the onus was thrown on the defendant, as owner of the car, to prove that the vehicle had not been used by him, or with his knowledge or consent.

[3.84] On appeal, Davitt P, on taking into account all the circumstances (including the fact that the owner did not guard his car 24 hours a day), was not prepared to hold that the District Justice was entitled to find the burden of proof

---

[89] *McGowan v Carville* [1960] IR 330.
[90] *Attorney General v Shorten* [1961] IR 304.

had shifted to the defendant. Davitt P's comment at one point in his judgment[91] is interesting:

> I confess that I do not feel at all happy about the application in criminal cases of what I have referred to ... the 'peculiar knowledge' principle ... I found it very hard to regard resorting to the 'peculiar knowledge' principle even in its modified form or to any similar principle as other than attempts to whittle down the presumption of innocence.

Davitt P distinguished this case from *McGowan* in that here there was no statutory provision involved and, hence deciding the issue by reference to common law principles, insisted the prosecution prove the case beyond all reasonable doubt.

[3.85] A rather different conclusion was reached by Davitt P in *Bridgett v Dowd*,[92] where the defendants were charged with carrying merchandise in a lorry without holding a merchandise licence. The complainant had observed the carrying only within an exempted area, but contended that once it was established the lorry had been carrying merchandise, and that the defendants owned the lorry and did not hold a merchandise licence, the onus then shifted to the defendants to show the merchandise had been carried on the occasion in question, exclusively within an exempted area. The District Justice dismissed the complaint but stated a case to the High Court.

[3.86] Davitt P felt, in light of *McGowan*, it was clear that in a prosecution for the offence of carrying goods without a merchandise licence, the onus of proving that the defendant has no such licence rests initially upon the prosecution:

> Once, however, it has been established that the defendant has no merchandise licence and that he has carried the merchandise by road in a mechanically propelled vehicle then if he is to escape liability, he must in my opinion bring himself within one of the exceptions which has the effect of relieving him of liability.

[3.87] It seems here, as in *McGowan*, that once the prima facie case is established against the defendant, the peculiar knowledge principle comes into operation to shift the burden of proof. This approach would seem to herald some support for the notion that what shifts to the defendant is in fact an evidential burden, which if not then discharged by the defendant, leads to the legal burden having been satisfied by the plaintiff.

---

[91] *Attorney General v Shorten* [1961] IR 304 at 309.
[92] *Bridgett v Dowd* [1961] IR 313.

[3.88] Although this approach is contrary to Lawton LJ's suggestion in *Edwards*[93] that it is the legal burden that moves, and there is some Irish judicial support for that view, academic opinion, in the main, has resisted a movement towards further development of exceptions to *Woolmington's* basic precept. Zuckerman,[94] most persuasively perhaps, feels this to be at best historically dubious and, moreover, to involve a departure from the placement of the burden of proof in criminal cases on the prosecution, in the context of very minor offences where very little evidence is required to discharge the burden of proof.

Standard of proof

[3.89] Phrases such as 'standard of proof' and 'quantum of proof' refer to the size of the legal burden of proof. The trier of fact decides whether the probative force of evidence presented to discharge the legal burden on a particular issue outweighs the evidence presented to show the contrary.

[3.90] In jury trials, the trial judge bears the responsibility to direct the jury as to the nature of that quantum or standard. The common law knows two standards of proof: civil cases requiring that of proof on the balance of probabilities and criminal cases requiring proof beyond reasonable doubt. The latter, higher, standard owes its rationale to the bias in our criminal justice system towards risking a guilty person's acquittal, rather than that an innocent one's conviction. An important aspect to this general standard is that when the legal burden is placed on an accused, in a criminal case, it is the civil standard which applies.

[3.91] The difficulty with such a system that allows standards of proof – as opposed to the scientific empiricism of something having been proven or not – is deciding when that standard has been reached. Any delineation or adjudication of that point may vary with the subjectivity of the individual concerned. For that reason, the judiciary have from time to time attempted to express what the particular standards translate into. Denning LJ is probably most notable for his effort to grapple with this difficulty in *Miller v Minister for Pensions*,[95] where he stated, in relation to the criminal standard, that:

> Proof beyond reasonable doubt does not mean proof beyond the shadow of doubt. The law would fail to protect the community if it admitted fanciful possibilities to deflect the course of justice. If the evidence is so strong against a man as to leave only a remote possibility in his favour which can be dismissed with the sentence 'of course it is possible but not in the least probable' the case is proved beyond reasonable doubt, but nothing short of that will suffice.

---

[93] *R v Edwards* [1975] QB 27.

[94] Zuckerman, *The Principles of Criminal Evidence* (Clarendon Press, 1989).

[95] *Miller v Minister for Pensions* [1947] 2 All ER 372.

In relation to the civil standard, Denning LJ commented that:

> If at the end of the case the evidence turns the scale definitely one way or the other, the tribunal must decide accordingly, but if the evidence is so evenly balanced that the tribunal is unable to come to a determinate conclusion one way or the other, then the man must be given the benefit of the doubt ... It must carry a reasonable degree of probability but not so high as in a criminal case ... If a tribunal can say 'we think it more probable than not', the burden is discharged but if the probabilities are equal it is not.

[3.92] In the Irish context, Kenny J in *People v Byrne*[96] commented in the Court of Criminal Appeal:

> In this case the trial judge used the words 'satisfied' and 'to your satisfaction' on many occasions when explaining the onus of proof. He then said that 'being satisfied' means the same thing as 'beyond a reasonable doubt'. This is not correct because one may be satisfied of something and still have a reasonable doubt.

Kenny J's enunciation of the correct charge to a jury in a criminal case was as follows:

> The correct charge to a jury is that they must be satisfied beyond reasonable doubt of the guilt of the accused, and it is helpful if that degree of proof is contrasted with that in a civil case. It is also essential, however, that the jury should be told that the accused is entitled to the benefit of the doubt, and that when two views on any part of the case are possible on the evidence they should adopt that which is favourable to the accused unless the state has established the other beyond reasonable doubt.

[3.93] It may be said that it is easier to establish what does not amount to an adequate explanation of the standard than what does: the comment of Megaw LJ in *R v Gray*[97] was to the effect that the description of 'reasonable doubt' as the sort of doubt which might affect you in the conduct of your everyday affairs, might suggest too low a standard to the jury. If the trial judge had referred to the sort of doubt which might affect the mind of a person in the conduct of important affairs, there could, he reasoned, be no proper criticism.

[3.94] The difficulties in giving further expression to an already abstract and vague criterion of proof or adjudication are obvious. Perhaps given the longevity of the provisions, and our familiarity as lawyers and laypersons with them, it is best to leave the phrases as they are, albeit subject to the vagaries of subjective interpretation, rather than encouraging what amounts to no more than further articulation of particular aspects of those subjective approaches.

---

[96] *People v Byrne* [1974] IR 1.
[97] *R v Gray* [1974] 58 Cr App Rep 177.

[3.95] In this regard, it is difficult to disagree with the statement of the English Court of Appeal in *R v Ching*:[98]

> We point out and emphasize that if judges stopped trying to define that which is almost impossible to define there would be fewer appeals. We hope there will not be any more for some considerable time.

[3.96] An endorsement of a trial judge's direction with regard to standard of proof was given in *People (DPP) v Kiely*.[99] The trial judge, in his direction to the jury, explained the difference between the civil and criminal standards of proof as follows:

> You will have a decision to make and an important decision and you will have to weigh it up. I must refer you to that, during your whole life, you are making decision after decision and they are in various categories. There is one category of decision which I will call of a passing or trivial nature. Will I go to the cinema tonight? Will I buy a lottery ticket? Will I look at the Late Late Show? ... All these things are little decisions that we make. They are not life changing decisions ... There is another kind of decision which is much more fundamental which we all again make. Are we going to get married or if we are already married are we going to leave our marriage partner and go with someone else? Are we going to sell our house in the rising property market? ... They are all decisions which we all have to make from time to time, not very often but we have to make them, but you make those decisions in a much more fundamental and careful way than the kind of decisions that you are going to watch the Late Late Show or you are going to buy a lottery ticket. They are totally different kinds of decisions. Now the civil standard of proof that I spoke about, the traffic case, injury at work, that kind of thing, you can equate that to the trivial kind of decision and the much more serious decision is equated with the criminal case, so, the difference between the trivial decision and the serious decision gives you some idea of the difference between the civil standards of proof which is lower and the criminal standard of proof which is much higher. I do not think I can explain it much better than that to you. It is very serious and you have to be satisfied beyond reasonable doubt, that it not mathematical doubt, but beyond reasonable doubt.

McGuinness J held that there could be no criticism of the trial judge's direction which she regarded as abundantly clear and comprehensive.

Tribunals; other contexts

[3.97] Occasions when the strict application of the general rule as to the standards of proof and their effect may well be departed from are provided by tribunal proceedings, and less obviously perhaps by instances on the civil side,

---

[98] *R v Ching* (1976) 63 Cr App Rep 7 at p 11.

[99] *People (DPP) v Kiely* (21 March 2001), CCA, McGuinness J.

when particular circumstances seem to warrant greater caution in reaching a determination on an issue. In other words the basic civil standard will never have to be less than satisfied, but may occasionally be augmented. Firstly, in the case of tribunals, rules of evidence may well be relaxed or not adhered to. No general provisions exist with regard to same, and (judicial) discretion as to satisfaction on the issues concerned is the standard mooted. It is interesting to note as an example of this, the statement of Lynch J in the *Report of Kerry Babies Tribunal* to the effect:

> With one exception ... the Tribunal finds facts only if the Tribunal is satisfied of such facts as a matter of *substantial probability.* This is a degree of proof in excess of the mere balance of probabilities and short of proof beyond reasonable doubt.

[3.98] Secondly, in the Goodman Tribunal, the standard adopted by Hamilton J was that of proof beyond reasonable doubt. It would seem that the civil standard is the benchmark, which on occasion may be raised for reasons of pragmatism or policy. Under the Residential Institutions Redress Act 2002, s 7,[100] 'Entitlement of Award', concerning the burden of proof, the standard of proof required is a lower one than that required by the civil standard – ie 'establishes to the satisfaction of the Board'.

This may be seen in the context of certain civil actions requiring higher standard of proof because of their wider implications for others, whether directly concerned in the action or not.

[3.99] In *Leahy v Corboy*,[101] in a situation where a legatee named in the will of a testator, who had also drafted a codicil to that will which increased the said legatee's bequest, Budd J, in the Supreme Court review of the case law (including *Fulton v Andrews*[102]), found the rules to be twofold:

(1)   The *onus probands* lies upon the party propounding a will and he must satisfy the conscience of the court that the instrument so propounded is the last will of a free and capable testator; and

(2)   if a party writes or prepares a will under which he takes a benefit that is a circumstance that ought generally to excite the suspicion of the court and calls upon it to be vigilant and jealous in examining the evidence in support of the instrument in favour of which it ought not to pronounce unless the suspicion is removed, and it is judicially satisfied that the paper as propounded does express the true will of the deceased.

---

[100] Residental Institution Redress Bill first presented in the Dáil on 12 June 2001 and passed on 28 March 2002. Section 7 was originally s 6 of the Bill.
[101] *Leahy v Corboy* [1969] IR 148.
[102] *Fulton v Andrews* (1875) LR 7 HL.

[3.100] The Supreme Court referred to *Windle v Nye*,[103] where Viscount Simonds stated that if a person who prepared a will for the testator takes a benefit under it, that fact creates a suspicion that must be removed by the person propounding the will. In all cases the court must be vigilant and jealous. The degree of suspicion will vary with the circumstances of the case. On the facts in this particular case, the Supreme Court felt the heavy burden of proof had not been satisfied.

[3.101] The case of *In the Matter of the Succession Act 1965, s 117 and in the Estate of IAC deceased; C and F v WC & TC*[104] concerned a challenge to the will of the deceased testatrix, who at the date of her death had been a widow with four surviving children. The plaintiff daughters of the deceased testatrix brought an application under s 117 of the Succession Act 1965, claiming that their mother had failed in her moral duty to make proper provision for them under the will according to her means. The High Court had upheld that claim. Finlay CJ in the Supreme Court adopted the statement of general principles, with regard to s 117, of Kenny J in *Re GM (deceased): FM & TAM*,[105] but added the following qualification:

> I am satisfied that the phrase contained in s 117(i) 'failed in his moral duty to make proper provision for the child in accordance with his means' places a relatively high onus of proof on an applicant for relief under the section. It is not apparently sufficient from these terms in the section to establish that the provision made for a child was not as great as it might have been, or that compared with generous bequests of other children or beneficiaries in the will, it appears ungenerous. The court should not, I consider, make an order under the section merely because it would on the facts proved have formed different testamentary dispositions. A positive failure in moral duty must be established.

[3.102] A further decision concerning wills and the standard of proof requisite is that of *Re Glynn (deceased)*.[106] The case provides an interesting insight into judicial assessment (and divergence) on the quantum of proof at trial, based on credibility of witnesses, and on appeal. The Succession Act 1965, s 77 requires that to be valid a will shall be made by a person who 'is of sound disposing mind', a legislative adoption of a judicial term requiring that the testator should know and approve the contents of the will and, at the time of execution of the will, be of sound mind, memory and understanding. The issue arose here in the context of a will made by William Glynn, the instructions of which were given

---

[103] *Windle v Nye* [1959] 1 WLR 284.
[104] *In the Matter of the Succession Act 1965, s 117 and in the Estate of IAC deceased; C and F v WC & TC* [1989] ILRM 815.
[105] *Re G M (deceased): FM & TAM* 106 ILTR 82 at 87.
[106] *Re Glynn (deceased)* [1990] 2 IR 326.

to a priest in the presence of a layperson prior to 5 October 1981, on which date the testator suffered a massive stroke. On 20 October, in the presence of those two same individuals, the purported execution of the will took place. Medical evidence was given to the effect that on that date it was practically impossible to communicate with the testator, and 'it may well be the case with this patient that he didn't understand what was being said to him'.[107] The two witnesses considered William Glynn knew what was going on and was capable of making a will.

[3.103] The President of the High Court, Hamilton P, admitted the will to probate. He noted that:

> Normally the legal presumption is in favour of the will of a deceased and in favour of the capacity of a testator to dispose of his property and to rebut this presumption, the clearest and most satisfactory evidence is necessary. However in a case like this when a person suffers a stroke which may affect his capacity, the onus shifts and lies on the party propounding the will. Having regard to the nature of the stroke suffered by the deceased and the disability resulting therefrom, there is a heavy onus on the defendant in this case to establish that on 20th October 1981, the deceased had the mental capacity to make a testamentary disposition of his property, that he had a sound disposing mind, that he was capable of comprehending the extent of his property, the nature of the claims of his sister, the plaintiff herein, and that he was disposing of his property.[108]

[3.104] He was satisfied that the two witnesses, Fr Donoghue and Mr Carter, had no interest in the disposition and their sole concern was to give effect to the testator's wishes as stated to them on a number of occasions. On appeal to the Supreme Court, that decision was upheld, Walsh J dissenting. Walsh J pointed out that although there was ample evidence to show that the document was in accordance with instructions given prior to the stroke: 'The question which arises for decision is whether at the time of the purported execution of the will the testator was of sound disposing mind'. Hamilton P had found that he was, on the basis of the evidence of Fr Donoghue and Mr Carter. However, Walsh J considered that to be the opinion of both of these gentlemen, but that opinion did not establish that the sick man knew what he was doing.

[3.105] Walsh J adopted the judgment in *Leahy v Corboy*[109] that nothing but firm medical evidence could suffice to discharge the onus of proving him to have been a capable testator. In that case, he pointed out the testator was a man who except during bouts of illness, had a reasonable degree of understanding although some difficulty in communicating. In the present case, the entire basis

---

[107] *Re Glynn (deceased)* [1990] 2 IR 326 at 328, McCarthy J.
[108] *Re Glynn (deceased)* [1990] 2 IR 326 at 330, Hamilton J.
[109] *Leahy v Corboy* [1969] IR 148 at 167.

of the finding that the deceased had the necessary understanding was based on an interpretation of his smiles and nods. No code of communication had been established to indicate he knew or approved the contents of what he was doing. Walsh J stated it was not the integrity or veracity of the witnesses which was in issue, but the correctness of their assessment of what was essentially a medical problem. In light of the medical evidence in this case, he felt it could not be proved that at the time of execution of the will the deceased was of sound, disposing mind.

[3.106] McCarthy J (Hederman J concurring) gave the majority judgment, however, and admitted the will to probate. He stated that:

> The learned President, who accepted the honesty and truthfulness of all of the witnesses, held that William did know what he was doing on 20 October 1981. This holding is an inference of secondary fact to be derived from the primary facts as found by the President who heard the witnesses ...

[3.107] Reference had been made to *Parker v Felgate*[110] as authority for the proposition that, although a person may no longer have the capacity to go over the whole transaction, if he can say that, having settled the business with a solicitor, he relies upon his having embodied the instructions in words, and accepts the paper as embodying it, that is sufficient. Similar authorities include *Re Wallace: Solicitor for the Duchy of Cornwall and Batten*,[111] where the document was executed without being read over to the testator, and *Perera v Perera*,[112] wherein McCarthy J considered that Lord McNaughton expressed a common sense and good public policy approach that if a person has given instructions to a solicitor to make a will and the solicitor prepares it in accordance with same, all that is necessary for it to be a good will if executed, is that the testator can accept the document put before him as embodying those instructions. McCarthy J further stated that:

> A duly attested will carries a presumption of due execution and testamentary capacity. That presumption was displaced because of the circumstances of the will in the instant case ... It is a fundamental matter of public policy that a testator's wishes should be carried out, however, at times, bizarre, eccentric or whimsical they may appear to be. One man's whimsy is another man's logic.
>
> ... The nub is William's capacity as of 20 October. If on that date he had been required to give instructions for the making of any sort of testamentary document, even as simple a one as the one in question, it may be that the validity of its execution may be challenged. That is not what he was doing, he was

---

[110] *Parker v Felgate* (1883) 8 PD 171.
[111] *Re Wallace: Solicitor for the Duchy of Cornwall and Batten* [1952] 2 TLR 925.
[112] *Perera v Perera* [1901] AC 304.

confirming instructions already given ... there was ample evidence before the President that the testator fully appreciated what was going on and that the terms of the document upon which he placed his mark fully represented what he wanted done with regard to his property. Admittedly the conclusion of the learned President is expressed as being that Fr Donoghue and Mr Carter had the opportunity to and did satisfy themselves as to this circumstance. That was not the issue, their opinion or conclusion is immaterial. It is a necessary inference, however, that the learned President came to the same conclusion and that consequently the will should stand.

[3.108] A case again illustrating an increased standard of proof, in a civil case where serious repercussions followed from the determination, is that of *Preston-Jones v Preston-Jones*,[113] which involved a husband petitioning for divorce on grounds of adultery. The husband had been absent from the UK from 17 August 1945 to 9 February 1946. On 13 August 1946 his wife gave birth to a normal child. The House of Lords accepted that in such cases, the standard of proof required by a petitioner in the case of an allegation of adultery was the criminal standard of proof beyond all reasonable doubt. This was so because of the gravity of the interests of the State and those of the child, as the effect of a *decree nisi* would be to bastardise the child.

[3.109] On the facts, as the husband had proven the child to have been born 360 days after he last had the opportunity of intercourse with his wife; and that the birth was a normal one, the court taking judicial notice of the normal period of gestation (nine months or 270 days) held as follows (*per* Lord McDermott):

> I do not think it open to doubt that a time must come when, with the period far in excess of the normal, the Court may properly regard its length as proving the wife's adultery beyond reasonable doubt and decree accordingly.

(Of course this decision raises issues as to where one draws the line: here it was 360 days. Ultimately, there was an acceptance by most of the judges that proof of an abnormal period of gestation threw an evidentiary burden on the wife in this instance).

[3.110] In *Lyons v Lyons*,[114] the standard applicable in relation to proof of adultery was deemed more stringent than is required of a plaintiff in other civil actions, but less stringent than beyond reasonable doubt. Cruelty has been adjudged to require proof on the balance of probabilities by the person alleging it (*O'Reardon v O'Reardon*[115]), the requisite standard being less than that in the context of the presumption of legitimacy and the policy considerations mooted

---

[113] *Preston-Jones v Preston-Jones* [1951] AC 391.
[114] *Lyons v Lyons* [1950] N1 181.
[115] *O'Reardon v O'Reardon* (February 1975, unreported), HC.

earlier. In the context of an application for nullity on the grounds of 'incapacity to form a caring marital relationship' in *RT v VP (orse VT)*,[116] Lardner J in dismissing the petition applied the standard of proof as expressed by Kenny J in *S v S*, ie, 'that the petitioner has to establish his or her case to a degree of probability or as Lord Birkenhead expressed it "must remove all serious doubt".'[117]

[3.111] A further variation on the 'standard of proof' on the civil side was considered in *Murphy v Green*.[118] Section 260 of the Mental Treatment Act 1945 requires the leave of the High Court as a precondition to the institution of proceedings under the Act. The High Court shall not give such leave unless there are 'substantial grounds' for contending that the person against whom the proceedings are to be brought acted in bad faith or without reasonable care. The interpretation of the section had come before the Supreme Court in *O'Dowd v North Western Health Board*.[119] O'Higgins CJ in that case was of the opinion that the section required something approaching a prima facie case. Griffin J felt the section put the onus of proof squarely on the person seeking to bring the action and the use of the word 'satisfied' indicated that the Oireachtas had in mind a somewhat higher standard of proof than that which a plaintiff must ordinarily discharge in a civil case. He referred to a statement by Denning LJ in *Richardson v London County Council*[120] with regard to the same words in the English Act 'there must be solid grounds for thinking that there was want of reasonable care or bad faith'. Parker LJ had stated: 'It is, I think, at the opposite end of the scale ... to a flimsy ground. It is something short of certainty, but something considerably more than bare suspicion'. Henchy J in *O'Dowd*[121] was of the opinion that 'the adjective "substantial" should be given ... a connotation of weight or solidity'.

[3.112] Finlay CJ in *Murphy v Green*[122] commented that it is reasonable to require a precondition of leave of the court, in the context of the Mental Treatment Act 1945, although it limits constitutional access to the courts. In that case, Finlay CJ stated that a prima facie standard would appear to be more consistent with the situation where a court is asked to adjudicate upon the state of the case at the conclusion of evidence adduced on behalf of a plaintiff and before a defendant has been given an opportunity to refute. To establish facts to

---

[116] *RT v VP (orse V T)* [1990] 1 IR 545.

[117] *S v S* (1 July 1976, unreported), SC at pp 4–5.

[118] *Murphy v Green* [1990] 2 IR 566.

[119] *O'Dowd v North Western Health Board* [1983] ILRM 186.

[120] *Richardson v London County Council* [1957] 1 WLR 751.

[121] *O'Dowd v North Western Health Board* [1983] ILRM 186 at 198.

[122] *Murphy v Green* [1990] 2 IR 566 at 572.

the satisfaction of the court, he was not satisfied that the intending plaintiff must prove them beyond a probability:

> I am satisfied that the use of the phrase 'substantial grounds' in this context ... would mean something more than probable or prima facie grounds. However, it is not necessary for the court to try and conclude at the end of the s 260 application, whether the plaintiff is, as a matter of probability, likely to succeed in his action.

[3.113] Griffin J having regard to the decision in *Re R Ltd*,[123] that restrictions on the general provision in Art 34 for the administration of justice should be strictly construed, changed his position in *Murphy v Green*, feeling that in *O'Dowd* he imposed a standard which was too high. He concluded that what is required by s 260 of the 1945 Act is that the applicant establishes, as a matter of probability, that there are substantial grounds for the contention that the defendant acted without reasonable care.

[3.114] O'Flaherty J stated:

> But even if the plaintiff established that he had a stateable case, that is not enough ... The test is not that he can contend (or assert) that he has substantial grounds but that the 'substantial grounds' which will help him prove his case ultimately do exist in fact. I would equate 'substantial grounds' with potentially credible evidence ... It is not necessary that the evidence should be so compelling as to make it certain (because that is to set too high a standard) that he will establish his case but the evidence must be there and must be demonstrated to be there to a credible extent before he should be permitted to bring his proceedings.

[3.115] An example of a case in which the burden having been placed on the accused was not satisfied (ie the requisite (civil) standard was not reached) is *DPP (Garda Malachy Crowley) v Connors*.[124] The case, stated by Hubert Wine DJ, was as to whether he was correct in dismissing a charge against the defendant on the grounds that s 22(3) of the Road Traffic (Amendment) Act 1978, requiring the Medical Bureau to forward a copy of the relevant certificate of analysis to the defendant (provider of the specimen), was not complied with.

[3.116] Lavan J adopted and applied the decision of Gannon J in *DPP v Ronnie Walsh*.[125] In that case, it was submitted the defendant should not be convicted since he had not received a copy of the certificate of blood alcohol level from the Medical Bureau of Road Safety. It had been returned 'not collected'. Gannon J construed s 22(3) of the 1978 Act firstly in terms of its ordinary meaning, resolving any ambiguity by considering other provisions of the Road

---

[123] *Re R Ltd* [1989] IR 176.
[124] *DPP (Garda Malachy Crowley) v Connors* (10 May 1990, unreported), HC, *per* Lavan J.
[125] *DPP v Ronnie Walsh* [1985] ILRM 243.

Traffic Acts in so far as they related to the matter. Gannon J went on to state that (*per* Lavan J):

> whether the statutory requirements in relation to the taking of a sample or specimen and in relation to the analysis thereof, and in relation to the results of such analysis, have been complied with are matters of proof which, but for s 21(4) and s 23(2) of the 1978 Act, would have to be undertaken by the prosecution.

He then pointed out that s 21(4) of the 1978 Act provides for the presumption, unless the contrary be shown, that the subsections in relation to the requirement for the taking of specimens and sending them to the Bureau, have been complied with. Section 23(2) of the 1978 Act provides that a certificate expressed to have been issued under s 22 shall, until the contrary is shown, be sufficient evidence of the facts certified to in it – and unless the contrary is shown – be sufficient evidence of compliance by the Bureau with requirements of the Act. Gannon J went on to state (*per* Lavan J) that these provisions:

> ... are in relief of the onus of proof which, because of the presumption of innocence in favour of an accused person, would otherwise be borne by the prosecution. It does not affect in any way the nature or performance of the functions of the Bureau. It does have the effect of casting upon the accused person the onus of establishing either from evidence adduced by the prosecution or the evidence given or called by him that there was a failure by the Bureau of compliance with the statutory requirements relating to its functions. Because this onus is then cast upon an accused person and having regard to the procedures prescribed in s 16(5) and s 21 it seems to me that an accused person, who has not received delivery from the Bureau of the copy certificate cannot rely on that fact alone as showing the contrary for the purposes of avoiding the effect of s 23(2).

For these reasons, Lavan J held that the determination of the District Justice in dismissing the case, was deemed not correct in law.

[3.117] In essence, therefore, while general standards of proof apply and a consensus exists as to their application, content and effect (although not necessarily as to the elucidation of same), variation in the spectrum of proof possible on the criminal side is limited to the occasion when an accused is fixed with the burden or onus of proof and liable to reach the civil standard. On the civil side, then, greater variety might accrue, although rarely reaching below the base standard, augmentation rather occurring in light of the 'gravity and public importance of the issues ... concerned'.[126]

---

[126] *Per* Lord McDermott in *Preston v Preston* [1951] AC 391.

Chapter 4

Illegally-Obtained Evidence

I'm telling you ... Joxer ... th' whole worl's ... in a terr ... ible state o' ... chassis!

O'Casey, *Juno and the Peacock* (MacMillan, 1980), p 73

Introduction

[4.01] The legal system is hugely dependent on witnesses, as we have seen, and so many of the rules of evidence relate to the giving of testimony. However, there is another branch of the rules of evidence which is equally significant and that relates to the manner in which evidence is obtained. In fact, this is an aspect of the law of evidence which consumes a great deal of the Irish courts' time. In general Irish courts consider that any breach of procedure in the manner in which evidence was obtained presupposes that the State cannot take advantage of that impropriety. This is not of course always or definitively the answer but serves to highlight the importance of the origins of the evidence for the courts' determination of admissibility and sets the scene for adjudication of what various interests and policy considerations might come in to play in determinations as to admission in given contexts.

[4.02] Consider the following hypothetical case:

Gardaí obtain a search warrant under the Misuse of Drugs Act 1977 to conduct a search for drugs of 25 Rathland Road, Dublin. They approach a house on 25 Rathland Road, which is subdivided into apartments. On approaching the house they hear a flushing noise, so they break down the door, forcibly enter the first floor flat and find Mary White, a tenant, talking to a visitor, John Black, who they search and find to have a quantity of cocaine in his pocket. Later on, during a search of out-pipes of the house, they find a number of small packages which, on further examination, are found to contain heroin.

If you consider the arguments for or against the admissibility of the evidence against Mary White and John Black, you also have to consider the basis for their involvement in the event – the difference in status and the role of the gardaí.

What is the justification for searching John Black? Does it matter that Mary White is a tenant? What about the misspelling in the warrant? Can a warrant allow gardaí to enter any of a series of premises at one address? Should it? Once evidence is found as here, should it go in at a subsequent trial regardless of the manner in which it was obtained? Would it have been different here if the gardaí had had no warrant? Would it be different if, in addition to not having a warrant, they had not heard flushing? Would a cry for help emerging from the premises have made a difference? What if all they had found was a small quantity of ham and baby food stolen from Dunnes Stores?

[4.03] Perennial issues highlighting problems central to the criminal justice system include the process of bringing an accused before a court and the attitude of the court to the pre-trial criminal procedure. The rules of evidence very often represent that attitude. Problems also arise with regard to the concept of admissibility (particularly on policy grounds) and resolution of that most 'contentious' political issue in the context of the criminal trial. It is that resolution which this chapter considers.

[4.04] Consideration thereof necessarily invokes questions as to the kind of criminal justice system we choose to operate within our jurisdiction, and the particular philosophical underpinning or rationale to which it claims adherence. The criminal justice system involves the most intimate confrontation between the individual and the state in our society, and so as the Law Reform Commission of Canada has identified 'is always on the cutting edge of the abuse of power'.[1] Hence the treatment of the individual caught within it, should be symptomatic or characteristic of the nature of that system.

[4.05] Our criminal justice system adheres to the trial model of an adversarial system: what Frank called the 'fight theory of justice'.[2] This operates on the premise that:

> [T]he best way for a court to discover the facts in a suit is to have each side strive as hard as it can, in a keenly partisan spirit, to bring to the court's attention, the evidence favourable to that side.

[4.06] In the criminal context, the protagonists are the state and the individual accused. The operative presumption adopted in the context of that criminal inquiry is one of 'innocent until proven guilty'. It is for the state to prove beyond all reasonable doubt that the accused is guilty of the offence alleged. Moreover, the bias of the system is such that it is allegedly preferred that nine guilty men go free, rather than one innocent be convicted. In the context of determining the issue of guilt, the court does not have regard to all evidence relevant to the issue before it. This is due most immediately to application of the rules of evidence, the concepts of relevance and admissibility and ultimately to the fact that, for various policy reasons over the years, the courts have found it possible to admit, or to rely on, certain types of evidence less frequently than others. Various

---

[1]   Law Reform Commission of Canada Report, *Our Criminal Law* Minister of Supply and Services, Canada. Ottowa 1976 at p 1.

[2]   Frank, *Courts on Trial: Myth and Reality in American Justice* (Princeton University Press, 1949), p 89.

interests and value judgments come into play in delineating the distinction between relevance and admissibility. One of these – the consideration of this chapter – relates to the desire that in the obtaining of evidence by agents of the state, pre-trial criminal procedures be observed. Hence, with varying degrees of strictness, the courts decline to admit what is termed 'illegally-obtained evidence', ie evidence obtained in breach of procedure. Yet these procedures bear no small relationship to the fundamental bias of our system and the interest it claims to serve.

[4.07] The balancing of interests involved includes a recognition that the interest of the public in combating crime must be counterbalanced by the need to secure the fair trial of an accused, the public interest in vindication of constitutional rights, and the operation of the rule of law. Overall, the system is characterised as 'due process' rather than 'crime control'. The 'due process' model purports to safeguard in the criminal context, those individual rights guaranteed to citizens in liberal democracies, and to centre on the extent to which state incursion on the individual is permissible.

Historical perspective: the criminal trial

[4.08] It is perhaps appropriate when considering the concept of inadmissibility on policy grounds in the criminal trial to view the matter in perspective, in order to adjudge its current role. In the context of the trial itself, the safeguarding of an accused's rights had early recognition. In eighteenth-century England, for example, the criminal law was characterised by a harsh regime, culminating very often in the death sentence. Hay notes that 'the number of capital statutes grew from about 50 to over 200 between the years 1688 and 1820. Almost all of them concerned offences against property'.[3]

[4.09] Against this background, the criminal trial became encrusted with a fair measure of procedural safeguards, to which strict adherence was then held. The credibility of the structure was thus ensured. As Douglas Hay commented:

> 'Justice' was an evocative word in the eighteenth century, and with good reason. The constitutional struggles of the seventeenth century had helped to establish the principles of the rule of law: that offences should be fixed, not indeterminate; that rules of evidence should be carefully observed; that the law should be administered by a bench that was both learned and honest ... Equally important were the strict procedural rules which were enforced in the high courts and at assizes, especially in capital cases. Moreover, most penal statutes were interpreted by the judges in an extremely narrow and formalistic fashion. In part

---

[3] Hay, 'Property, Authority and the Criminal Law' in Hay *et al* (eds), *Albion's Fatal Tree: Crime and Society in Eighteenth Century England* (Pantheon, 1975), 17 at p 18.

this was based on seventeenth-century practice, but as more capital statutes were passed in the eighteenth century the bench reacted with an increasingly narrow interpretation ... If a name or date was incorrect, or if the accused was described as a 'farmer' rather than the approved term 'yeoman', the prosecution could fail ... These formalisms in the criminal law seemed ridiculous to contemporary critics, and to many later historians. Their argument was (and is) that the criminal law, to be effective, must be known and determinate, instead of capricious and obscure. Prosecutors resented the waste of their time and money lost on a technicality, thieves were said to mock courts which allowed them to escape through so many verbal loopholes. But it seems likely that the mass of Englishmen drew other conclusions from the practice. The punctilious attention to forms, the dispassionate and legalistic exchanges between counsel and the judge, argued that those administering and using the laws submitted to its rule ...[4]

Hay's ultimate thesis is that this absurd formalism was part of the strength of the law as an ideology, which later he alleges was class-based. Eighteenth-century formalism is thus revealed by Hay as instrumental in the oppression of the working classes.

Twenty-first-century formalism, or adherence to procedure, in the criminal justice context, has ostensibly a different function: the limitation of state incursion on the individual. The ideology is that of the criminal justice regime adhering to the aforementioned 'due process' model.

[4.10] The historical perspective illustrates the beginnings of the precedent of a criminal justice system encrusted with procedure. The current rationale of such procedure is now that of regulating state power, and the apparent inequality between citizens and the state, in the context of a criminal trial. Yet the criminal justice system had its origins in a very harsh regime: one where the accused was not competent, for some considerable time, as a witness in his own trial. Even when competent, he invariably came from the poorer sectors of society, was badly educated and so ill-equipped to put forward a defence or, in the absence of a legal aid scheme, to afford legal representation. If conviction ensued (as was, therefore, almost inevitable), very many of the offences merited the death penalty.

[4.11] It can be argued that current conditions require a different system of criminal justice: one whose procedures do not so jealously guard the rights of the accused. In a democracy, however, any such debate should be an open and full one, mindful of the constitutional guarantees to citizens, and conscious of the need to develop a structure with an inherent logic – a system of checks and

---

[4] Hay 'Property, Authority and the Criminal Law' in Hay *et al* (eds), *Albion's Fatal Tree: Crime and Society in Eighteenth Century England* (Pantheon, 1975), 17 at p 32.

balances to ensure overall equity to the citizens caught within it. This is what liberal democracy guarantees, after all.

[4.12] Recent events may suggest, however, that in the context of the Irish criminal justice system, change has occurred in the absence of debate and under the guise of adjustments of no substantive effect. Such adjustment or mutation can be observed in the context of recent pronouncements by the Irish courts on the issue of the admissibility of illegally or unconstitutionally obtained evidence.

[4.13] Prior to examining this, however, it is useful to set out the current parameters on police use of powers of incursion on the liberty and or freedoms of the individual citizen. These can usefully be termed powers of search and seizure, as in this context one is talking of the admissibility of evidence obtained by force in an unlawful or invalid search, rather than a process of interrogation which results in confession-type evidence. Although the latter similarly involves a constitutional dimension, it is further complicated by the requirement of 'voluntariness' and will be considered separately together with police powers of arrest and detention and the regulation thereof.

Search and seizure

[4.14] *Consent* of the person concerned can of course be lawful justification for a search by a police officer. *Statutory authority* may also provide a power of search short of arrest. In *O'Callaghan v Ireland*[5] such a statutory power, short of arrest under s 23 of the Misuse of Drugs Act 1977 (as amended by s 12 of the Misuse of Drugs Act 1984), was upheld under a constitutional challenge. The Supreme Court held such persons did have all rights accruing on arrest.

[4.15] A decision which seems to indicate a possible implied statutory power or common law power short of arrest is *DPP v Fagan*.[6] Carney J held that An Garda Síochána had both an implied statutory power under the Road Traffic Acts and a common law power to operate random road traffic checks involving the stopping of vehicles, even where the gardaí did not suspect the drivers of any criminal offence. The Supreme Court confirmed on appeal (Denham J dissenting) that such a power existed at common law.

[4.16] *On arrest*, a person can be searched for the protection of the arresting officer. His immediate environment may also be searched (*Dillon v O'Brien and Davis*[7]). In *Jennings v Quinn*,[8] O'Keeffe J outlined in the High Court the parameters of police powers of search and seizure of material in the aftermath of a lawful arrest. Police can take:

---

[5]   *O'Callaghan v Ireland* [1994] 1 IR 555.
[6]   *DPP v Fagan* [1993] 2 IR 95.
[7]   *Dillon v O'Brien & Davis* (1897) 20 LR Ir 300.
[8]   *Jennings v Quinn* [1968] IR 305 at 309.

(i)   evidence in support of the crime charged on which the arrest is made;

(ii)   evidence in support of any crime charged or then in contemplation against the person; and

(iii) evidence reasonably believed to be stolen property or to be property unlawfully in possession of that person.

[4.17] This can be contrasted with *Jeffrey v Black*[9] where Mr Black was arrested because he stole a sandwich from a pub. Before being brought to the police station and charged, however, the police officers brought him to his home where they found cannabis. The evidence on the charge of possession of cannabis was deemed inadmissible.

[4.18] *People v McFadden*[10] emphasised the importance of informing a person of the reason why they are being searched. Here the individual accused had been arrested on suspicion of drunken driving and consented to being searched, but objected when gardaí began to search his wallet. They proceeded with the search and found a document with information on the movements of a superintendent in the RUC. He was convicted in the Special Criminal Court on the basis of this information alone of being in possession of information likely to be useful to an unlawful organisation in the commission of a serious offence. He appealed on the basis that the search for the document was unlawful. The Court of Criminal Appeal held that a garda could not search a person without the consent of the arrested person unless he informed the person of the legal justification for the search.[11] Here the failure to inform the accused was felt to affect the lawfulness of the custody of the accused or the admissibility of the evidence and so the conviction was quashed. Keane CJ stated:[12]

> The failure of the garda in this case to give any explanation to the accused as to why his wallet was being searched, at a stage when it was clear to him that the accused was objecting to his search of the wallet, could not be regarded as a trivial or inconsequential departure from the Regulations of 1987. A breach of the fundamental requirement of our law that a police officer who is carrying out a search of a person without his consent informs that person of the legal justification for so interfering with his constitutional rights cannot, in the view of the court, be considered as of such little importance as to justify a departure from the Regulations.

---

[9]   *Jeffrey v Black* (1978) 1 All ER 555.
[10] *People v McFadden* [2003] 2 IR 105.
[11] *DPP v Rooney* [1992] 2 IR 7; *DPP v O'Donnell* [1995] 3 IR 551 followed.
[12] *People v McFadden* [2003] 2 IR 105 at 112.

Search warrants

[4.19] Search warrants are probably the most common justification for search and seizure. Traditionally, search warrants were very specific and limited exceptions made to the historically important principle of the common law that 'a man's home is his castle'. In *Leach v Money*,[13] the concept of a general warrant was rejected, as the courts had a horror of the 'general ransack', and in *Entick v Carrington*[14] the concept of a warrant issued on grounds of 'state necessity' was rejected. In general, a search warrant was 'spent' when used once, and could not be used again. However, many warrants are now exceptionally and specifically provided to 'live' for a specified time. An early example of such an exception is the Misuse of Drugs Act 1977, s 26(2), which allows for the execution of a warrant 'at any time or times within one month from the date of issue of the warrant'.

[4.20] With regard to the use of a premises for the purposes of prostitution and living on the earnings of prostitution, s 10(2) of the Criminal Law (Sexual Offences) Act 1993 also provides that a District Court can issue a warrant authorising a search of such premises 'at any time or times within one month from the date of issue of the warrant'.

[4.21] Recent legislative changes to the provisions regarding the issue of search warrants include changes to their traditional specificity (ie warrants are now more broad sweeping in terms of the powers they confer), their longevity and their issuance, in that provision is made for avoidance of the judicial imprimatur in granting a warrant (ie in circumstances of urgency or necessity they can be issued by gardaí of a certain rank). In that case, they generally do not 'live' for as long, but the notion of independent (ie judicial) scrutiny of the justification for such search is lost.

[4.22] It is worth examining some of the more recent provisions with regard to changes in powers of search under warrant, in terms of the powers granted to the police and agencies such as the Criminal Assets Bureau (CAB) in order to note the areas where such powers of search and seizure have increased. The manner in which broad-sweeping powers of search have moved from such limited areas of concern, to gradually (as those areas increase) overwhelm the whole, is remarkable, and typical of a piecemeal approach which facilitates change incrementally, without the need to address therefore the implications for the whole of the system. These implications relate to privacy, property rights, self-incrimination and the role of the court in safeguarding civil liberties.

---

[13] *Leach v Money* (1765) 19 St Jr 1001.
[14] *Entick v Carrington* (1795) 2 Wils 275.

[4.23] The gradual diminishing in importance of the role of the judiciary as a 'brake' on police action is also perhaps a product of state anxiety to avoid the implications of arguments which led to the loss of evidence at trial (inadmissibility) because of the fragility of the judicial role – as witnessed in *Kenny* etc (see paras **4.68–4.69** below). Yet avoidance of the role of the Peace Commissioners or District Court judges as reviewers of 'police suspicion' by providing for a power for garda issuance of a warrant in certain situation, in an effort to circumvent defence attacks on whether the district judge or PC was truly satisfied regarding the existence of reasonable grounds for suspicion, results in a loss of the only independent review of the police action in this most highly charged area for individual rights.

Warrants – recent changes

[4.24] Traditionally, as has been shown, warrants had to be specific, eg to search for stolen goods or drugs. As they had been issued on the basis of a reasonable suspicion, this was a logical extension which also served to ensure not just limitations in terms of state intrusion on individuals by guarding against unwarranted interference but also the avoidance of over-extensive interference. In their original incarnation, therefore, search warrants were specific and were limited in terms of their life span. That is to say that in general, once used, a warrant was no longer valid.

Recent changes have ensured that warrants now allow gardaí to do rather more than traditionally; what they can take, for instance, under an authorised search has increased. There is also the phenomenon of warrants which stay 'live' for a while. For example under Misuse of Drugs Act 1977, s 26 the warrant can be used over the course of a month. The third change is in relation to the issuance of a warrant. Traditionally, there had to be judicial imprimatur for a warrant to issue. It wasn't sufficient for gardaí simply to have a suspicion: there had to scrutiny of that suspicion to the extent that there was judicial satisfaction that there was a basis for the grounding of the warrant.

[4.25] Moreover, as the courts said there should not be merely a rubber-stamping of warrants by judiciary, it was evident that this was seen to be an important check on the police power of entry with warrant. Increasingly, however, the role of the judiciary in the granting of warrants is under attack to the extent that it has diminished. On occasion a Peace Commissioner would be stated to suffice, but increasingly, and rather more worryingly, and starting with such provision in subversion-related legislation, eg Offences against the State Acts, gardaí of a certain rank were in some circumstances allowed to issue a warrant. Generally, this is specified to be in cases of urgency, but though limited, it is becoming more frequently employed. The difficulty with such increasingly prevalent provision is that it removes the independent scrutiny of the judiciary from the issuance of the warrant.

Provisions regarding issuance of search warrants

Search warrants in relation to arrestable offences

[4.26] Section 6 of the Criminal Justice Act 2006 replaced a previous provision (s 10) under the Criminal Justice (Miscellaneous Provisions) Act 1997 which provided for warrants in relation to *serious* offences. Section 6 of the 2006 Act provides for the issuance of a warrant in circumstances where there are reasonable grounds for suspecting evidence in relation to commission of an 'arrestable' offence. Hence such a warrant can issue where there is evidence of the commission of an 'arrestable' offence, ie an offence which merits five years' imprisonment or more, which is in effect any criminal offence of any substance. The provision enables the police to search a place and any person found at that place and extends that power beyond just the remit of serious offences which had been enabled by the 1997 legislation.

[4.27] Section 6 provides that s 10 of the Criminal Justice (Miscellaneous Provisions) Act 1997 is amended by the substitution of the following for s 10:

> (1) If a judge of the District Court is satisfied by information on oath of a member, not below the rank of sergeant, that there are reasonable grounds for suspecting that evidence of, or relating to, the commission of an arrestable offence is to be found in any place, the judge may issue a warrant for the search of that place and any persons found at that place.

Subsection (2)(a) authorises a named member together with other persons to enter at any time or times within one week of the date of issue of the warrant the place named on the warrant; (b) to search it and any persons found at that place; and (c) to seize anything found at that place or anything found in the possession of a person present that that member believes to be evidence of or relating to, the commission of an arrestable offence.

Subsection (3) enables a member acting under the authority of a search warrant under that section (a) to require any person present to give the member his or her name and address; and to (b) arrest without warrant any person who obstructs or fails to comply.

It can be seen that the powers of the police under this section are considerable. It is notable that this provision still maintains judicial input in that a judge of the District Court must issue the warrant.

Search warrants for entry for the purpose of arrest

[4.28] A second provision that broadens and strengthens the powers issuing under a warrant is the Criminal Law Act 1997, s 6. That section provides for warrants for entry for the purposes of arrest follows:

> (1) For the purpose of arresting a person on foot of a warrant of arrest or an order of committal, a member of the Garda Síochána may enter (if need be, by use of reasonable force) and search any premises (including a dwelling) where the person is or where the member, with reasonable cause, suspects that person to be, and such warrant or order may be executed in accordance with section 5.
>
> (2) For the purpose of arresting a person without a warrant for an arrestable offence a member of the Garda Síochána may enter (if need be, by use of reasonable force) and search any premises (including a dwelling) where that person is or where the member 'with reasonable cause' suspects that person to be, and where the premises is a dwelling the member shall not, unless acting with the consent of an occupier of the dwelling or other person who appears to the member to be in charge of the dwelling, enter that dwelling unless—
>
> (a)   he or she or another such member has observed the person within or entering the dwelling, or
>
> (b)   he or she, with reasonable cause, suspects that before a warrant of arrest could be obtained the person will either abscond for the purpose of avoiding justice or will obstruct the course of justice, or
>
> (c)   he or she, with reasonable cause, suspects that before a warrant of arrest could be obtained the person would commit an arrestable offence, or
>
> (d)   the person ordinarily resides at that dwelling.
>
> (3) Without prejudice to any express amendment or repeal made by this Act, this section shall not affect the operation of any enactment or rule of law relating to powers of search or powers of arrest.

This warrant, in allowing for a power of entry effectively in 'hot pursuit', is remarkable by contrast with traditional jurisprudence. Its origin is also notable in that it was introduced in direct response to *Freeman v DPP*[15] where constitutionally such an entry was deemed prohibited.

[4.29] With a warrant a garda may now enter by use of reasonable force any premises where that person is, or is suspected to be, and search that premises, including a dwelling. If they don't have a warrant, they can still for the purposes of arresting someone enter any premises (with force if necessary) and search that premises (including a dwelling) where the person is or they reasonably suspect the person to be. Where the premises is a dwelling, they are not to enter

---

[15]   *Freeman v DPP* [1996] 3 IR 565.

without the consent of the owner *unless* they saw the person enter the dwelling or observed them within the dwelling, or they suspect that the person will abscond, or will commit an 'arrestable' offence before a warrant can be obtained, or that the person ordinarily resides at that dwelling.

That provision under the 1997 Act was introduced directly as a result of a decision of the courts in the case of *Freeman v DPP*[16] where the absence of such a power was noted by the courts and picked up by the legislature even though on the facts in *Freeman*, the result was the same.

Warrants for the Criminal Assets Bureau in relation to the proceeds of crime

[4.30] The Criminal Assets Bureau Act 1996, s 14 (as amended by the Criminal Justice Act 2006, s 190), provides:

(1) that a judge of the District Court, when satisfied (and not simply 'on hearing' as in the original provision in the 1996 Act) by information on oath given by a Bureau officer that there are reasonable grounds for suspecting that evidence of or relating to assets or proceeds deriving from criminal conduct (not activities as previously) or to their identity or whereabouts to be found in any place, the Judge may issue a warrant for the search of that place and any person found at that place.

[4.31] The remainder of s 14 continues:

(2) A bureau officer who is a member of the Garda Síochána not below the rank of superintendent may, subject to subsection (3), if he or she is satisfied that there are reasonable grounds for suspecting that evidence of or relating to assets proceeds deriving from criminal activities, or to their identity or whereabouts is to be found in any place, issue a warrant for the search of that place and any person found at that place.

(3) A bureau officer who is a member of the Garda Síochána not below the rank of superintendent shall not issue a search warrant under this section unless he or she is satisfied that circumstances giving rise to the need for the immediate issue of the search warrant would render it impracticable to apply to a judge of the District Court under this section for a search warrant.

(4) Subject to subsection (5), a warrant under this section shall be expressed to and shall operate to authorise a named bureau officer who is a member of the Garda Síochána, accompanied by such other persons as the bureau officer thinks necessary, to enter, within one week of the date of issuing of the warrant (if necessary by the use of reasonable force), the place named in the warrant, and to search it and any person found at that place and seize and retain any material found at that place, or any material found in the possession of a person found present at that place at the time of the search, which the officer believes to be

---

[16] *Freeman v DPP* [1996] 3 IR 565 below.

evidence of or relating to assets or proceeds deriving from criminal activities, or to their identity or whereabouts.

(5) Notwithstanding subsection (4), a search warrant issued under subsection (3) shall cease to have effect after a period of 24 hours has elapsed from the time of the issue of the warrant.

(6) A bureau officer who is a member of the Garda Síochána acting under the authority of a warrant under this section may—

(a) require any person present at the place where the search is carried out to give to the officer the person's name and address, and

(b) arrest without warrant any person who:

(i) obstructs or attempts to obstruct that officer or any person accompanying that officer in the carrying out of his or her duties,

(ii) fails to comply with a requirement under paragraph (a), or

(iii) gives a name or address which the officer has reasonable cause for believing is false or misleading.

(7) A person who obstructs or attempts to obstruct a person acting under the authority of a warrant under this section, who fails to comply with a requirement under subsection (6)(a) or who gives a false or misleading name or address to a bureau officer who is a member of the Garda Síochána, shall be guilty of an offence and shall be liable on summary conviction to a fine not exceeding £1,500, or to imprisonment for a period not exceeding 6 months, or to both.

(8) The power to issue a warrant under this section is in addition to and not in substitution for any other power to issue a warrant for the search of any place or person.

(9) In this section 'place' includes a dwelling.'

The CAB warrant was specifically drawn up to facilitate its officers with the widest powers of search and seizure. In addition to the judicial power, there is a garda power to issue a warrant, and accompanying wide-ranging powers in relation to those on the premises in question.

Warrants for the purposes of drug trafficking

[4.32] The Criminal Justice (Drug Trafficking) Act 1996, s 8 provides for the issuing of search warrants by a member of An Garda Síochána not below the rank of Superintendent under s 26 of the Misuse of Drugs Act 1977, where he is satisfied:

(a) that the warrant is necessary for the proper investigation of the suspected drug trafficking offence, and

(b)   that circumstances of urgency giving rise to the need for the immediate issue of the search warrant would render it impractical to apply to a District Court Judge or Peace Commissioner.

This demonstrates the avoidance, once more, of judicial review of garda suspicion or opinion before necessary issuance of a warrant.

[4.33] The Court of Criminal Appeal decision of *People (DPP) v Byrne*[17] is significant as it involves consideration of just such an issuance of a warrant by a Chief Superintendent. The accused had been convicted under the Misuse of Drugs Act 1977 in respect of drugs found under a search warrant issued by a Chief Superintendent in accordance with s 8(2) of the Criminal Justice (Drug Trafficking) Act 1996. He had been sentenced to 10 years' imprisonment. The sole ground of appeal was that the search warrant was invalid. Although the appeal was unsuccessful, some interesting comments were made by Hardiman J in relation to the power of a Chief Superintendent to issue a search warrant. Although the point raised by the matter was constitutionally significant and decided in favour of the applicant, the court was satisfied that no miscarriage of justice had occurred in the case and so confirmed the conviction under s 3(1)(a) of the Criminal Procedure Act 1993.

[4.34] Hardiman J's judgment points out that the case of *Byrne v Grey*[18] has emphasised the constitutional importance of proper procedures in relation to searches, particularly of private dwellings. That case had considered the argument that it was unconstitutional to have a warrant issued by a Peace Commissioner, who is a non-judicial personage, rather than a judge and rejected it, stressing, however, that the Peace Commissioner was an independent person who must be satisfied of the necessary matters by information on oath.[19]

Hardiman J goes on to then consider the further provision here of the power of a Garda Chief Superintendent or Superintendent to issue a warrant and comments[20] that 'the power of a garda chief superintendent or superintendent to issue a search warrant is by way of a further exception and is an emergency provision, and cannot be regarded as anything other than an emergency provision.' He later continues:[21]

> …[I]t is not the case that An Garda Síochána are free to choose whether they will apply for a warrant to a judge, to a peace commissioner or to a superintendent. They *must* apply to a judge or a peace commissioner unless the very limited circumstances which permit them to apply to a superintendent are present. These

---

[17] *People (DPP) v Byrne* [2003] 4 IR 423.

[18] *Byrne v Grey* [1988] IR 31.

[19] *People (DPP) v Byrne* [2003] 4 IR 423 at 426, *per* Hardiman J.

[20] *People (DPP) v Byrne* [2003] 4 IR 423 at 427.

[21] *People (DPP) v Byrne* [2003] 4 IR 423 at 427–428.

circumstances must be *demonstrated* to be present for the superintendent's warrant to be valid ... We hope that the indication that this court has very clearly given, that there is an obligation to apply in priority to a district judge or a peace commissioner before seeking a warrant elsewhere and that it is doubtful whether permitting a situation of urgency to arise before seeking a warrant where one might easily have forestalled it is proper compliance with section 8(2) of the Act of 1996, will be sufficient to prevent difficulties arising in the future.

Warrants for the purpose of surveillance

[4.35] The most recent provision regarding the issuance of warrants relates to the now newly regulated area of activity-surveillance. Under the Criminal Justice (Surveillance) Act 2009,[22] s 4 makes provision whereby a superior officer of an Garda Síochána may apply to a judge for a surveillance warrant. The surveillance must relate to the investigation of an arrestable offence or concern the security of the state. Authority is given to enter a premises by force if necessary. Section 5 provides for authorisation by a District Court judge on oath on an ex parte basis which will allow an authorised member or officer to enter a property (by force of necessary) for the purpose of surveillance. Such authority is valid for up to three months and renewable (s 6). In urgent situations to prevent a person absconding to avoid justice, the possible destruction of evidence or when the security of the state would be compromised a superior officer may give approval for surveillance for up to 72 hours (s 7).

[4.36] Section 8 provides for internal tracking device use for up to 4 months where judicial authorisation is not necessary for their use but superior officer approval required. Section 14 provides that evidence obtained by means of surveillance notwithstanding any error or omission on the authorisation or written record or failure by member/officer to comply with the requirements of the authorisation/written record is admissible. This is an interesting attempt to avoid the scrutiny of the courts in terms of application of the *O'Brien* formula. It is reminiscent of an attempt in s 13 of the Criminal Justice (Amendment) Act 2009 to make similar provision with regard to organised crime offences under the Criminal Justice Act 2006 by adding a section (s 74B) which 'confirms that a court may exclude evidence if in the opinion of the court the prejudicial effect of the evidence outweighs its probative value'. The latter begs the question – as if such confirmation were needed, but also raises the issue of that being the only basis of exclusion as the reach of the courts under the *O'Brien* formula is greater (see paras **4.50–4.51**).

[4.37] The Criminal Justice (Surveillance) Bill (introduced in February 2009) stated in the explanatory memorandum that its purpose 'is to buttress the work

---

[22] No 10 of 2009.

of the Garda Síochána … in the prevention and detection of serious crime and in safeguarding the security of the State against subversion and terrorism.' It later states that 'the Bill ensures that any possible legal obstacles to the admissibility of such material in criminal trials are removed in cases involving arrestable offences.' Hence it is perhaps unsurprising that a key section in the Act deals with the admissibility of evidence gained by surveillance.

[4.38] The regime put in place is one whereby prior authorisation by a District Court judge will be required and will last for up to three months, renewable on application, and where in urgent circumstances surveillance can take place without court authorisation for 72 hours, on the authority of a superior officer. This is similar to other areas –the development of law on warrants and also arrest – so that particular offences (mention of terrorism and subversion here) sets the context for use and there is provision for the authorisation to 'live' a while, and an alternate to obtenance through judicial oversight.

It is provided under s 14 that (s 14(3)(a)) 'notwithstanding any error or omission on the face of the authorisation or written record of approval concerned' or (s 14(4)(a)) 'notwithstanding any failure [by a member or officer]… to comply with a requirement of the authorisation or approval' such evidence is admissible if the court decides that—

(i)   the error or omission/failure concerned was inadvertent or the member or officer acted in good faith and that the failure was inadvertent and

(ii)   the information or document ought to be admitted in the interest of justice.

[4.39] The court is to have regard to the following matter in so deciding:

(i)   whether the error or omission/ or failure concerned was serious or merely technical in nature;

(ii)   the nature of any right infringed by the obtaining of the information or document concerned;

(iii)   whether there were circumstances of urgency;

(iv)   the possible prejudicial effect of the information or document concerned;

(v)   the probative value of the information or document concerned.

It remains to be seen whether such provision survives constitutional scrutiny. If it does it will certainly ensure a loosening of the strictures of *Kenny* in the very early pre-trial process and a narrower approach to exclusion. Once again it presupposes a knowable content to 'in the interest of justice' which is unrelated to prior jurisprudence. In like manner to 'in the public interest' that latter needs some further elucidation by the courts. It is useful to reflect on some European

Court of Human Rights jurisprudence here to assess the extent to which such provision comes within the rubric of fairness.

[4.40] The European Court of Human Rights (ECt HR) has made it clear that they require judicial supervision of warrants in *Kopp v Switzerland*[23] and *Valenzuela Contreras v Spain*[24] where they held there was a breach of art 8 as the surveillance legislation lacked judicial supervision. It is also notable that the exclusion of cameras from the definition of surveillance devices under the Irish legislation (s 1 of the 2009 Act) may be questionable. The Law Reform Commission and the recent observations of the Irish Human Rights Commission[25] would support its inclusion. In *Friedl v Austria*,[26] the European Commission for Human Rights rejected a claim of a breach of art 8 in the context of video recording of a demonstration but there the Austrian authorities had compensated Mr Fiedl and destroyed the evidence. In *Perry*,[27] the European Court ruled that material which is obtained from cameras or recordings and stored for future use can only be justified under art 8 if done in accordance with the law. The absence of any such oversight regarding cameras in the context of policing in Ireland given its exclusion from the 2009 Act would seem problematic in that light.

[4.41] In *Klass v Germany*[28] a number of lawyers and a judge claimed the German G10 Act was contrary to the Convention. The ECt HR required surveillance to have adequate measures against abuse and considered each case on its merits.

[4.42] In *Weber & Savaria v Germany*[29] the ECt HR held German law complied with art 8 of the ECHR. Weber was a freelance journalist working for German media investigating arms trafficking. Savaria took messages for her while she was away. They argued that the German legislation – (Fight Against Crime Act 1994 which amended the G10 Act) was contrary to art 8. The Court noted that the G10 Act specified the offences concerned, the category of people, and satisfied minimum standards with regard to limits on duration, use and storage, destruction etc. The Court was therefore satisfied that the German legislation was not contrary to art 8. The significant issue here is the presence of regulation.

---

[23] *Kopp v Switzerland* [1998-II 27 EHRR 91.

[24] *Valenzuela Contreras v Spain* [1999] 28 EHRR 483.

[25] Law Reform Commission LRC 57-1998 Report on Privacy: Surveillance and the Interception of Communications (Dublin 1998); Irish Human Rights Commission: Observations on the Criminal Justice (Surveillance) Bill 2009 May 2009.

[26] *Friedl v Austria* Applic 15225/89 (26 January 1995).

[27] *Perry v United Kingdom* (2004) 39 EHRR 76.

[28] *Klass v Germany* A28 (1978) 2 EHRR 214.

[29] *Weber & Savaria v Germany* (2008) 46 EHRR 515.

[4.43] In *Liberty & Ors v UK*[30] the Ministry of Defence had a facility which monitored all telephone fax & email coming from Dublin/London to the Continent. The applicants (Liberty, British Irish Rights Watch and the ICCL) were in regular telephone contact with each other and would have provided legal advice. They alleged such monitoring was contrary to art 8 on the basis that the interception was not accessible and foreseeable. The case involved blanket monitoring (using catch words to target surveillance). The Court found terms such as 'national security' and 'preventing and detecting serious crime' too general and the relevant legislation insufficiently clear on the procedure for selecting storing destroying intercepted material and therefore was contrary to art 8.

Therefore it can be seen that the ECt HR at a minimum requires clarity in order for the requirements of forseeability and accessibility to be complied with. The question is whether the Irish 2009 Act meets that standard.

[4.44] Together with legislative moves such as the further elevation of garda opinion evidence in the Criminal Justice (Amendment) Act 2009, the pressure will be on the judiciary and their ability to square the circle of fairness and the legislature's moves to combat crime ostensibly in the 'public interest'.

Although the rules in relation to the issuance of warrants may have been liberalised by recent changes in legislation (often in the context of particular types of offences, eg drug trafficking, criminal assets, war on organised crime etc), it is also evident that the courts' jurisprudence, ie what courts do with the issue of the admissibility of evidence thereby obtained, is still of considerable import. Hence it is to that judicial consideration that we now turn moving from older initial comparative positions to more recent only to understand the issues underneath.

Judicial approach – historical and comparative

[4.45] The proliferation of specific and more extensive provisions in relation to warrants for particular offences, targeting certain areas of crime or facilitating bodies such as CAB, will undoubtedly continue. As rules relating to admissibility of evidence, and in particular illegally-obtained evidence, focus on abuse or breach of procedure, the increasing complexity and variety of procedures renders this a more complicated task. Scrutiny of the grounds for issuance of a warrant, by reviewing the role of the Peace Commissioner or judge, may now in many cases be obviated by the role of the issuing garda officer. Implications of such changes for the role of the reviewing courts will only then

---

[30] *Liberty & Ors v UK* (2009) 48 EHRR 1.

emerge. To gain an insight into potential development here, an historical and comparative perspective on the possible divergent views of the courts is useful.

Approach of the English courts

[4.46] Traditional judicial approach in England could be epitomised in the statement 'It matters not how you get it, if you steal it even, it would be admissible in evidence'.[31] A change of approach with regard to the admissibility of illegally-obtained evidence was then introduced in that jurisdiction and found in the Police and Criminal Evidence Act 1984, s 78, which provides:

> In any proceedings the Court may refuse to allow evidence on which the prosecution proposes to rely to be given if it appears to the Court that, having regard to all the circumstances, including the circumstances in which the evidence was obtained, the admission of the evidence would have such an adverse effect on the fairness of the proceedings, that the Court ought not to admit it.

[4.47] In *R v Mason*[32] the Court of Appeal commented that although the court's role was not to discipline the police, the 'hood winking' of the client and his solicitor in this case (by informing them falsely that the police had forensic evidence implicating the accused) necessitated exclusion of the evidence thereby obtained. The basis for exclusion in *Mason* was that provision in the Police and Criminal Evidence Act 1984 (s 78) which was said to encapsulate the English courts' previous discretion at common law. The advent of the Human Rights Act 1998 has meant an impact, as noted by Ashworth, mainly felt in criminal procedure and evidence.[33] However, the English courts have followed the House of Lords' interpretation of *Khan v UK*,[34] that the obtaining of evidence by violation of another Convention right does not render a trial unfair under art 6, and that it is always a question of judicial discretion under s 78. However, the decision in *A v Secretary of State for the Home Department*[35] sees the House of Lords distancing itself where torture is involved so that a fair trial under art 6 would not be possible where evidence was obtained by torture contrary to art 3.[36]

---

[31] Crompton J in *R v Leatham* (1861) 8 Cox CC 498 at 503.

[32] *R v Mason* [1988] 1 WLR 139.

[33] Ashworth, 'Criminal Proceedings after the Human Rights Act: the First Year' [2001] *Crim LR* 855.

[34] *Khan v UK* (2000) Crim LR 684.

[35] *A v Secretary of State for the Home Department* [2005] UKHL 71.

[36] See further Ashworth, 'Security Terrorism and Human Rights' in Goold & Lazarus *Security & Human Rights* (Hart Oxford, 2007), 203.

Approach of the United States courts

[4.48] The exclusionary rule in relation to illegally-obtained evidence in the United States was developed initially in *Boyd v US*[37] in relation to forfeiture proceedings. *Weeks v US*[38] extended the doctrine to federal criminal trials, and *Mapp v Ohio*[39] to state criminal trials. Furthermore, the doctrine of the 'fruit of the poisoned tree' in the United States, operated to exclude evidence obtained indirectly in consequence of a constitutional violation. The rationale for the exclusionary rule was based firmly in the notion of the deterrence of unacceptable violation of constitutional rights by the police:

> Only by exclusion can we impress upon the zealous prosecutor that violation of the constitution will do him no good. And only when that point is driven home can the prosecutor be expected to emphasise the importance of observing constitutional demands in his instructions to the police.[40]

The United States Supreme Court became less enamoured of the exclusionary rule, however, and in a number of decisions has somewhat reduced its monolithic effect. For example, if the court determined that the rationale of the rule – deterrence – would not be effected in a given case, the evidence would be admitted, notwithstanding the breach of constitutional rights involved.

[4.49] This was the situation in *US v Leon*[41] where the warrant was invalid but the officers acted in good faith. Exclusion of the evidence obtained thereunder would not have any deterrence effect, hence a 'good faith' exception was carved out to the exclusionary rule.

Approach of the Irish courts

[4.50] The yardstick by which the Irish courts determine admissibility of illegally-obtained evidence is *People (AG) v O'Brien*.[42] The search warrant used in *People (AG) v O'Brien* contained an error in relation to the name of the street. The search was deemed illegal – so incorporating a discretion on the part of the trial judge to admit or exclude the evidence. A distinction was drawn by the court between 'mere illegality' which could facilitate admissibility, and a breach of constitutional rights which would exclude evidence.

[4.51] The Supreme Court held that evidence obtained in 'deliberate and conscious' breach of constitutional rights was inadmissible, save in

---

[37] *Boyd v US* (1866) 116 US 616.
[38] *Weeks v US* (1914) 332 US 383.
[39] *Mapp v Ohio* (1961) 367 US 643.
[40] Murphy J (dissenting) in *Wolfe v Colorado* (1949) 338 US 25 at 41.
[41] *US v Leon* (1983) 468 US 879.
[42] *People (AG) v O'Brien* [1965] IR 142.

'extraordinary excusing circumstances'. Although Kingsmill Moore J was reluctant to define the latter, Walsh J was of the opinion that they would include circumstances such as the imminent destruction of vital evidence, or the need to rescue a victim in peril. He also placed in the excusable category evidence obtained by a search incidental to and contemporaneous with a lawful arrest, although made without a valid search warrant. If a breach involved a mere illegality, the trial judge had a discretion as to whether to exclude the evidence. The considerations then to be invoked, *per* Kingsmill Moore J, were as follows:

> Was the illegal action intentional or unintentional, and if unintentional was it the result of an ad hoc decision or does it represent a settled or deliberate policy? Was it illegality of a trivial and technical nature or was it a serious invasion of important rights, the recurrence of which would involve a real danger to necessary freedom? Were there circumstances of urgency or emergency which provide some excuse for the action?[43]

[4.52] In *People v Shaw*,[44] Griffin J suggested that the *O'Brien* ratio was confined to real evidence. In *People v Lynch*, Higgins CJ, however, castigated this suggestion and reasserted that, in fact, the *O'Brien* ratio covered both real and confession evidence.[45]

[4.53] In *Trimbole v Governor of Mountjoy Prison*[46] the applicant was arrested at 2 pm on 25 October 1984 under s 30 of the Offences Against the State Act 1939. On 26 October an additional 24 hours' detention was sanctioned. At 3 pm on 26 October, an application was made to the High Court. Egan J was satisfied no genuine suspicion could have been formed by gardaí regarding possession of firearms or ammunition. An order for release was granted. A short while later, the applicant was arrested on foot of a provisional warrant under s 27 of the Extradition Act 1965. On 26 October 1984 the government had made an order applying the Extradition Act 1965 to Australia as and from then. The applicant was brought before the District Court and remanded in custody. On 21 November 1984 the Minister made order for extradition. Egan J commented:[47]

> the only rational explanation for the s 30 arrest on 25th October 1984 was to ensure that the applicant would be available for arrest and detention when Part II of the 1965 Act would apply to the Commonwealth of Australia. There was a gross misuse of s 30 which amounted to a conscious and deliberate violation of constitutional rights. There were no extraordinary excusing circumstances.

---

43 *People v O'Brien* [1965] IR 142 at 160.
44 *People v Shaw* [1982] IR 1 at 59–60.
45 *People v Lynch* [1982] IR 64 at 77–78. Also at [1981] ILRM 389 at 395.
46 *Trimbole v Governor of Mountjoy Prison* [1985] ILRM 465.
47 *Trimbole v Governor of Mountjoy Prison* [1985] ILRM 465 at 479.

[4.54] The decision was upheld on appeal to the Supreme Court where Finlay CJ (Henchy, Griffin, Hederman JJ concurring) stated:[48]

> I am satisfied that from those decisions (*State (Quinn) v Ryan* [1965] IR 70; *People (AG) v O'Brien* [1965] IR 342; *People v Madden* [1977] IR 336; *People v Lynch* [1982] IR 64) certain principles can be deduced. They are:
>
> The Courts have not only an inherent jurisdiction but a positive duty:
>
> (i)   To protect persons against the invasion of their constitutional rights.
>
> (ii)   If invasion has occurred, to restore as far as possible the person so damaged to the position in which he would be if his rights had not been invaded; and
>
> (iii) To ensure as far as possible that persons acting on behalf of the Executive who consciously and deliberately violate the constitutional right of citizens do not for themselves or their superiors obtain the planned results of that invasion
>
> ... I am satisfied that this principle of our law is of wider application than merely to either the question of the admissibility of evidence or to the question of the punishment of persons for contempt of Court by unconstitutional action.

[4.55] Recent consideration of impropriety of action on the part of the gardaí occured in *People (DPP) & O'Toole*.[49] O'Toole was charged with knowingly being involved in the importation of cocaine at Kinsale harbour where large quantities had been found on board a yacht which he had with others sailed to Kinsale. One argument made on appeal alleged that there had been a conspiracy on behalf of two State agencies – An Garda Síochána and Customs – in order to facilitate the obtaining of the evidence. O'Toole alleged he was unlawfully detained on the yacht as a device to keep him away while a search of his hotel room in Kinsale took place. Similar to the *Trimbole* case, it was argued that O'Toole was being kept without justification in order to facilitate a search of the hotel room. It was alleged that these actions of Customs allowed gardaí to obtain a search warrant. The argument was unsuccessful and it was held on appeal that he went with a customs officer to the boat – supposedly to get his passport – voluntarily. The court found in fact that he had engineered his presence on the boat, as his passport was in his pocket all along.

[4.56] Another case dealing with a 'trick' allegation is *DPP v Costigan*.[50] Costigan had been convicted of the murder of Christine Quinn who had been found stabbed about 35 times at her home in Kilkenny. Blood spatters had been

---

[48] *Trimbole v Governor of Mountjoy Prison* [1985] ILRM 465 at 484.
[49] *People (DPP) & O'Toole* (25 March 2003), CCA.
[50] *DPP v Costigan* [2006] IECCA 57.

found in the course of forensic examination of her home and the prosecution connected the applicant with the premises on the basis of Costigan's DNA evidence, which when presented matched the stains upstairs in Ms Quinn's house.

[4.57] Costigan appealed on the basis that the trial judge had erred in admitting the blood sample taken from him. When the sample was taken, Costigan was 16 years old and it was argued that there was no informed consent given by his father (his guardian) as to the taking of blood. It was also alleged that the father had consented on the basis that one of the guards had assured him that Costigan was not a suspect and so had secured the blood sample by a ruse or a trick, which should not be admitted because of the illegal or unfair manner in which it was obtained. The court took the view that there had not been such a trick. Macken J[51] delivered the judgment of the court:

> In the view of the court there was, on the evidence, no such assurance given to the Applicant or his father of the type contended for. On the contrary there was evidence upon which the learned trial judge was entitled properly to conclude that there was no ruse or tricks used by members of the Garda such as to induce the Applicant's father to consent to the taking of the Applicant's blood sample when he or his father would otherwise have refused. The Court finds therefore that the trial judge committed no error of law in finding that the consent was not procured by means of a ruse or trick, there being ample evidence to support such a finding.

[4.58] In the context of the Irish courts' approach to illegally-obtained evidence, an increased willingness to admit evidence under the *O'Brien* formula is evident on occasion, which leads to a certain inconsistency between the decisions. Some decisions are particularly interesting in this regard.

[4.59] *DPP v Lawless*[52] involved a conviction under the Misuse of Drugs Act 1977. Police went to flats in Dublin with a warrant under the said Act and using the necessary force, entered. The applicant was in the lavatory, where the noise of flushing was heard. Detectives found a quantity of heroin in the manhole. The warrant was deemed defective. It was held that as the warrant was defective, the entry and search of premises was unlawful. However, as the accused was not a tenant of the flat, no breach of his constitutional rights occurred. But even if there had been a breach of constitutional rights, the court held that it was not a conscious and deliberate violation. There was no evidence of deliberate deceit or illegality, no policy to disregard the provisions of the Constitution or conduct searches without a warrant (*per O'Brien*). Even if it was a deliberate and

---

[51] *DPP v Costigan* [2006] IECCA 57 at p 7/14.
[52] *DPP v Lawless* (28 November 1985, unreported), CCA, *per* Keane, McCarthy, O'Hanlon JJ.

conscious violation, however, there were 'extraordinary excusing circumstances' – the need to prevent the imminent destruction of vital evidence. It can be seen that on any possible construction of the facts, the evidence goes in. This demonstrates the flexibility of the formula laid down in *O'Brien.*

[4.60] In the *DPP v Bowes*[53] a similar issue arose. This case involved an appeal against conviction of an offence of being in possession of heroin with intent to supply, at an address in Crumlin, Dublin. At trial the prosecution did not intend to prove that they had a search warrant. When they went to the premises at Clogher Road in Crumlin and found Bowes apparently in possession of heroin, they claimed that they were not obliged to have a search warrant because Bowes did not live there, and that there was therefore no breach of his constitutional rights to the inviolability of dwelling.

[4.61] There was evidence that this was a house not in any sense owned by Bowes, but owned by his parents. His sister lived there on occasion, as did a brother and the parents. There were two bedrooms upstairs in the premises, only one of which was in use. It was said to be used by the sister when she was living there. There was also evidence that when he was asked his address by gardaí, Bowes gave his address as 9 Durrow Road in Crumlin, which was where he had lived when he left his parents' house when he married. Now separated, he moved to various addresses, depending on the women he was involved with at the time. Bowes was not someone who appeared to reside for any great length of time at one address. When asked his address, he would give his matrimonial home address. His sister gave evidence that he was living at the parents' house in Clogher Road and that he resided in the front room. Garda evidence was that no-one could live in the front room, as there were various bags and so forth dumped there, and so it was not in a habitable state. Gardaí said it was in a derelict state.

[4.62] On the basis of this evidence, the trial judge had concluded that it was not the dwelling-house of Bowes within the meaning of the Constitution. On appeal, Keane CJ[54] reasoned in delivering the judgment of the court:

> The fact that he may have visited there occasionally, and perhaps even stayed overnight occasionally, does not mean that it was his dwelling house and there was nothing permanent in the nature of his residence there which could possibly make it his dwelling house in constitutional terms. Nor was he in the position of a member of the family who simply lived there who might not enjoy the legal ownership of the house but who as a member of the family living there with the rest of the family would be regarded as entitled to constitutional protection under Article 40.5. That was the finding of the trial judge. This court is satisfied that

---

[53] *DPP v Bowes* (25 February 2002), CCA, *per* Keane CJ.
[54] *DPP v Bowes* (25 February 2002), CCA, *per* Keane CJ at 4/6.

that was the conclusion he was perfectly entitled to arrive at on the evidence. It is clear that he applied the appropriate legal test in deciding whether this was the dwelling house of the applicant or whether he was simply a transient visitor to the house. That being the appropriate legal test, it is then a matter for the trial judge to determine on the facts and there is undoubtedly, ample evidence to support the conclusion he arrived at.

The distinction made by Keane J between those residing permanently in a dwelling-house and/or transient visitors establishes that there are two ways you can have an interest in the dwelling: through being the owner (or tenant) or through living there permanently as part of the family, even without such ownership or legal entitlement as under a lease.

[4.63] In *DPP v McMahon, McMeel and Wright*[55] the owners of a licensed premises were charged and convicted of offences against the Gaming and Lotteries Act 1956. The gardaí had made observations leading to evidence of the offences, without having identified themselves as guards or having a search warrant. It was held that the gardaí on entering premises were outside the implied invitation of the owner of the premises. Therefore, in law, they were trespassers. However, entering as a trespasser the public portion of a licenced premises, which is open for trade, does not, the court held, constitute any invasion or infringement of the constitutional rights of the owner. Thus, it was a question of the admissibility of illegally-obtained evidence, which according to the majority judgment of Kingsmill Moore J in *AG v O'Brien*, is dependent on the court's discretion. Therefore, in balancing the public interest that the crime should be detected against the undesirability of using improper methods, particular importance was attached to the fact that gardaí, in entering the public houses to view the machines, were trespassers only; they were not involved in any criminal or opprobrious conduct, and that the offence of permitting gaming on licensed premises might be considered as one with grave social consequences. The definition of the breach here as mere illegality by the court was crucial, and facilitated the subsequent admissibility of the evidence in accordance with the court's discretion. The view taken of the gravity of the offences involved was ultimately vital in determining admissibility.

[4.64] In *DPP v Gaffney*[56] the accused's failure to stop at a garda checkpoint resulted in a car chase to his home. Gardaí called on the accused to stop; he refused and entered the house. On two occasions, the accused's brother refused the gardaí entry, and on the second of these, he was arrested. The question arose as to whether the accused's response to a knock, 'Yes, in here,' constituted an

---

[55] *DPP v McMahon, McMeel and Wright* [1987] ILRM 86.
[56] *DPP v Gaffney* [1987] IR 173.

invitation to the gardaí to enter. It was held that in view of the fact the gardaí had twice been expressly refused entry and that there had been no express invitation, an invitation cannot be presumed simply because there was no refusal. Hence the gardaí were trespassers and their entry was in violation of Art 40.5 (inviolability of the dwelling) and the arrest of the accused was deemed unlawful.

[4.65] In *DPP v McCreesh*[57] a similar factual situation arose but this time the accused was arrested on the driveway leading into his house. Nonetheless, the court held the same constitutional protection applied, and being without authority, the garda invasion of the property tainted the evidence obtained after the arrest. The careful attitude of the courts towards the right of householders in these cases contrasts sharply with the approach to tenants in *Lawless* and publicans in *McMahon*. The seriousness with which the relevant offences were viewed in both these cases (drugs, gaming) may also have been a factor, although drink-driving is certainly now viewed as a grave offence. The legislation did, however, respond to amend the law in accordance with the lacunae identified by the court in *Gaffney* and *McCreesh*. This situation has now been the subject of attention in the Road Traffic Act 1994. Sections 10 and 11 provide for a power on the part of gardaí to arrest without warrant in relation to 'drink-driving' offences. Section 39 provides for a power to enter a dwelling in relation to 'hit and run' offences. (Section 106(3)(a) also gives a power to arrest without warrant in relation to same.) A power to enter the curtilage of a dwelling is also provided for in this section. This applies to 'drink-driving' offences, as does the power to enter a hospital to obtain a specimen. The burden of proof with regard to consumption of alcohol after an incident (the so-called 'hipflask' defence) is placed on the accused under s 20 of the 1994 Act, as is that regarding a defence to a refusal to permit the taking of specimen of blood or breath (s 23).

[4.66] In *DPP v Forbes*[58] the Supreme Court held that there is an implied permission on the part of every householder with regard to entry onto the forecourt of the premises. This may be rebutted but was not here – therefore, the arrest of the defendant for drunken driving on a third party's property (driveway of a private house) was valid.

[4.67] In *DPP v Delaney*[59] gardaí had observed the defendant driving erratically on a public road and pursued him. The defendant had entered the premises of his brother and entered the dwelling house. The gardaí had forcefully entered the house and arrested him on suspicion of drunken driving under s 49(8) of the

[57] *DPP v McCreesh* [1992] 2 IR 239.
[58] *DPP v Forbes* [1994] 2 IR 542.
[59] *DPP v Delaney* (27 January 2003, unreported), HC, Ó Caoimh J.

Road Traffic Act 1961.The defendant argued that the arrest was unlawful as the gardaí had no permission, express or implied, to enter the dwelling. The prosecution argued that there was no breach of the defendant's right under Art 40.5 as the dwelling was not his. The court held that there was no express or implied authority to enter and s 39(2) of the Road Traffic Act 1961 did not confer a power to enter a dwelling without warrant for the purpose of carrying out an arrest. Although the defendant could not claim breach of his right to the dwelling as the dwelling was not his, the court held that he had been deprived of liberty otherwise than in accordance with the law and so the prosecution must fail as the court did not have discretion to admit such evidence.

[4.68] The high water mark in terms of an exclusionary approach by the Irish courts is probably found in *Kenny*. In *People (DPP) v Kenny*[60] garda surveillance of a flat in Rathmines, Dublin, led to a telephone request to obtain a search warrant under s 26(1) of the Misuse of Drugs Act 1977. The standard form used to obtain the warrant did not give the issuing Peace Commissioner facts sufficient to satisfy him as to the presence of reasonable grounds for suspicion. The gardaí used the warrant to obtain entry to the flat in question, where they found a quantity of controlled drugs, for which the accused took responsibility. The accused was convicted and sentenced to five years' imprisonment. The Court of Criminal Appeal certified a point of law of exceptional public importance for the Supreme Court, namely whether the forcible entry of the accused's home by the gardaí on foot of an invalid search warrant constituted a deliberate and conscious violation of the accused's constitutional rights such as to render any evidence obtained thereby inadmissible at his trial. The Supreme Court held that the warrant was invalid and so breached Art 40.5 of the Constitution. Further, the breach was deliberate and conscious, as it was immaterial whether the person carrying out the breach was aware it was illegal, or it amounted to a breach of constitutional rights. There were no extraordinary excusing circumstances. Hence, the evidence was inadmissible at the trial. *Kenny* specifically refused to follow the 'good faith' exception endorsed by the United States Supreme Court in *Leon*[61] and so the absolute protectionist principle (not a deterrence one) was endorsed as the rationale for exclusion under Irish law.

[4.69] Finlay CJ's[62] explanation of the rationale behind the exclusionary rule as he saw it, is significant as a judicial exposition of the principle lying behind the rule:

---

[60] *People (DPP) v Kenny* [1990] ILRM 569.
[61] *US v Leon* (1983) 468 US 897.
[62] *People (DPP) v Kenny* [1990] ILRM 569 at 578–579.

The duty of the court, pursuant to Article 40.3.1° of the Constitution is as far as practicable to defend and vindicate such rights.

As between two alternative rules or principles governing the exclusion of evidence obtained as a result of the invasion of the personal rights of the citizen, the court has, it seems to me, an obligation to choose the principle which is likely to provide a stronger and more effective defence and vindication of the right concerned.

To exclude only evidence obtained by a person who knows or ought reasonably to know that he is invading a constitutional right is to impose a negative deterrent. It is clearly effective to dissuade a policeman from acting in a manner which he knows is unconstitutional or from acting in a manner reckless as to whether his conduct is or is not unconstitutional.

To apply, on the other hand, the absolute protection rule of exclusion whilst providing also that negative deterrent, incorporates as well a positive encouragement to those in authority over the crime prevention and detection services of the State to consider in detail the personal rights of citizens as set out in the Constitution, and the effect of their powers of arrest, detention, search and questioning in relation to such rights.

It seems to me to be an inescapable conclusion that a principle of exclusion which contains both negative and positive force is likely to protect constitutional rights in more instances than is a principle with negative consequences only.

The exclusion of evidence on the basis that it results from unconstitutional conduct, like every other exclusionary rule, suffers from the marked disadvantage that it constitutes a potential limitation of the capacity of the courts to arrive at the truth and so most effectively to administer justice.

I appreciate the anomalies which may occur by reason of the application of the absolute protection rule to criminal cases.

The detection of crime and the conviction of guilty persons, no matter how important they may be in relation to the ordering of society, cannot, however, in my view, outweigh the unambiguously expressed constitutional obligation 'as far as practicable to defend and vindicate the personal rights of the citizen'.

(emphasis added)

Finlay CJ here takes an absolute protection approach. It is not just about deterrence; it is about the protection of constitutional rights. There is also here a strong statement about the courts monitoring the police, together with a particular interpretation of the importance of the ordering of society versus the personal rights of the citizen.

[4.70] *DPP v Yamanoha*[63] followed *Kenny* where a warrant was issued in relation to a hotel room under s 26 of the Misuse of Drugs Act 1977 (as amended by s 13 of the Misuse of Drugs Act 1984). The warrant was challenged on the basis that the information on oath was confined to reciting that the Detective Sergeant had reasonable grounds and was not sufficient. The DPP contended that oral evidence was given as well. However, as that was unsworn, the warrant was deemed invalid and the evidence excluded.

[4.71] In *DPP v Dunne*,[64] a warrant under s 26 of the 1997 Act was again deemed invalid, as the words 'is on the premises' were deleted from it. Carney J held that if the inviolability of the dwelling is to be set aside by a printed form, it should be clear.

Given the due process approach of the Supreme Court in *Kenny*, subsequent decisions can be reviewed with a view to ascertaining whether that is a necessary function of the *O'Brien* formula, or merely illustrative of its malleability. From the latter perspective, all manner of decisions and applications to facts facilitate exclusion and inclusion, and so demonstrate its elasticity.

[4.72] In *People (DPP) v Balfe*,[65] s 42(1) of the Larceny Act 1916 provided the basis for the issue of a search warrant. Here, the address on the information was incorrect, the date of the larceny was incorrect and the name 'Eddie Balfe' was incorrect. The Criminal Court of Appeal held the defect was similar to and fell within *O'Brien* rather than *Kenny*, and that the evidence seized, therefore, was properly admitted.

[4.73] In *DPP v Owens*[66] the Supreme Court endorsed the focus on the importance of the role of the Peace Commissioner, which had been evident in *Kenny*. The intermediary role played by the Peace Commissioner, ensuring that garda suspicion is not merely 'rubber-stamped' for issuance of a warrant, is a guarantee of a safeguard for individual rights which is preventative, being prior to rights invasion, rather than curative, at trial. The facts in *Owens* concerned a situation where gardaí acting on information received, that robbery proceeds might be at a particular premises in Dublin, obtained a warrant to search that premises from a Peace Commissioner. The gardaí went to the premises, where the door was opened by the accused, and conducted a search but found nothing incriminating. Nonetheless, on the basis of confidential information received, they believed Owens was responsible for the robbery and arrested him and brought him to Ballymun Garda Station where he was detained under s 4 of the Criminal Justice Act 1984 and where he made an incriminating statement consisting of the principal evidence against him. The defence challenged the

---

[63] *DPP v Yamanoha* [1994] 1 IR 565.
[64] *DPP v Dunne* [1994] 2 IR 537.
[65] *People (DPP) v Balfe* [1998] 4 IR 50.
[66] *DPP v Owens* [1999] IESC 107.

validity of the search warrant, arguing the entry was illegal, the arrest and detention invalid and the evidence consequently inadmissible.

[4.74] At the date of issuance of the warrant, the Peace Commissioner was 85 years old, and at the date of the trial was too ill to go to court to explain his state of mind at the time he issued the warrant. The trial judge felt bound by *People (DPP) v Byrne*[67] to hold that the Peace Commissioner's signature was not sufficient to establish the validity of the warrant and that the Peace Commissioner must be present in person to prove his state of mind and to be available for cross-examination by the defence. *People (DPP) v Byrne*[68] concerned the extension of the detention of the accused under s 30 of the Offences Against the State Act 1939 by a Chief Superintendent who was no longer alive at the date of trial. Hence the Supreme Court upheld the trial judge's determination that an overriding statement made during that extended period was therefore inadmissible.

In *Owens*, the Supreme Court held to the same effect, ie that a search warrant is a document which may affect constitutional rights and does not speak for itself in a criminal trial. As seen in the review of provisions regarding warrants, the recent phenomenon whereby warrants can increasingly (at least in certain circumstances) be issued by the gardaí themselves, obviates to some extent many of the difficulties – and safeguards – provided by that additional layer of supervision and proof. There remain, however, occasional reminders of judicial scrutiny of powers of search.

[4.75] Until the Supreme Court decision in *Kenny* not too much attention had focused on the role of those charged with issuance of the search warrant, in other words the role of the Peace Commissioner or District Justice. It became hugely significantly in *Kenny* and other subsequent cases, as seen above. This led to greater scrutiny overall of the issuance process as seen in the next two cases.

[4.76] In *People (DPP) v Tallant*[69] the facts involved a conviction of possession of heroin and cannabis. The issue on appeal dealt with the issuance of the warrant under s 26 of the Misuse of Drugs Act 1977. A question was raised as to the enquiries made by the District Judge to satisfy himself that there was sufficient basis for the issuance. The gardaí said they had received confidential information to ground their issuance and the defence had argued that there was insufficient evidence before the District Court to entitle the District Justice to issue the warrants. The court was happy that in this case the totality of evidence given was sufficient. Fennelly J commented:[70]

---

[67] *People (DPP) v Byrne* [1989] ILRM 613.

[68] *People (DPP) v Byrne* [1989] ILRM 613.

[69] *People (DPP) v Tallant* (19 March 2003, unreported), CCA, Fennelly J.

[70] *People (DPP) v Tallant* (19 March 2003, unreported), CCA at 5.

[I]t is accepted by this court, the constitutional protection of the integrity of the home of the individual immediately comes into play and the court must be vigilant to ensure there is not any undue or improper invasion of that constitutional right to the sacrosanct character of the home of the person who is an individual citizen. On the other hand, of course, the Gardaí are engaged in carrying out their public duty to investigate crime and a *proper balance* has to be struck between those two objectives; so in collecting evidence all proper respect has to be accorded to the protection of the constitutional right of every individual citizen in respect of his home and therefore any invasion of that must take place only on the basis that the proper judicial procedures have been carried out. (Emphasis added.)

The court takes the view following *Kenny* here that the District Judge had before him evidence and he acted judicially – he did not simply take it and rubber-stamp it. The case serves as a reminder of the important role of the judiciary in terms of reviewing garda suspicion.

[4.77] The case of *DPP v Curtin*[71] is a decision again focusing on the processing of issuance and execution of a warrant. The accused was charged with the offence of knowingly having in his possession child pornography at his home in Tralee on 27 May 2002. An issue arose as to the validity of the search warrant, and therefore as to the admissibility of evidence. The warrant had been issued under s 7(2) of the Child Trafficking and Pornography Act 1998, which provided that the named member could enter the accused's home within seven days of the date thereof. The warrant was issued on 20 May 2002 and, if one includes 20 May 2002 in the calculation, the search warrant had been acted upon in its eighth day when it had expired. The accused's argument was that the warrant was spent and so, in accordance with the Supreme Court decision in *Kenny*, the search was in breach of the accused's constitutional rights and the fruits of the search were inadmissible. The prosecution argued that as under this Act an application had to be made to a District Court judge (there was no provision to apply to a Peace Commissioner), more time was needed to apply to a District Court judge and so more time was needed for the gardaí to execute the warrant, therefore the day of its issue should not be included. None of the arguments appeared to Judge Moran to have any merit at all. He pointed out that there is no time stamp on a warrant, just a date. Judge Moran concluded:[72]

There is no doubt that on a proper interpretation of s 7 of the Child Trafficking and Pornography Act 1998, having regard to s 11(h) of the Interpretation Act 1937, in the present day, the day on which the search warrant was issued has to be included in the reckoning and since the warrant was issued on 20th May, 2002, it

---

[71] *DPP v Curtin* (23 April 2004, unreported), CCC.
[72] *DPP v Curtin* (23 April 2004, unreported), CCC at 3–7.

expired on midnight of the day ending on 26th May, 2002. Accordingly, it was spent when the Gardaí Síochána purported to rely on it in their search of the accused's home on 27th May 2002.

[4.78] The second argument he considered then was as to the consequence of the search warrant being spent at the relevant time. He noted that the prosecution and defence were agreed that the law was to be found in *People v Kenny*. Moran J noted further that there was a difference there between members of the Supreme Court in that a minority of two felt the gardaí must be aware their actions are illegal or unconstitutional before they can amount to a conscious breach. However, he concluded that 'the majority of three judges held that the reference to unintentional or accidental acts meant that the acts themselves must be unintentional or accidental and the words do not refer to the state of mind of the gardaí involved.'[73]

[4.79] If the Irish Supreme Court in *Kenny* had by contrast accepted *US v Leon* as a persuasive precedent, to the effect that there was a good faith exception, it would have covered precisely this kind of scenario, because the gardaí could have argued that they were unaware of the warrant's invalidity. Instead, however, the Supreme Court took a protectionist stance which mandated Moran J's decision here.

[4.80] Judge Moran quoted quite extensively from *Kenny* and concluded, in applying the principles in *Kenny*:[74]

> As in the *Kenny* case there was a violation of the accused's constitutional rights committed by acts by the Garda Síochána which were not unintentional or accidental. There is one similarity between the acts of the Garda Síochána in the *Kenny* case and the present case and that is in both cases the Garda Síochána may not have known that they were necessarily infringing such constitutional rights. As to the other leg by which evidence might be rendered admissible, it has been conceded by ... the prosecution that there are no extraordinary excusing circumstances justifying the admission of the evidence in question.

Hence there is a fairly straightforward application of *Kenny* in *Curtin*. Judge Moran takes the opportunity to comment on this to the extent that anyone in the DPP's office might have anticipated and known that there was going to be such a problem in this case. His comment on this issue is an interesting one in terms of court censure of not just police but prosecutorial policy – reminiscent of US Supreme Court judge's reference to the exclusionary rule 'impressing upon the zealous prosecutor' that it would not avail them to infringe the accused's constitutional rights[75] – Moran J stated:[76]

---

[73] *DPP v Curtin* (23 April 2004, unreported), CCC at 4–7.
[74] *DPP v Curtin* (23 April 2004, unreported), CCC at 6–7.

Before concluding I would like to refer to the fact that the prosecution in bringing this case to trial must have known, or at least ought to have known, that on any reasonable interpretation of the issues, any judge in any court would have excluded the relevant evidence. This has to be so, given the untenable and nonsensical submission made on behalf of the prosecution.

In such circumstances I think it unfair and unreasonable to impose on me the task of presiding at the trial of a colleague when the prosecution knew, or ought to have known, that I would have to arrive at this result.

Force of circumstances as the assigned judge in this Circuit in Co Kerry obliges me to preside at this trial. I said last Tuesday, on the first day of the trial, that I would preside 'without fear or favour' and that is what I intended, and still intend, to do. My duties as a judge oblige me to give no favour to the accused.

At the same time, I cannot be expected to treat him more unfavourably than I would any other accused. For me to do so would be grotesque.

It is important to emphasise that, at all times this accused has been treated exactly the same as any other accused appearing in this court and he, the accused, will continue to be so treated until this trial is concluded.

In conclusion, for the reasons I have explained, there is no alternative but to find:

1. that, the particular warrant had expired by the time of the search,

2. that, the actions of the Garda Síochána at the material time were not unintentional or accidental, and

3. that, as conceded by the prosecution, there are no extraordinary excusing circumstances which would justify the admission of the evidence. Accordingly, evidence of the search and of what was found in the search is inadmissible and cannot go before the jury ... The law is crystal clear. The issue could not have been simpler and it was wrong for the prosecution to bring this case to trial when they knew, or ought to have known, that this finding would be the inevitable result.

[4.81] *Hanahoe v Hussey*[77] involved a situation where, although a discovery order could have been made under s 63 of the Criminal Justice Act 1994, s 64(1) of the Criminal Justice Act 1994 also made provision for a search warrant. On evidence presented with regard to the danger of the targeted individual interfering with the ability of the solicitors firm concerned to comply with a discovery order, a search warrant was granted in relation to the applicant solicitors' premises under s 64(1), rather than said discovery order. The media were present at the execution of the warrant. On application for *certiorari*, the

---

[75] Murphy J (dissenting) in *Wolfe v Colorado* (1949) 338 US 25 at 41.

[76] *DPP v Curtin* (23 April 2004, unreported), CCC at 6–7.

[77] *Hanahoe v Hussey* [1998] 3 IR 69.

issue came to the High Court, where it was held that any intrusion on the personal rights of citizens and the inviolability of the dwelling must be closely scrutinised and justified. The District Justice must be satisfied as to the need for the issuance of a warrant (and not just rely on garda averment), while the publicity attending the search warrant would not in itself invalidate the warrant, there was a duty of care on the part of the gardaí to the citizen about such information becoming public. The court noted that the provisions under the Criminal Justice Act 1994 (a precursor of the Criminal Assets Bureau provisions) greatly extended the power to grant search warrants. Whereas hitherto persons subject to search warrants were essentially suspects, it contemplated the obtaining of documentation from wholly innocent third parties, which was 'a new and serious invasion of constitutional rights including the invasion of privacy and possibly the invasion of confidential relationships'.[78] The court awarded damages here due to the resultant 'media circus' which had caused the applicants harm.

[4.82] In terms of subsequent provisions extending provision with regard to search warrants, Kinlen J's comment is worthy of note:[79]

> The primary concern of the judge ... must be so far as is practicable, to protect the rights of the citizen. We live in an era of fantastic and intrusive invasions of privacy. The State, the media and the many electronic devices have combined in a growing and worrying assertion that the invasion is allowable because of the battle against crime and corruption and also based on the alleged 'public's right to know'. These invasions are increasing but the courts must be the restraining arm to protect privacy and only allow invasion into privacy where on balance it can be justified.

[4.83] In *DPP v Delaney*[80] Sergeant M and nine gardaí were at the scene of a disturbance where a crowd was threatening to burn down a flat. The appellants had barricaded themselves in and were armed. Two women claimed there were children in the flat. The sergeant felt he had a right to enter for the safety of the children and the interests of the persons in the flat, because of the mob. In the High Court, Morris J said entry was justified: (1) if there was the implied consent of the owner; and (2) to protect the constitutional right to life of those in the flat. The Supreme Court held that, provided the sergeant acted bona fide in the belief he should enter the dwelling to safeguard life and limb, there was no breach of the Constitution.

---

78   *Hanahoe v Hussey* [1998] 3 IR 65 at 94.
79   *Hanahoe v Hussey* [1998] 3 IR 65 at 96.
80   *DPP v Delaney* [1997] 3 IR 453.

[4.84] *Freeman v DPP*[81] concerned s 41 of the Larceny Act 1916, which provides that any person committing an offence under the Act may be apprehended without warrant. Two gardaí received information that the appellant and two other men were seen unloading goods from a van into the appellant's house. There was a van outside the house and three men, including the appellant, at the porch. They saw the gardaí and ran into the house. The gardaí pursued using the key in the door. There were cigarettes, spirits etc in the room. The appellant ran out of the house onto the street where he was arrested under s 41. Subsequent to the arrest, a search warrant was obtained. A number of shoes were shown to have been in contact with the surface in the shop from where the goods in the van were stolen. A challenge was made to the arrest and admissibility of the evidence. In the High Court, Carney J held that the appellant's presence in a public place was induced by the unconstitutional entry into the dwelling, and hence the arrest was invalid. The exclusionary rule, he stated, did not as a corollary entitle the state to breach constitutional rights in extraordinary excusing circumstances – it was to protect the rights of citizens including the inviolability of the dwelling. In the circumstances, however, it was held that the appellant was *in flagrante delicto* and the dwelling was being used in the commission of an offence. The trial judge could, therefore, exercise discretion to admit evidence obtained as a result of an illegal entry and unlawful arrest under extraordinary excusing circumstances (*per Lawless*). In any event, there was deemed to be ample evidence grounding the search warrant independent of the unconstitutional entry.

[4.85] It is worth quoting from Carney J's judgment:[82]

> The appellant challenges the legality of his initial arrest, arguing that the entry of the Gardaí into his home was unauthorised by law and in breach of his constitutional rights under Article 40, section 5. Accordingly, it is submitted, his arrest, although in a public place, was unlawful, as his presence outside was induced by the gardaí illegally entering his dwelling. The appellant further argued that all evidence obtained as a result of this entry was inadmissible at trial as being obtained in conscious and deliberate violation of his constitutional rights, as was his subsequent detention under s 4 of the Criminal Justice Act 1984.

The prosecution had argued that s 41 of the Larceny Act 1916 would justify entry to the house but the High Court had regard to the terms of Art 40.5 and the provision that the dwelling house of every citizen is inviolable save in accordance with law. Carney J further stated:[83]

---

[81] *Freeman v DPP* [1996] 3 IR 565.
[82] *Freeman v DPP* [1996] 3 IR 565 at 570.
[83] *Freeman v DPP* [1996] 3 IR 565 at 574–575.

Can it be said the Constitution requires s 41 to be interpreted narrowly so as not to entrench on Article 40, s 5 rights without *express* statutory authority? It seems to me that it does so require. Given that the Constitution has elevated the Common Law right to the constitutional plane, in clear and unqualified terms, any interference with that constitutional right must be given expressed statutory effect. Accordingly, the initial arrest of the appellant was not authorised by s 41 … and consequently was unconstitutional in that it breached Article 40, section 5. In reaching this conclusion, I do not lose sight of the fact that in the circumstances of this case, the appellant was arrested in a public place, having gone out of his dwelling. I accept, however, the appellant's contention that insofar as his fleeing was induced by the wrongful presence of the gardaí, it is coloured by their unlawful entry.

Hence he concluded that the entry was unlawful and the arrest was not valid.

[4.86] Carney J also referred to the rationale behind the decision in *Kenny* and went on to look at whether there were any extraordinary excusing circumstances in the case before him, pointing out that:

[T]o attribute too wide a scope to the exception in the case of the imminent destruction of evidence may undermine the rationale of a rule which by its nature is invoked in circumstances where well-meaning haste on the part of the gardaí may lead to unconstitutional acts. The Supreme Court in … [*Kenny*] … held that knowledge or understanding on the part of the gardaí that they were invading constitutional rights is unnecessary. Thus, to excuse unconstitutional behaviour merely because it was designed to garner vital evidence is to adopt a lesser standard than established in … [*Kenny*]. Yet, it is hard to think of circumstances more apt to come within Walsh J's exception [in *O'Brien*] than the facts of this case: the gardaí came upon the appellant and his associate *in flagrante delicto*; there simply was not enough time for the gardaí to obtain the necessary search warrant. The dwelling house itself was being employed in the course of committing an offence. I hold that in the peculiar circumstances of this case there was material on which the District Court Judge could exercise his discretion to admit this evidence. [84]

[4.87] Even though in *Freeman* there was found to be an unconstitutional breach of the accused's rights, the evidence went in under the exception of extraordinary excusing circumstances to prevent destruction of vital evidence. Carney J made it quite clear, however, that the gardaí had no power to enter 'in hot pursuit' and so unless there was a situation as dramatic as this one, they could not go in and make a lawful arrest.

[4.88] Although in *Freeman* the evidence was admitted due to extraordinary excusing circumstances, in the aftermath of this decision s 6 of the Criminal

---

[84] *Freeman v DPP* [1996] 3 IR 565 at 576.

Law Act 1997 was introduced, which made provision for just such 'hot pursuit' entries for the purpose of arrest in *every* case, not just where there are such extraordinary excusing circumstances. The introduction of this legislative provision shows the interface between legislative facilitation of greater police powers in this area, running alongside judicial vindication of due process rights. It can also be said to demonstrate another application of the particular (exception) to the general process, ie that which was first allowed in one exceptional circumstance becomes the norm.

[4.89] In *People v McCann*,[85] the defendant had been convicted of the murder of his wife and foster child at their family home. They had died in a deliberate arson attack. It was argued that the forensic evidence gathered by the prosecution from the burnt-out dwelling, without McCann's consent, was a breach of his constitutional rights. It was also argued that his arrest in the private residential area of his business premises (a pub) was not consented to, and hence unlawful. The Court of Criminal Appeal held that the gardaí had a duty to investigate. McCann had made extensive representations to them about the ongoing investigation, which therefore implied consent. It was also queried whether a burnt-out house was 'a dwelling' for these purposes and, in any event, whether there were extraordinary excusing circumstances (ie, the need to preserve vital evidence). With regard to the locale of the arrest, the court held that there was no forcible entry and an implied invitation.

[4.90] In *Simple v Revenue Commissioners*[86] the Supreme Court (Keane CJ, Barrington J) held that, given the draconian nature of the powers concerned – in this case, under Customs legislation – a warrant could not be regarded as valid when it carries on its face a statement that it had been issued on a basis not in fact authorised by statute (ie the customs officer, not the District Justice, was satisfied of the evidence of 'reasonable grounds'). Barron J (dissenting) held the warrant was merely ineffective, not invalid.

Causation

[4.91] In *Walsh v O'Buachalla*[87] the defendant was convicted of driving over the limit. In custody he did not contact a solicitor until a doctor came to take a sample, when he then asked to do so. The gardaí refused this request as they saw it as a delaying tactic. Blayney J held that there was no causal connection between the infringement and obtaining the evidence. The evidence here was obtained after the violation but not as a result. There was a requirement by law to give a specimen.

---

[85] *People v McCann* [1998] 4 IR 397.
[86] *Simple v Revenue Commissioners* [2000] 2 IR 243.
[87] *Walsh v Ó Buachalla* [1991] 1IR 56.

'Fruit of the poisoned tree'

[4.92] In *People (DPP) v O'Donnell*[88] the defendant was travelling in a van and was stopped by gardaí who recognised him as a suspected IRA member. At the request of gardaí, the defendant stepped out of the van and was told he was to be searched under s 30 of the 1939 Act. The gardaí found a walkie-talkie in his right-hand pocket. The gardaí attempted to search his left-hand-pocket and the defendant resisted. The gardaí cautioned him, and arrested him under s 30 on suspicion of membership. The defendant gave them a parcel containing explosives from his left-hand pocket. It was submitted on appeal that, although gardaí informed the applicant that he was suspected of being a member of an illegal organisation before they searched his pocket, failure to do so before searching his right-hand pocket tainted everything subsequently. The Court of Criminal Appeal affirmed the conviction, holding that evidence following a deliberate and conscious breach was only excluded if obtained as a result of that breach and if a causative link existed between the breach and obtaining evidence. Even if it were conceded that the search of a right-hand pocket was unlawful, there was no casual connection between that search and the later search of a pocket containing explosives.

Conclusion

[4.93] Admissibility of illegally-obtained evidence, in the context of the use or abuse of the pre-trial process, has been the subject of changing judicial attitude. In Ireland, the *O'Brien* formula, although still the applicable criterion to determine admissibility, has been seen to demonstrate a considerable facility for inclusion or exclusion of evidence. Given the recent proliferation of ever more extensive powers of intrusion, it may be that the courts will become more vigilant (Kinlen J in *Hanahoe*) in terms of scrutiny of these powers. However, that is in a context where with increasing avoidance of independent review of garda suspicion, the scope for judicial scrutiny is narrowed. It may also emerge that the facility for accommodation is so great in the original *O'Brien* yardstick of judgment, that only the appearance of rights vindication will be maintained.

There is some evidence that the reign of the exclusionary rule in the Irish criminal process may be on the wane. In *Curtin v Dáil Éireann*[89] the Supreme Court – albeit in the context of proceedings separate from that of a criminal trial – sanctioned what might be categorised as an independent source exception to the exclusionary rule. The case concerned the use by an Oireachtas Committee of evidence which had previously been deemed unconstitutionally obtained in a

---

[88] *People (DPP) v O'Donnell* [1995] 3 IR 551.
[89] *Curtin v Dáil Éireann* [2006] 2 IR 556.

criminal trial. The Supreme Court rejected an argument that the computer evidence so obtained was inadmissible.

Murray CJ:

> "The exclusionary rule is concerned with the admissibility of evidence unconstitutionally obtained at the criminal trial of that citizen. It does not state that it is inadmissible for all time and in all contexts."[90]

[4.94] *DPP v Cash*[91] provides a useful postscript to discussion of illegally-obtained evidence in terms of giving an indication of how precedents can be read differently, as well as providing an insight into policy dimensions changing over time in this area. The facts here concerned a woman calling gardaí to her home in Dublin, where a bedroom window had been smashed and property stolen. The gardaí duly called in fingerprint experts who found prints on the smashed glass (prints 2). Two months later, Cash was arrested on suspicion of committing the burglary. The basis for his arrest was that there was a match between prints 2 and prints 1, which latter were already held in the garda technical bureau. Cash was under 18 years and so his mother signed a consent and a third set of prints was taken (prints 3). The latter matched the ones from the window frame (prints 2). There was no clarity as to the basis on which prints 1 had been obtained. Prints can either be obtained by consent or under s 6 of the Criminal Justice Act 1994 where someone can be required to give prints. If required under s 6, they must then be destroyed after a certain period of time. If obtained by consent, however, there is no obligation to destroy them. The issue here, therefore, relates to whether, as the accused asserted, there is an onus on the state to show the lawful history of any piece of evidence put before a criminal court and that any step in the criminal process, including arrest, must be shown to have been taken by the state on foot of evidence lawfully obtained.

[4.95] A case was stated to the High Court and Charleton J took the opportunity to deliver a lengthy judgment, reviewing the jurisprudence of illegally-obtained evidence from *O'Brien* through the next 25 years. Mr Justice Charleton then commented:

> The only exception to the principles excusing a deliberate and conscious breach of a constitutional right of the accused, enunciated by Kingsmill Moore J, was that it eventually came to be held that an unlawful entry for the purposes of arrest would cause both that arrest and anything seized in the course of the entry to be classified as an invasion of constitutional rights and accordingly excluded.[92]

[4.96] Referring to *People (DPP) v Lawless*,[93] he pointed out that:

---

[90]   *Curtin v Dáil Éireann* [2006] 2 IR 556 at 607 *per* Murray CJ.
[91]   *DPP v Cash* [2007] IEHC 108, Charleton J.
[92]   *DPP v Cash* [2007] IEHC 108 at para 21.

In practice, an unnoticed mistake in a warrant never had the effect, in the 25 years subsequent to the Supreme Court decision in *O'Brien's* case of automatically causing the exclusion of evidence. Judicial discretion decided whether the evidence was to be admitted. In principle, the nature of the crime and the infringement was balanced against each other.[94]

[4.97] That situation, Charleton J said, ended as a result of *People (DPP) v Kenny*. He pointed out that Finlay CJ and the majority in that case held that it was immaterial whether the police officer was aware that what he was doing was in breach of constitutional rights. Charleton J stated:

> This reversed the line of authority that had always been applied by the courts to the effect that a conscious and deliberate violation of someone's constitutional rights required that the act should be done deliberately with a consciousness that the effect of it would be to unlawfully invade someone's dwelling or to deprive them of their liberty or whatever constitutional right was infringed by the impugned action. A mistake of law did not excuse, of itself, such an action; once it was deliberate. As the *Lawless* case indicates clearly, mistakes had never been found to fit within the category of action that required the automatic exclusion of evidence.[95]

[4.98] Charleton J then quoted extensively from Lynch and Griffin JJ, dissenting, in *Kenny*. Mr Justice Charleton reviewed the effects of *Kenny* and identified three practical consequences of that decision:[96]

1. every error on the part of the agents of the state that takes their action outside the strict letter of the law causes the exclusion at trial of any evidence which results therefrom;

2. every breach of the accused person's rights is always pleaded at trial as an infringement of the Constitution; and

3. it has become practically impossible to say when a constitutional right begins and ends.

[4.99] He cited as an instance of this *People (DPP) v Dillon*,[97] where a garda who took a mobile telephone from an arrested person answered the phone when it rang and pretended to be involved in drug activity. He thereby made an arrangement to meet the caller at an agreed location and when the accused turned up, he was in possession of heroin. The action by the garda was held to be unlawful, the Court of Criminal Appeal saying the garda should have applied for

---

93 *People (DPP) v Lawless* (28 November 1985, unreported), CCA.
94 *DPP v Cash* [2007] IEHC 108 at para 23.
95 *DPP v Cash* [2007] IEHC 108 at para 23.
96 *DPP v Cash* [2007] IEHC 108 at para 25, 27, 29.
97 *People (DPP) v Dillon* [2002] 4 IR 501.

a warrant before intercepting the communication. Charleton J commented that this indicated that 'the entire focus is on the accused and his rights; the right of the community to live safely has receded out of view.'

[4.100] Returning to the specific facts in the case before him, Charleton J then focused on the law governing fingerprints. He differentiated between physical evidence, such as a fingerprint, which is he said was different from a confession in that fingerprint evidence is not affected by the mood of a suspect giving same. He found some support for same in *Costigan* where, however, it was found that there was no trick and a valid consent, and in Murray CJ's judgment in *People (DPP) v Boyce,*[98] which again dealt with voluntarily obtained forensic samples. Charleton J said that he would be reluctant to hold that a constitutional right to privacy extended to the map of one's DNA, one's fingerprints or the chemical composition of blood or urine. He conceded, however, that he may be bound to so hold[99].

[4.101] He then turned 'to consider whether there is any room left for a *balancing of rights* where a mistaken violation of the constitutional rights of an accused person, for example to total privacy, has occurred.' Charleton J pointed out that in *O'Brien* the competing interests identified were both related to the community: interest in the prosecution of crime and interest in the maintenance of legal rules in the detection of crime. In *Kenny* the sole interest identified, he said, was that of ensuring proper police conduct. According to Charleton J: 'there are more than the rights of the accused involved in every criminal prosecution'.[100]

[4.102] Charleton J noted that 'there is a balance ... to be struck between the competing rights of the accused to have the law observed and that of the community to have social order maintained.'[101] He went on to refer to the European Convention on Human Rights (ECHR) and a number of decisions thereunder. The fact that the ECHR does not require the exclusion of unlawfully obtained evidence, but leaves such issue to the discretion of states, as well as the fact that Ireland's domestic constitutional regime may require a higher standard of rights defence than the ECHR regime is not addressed. In contrast, Charleton J concluded:

> I consider that a rule providing for the automatic exclusion of evidence obtained
> in consequence of any mistake that infringes any constitutional right of an

---

[98] *People (DPP) v Boyce* [2005] IECCA 143.
[99] *DPP v Cash* [2007] IEHC 108 at para 41.
[100] *DPP v Cash* [2007] IEHC 108 at para 42.
[101] *DPP v Cash* [2007] IEHC 108 at para 43.

accused, may be incompatible with Ireland's obligations to provide, for both accused and the community, a fair disposal of criminal charges.[102]

This is an interesting juxtaposition of the fair trial onus on Ireland under the ECHR, which is effectively using it to read down previously established rights of accused persons. Charleton J also refers to a number of English court decisions, again without reference to the fact that that jurisdiction would traditionally not have offered a strong protection of constitutional rights for the accused and is only recently absorbing the ECHR compliance requirements.

[4.103] Ultimately, this lead Charleton J to a statement as to what he thought should be possible in terms of fairness construction in this area of improperly obtained evidence by Irish courts:

> In my judgement it should now be possible, in considering whether to exclude evidence which has been unlawfully obtained, to take into account factors other than the isolated interests of the accused, divorced from any other consideration. Criminal trials are about the rights and obligations of the entire community; of which the accused and the victim are members. It is not a function of the criminal courts to discipline police officers by causing the exclusion of evidence. Sometimes, however, the balancing of competing interests requires that exclusion in the overall interests of the administration of justice. The cases of *JT* and *B* and *X and Y* make it clear that the victim, being the subject of a crime, can have interests which should be weighed in the balance as well as that of the accused. But I would hold that the primary interest in the prosecution of crime is the maintenance of social order under the Constitution as provided for in the Preamble.[103]

His selection of those precedents is interesting in so far as *JT* and *B* are historic sex abuse cases, and *X & Y* are cases involving rape and burglary. He then went on to assert that Ireland is the only country with a common law heritage that does not apply a balancing exercise as to the exclusion of unlawfully obtained evidence.[104]

[4.104] Mr Justice Charlton's conclusions follow his particular take on Irish jurisprudence as well as on both European and common law precedent, including his characterisation of the *Kenny* decision by which he accepted he was bound as '[a] rule which remorselessly excludes evidence obtained through an illegality occurring by a mistake [and] does not commend itself to the proper ordering of society which is the purpose of the criminal law.'[105] He continued in

---

[102] *DPP v Cash* [2007] IEHC 108 at para 45.
[103] *DPP v Cash* [2007] IEHC 108 at para 50.
[104] *DPP v Cash* [2007] IEHC 108 at para 58.
[105] *DPP v Cash* [2007] IEHC 108 at para 65.

a paragraph that is worth quoting in full as it illustrates with aplomb the importance of context:

> Any system of the exclusion of improperly obtained evidence must be implemented on the basis of a balancing of interests. The two most fundamental competing interests, in that regard, are those of society and the accused. I would also place the rights of the victim in the balance. I note, in writing this judgment, that the third anniversary of March 2004 train bombings in Madrid is being marked. That atrocity led to the death of 191 commuters making their way to work and was inspired, apparently, because of the involvement of Spain in a foreign policy with which an international terrorist organisation did not agree. It is entirely conceivable, were the same thing to occur in Ireland, that vital evidence that might lead to the conviction of the perpetrators might have been uncovered through the infringement of someone's privacy as they spoke on the telephone or as a result of the comparison of DNA samples which the prosecution could not strictly prove were obtained by consent through the proper exercise of statutory powers. The original test, as propounded by the Supreme Court in *O'Brien's* case would have allowed for a balancing of the rights of the parties. In particular, the gravity of the defence and the nature of the infringement by the State authorities would have been taken into account. The current rule, as set forth by the Supreme Court in *Kenny's* case, automatically requires the exclusion of any evidence obtained through a mistake which has the accidental, and therefore unintended, result of infringing any constitutional right of one individual, namely the accused. The entire rationale of the original Supreme Court decision in the *O'Brien's* case is undermined by *Kenny's* case. The principle that extraordinary excusing circumstances can allow for the admission of evidence obtained in breach of a constitutional right can no longer be applied. It is an impossibility to make a mistake while, at the same time, acting to rescue a victim in peril or prevent the destruction of vital evidence. The whole rationale for a balanced rule with exceptions, set out in *O'Brien's* case has been replaced ... There can be no doubt that exclusion is sometimes the only correct response to egregious police misconduct. The admission of evidence obtained in flagrant violation of fundamental rights without excusing circumstances can amount to an attack on the very administration of justice. The problem identified, however, is the isolation of the rule of exclusion formulated in *Kenny's* case from any principle of balance as otherwise operated within the constitutional scheme.[106]

Charleton J ultimately concluded that the District Court was bound by *Kenny* but that 'that decision should not be extended as to its effects to require the prosecution to prove that every element of an investigation was entirely proper and in accordance with statutory powers.'

[4.105] This is an interesting, not to say landmark, decision as it gives an indication of where the courts may go, the elasticity of the *O'Brien* formula and

---

[106] *DPP v Cash* [2007] IEHC 108 at para 66–67.

the influence of current conditions and contexts factual, and otherwise, when decisions are made. It may also provide an instance of that dialogue between courts and legislature; as the Criminal Justice (Surveillance) Act 2009 surely demonstrates that someone was listening in relation to strengthening state powers of eavesdropping referred to here.

That the *O'Brien* yardstick itself as the measure of acceptability may be under pressure is evident not just from judicial commentary such as that seen above in *Cash*; but also in the statutory provision found in the Criminal Justice (Amendment) Act 2009, s 13 and the Criminal Justice (Surveillance) Act 2009, s 14 which tends to either proffer an alternate test as in the former's allusion to prejudicial effect versus probative value, or circumvent scrutiny on admissibility altogether as is the case in the latter's provision that the material, whatever breaches, is admissible.

[4.106] An indication of how and where this area might develop is provided by the Balance in the Criminal Law Review Group (Final Report 2007). Obviously that Group's very establishment and its raison d'être is to provide an opportunity for the exchange of views and policy influence on legislation, but there is a level of influence on the court jurisprudence itself anticipated here which is somewhat less subtle than instances of earlier such detected influences on judicial decisions (*Donnelly* etc – see ch **5**).

[4.107] Section 21 of the Criminal Justice Act 2006 Act, which came into force on 1 August 2006, inserted a new s 34 in the Criminal Procedure Act 1967 whereby a decision of a trial judge to exclude evidence on the basis of *Kenny* may in the event of an acquittal be the subject of a reference to the Supreme Court. This, the Balance in the Criminal Law Review Group notes, may result in a reconsideration of the law on illegally-obtained evidence. The Group moreover is not slow to offer a view on what that might comprise. A majority of the Group considers 'that the most satisfactory approach would be to see whether the appeal provisions of the Criminal Justice Act 2006 would give the Supreme Court an opportunity, in the appropriate case, of revisiting its jurisprudence and of moving towards the discretionary approach'.[107] The Report goes on: 'We would wish to see a situation where the court would have a discretion to admit unconstitutionally obtained evidence or not, having regard to the totality of the circumstances and in particular the rights of the victim.'[108]

[4.108] The Group's Chairman Gerard Hogan agrees with the majority that the operation of the exclusionary rule may result in the exclusion of highly probative

---

[107] Balance in the Criminal Law Review Group *Final Report*, Department of Justice, Equality and Law Reform (2007), p 164.

[108] Balance in the Criminal Law Review Group Report, p 165.

evidence, but does not agree that by reason of that fact alone it ought to be modified:

> [I]f the occasional exclusion of otherwise relevant evidence is the price of respecting … constitutional rights, then that is a price society should be prepared to pay in the interests of upholding the values solemnly enshrined in our highest law, even if one unfortunate consequence is that a particular victim may feel that 'their' case has not been fairly dealt with.[109]

[4.109] Whereas the majority show particular vulnerability for the vagaries of the moment as their preference is for 'a discretion to admit unconstitutionally obtained evidence or not, having regard to the totality of the circumstances and in particular *the rights of the victim*' (emphasis added),[110] his dissenting view shows no such regard for popular sentiment:

> The Supreme Court is the ultimate arbiter under our constitutional system of the manner in which the constitutional rights of citizenry is to be protected. This sometimes produces results which are not popular with the general public. But the whole theory of the Constitution is that certain fundamental rights – such as free speech, habeas corpus, personal liberty, fair trial and religious freedom – are not dependent on the whim of a legislative majority or the protestations of a populist media.[111]

It will be interesting to see how that spectrum of views is reflected in the approach of the Irish courts. Of course if the latest legislative seeds in the 2009 Acts bear fruit either the opportunity for judicial comment or its extent may be absent or greatly circumscribed.

---

[109] Balance in the Criminal Law Review Group Report, p 287.
[110] Balance in the Criminal Law Review Group Report, p 165.
[111] Balance in the Criminal Law Review Group Report, p 292.

Chapter 5

Witness System: Competence and Compellability

Cross-examination is an adversarial war of words, sequences, and ideas, a war in
which capability to finesse reality through talk represents the ultimate weapon of
domination. When considering the reproduction of rape as a criminal social fact,
I am looking at how a woman's experience of violation is transformed into
routine consensual sex through the organization of courtroom linguistic practice,
and not at how that violation is subjectively experienced through the meanings
and intentions of individual victims, rapists, or administrators of justice. In very
tacit and taken for granted fashion, language categorizes, objectives, and
legitimates our interpretations about social reality, sustaining some versions
while disqualifying others, and conceals the hierarchical arrangements and
sexual differences between men and women. Language is a system of power for
those who control it, and, in the context of the rape trial, talking power transforms
the subjective violation of the victim, the victim's experience of sexual terror,
into an objectivity: namely, consensual sex ...

Because of procedural and evidentiary strictures in court, blame work is
conducted inferentially through powerful procedures of talk and sensemaking
practices. But access to these procedures is not equally distributed across social
position. Attorneys and victims possess differential access to the procedures of
talk. The defense attorney possesses the linguistic and sequential capital to make
his/her account 'count' relative to the victim. Attorneys control the topic, the
syntactic form of questions, and the sequential resources with which to
manipulate words, utterances, and turns as microtechniques of disciplinary
power. When interlaced and synchronised with patriarchal ideology – ideas about
sexual access and practice – these power mechanisms generate the accusatory
sense of what happened during the rape incident; they thereby reproduce the
constraining and enabling facticity facts constructed locally in context of both
rape and the legal order.

Matoesian, *Reproducing Rape: Domination through Talk in the Courtroom*
(1993).

Competence and compellability

[5.01] Given the centrality of testimonial evidence to our system of legal
adjudication, it is appropriate to examine together both the manner in which
such testimony is elicited from a witness, and the criteria by reference to which a
witness's ability to testify is adjudged.

Process of elicitation of testimony

Examination-in-chief

[5.02] Assuming a witness to be both competent and compellable, the procedure by which testimony is elicited from that witness is as follows. The witness is firstly sworn in. That witness then gives testimony by means of the process of examination by counsel for that party on whose behalf the witness is being called. Examination-in-chief is the means whereby the witness tells whatever relevant evidence he has to proffer. It is not as simple as a witness merely telling the story as s/he saw it. In the course of eliciting the information from the witness, counsel may not ask leading questions of his own witness. There are, however, exceptions to this situation:

(1)   in relation to non-contentious issues;

(2)   in order to identify persons, or things in court; and

(3)   in relation to hostile witnesses.

Cross-examination

[5.03] Cross-examination is then carried out by counsel for the other side. It is therefore a much less regulated procedure, and has been described as 'the most effective weapon yet devised to test truth'[1]. In the course of such cross-examination, counsel can ask any leading questions. However, if the question is deemed to be a collateral question, the witness's answer to such a question is final. There are exceptions to this in relation to a defendant's previous convictions (Criminal Justice Procedure Act 1866, s 6) and the question of bias (for example, the witness's relation to the accused).

[5.04] With regard to the finality of collateral questions, it is interesting to note a decision of the Court of Criminal Appeal *DPP v Patrick Barr*[2] endorsing same in refusing to allow an appeal against convictions of indecent assault and buggery based on the discovery of evidence which could have been put to the complainant in cross-examination. The evidence concerned involved the familiarity of the complainant with the Phoenix Park, and in particular the scene of the crime. The Court, on viewing the transcript as a whole, doubted if there had, in fact, been any inconsistency on the part of the complainant, and in any event felt pursuance of the issue would have been to seek to contradict a witness on a collateral fact:

---

[1]   Wigmore, *A Treatise on the Anglo American Statem of Evidence in Trials at common law* (3rd edn, Little Brown & Co, 1940) Vol 5 (Chadbourne revision) para 1367.

[2]   *DPP v Patrick Barr* (2 March 1992, unreported), CCA, *ex temp* (O'Flaherty J).

It seems to the Court that there is a sound general rule, based on the desirability of avoiding a multiplicity of issues, that the answers given by a witness to questions put to him in cross-examination concerning collateral facts must be treated as final. They may or may not be accepted by the jury, but the crossexaminer must take them for better or worse and cannot contradict them by other evidence.

[5.05] A witness's own prior statements if inconsistent can be put to him/her in cross examination. This was recently confirmed in *O'Callaghan v Mahon*[3] in the context of tribunal proceedings:

Hardiman J:[4]

In my view it is a matter of common justice and indeed common sense, that a witness who makes a grave allegation against another may be contradicted out of his own mouth where that is possible. If a right to do this were not assured, cross examination would be gravely hampered and even subverted. It is a statement of the obvious to say that the credibility of a particular statement made by a particular person is reduced or destroyed if he has made a contradictory statement on a previoius occasion, unless that can be explained in some way. Conversely, consistency enhances the credibility of a statement.

[5.06] The strength of the entitlement and basis for cross-examination, and its centrality to our process of legal adjudication, is illustrated by the decision of *O'Brien v DJ Ruane and Attorney General.*[5] The applicant here was arrested under s 21 of the Road Traffic (Amendment) Act 1978, which provides that it shall be presumed, until the contrary is proven, that the statutory procedure has been complied with. The applicant's solicitor cross-examined the prosecuting garda sergeant in regard to compliance with s 21. Objection by the prosecution to the effect that such a general question was not permissible having regard to sub-s 4 was upheld by the District Justice.

[5.07] Lynch J in the High Court, however, held that although the cross-examination was a 'fishing cross-examination' in the sense that the solicitor for the applicant was not in a position to show any particular non-compliance with s 21 unless something should be elicited in the course of same, it was allowable. Lynch J was of the opinion that:

It seems to me ... that the defending solicitor is entitled to enquire in a general way as to what happened to his client from the time he was brought to the Garda Station in relation to the taking of specimens and the treatment of such specimens in order to see whether compliance with s 21 was observed. I think he may do this in a general way ...

---

3   *O'Callaghan v Mahon* [2006] 2 IR 32.
4   *O'Callaghan v Mahon* [2006] 2 IR 32 at 58 *per* Hardiman J.
5   *O'Brien v DJ Ruane and AG* [1989] ILRM 732.

... Of course on the other hand the District Justice must be entitled to control cross-examination and keep it within reasonable bounds. If, for example, the general sort of cross-examination seemed to go on repetitively, the District Justice, would clearly be entitled to say: that's enough of that. You have made your point. But he must allow some reasonable general enquiry as to what procedures were in fact done and followed in the Garda station so that the defending solicitor, even in the absence of any specific allegation of a contravention of the requirements of s 21, may ensure that these requirements were complied with.[6]

Re-examination

[5.08] The third process of eliciting information is called re-examination. This again is carried out by the party tendering that witness. Re-examination is not, however, a second chance at examination-in-chief. It must be strictly confined to matters which have arisen in the course of cross-examination. For this reason counsel may or may not opt in given cases for re-examination. In the same manner, a facility for the other party to opt for a reply, with similar restrictions, may or may not be exercised.

Hostile witnesses

[5.09] A distinction should be drawn between unfavourable witnesses and hostile witnesses. An unfavourable witness is one who is called to prove a particular fact, and fails to do so. A hostile witness, on the other hand, is one not desirous of telling the truth at the instance of the party who called him. While the general rule is that a party cannot impeach his own witness, this rule applies in relation to unfavourable witnesses, but not in relation to those deemed to be hostile. The trial judge decides whether a witness can be treated as hostile.[7] In making his determination, the trial judge considers the following: the witness's demeanour, the terms of any inconsistent statement made by that witness and the circumstances in which it was made. The decision is taken in the absence of the jury. Should the witness be declared hostile, the examination-in-chief then takes on the format of cross-examination. The witness may be asked leading questions, challenged as to his means of knowledge, and asked whether on another occasion he had made a statement which differed materially from, or contradicted, the one made in the witness box. This latter statement, however, does not, due to the operation of the rule against hearsay,[8] constitute evidence of any facts referred to in that statement, but only constitutes evidence going to that witness's credibility.[9]

---

[6] *O'Brien v DJ Ruane and AG* [1989] ILRM 732 at 734.
[7] *The People (AG) v Hannigan* [1941] IR 252.
[8] See Ch 9.
[9] *People (AG) v Taylor* [1974] IR 97.

Calling of witnesses

[5.10] In general, a party is free to call any witnesses, provided that once called they are confined to evidence which is relevant and admissible. Their ability to provide such is generally not determined in advance. However, there may be circumstances where a judge may query the purpose of calling a witness, and so refuse to permit that witness to be called if satisfied that he has no relevant evidence to offer.

[5.11] In *Herron v Haughton*,[10] the appellant was prosecuted for failure to have a tax disc displayed and to wear a seatbelt. Her defence alleged a campaign of harassment by the Gardaí. She wished to call the prosecuting solicitor, and when asked why by the District Judge, explained that he was a party to the conspiracy. The District Justice refused to allow her to call that witness as he regarded the allegation irrelevant to the proceedings. Geoghegan J in the Supreme Court took the view that it was perfectly in order for a trial judge to refuse a witness to be called for frivolous or irrelevant reasons and that the obligation to ensure a fair trial obliges him to probe the purpose for which a witness is called.

Elicitation of testimony

[5.12] At common law a general rule existed that if a person was capable of giving testimony, that person had a duty to do so, and was often compellable to give same. Evidence is usually taken on oath from a witness. The oath may take any form the witness wishes and unsworn evidence is also allowed, particularly in the case of children.

[5.13] Witnesses are examined-in-chief by the party calling them (during which process they may not be asked leading questions), then cross-examined by the other side (who can ask leading questions) and then re-examined on issues arising in the course of the latter.

Competence of witnesses

Physical disability

[5.14] If persons with a physical disability are capable of giving evidence by whatever means, it will be treated as admissible.

Mental disability

[5.15] The judge must be satisfied that persons of defective intellect can give an intelligible account and so give unsworn evidence under s 27(3) of the Criminal Evidence Act 1992.[11]

---

[10] *Herron v Haughton* [2000] IESC 57.
[11] *O'Sullivan v Hamill* [1999] 3 IR 9.

Children's evidence

[5.16] The Criminal Evidence Act 1992, s 27 provides:

> (1) Notwithstanding any enactment, in any criminal proceedings the evidence of a person under 14 years of age may be received otherwise than on oath or affirmation if the court is satisfied that he is capable of giving an intelligible account of events which are relevant to those proceedings.

> (2) If any person whose evidence is received as aforesaid makes a statement material in the proceedings concerned which he knows to be false or does not believe to be true, he shall be guilty of an offence and on conviction shall be liable to be dealt with as if he had been guilty of perjury.

> (3) Subsection (1) shall apply to a person with mental handicap who has reached the age of 14 years as it applies to a person under that age.

[5.17] The 1992 Act changed the manner of receipt of children's evidence by introducing live television link and video testimony. These are similar to changes made in England, on the basis of the *Pigot Committee Report*,[12] and here follow on recommendations of the Law Reform Commission.[13] The reasoning behind the changes relating to the reception of children's testimony are elucidated by the Law Reform Commission in its consultation paper, *Child Sexual Abuse*. In the consultation paper the reasons for that change were elucidated as follows:

> The relief of trauma to the child, is the Commission's paramount objective in making provisional recommendations for reform in this Paper. In making our recommendations, however, we must ensure that the defendant is not asked to pay too high a price for the attainment of that objective. If, for example, the defendant is to lose his right to cross-examine, it is vital that there be great confidence in the reliability of the evidence in question ... While in this Paper we are not treating child witnesses as inherently unreliable, we nevertheless place great store firstly on the court's assessing their competence before they can give evidence and secondly on the defendant's right to cross-examine.

> Confrontation and cross-examination are indelible characteristics of the adversarial system as normally operated. The quest is for immediacy tempered with accuracy. The law leans against the secondhand as stale and potentially unreliable. But the use of modern technology asks searching questions of the traditional system and can be accommodated to the advantage of the system. The law must provide for the keeping of records on computer chip or micro-film. In turn, these records should prove much more accurate and reliable than records

---

[12] Pigot, *Report of the Advisory Group on Video-Recorded Evidence* (HMSO, 1990).

[13] Law Reform Commission, *Consultation Paper on Child Sexual Abuse* (1989). Ireland, *Report on Child Sexual Abuse* (1990).

compiled by hand, which compilation has subsequently to be recalled in evidence.

Modern TV and video technology raise serious questions as to the desirability of the Rule against Hearsay. A video recording not only preserves the *ipsissima* of the questions and answers, the pauses and the vocal inflexions, but also the facial expressions and body languages of the witness being recorded. The availability of closed circuit television can take a witness out of an oppressive atmosphere while preserving the immediacy of a trial and can even provide for the 'live' participation in a trial of a witness in another jurisdiction or continent. In fact the use of a live video-link cannot truly be regarded as tendering an out-of-court statement except to the extent that the witness is not physically present.[14]

[5.18] The facility for live television link (s 13), video testimony (ss 15, 16) and evidence through an intermediary (s 14) in certain criminal proceedings is also found in Part III of the 1992 Act and is quite radical in departing from oral testimony being given by witnesses in the presence of the accused, subject to the sanction of the oath and cross-examination. However, the provisions themselves mandate (s 14) that the court operates same on the basis of the 'interests of justice', and s 16(2)(b), in the context of video recording, specifically states that the court should have regard to all the circumstances, including any risk that its admission will result in unfairness to the accused.

[5.19] The constitutionality of this provision was upheld in *Donnelly v AG.*[15] The impugned provisions were those which facilitated the elicitation or giving of testimony by sexual offence victims, particularly children, by means of a live video link, but at the trial judge's discretion applied also to vulnerable witnesses in such cases.[16] The plaintiff claimed that it interfered with his right to a fair trial. It was argued that the plaintiff had a constitutional right physically to confront his accused in open court, and that the presumption of trauma created for child witnesses testifying in such circumstances placed an unconstitutional and unfair burden of proof on an accused who would have to prove the child capable of testifying in open court. The constitutional provisions referred to were Arts 38.1, 38.5, 40.3, and 40.1.

[5.20] Costello J in the High Court dismissed the applicant's claim, quoting from O'Higgins CJ in *State (Healy) v Donoghue*[17] that "[t]he general view of what

---

[14] Law Reform Commission, *Consultation Paper Child Sexual Abuse* (1989), pp 144–146.

[15] *Donnelly v AG* [1998] 1 IR 321.

[16] Part 3 of the Act applies to sexual offences and offences involving violence or the threat of violence to a person (s 12). This facility has recently been extended to apply in relation to witnesses subject to intimidation, particularly in the context of organised crime. See Criminal Justice Act 1999, s 39.

[17] *The State (Healy) v Donoghue* [1976]IR 325.

was fair and proper in relation to criminal trials has always been the subject of change and development. Rules of evidence and rules of procedure gradually evolved as notions of fairness developed".[18]

[5.21] In the Supreme Court in *Donnelly v Ireland*, Hamilton CJ noted[19] that it was well established in our constitutional jurisprudence that an accused person's right to a fair trial was 'one of the most fundamental constitutional rights accorded to persons and that in so far as it is possible or desirable to construct a hierarchy of constitutional rights it is a superior right.'[20]

[5.22] Relating these concepts to the question before him in *Donnelly,* Hamilton CJ noted that an essential ingredient in the concept of fair procedures was that an accused person should have the opportunity to 'hear and test by examination the evidence offered by or on behalf of his accuser'. The plaintiff in these proceedings submitted that this right to test by examination the evidence offered against him to be effective and to give him the opportunity to defend himself adequately, necessarily implied and required that the witness should give evidence in his presence and that the witness, when giving evidence, should physically confront him. In *White v Ireland* the High Court had held that the right to 'eyeball to eyeball' did not exist.[21]

[5.23] Having reviewed the United States case law,[22] Hamilton CJ noted that although the confrontation clause was clear and specific, it did not give to

---

18 *Per* Costello P in *Donnelly v Ireland* [1998] 1IR 321 at 333 (HC) quoting O'Higgins CJ in *The State Healy v Donoghue* [1976] IR 325 at 349. Costello J in *Donnelly* noted how the procedure operated as documented previously by the Court in *White v Ireland* [1995] 2 IR 268. It is interesting that Costello J makes copious reference to context here and, refers in particular, to Law Reform Commission documentation and reports on sexual abuse.

19 *Donnelly v Ireland* [1998] 1 IR 321 at 348–349.

20 He noted in particular statements regarding the importance of the guarantee of basic fairness in the Constitution in *Re Haughey* [1971] IR 217 at 264, *State (Healy) v Donaghue* [1976] IR 325 at 335–336 and *Donnelly v Ireland* [1998] 1 IR 321 at 348–349 *per* Hamilton CJ.

21 *White v Ireland* [1995] 2 IR 268.

22 Hamilton CJ referred to the judgments in two cases decided by the Supreme Court of the United States of America: *Coy v Iowa* (1987) 487 US 1012 and *Maryland v Craig* (1989) 497 US 836, but commented that these cases turned upon differently worded constitutional statutory provisions to those under examination in the then present case. Nevertheless, they contained certain discussions of principle which he found useful. He referred to the Sixth Amendment of the American Constitution which provides as follows:

    in all criminal prosecutions, the accused shall enjoy the right to a speedy and public trial, by an impartial jury of the State and district wherein the crime shall have been committed, which district shall have been previously ascertained by law, and to be informed of the nature and cause of the accusation; to be confronted with the witnesses against him; to have compulsory process for obtaining witnesses in his favour, and to have the Assistance of Counsel for his defence.

criminal defendants the absolute right to a face-to-face meeting with witnesses against them:

> [T]he Constitution of Ireland, 1937, contains no specific right such as that guaranteed in the confrontation clause, [but] the central concern of the requirements of due process and fair procedures is the same, that is to ensure the fairness of the trial of an accused person. This undoubtedly involves the rigorous testing by cross-examination of the evidence against him or her.[23]

[5.24] The logic of Hamilton CJ's reasoning stems from what the impugned provisions do not do in order to save those provisions:

> The impugned provisions of the Act of 1992 do not restrict in any way the rights of an accused person as established by the constitutional jurisprudence of this Court ... What they do permit in the case of proceedings for the offences set forth in s 12 of the Act of 1992 is the giving of evidence by persons under 17 years (unless the court sees good reason to the contrary) and by any other person, with the leave of the court, through a live television link. It is accepted that the reason for the procedure permitted by s 13 of the Act of 1992 was that it is generally accepted that young persons under the age of 17 are likely to be traumatised by the experience of giving evidence in court and that its purpose is to minimise such trauma.[24]

Hamilton CJ concluded that therefore:

> ... the assessment of such credibility does not require that the witness should be required to give evidence in the physical presence of the accused person and that the requirements of fair procedures are adequately fulfilled by requiring that the witness give evidence on oath and be subjected to cross-examination and that the judge and jury have ample opportunity to observe the demeanour of the witness while giving evidence and being subjected to cross-examination. In this way, an accused person's right to a fair trial is adequately protected and vindicated.

> Such right does not include the right in all circumstances to require that the evidence be given in his physical presence and consequently there is no such constitutional right.[25]

[5.25] Hamilton CJ's circular reasoning is resonant of that found to exist in the legislature's enactments in this area, typified in the qualification (as here) that the provision be invoked 'in the interests of justice' or without detriment to 'fairness to the accused'. This perspective gives the view that the existence of this provision quiescent in the legislation (arguably precisely because there is such a problem with the relevant change) is invoked and relied upon by the judiciary, thereby copper fastening the lack of a correlation or relationship

---

[23] *Donnelly v Ireland* [1998] 1 IR 321 at 356–357.

[24] *Donnelly v Ireland* [1998] 1 IR 321 at 356–357.

[25] *Donnelly v Ireland* [1998] 1 IR 321 at 357.

between what was changed and what is now fair. There could hardly be a greater irony: the legislation is 'saved' because the judiciary need not invoke it where it would be unfair to do so – hence it is potentially unfair. Hamilton CJ's reasoning along these contradictory lines is as follows:[26]

> The accused person's right to a fair trial is further protected by the fact that it is open to the court not to permit the giving of evidence by a young person through a live television link if the accused person establishes that 'there is good reason to the contrary' and that the leave of the court is required before any other person may give evidence in this manner. A judge considering either of these issues will be obliged to have regard to the accused person's right to a fair trial.

[5.26] The reasoning is familiar from earlier terrorist cases – the individual's rights are underscored and their importance emphasised, but the limited nature of the provision impugned (indicated by what it does not do) is invoked to save it. The linkage is a familiar one: moving from what the provision does not do, through what safeguards do exist, here augmented with the 'goodness' of the victim (as opposed to simply the need or safety of the State), which is set in opposition to the individual accused, all to the same effect. Over-familiarity or perhaps cynicism with regard to the State and State entities may mean it no longer has as much purchase as hitherto, so the invocation of the victim poses a nice substitute to bolster State power, supposedly in the interests of the victim, who may prove in fact be merely another pawn in the 'law and order' momentum.

[5.27] The 1992 Act's mechanism for elicitation of the testimony of children is as follows: evidence can be given through live television link[27] or through an intermediary[28] and provision is made for the admissibility of hearsay evidence when the court considers the child unable to give evidence by reason of age or that it would not be in the interests of the welfare of the child.[29] Such evidence will not be admitted, however, if not in the 'interests of justice'[30] or where it would result in 'unfairness to any of the parties'.[31] Oath or affirmation is not necessary for child witnesses where the child is under 14 years of age and the court is satisfied that the child 'is capable of giving an intelligible account of events'.[32] The 1992 Act's provision for the reception of children's evidence in criminal cases was extended to civil cases under the rubric of the Children Act

---

[26] *Donnelly v Ireland* [1998] 1 IR 321 at 357.
[27] Criminal Evidence Act 1992, s 21.
[28] Criminal Evidence Act 1992, s 22.
[29] Criminal Evidence Act 1992, s 23(1)(a) and (b).
[30] Criminal Evidence Act 1992, s 23(1)(a).
[31] Criminal Evidence Act 1992, s 23(1)(b).
[32] Criminal Evidence Act 1992, s 28.

1997. Part III of that Act applies to civil proceedings before any court concerning the welfare of a child, and civil proceedings concerning the welfare of a person who has a mental disability such that he or she is not able to live independently.

[5.28] This particular 'exceptional' provision once introduced (the 1992 Act) and sanctioned (*Donnelly*) became normalised as the facility to give evidence through a live television link granted to children and other vulnerable witnesses was extended by the Criminal Justice Act 1999, s 39, to a person other than the accused with leave of the court.[33] Under s 39(2) the court order granted leave if 'satisfied that the person is likely to be in fear or subject to intimidation in giving evidence otherwise'. The most recent proposed extension of the ambit of that provision is under the Criminal Procedure Bill 2009 in the context of a change in the law to allow victim impact statements to be given by the family members of victims of homicide. Provision is to be made to amend the Criminal Justice Act 1993 (which provides for victim impact statements) to allow a child, person with mental disorder or any other person with leave of the court to make a victim impact statement by live tv link.[34]

Reform

Children

[5.29] Article 12 of the UN Convention on the Rights of the Child (UNCRC) provides that the child has a right to be heard in all matters affecting him or her with due regard to his or her age and maturity. The *Report of the Special Rapporteur on Child Protection*[35] states that the 1992 Act and the Children Act 1997 are 'landmark pieces of legislation in this regard'. It says:

> Under the Criminal Evidence Act 1992 it is now possible for children to give evidence otherwise than on oath if the child is deemed capable of giving an intelligible account of the events. Evidence can be given via the medium of video recording or television link. Questions can be put to the child witness using anatomically correct dolls or through an interpreter.

This report also, however, notes that:

> [t]he main difficulty in respect of vulnerable witnesses has always been cross-examination. It is self evident to state that cross-examination is central to the adversarial system, but the manner of its operation is an issue of live concern where vulnerable child witnesses are concerned ... [T]here is a fear that further

---

[33] Criminal Evidence Act 1992, s 39(1).
[34] Section 5 Criminal Procedure Bill 2009 amending 1993 Act by insertion of s 5A.
[35] A Report submitted to the Oireachtas – Geoffrey Shannon (Nov 2007) at para 5.3.1.

reform in this field could be deemed unconstitutional in respect of fair procedures and due process rights of the accused.[36]

With regard to competency of child witnesses, that report makes the point that instead of requiring competency to be proved as at present, a reversal of this requirement would given greater effect to art 12 of UNCRC.[37] This is the situation in the UK.[38]

[5.30] Further, the Report points out that there is no express rule in Irish law prohibiting the cross-examination of a child witness in a sexual offence case by an unrepresented accused (such does exist in the UK – Criminal Justice Act 1991, s 55).[39] The Report refers to provision in Germany where witnesses under 16 are examined only by the presiding judge. The solution suggested by the rapporteur is to put judicial intervention in questioning of child witnesses on a sound statutory basis:

> This would give the judge the ability, inherent within him/her by the nature of the judicial power, to rule out any question deemed inappropriate for the witness as well as the capability to put his/her own questions to the witness should any matter require clarification.[40]

An example of a case where some of these issues arose is *DPP v T*.[41] The case was the first time anatomically correct dolls were used. The witness was an 18 year-old girl with Down Syndrome whose father was charged with various offences. He insisted on running the trial himself including cross-examining of her as witness.

[5.31] The provisions mentioned above from the 1992 Act relate to criminal trials, not civil cases. *Mapp v Gilhooley*[42] made it clear that there was no such provision in civil actions. Eventually, the Children Act 1997, s 28 provided that a child in a civil case could give testimony as long as they could give an intelligible account. Section 21 of the 1997 Act allowed the evidence of children to be given by live TV link in civil cases. Section 22 allowed questions to be put through an intermediary in civil cases. That Act also allowed for the admission of hearsay evidence regarding child welfare.[43]

---

[36] At para 5.3.1.

[37] At para 5.3.2.

[38] Youth & Criminal Evidence Act 1999 c.23, s 53.

[39] A Report submitted to the Oireachtas – Geoffrey Shannon (Nov 2007) at para 5.3.3.

[40] At para 5.3.3, p 61.

[41] *DPP v T* (27 July 1998, unreported), CCA.

[42] *Mapp v Gilhooley* [1991] ILRM 695.

[43] Children Act 1997, s 23.

[5.32] The need for constant review and assessment of this area of the law is evident from ongoing research. Bala *et al*[44] point out that, '[r]ecent psychological research raises serious questions … for assessing the competency of child witnesses.'

[5.33] In their study of 192 maltreated children, Lyon and Saywitz found that children who had been neglected or abused often showed developmental delays due to the treatment they suffered. These delays make it more difficult to qualify the very group of children who are most likely to be called as witnesses. Although these children present seriously delayed vocabulary skills, most maltreated children by age five have a basic understanding of the meaning and the immorality of lying. However, the capacity of children to demonstrate their understanding is dependent on the manner in which they are questioned.

Other vulnerable witnesses

[5.34] Once there was a notion that witnesses could testify outside court, it was rolled out to other witnesses, except the accused, under s 39 of the Criminal Justice Act 1999 with the permission of the court. That section provides that any person other than the accused may give evidence via a television link. This will be with the leave of the court where it is satisfied the person is likely to be in fear or subject to intimidation.

Inappropriate questions on cross-examination

[5.35] Inappropriate questions are considered in *People (DPP) v DR*[45] where the question posed to the accused in cross-examination by the prosecution was whether the complainant was either lying or perjuring herself. Counsel for the accused had objected and on appeal the Court of Criminal Appeal commented:[46]

> The law is not as simple as that. There may be many good reasons why a jury, while satisfied that the complainant is telling the truth according to her, might still consider her evidence unreliable and might without any stain on the complainant's character as it were, acquit the applicant and it appears to this Court that the advancement of justice in a trial is not helped by forcing a witness to take up so extreme an attitude particularly in relation to a question like perjury and the Court thinks that counsel for the applicant was right to take the stand which he did take and to persist in his objection. We all know that in the course of conducting trials situations arise where a clash takes place between two sides both of whom cannot be telling the truth and counsel's job is to test the veracity of the opposing party's witnesses but it is difficult to envisage that in the normal

---

[44] Bala, Lee, Lindsay & Talwar, 'A Legal and Psychological Critique of the Present Approach to the Assessment of the Competence of Child Witnesses' [2000] 38 (No 3) Os HLJ 409 at 442.

[45] *People (DPP) v DR* [1998] 2 IR 106.

[46] *People (DPP) v DR* [1998] 2 IR 106 at 110–111 *per* Barrington J.

run of a case he will be justified in putting to a witness: does that mean that the other witness is committing perjury? It is a situation which counsel should in the proper conduct of a cross-examination avoid although he may of course clearly raise the clear suggestion that the witness is not telling the truth or is not reliable.

In the event, the CCA determined that the trial judge undid the damage and so the incident did not have any real impact on the trial.

Criminal Justice Act 2006

[5.36] The most recent change in relation to witnesses that builds on this notion of witnesses being permitted to give testimony otherwise than on oath, in court and subject to cross-examination, is found in the Criminal Justice Act 2006. The Act's title gives an indication of its genesis which again lies in a particular context of perceived difficulty:

> An Act to amend and extend the powers of the Garda Síochána in relation to the investigation of offences; to amend criminal law procedure in other respects including provision for the admissibility in evidence of certain witness statements, an extension of the circumstances in which the Attorney General in any case or, if he or she is a prosecuting attorney in a trial, the Director of Public Prosecutions may refer a question of law to the Supreme Court for determination or take an appeal in criminal proceedings, provision for offences relating to organised crime ...

This is really the first piece of legislation to respond to the phenomenon of 'organised' crime through modification of the criminal process (earlier moves had focussed on confiscation proceedings). The impetus behind it was to ease the task of the prosecution in these cases. This is the same impetus that led to the 1992 Act where there was a worry about the inability to successfully prosecute sexual offences perpetrated against children because of issues relating to their competency. The concern driving the later Act is a perceived inability to prosecute organised crime activity because of the retraction of witness statements. A number of cases in Limerick had collapsed because a number of witnesses refused to give testimony.[47] Because of that, provisions to ease the giving of testimony by these witnesses were introduced.

[5.37] Part 3 of the Criminal Justice Act 2006 deals with the admissibility of certain witness statements. Section 16 provides:

---

[47] Prime amongst these was the case against Liam Keane which collapsed and was marked by his leaving the court room and giving a two-fingered salute to the waiting media, which received broad publication and was interpreted as being symptomatic of the attitude to the trial system amongst those engaged in gang and organised crime activities. (2003) Irish Times, 6 November, pp 6–7.

(1) Where a person has been sent forward for trial for an arrestable offence, a statement relevant to the proceedings made by a witness ... may, with the leave of the court, be admitted as evidence of any fact mentioned in it if the witness, although available for cross-examination-

(a) refuses to give evidence,

(b) denies making the statement, or

(c) gives evidence which is materially inconsistent with it.

The statement will be admitted if the court is satisfied under s 16(2)(b):

(i) that direct oral evidence of the fact concerned would be admissible in the proceedings,

(ii) that it was made voluntarily, and

(iii) that it is reliable,

and

(c) either—

(i) the statement was given on oath or affirmation or contains a statutory declaration by the witness to the effect that the statement is true to the best of his or her knowledge or belief, or

(ii) the court is otherwise satisfied that when the statement was made the witness understood the requirement to tell the truth.

[5.38] The latter is surely an unusual substitute for the sanctity of the oath/ affirmation? Section 16(3) provides that when a court is deciding whether a statement is reliable, it should have regard to the following:

(a) whether it was given on oath or affirmation or was video-recorded, or

(b) whether there is other evidence to support its reliability.

The court is also to look at any explanation or denial by the witness.

[5.39] Finally, the statement will not be admitted if the court is of the opinion (s 16(4)):

(a) having had regard to all the circumstances, including any risk that its admission would be unfair to the accused or, if there are more than one accused, to any of them, that in the interests of justice it ought not to be so admitted, or

(b) that its admission is unnecessary, having regard to other evidence given in the proceedings.

It is extraordinary that once again the operation of the change is to be 'finessed' by the courts in accordance with the 'interests of justice' again without assuming that there might have been a correlation between that concept and the evidentiary rule (here of a witness testifying under oath in court) which is now changed. This is familiar territory from other statutory changes. There is no specific reference here to 'fairness to the accused'. Is that perhaps significant? What is the connection between fairness to the accused and the interests of justice? Are they actually compatible? This provision constitutes a fairly broad-sweeping and major change to our system.

[5.40] Section 19 provides in relation to video-recording that the Minister can decide on the retention, and the period of retention, of tapes. Any failure of the Gardaí to comply with those regulations shall be subject to the power of the courts generally to include and exclude evidence. This change represents much greater provision for the giving of testimony other than under oath, present in the witness box, through a video link or via a statement.

Defendant's spouse as a witness

[5.41] There existed a general rule at common law that a spouse was not competent as a witness for the prosecution at a criminal trial. The rule extended to the joint trial situation, so that even if the evidence of a spouse was only against the co-accused, the spouse was not permitted to testify. The rationale of the rule lay in the public policy of upholding marriage. Inroads were made into this rule both at common law, and by statute.

[5.42] This area of law has now been substantially amended by the Criminal Evidence 1992. Part IV of that Act provides for the competence of the spouse of an accused as a prosecution witness in any criminal proceedings (s 21). The spouse of an accused is also rendered compellable as a prosecution witness in certain instances. Section 22 of the 1992 Act provides that the spouse of an accused shall be compellable as a prosecution witness in the case of a violent or sexual offence against the spouse, a child of the spouse or accused, or any person who at the material time was under 17 years of age, or any sexual offence against a child of the spouse or accused or person under 17 years, or an attempt or conspiracy to commit either.

[5.43] This change in the law with regard to spousal competence and compellability was preceded, and mandated to some degree, by the Irish Court of Criminal Appeal in *DPP v T*,[48] where the Court found reason in the Constitution's protection of the family (Art 41), together with its vindication of personal rights (Art 40.3) – and in particular those rights of individual family members – to render a spouse competent in cases where personal violence had been perpetrated upon a member of that family by the other spouse. In that case, where the mother of a Down Syndrome child was not rendered competent by statutory exception in the case of a charge of incest against the child's father

---

[48] *DPP v T* (27 July 1998, unreported), CCA.

(now separated from his wife), Walsh J deemed the spouse to be rendered both competent and compellable.

[5.44] Section 23 of the 1992 Act provides for the compellability of a spouse or former spouse of an accused to give evidence at the insistence of the accused (in so far as they may be charged in the same proceedings (s 25)). Section 24 provides for the compellability to give evidence at the insistence of a co-accused in the same circumstances providing for compellability as a prosecution witness.

The accused as a prosecution witness

[5.45] The accused is not competent as a prosecution witness, with the exception of the Public Nuisance Act 1887. When there is more than one defendant, they cannot give evidence against one another. However, by means of various technical devices the prosecution can get around this prohibition:

(1) If no evidence is offered against an accused and he is acquitted, the defence of *autre fois acquit* operates as a bar against possible subsequent prosecution and the individual concerned is free to testify against the other accused.

(2) The prosecution can *nolle prosequi* the charges preferred against an accused, which protects the accused de facto from the possibility of a trial on the same charges again. The accused is once more free to testify against others.

(3) If the accuseds are not tried together and one pleads guilty and is sentenced, the latter is then free to give evidence against others.

(4) When the accused has been found guilty and sentenced he may give evidence against other(s).

Diplomats and prosecution witnesses

[5.46] Under the Geneva Convention and the Diplomatic Relations Immunity Act 1962, a diplomat cannot be compelled to give evidence. This provision is also extended to cover his or her family, provided they are not nationals of the deciding state. This rule also applies to mission members in Ireland. The Diplomatic Relations and Immunities (Amendment) Act 1976, s 1 provides that the government may by order extend immunity to international bodies, persons etc under an international agreement to which the state or the government is or intends to become a party.

Chapter 6

Witness System: Corroboration

Corroborative Evidence

[6.01] The major question when considering a corroboration requirement is what kind of evidence is corroborative or satisfies the said requirement. The authority here is *R v Baskerville*,[1] where Reading LCJ defined corroboration as

> independent testimony which affects the accused by connecting or tending to connect him with the crime. In other words it must be evidence which implicates him, that is, which confirms in some material particular not only the evidence that the crime has been committed, but also that the prisoner committed it.

[6.02] In *People (Attorney General) v Williams*,[2] Sullivan CJ formulated corroborative evidence as 'independent evidence of material circumstances tending to implicate the accused in the commission of the crime with which he was charged'. A straightforward example of the application of this definition is found in *R v Gregg*[3] in the context of a charge of rape. The fact that the victim here was found to be suffering from a particular type of venereal disease soon after the offence, and that the accused at the time of the offence suffered from that particular venereal disease, constituted corroboration.[4]

[6.03] An important qualification here is the fact that a witness cannot corroborate herself. So, for example, a witness cannot corroborate herself by an early complaint in a rape case.[5] Yet, if the danger that is being averted by the requirement is one of fabrication, would logic not seem to dictate that the jury be permitted to take account of anything indicating that the story is not fabricated?

---

1. *R v Baskerville* [1916] 2KB 658 at 667. This was recently confirmed as the authority in Irish law in *DPP v Gilligan* [2006] 1 IR 107.
2. *People (AG) v Williams* [1940] IR 195 at 200, confirmed in *People (AG) v Trayers* [1956] IR 110 at 114.
3. *R v Gregg* (1934) 24 Cr App Rep 13.
4. The presence of the venereal disease would, of course, only constitute corroboration of the act of intercourse, the subject matter of the alleged offence. The development of DNA fingerprinting has considerable significance for this area of the law. See also Fennell, 'Genetic Fingerprinting for Sexual Offences' (1988) *Irish Medical Times* 18 and Fennell, 'DNA Profiling, Hidden Agendas' (1991) 1 *Irish Criminal Law Journal* 34.
5. *R v Christie* [1914] AC 557.

[6.04] In *R v Redpath*,[6] the distressed condition of the victim was deemed capable of constituting corroboration, although its probative worth was greater if it was witnessed by an independent witness. Similarly, in *R v Zielinski*,[7] the evidence of the victim's son as to the distressed condition of the victim a few minutes after the appellant left, was held to constitute corroborative evidence.

[6.05] Where difficulty readily arises in this area is in relation to the trial judge's direction as to the finding of corroborative evidence. The present position is one in the context of sexual offence complaints, for example, which allows the avenue of defence to the accused, whereby admission of all actions up to the act of the intercourse itself undermines the potential corroborative value of evidence of a struggle (torn clothing etc). This is because the accused, by alleging last-minute consent on the part of the victim, can force corroboration as to the issue of consent itself. Hence, evidence of an earlier struggle, which would have had corroborative value had the defence put forward been one of alibi or a denial of the act of intercourse, is of no avail.

[6.06] Selective defence tactics can, therefore, manipulate the corroboration requirement to render the prosecution's task extremely and artificially difficult. In turn, this further complicates the roles of the judge and jury at trial, and creates a fertile source of appeals. In *People (DPP) v Collins*[8] the applicant had been convicted of one offence of unlawful sexual intercourse contrary to s 1(1) of the Criminal Law (Amendment) Act 1935. The details of that offence were that he met with the complainant outside her school in his car, and they drove to his house where the alleged sexual intercourse took place in his bedroom. The trial judge had given a corroboration warning to the jury and then commented on the evidence to the effect, as counsel for the applicant alleged, that the description of the windows and curtains in the bedroom given by the complainant, if accepted, amounted to corroboration of her story. The Court of Criminal Appeal held that this was the direction given and that the trial judge was wrong in conveying to the jury that the complainant's evidence regarding the windows and curtains was capable of constituting corroboration, citing the *Baskerville*[9] definition that the evidence 'must be independent testimony to connect (the accused) with the crime.'

[6.07] Difficulties with a restrictive definition of corroboration were identified in *People (DPP) v Meehan*[10] where the Court of Criminal Appeal (judgment

---

6   *R v Redpath* (1962) 46 Cr App Rep 319.
7   *R v Zielinski* (1950) 34 Cr App Rep 193.
8   *People (DPP) v Collins* (22 April 2002), CCA, Murray, Barr, Kinlen JJ.
9   *R v Baskerville* [1916] 2 KB 658 at 667 *per* Reading LCJ.
10 *People (DPP) v Meehan* [2006] 3 IR 468.

delivered by Kearns J) opted to emphasise that a more flexible approach to the definition of corroboration than that drawn by the traditional *Baskerville* formula was supported by the Irish case law, as well as being consistent with developments in other jurisdictions.[11] The Court of Criminal Appeal in *Meehan*[12] criticised the *Baskerville* approach as one which relates unreliability to classes of persons – accomplices, children, sexual complainants – rather than to the circumstances of the case, which is in itself a type of stereotyping. Kearns J found support for a more flexible approach to *Baskerville* in *AG v Levinson*,[13] *People (DPP) v Murphy*[14] and *People (DPP) v Gilligan*:[15]

> In recent years the Courts have shown themselves more prepared, at least in sexual offence cases, to evaluate various evidential facts cumulatively as partial or complete corroboration of a complainant's account, even where the corroborative value of each established fact is low.[16]

[6.08] Thus in *People (DPP) v Reid*,[17] the court identified as potentially corroborative of the complainant's testimony the state of her genitalia, the high volume of the accused's television set at the time of the alleged offence, and the distressed state of the complainant observed by her parents in the aftermath. In *People v Murphy*[18] the court considered evidence that the accused's trousers had been dirtied to be potentially corroborative of the complainant's allegation that a fracas had taken place on the way home from a disco.

[6.09] The Court of Criminal Appeal in *Meehan* did not feel the need to abandon *Baskerville* but rather qualify it 'towards a more common sense interpretation of what the requirement of corroboration should be'.[19] Moreover, they point out that any re-evaluation of *Baskerville* would have to acknowledge the different world described by Denham J in *Gilligan*, which they say is 'light years away' from that when *Baskerville* was decided. Kearns J:[20]

> Modern Ireland is awash with illegal drugs and beset with the enormous social problems which attend their use. Gangland killings in connection with that trade have virtually become a daily occurrence. A witness protection programme may

---

[11] For example, Supreme Court of Canada in *Vetrovec v The Queen* [1982] 1SCR 811 and Australia in *Jenkins v The Queen* [2004] HCA 57.

[12] *People (DPP) v Meehan* [2006] 3 IR 468 at 490.

[13] *AG v Levinson* [1932] IR 158.

[14] *People (DPP) v Murphy* [2005] 2 IR 125.

[15] *People (DPP) v Gilligan* [2006] 1 IR 107.

[16] *People (DPP) v Meehan* [2006] 3 IR 468 at 493.

[17] *People (DPP) v Reid* [1993] 2 IR 186.

[18] *People v Murphy* (3 November 1997, unreported), CCA.

[19] *People (DPP) v Meehan* [2006] 3 IR 468 at 495.

[20] *People (DPP) v Meehan* [2006] 3 IR 468 at 495–6.

well provide one of the few effective ways of dealing with these activities, a consideration which must be kept in mind if *the community's right to see serious crime being prosecuted is to be respected*. Evidence emanating from witnesses in such a programme is not automatically to be scorned or discounted. It is, and always will be, evidence which must be treated with caution. However, if and when satisfied in a particular case that it is credible, a court should be free to act on it. This court is of the view that a more flexible approach to the whole issue of corroboration beyond the narrow formalistic definition of *Rex v Baskerville* is entirely open on the decided cases in this jurisdiction and in the particular circumstances adverted to by Denham J ... [in *Gilligan*] ... The court believes in any event that the formula of words adopted in *Rex v Baskerville* to define corroboration, including as it does the words 'tending to connect him with the crime', leaves a considerable margin of discretion with any court dealing with issues of corroboration to decide what may or may not constitute corroboration. [Emphasis added.]

Doctrine of recent complaint

[6.10] The 'doctrine of recent complaint' does allow for the introduction of evidence of a complaint made by the victim of a sexual offence in the aftermath of the incident. The evidence may not amount to corroboration, yet does go to the issue of the witness's credibility.

[6.11] In *DPP v Brophy*,[21] the accused had been convicted of the indecent assault of a fourteen-year-old schoolgirl, and appealed *inter alia* on the grounds that the trial judge had erred in law in refusing an application to have the jury discharged following the giving of inadmissible evidence of complaint.

[6.12] The facts, in brief, concerned allegations of an incident of indecent assault occurring at the home of the accused on 28 December 1989. The complainant had later informed her father and some friends of the incident, but had not informed her mother or others immediately after the alleged incident. The prosecution accepted that since the complaint had not been made at the first opportunity, they should not give the terms, but only the fact of complaint. The Court of Criminal Appeal had to consider, then, whether evidence of the fact of the making of a complaint was admissible in circumstances where it was conceded that the complaint was not made at the first opportunity that reasonably presented itself. Considering the history of admissibility of complaints in sexual cases, O'Flaherty J noted it was only the *fact* of complaint that was admissible, until in *R v Lillyman*,[22] the court extended admissibility of a complaint to its terms. O'Flaherty J continued:

---

[21] *DPP v Brophy* [1992] ILRM 709.
[22] *R v Lillyman* [1896] 2 QB 167.

It seems to the court therefore, that either evidence of a complaint having been made, is admissible, or it is not. If it is admissible, then, subject to the discretion of the trial judge to prevent unnecessary prejudicial repetition, the terms of the complaint are also admissible ... there seems no room for half measures in regard to this; either the fact of a complaint is admissible or it is not.'

[6.13] O'Flaherty J[23] then summarised the law on the topic of admissibility of complaints:

(a)   Complaints may only be proved in criminal prosecutions for a sexual offence.

(b)   The complaint must have been made as speedily as could reasonably be expected and in a voluntary fashion, not as a result of any inducements or exhortations. Once evidence of the making of a complaint is admissible then particulars of the complaint may also be proved.

(c)   It should always be made clear to the jury that such evidence is not evidence of the facts on which the complaint is based but to show that the victim's conduct in so complaining was consistent with her testimony.

(d)   While there is mention in one of the older cases, *R v Osborne*[1905] 1 KB 551 of a complaint being corroborative of the complainant's credibility, this does not mean that such a complaint amounts to corroboration of her testimony in the legal sense of that term but as pointing to the consistency of her testimony. Corroboration in the strict sense involves independent evidence, that is evidence other than the complainant's evidence.

(e)   The law on complaints should not be confused with what takes place once the police institute their inquiries. That is a separate matter. A complaint made to the police may, as such, be admissible or not under the guidelines set out above but just because a complaint is not made at the first opportunity to the police does not, of course, inhibit their inquires. Indeed a complaint to the police may be made by someone other than the injured party.

O'Flaherty J noted that in this case the prosecution had conceded the complaint was not made as speedily as possible: 'since the prosecution was clearly of the view that the terms of the complaint were not admissible the fact of the complaint should not have been admitted either'.

[6.14] In this case, in fact, the Court of Criminal Appeal went further, interfering with the trial judge's decision not to order a discharge of the jury in light of the admission of the evidence. *Per* O'Flaherty J:

The judge ruled that he would not discharge the jury, and, in the ordinary way, the discharging of a jury in any trial must be a very extreme remedy but we are of

---

[23]   *DPP v Brophy* [1992] ILRM 709 at 716.

the opinion that in this case where the prosecution depended on the uncorroborated evidence of the complainant, the requirement that a balance had to be kept to preserve fairness in the trial – since the evidence was so minimal – required that the jury should have been discharged when this evidence got in.

[6.15] This and the earlier cases may be examples of what Pattenden[24] asserts is the greater willingness on the part of appeal courts to interfere with the exercise of a trial judge's discretion, even if that is not what she terms an 'overt' discretion (ie is in fact dictated by rules or criteria, however vague, and so constitutes a question of admissibility – of law – readily interfered with on appeal). In *People (DPP) v Synott*,[25] Finlay CJ, relying on Brophy,[26] held that a complaint made after a year by a child was not admissible. More recently, however, a series of cases have made it clear that delay (in terms of complaint and prosecution) will not necessarily lead to prohibition of evidence in the case of historic sex abuse claims (see, eg, *G v DPP*[27]).

[6.16] In *People (DPP) v Gavin*[28] there was an inconsistency between the complainant's own evidence at the trial and the garda evidence of the complainant. In the complaint it was stated that the complainant awoke to discover the appellant in his bed, with his hand on the complainant's groin. This was not stated in the complainant's evidence. According to McGuinness J, it is clear from *Brophy* that the purpose of allowing the evidence of complaint is to demonstrate the consistency of the complainant. Here the complaint met the criterion of being voluntary and made at an early stage, but not that of being consistent with the complainant's evidence at trial and so should not have been admitted. It should, in any event, have been made clear by the trial judge that the complaint does not amount to corroboration.

[6.17] In *People (DPP) v Jethi*[29] inconsistencies between complaint and evidence were characterised by the court as minor in nature and, because on the central issue of consent they were clear and consistent, the complaint was admissible.

[6.18] In *People (DPP) v MA*,[30] the appeal was on the basis that the trial judge had omitted to explain to the jury that the purpose of admitting the complaint in a rape trial was to show consistency of account and not to prove the fact of a

---

[24] Pattenden, *Judicial Discretion and Criminal Litigation* (2nd edn, Clarendon, 1990), pp 6–7.

[25] *People (DPP) v Synott* (29 May 1992, unreported), CCA.

[26] *DPP v Brophy* [1992] ILRM 709.

[27] *G v DPP* [1994] 1 IR 374.

[28] *People (DPP) v Gavin* [2000] 4 IR 557.

[29] *People (DPP) v Jethi* (7 February 2000, unreported), CCA, Barrington J *ex temp.*

[30] *People (DPP) v MA* [2002] 2 IR 601.

complaint itself, nor for the purpose of proving the rape. Nor, indeed, did it constitute corroboration.

Corroboration required as a matter of law

[6.19] The Treason Act 1939, ss 14 and 22, states that corroboration is required as a matter of law in regard to the charge of perpetrating the act of treason or aiding, abetting or harbouring the perpetrator of same.

[6.20] The Road Traffic Act 1961, s 105, states that corroboration is required as a matter of law in regard to offences involving the proof of speed at which a person was driving under the Road Traffic Act. Section 105(a) states that: 'the uncorroborated evidence of one witness stating his opinion as to that speed shall not be accepted as proof of that speed'. Paragraph (b) of that section goes on to allow evidence of speed to be established *prima facie* by a watch or electronic or other apparatus. Section 44 of the Road Traffic Act 1994 extended that to photographic apparatus.

[6.21] Section 105 was considered in *People (DPP) v Connaughton*,[31] where the applicant had been convicted of dangerous driving causing serious bodily harm. The appeal on the basis of section 105 objected to the admissibility of the evidence of a number of witnesses who gave evidence that the applicant had been driving at speed. It was held, however, that the section was not relevant, as their evidence was confined to a general impression of speed, and no witness has testified as to an enumerated speed of the applicant.

[6.22] The above are the instances when corroboration is required as a matter of law because of statutory provisions. There is one instance when corroboration is required as a matter of law at common law, and that is the crime of perjury. In other words, no one can be convicted of perjury without some kind of corroborative evidence being produced by the prosecution.

Corroboration required as a matter of practice

[6.23] This area has been the subject of much change. Whereas previously all evidence which required corroboration as a matter of practice, or at least a warning to the jury, met with that requirement on every occasion such evidence was presented, reform of this area of the law has meant that certain categories (sexual offence/children) have been removed from this category to the extent that the requirement to give such a warning now constitutes a discretion on the part of the trial judge. Justification for caution in respect of these witnesses varies from the characteristics of the witnesses to the nature of the offence

---

[31] *People (DPP) v Connaughton* (5 April 2001, unreported), CCA.

charged. The latter comprises sexual offence victims' evidence, for example, while an instance of evidence which requires corroboration as a matter of practice, because of the characteristics of the witness, is accomplice evidence.

Accomplices

[6.24] The first category of witnesses where corroboration is required as a matter of practice, or at least a warning to the jury is required as a matter of practice, is that of accomplice evidence. The definition of accomplices for the purpose of the rule is that of the House of Lords in *Davies v DPP*,[32] where Simonds LC stated:

> There is in the authorities no formal definition of the term accomplice ... On the cases it would appear that the following persons if called as witnesses for the prosecution, have been treated as falling within the category:
>
> (1) persons who are *participis criminis* in respect of the actual crime charged, whether as principals or accessories before or after the fact (in felonies) or persons committing, procuring or aiding and abetting (in the case of misdemeanour). This is surely the natural and primary meaning of the term 'accomplice'. But in two cases persons falling strictly outside the ambit of this category have, in particular decisions, been held to be accomplices for the purpose of the rule: viz:
>
> (2) Receivers have been held to be accomplices of the thieves from whom they receive goods on the trial of the latter for larceny ...
>
> (3) When X has been charged with a specific offence on a particular occasion and evidence is admissible and has been admitted, of his having committed crimes of this identical type on other occasions as proving system and intent and negativing accident in such cases the court has held that in relation to such other offences, if evidence of them were given by parties to them the evidence of such other parties should not be left to the jury without a warning that it is dangerous to accept it without corroboration ...

The House of Lords in *Davies*, although on the facts held the failure to give the warning as insignificant on the basis that there was no evidence that the witness was a participant, also said the requirement, in relation to the warning, was a rule of practice akin to a rule of law.

[6.25] It is important to remember that evidence given by a witness who has already been convicted remains accomplice evidence (*Davies*). The test is not whether the witness is subject to conviction at the time of testifying but whether he has become liable to prosecution as a result of the events in issue. Even if the witness is acquitted, he may be an accomplice, as the acquittal may have been

---

[32] *Davies v DPP* [1954] AC 378 at 400.

wrong. In *Davies* the witness had been acquitted of murder but he was not an accomplice because there was little evidence against him and the Crown had offered none.

[6.26] Schools of thought vary in relation to the ambit of the definition of 'accomplice' in this context. In the *King*[33] case, the appellant had been convicted of living on the immoral earnings of a prostitute. It was contended that the latter's evidence was accomplice evidence and that there should have been a warning in relation to same. The Lord Chief Justice commented that there was no evidence that she was an accomplice, and seemed to indicate that if someone were not charged or implicated in relation to the charge before the court, that person was not an accomplice for the purposes of the rule.

[6.27] This narrow approach was criticised in *McNee v Kay*,[34] where School J recommended a wider definition of accomplice. The true principle, he stated, was that a person was an accomplice who was chargeable in relation to the same offence as those in the charge proferred against the accused, and would be, if convicted, liable to such punishment as might tempt him to lie or fabricate in regard to the accused, and, secondly, if not doing it for the accused, could well be testifying to deflect prosecution from himself. The focus of this approach, then, is essentially that of the interest the accomplice has in giving this evidence, which, after all, forms part of the rationale of the corroboration requirement in this context in the first place.

[6.28] In the Irish context, it has been held that a 'police spy' who participates in the entrapment of the criminal (the accused) is in law not an accomplice. Thus, a distinction is drawn between someone who acts as 'agent provocateur' and an accomplice (*Dental Board v O'Callaghan*).[35]

[6.29] In *AG v Linehan*,[36] the Irish courts considered, but did not feel it necessary to lay down, a definition of accomplice. The facts involved a woman who had been charged with the murder of her granddaughter's illegitimate child. The case against her depended on the granddaughter's evidence, the latter having been tried and acquitted. The granddaughter's evidence was uncorroborated and showed she could have been involved. The court felt a warning should have been given in those circumstances, but felt a narrow and precise definition of accomplice should be avoided. The court did indicate that a principal or accessory to a crime would be an accomplice for the purposes of the rule, and the warning should apply.

---

[33] *R v King* (1914) 10 Cr App Rep 117.

[34] *McNee v Kay* (1953) VLR 520.

[35] *Dental Board v O'Callaghan* [1969] IR 181.

[36] *AG v Linehan* [1929] IR 19.

[6.30] The Court of Criminal Appeal, in *People (DPP) v Murtagh*,[37] held that in a prosecution for the offence of subornation of perjury, the perjurer is an accomplice of the suborner, and the trial judge must warn the jury that, although they may convict on the evidence of an accomplice, it is dangerous to do so unless it is corroborated. Likewise, in a prosecution for an offence of attempting to pervert the course of justice by inciting another person to make a false statement to the gardaí, that other person, by allowing himself to be incited, is an accomplice to the accused's crime and the same warning must be given.

[6.31] In *People (DPP) v Hogan*,[38] with regard to the necessity of giving a warning in relation to the dangers attendant on the evidence of an accomplice, the court emphasised that the purpose of pointing to the need for corroboration was not to confirm the accomplice's account but to find whether it implicates the accused in the crime with which he is charged.

[6.32] In *People (DPP) v Meehan*[39] Juliette Bowden, the wife of Charles Bowden (the Witness Protection Programme participant), while not herself charged or convicted of any offence related to the events of the case, was so clearly identified with those who were members of the drug importation gang that her evidence was treated on the same basis as that of an accomplice. This is evidence of an approach that is flexible enough to accommodate a cautious approach where the rationale or reasoning for caution may be present and the same as that in relation to an accomplice, although the definition of an accomplice may not be met.

[6.33] The Irish approach to the warning, would seem to be one where the format of same can vary from case to case. The degree of gravity and complicity may vary, and in as much as complicity will vary, so will the strength of the warning.

[6.34] One issue that has led to some difficulty is that of who decides when the witness is an accomplice. Cross[40] postulates that there are three potential situations here. Firstly, where there is no evidence that the witness is an accomplice, and hence no warning is necessary. Secondly, the English authorities have indicated that the matter may have to be left to a jury with a warning to the effect that if they think a witness is an accomplice, they should be cautious before convicting. Thirdly, it has been stated that in some cases the trial judge will direct that a particular witness is an accomplice because of the weight of the evidence proferred.

---

[37] *People (DPP) v Murtagh* [1990] 1 IR 339.
[38] *People (DPP) v Hogan* (21 January 1994, unreported), CCA.
[39] *People (DPP) v Meehan* (29 July 1999, unreported), SCC.
[40] *Cross on Evidence* (7th edn, Butterworths, 1990), pp 219–222.

[6.35] In *People (AG) v Carney*,[41] the defendants were jointly charged with shop-breaking and receiving stolen goods. They were convicted on a charge of receiving. The trial judge left the question to the jury as to whether the witness against them was an accomplice or not. The Supreme Court felt that it was not proper to leave to the jury the issue of whether the witness was an accomplice. The nature of the warning to the jury should not have been dependent on whether the witness was an accomplice or not, but should have been absolute and unconditional.

[6.36] O'Byrne J for the majority, based his view on a reasonable view of the evidence. The witness was an accomplice within the meaning of *Linehan*, being involved in the crime either as a principal or accessory. The majority were satisfied that in the circumstances, the trial judge should not have left the issue to the jury, but should have given an absolute and unconditional warning. Dixon J dissented, holding that it was for the jury to decide whether the witness was an accomplice. While the trial judge should have put the view more forcibly as to who was an accomplice, the issue was for the jury to decide.

[6.37] An example of an instance of corroboration in relation to accomplices is given in *R v Cramp*,[42] where the silence of the accused, when a reply was to be expected, was held to corroborate the testimony of a girl whose miscarriage was alleged to have been attempted by the accused. The silence of the accused was in response to the girl's father's statement, 'I have here those things you gave my daughter to produce abortion'.

[6.38] An important rule in the context of accomplice evidence is the rule against mutual corroboration. One accomplice cannot corroborate another (*R v Gay*,[43] confirming the earlier decision to that effect in *R v Noakes*[44]). This rule was disapproved of in the context of children in *DPP v Hester*.[45]

[6.39] In *DPP v Kilbourne*,[46] a case which involved two groups of young boys, against which the accused had allegedly perpetrated assaults in 1970 and 1971, the court felt that, while children within each group could not corroborate each other, members of one group could corroborate members of the other group. To this extent, therefore, that 'third' category of witnesses considered to be accomplices could corroborate each other. In *Kilbourne*, Halisham LJ stated that:

---

[41] *People (AG) v Carney* [1955] IR 324.

[42] *R v Cramp* (1880) 5 QB 307.

[43] *R v Gay* (1909) 2 CR App Rep 327.

[44] *R v Noakes* (1832).

[45] *DPP v Hester* [1973] AC 297.

[46] *DPP v Kilbourne* [1973] AC 728 at 747.

[The rule against mutual corroboration] ... applies to those in the first and second of Lord Simond LC's categories and to many other cases where witnesses are not or may not be accomplices. It does not necessarily apply to all witnesses in the same case who may deserve to be categorised as 'accomplice'. In particular it does not necessarily apply to accomplices of Lord Simond LC's third class where they give independent evidence of separate incidents, and where the circumstances are such as to exclude the danger of a jointly fabricated story.

[6.40] The abolition of the rule against mutual corroboration was proposed by the English Criminal Law Reform Committee.[47] The Criminal Justice and Public Order Act 1994, s 32(1) abolished the warning requirement in relation to alleged accomplices and complainants in sexual cases. There are now very few cases where corroboration is a legal requirement under English law and none where a judge is required to give a corroboration warning.[48] Nevertheless, there may well be greater justification for the rule against mutual corroboration's continuance in the context of accomplices than in that of children, because the factors making it dangerous to rely on the evidence of both types of witnesses are different. Whereas accomplices may tend to tell the same lie, ie one against the accused, there is no reason to suppose that children's imaginations should lead to the same untruth.

[6.41] Quite often, if a witness is tendered who qualifies to be considered as an accomplice, that witness may have struck a deal guaranteeing immunity from prosecution with the authorities. In England, it is only the Crown that has such authority; in Ireland only the DPP should give an offer of immunity, not the gardaí. Should the latter make such an offer, it would probably amount to an 'inducement'.

[6.42] In the New Zealand case of *R v Weightman*,[49] the witness was given such immunity from prosecution in return for his testimony. He was deemed an accomplice, and it was suggested that in addition to the normal warning, the jury should be told he was escaping prosecution because of his testimony.

[6.43] The supergrass phenomenon in Northern Ireland led to the issue of accomplice evidence being the subject of scrutiny by Tony Gifford QC, who conducted an investigation under the auspices of the Cobden Trust in 1984. The terms of reference of the inquiry were as follows:

---

[47] Criminal Law Revision Committee, Eleventh Report, *Evidence (General)* (1972) Cm 4991, paras 186–188.

[48] See further Dennis *The Law of Evidence* (3rd edn, Thomson Sweet & Maxwell, 2007) at 643.

[49] *R v Weightman* [1978] 1 NZLR 79.

i. Whether and in what circumstances the interests of justice can be served by the uncorroborated evidence of accomplices in criminal trials in the United Kingdom.

ii. What particular considerations arise from the use of such evidence in non-jury trials in Northern Ireland.

iii. What consequences may the keeping of such accomplices and their families in protective custody have for their interests and the interests of justice generally.[50]

[6.44] Gifford QC concluded from his survey that the use of supergrass evidence can lead and has led to the telling of lies and to the conviction of the innocent. He felt the use of supergrasses in Northern Ireland had discredited the judicial institutions and, in the context of Northern Ireland, recommended the abolition of the Diplock Court system, the restoration of the jury and the warning of the latter by the trial judge of the dangers involved. Should the Diplock Court system continue, however, Gifford recommended that there should be no further grant of immunity from prosecution to those who have been repeatedly involved in serious terrorist crimes;[51] and that the uncorroborated evidence of a supergrass should not be accepted as a valid basis for convicting a defendant in a non-jury court. Gifford felt that defendants should no longer be convicted on uncorroborated supergrass evidence, prosecutions should not in such cases be initiated by the DPP, trial judges should adopt the criterion that it is highly dangerous and wrong to convict on the uncorroborated evidence of a supergrass and the Court of Appeal should, when faced with that uncorroborated evidence, examine very carefully whether the convictions which have been recommended are safe and satisfactory.[52] His final recommendation was that parliament should legislate to provide safeguards for the Diplock system by a simple measure which provides that in a Diplock Court there must, as a matter of law, be corroboration of the evidence of an accomplice.

[6.45] What is interesting about Gifford's report is the extent to which he distinguishes supergrass evidence from accomplice evidence in general, and in that context justifies a stronger corroboration requirement in relation to that species of accomplice. What the report does not address is the issue of the rationale of the corroboration requirement in relation to accomplices generally, in the first place.

---

[50] Gifford, *Supergrasses: the Use of Accomplice Evidence in Northern Ireland* (Cobden Trust, 1984).

[51] Gifford, *Supergrasses: the Use of Accomplice Evidence in Northern Ireland* (Cobden Trust, 1984), para 98 at p 35.

[52] Gifford, *Supergrasses: the Use of Accomplice Evidence in Northern Ireland* (Cobden Trust, 1984), paras 100–102 at p 36.

[6.46] In *R v Turner*[53] Lawton LJ addressed the issue of the corroboration requirement in the context of a witness testifying against the perpetrators of a bank robbery, which offence the witness himself was involved in. The evidence of the witness had been secured by virtue of a deal granting immunity, given by the DPP, to him for those crimes. Lawton LJ addressed the historical issue of the corroboration requirement in relation to accomplices, first rejecting the contention on the part of the defence that such witnesses were not competent in such circumstances. Lawton LJ commented that there could be no doubt at common law that an accomplice who gave evidence for the Crown in the expectation of getting a pardon for doing so, was a competent witness. The nineteenth century contribution to this topic, he noted, was to introduce a rule of practice that judges should warn juries of the dangers of convicting on the uncorroborated evidence of accomplices. In this century that practice became a rule of law.

[6.47] In relation to whether the trial judge should exercise his discretion to exclude such testimony, Lawton LJ stated that:

> If the inducement is very powerful, the judge may decide to exercise his discretion; but when doing so he must take into consideration all factors, including those affecting the public. It is in the interests of the public that criminals should be brought to justice; and the more serious the crimes the greater is the need for justice to be done. Employing Queen's evidence to accomplish this end is distasteful and has been distasteful for at least 300 years to judges, lawyers and members of the public. It is, however, no part of our function to add to the weight of ethical condemnation or to dissipate it. We are concerned to decide what the law is and whether the judge should, as a matter of discretion, have excluded Smalls' evidence, and whether, having admitted it, he gave the jury an adequate warning about acting on it.[54]

[6.48] Lawton LJ did continue to consider the witness's (Small's) position in this case when he gave evidence and noted that all charges preferred against him had already been terminated at that stage. There was no real likelihood of his being prosecuted if he refused to give evidence. These facts would have justified the judge in refusing to exercise his discretion to exclude Small's evidence had he been so requested. Lawton LJ further found that there was no question but that the judge had given adequate direction to the jury as to the danger of Small's evidence and the need for corroboration. He concluded:

> Further, if the jury found Small's to be a credible witness, as they did, and there was independent evidence supporting him we can find no reason for adjudging that verdict based on his evidence were unsafe or unsatisfactory.

---

[53]   *R v Turner* (1975) 61 Cr App Rep 67.
[54]   *R v Turner* (1975) 61 Cr App Rep 67 at 79.

However, Lawton LJ then issued the following caution:

> Undertakings of immunity from prosecution may have to be given in the public interest. They should never be given by the police. The Director should give them most sparingly; and in cases involving grave crimes it would be prudent of him to consult the law officers before making any promises. In saying what we have, we should not be taken as doubting the well-established practice of calling accomplices on behalf of the Crown who have been charged in the same indictment as the accused and who have pleaded guilty.

[6.49] Whereas the requirement was mandatory if an accomplice gave evidence for the prosecution, it was discretionary if he did so on his own behalf *(R v Bagley*[55]). In *Muff*,[56] the Court of Appeal held that, in deciding whether to give the warning, the judge must weigh the difficulties of achieving a fair trial of the defendant who has given evidence implicating another defendant, against the risk that the trial of a person implicated by that evidence will not be fair unless a warning is given.

[6.50] In England, parliament abolished the warning requirement for children in s 34(2) of the Criminal Justice Act 1988, and for accomplices and complainants in s 32(1) of the Criminal Justice (Public Order) Act 1994.

[6.51] In Ireland it is notable that the Criminal Law (Rape) (Amendment) Act 1990 and the Criminal Evidence Act 1992 amended the corroboration requirement in relation to sexual offences complainants and children respectively – but not accomplices. Indeed in *People (DPP) v Hogan*,[57] the Court of Criminal Appeal emphasised 'that the purpose of pointing to the need for corroboration was not to confirm the accomplice's account but to find whether it implicated the accused in the crime with which he was charged.' This represents adherence to the traditional application and meaning of corroboration in the context of accomplices and is a useful litmus test for some of the more recent accomplice evidence cases.

[6.52] An issue has arisen in particular in Ireland in the context of accomplice evidence and corroboration, of whether that warning needs to be *strengthened* in the context of those who have done a deal with the state in return for their testimony. This was evident in cases in the aftermath of the killing of journalist Veronica Guerin and the subsequent introduction of a Witness Protection Programme in the Irish state.

---

[55] *R v Bagley* [1980] *CrimLR* 572, CA.

[56] *Muff v R* (2 November 1979, unreported), CA.

[57] *People (DPP) v Hogan* (21 January 1994, unreported), CCA.

Evidence of witnesses in Witness Protection Programme

[6.53] The following cases concern the evidence of those who are participants in the state's witness protection programme. The charges are generally (though not exclusively) related to the killing of Veronica Guerin and the forum is the non-jury Special Criminal Court. Both of these are significant factors. The cases are:

1. *The People v Ward (Special Criminal Court)*;[58]

2. *People (DPP) v Ward (Court of Criminal Appeal)*;[59]

3. *DPP v Brian Meehan(Special Criminal Court)*[60]

4. *People (DPP) v Patrick Holland (Court of Criminal Appeal)*;[61] and

5. *People (DPP) v Gilligan (Supreme Court)*.[62]

[6.54] *In DPP v Ward*,[63] *DPP v Holland*[64] and *DPP v Meehan*[65] the use of accomplice evidence through the medium of the state's Witness Protection Programme was sanctioned. The Special Criminal Court refused to accept that any particular warning was required in relation to such participants, apart from the standard warning in relation to accomplices.

[6.55] The aftermath of the killing of Veronica Guerin led to the introduction of the so-called 'crime package' (drug trafficking, Criminal Assets Bureau and proceeds of crime legislation). The opening paragraph of the Special Criminal Court judgment in Ward recounting the murder of Veronica Guerin gives a useful indication of that context. *Per* Barr J:[66]

> On 26 June 1996, Ms Veronica Guerin, a distinguished brave journalist who specialised in the investigation of crime, was brutally murdered when she was riddled with bullets as she sat in her car waiting for traffic lights to change at the Naas Road junction, Clondalkin, Dublin. Eyewitnesses have established that, as the victim waited at the lights, a motorcycle on which there were two persons, drew up alongside her. The rider and the pillion passenger both wore full-sized helmets which concealed their faces. The pillion passenger broke a window in the driver's door and fired six bullets at point blank range into the car. All struck the victim and caused fatal injuries from which it is probable that she died within seconds. Thereupon the motorcycle sped away and disappeared. The accused has

---

58 *People (DPP) v Ward* (27 November 1998), SCC, Barr J.
59 *People (DPP) v Ward* (22 March 2002, unreported), CCA, Murphy J.
60 *People (DPP) v Meehan* (29 July 1999, unreported), SCC; CCA [2006] 3 IR 468
61 *People (DPP) v Holland* (15 June 1998, unreported), CCA, Barrington J.
62 *People (DPP) v Gilligan* (15 March 2001, unreported), SCC and [2006] 1 IR 107 (SC).
63 *People (DPP) v Ward* [1998] IEHC 154.
64 *People (DPP) v Holland* (15 June 1998, unreported), CCA.
65 *People (DPP) v Meehan* (29 July 1999, unreported), SCC CCA [2006] 3 IR 468
66 *People (DPP) v Ward* (27 November 1998), SCC, Barr J at p 1 of 39.

been charged with the murder of Ms. Guerin. The prosecution does not contend that he was the gunman or the motorcyclist or that he was present at the scene of the crime. The case against him is that he participated in the planning of the murder and that pursuant to such plans he played an important role in the crime by receiving from the killers very soon after the event the motorcycle and the gun which they had used and both of which he had disposed of thereafter. The evidence against the accused comprises verbal admissions allegedly made by him while in police custody following arrest under Section 30 of the Offences against the State Act 1939, on 16 October 1996, and the testimony of Charles Bowden, an accomplice whose evidence supports and establishes the accused was an accessory before the fact of Ms. Guerin's murder.

[6.56] The statement makes it clear that Paul Ward was not being charged as a principal but as an accessory before and after the facts, and it is clear the case against him involved a number of verbal admissions that he allegedly made during interrogation combined with the evidence of Charles Bowden, an accomplice. Hence this case will also be important for consideration regarding confession evidence. The judgment looks at verbal admission first and then looks at Charles Bowden's evidence, the latter being the state witness, accomplice and Witness Protection Programme participant. A number of Ward's statements were later denied. The court noted he was an experienced s 30 detainee but he was also a heroin addict and in the course of interrogation his girlfriend and his mother were brought in to the interrogation by the gardaí. This was not at the request of Ward and the courts were critical about why this was done. Was it to put pressure on Ward? As a result of the way in which he was treated during interrogation, the Special Criminal Court determined that they would not look at his confession statements. They looked into the conditions of how they were obtained (see paras **9.143** *et seq* on confession evidence) and decided not to admit them. As this was a non-jury trial (rather it was a trial by three judges alone in the Special Criminal Court), the judges made this determination themselves as arbiters of law (not one where the jury was absent for that legal argument) and then instructed themselves in their additional capacities as arbiters of fact to ignore that evidence. They were then put in the position of relying solely on the evidence of Charles Bowden.

[6.57] Again the courts' reasoning, as revealed in Barr J's judgment,[67] is insightful:

> The second leg of the prosecution case against the accused is the evidence of Charles Bowden an admitted accomplice in the murder of Ms. Guerin who also implicated the accused as one of those who participated in the planning of the murder and who he alleges in the course of that plan provided a crucial back-up

---

[67] *People (DPP) v Ward* (27 November 1998), SCC, Barr J at p18/39.

service for the actual killers by taking charge of the gun and motorcycle used in the crime at his home at 113 Walkinstown Road soon after the event and subsequently spoke to both. What may have been the motorcycle in question was later to be found in the river Liffey. The gun was never found and no information emerged at the trial as to what became of it. There is no doubt that at all times the gardaí have been anxious to trace the weapon.

[6.58] The first question for the court was Bowden's credibility and his status in the case. Barr J asked whether he was a common or garden accomplice or one of a category of accomplices found in similar cases in courts in Northern Ireland, a supergrass. Mr McEntee, counsel representing Ward, had contended that Bowden was akin to a supergrass and referred the court to the decision of *Queen v Steenson*[68] where Lord Chief Justice Lowry had approached the evidence of Kirkpatrick (a supergrass) with great reserve and suspicion. In the course of his judgment Lord Lowry had approved an earlier judgment of Lord Justice Hutton in the *Crown v Crumley*, an unreported supergrass case where Lord Hutton's stated:

> It is essential for a judge to warn juries and to remember if he is the tribunal of fact that it is dangerous to convict any accused on any count of an indictment on the evidence of an accomplice if uncorroborated as to that accused and as to that count. But a supergrass is no ordinary criminal and no ordinary accomplice. Therefore the extent that what is known about the supergrass's character and situation increases the probability that he would be an unreliable witness. The danger of acting on his uncorroborated evidence is increased. In this case, as in so many similar cases, we are confronted with a witness who, by his own admission, was a man of lawless character, a member of an unlawful organisation dedicated to violence and the principle that the end justifies any means including indiscriminate murder and a person who has wholeheartedly engaged in all the activities of that organisation. He is not just a cornered criminal who is reluctantly disgorging information to save himself from enduring the penalty of perhaps one moderately serious crime. But he has volunteered a veritable mass of damning information against men whom he alleges to have been his confederates to whom and with whom he is bound by an oath to further a joint cause which he no doubt regarded as patriotic. His motive may be fear, despair or hope of an enormously improved life for the future or a mixture of all three. Wherever the truth lies, his motive is extremely powerful. It is manifest that the evidence of such a witness must stand up successfully to the sternest criteria before it can be accepted and become the sole basis for being satisfied beyond reasonable doubt that the accused is guilty of any offence charged against him.[69]

---

[68] *Queen v Steenson and others* [1986] 17 NIBJ 36.
[69] *Crown v Crumley* [1984, unreported) quoted with approval by Lord Lowry LCJ in *Queen v Steenson and others* [1986] 17 NIBJ 36 at 45.

The essence of this approach is one which says that a witness who has made a deal has to be approached with even more caution that one who has not; a supergrass is no ordinary criminal or accomplice. But there is a distinction: whereas supergrasses were brought in to testify against more than one accused, arguably Bowden here was on his first outing, although he later reappeared in other cases involving Meehan and Gilligan. Another distinction, arguably, is the organisation element of it; the reference to 'patriotic duty' makes the point that a rather more tightly regarded organisational basis than in Ward's case may have been present.

[6.59] Some elements are, however, similar. In both cases, the witnesses are trying to do the best deal possible to secure a new life: Bowden and others are dependent on the state for this. That would argue that the Special Criminal Court here should treat Bowden the same way as the Northern Irish courts would supergrasses and that is to take even more care, bringing in sterner criteria. This might be seen to be particularly so here given that the confessions are not admissible and the accomplice evidence is the sole basis of conviction here. Nonetheless the Special Criminal Court in *Ward* reasoned as follows:[70]

> This court is satisfied that Charles Bowden is not a supergrass in the sense envisaged by Hutton L. J. but when admitting his own part in the Guerin murder and in implicating others in that crime, including the accused, he furnished information to the police as a cornered criminal to extricate himself in part at least from a grievous situation in which he found himself.

[6.60] The Special Criminal Court concluded[71] that Bowden was without doubt:

> without doubt a self-serving, deeply avaricious, and potentially vicious criminal. On his own admission he is a liar, and the Court readily accepts that he would lie without hesitation and regardless of the consequences for others if he perceived it to be in his own interest to do so. The court fully appreciates that assessment of his evidence must be made with great caution and with the foregoing firmly in mind.

[6.61] They then scrutinised his evidence, and one might anticipate that they were going to be cautious with Bowden:[72]

> Mr Bowden is an intelligent man. The court is satisfied that the reason for his conversion to the alleged truth had nothing to do with remorse as he contends but is the product of a cold dispassionate assessment of his grievous situation at that time and amounted to a decision on his part to extricate himself as best he could from what he probably perceived to be the reality of the situation then... The

---

[70] *Per* Barr J in *People (DPP) v Ward* (27 November 1998), SCC, at p 20/39.
[71] *Per* Barr J in *People (DPP) v Ward* (27 November 1998), SCC, Barr J at p 22/39.
[72] *People (DPP) v Ward* (27 November 1998), SCC at pp 24–25/39.

court is satisfied that Bowden was motivated by self-interest in voluntarily admitting his own involvement and that of others in the murder of Ms. Guerin. The conclusion is inescapable that he would have perceived himself as being at high risk of conviction for the murder of Ms. Guerin; that all his money would be lost, and that after conviction his bargaining position might very well be reduced to zero. He had every reason to seek to bail himself out of that dreadful situation as best he could, and soon. He did so. He has agreed to turn State evidence in this and other related trials in return for a written undertaking from the DPP not to prosecute him for the murder of Ms. Guerin. He has also obtained modest prison sentences having pleaded guilty to major drugs and arms crimes. He has secured special concessions while in prison and his wife and children have been given the benefit of the Witness Protection Programme. Although not yet finally negotiated, it seems likely that when Bowden serves his sentences or earlier, he will be released and set up with a new identity in a foreign country and some money in lieu of his substantial ill-gotten gains will be provided for him. It seems that he has made what from his perspective appears to have been probably the best bargain he could hope to achieve from the State in all the circumstances.

However, there is no doubt Bowden would also appreciate, that to achieve the foregoing advantages, it would be in his best interest to tell the truth about all the relevant details known to him relating to the murder and also the Gilligan criminal business enterprise. He is clever enough to realise and he has been told in terms that the information he has furnished will be thoroughly checked out. He knows if he is found to be lying as to any material fact, much of the situation he has established for himself and his family may be jeopardised. The Court accepts that Bowden is fully aware that it is in his best interests to tell the truth about those involved in the murder and he is likely to have done so unless on any issue crucial to the case against the accused, Paul Ward, it appeared to him, Bowden, that it was or might be in his interests to lie and wrongly implicate the accused. If in assessing the evidence the court has a reasonable doubt that that might then be so then Bowden's evidence against the accused would be fatally flawed and would have to be rejected. In the final analysis, that is the net issue in the case.

The evidence given by Bowden about the Gilligan business enterprise, and the major part played by him and others including the accused and Brian Meehan in it, has been corroborated and supported in its essentials by the accused in evidence. It seems therefore that he, Bowden, has told the truth about these matters.

The court concludes:[73]

The end result is that up to an advanced point in the narrative relating to the murder of Ms. Guerin, Charles Bowden appears to have been giving a truthful account of events which is substantially corroborated or is unchallenged by the accused.

---

[73] *People (DPP) v Ward* (27 November 1998), SCC at p.31/39.

The positing here of an alternative to corroboration being that of the evidence remaining unchallenged by the accused is interesting and questionable.

[6.62] Later on the Special Criminal Court concluded: '[a]ll in all Bowden's evidence about the accused' involvement in the crime has a strong ring of truth about it.'[74] They then came to the question which was at the root of this case: was there any basis on which the court might reasonably suspect that Bowden had an interest to lie about the accused and wrongly implicate him in the crime of murdering of Ms Guerin?

> [I]f on assessment of the evidence the court has a reasonable doubt that that might be so, then Bowden's evidence against the accused must be rejected. The court can find nothing in the evidence that raises suspicion. The court has carefully considered all the evidence and can find nothing in it which might support a contention that Bowden had a motive of self-interest to implicate the accused in the crime. The court bears in mind that, apart from the gun, there was the question of disposing of the motorcycle. There is not the slightest suggestion Bowden or anyone else, other than the accused, had a responsibility in that regard. The court is satisfied beyond reasonable doubt that Bowden's evidence implicating the accused in the crime is correct and ought to be regarded as truthful.[75]

The court convicted Ward and that conviction was appealed. Some issues on appeal related to Bowden's evidence; unsurprisingly, as the prosecution and conviction rested primarily on that evidence. Indeed, Murphy J, delivering the judgment of the Court of Criminal Appeal, commented that 'the case of the prosecution consisted virtually, if not entirely, of the evidence given by Mr Charles Bowden'.[76]

[6.63] In consideration of the appeal, the Court of Criminal Appeal pointed out:[77]

> Numerous other facets of the conduct and character of Charles Bowden were explored in cross-examination with a view to establishing and illustrating – as it did – that Bowden lied and lied again and again. This is not merely the submission made on the part of the defence. It was the unequivocal finding of the Special Criminal Court and it was the frank and unavoidable admission of Mr Bowden himself that he was an inveterate liar. In addition to lies, the cross-examination exposed a variety of errors and inaccuracies in the evidence given against the accused. Some of these were of particular importance. The credibility of Charles Bowden as a witness was further compromised by the fact that he was

---

[74] *People (DPP) v Ward* (27 November 1998), SCC at p 32/39.

[75] *People (DPP) v Ward* (27 November 1998), SCC at p 33–34/39.

[76] *People (DPP) v Ward* (22 March 2002, unreported), CCA, Murphy J at p 5/20.

[77] *People (DPP) v Ward* (22 March 2002, unreported), CCA, Murphy J at p 12/20.

an accomplice in the particular crime of which Paul Ward was accused. But he was much more than that. He was a witness to whom immunity was granted in respect of a murder to which he had, in effect, confessed and in addition he, his wife and his children were, understandably, afforded the benefit of the witness protection programme under which he was to be given the opportunity of living in a different jurisdiction with a new identify and some unspecified income. The law has always recognised that the evidence of an accomplice – even an accomplice who appears to be a credible witness – must be corroborated from independent sources or alternatively that the jury should be warned, or a tribunal of fact reminded, of the danger of convicting without such corroboration. Whether or not Charles Bowden fell within the category comprised in the slang expression '*supergrass*', clearly his general lack of credibility and his position as a criminal negotiating with the authorities to secure advantages for himself at the expense of his former friends and criminal associates did require that his evidence be considered with the utmost care.

Murphy J then continued to state that there was no doubt that the Special Criminal Court clearly and correctly recognised Bowden's lack of credibility and the problems to which that gave rise. (He quoted from the section of the judgment where Bowden is described as deeply avaricious.) However, undoubtedly the indication here is that Murphy J took a colder view of the evidence which was tendered and was more cautious of even regular accomplice evidence.

[6.64] Ultimately, the trial court had, notwithstanding the 'serious shortcomings' of Mr Bowden as a credible witness, expressed itself satisfied beyond reasonable doubt that the accused was guilty as charged. Murphy J[78] commented on the reasoning of the lower court:

> The court did not base its conclusion on the manner in which Mr Bowden gave his evidence or his demeanour. Instead it examined the logic of Mr Bowden's position. It fully accepted Bowden would lie and lie readily and unhesitatingly to protect his own interests irrespective of the consequence for others. The court then raised the question what interest would Bowden have for lying so he could implicate Ward. It could find none. Indeed their view to that extent is supported by Ward himself who was unable to suggest there was any difference between himself and Bowden or that the latter bore him any ill will. The importance to Mr Bowden of telling the truth (or at any rate not lying) in relation to Paul Ward was emphasised by the Special Criminal Court at p 25 of the judgment where the President said:-
>
>> He knows that if he is found to be lying much of the situation he established for himself and his family may be jeopardised.

---

[78] *People (DPP) v Ward* (22 March 2002, unreported), CCA, Murphy J at p 14–15/20.

That analysis underscores the vulnerability of Mr Bowden's position but does not explain who would determine whether Mr Bowden was lying, or by reference to what standard. Mr Bowden had made statements to the gardaí which supported – but did not coincide – with the statements allegedl to have been taken by the gardaí. Would a departure from those statements be regarded as a lie that would jeopardise the future of Mr Bowden? Certainly it is questionable whether one could be confident of eliminating all factors which would motivate and encourage liars, such as Mr Bowden, so as to justify a belief beyond all reasonable doubt in any evidence given by him.

In reading the record of the evidence, the Court of Criminal Appeal cannot assess the credibility of Charles Bowden nor the cogency of evidence of primary facts, or of inferences of fact which were dependent upon the credibility of Charles Bowden. The function of the Court of Criminal Appeal is to consider whether, in relation to the several grounds of appeal the evidence accepted by the Special Criminal Court, on its assessment of the credibility of the witnesses, fairly and properly supports the finding of that court, and whether inferences drawn as disclosed on the transcript were fairly and properly drawn, having regard to the onus of proof which lies on the prosecution ... However, a decision based on an error of law or logic, or a demonstrable misapprehension of a known fact, must be susceptible of correction.'

[6.65] The implication is clear that Murphy J does not completely accept the notion that you can discount any difficulty because of the interests Bowden had in securing a deal for his family. He did not see Bowden in court or witness his demeanour, however, so he would not interfere in the Special Criminal Court's assessment, but the implication is that he may well have gone the other way.

[6.66] Returning to the trial, the Special Criminal Court in their judgment made reference to the fact that the motorcycle was disposed of by Ward, having been brought to his house in Walkinstown. The difficulty here is that there was no evidence that the bike had been brought to his house. The only evidence that had suggested this was the statement allegedly made by Ward during interrogation. The Special Criminal Court had excluded those statements as being either involuntary or fabricated by the gardaí. However, it would appear that the trial judges had got confused and, having excluded that evidence, had evidently not completely wiped it from their minds. Murphy J commented:[79]

The reality of the matter would appear to be that the Special Criminal Court was misled by the confusing evidence and voluminous documentation placed before it. The statement that the motorcycle and the gun had been brought to the premises in Walkinstown was alleged to have been made by Ward to the gardaí. That statement had been accepted in evidence and referred to throughout the course of the trial. It was only when judgment was delivered that the court

---

[79] *People (DPP) v Ward* (22 March 2002, unreported), CCA, at pp 18–19.

excluded from its consideration the statements alleged to have been made to the gardaí which were then rejected ... The contention that both the bike and the gun were [delivered to the premises at Walkinstown] ... was not supported by the evidence. This court would not be justified in assuming that the Special Criminal Court was or could have been satisfied that the gun was received by Mr Ward and the bike was not.

[6.67] On appeal, it became clear then that the Special Criminal Court misled itself. It paid attention to something in the evidence which had been excluded. This is undoubtedly a function of the fact that corroboration rules in general and the accomplice rule in particular here presumes, and indeed is predicated upon, a division of function between trier of fact and trier of law – as is the case in a jury trial. This is not the position in the non-jury Special Criminal Court and is self-evidently a potential problem wherever no jury exists. That problem has manifested itself here in the Special Criminal Court misleading itself.

[6.68] A further issue which arose on appeal was that the defence had asked for a number of transcripts of later cases (*Meehan* and *Gilligan*[80] in particular) to be admitted, which was unusual. The reason they did this was because Bowden had testified in those cases also, and they made the argument that he had there contradicted what he had said earlier in testimony. Murphy J commented on this as follows:[81]

> It is difficult to see any circumstance in which a finding made in a subsequent case in any court, as to the character and integrity of any witness or party could be evidence on appeal. However, there are extreme cases in which facts established in later cases may so undermine the basis on which an earlier case has been decided, that it would be appropriate to have regard to the later cases on an appeal in the former ... It was impossible in the present case to identify any comparable far-reaching breach of fair procedures and much of the evidence which it was sought to introduce merely went to the credibility of the State's only material witness. However to avoid any possible injustice, this Court permitted the applicant to extract material from the transcripts in the two subsequent trials relating to certain specified topics which might have had the capacity to undermine the substance of a fair trial. In fact the evidence adduced was not material to this court in reaching its decision but it might be said that it illustrated further, if that were necessary, the difficulties of ensuring the integrity of the evidence of an accomplice whose evidence is such that he must be admitted to a witness protection programme.

---

[80] *DPP v Meehan* (29 July 1999, unreported), SCC; *DPP v Gilligan* (15 March 2001, unreported), SCC.

[81] *People (DPP) v Ward* (22 March 2002, unreported), CCA, at pp 19–20.

[6.69] That point – that the later cases illustrate further the difficulty of ensuring the integrity of the evidence of an accomplice whose evidence is such that he must be admitted to a Witness Protection Programme – is a more significant marker of the need for special caution in these cases and the fact that it emerged from a situation where the later evidence of an accomplice, who was part of a Witness Protection Programme was available for comparison and led to this comment, gives it particular bite. The only comforting factor that emerged from the case (and was noted by Murphy J) is that the availability of a reasoned judgment from the non-jury court facilitated an appeal here, where a verdict of a jury (non-reasoned) would not. Some might view that as cold comfort indeed.

[6.70] There are a number of interesting things about *Ward's* case:

1. The Irish courts had turned their face against treating Witness Protection Programme participant evidence as being anything other than regular accomplice evidence. There is more than a suggestion in Murphy J's judgment of the Court of Criminal Appeal of an appreciation of the need for more caution.

2. It is also clear that there is a difficulty with a non-jury court in terms of applying rules of evidence in the context of confessions and, arguably, accomplice testimony.

3. To some extent, the finding of corroboration is said by the Special Criminal Court to lie in the accused's testimony. Corroboration is supposed to be independent testimony but in *Ward* the only source was Ward himself. This is quite apart from the fact that evidence from his statements was considered, which should not have been.

[6.71] In *People (DPP) v Holland*[82] the Court of Criminal Appeal again manifested a great deal of trust in the Special Criminal Court warning itself. Barrington J,[83] delivering the judgment of the court, said that:

> it is quite clear from the evidence that the accomplice in this particular case was one in relation to whom a Court was entitled to have the greatest reservations but again it is clear that the Court which tried the case was a Court of three Senior and experienced judges and it is not necessary for them to repeat again that they are warning themselves. If they say they have warned themselves of the dangers of acting on the uncorroborated testimony of this accomplice [Russell Warren], then it appears to us that we must accept that they mean what they say.

[6.72] In *People (DPP) v Meehan*[84] the Court of Criminal Appeal emphasised that corroboration is not a prerequisite to a conviction where the main evidence

---

[82] *People (DPP) v Holland* (15 June 1998, unreported), CCA, Barrington J.
[83] *People (DPP) v Holland* (15 June 1998, unreported), CCA at 9–13.
[84] *People (DPP) v Meehan* [2006] 3 IR 468. CCA

against the accused was that of an accomplice. It was a corroboration warning, not corroboration, that was the mandatory requirement. Here Russell Warren gave evidence against Meehan and his evidence was held to be corroborated by the telephone traffic between Warren and the accused. Significantly, with regard to the definition of corroboration, the Court of Criminal Appeal found a more flexible approach than that taken in *Baskerville* was open to it on the basis of the Irish case law.

[6.73] In the decision of *DPP v Gilligan*[85] detailed consideration was given to the overall existence of and practice surrounding the Witness Protection Programme. This deserves some consideration because of its implications for corroboration generally in relation to accomplice evidence, particularly where it is obtained through an arrangement with the state in exchange for testimony.

[6.74] At the accused's trial in the Special Criminal Court, on charges of the murder of Veronica Guerin and several offences regarding the importation of drugs, three witnesses were called who were alleged accomplices of the accused and were also part of a state Witness Protection Programme. The three witnesses were John Dunne, Charles Bowden and Russell Warren. The Special Criminal Court considered the very many arguments the defence had made in relation to the fragility of the evidence of these witnesses. The court took the view that Bowden and Warren were 'compromised witnesses' and that it should have grave reservations about the truthfulness of any piece of evidence that either of these men gave in the witness box. Nevertheless, the court did not accept that 'there was no vestige of truth in their evidence.' The Special Criminal Court ultimately convicted Gilligan only on drugs importation offences, not on Guerin's murder, due to insufficient corroboration of evidence. The accused appealed. In the appeal the submission was made that the evidence of witnesses in the Witness Protection Programme should be rejected entirely on the basis *inter alia* that: the witnesses had received money which could have been the proceeds of crime, they perceived their situation to be performance related, they had been interviewed by the gardaí and no record had been kept and they were never charged with serious offences where evidence against them existed. The state argued that evidence from those in such a programme was the same as any other and that if its probative value outweighed prejudicial effect, it should be admitted. The points of law certified on appeal were:

(1)   In what circumstances was evidence obtained from witnesses in a state Witness Protection Programme inadmissible and/or inconsistent with trial in due course of law?

(2)   Was corroboration as *per Baskerville* required?

---

[85]   *DPP v Gilligan* [2006] 1 IR 107.

[6.75] The Supreme Court took the view that the normal rules relating to accomplice evidence applied here and that as long as the trier of fact held the corroboration warning in mind, they might convict on the basis of same. They also felt that, there being no jury, once the trial court had indicated that it had read the relevant case law, there was no necessity to state expressly that it was warning itself.

[6.76] The comments in the judgments with regard to the Witness Protection Programme are interesting:

Regarding the first certified question, Denham J[86] opined:

A decision to establish a witness protection programme may be taken by the executive and/or the legislative organs of the State. However, it is the duty of the judicial branch of government to protect the constitutional right of fair trial, the right to due process. In carrying out this duty the court may have to balance competing rights, to consider the rights of different persons and groups of persons and of the community. It is necessary to analyse the situation to see if there has been an unfair process, or breach of constitutional rights of any person.'

[6.77] Reviewing those principles and case law under Art 38.1 (*Breathnach, Trimbole, State (Healy) v O'Donoghue*), Denham J concluded:[87]

While applying these principles to protect the rights of an accused the court will also have regard to the right of the people that offences be prosecuted. This may require the court to balance competing rights. On a hierarchy of constitutional rights, the accused's right to a fair trial is superior to the community's right to have the matter prosecuted: Z v *Director of Public Prosecutions* [1994] IR 465. The rights of the people is also part of the equation. This incorporates the right to have an accused prosecuted; the right to have a fair trial system in the community; and to guard against unfair trials which may lead to miscarriages of justice. The position of victims (and their families) should not be excluded from this equation either.

Thus in these few words of Art 38.1 is the root of our justice system, of a fair trial system. The balance and re-casting of the fairness equation here is most significant.

[6.78] Traditionally, the only concern was about the accused. Here the right of the people is considered important and their right to ensure that the accused has a fair trial. For the first time in any of these fair trial cases, the position of the victim is judged sufficiently important to also become part of the conceptual and

---

[86] *DPP v Gilligan* [2006] 1 IR 107 at 135.
[87] *DPP v Gilligan* [2006] 1 IR 107 at 137.

definitional framework of fairness. Denham J[88] then looked at the issue of the warning to be required:

> In contemplating the position of evidence from persons in a witness protection programme the law relating to the testimony of an accomplice is a useful analogy. The evidence of an accomplice is admissible and may ground a conviction even if there is no corroborating evidence. However it has been well settled in Irish common law that there should be a warning given to the jury of the danger of convicting on such evidence, absent corroborating evidence [*Dental Board v O'Callaghan* [1969] IR 181] ...

> The rationale behind the common law rule requiring a warning before acting on the uncorroborated evidence of an accomplice applies equally to the evidence of a person in, or who is going to join, a witness protection programme. There is a danger the witness may not be telling the truth in the hope of receiving benefits. In relation to the witness protection programme this applies also to expectations the witness may have into the future for him or herself and their family. Thus there is the danger the witness may seek to obtain additional benefits by his or her evidence. There are dangers especially where there has been a grant of immunity and/or the prosecution has supported the giving of a light sentence. These and other factors may arise in relation to witnesses in a witness protection programme.

> I am satisfied to ensure a fair trial the same approach should be taken to evidence given by a witness in a witness protection programme as to be given by an accomplice ... [T]here is no rule of law to the effect that the uncorroborated evidence of a person in or going into a witness protection programme must be rejected. The rule should be that the trier of fact must clearly bear in mind and be warned that it is dangerous to convict on the evidence of such a witness unless it is corroborated; but having borne that in mind and having given due weight to the warning ... then the trier of fact may act upon the evidence and convict.

[6.79] Looking to the definition of corroboration, the court endorsed *Baskerville* and noted there were three strands to corroborative evidence, ie that it:

1. tends to implicate the accused;

2. should be independent of the evidence which makes the corroboration desirable; and

3. should be credible.

[6.80] The Supreme Court[89] concluded that:

> it is clear from the judgment that the trial judge was aware of the dangers of convicting on evidence from a person who was both in a witness protection

---

[88] *DPP v Gilligan* [2006] 1 IR 107 at 138.
[89] *DPP v Gilligan* [2006] 1 IR 107 at 143 *per* Denham J.

programme and who was an accomplice. The trial court referred repeatedly to compromising facts and regarded the evidence cautiously. It took a different view in its assessment of the different witnesses. This illustrates that the application of the law as to corroboration is quintessentially a matter for the trier of fact after the appropriate warning is given.

[6.81] Denham J[90] then commented on the Witness Protection Programme, its dangers and benefits, and referred to the changing nature of crime in Ireland and the response to it:

> The situations which have given rise to such a programme are not unique to Ireland, they include organised crime, gang warfare, drug trafficking, and significant funds entering the criminal world by criminal activity such as selling drugs illegally. It has been determined in other jurisdictions that it was necessary to protect witnesses who give evidence of such activities. It is not unusual that a witness in a witness protection programme be both a member of the programme and an accomplice. Counsel for the accused did not seriously argue that there could not be a witness protection programme … but rather made submissions on the way the programme applicable to this case was organised and applied.

> [This] … was the first such programme in the State and there is no doubt it was undoubtedly not well organised or executed. It had deficiencies. However, the fact that it was not organised … the fact that it was not a perfect programme, is not immediately fatal.

[6.82] Denham J then considered these facts and circumstances and whether they rendered the trial unfair or not. She came to the conclusion that there is no doubt that payments of money being the proceeds of crime should not be made to accomplices expected to give evidence, but pointed out that the trial court held that it did not find that there had been a lack of bona fide by the members of An Garda Síochána. She stated that, '[t]here is no issue in this case of the executive consciously and deliberately violating constitutional rights. Thus the modern case-law commencing with The *People (Attorney General) v O'Brien* does not arise.'[91]

[6.83] This is an extraordinary sleight of hand, which allows the case law regarding fair trial and the approach in *O'Brien* and *Kenny* to be sidelined because of good intent or lack of bad – surely in direct contradiction to *Kenny*? Irish courts after all do care about how evidence is obtained. Evidence will not be admitted on occasion because of the manner in which it was obtained. The argument here is that the Witness Protection Programme was badly constructed and run and that the state should not be allowed to take advantage of that. Denham J sidestepped that issue by saying there was no deliberate breach of

---

[90] *DPP v Gilligan* [2006] 1 IR 107 at 143.
[91] *DPP v Gilligan* [2006] 1 IR 107 at 147.

constitutional rights, but earlier case law would have indicated that was not relevant. She regretted aspects of the procedures followed here[92] but did not find they compromised the entire criminal process. With regard to the warning, she decided that adequate care was taken by the trial court and addressed the fact that it is not necessary for Special Criminal Court judges to warn themselves:

> In this case the issue of the warning to be given as to the dangers of convicting on uncorroborated evidence was argued in the trial court. As the trial court was the trier of fact, there being no jury, once the trial court indicated it had read the relevant case law (as it did) I am satisfied there was no necessity for the trial court to state expressly that it was warning itself of the dangers of so convicting. The President of the trial court stated that the members of the trial court had read the relevant judgments. It was inferred throughout the judgment, in its method of analysing and by accepting or rejecting evidence, that the trial court was manifestly aware of the dangers of relying of such evidence where it was uncorroborated. The very tests established by the trial court as to the evidence of the three witnesses indicated this. So an express warning to itself would have been tautologous once it was clear the trial court was aware of the dangers of convicting on the uncorroborated evidence of a witness.[93]

[6.84] To some extent it might be seen as logical that it is not necessary for judges who are triers of fact to warn themselves. The rule undoubtedly exposes the artificiality of a rule of evidence that is dependent on a division between trier of fact and trier of law. That rule does not operate effectively when judges are sitting alone. It could, of course, be argued that the application of such a rule of evidence is in any event cosmetic. This statement goes further however. It says there is no need to go through even that pretence: You are judges, you know the rule. Ultimately, Denham J[94] concluded with a, perhaps unsurprising, contextual note:

> In an ideal world there would be no need for witnesses who are in a witness protection programme or who were accomplices of an accused. The development of a witness protection programme is a reflection of a need arising in our times. It is a consequence of a society where there are gangs, drug trafficking, violence and death, and very significant sums of money being made from criminal activity. Many cases, such as this, could not be brought unless there was evidence from an accomplice or a person in a witness protection programme. Of course the fact that a prosecution could not proceed without evidence of a witness in a witness protection programme is not determinative.

---

[92] *DPP v Gilligan* [2006] 1 IR 107 at 149.
[93] *DPP v Gilligan* [2006] 1 IR 107 at 158 *per* Denham J.
[94] *DPP v Gilligan* [2006] 1 IR 107 at 162.

It is for the executive or the legislature to establish a witness protection programme. The Director of Public Prosecutions having made the choice to use such a witness, it is for the courts to ensure that there is a fair trial.

[6.85] Were the challenges of gangs, violence and illicit money not ever thus, however, and is the challenge not precisely that of squaring those challenges with method and fair trial? The final statement of our Supreme Court on the issue is one of finessing such fairness to the exigencies of the moment rather than setting a marker which will last over time. Denham J:[95]

> In conclusion, evidence may be obtained from witnesses in a State witness protection programme, but such evidence is subject to the law and the Constitution. A warning should be given to the jury of the dangers of convicting on such evidence without corroboration ... Once such warning is given it is open to the trier of fact to make a finding of fact with or without corroborative evidence. Corroborative evidence should tend to implicate the accused in the commission of the offence, it should be independent of the evidence which makes corroborative evidence desirable ... and it should be credible.

The appeal of the accused was thus dismissed.

[6.86] What can one conclude from this series of cases regarding the Witness Protection Programme? Some jurisdictions consider special care is needed in relation to receipt of evidence from witnesses in protection programmes (this was particularly evident in Northern Ireland). In this jurisdiction, inevitably, most cases involving witnesses from the Witness Protection Programme will go directly to the Special Criminal Court because the DPP has determined that justice cannot be done in the ordinary courts. The Special Criminal Court has a difficulty with some of the rules of evidence that presuppose a division between trier of evidence and trier of law. In that context, are the courts being genuinely cautious with regard to this evidence? Have these cases been established beyond a reasonable doubt built on, some would say, the fragile ground of accomplice evidence? Certainly the accomplice evidence rule itself is endorsed by the Supreme Court. Whereas some jurisdictions have done away with the requirement of caution in relation to accomplices, in Ireland it remains the only traditional type of witness requirement retaining the corroborative requirement.

[6.87] But there is no additional augmentation for Witness Protection Programme participants and arguably it is only that phenomenon that has secured and continued the accomplice requirement, though Denham J quite clearly enunciates two characteristics of the witnesses: accomplices and those in the Witness Protection Programme. Nonetheless, the classification of danger at the mere level of accomplice here, the adjudication of fairness to include public/

---

[95] *DPP v Gilligan* [2006] 1 IR 107 at 163.

victim interest, the asserted relevance of garda bona fides and the use of contextualised arguments to justify state action bode ill for the accused's rights in this arena. The additional remit of the Special Criminal Court under the recent Criminal Justic (Amendment) Act 2009 can only serve to increase the occasion for similar adjudication.

Corroboration requirement in relation to confession evidence

[6.88] Section 10 of Criminal Procedure Act 1993 introduced an additional corroboration requirement into Irish law, just as it seemed as though such stylised requirements for caution were going out of fashion elsewhere (children and sexual offences victims having had their requirements lessened):

> Subsection 1 provides 'where at a trial of a person on indictment, evidence is given of a confession made by that person and that evidence is not corroborated, the judge shall advise the jury to have due regard to the absence of corroboration'; and

> Subsection 2 provides that it 'shall not be necessary for a judge to use any particular form of words under this section.'

[6.89] This legislative provision was seen to introduce a requirement in these cases that at least a warning be given to the jury. It therefore placed confessions in the same category as accomplices. The reason for this came about in part at least due to miscarriages of justice because of an overreliance on confession evidence (Guildford Four and Birmingham Six, for example). Until 1993, there was no such need for a warning under Irish law where someone had just a confession proffered in evidence against them. There were, nonetheless, quite a number of cases where someone had been convicted on the basis of a confession alone and the O'Briain Commission[96] had estimated that some 80% of criminal trials in Ireland turned on the admission of confession evidence, which gives an indication of the prevalence of confession-type evidence in the courts.

[6.90] There had also been a number of Irish cases where it had became evident on appeal that a conviction based on a confession was erroneous. One such case was *People v Lynch*.[97] Lynch had been charged and convicted of the murder of Vera Cullen. He did odd jobs for his landlord in various properties around Dublin. He found Cullen's body, reported it to the gardaí and spent 22 hours with them being questioned, at the end of which he confessed to having strangled Cullen. He appealed on the basis that the period of questioning had been oppressive and that the statement was not voluntary. Although the case is

---

[96] Committee to Recommend Certain Safeguard for persons in custody and for member of An Garda Síochána (Chairman: Hon Mr J Barra O'Briain), Dublin: Stationary Office (1978).

[97] *People v Lynch* [1982] IR 64.

mainly referred to in that context, it is noteworthy that in the course of the appeal it became evident that his claim that he had seen two people pushing a red Renault car near Cullen's house could be substantiated and that it established that he did not come within the time period when Cullen was killed. His conviction was overturned on the basis of the voluntariness of the confession but this case also underpins the rationale for a corroboration warning in cases such as his where there was no other evidence except a confession.

The main distinguishing feature of this second category of instances requiring corroboration or a warning to the jury as a matter of practice, as opposed to the earlier category requiring corroboration as a matter of law, is that in the former instance the jury has a right to convict despite the absence of corroborative evidence.

Visual identification evidence

[6.91] The third category of evidence (or an extension of the second) that requires corroboration to any degree, is one more recently developed by the judiciary – that of visual identification evidence. It merits separate consideration, in that it represents the most recent addition to this catalogue of evidence demanding corroboration, and requires it to a separate and different extent to those considered hitherto.

Rationale

[6.92] Perhaps the least contentious of those categories of evidence requiring corroboration to some degree, are those cases involving visual identification evidence. The rationale for the requirement in this instance is expressed variously in the dangers of defective memory; inadequate opportunity for recognition (the witness may have had only a fleeting glimpse of the individual in question); the likelihood a witness may have been overly influenced by tendered photographs or identikits; the possibility that the witness may err in relation to outsiders ('they all look alike to me' syndrome); and the likelihood of stubborn pride, in that the witness once committed to identifying the accused may be loath to reconsider. Finally, the usual way of overcoming risk in the context of testimonial error (that of cross-examination) is not all that effective in this context, an identification being either wrong or right, and not all that susceptible to that 'greatest legal engine ever invented for the discovery of truth'.[98]

---

[98] Wigmore, *A Treatise on the Anglo American System of Evidence in Trials at Common Law* (3rd edn, Boston: Little Brown & Co, 1940) Vol 5 (Chadbourne revision) par 1367.

The requirement

[6.93] The formulation of the corroboration requirement in relation to visual identification evidence occurred in the Supreme Court of Ireland in the decision of *People v Casey (No 2)*.[99] Casey had been convicted of assault and sentenced to four years' penal servitude. In the Court of Criminal Appeal, Casey challenged the veracity of the visual identification by witnesses to whom he was not previously known. One witness was a boy of eleven years; the other had caught a momentary view in the light of the headlamps of a car. On a point of law of public importance, the issue went to the Supreme Court. Kingsmill Moore J, delivering judgment, held that there should be a general warning given in all cases wholly or substantially dependent on visual identification evidence. He then formulated the direction that the trial judge should give the jury in such cases, as follows:

> We are of opinion that juries ... may not be fully aware of the dangers involved in visual identification nor of the considerable number of cases in which such identification has been proved to be erroneous; and also that they may be inclined to attribute too much probative effect to the test of an identification parade. In our opinion it is desirable that in all cases, where the verdict depends substantially on the correctness of an identification, their attention should be called in general terms to the fact that in a number of instances such identification has proved erroneous, to the possibilities of mistake in the case before them and to the necessity of caution. Nor do we think that such warning should be confined to cases where the identification is that of only one witness. Experience has shown that mistakes can occur where two or more witnesses have made positive identifications ...[100]

[6.94] The Irish courts were quite progressive in delineating such a requirement in relation to visual identification evidence. It was certainly true that such evidence had been found to be faulty on a number of occasions in the past, and had led to several (some quite notorious) false convictions. Indeed the Criminal Law Revision Committee in England, in its *Eleventh Report*,[101] regarded mistaken identification as by far the greatest cause of actual or possible wrong convictions. The English courts, however, showed an initial reluctance to impose such a requirement in these cases. In *Arthurs v AG for Northern Ireland*,[102] a case involving the identification by an RUC constable of the accused – at night and in the midst of a riot, hardly a situation conducive to a clear appraisal of

---

[99] *People v Casey (No 2)* [1963] IR 33.

[100] *People v Casey (No 2)* [1963] IR 33 at 38.

[101] Criminal Law Revision Committee, Eleventh Report, *Evidence (General)* (1972) Cm 4991 at para 196.

[102] *Arthurs v AG for Northern Ireland* (1971) 55 Cr App Rep 161.

identity – the House of Lords refused to impose such a requirement. They felt it undesirable to lay down that a general warning must be given where the case against the defendant depends wholly or substantially on identification evidence.

[6.95] In the subsequent decision of *R v Turnbull*,[103] however, the English courts relented, and laid down quite elaborate guidelines as to the manner in which they would approach the matter of visual identity and recognition in the future. Widgery LCJ initially set out and adopted the *Casey* requirement, namely, where the case against the accused depends wholly or substantially on eye-witness identification, which is alleged to be mistaken, the judge should warn the jury of the special need for caution. The court continued, that not only should the judge give the simple warning, but also the reasons for the warning should be explained to the jury. Widgery LCJ felt it should be pointed out that it is possible that a witness who sounds convincing has, in fact, made a mistake. The trial judge should direct the jury to examine the circumstances of the case in a minute fashion. There is also a duty on the prosecution, if there is a material discrepancy between the description given by a witness shortly after first sight of the culprit and the actual appearance of the accused, to furnish same to the accused. Likewise, if the accused asks for a description, he should be given it.

[6.96] The guidelines further indicate that the trial judge should remind the jury of any specific weaknesses in the prosecution evidence. Where the identification evidence is good, and a warning as to caution is given, then the trial judge can leave the jury to act. Where the identification evidence is of a poor quality, the trial judge should withdraw the case from the jury and direct an acquittal unless there is evidence supporting the identification. This supporting evidence would take the form of corroboration, or any other evidence which supports the identification evidence. The trial judge should always point to evidence which does, and evidence which does not, corroborate identification evidence. Finally, it was emphasised that the absence of the accused from the witness box is not evidence of anything, although the jury may take into account the fact that the identification has not been contradicted. The setting up of a false alibi, or telling lies, is not of itself proof that the accused was where the identifying witness says he was. Failure to follow these guidelines, the House concluded, is likely to result in a conviction being quashed.

[6.97] The Irish Court of Criminal Appeal in the decision of *People v Strafford*,[104] held that the warning in this context extended to cases of recognition (where the witness was previously acquainted with the appearance of the accused), and cited the guidelines laid down in the *Turnbull* decision. A

---

[103] *R v Turnbull* [1977] QB 224.
[104] *People v Strafford* [1983] IR 165.

decision of the Privy Council in *Scott v R*[105] confirmed the necessity of a direction by the trial judge on the issue of identification evidence.

The decisions in *Casey* and *Turnbull* lay down general principles, the application and relevance of which will depend on the particular facts of any given case.

[6.98] In the *People v Wallace*[106] the Irish Court of Criminal Appeal emphasised that if there are a number of counts on an indictment, and visual identification is an issue at trial, it is the duty of the trial judge to comment upon the visual identification, and draw the jury's attention to those courts to which it relates.

[6.99] The strength of the warning, similarly, will vary with the facts. In *People v Fagan*,[107] the accused had been convicted of the robbery of a garage attendant. The robbery had been carried out by two men, one of whom was masked. The attendant was brought to the District Court by the gardaí, and informed that he would there see the person who carried out the robbery. In these circumstances the attendant identified the accused. The trial judge gave a warning to the jury, in accordance with *Casey*. The Court of Criminal Appeal found that, having regard to the circumstances of the case, a much stronger warning should have been given.

[6.100] With regard to the manner in which the police obtain visual identification evidence, it is interesting to note that in *People v Mill*,[108] it was stated that gardaí can go around with a number of photos and show them to the victim of the crime for the purpose of identifying the culprit. The prosecution cannot, however, introduce these at trial, and they can only go into evidence if they are referred to in cross-examination.

[6.101] With regard to the conduct of identification parades, a decision of the Court of Criminal Appeal is instructive. In *People (DPP) v O'Reilly*,[109] that court laid down parameters with regard to the necessity for, and the conduct of, such parades. The applicant had been convicted of larceny and sentenced to four years' penal servitude. He applied for leave to appeal the conviction and sentence. Identification evidence was given by a woman aged 81 years, whose description of the perpetrator was 'a stout butt or a fair haired man' with 'a most notorious, and awful face'. The gardaí had brought that witness to the main street in Edgeworthstown (at or near the courthouse) to ascertain if she could identify anyone. She identified the applicant. The defence argued that evidence

---

[105] *Scott v R* [1989] 2 All ER 305.
[106] *People v Wallace* (22 November 1982, unreported), CCA.
[107] *People v Fagan* (1974) 1 Frewen 375, CCA.
[108] *People v Mill* [1957] IR 106.
[109] *People (DPP) v O'Reilly* [1990] 2 IR 415.

of identification should not have been admitted in the absence of a satisfactory explanation as to why a formal identification parade was not held, that fairness directs that no convenient shortcuts be taken by the state in obtaining evidence if it affects a defendant's ability to test the evidence adduced by the prosecution and that there were valuable safeguards which applied to the holding of formal identification parades, and one should be held unless there was a good reason for not doing so. The case was further complicated by the fact that photographs of the applicant were shown to the injured party, prior to the identification. The defence also contended that the *Casey* warning should not have been given in a general manner, but applied to the particular facts of the case.

[6.102] O'Flaherty J, delivering the judgment of the court, noted that the investigating garda had stated that in 23 years in the force he had never held an identification parade, and, in fact, felt that an informal identification was fairer to the accused because of the difficulty in picking someone out on a street with any number of other people around. In relation to the latter, O'Flaherty J noted that the garda was yet unable to give any description of any person on the street that morning. The court noted that in *People (AG) v Fagan*,[110] the fact that the applicant was not living at home, and so not always readily available for holding an identification parade, was deemed a less than satisfactory explanation for failure to hold same.

[6.103] O'Flaherty J noted in *People (AG) v Martin*,[111] that the Supreme Court had stated there was no rule of law or practice that required visual identification to be by means of an identification parade; each case must be considered on its facts. The Supreme Court had there acknowledged that other types of identification might in certain circumstances be fairer, and more dependable, than a formal identification parade, which, because of its surroundings, atmosphere, range of choice and limited opportunity for observation, might be less than satisfactory in achieving a reliable identification. The acceptability of such an alternative method would depend on the circumstances of the case.

[6.104] The reason given in *O'Reilly* for the failure to hold a parade was that it might be 'more beneficial' to the defendant not to hold one. While accepting that it was right that those involved in the prosecution should be scrupulous in looking to the rights of the accused, O'Flaherty J nonetheless felt the decision as to what is most beneficial for an accused in the preparation and conduct of his defence, must be primarily a matter for the accused and his legal advisor.

---

[110] *People (AG) v Fagan* (1974) 1 Frewen 375.
[111] *People (AG) v Martin* [1956] IR 22.

[6.105] O'Flaherty J acknowledged that there would be circumstances where – for reasons of the singular appearance of the accused, the witness's previous acquaintance with him or the unco-operative attitude of the suspect – the holding of an identification parade might be impossible or redundant (although a warning would still be given *per Casey*). This case, however, he reasoned, was clearly one where the court would require the holding of an identification parade. Such formal parades were an important filter for both prosecution and defence, and enabled the accused (and his legal advisor) to object to its composition if it were perceived to be unfair. Similarly, the court of trial would have the benefit of the description of same. By contrast, in the case of an informal identification, the accused had no input, was unlikely to be even aware of its happening, and might, therefore, be seriously inhibited in challenging its fairness at trial.

The court emphasised that the result of the identification in the parade was not, however, conclusive, and confirmed the application of the *Casey* warning to same.

Counsel for the applicant pointed out that the way in which such identification parades were held was in no doubt: eight or nine people similar in age, height, appearance, dress, and walk of life to the suspect should be assembled, supervised by an independent garda (ie not involved in the case), and full details should be kept of the descriptions of those in the parade, the witness not having an opportunity to see the suspect in advance of the parade. O'Flaherty J[112] further commented:

> This is not intended to be an exhaustive list for such parades and on occasion, the way in which an identification parade has been held has itself been subject to criticism (see eg *People (AG) v Michael O'Driscoll* (1972) 3 Frewen 351).

[6.106] Of interest is the concern expressed by the court at the fact that photographs (including one of the accused) were shown to the injured party prior to her visit to Edgeworthstown. This further substantiated the court's fears that this was an identification obtained in unusual and doubtful circumstances, which rendered the conviction unsafe. Indeed the court felt the trial judge's ruling should have been sought on the admissibility of the identification obtained in such frail circumstances.

[6.107] With regard to the appeal on the ground of the trial judge's failure to adequately warn the jury in accordance with *Casey* of the danger of acting on uncorroborated visual identification evidence, the court acknowledged the danger that the direction might be treated as a 'stereotyped formula'. While the court felt that the trial judge here had complied fully with the first part of the

---

[112] *People (AG) v O'Reilly* [1990] 2 IR 415 at 420.

direction and went on to deal with the particular circumstances in which the injured party observed the accused man, he should have given firmer guidance to the jury as regards the particular infirmities that affected this case, namely, the fact that the lady was elderly, in a state of shock, suffered a good deal of pain from an arthritic condition and had only a short period in which to observe the perpetrators. Further, the trial judge should have highlighted the deficiencies to the jury in the actual identification that was made at Edgeworthstown.

[6.108] O'Flaherty J pointed out that this was a case that required the holding of an identification parade. An important distinction between an informal and formal identification is that, in the latter, the accused has full knowledge of its composition and may object if it is perceived to be unfair. The court has a detailed account of same. However, the *Casey* warning is still required. The court also pointed to the fact that here the witness was shown photographs (including one of the accused) prior to her visit to Edgeworthstown. This added weight to the court's concern and indicated that the trial judge's ruling should have been sought on the admissibility of the identification evidence obtained in such frail circumstances. Furthermore, the Supreme Court emphasised that the *Casey* warning should not be treated as a 'stereotyped' formula. In this case, the trial judge's direction should have been much more specific as regards the danger of acting on the evidence of Mrs Farrell. The only difference between this and *Fagan's* case was that the witness in the latter was shaken under cross-examination. Mrs Farrell was made of sterner stuff.

> However, it is central to the need to give warnings in cases of visual identification that people young and old, tend to be certain. If they are not certain their evidence will fall to the ground anyway. No matter how certain a witness appears to be, the requirement laid down in *Casey* ... remains.[113]

[6.109] This confirmation on the part of the Irish courts of the inherently fallible nature of visual identification evidence, the necessity for caution in relation to same, and the confirmation of the *Casey* warning are significant. It is in contrast with other perceived judicial rejection or abolition of the corroboration requirement (witness decisions such as *R v Spencer*,[114] *R v Bagshaw*,[115] *R v Chance*[116] etc). The reason for the strength of judicial support for the warning in relation to cases substantially dependent on visual identification evidence,[117] may lie in the availability of empirical evidence substantiating such a requirement. This, coupled with the difficulty of countering this type of

---

[113] *People (AG) v O'Reilly* [1990] 2 IR 415 at 424, *per* O'Flaherty J.

[114] *R v Spencer* [1985] 1 All ER 673.

[115] *R v Bagshaw* [1984] 1 WLR 477.

[116] *R v Chance* [1988] QB 932.

[117] See also the Privy Council decision in *R v Scott* [1983] IR 165.

evidence by cross-examination (see O'Flaherty J's comment with regard to the certainty of witnesses), may explain the judicial desire to maintain this requirement, and indeed avoid the 'ritualistic incantation' of a stereotyped formula.

[6.110] Of additional interest for the Irish law of criminal procedure is O'Flaherty J's recognition in *O'Reilly* of the inherently adversarial nature of the process, the conflict of interest between prosecution and defence and the requirement of 'fairness' to the accused in the pre-trial process – an element of which may well be the holding of a formal identification parade. (This follows the concept of 'fairness' *per Healy* as including a right to counsel.)

[6.111] Contrasting with the decision in *O'Reilly* is the subsequent Court of Criminal Appeal decision in *People (DPP) v O'Callaghan*,[118] where the characteristics of the identifying witness strengthened the case. This case concerned charges of robbery and larceny arising out of an armed hold-up of a bank in Dublin. It was contended that the evidence was inadequate to support a conviction, particularly in relation to the purported identification of the applicant, and that the trial judge had insufficiently warned the jury in relation to same.

[6.112] The witness called to give evidence of identification was a security officer. He had the robber in sight for a few seconds prior to being made lie on the floor. A video recorder had recorded the incident and, on seeing it twice, it occurred to the witness that the man was one of two men who had aroused his suspicions two days before the robbery. On looking at the video of that earlier day, he claimed to be able to identify the applicant. The jury saw both videos. The applicant had been in disguise on the day of the robbery.

[6.113] The trial judge had refused an application to withdraw the case from the jury. O'Hanlon J upheld that decision. He pointed out that this witness was not:

> a mere casual passer-by, but a security officer who had worked in the bank for over a year prior to the robbery ...

> If such a witness in such circumstances gives positive evidence on which he is not shaken on cross-examination ... it appears to this Court that it was proper to leave to the jury to decide whether they were convinced as to the truthfulness and reliability of his evidence.

[6.114] Given the fact that identification evidence is perhaps the least contentious area of the law with regard to corroboration, and in light of the recent endorsement by the judiciary of the necessity for caution in regard for same, it is perhaps curious that s 17 of the Criminal Evidence Act 1992 provides

---

[118] *People (DPP) v O'Callaghan* (30 July 1990, unreported), CCA, *per* O'Hanlon J.

that in the case of a person accused of a sexual offence, or offence involving violence or the threat of violence, where the victim is under 17 years of age, and the identifying witness is the victim or other person under that age, it shall be presumed, until the contrary is proven, that the person so identified, is the accused (s 17(1)).

[6.115] In *People v Duff*,[119] the optimum method of visual identification was noted to be by means of an identification parade. In *DPP v Cooney*,[120] the Supreme Court held, however, that while dock identifications were undesirable and unsatisfactory, they may be admitted by the trial judge with a specific warning to the jury of acting on same. This was confirmed in *DPP v Meehan*,[121] where the dock identification had the added weakness of being provided by an accomplice and the non-jury court involved the judges warning themselves as arbiters of fact.

[6.116] In *DPP v Gilligan*[122] the accused had argued that the identification of the accused by John Dunne was a dock identification, that it was inappropriate to admit such evidence and that it was neither corroborated nor confirmed. The Supreme Court affirmed the trial court's finding that John Dunne's identification of the accused was recognition rather than a dock identification. It took the view that because of the circumstances of the case (Gilligan had been returned to Ireland on foot of rendition proceedings), an identification parade was not possible. The court reasoned (*per* Denham J[123]) that:

> it was open to the prosecution to provide evidence of identity in court. The evidence in this case was not a dock identification. John Dunne gave evidence of meeting the accused previously on at least five occasions ... The fact that the meetings were several years earlier does not prevent their admission as evidence of recognition, although it may be a factor to weigh in considering the evidence.

> I am satisfied that the situation in this case was one of recognition, not a dock identification. I would apply also the words of O'Flaherty J in *The People (Director of Public Prosecution) v O'Reilly* where he pointed out that the holding of an identification parade would probably be a redundant exercise if the witness knows the suspect previously.

---

[119] *People v Duff* [1995] 3 IR 296.

[120] *DPP v Cooney* [1997] 3 IR 205.

[121] *DPP v Meehan* (29 July 1999, unreported), SCC; CCA [2006] 3 IR 468

[122] *DPP v Gilligan* [2006] IR 107.

[123] *DPP v Gilligan* [2006] IR 107 at 158.

Discretion to give warning

Sexual offences

[6.117] Whereas formerly the evidence of a complainant in a 'sexual offence' action was deemed to require corroboration as a matter of practice, or at least a warning to the jury as to the dangers of acting on such evidence, since the passing of the Criminal Law (Rape) (Amendment) Act 1990, this position has been altered.

[6.118] Under s 7 of the Criminal Law (Rape) (Amendment) Act 1990, the trial judge in such a case has a discretion as to whether to give such a warning or not. The warning remains the traditional one in relation to sexual complainants, although no particular form of words need be utilised. The extent to which this judicial discretion to issue the warning in relation to sexual complainants would be exercised, would, of course, determine the effectiveness of this mechanism of reform.

[6.119] It seemed as though the resurgence of the warning in practice through the exercise of judicial discretion was realised by the Court of Criminal Appeal judgment in *People (DPP) v Molloy*,[124] where Flood J criticised the failure of the trial judge to give a warning, as was 'prudent practice' in a sexual offence case. However, in *People (DPP) v JEM*,[125] Denham J referred to the English decision of *R v Makanjoula*[126] with approval. There, the English Court of Appeal had trenchantly rejected the notion that the warning had any continued existence in the aftermath of s 32(1) of the Criminal Justice (Public Order) Act 1994, which removed mandatory corroboration warning for accomplices and sexual offence victims. Although s 7 of the 1990 Act did not contain the same wording, Denham J stated that the legal principle underpinning the two statutes was similar. She endorsed the following principles laid down in that case:

> (1) Section 32(1) abrogated the requirement to give a corroboration direction in respect of an alleged accomplice or a complainant of a sexual offence simply because a witness falls into one of those categories.

> (2) It is a matter for the judge's discretion what, if any, warning he considers appropriate in respect of such a witness, as indeed in respect of any other witness in whatever type of case. Whether he chooses to give a warning and in what terms will depend on the circumstances of the case, the issues raised and the content and quality of the witnesses' evidence.

---

[124] *People (DPP) v Molloy* (28 July 1995, unreported), CCA.
[125] *People (DPP) v JEM* [2001] 4 IR 385.
[126] *R v Makanjoula* [1995] 3 All ER 730.

(3) In some cases, it may be appropriate for the judge to warn the jury to exercise caution before acting upon the unsupported evidence of a witness. This will not be so simply because the witness is the complainant of a sexual offence nor will it necessarily be so because a witness is alleged to be an accomplice. There may be an evidential basis for suggesting that the evidence of the witness may be unreliable. An evidential basis does not include mere suggestions by cross-examining counsel.

(4) If any question arises as to whether the judge should give a special warning in respect of a witness, it is desirable that the question be resolved by discussion with counsel in the absence of the jury before final speeches.

(5) Where the judge does decide to give some warning in respect of a witness, it will be appropriate to do so as part of the judge's review of the evidence and his comments as to how the jury should evaluate it rather than as a set piece legal direction.

(6) Where some warning is required, it will be for the judge to decide the strengths and terms of the warning. It does not have to be invested with the whole florid regime of the old corroboration rules.

(7) ... Attempts to re-impose the straightjacket of the old corroboration rules are strongly to be deprecated.[127]

[6.120] In *People (DPP) v C*[128] an appeal against conviction on a charge of rape on the basis of the trial judge's failure to give a corroboration warning failed, the Court of Criminal Appeal emphasising that it was no longer a rule of law or practice that a jury be warned of the danger of convicting on the uncorroborated evidence of a complainant in a sexual offence trial by reason of the nature of the offence. Murray J was satisfied that it had not been demonstrated to the court that there was any ground on which the trial judge could be said to have exercised his discretion improperly in this case.

Children's evidence

[6.121] The requirement that children's evidence be corroborated was abolished by s 28 of the Criminal Evidence Act 1992. It was replaced by a judicial discretion to give such a warning, and no particular form of words is necessary to do so. Section 28 provides:

(1) The requirement in section 30 of the Children Act, 1908, of corroboration of unsworn evidence of a child given under that section is hereby abolished.

(2)(a) Any requirement that at a trial on indictment the jury be given a warning by the judge about convicting the accused on the uncorroborated evidence

---

[127] *People (DPP) v JEM* [2001] 4 IR 385 at 401–402. The final eighth principle with regard to interference with a trial judge's discretion was not endorsed by Denham J.
[128] *People (DPP) v C* [2001] 3 IR 345.

of a child is also hereby abolished in relation to cases where such a warning is required by reason only that the evidence is the evidence of a child and it shall be for the judge to decide, in his discretion, having regard to all the evidence given, whether the jury should be given the warning.

(b) If a judge decides, in his discretion, to give such a warning as aforesaid, it shall not be necessary to use any particular form of words to do so.

(3) Unsworn evidence received by virtue of section 27 may corroborate evidence (sworn or unsworn) given by any other person.

[6.122] This provision, like the Criminal Evidence Act 1992 which weakened the corroboration rule in relation to sexual offences, gives the judiciary a discretion as to whether to give such a warning to the jury. The application of the said corroboration rule in relation to accomplices remains at full strength, but would seem to be somewhat cosmetic in effect, as evidenced by the *Holland*[129] and *Ward*[130] cases. Moreover, the application of the rules of evidence in the Special Criminal Court suffers from the artificiality of judges instructing themselves to be cautious of accomplice evidence, for example, or to ignore evidence as in the case of excluded confessions (eg *Ward*). Yet there may yet be strength in corroboration rules.

They haven't gone away, you know ...

[6.123] Much has been made of the influence of rules of evidence arising from the popular mood, perhaps, to solidify into legal rule, or gradually permeating existing rules in the aftermath of legislative change, thus changing assumptions regarding credibility. Such changes can enter the legal culture rather slowly, in terms of influencing fact determination. Once integrated, however, they may be correspondingly difficult to uproot. Ironically, Althouse's point[131] with regard to the difficulty of effecting a legislative change prior to a cultural one, can be made by reference to the Irish position on corroboration – ie after its removal or weakening, it continues to emerges as a player in the courts' adjudication. *DPP v Finnerty*[132] is a case in point. The factual scenario was that of a sexual offence: the alleged rape of a student after a disco. The defendant claimed they had met after the disco and that the intercourse was consensual. At trial, a corroboration warning was given by the trial judge. On appeal it was commented that, '[n]o criticism has been, or could be, made of those aspects of his charge'.[133]

---

[129] *DPP v Holland* (15 June 1998, unreported), HC.
[130] *DPP v Ward* (23 October 1998, unreported), HC.
[131] Althouse, 'Thelma and Louise and the Law: Do Rape Shield Rules Matter?' [1992] *Loyola LR* 757 at 772.
[132] *DPP v Finnerty* [1999] 4 IR 364.
[133] *DPP v Finnerty* [1999] 4 IR 364 at 372–373 (*per* Keane J).

[6.124] *Finnerty* illustrates how a once crystallised perspective on credibility prevails, even through legislative change, because of judicial adherence to its original precepts.[134] However, even when that transition is complete, a case can be found being made for its re-emergence. The re-emergence of rules of evidence encapsulating scepticism and caution may not in this context seem unjustifiable or indeed unwelcome. This is despite the fact that their origins may be dubious, or the rumours of their demise greatly exaggerated. There are signs of disenchantment with 'received wisdom' and assumptions of veracity on the part of the victim. Ironically, this manifested itself in a renewed argument for the re-introduction of corroboration in Ireland, in the face of its comparatively recent legislative reform.

[6.125] In *P O'C v DPP*,[135] where an order of prohibition on the grounds of delay was granted, the applicant was charged with five counts of indecently assaulting PK at dates unknown from 1 January 1982 to 31 December 1983. The applicant was a violin teacher, and the incidents allegedly took place in a music room, a significant factor being the existence of a facility to lock same, something that was difficult for the applicant to obtain evidence of after the delay – grounds for prohibition. Of specific interest in terms of the rules of evidence, and the impact or influence of popular culture, is the judgment of Hardiman J. He referred to the fact that corroboration requirement in sexual cases was abolished by s 7 of the Rape Amendment Act 1990 and the Criminal Evidence Act 1992, s 27, and commented:

> It may well be that these pieces of legislation were enacted before the prosecution of very old offences became routine as it now is. Cases which will be tried more than ten years after the offences are alleged to have been committed are very common, and a twenty to twenty five year interval is by no means uncommon. My personal experience extends to a case proposed to be prosecuted more than 46 years after the alleged offences and one has heard of an interval of more than 52 years. These, even the shorter periods, are remarkable lengths of time. They appear to me of themselves, and independently of the Director's reliance on possible unspecified 'directions' of a trial judge, to require serious consideration of what can or should be said to a jury in these cases. At present, one cannot be sure that any direction or warning will be given ... A plausible and sympathetic witness is not necessarily telling the truth, nor a furtive and cowed one lying. The very pressures of litigation of this sort, so deeply personal and

---

[134] Birch, 'Corroboration: Goodbye to All That?' [1995] *Crim LR* 524. In earlier consideration of reform of the corroboration requirement by s 32(1) of the Criminal Justice (Public Order) Act 1994, Birch had expressed an appreciation of the value of *Beck* [1982] 1 WLR 461, which creates a witness specific obligation, arising only if material to suggest a particular witness's evidence may be tainted by improper motive.

[135] *P O'C v DPP* [2000] 3 IR 87.

perhaps central to a complainant's self worth on the one hand and so threatening of prolonged imprisonment, life long stigmatisation and financial and familial catastrophe on the other, in themselves have the potential drastically to alter the witnesses' presentation and effect. To permit such prosecutions, in the absence of any scope for corroboration or contradiction after one, two or more decades is, to say the least, to venture into uncharted territory where the normal forensic safeguards are gravely attenuated. The process of the trial itself may be a life altering event for one or both parties and their families, and rarely for the better. In these circumstances it appears to me that there is in each case a point at which a trial in those circumstances 'puts justice to the hazard' so that the issue of guilt or innocence is 'beyond the risk of fair litigations'.[136]

Hardiman J clearly makes a case for the 'reclaiming' of corroboration in this context.

[6.126] It was clear that within a decade of the reform of the 1990 Act, the corroboration requirement was alive and well and the warning was being given in the case of evidence in sexual offences cases. There may, however, as noted in *Meehan*, have been a corresponding weakening of the *Baskerville* definition of same. There was also emerging an increasing number of historic sex abuse cases – a trickle that by the twenty-first century would become a flood. These cases presented two issues or grounds of concern: the allegation of sexual offence and the issue of delay, the latter because generally an allegation was now being made about something which happened a long time ago. There were two issues regarding corroboration in the context of these cases: the question of whether to give a warning because of their nature as sexual offence cases (the exercise of that particular judicial discretion left in the wake of the 1990 Act) and the development of a new basis for warning because of the factor of delay.

Constructions of 'fairness'

The context of sexual offences

[6.127] Recent decisions in the context of sexual offences in Ireland and England reveal, in the context of credibility and relevance assessment, the influence on or mitigation of traditional notions of fairness by popular culture. A movement, for example, from automatic suspicion to automatic belief of certain victims not only has powerful implication in terms of the determination of guilt or innocence at trial, but also reveals the genesis of evidentiary rules and their justifying or ostensible underlying rationale.

[6.128] The cultural and legal context with regard to sexual offences has undergone somewhat of a sea-change in recent times. This has resulted in

---

[136] *P O'C v DPP* [2000] 3 IR 87 at 20–21, *per* Hardiman J.

legislative activity introducing changes in criminal procedure, which in England culminated in the Youth Justice and Criminal Evidence Act 1999, which aimed to be more cognisant of the special needs of child and vulnerable adult witnesses.[137] In Ireland, the facilitation of live television link and video testimony by witnesses was introduced by the Criminal Evidence Act 1992,[138] which Act also weakened the corroboration rule in relation to sexual offences, giving the judiciary discretion as to whether to give such a warning to the jury.[139] Each of these changes emanates from what might be categorised as a 'pro-victim' approach – introducing changes to facilitate prosecution and ease the giving of testimony by witnesses.

[6.129] Whether fact-finding itself and the judicial construction of fairness is then influenced by this sway from accused to victim, or whether it results in a judicial mandate to pull against the tides of current wisdom, may be revealed in relevant case law. In sexual offences cases, issues such as credibility (of the victim) and relevance (of sexual history evidence) are obviously core to determination of the ultimate issue at trial. When these are in turn constructed in accordance with judicial views of what is 'fair', it can be seen whether the motivation to do justice for adult and child victims clashes with that of the fair trial rights of the accused. Such issues are central to sexual offences cases such as the English House of Lords decision regarding rape shield rules and fair trial rights in *A*[140] and the Canadian Supreme Court decision regarding access to a rape complainant's counselling and medical records in *R v O'Connor*.[141] In *Regina v A* the House of Lords had an opportunity to directly assess victim or witness accommodation in the context of fair trial rights of the accused, as mandated by the Human Rights Act 1998. The central concern here was the accommodation of the rape shield provisions under the Youth Justice and Criminal Evidence Act 1999 with the concept of fair trial guaranteed to the accused under the ECHR. Section 41 of the 1999 Act prohibited the giving of evidence and cross-examination about any sexual behaviour of the complainant except with leave of the court. Leave could be given in very limited

---

[137] See Hoyano, 'Variations on a Theme by Pigot: Special Measures Directions for Child Witnesses' [2000] *CrimLR* 250 at 273.

[138] This facility was extended to intimidated or vulnerable witnesses by the Criminal Justice Act 1999. Separate legal representation for rape victims is also provided for under the Sexual Offenders Act 2001, s 34 of which allows for legal representation of complainants in relation to the accused's application for cross-examination on past sexual history.

[139] Moreover the application of the rules of evidence in the Special Criminal Court suffers from the artificiality of judges instructing themselves to be cautious of accomplice evidence, for example, or to ignore evidence as in the case of excluded confessions (eg *Ward*).

[140] *Regina v A* UKHL 25.

[141] *R v O'Connor* [1995] 4 SCR 411.

circumstances: where the sexual behaviour is alleged to have taken place 'at about the same time' as that before the court (s 41(3)(b)) and where it is 'so similar' to that before the court that it cannot be explained as coincidence (s 41(3)(c)). Neither of these would avail the defendant in this case. The legislative objective in introducing the rape shield provisions was identified as that of eliminating the 'twin myths' that if the complainant had had sexual intercourse with third parties, she would be more likely to have consented to intercourse with the defendant, and that such a complainant would be less worthy of belief than a woman of unblemished chastity. In terms of the result (aside from the implications of the court's avoidance of a declaration of incompatibility), superficially, it might appear that the fair trial considerations – and in particular fairness to the accused – won out, as the decision of the majority of the court in *A* was that evidence of the complainant's past sexual history with the accused should not be excluded if it is so relevant to the issue of consent that to exclude it would endanger the fairness of the trial under art 6 of the Convention. Irish 'rights' adjudication in the context of (historical) sex abuse cases operates in a climate of public opinion that is emotionally charged in relation to all sexual offenders, and particularly child sexual abusers, and offers a similar occasion to test the mettle of guarantees of fairness or to estimate the variable nature of rules of evidence in the face of policy considerations.

Historic sex abuse cases

[6.130] In Ireland, the constitutional guarantee of fair procedure includes that of a right to expeditious trial. In *DPP v Byrne*[142] Denham J[143] commented that 'whereas there is no specific constitutional right to a speedy trial, there is an implied right to reasonable expedition under the due process clause. An accused is entitled to have a trial free of abuse of process.' Chief Justice Finlay in that same case[144] quoted O'Higgins J in *State (Healy) v Donoghue*[145] to the effect that 'the importance of the protection of the right to a trial with reasonable expedition is not in any way lessened by the fact that the constitutional origins of it in our law arose from the general provision for a trial in due course of law rather than from a separate express provision of a right to a speedy trial.'

[6.131] Recent resolution of the concepts of fairness and delay in the context of prosecution of historic sex abuse in Ireland has revealed competing tensions in

---

[142] *DPP v Byrne* [1994] 2 IR 236. The Supreme Court in a 3:2 decision in relation to a drunken driving charge rejected an application to prohibit the trial of the offence. There had been a ten-month delay, which had led to a dismissal in the District Court for reasons of delay.

[143] *DPP v Byrne* [1994] 2 IR 236 at 260.

[144] *DPP v Byrne* [1994] 2 IR 236 at 244.

[145] *State (Healy) v Donoghue* [1976] IR 325 at 375.

judicial prioritisation and identification of the standpoints therein: that of victim, accused, community and state. The 'balance' constructed between these identified standpoints and the treatment of historic sex abuse allegations within the confines of the general precepts of the criminal justice system (particularly expeditious trial) offer a perspective on both fairness and credibility issues.

[6.132] Initial differences were marked out, for example, in *G v DPP*,[146] which concerned 27 charges related to the period 1967–1981 involving offences against young women. In 1993 the accused was charged and sought leave to apply for judicial review on grounds of lapse of time. In relation to delay in sexual offences against young children, Finlay CJ's comments marked the beginnings of a recognition on the part of the Irish courts that because of the feature of domination in particular, an exception to the general requirement of expeditious justice is created:

> In cases in general of sexual harassment or interference with young children, the perpetrator may, if he or she is related to or has a particular relationship of domination with the child concerned, by that domination or by threats or intimidation prevent that child from reporting the offence. The Court asked to prohibit the trial of a person on such offences, even after a very long time, might well be satisfied and justified in reaching a decision that the extent to which the applicant had contributed to the delay in the revealing of the offences and their subsequent reporting to the prosecution authorities meant that as a matter of justice he should not be entitled to the order.[147]

Denham J in that same case, however, cautioned victims as to what they might seek:

> A trial in a court of law is not an exercise in vengeance but is a trial in due course of law in the pursuit of justice on behalf of the community ... When women and children come to the legal system it would be disservice to them if it were perceived that they sought vengeance rather than the rule of law and justice.[148]

The accused's interest in fairness, therefore, is tempered by the role he *may* have had in causing the delay.

[6.133] There is also evidence of the community's pursuit of justice through the vindication of victims' interests. This identification of the 'community' with victims' rights is evident in *EO'R v DPP*,[149] which concerned charges made against the accused in March 1993 in relation to sexual offences against three young women, which were alleged to have occurred between 1978 and 1986,

---

[146] *G v DPP* [1994] 1 IR 374. He was successful on grounds of delay.

[147] *G v DPP* [1994] 1 IR 374 at 380, Finlay CJ.

[148] *G v DPP* [1994] 1 IR 374 at 381, Denham J.

[149] *E O'R v DPP* (21 December 1995, unreported), HC, Keane J.

and one in the period 1982 to 1986. A challenge on the grounds of delay was successful in the High Court where Keane J[150] stated that 'what is beyond doubt is that where that community right conflicts with due process, it is the latter right which must prevail.'

Keane J noted that jurisprudence had developed to the effect that in the case of a charge of sexual abuse of children, special considerations apply. These include the reluctance of young children to accuse persons in authority,[151] which reluctance may be exacerbated by threats, and the fact that the accused may be responsible for the delay.[152] In application of the *general principles* identified to the facts of the case at hand, including that of the relationship between the applicant and complainants, however, Keane J pointed out that this must be seen in the context of their respective ages (difference: 4–11 years) and that the possibility of a relationship of domination is markedly lessened as they were not living in the home. Keane J concluded, therefore, that the interests of the accused must prevail here, although his identification of the victims' interests with that of the public is clear:

> Whatever decision a judge arrives at in a case such as this, there is the possibility of injustice: injustice to the complainants and the public whom the court must protect if the proceedings are stayed where the accused was indeed guilty of the offences, and injustice to the accused if he is exposed to the dangerous ordeal of an unavoidably unfair trial. I am satisfied there is a real and serious risk of unfair trial that cannot be avoided by any ruling or direction that may be given by judge.[153]

[6.134] This identification of community or public interests with those of the victim, to the detriment of the accused, reached its pinnacle in *B v DPP*[154] where the defendant was charged in 1993 in relation to offences allegedly perpetrated

---

[150] *E O'R v DPP* (21 December 1995), HC, Keane J at p 12.

[151] In *Hogan v President of Circuit Court* [1994] 2 IR 513, Finlay J had identified these.

[152] Keane J noted that in the English case *LPB* (1990/1) Criminal Appeal Reps, Judge J had stated that it would be difficult to envisage any circumstances where delay in a complaint of child abuse would lead to abuse of the court process. Keane J did not, however, agree and commented that such would be at variance with the need to have regard to particular circumstances and the paramount nature of due process guarantees. *E O'R v DPP* (21 December 1995, unreported), HC, Keane J at p 18.

[153] *E O'R v DPP* (21 December 1995, unreported), HC, Keane J at p 22. On appeal to the Supreme Court, however, O'Flaherty J interpreted Keane J's decision as being one that meant the accused was going to find it difficult to defend the case. O'Flaherty J commented that this is so in every case of this kind, even if there is no significant delay, and therefore held this not to be a case where the court was entitled to prohibit the continuation of proceedings. The effect was to prefer the continuation of proceedings over fairness to the accused.

[154] *B v DPP* [1977] 2 ILRM 118 (SC), Denham J.

against his daughter between 1963 and 1973. In 1982 his wife had obtained a barring order against the defendant and in 1991 she had died. An order of prohibition on grounds of delay was refused.[155] In reaching the decision as to whether this particular delay of between 20 and 30 years, acknowledged as 'an inordinate length of time',[156] would prejudice the fair trial of the defendant, Denham J placed heavy emphasis on domination:[157]

> The events in this case are governed by what the learned trial judge described as B's: 'violent, dominant and menacing personality'. This dominance is the kernel reason for the delay and the factor carrying most weight.

In dismissing the appeal, Denham J placed the community rights in opposition to those of the accused:

> In weighing up the community's right to proceed with this prosecution as against the other factors ... it is clear that B has not discharged the onus of establishing that arising out of the delay there is a real risk that he would not obtain a fair trial, that the trial would be unfair as a consequence of the delay between the dates of the alleged events and the postponed trial.[158]

[6.135] Decisions of the Irish courts such as these reveal the acceptance of the role and input of the victim into the criminal trial. Although there is occasional vindication of the priority of the accused's rights in the hierarchy of balance, it is only of occasional and limited effect.[159] The overarching theme is revealed as an accommodation of the prosecution and pursuit of victims' interests, seen to be in the public interest, with the presumptions of domination prevailing over innocence rights. In credibility and fact-finding terms, the popular context – one increasingly intolerant of sexual offences, particularly those perpetrated

---

[155] On appeal, Denham J identified the particular factors to be considered in this case: the relationships in question, the matter of domination, the question of who delayed, the nature of the offence (namely alleged abuse in the home), a possible alibi, the witnesses and the question of an admission of guilt. In looking at each of those factors, domination received much, if not most, attention. Denham J commented: 'This dominion places this (and similar cases) in a special category as by the said control the accused's actions prevented the complainant's taking steps so that the prosecution could proceed within a more usual timeframe. B is barred from arguing that the delay is unreasonable while such dominion existed. Any delay that continued during this time of dominion is reasonable. Consequently any prosecution commenced within that time or within a reasonable time thereafter, is commenced with reasonable expedition.' *B v DPP* [1977] 2 ILRM 118 at 133.

[156] *B v DPP* [1977] 2 ILRM 118 at 132.

[157] Denham J relied here on the evidence of the psychologist in this case. The psychologist was not, however, cross-examined on his affidavit: *B v DPP* [1977] 2 ILRM 116 at 128, 129.

[158] *B v DPP* [1977] 2 ILRM 118 at 133–4.

[159] *G v DPP* [1994] 1 IR 374 and *E O'R v DPP* (21 December 1995, unreported), HC, Keane J, for example.

against young children – is directly influential in supporting the admissibility of psychological expert evidence to explain delay and analyse victim response. Quite literally the expert evidence *is* admissible dependent on the status of that specialty and its standing in our community.[160] In other words community deference ensures a greater degree of respect and notice to that which is deferred to.

The 're-claiming' of corroboration

[6.136] If assumptions of the veracity of victims' statements have reached an orthodoxy, it may be inevitable that in order to express caution, the judiciary may bring about the rehabilitation of rules relating to suspicion of credibility and veracity in those contexts. This can in turn be interpreted as typical of judicial fondness for rules of their own creation, or their adherence to their discretion, but should in fact be taken more seriously in terms of the dynamics of evidentiary rules, fact-finding and popular contexts or beliefs. It may in fact say more about the role and rationale of rules of evidence than we at first realise or indeed later truly develop.

[6.137] The beginning of this realisation that a presumption of the credibility of victims in cases of historic sex abuse has hardened to an orthodoxy in Ireland is found in *PC v DPP*.[161] The facts concerned the arrest of the defendant in 1995 in relation to allegations of sexual offences perpetrated between 1982 and 1984 against a young woman. The defendant had been the coach driver who transported schoolgirls to a pool. His relationship with the victim had been ended by her when he commented that it would be legal when she was 16, causing her to appreciate the illegality. There were two periods of delay here: 1980–88 and 1988–95. The victim had meantime gone to university and obtained a Masters Degree. McGuinness J did not find evidence of the type of 'dominion' dealt with in B's case and, although the experts[162] Mr Carroll and Ms Fitzmaurice did describe a type of 'kindly' domination, she suggested 'their

---

[160] See para **[1.11]**.

[161] *PC v DPP* [1999] 2 IR 25, McGuinness J.

[162] By contrast with Denham J's reliance on the expert's testimony in *B*, McGuinness J was critical of the experts testifying in the case. Ms Fitzpatrick, she commented, 'had great difficulty in elaborating with any degree of logic or scientific method what lay behind [theories on the effect of child abuse]. She was vague about the nature of the organisation from which she had obtained her qualifications and also about the process whereby she treated those whom she counselled ... I had difficulty in accepting that she was sufficiently qualified to be an expert witness as to what lay behind AM's delay in making her complaint to the gardaí in this particular case.' [1999] 2 IR 25 at 35. (contd/)

views contain[ed] an element of rationalisation by hindsight'.[163] In terms of the relationship between assumptions of dominion and the presumption of innocence, McGuinness J commented[164] that:

> [t]his court cannot accept that a situation of dominion exists automatically in all cases where a person is accused of sexual offences. The presumption of innocence has to play a part in the Court's considerations and the court must base its decision on the actual evidence before it.

[6.138] In a neat juxtaposition, McGuinness J linked the current orthodoxy with that of the past, finding both equally reprehensible. First she identified that which was current:

> ...I consider that there may be a danger that *B v DPP* and the unreported cases to which I have also been referred might be taken as authority for the proposition that in all cases where an accused is charged with sexual abuse of a child or young person which took place some years ago, any claimed prejudice on account of delay can be negatived by a claim that the accused exercised 'dominion' over the complainant.[165]

She then related this directly to the equally abhorrent automatic disbelief which pertained in relation to all sexual offence complainants:

> In years gone by, accusations of rape or any kind of sexual assault were treated with considerable suspicion. The orthodox view was that accusations of rape and sexual assault by women against men were 'easy to make and hard to disprove' and Judges were required to give stern warnings in their charge to the jury of the need for corroboration and the dangers attached to convicting on the evidence of the complainant alone.
>
> No one to-day would support the orthodoxy of the past and there has been a great increase in the psychological understanding of sexual offences generally. Nevertheless it would be unfortunate if the discredited orthodoxy of the past were to be replaced with an equally rigid orthodox view that in all cases of delay in making complaints of sexual abuse the delay can automatically be negatived by dominion.[166]

---

[162] (\contd) The affidavit of Mr Alex Carroll, Senior Clinical Psychologist employed by the Midlands Health Board, she found 'extremely close both in content and actual wording' to the affidavit sworn by him in *DO'R v DPP* [1997] 2 IR 273 although the facts of the case were very different. The fact that he relied on a statement provided by the gardaí for the victim's history rather than going through it with her himself, did not strike McGuinness J 'as the most desirable way of carrying out an in-depth psychological assessment in a matter of such crucial importance to both the complainant and the accused' [1999] 2 IR 25 at 36.

[163] *PC v DPP* [1999] 2 IR 25 at 40.

[164] *PC v DPP* [1999] 2 IR 25 at 40.

[165] *PC v DPP* [1999] 2 IR 25 at 43.

[166] *PC v DPP* [1999] 2 IR 25 at 43.

The applicant was held to have established his claim and the order of prohibition granted.[167] This was, however, reversed on appeal to the Supreme Court.

[6.139] There Denham J identified the 'fundamental principles' involved, which had to be 'weighed and *balanced* by the court'[168] (emphasis added). She noted:

> ...the community's right to legal issues being determined in the courts; to have criminal charges processed through the courts; the right and duty of the prosecutor to bring to the courts for adjudication allegations of serious child sexual abuse alleged to have taken place; the community's right to have its society protected, especially its most vulnerable – children. Also at the core of this case is the rule of law; the right of the applicant to a fair trial; the right of the community to the rule of law for all, including the applicant.[169]

In terms of the identification of standpoints within the criminal justice system, the community's identification with the vindication of the interest of the victim is in contrast to the failure to identify the interest of the community in the accused's right to a fair trial – the only indication of a commonality between accused and community being in the rule of law, which could, after all, cut both ways. Denham J differed from the trial judge also with regard to the presence of dominance and the interpretation of the expert evidence, deciding the applicant 'may not profit from alleged illegal actions.'[170]

[6.140] It is regarding the question of whether the simple efflux of time had prejudiced the applicant's chance of a fair trial, however, that her comments were most revealing: 'A trial of charges of this type, in the circumstances described, is in fact a trial of the credibility of the witnesses.'[171] Denham J held that the applicant had not 'distinguished his case from the growing body of case law which has permitted delayed prosecutions for child sexual abuse to proceed. No factor takes his case out of the *norm* of this common law, or establishes that a constitutional right will be breached.'[172] (Emphasis added.)

[6.141] The crucial point missed here is that credibility issues do change over time, as do cultural and societal norms. While the latter is acknowledged, and

---

[167] A number of cases where the exception was applied, and so prohibition on grounds of delay refused, include: *DO'R v DPP* [1997] 2IR 273 (High Court decision *per* Kelly J); *PD v DPP & Ors* (19 March 1997, unreported), HC, *per* McCracken J) and *DC v DPP & O'Leary* (31 October 1997, unreported), SC, *per* Geoghegan J). In others, it was nonetheless granted: *PW v DPP* (27 November 1997), HC, *per* Flood J; *Fitzpatrick v DPP* (5 December 1997, unreported), HC, *per* McCracken J).

[168] *PC v DPP* [1999] 2 IR 25 at 61 (Supreme Court).

[169] *PC v DPP* [1999] 2 IR 25 at 61.

[170] *PC v DPP* [1999] 2 IR 25 at 63.

[171] *PC v DPP* [1999] 2 IR 25 at 63.

[172] *PC v DPP* [1999] 2 IR 25 at 63.

hence legitimate to that degree, the former may remain hidden and unappreciated in its effect. It is precisely relevant that if the individual here had been tried at the time of the alleged offences, he would have had not only no temporal obstacles to overcome, but avoided current cultural obstacles. The victim might also have faced additional hurdles at that time, equally illegitimate perhaps, but again adding to the advantages held by an accused. If it is not right to place credibility barriers in front of certain victims (as then), is it not similarly unacceptable to place them at the door of certain accused now? Supporting the centrality of credibility here, Keane CJ, with regard to the issue of fair trial, found that '[h]ad this case been tried ten years ago, the issue for the jury would essentially have been one as to the credibility of the complainant and, if he gave evidence, of the applicant.'[173]

[6.142] That issue of credibility and norms regarding these cases begs the very question of how different the temporal and popular cultural climate is now than it might have been ten years ago? The legal and cultural context of belief regarding these kinds of cases has greatly changed. The prosecution task regarding such offences has been eased by the availability – and admissibility – of expert testimony, the removal of the corroboration requirement and the facilitating of witness testimony through live television link and video provision. Moreover, the public, and hence jury, view of such cases has simply transformed.

[6.143] Popular wisdom which would have leaned in the past in the opposite direction, now leans in a pro-prosecution direction and hence accommodates the victim's voice at the expense of the defendant's claim to a fair trial. Within the confines of sexual offences, there is a current consistency of opposition between state and the individual accused, community and the accused, victim and the accused. The orthodoxy of the past has, therefore, turned full circle on fairness.

[6.144] The particular nature of judicial reflection, is such that it occurs in a specific context where partial sightedness may tolerate departure from traditional norms. This facilitates a judicial role which may continue to pledge allegiance formally and visibly to such concepts as fairness, (thereby ensuring the appearance of their continuity) despite the reality of changes on the ground. Ultimately however this may result in a schism being created between formal values and actual application in fact. This then may prove a fertile breeding ground for future and further divergence, and ultimate paradigm collapse as the values we pledge allegiance to are hollowed out.

---

[173] *PC v DPP* [1999] 2 IR 25 at 70.

[6.145] To the extent that it goes against the grain of popular sentiment, McGuinness J's decision in *PC v DPP*[174] serves as a litmus test for the meaning of justice as fairness in context. Ironically, (in the face of its comparatively recent legislative reform) it is this disenchantment with 'received wisdom' and assumptions of verity on the part of the victim which has manifested in a renewed argument for the re-introduction of corroboration.

[6.146] In *J O'C v DPP*[175] the applicant was a retired guard of 69 years of age who was charged with 16 counts of indecent assault between 1974 and 1978 when the complainant, C O'S, was between 10 and 13 years of age. Her father was a retired Sergeant and the families were next-door neighbours at the time of the alleged offences. The applicant's wife had died in 1993 and so was unavailable to give valuable evidence regarding frequency of visits etc. The applicant suffered from ill health and medical evidence suggested he would have great difficulty in coping with the stress of a trial. A consultant psychologist gave evidence that the delay of C O'S was 'reasonable'. The president of the High Court had accepted that a number of factors here militated against a fair trial.

[6.147] On appeal, Keane CJ pointed out that the court must decide whether as a matter of probability, assuming the complaint to be truthful, the delay in making it was referable to the accused's own actions. Given the respective ages and the fact that the accused was not only considerably older, but a person in authority, this was classically a case where the child might not be willing to make a complaint.[176] With regard to the hierarchy of interests here, Keane CJ pointed out that, '[e]ven in cases where, assuming, as one must do for the purpose of the application, that the complaints are true, the court finds that the delay is essentially due to the applicant's own conduct, there remains the paramount necessity to ensure that the applicant receives a trial in due course of law.'[177] He found that the President of the High Court was not correct in drawing inferences that the degree of prejudice here was such as would lead to a real and serious risk of an unfair trial. With regard to the court's approach to proceedings such as these, Keane CJ was clear that 'the court must proceed on the assumption that the allegations are well founded and, to that only and solely in the context of these specific proceedings, the presumption of innocence does not apply.'[178]

---

[174] *PC v DPP* [1999] 2 IR 25.

[175] *J O'C v DPP* [2000] 3 IR 478.

[176] *J O'C v DPP* [2000] 3 IR 478 at 485 *per* Keane CJ.

[177] *J O'C v DPP* [2000] 3 IR 478 at 485.

[178] *J O'C v DPP* [2000] 3 IR 478 at 486 *per* Keane CJ.

[6.148] Murphy J stated that in the absence of delay on the part of the state or prosecution, the onus was on the applicant to prove that a fair trial was impossible. This was not done here and so he also dismissed the application. Hardiman J in a lengthy judgment dissented. He pointed out that the inability to test evidence in sex abuse cases due to the lapse of time is compounded by two factors: no general requirement of corroboration and the practical pressure on the defendant to answer questions. With regard to the special category status of such cases, Hardiman J endorsed this for another reason, that of 'the chilling and destructive effect which a long lapse of time may have on the ability even of an innocent person to defend himself.'[179] It is with regard to the presumption of innocence, however, that his disagreement with the jurisprudence to date was most profound:

> I cannot subscribe to the proposition that the presumption of innocence applies only in the actual trial of criminal proceeding or is capable of suspension for any purpose relating to the trial, such as the disposal of injunctive proceeding like the present ones.
>
> … [T]here is … no basis whatever for assuming the truth of the allegations against the accused prior to conviction, for any purpose or on any proceeding. This assumption, even for a limited purpose, is a much greater step than merely not applying the presumption, great as that is in itself. It involves assuming the contrary.[180]

[6.149] Hardiman J reiterated that the real issue was whether there was a real risk that the applicant would not receive a fair trial. In that he was *at idem* with the others, but begged to differ in so far as he did not see it necessary 'to assume for any purpose that the allegations of the complainant are true.'[181] He would restrain the prosecution. Hardiman J also commented that he found the nature of the examination by the psychologist here to have been 'gravely inadequate'.[182] This is a theme of his judgments in the area in so far as criticism of the expert witnesses or the presentation of the evidence and their area of research or expertise was inadequate. In *NC v DPP*[183] this was reflected in the unavailability of the hypnotist under whose ministrations the complainant revived her memory of the events forming the basis of the complaint, this also triggering the other complaints made by her sister. Here the trial would have taken place 40 years and 10 months after the first alleged assault. Hardiman J, granting the application to restrain prosecution, pointed out that there was therefore no

---

[179] *J O'C v DPP* [2000] 3 IR 478 at 514 *per* Hardiman J.
[180] *J O'C v DPP* [2000] 3 IR 478 at 517 *per* Hardiman J.
[181] *J O'C v DPP* [2000] 3 IR 478 at 521.
[182] *J O'C v DPP* [2000] 3 IR 478 at 527.
[183] *NC v DPP* [2001] IESC 54.

effective test or control of the mechanism of alleged recovery, rendering this a situation 'fraught with the risk of unfairness'.

[6.150] Subsequently, vindication of that stance was given in *JL v DPP*[184] by McGuinness J, who said Hardiman J's experiences accorded with her own in the Central Criminal Court.[185] There was also, in that case, vindication of the presumption of innocence, with Keane J concluding:

> Given the presumption of innocence to which, at this stage of the inquiry, the applicant is entitled, I am satisfied that he has discharged the onus ... that there is a real and serious risk of an unfair trial.[186]

McGuinness J also stated:

> I do not accept, however, that the presumption of innocence plays no part in the decision which must be made by the court in this case ... While for the purposes of looking at the reasons for a complainant's delay in reporting a sexual assault to the gardaí an assumption as to the truth of her allegations may be made, when the court subsequently considers whether there is a real risk of an unfair trial it is a trial based on the presumption of innocence that is in question. By this approach the court will hold the balance between a situation in which it would be impossible to try any accused of sexual offences against children where delay in reporting had occurred, and the equally undesirable situation where all persons accused of sexual offences against children would have to face trial no matter how long the time was which had elapsed since the alleged offence and no matter how great was the danger of an unfair trial.

[6.151] *DPP v Gentlemen*[187] was a case involving a number of counts of indecent assault in relation to a young boy, alleged to have been the pupil of the accused teacher, where 22 years had elapsed since the alleged offending conduct had taken place. There was no corroboration of the applicant's allegation, which the court noted to be frequently a feature of these cases. The trial judge had exercised his discretion to give a warning (under s 7 of the Criminal Law (Rape) (Amendment) Act 1990). Once exercised, Keane CJ pointed out that the appellate court was entitled to consider whether, in all the circumstances, he gave the appropriate warning.

---

[184] *JL v DPP* [2000] 3 IR 122. The applicant here was charged with three counts of rape, indecent assault and buggery of J O'R (female) on a date unknown between 1 June 1979 and 30 September 1980. The High Court had dismissed an application to restrain the trial because of delay, leading to the Supreme Court appeal. Evidence (not contradicted) of a psychologist was presented. Keane J identified two special features not typically present in cases of alleged child abuse: complaint was about one incident only and, as in *P O'C v DPP*, the applicant claimed inability to construct a defence through passage of time.

[185] *JL v DPP* [2000] 3 IR 122 at 133, McGuinness J.

[186] *JL v DPP* [2000] 3 IR 122 at 126–127, Keane J.

[187] *DPP v Robert Gentlemen* (25 February 2002, unreported), CCA.

[6.152] The Court of Criminal Appeal commented that this was obviously a case where a trial judge would give a warning for three reasons: (i) the absence of corroboration of the applicant's story; (ii) the fact that 22 years had elapsed; and (iii) no act or complaint was made at the time. The Court (Keane CJ) found the warning not to have been adequate, specifically because it did not indicate to the jury why the law considers it dangerous to convict, that it is one person's word against another, and it had not been explained that this is not some formalistic requirement but a 'real and important requirement based on the experience of the courts that must be exercised'.[188]

[6.153] Since the change in the law in 1990 the corroboration requirement has not gone away in the context of sexual offences generally. However, the following two historic sexual abuse cases clarify whether a separate and an independent corroboration requirement has developed with regard to such cases.

[6.154] *People (DPP) v LG*[189] concerned an allegation of rape and indecent assault in relation to two of the accused's sisters between July 1973 and June 1978 and other dates unknown. One sister was between 8 and 13 years at the time; the other between 4 and 6 years. All the offences were alleged to have taken place in their Dublin home, where 12 children were living in very poor circumstances. By the time the allegations were made, a lot of possible witnesses had died, including the mother. Following conviction and on appeal one of the issues raised was whether the trial judge dealt adequately with corroboration and delay and specifically whether those issues should have been dealt with separately in the trial judge's charge to the jury and should not have been conflated as they were in this case.

[6.155] The trial judge's initial direction was:

> You have already heard from counsel of the problems relating to matters which go back to 1973. There are of course problems with regard to delays in prosecution and these have been referred to by counsel for the defence. You must balance that with the difficulty that the complainants had first in coming to realise what happened. Remember it happened when they were minors and indeed their evidence – certainly the evidence of one of them – was that she had tried to put it out of her mind.[190]

At the end of that direction, counsel for the accused asked for more direction on the issue of corroboration. The trial judge recalled the jury and stated as follows:

> And finally, I spoke to you about corroboration and I would add that you should be cautious with regard to any finding that is from a long time in the past. There

---

[188] *DPP v Robert Gentlemen* (25 February 2002, unreported), CCA Keane CJ at 7.
[189] *People (DPP) v LG* [2003] 2 IR 517.
[190] *People (DPP) v LG* [2003] 2 IR 517 at 528 *per* Keane CJ.

is always that difficulty but I think I have mentioned the difficulty with regard to the timing of these charges going back to 1973. Just again to state: be cautious in terms of evidence that is from so long ago on anybody's evidence.

[6.156] The Court of Criminal Appeal took a poor view of the adequacy of that direction. Chief Justice Keane stated:[191]

> The court is satisfied that, given the very significant delay of 27 years that had elapsed in this case, these could not on any view be regarded as adequate warnings to the jury of the dangers of a conviction in respect of any of the counts after so great a lapse of time. There was no indication to the jury of the problems that this inevitably would create for the defence in preparing for the trial, including the death of one of the members of the family and the difficulty for the accused in assembling evidence as to whether he was in fact living at the house at the time the episodes were alleged to have occurred. Those were incidents of possible prejudice which were specific to these proceedings and of which the jury should have been reminded by the trial judge. The jury should also have been told by the trial judge that, in assessing the credibility of both complainants, they would have to bear in mind that they had not complained to the gardaí until more than 20 years had elapsed. Nor were they told that, while on one view it was understandable that no complaint had been made while the complainants were still children or adolescents, there was no satisfactory explanation given as to the delay which ensued from 1986 until 1997 in making any complaint, although it was obvious at that stage they were not in any sense under the dominion of the accused. The jury should also have been reminded that, even in respect of the earlier period of delay prior to 1986, the respective ages of the complainants and the accused, and the fact that the latter was not living in the house from 1979 onwards, made it is extremely unlikely that any question of a relationship of dominion between the complainants and the accused could have arisen which might have explained the failure to complain during that period.

Keane CJ concluded that 'on no view could the directions of the trial judge on the question of delay be regarded as adequate.'[192]

[6.157] The Court of Criminal Appeal then moved to consider the issue of corroboration in relation to sexual offences and a separate issue of a warning under that heading. The court noted that, although he was not obliged to do so, the trial judge had treated this as a case where he should warn the jury as to the dangers of convicting the accused in a case of this nature in the absence of any corroboration. His warning was as follows:

> Because of the serious nature of these charges, counsel has already told you that the law is that it was necessary to have corroboration, that is, supporting

---

[191] *People (DPP) v LG* [2003] 2 IR 517 at 528–529.
[192] *People (DPP) v LG* [2003] 2 IR 517 at 529.

evidence. The nature, of course, of both sexual assault and indeed of rape are such that they occur when there are no other witnesses, or usually when there are no other witnesses. The position with regard to corroboration is that it is now no longer necessary and it is important that I remind you that it is no longer necessary. However, that does not mean that in relation to incidents which have occurred many, many years ago, it is appropriate that I give you a warning with regard to time. The experience of the courts has shown that it is often unsafe to act on the uncorroborated evidence of a witness. The law is that we do not need it. Nonetheless, it seems appropriate that I caution you with regard to simply accepting evidence where the surrounding circumstances are difficult to ascertain, where there are problems with regard to recollection and other matters, such as timing. Again, this is not essential but is important to bear in mind as part of the circumstances of the matter.

[6.158] The Court of Criminal Appeal noted that the trial judge overlooked the fact that he never had to give a corroboration warning as a matter of law – the change effected in 1990 was the abolition of the requirement to give a warning in such cases. That in itself the Court of Criminal Appeal noted would not give rise to a problem in this case. But an issue does arise with regard to the failure to give a separate warning:

> … it must be said that the warning he did give was, in its terms, linked to the question of delay. The latter is of course an entirely separate matter in respect of which … a separate and distinct warning was required … [T]he issues of corroboration and delay should be dealt with separately and not conflated as they were.[193]

[6.159] Support for this is found in *People (DPP) v Hernon*,[194] which confirmed that issues of corroboration and delay should be dealt with separately and not conflated and that a distinct warning is necessary in relation to delay. Corroboration would then seem to have some life in it, with this separate and distinct heading emerging.

[6.160] This was further confirmed in *People v PJ*,[195] which concerned charges of rape and indecent assault allegedly perpetrated in the 1970s. The applicant's niece was the complainant. She was between 4 and 10 years and he was between 13 and 20 years at the time. He was convicted but appealed on the basis of the trial judge's failure to give a full corroboration warning and a failure to deal fully and properly with the issue of delay. McGuinness J gave the judgment of the Court of Criminal Appeal. The court found that there was no distinction made between the issue of corroboration and that of delay. There was no clear

---

[193] *People (DPP) v LG* [2003] 2 IR 517 at 530 (Keane CJ).

[194] *People (DPP) v Hernon* (3 December 2001, unreported), CCA.

[195] *People v PJ* [2003] 3 IR 550.

warning given to the jury about the difficulties in a trial relating to offences which occurred many years ago. The Court of Criminal Appeal made the point that the issues of corroboration and delay are distinct. In relation to sexual offences, they noted that since the 1990 Act it is no longer mandatory to give a corroboration warning but that '[i]t may still, however, be desirable in particular cases.'[196] McGuinness J quotes Keane J in *People (DPP) & Reid*:[197]

> Notwithstanding the new legislation, there will still be cases in which trial judges will consider it desirable to warn the jury as to the dangers of convicting on the uncorroborated evidence of the complainant. The Court considers it may be of assistance, in such cases, to direct the jury's attention to those aspects of the evidence which are capable of corroborating the complainant's version.

McGuinness J continued to comment on this case:[198]

> In the instant case the trial judge was certainly justified in giving a corroboration warning. The complainant's evidence was not corroborated in any way, it contained a number of inconsistencies and was vague in some respects, especially in regard to dates. The offences were alleged to have taken place in a house with many inhabitants, and no evidence was given as to physical injuries which might have been suffered by the complainant as a result of repeated rape.

[6.161] The Court of Criminal Appeal then went through a lot of the older cases in relation to the requirement of warning in sexual offence cases, noting that their reasoning is uncomfortable in the modern age:

> The warning is no longer mandatory and much of the general tenor of the judgments in the older cases would not readily be acceptable today, but once a trial judge has elected to give a warning, it seems to us that the necessity remains for that warning to be clear and unmistakable.[199]

McGuinness J further noted that, although the cases referred to on the warning:

> [a]re pre-1990 cases ... where in the context of the present law a discretionary warning is given, it is still in our view necessary for the meaning of corroboration to be made clear to the jury.

> The wording used by the trial judge in the instant case was not calculated to convey any clear message to the jury. No proper effort was made to define what in law is meant by corroboration, nor was it explained in detail how a lack of corroboration might affect the jury's view of the evidence. It is hard to understand what assistance can be gained from saying that the fact that there is no corroboration is not the complainant's fault.[200]

---

[196] *People v PJ* [2003] 3 IR 550 at 566, *per* McGuinness J.
[197] *People (DPP) & Reid* [1993] 2 IR 186 at 197.
[198] *People v PJ* [2003] 3 IR 550 at 566.
[199] *People v PJ* [2003] 3 IR 550 at 567.
[200] *People v PJ* [2003] 3 IR 550 at 568.

[6.162] Therefore the court concluded that the warning in relation to it being a sexual offence was unsatisfactory. The court then turned to address the issue of delay. They pointed out that, '[i]t has again and again been pointed out that trial judges are obliged to issue appropriate directions and rulings to avoid the possible prejudicial effect of delay in sexual abuse cases.'[201]

[6.163] They noted that in the *People (DPP) v RB*[202] the full text of the trial judge's charge on the difficulties caused by delay was set out and approved by the Court of Criminal Appeal. This was that direction of Judge Haugh to the jury:

> I now want to move from the general, not totally to the particular, but to this kind of case. You have heard in this case, and it is undoubtedly a further difficulty for the case, but this is a case of an old complaint. The events that you have to decide here are alleged to have occurred more than fifteen years ago. It obviously makes the task for a jury and the task for a court in trying these cases a lot more difficult. As Mr McKeon says they normally degenerate into one man's word against another, a 'you did, I didn't, you did, I didn't' kind of contest and that is because when you are dealing with old complaints, you are dealing with events from a long time ago and for the very reason that they are so old they generally lack precision, they generally lack detail. And it is in precision and in detail that cross-examinations generally take place. Witnesses seldom change their stories and admit that what they have said was a fabrication or a lie. You probe looking for the truth by questioning people in detail. If there are contests, as there is in this case or any case where there is a plea of not guilty, again it is much easier to defend an allegation where there is detail alleged against you. If somebody alleged that any one of you had assault me in the middle eighties and left it no more than that, it is very, very hard for you to defend it. I think that it would be accepted by all of you and it is, no doubt, so. But if I had complained that one of you had assaulted me last July, if I had complained that one of you had assaulted me on 17th of July, the chances are you would be able to work out your whereabouts at the time, and who can vouch for you at that time, and be able to grapple with issues on the basis of detail. You will be able to look up your diaries maybe, if you keep them, or check with your employers if you have them and you may have been on holidays. But how can a person be expected to attack the allegation, to contest the allegation with any subtlety, with any detail, with any forensic form of attack, if all you are told about it is that you did it about fifteen years ago on some date unknown over a period of eighteen months? That, I suggest to you, makes it far harder to defend it than it is to prosecute it. In fact to prosecute it is easier if you do not nail your colours to the mast because there is less you can be cross-examined on. But the law does not say that stale cases, old cases, cannot be tried. But what I must tell you is that an accused person cannot

---

[201] *People v PJ* [2003] 3 IR 550 at 568.

[202] *People (DPP) v RB* (12 February 2003, unreported), CCA, Denham J.

in your minds or in your consideration be disadvantaged because the case is old, because the complaint is related to events from a long time ago. You have to be all the more careful and it should be much harder to satisfy you in relation to an event that is phrased in a general and vague way rather than an event which carries details or particulars. You cannot let the fact that Mr B. is handicapped by reason of the lack of precision in the charge cause you to come easier to a decision adverse to him. The State should not take benefit from old cases. Their life should not be made easier by bringing old cases. Juries must, with their hand on their heart, recognise the huge difficulty that accused persons have of dealing with old cases and be all the more careful and take that into account when arriving at a decision.[203]

[6.164] That direction was endorsed by the court in *RB* and again here in *PJ* the Court of Criminal Appeal decided that, by contrast, the direction of the trial judge was inadequate. The conviction was quashed. A specific comment on the circumstances of this case was as follows and indicates how the appeal court felt the trial judge should have warned the jury:

> In the instant case, very specific problems were caused by the fact that the complainant did not raise her complaint to the gardaí until some 25 years after the alleged offences occurred. The most important of these difficulties resulted from the fact that both the complainant's mother and, more crucially still, her grandmother had died before any complaint was made.[204]

There was also some conflicting and some unavailable medical evidence. Therefore, the court was satisfied that the direction given by the trial judge in regard to corroboration and delay was not adequate and so the trial was unsatisfactory in that respect.

[6.165] It seems then that we have now developed a separate corroboration requirement in the context of delay, particularly in relation to historic sexual abuse cases. It shows there is still life in these rules which are developed over the years. They are a creature of the kind of cases which come before the courts. With an increasing number of sex abuses cases, the courts start thinking about how to treat them and rules are developed in that light. With cases involving witness protection, courts have to decide how to deal with accomplice evidence. Do we strengthen the warning or not? The rules are very much a product of what is coming before the courts.

[6.166] Corroboration rules are the most technical of evidentiary rules. They deal with how to direct juries, satisfy requirements, provide perfect material for appeals by asking questions such as: Did the trial judge give warning(s)? Was

---

[203] *People v PJ* [2003] 3 IR 550 at 569–570 *per* McGuinness J, quoting Haugh J, as quoted by Denham J in *People (DPP) v RB* (12 February 2003, unreported), CCA, pp 8 and 19.

[204] *People v PJ* [2003] 3 IR 550 at 570.

the warning appropriate and adequate and separate under each heading required and not conflated?

[6.167] At base it is all about crystallizing assumptions about credibility: doubting certain categories of people and certain categories of evidence, believing others and sometimes, particularly regarding confession evidence and visual identification evidence, giving the jury the benefit of the court's experience by saying: 'You need to be careful here. It might be probative, confession might sound great, but it has been the experience of the courts/ science etc that people make mistakes with identification.' In the context of historic sex abuse cases, McGuinness J's reminder is a striking one that just as it was unacceptable in the past to completely doubt women who alleged rape, it would be as bad to have the other extreme and believe them entirely when they make allegations thirty years after an alleged offence.

[6.168] It is the certainty, the assumption, that needs shaking – ironically that is what corroboration rules both emerge from and challenge. A judge always has the ability to point out if a witness lies on the stand or if there are inconsistencies with a witness's statement. This can be pointed out to the jury. The system allows us to comment on particular witnesses because they show themselves to be unreliable. This, however, is very different. This is fastening onto them an extra requirement because of the *type* of witness they are or the *kind* of evidence it is. There are lots of other types of witnesses and evidence which do not have a corroboration requirement attaching to them: anyone with a history of mental illness, for example. This was considered in a series of cases (*Bagshaw* and *Spencer*)[205] in England involving allegations of maltreatment of patients in institutions. Patients testified against those running the institutions. The English Court of Appeal was faced with the issue of how to treat these people who all had differing ranges of mental illness. The question arose of whether there should be a warning requirement? The defence argued that there should be, yet the court did not create a warning requirement. Commentators afterwards said it was unusual then that those with a mental illness were thereby deemed more credible than, say, sexual offence complainants.

[6.169] We have had other examples of commentary with regard to categories of people and credibility. In the Kerry Babies Tribunal Report, for example, Judge Lynch remarked that the familiarity of the gardaí with giving testimony may lead to a situation where they are less inclined to be impressed than ordinary citizens by the requirement to take the oath. Gardaí would be attending court frequently and might have a more casual attitude to giving testimony. It is certainly true that there is no requirement fastened on to those involved in law

---

[205] *R v Bagshaw* [1984] 1 WLR 477 and *R v Spencer* [1985] 1 All ER 673.

enforcement or to police officers. It is useful to reflect on the changes to the law which have occurred and think about how the rules which emerge have evolved, and in that light to consider if they still (justifiably) give cause for pause.

[6.170] The Irish courts, therefore, have turned full circle: the exception carved out to the principle of expeditious justice, invoking assumptions of credibility and proof to the detriment of the accused's fair trial rights, and the presumption of innocence, turning to the judicial rejection of received wisdom and vindication of fair trial rights for the accused.

Impact of Strasbourg jurisprudence on fair trial

[6.171] Ashworth,[206] in an article assessing the impact of the Human Rights Act 1998 on criminal proceedings in its first year, estimated it has mainly been felt in criminal procedure and evidence. Ashworth[207] had earlier made evident his dislike of the practice of 'balancing' rights in the context of such proceedings:

> The scourge of many debates about criminal justice policy is the concept of 'balance' ... The principled approach to criminal justice ... is explicitly normative. It sets out various rights and principles that ought to be safeguarded ... One consequence of the Human Rights Bill 1998 will be to bring rights into a central position.

With regard to assessments of art 6 fair trial rights and the particular 'balancing' exercises beloved of members of the judiciary, he reminds us that art 6 is a strong right – unlike say arts 8–11, which are qualified rights.

[6.172] Hence his warning with regard to this kind of reasoning in that context:[208]

> Any argument to the effect that a right implied into Article 6 should be restricted out of deference to the 'public interest' should be required to be at least as strong, and probably stronger, than a similar argument for justifying interference with one of the qualified rights under Articles 8–11. The right to a fair trial and its constituent elements should surely be given a greater weight, in such calculations ... [T]he Strasbourg decisions refer frequently to one doctrine ... that no restriction should be such as to 'destroy the very essence of the right'. This doctrine places distinct limits on 'public interest' balancing of the kind that some British Judges have found attractive.

---

[206] Ashworth, 'Criminal Proceedings after the Human Rights Act: The First Year' [2001] CrimLR 855.

[207] Ashworth, *The Criminal Process* (2nd edn), p 307.

[208] Ashworth, 'Criminal Proceedings after the Human Rights Act: The First Year' [2001] CrimLR 855 at 856.

Ashworth makes the further point that to accept that these rights are not absolute is 'not to concede that they may be 'balanced away' by being compared with a general public interest and put in second place.'[209]

[6.173] In this context of consideration of present and future implications of the shape of evidentiary decision making as influenced by the dictates of constitutional and Convention parameters, it is apposite to remind ourselves of Garland's[210] perception of the role of penalty – for which can be substituted that of the trial process generally:

> [It]…communicates meaning not just about crime and punishment but also about power, authority, legitimacy, normality, morality, personhood, social relations, and a host of other tangential matters. [They] … are part of an authoritative, institutional discourse which seeks to organise our moral and political understanding and to educate our sentiments and sensibilities. They provide a continuous repetitive set of instructions as to how we should think about good and evil, normal and pathological, legitimate and illegitimate, order and disorder. Through their judgment, condemnations, and classifications they teach us (and persuade us) how to judge, what to condemn, and how to classify, and they supply a set of languages, idioms, and vocabularies with which to do so…In short, the practices, institutions and discourses of penalty all *signify* and the meanings which are conveyed thereby tend to outrun the immediacies of crime and punishment and 'speak of' broader and more extended issues.

Within the Irish and English contexts, there is evident judicial scepticism regarding recent changes to criminal procedure to accommodate witnesses, other than the accused, in terms of implications held for fair trial rights. On the other hand, prosecutorial bias is evident in the legislature's, and the popular, view regarding certain offences – now including those of sexual offences and historic sex abuse claims.[211]

[6.174] Hardiman J has counselled caution in the face of historic sex abuse claims, and McGuinness J has correctly identified a parallel equally reprehensible to that previously applicable to sex abuse victims, which is now affecting the accused. The construction of fairness in sexual offences, it is suggested, may have resulted in the accused's presumption of innocence being usurped by a presumption of guilt. 'Fairness' in the House of Lord's decision in

---

[209] Ashworth, 'Criminal Proceedings after the Human Rights Act: The First Year' [2001] CrimLR 855 at 866–7.

[210] Garland, 'Punishment as a Cultural Agent' in *Punishment in Modern Society* (Oxford University Press, 2001), p 252–3.

[211] See generally re recovered memory/false memory debate: Nachson, 'Truthfulness, Deception and Self-Deception in Recovering True and false memories of Child Sexual Abuse' [2001] Vol 8 *Int Rev of Victimology* 1–18.

A[212] operated to include evidence previously excluded under legislation with a victims' rights mandate. Yet in A the House of Lords invoked the triple danger of the opposition of the accused and victims' rights in the criminal justice system; deference to popular legislative sentiment; and, although de facto vindicating the accused here, raising the spectre of future 'contextual sensitivity' in rights evaluation.

[6.175] A possible solution emerges in *P O'C*,[213] which revived a rule of evidence cautious of credibility (corroboration) in a context where a judicially carved exception to expeditiousness in cases of historic sex abuse was predicated on victims' needs. Fairness is revealed as a moveable feast dependent on legislative desire and popular wisdom, even to the extent of influencing judicial construction of fair trial needs in context. Certainly one might question whether the mechanism for implementation used – judicial mandates regarding fairness – provides an adequate vindication of an accused's fair trial rights.

[6.176] European precedents invoked in *Brown v Stott*,[214] and *Kebilene*,[215] where *Murray*[216] is consistently preferred to *Saunders*,[217] indicate that those decisions vindicating fair trial rights are purely symbolic. Article 6 may not offer any protection for those who are seen as abhorrent – the victims of current witch-hunts and collective wisdom. There has certainly been ample evidence of the accommodation of victims' rights at the expense of those of the accused. The solution here may not lie, however, in rights discourse and the dictates of fair trial, but in our approach to fact-finding itself. In adjudging whether judgments like Hardiman J's are to be welcomed, one has to estimate whether it will either be drowned in the rush of certainty and belief or worse invoked merely to reassure as to the prevailing and overarching nature of justice.

[6.177] Yet taking the current culture into account, one can certainly argue for a pro-accused approach in interpreting the 'story' of a criminal trial. Any crime that is currently the subject of a perceived 'crisis' or 'witch-hunt', whose perpetrators are thus distanced from all fact-finders (jury, judge, legislator and public) arguably requires an adjustment in terms of credibility issues, as at a fundamental level we cannot recognise their 'story' – it literally makes no sense in equal measure as the opposing tale does. To make such an assumption may undoubtedly be uncomfortable for us as a society collectively and individually,

---

[212] *Regina v A UK* [2002 1 AC 45 HL .

[213] *P O'C v DPP* [2000] 3 IR 87.

[214] *Brown v Stott* [2003] 1 AC 681.

[215] *R v DPP ex p Kebilene* [2000] 2 AC 326.

[216] *Murray v United Kingdom* (1996) 22 EHRR 29.

[217] *Saunders v United Kingdom* (1997) 23 EHRR 313.

as we do not like these people and are not 'like' them. On the other hand, not to do so and to risk using the criminal process to draw that distinction is not just wrong, it is a travesty and a perversion of justice. It is surely to those whom we regard as perverse that we owe most, or we pervert not only the course of justice but, by definition, ourselves. The rules of evidence are often criticised as being of another climate or time. It may be, however, that it is *precisely* when they reject the certainties or tenor of our own culture and values, that they are necessary to counter-balance our prejudices as fact-finders.

[6.178] To leave matters subject to the exercise of judicial discretion on an individual basis, or subject to community feeling, manifest through the jury on occasion when they feel so moved, will most likely result in the issue being determined by such non-identification with the victim or accused – the prostitute, drug dealer, paedophile, rapist – those currently furthest from us and so 'other'. The avoidance of 'scapegoating' and arbitrary justice requires rooting the rules of evidence and fact-determination in a pro-accused, pro-defence rights bias, which may be the only guarantee of justice in the aftermath of witch-hunts. The reliance on judicial watchfulness alone – even with an increased rights mandate – does not prove a sufficient or, despite the evidence of the Irish courts' periodic breaks with legislative and public consensus, constant guarantee.

[6.179] The inevitable constraints of fact determination and application of evidentiary rules – not least the adjudication of fairness – require more than is promised by a judicial mandate of fair trial. An overarching remit, applicable in all contexts, but most particularly those of current 'popular' concern, to vindicate the accused's rights through application of the rules of evidence directing finders of fact to err on the side of the accused, may indeed be a pre-condition to justice.

Chapter 7

Opinion Evidence

Pansy was really a blank page, a pure white surface, successfully kept so; she had neither art, nor guile, nor temper, nor talent – only two or three small exquisite instincts: for knowing a friend, for avoiding a mistake, for taking care of an old toy or a new frock.

James, *The Portrait of a Lady*

Introduction

[7.01] The rule in relation to the admissibility of evidence of opinion on the part of a witness is yet another exclusionary rule. The general rule is that which provides that witnesses must speak only to the facts which they have observed, and not of the inferences which they have drawn from such facts. In particular, the justification for this exclusionary rule lies in the fact that for a witness to draw conclusions and form opinions in regard to proved facts would constitute a usurpation of the function of the jury as trier of fact.

[7.02] Exceptions to the general rule do exist, however, and not unusually in this branch of the law, they are often more powerful in effect than the rule itself. The exceptions are twofold:

(1) 'Expert' witnesses can give opinion evidence. The motivation for calling such witnesses is, of course, to benefit from the expertise of their opinion, and they are generally stated to be permitted to opine on matters of science and art.

(2) Secondly, non-expert witnesses may, in certain circumstances, give what might be regarded as opinion evidence. This type of evidence is mostly received because it would be virtually impossible for the witness to confine himself to the observed facts, and so leave the inference to the jury. Examples of this occurring include testimony that the accused had been drinking, the identification of a person's belongings and handwriting, the speed of a vehicle, the age of a person and the state of the weather. For example, in *R v German*,[1] the accused was charged with dangerous driving and driving while intoxicated, and a lay person was allowed to testify with regard to same.

---

[1] *R v German* [1947] 4 DLR 68.

Expert evidence

[7.03] With regard to expert evidence, Roberts and Zuckerman state that:

> The longstanding relationship between law and science, like any partnership of enduring value, is infused with a certain creative tension, and there have been some rough patches and the odd unsavoury incident. The reputation of forensic science has not entirely recovered from its association with several of the high profile miscarriages of justice that came to light in the late 1980s ... Problems with expert evidence tend to materialize when people are seduced into thinking that science is an evidentiary panacea, devoid of blind spots, limitations and special challenges of its own. The implication of scientific evidence in so many notorious miscarriage of justice ought to serve as a dramatic reminder of what can, and sometimes does, go wrong when courts are beguiled by flaky expertise or place too much faith in the wrong kinds of science.[2]

Qualification

[7.04] In order to qualify for consideration as an expert witness capable of giving opinion evidence, it was not traditionally required that the expertise take a professional format. In *R v Silverlock*,[3] a solicitor with 'a bit of an interest in handwriting' was allowed to testify. However, as specialisation has increased, and designation of expertise status perhaps became correspondingly more elusive, witnesses tendered must be shown to have acquired more than just a little knowledge before coming within this category.

[7.05] In the Canadian case of *R v Kuzmack*,[4] for instance, the accused was charged with murder. His defence was that the victim had a knife when he grabbed her, hence the killing was an accident. A doctor's testimony to the effect that the wounds on her hands were sustained while defending herself was not allowed on the basis that that doctor was not an expert on wounds or forensic medicine.

[7.06] In regard to handwriting evidence, another Canadian case (*Pitre v R*[5]) held it necessary to prove that there was regular correspondence with the witness, ie the witness must have been acquainted with the person's handwriting if not with the writer.

[7.07] In *Poynton v Poynton*,[6] Madden J differentiated in the case of evidence regarding to the medical incapacity of a testator between that of a lay or

---

2   Roberts and Zuckerman, *Criminal Evidence* (OUP, 2004), pp 291–2.
3   *R v Silverlock* [1894] 2 QB 766.
4   *R v Kuzmack* (1955) 111 CCC 1, 20 CR 377, [1955] SCR 293.
5   *Pitre v R* (1933) SCR 69.
6   *Poynton v Poynton* (1903) 37 ILTR 54.

nonmedical person (here, such witnesses being the testator's brother-in-law and a clergyman) and that of a doctor. A similar distinction was drawn by Walsh J (dissenting) in the Supreme Court decision of *Glynn*,[7] with regard to evidence pertaining to whether, at the time of execution of a will, the deceased was of sound mind.

[7.08] In general, the modern rule can be said to be that the opinions of skilled witnesses are admissible when the person who is giving the opinion has a particular expertise or experience in the relevant area, which is based on a special study or his day-to-day experience. The burden of proof with regard to such expertise on the part of a witness rests with the person tendering such witness in evidence. In adducing evidence by an expert witness, certain principles must be observed. The witness gives evidence under oath during examination-in-chief having first established his credentials, on which he may, if the other side does not object, be led. He can then be cross-examined by the other side. A prosecution for perjury may ensue if he gives evidence of an opinion he did not *bona fide* hold.

[7.09] Developments in society and the increasing specialisation of knowledge, have meant an increase in the tendering of expertise in the course of any litigation. The burgeoning use of expertise has spawned candidates – in the form of expert witnesses – for both sides. It is unusual to see even the more mundane 'running-down' action without experts of various hues – engineers, medical consultants etc – ranged on both sides. This poses some difficulties for the role of the adjudicators in the process (the judge as to admissibility: the jury as to credibility) and a challenge to counsel on cross-examination.

[7.10] In relation to the issue of whether jurors are capable, or indeed entitled, to choose between conflicting experts on an issue which, by definition, they are not themselves fully competent, the Australian High Court has recently vindicated the role of the jury in this context and their entitlement to so choose. In *Velveski v The Queen*,[8] on the trial of the applicant for the murder of his wife and their children, where medical and pathological evidence had been tendered with regard to whether wounds were self-inflicted, the High Court held that the fact that there was conflicting evidence did not mean the case should be withdrawn from the jury:

> Juries are frequently called upon to resolve conflicts between experts. They have done so from the inception of jury trials. Expert evidence does not, as a matter of law, fall into two categories: difficult and sophisticated expert evidence giving rise to conflicts which a jury may not and should not be allowed to resolve; and

---

[7] *Re Glynn (decd); Glynn v Glynn* [1990] 2 IR 326 at 335.
[8] *Velveski v The Queen* [2002] 76 ALJR 402.

simple and unsophisticated expert evidence which they can. Nor is it the law, that simply because there is a conflict in respect of difficult and sophisticated expert evidence, even with respect to an important, indeed critical matter, its resolution should for that reason alone be regarded by the appellate court as having been beyond the capacity of the jury to resolve.[9]

[7.11] In terms of accessibility and comprehension of expert evidence, improvement with regard to complex fraud trials, for example, is provided by the Criminal Justice (Theft and Fraud) Offences Act 2001, s 57 of which provides that in trials on indictment under that Act, transcripts of the whole or any of the evidence, including documentation from accountants explaining transactions, may be given to the jury.

[7.12] In relation to the issue of when such expertise is admissible or desirable, Zuckerman[10] states that a judge determining whether expert opinion should be accepted on a certain matter must consider the state of public opinion on the point:

> If the community has come to defer to professional standards on the matters in question, the courts will normally follow suit. Medical evidence is admissible on matters of health because we accept the authority of the medical profession in this regard.

[7.13] The theory as to the purpose or effect of the expert evidence when so admitted is interesting. In *Davie v Edinburgh Magistrates*,[11] Cooper LJ put the classic theory as follows:

> [T]heir duty is to furnish the judge or jury with the necessary scientific criteria for testing the accuracy of their conclusions, so as to enable the judge *or* jury to form their own independent judgment by the application of these criteria to the facts proved in evidence.

Of course, the extent to which this theory is effective in practice is muted by the presentation by the other party to the action of completely contrary opinion evidence, leaving the jury to choose between them. Taylor stated that:

> It is often quite surprising to see with what facility, and to what an extent their [experts'] views can be made to correspond with the wishes or the interests of the parties who call them. They do not, indeed, wilfully misrepresent what they think but their judgments become so warped by their regarding the subject in one point of view, that even when conscientiously disposed they are incapable of forming independent opinion.[12]

---

9   *Velveski v The Queen* [2002] 76 ALJR 402 at 433, *per* Gummow and Callinan JJ.

10 Zuckerman, *The Principles of Criminal Evidence* (Clarendon Law Series, 1989), p 67.

11 *Davie v Edinburgh Magistrates* (1953) SC 34.

12 Taylor, *A Treatise on the Law of Evidence* (12th edn by Croom-Johnson and Bridgman, Sweet & Maxwell, 1931), p 59.

[7.14] In the United States, the test for admissibility of expert opinion was the general acceptance of that technique or science within the scientific community, the so-called '*Frye* test', laid down in *Frye v US*.[13] In *Daubert v Merrell Dow Pharmaceuticals*,[14] the US Supreme Court rejected that standard in favour of the court ensuring that the expert's testimony both rests on a reliable foundation and is relevant to the task at hand. This would involve consideration of:

(i)   whether the theory or technique can be (and has been) tested;

(ii)   whether it has been subjected to peer review and publication;

(iii)   its known or potential error rate;

(iv)   the existence and maintenance of standards controlling its operation; and

(v)   whether it has attracted widespread acceptance within a relevant scientific community.

[7.15] In 1999 the US Supreme Court in *Kumho Tire Co Ltd et al v Carmichael*[15] held that *Daubert*'s requirement of reliability not only applied to scientific experts, but to all experts. Under *Daubert* and *Kumho* the opinion of the expert must be based on reliable methodology or analysis and not subjective belief or unsupported speculation. Reliability of expert testimony is as important as the relevance of the expert testimony.

[7.16] Expert testimony, in theory, is called to assist the jury in their adjudication. In practice, the jury must choose between varying expert opinions on matters on which they have been deemed to require expert assistance. What criteria do they then use to make their choice? Often it is the personality and presentation of the particular experts – hence the search for witnesses skilled in the presentation of their expertise. The significance of an opportunity to rebut an expert's opinion was raised to some degree in the case of *DPP v Smith*.[16] It was argued here *inter alia* that the evidence of the handwriting expert called by the prosecution differed at the hearing from the book of evidence, to the prejudice of the accused, yet did not allow then for the accused to get his own expert witness to put forward the opposite point of view. In the circumstances, the court felt it did not involve a real danger of wrong conviction.

---

[13]   *Frye v US* 54 App DC 46, 47, 293 F 1013,1014.

[14]   *Daubert v Merrell Dow Pharmaceuticals* 509 US 579.

[15]   *Kumho Tire Co Ltd et al v Carmichael* (1999) 119 SC 1167.

[16]   *DPP v Smith* (5 November 1990, unreported), CCA, Finlay CJ, *ex temp*.

The Ultimate Issue Rule

[7.17] Related to the importance of expert witnesses is the issue as to the determination of the 'ultimate issue' at trial. The theory of adjudication is such that it is for the jury or arbiter of fact to determine. Thus, the opinion of a witness, if given, is not the final word on any issue that is the prerogative of the arbiter of fact in that case. So, for example, if expert testimony has been tendered on identical characteristics of fingerprints, it is for the jury to decide, on examination of the evidence, whether they are indeed identical. In other words, they may choose to act on the evidence before them, but the expert witnesses' testimony is not conclusive. They must themselves be satisfied. Difficulties may arise with regard to that particular choice, if there is a conflict of expert opinion.

[7.18] The statement that it is for the jury to determine the ultimate issue is not without complete effect, however, because if the subject is one upon which the jury is capable of forming an opinion without the aid of an expert, expert evidence is not admissible. For example, if the defence of insanity is not raised, but the defence seeks to adduce evidence in the form of expert testimony as to the likely state of mind of the accused at the time of the incident, that is inadmissible as evidence of *mens rea*, which is a matter entirely for the jury and within their competence. In *R v Chard*,[17] Rossville LJ held that in the absence of an insanity defence, it was simply a matter for the jury on the evidence presented whether in fact the requisite *mens rea* was present. In *R v Turner*,[18] the trial judge rejected expert psychiatric evidence as to the likelihood of the accused being provoked by his girlfriend's admission of infidelity (this evidence had been tendered to support a defence of provocation to murder). This ruling was upheld on appeal. Lawton LJ explained the rationale for rejection as follows:

> If on the proven facts a judge or jury can form their own conclusions without [expert] help, then the opinion of an expert is unnecessary. In such a case if it is given dressed up in scientific jargon it may make judgment more difficult. The fact that an expert witness has impressive scientific qualifications does not by that fact alone make his opinion on matters of human nature and behaviour within the limits of normality any more helpful than that of the jurors themselves; but there is a danger that they may think it does.

[7.19] The reluctance of the courts to admit evidence of an expert on a matter which the jury or lay person is considered competent is understandable, not only for the purpose of vindicating the role and function of the jury, but also that of upholding the rationale of legal adjudication by lawyers and lay persons – not

---

17 *R v Chard* (1972) 57 Cr App Rep 268.
18 *R v Turner* [1975] 1 All ER 70.

experts. Should experts be deemed capable of giving definitive opinion conclusive of certain issues in a trial, the dawn of 'trial by psychiatrist' or 'trial by scientist' would not be very far away, but we may not yet be ready to concede that position without justification. For this reason, expert testimony or opinion evidence as to the ultimate issue has not been allowed. Some inroads have, on occasion, been made on this rule, but may be indicative of the time period in which the decisions were made, where courts were not yet overly familiar with, and so did not remain underwhelmed by the tendering of expertise.

[7.20] In *DPP v A & BC Chewing Gum Ltd*,[19] on a charge of obscenity against the defendant manufacturers who had provided a range of graphically violent war picture cards to distribute with their produce, evidence of child psychiatrists was allowable as to whether that material was likely to corrupt and deprave (this being the legal test or criteria for obscenity). Similarly, in *Lowery v R*,[20] the trial judge was adjudged to have correctly admitted evidence of a psychiatrist on behalf of one of the accused, to the effect that one of the two accused persons was more likely than the other to have committed the crime in question.

[7.21] By contrast, in the case of *R v Anderson & Neville*,[21] on the trial of the magazine 'Oz' for obscenity, a witness for the defence testified to show that the article in question was not obscene, as it did not have a tendency to corrupt and deprave. Widgery J excluded the evidence on the ground that whether 'an article is obscene or not is a question exclusively for the jury, and expert evidence should not be admitted as to whether it is obscene or not. The courts must relate the facts of the case to the standard'.

[7.22] In *DPP v Kehoe*[22] that very same issue was addressed by the Irish courts. The facts of the case involved the accused's killing of PH, his former best friend, who now had a relationship with the mother of the accused's child. The defence to the charge of murder was provocation. O'Flaherty J, delivering the judgment of the Court of Criminal Appeal, found that the expert witness here was not called to establish a defence of insanity or any form of mental illness or derangement that might have occurred by the accused's use of drugs and alcohol in regard to which it appeared he had become dependent.[23] He could not, according to the Court, give any relevant admissible evidence in relation to state of mind, temperament etc, that the accused himself could not do. However, according to the Court:[24]

---

[19] *DPP v A & BC Chewing Gum Ltd* [1968] 1 QB 159.
[20] *Lowery v R* [1974] AC 85.
[21] *R v Anderson & Neville* [1971] 3 All ER 1152.
[22] *DPP v Kehoe* [1992] ILRM 481.
[23] *DPP v Kehoe* [1992] ILRM 481 at 484.
[24] *DPP v Kehoe* [1992] ILRM 481 at 484.

... he attempted to do so, and his approach ... was to say that he had a great deal of experience of people who had been through emotional upset, people who had become involved with drink and drugs, and so forth, and that, therefore, he was in a strong position to give a clinical pronouncement on the reality of the defence that the accused man was putting forward.

[7.23] O'Flaherty J commented that:

While the evidence of a psychiatrist is, undoubtedly, relevant and admissible in such circumstances, as it will be if the defence of diminished responsibility or such is given recognition in our law it is clear to the Court that Dr Behan could not in this case give any relevant, admissible evidence in relation to the state of mind, the temperament and those other matters that are referred to in *MacEoin's* case, that the accused could not do himself.

There is no doubt that Dr Behan was attempting to articulate in a fuller way what the accused has stated, rather briefly, viz his annoyance and upset but on which he based his defence of provocation.

The Court is of the opinion that the accused's defence was properly to be considered by the jury without such elaboration and that, further, in the course of his evidence it is clear that Dr Behan overstepped the mark in saying that he believed the accused did not have an intention to kill and that the accused was telling the truth. These are clearly matters foursquare within the jury's function and a witness no more than the trial judge or anyone else is not entitled to trespass on what is the jury's function.

[7.24] O'Flaherty J noted that this had been recently emphasised by the Supreme Court in *People (DPP) v Egan*[25] and concluded, therefore:

So, it appears to the Court, that the correct approach, where there is any doubt in the matter, is for the defence to canvass the view of the trial judge in the first instance as to whether psychiatric evidence is properly admissible, because the view of Court is that this was not a case for the admission of psychiatric evidence, and it would appear to be, as far as criminal cases are concerned, properly to be confined to the matters already mentioned, such as the defence of insanity or the like.

O'Flaherty J noted that the issue was considered by the English Court of Appeal in *R v Turner*,[26] where the evidence of a psychiatrist was tendered in support of a provocation defence put forward by an accused on the basis of his girlfriend's allegations regarding her relations with other men. The court there took the view that these matters were well within ordinary human experience and the capabilities of the jury. The law in Ireland, stated O'Flaherty J, is the same.

---

[25] *People (DPP) v Egan* [1990] ILRM 780.
[26] *R v Turner* [1975] QB 834.

[7.25] The *Turner* rule has been reconsidered in Australia in *Murphy v Queen*:[27]

> In *R v Turner* Lawton LJ expressed the basis upon which expert evidence is received in terms about which there can be no quarrel: 'An expert's opinion is admissible to furnish the court with scientific information which is likely to be outside the experience and knowledge of a judge or jury.' Later Lawton LJ added some remarks which may not be so unquestionable: 'Jurors do not need psychiatrists to tell them how ordinary folk who are not suffering from any mental illness are likely to react to the stresses and strains of life.' There are difficulties with such a statement. To begin with, it assumes that 'ordinary' or 'normal' has some clearly understood meaning and, as a corollary, that the distinction between normal and abnormal is well recognised. Further, it assumes that the common sense of jurors is an adequate guide to the conduct of people who are 'normal' even though they may suffer from some relevant disability. And it assumes that the experience of psychiatrists (or, as in the present case, psychologists) extends only to those who are 'abnormal.' None of these assumptions will stand close scrutiny.

DPP v Kehoe is significant in restricting the evidence of an expert to matters without the jury's function – *mens rea*, credibility etc – and also restricting the admissibility of opinion evidence in relation to mental or emotional disturbance short of an insanity defence, very much in line with *Turner* and distinct from the decision in the Australian case of *Murphy*.

[7.26] The English courts, since *Turner*, have allowed expert testimony where the evidence would be beyond the normal experience of the jury. In *R v Toner*,[28] evidence that a mild hypoglycaemic attack could have negative specific intent required for a charge of grievous bodily harm was allowed. In *R v Ward*[29] the Court of Appeal allowed psychiatric or psychological testimony that the defendant, while not suffering from a mental illness, was suffering from a personality disorder so serious as to be described as a mental disorder, if such evidence demonstrated the unreliability of the defendant's confession.

[7.27] In *People (DPP) v Yasuf Ali Abdi*[30] the defendant appealed his conviction of murder of his baby son on the basis that an expert witness, a psychiatrist, had gone beyond their remit in suggesting the defendant's alleged actions were motivated by his inability to accept that he would not be able to rear his child in his faith and his fear of loss of custody. The Court of Criminal Appeal, however, held that unlike *Egan*[31] and *Keogh*,[32] where the issue was reliance on

---

[27] *Murphy v Queen* (1988–89) 167 CLR 94 at 110.
[28] *R v Toner* 93 Cr App R 382.
[29] *R v Ward* 96 Cr App R 1.
[30] *People (DPP) v Yasuf Ali Abdi* [2004] IECCA 47.
[31] *People (DPP) v Egan* [1990] ILRM 780.
[32] *People (DPP) v Keogh* [1992] ILRM 481.

provocation which is plainly a matter for the jury, here insanity was specifically pleaded and the defence had called expert witnesses to establish it. The prosecution was, therefore, entitled to counter with their own expert witness.

The common knowledge rule

[7.28] This rule militates against allowing expert evidence on matters of common knowledge. Of course the issue is what lies outside that boundary. The Law Reform Commission[33] provisionally recommends that this rule should not be abolished.

The ultimate issue rule together with the common knowledge rule work to maintain the role of the jury. The ultimate issue rule has arisen in nullity proceedings. The medical inspector will be called to testify as to whether the parties had the mental capacity to enter into marriage, which is the issue at stake in such cases. The court does, however, retain the power to reject their view, although Budd J in *S(J) v S(C)*[34] acknowledges their evidence is an opinion 'verging on the ultimate issue'. The Law Reform Commission in Ireland provisionally recommends that the ultimate issue rule should not be abolished and that the courts should continue to be entitled to allow expert evidence to inform and educate Judge and jury about the background to the ultimate issue where necessary, whilst emphasising that the ultimate decision on such issues is for the court and not the expert.[35]

Expert and non-expert opinion evidence of fact

[7.29] In *People (DPP) v Buckley*[36] the issue arose as to whether, in the absence of a certificate of analysis from the forensic laboratory, the defendant's admission as to the fact that the substance in his pocket was cannabis was sufficient. Charleton J held that 'the qualities of cannabis are not now so unusual as to put it in a different category so that expert evidence of its presence is always required.'[37]

[7.30] It is significant that the designation of expert status and receipt of opinion evidence is facilitated in the context of drugs or organised crime with the ease one has come to expect in such contexts, whatever strict application of the rules of evidence might have been thought to imply. In *People (DPP) v Gilligan*,[38]

---

[33] Law Reform Commission, *Consultation Paper on Expert Evidence* (LRC CP 52–2008), p 78, para 2.192.

[34] *S(J) v S(C)* [1997] 2 IR 506.

[35] Law Reform Commission Consultation Paper *Expert Evidence* (LRC CP 52–2008), at paras 2.242 and 2.243.

[36] *People (DPP) v Buckley* [2007] IEHC 150.

[37] *People (DPP) v Buckley* [2007] IEHC 150, para 16.

[38] *People (DPP) v Gilligan* (22 March 2002, unreported), SCC.

John Gilligan having been convicted of drug trafficking offences, the Special Criminal Court under s 4 of the Criminal Justice Act 1994 as amended by s 25 of the Criminal Justice Act 1999, had to determine whether he had benefitted from the drug trafficking. The Court had to determine the cost, amount, expenses, consideration received and profit in the activities. Assistant Commissioner Tony Hickey was regarded by the Court:

> as a person with considerable experience in the field of investigating illicit drug trafficking and, in light of that experience, was in the view of the court a person with a wealth of knowledge of all aspects of illicit drug trafficking.[39]

The Court concluded that he was therefore:

> a person who is well qualified to express a credible opinion or belief on the subject; so much so, that the Court is entitled to regard such opinion and belief as admissible evidence for the purpose of supplying the Court with information which is outside the range and knowledge of the Court.[40]

[7.31] In *People (DPP) v Fox*,[41] evidence of a handwriting expert was put forward by the prosecution to establish that it was the accused's signature which appeared on a passport application form that was alleged to have been a forgery. The court quoted from and adopted the principles laid down in *Dowie v Edinburgh Corporation*[42] with reference to the role of the expert:

> Their duty is to furnish the judge or jury with the necessary scientific criteria for testing the accuracy of their conclusions so as to enable the judge or jury to form their own independent judgment by the application of these criteria to the facts proved in evidence. Scientific evidence if intelligible, convincing and tested becomes a factor and often an important factor for consideration, along with the whole other evidence in the case. But the decision is for the judge or jury. In particular the bare *ipso dixit* of a scientist, however eminent, upon the issue in controversy will normally carry little weight for it cannot be tested by cross-examination or independently appraised and the parties have invoked the decision of the judicial tribunal and not an oracular pronouncement by an expert.

In this case, the court noted that the evidence presented was not backed by any scientific criteria enabling the accuracy of its conclusions to be tested. Normally, various aspects of writing similarities and dissimilarities would be testified to, which would have enabled testing by the defence. The expert witness also relied solely on lower case writing and gave no explanation for same. Hence the expert evidence was rejected by the court.

---

[39] *People (DPP) v Gilligan* (22 March 2002, unreported), SCC.
[40] *People (DPP) v Gilligan* (22 March 2002, unreported), SCC.
[41] *People (DPP) v Fox* (23 January 2002, unreported), SCC.
[42] *Dowie v Edinburgh Corporation* [1953] SLT 54.

Defence access to evidence and the duty to preserve evidence

[7.32] With regard to access to material on which to conduct tests and testify, the Irish courts have seen such as being a prerequisite to fair procedure. In *Murphy v DPP*,[43] where a fingerprint expert for the defence wished to examine the car in which the alleged offences were carried out, the fact that the car had been disposed of and was now unavailable was held to amount to a breach of fair procedure.

[7.33] In *Mitchell v DPP*,[44] it was held that there was no duty to retain all CCTV recordings, although there will be cases where the gardaí are obliged to inform the defence of the existence of video evidence and of any intention to destroy it. In *Braddish v DPP*[45] Hardiman J noted:

> It is the duty of the gardaí, arising from their unique investigative role, to seek out and preserve all evidence having a bearing or potential bearing on the issue of guilt or innocence. This is so whether the prosecution proposes to rely on the evidence or not, and regardless of whether it assists the case the prosecution is advancing or not.

[7.34] In *Dunne v DPP*,[46] the only evidence against the appellant on a charge of robbery of a filling station was an alleged signed admission. The prosecution was unable to produce any tapes to the defence when requested, although a number of video cameras covered the station. The High Court had taken the view that it was more likely than not that the gardaí had been given the tapes by the station, but refused relief on the basis of the delay from the date of the offence (January 1998) and the defence's request for them (January 1999). Hardiman J delivered the majority judgment of the Supreme Court, emphasising the duty of the gardaí not simply to preserve evidence, but to seek it out. Hardiman J emphasised that the test applied is whether or not there is a real risk that the applicant will not receive a fair trial. This is a lower standard than the English test of establishing that the defendant cannot receive a fair trial, a standard he characterised as one extraordinarily favourable to the prosecution, and one which involves the English courts looking for bad faith on the part of the authorities. This is not the case in Ireland, and once again fairness is invoked here:

> The *"real risk* of an unfair trial" … does not necessarily involve blaming any person. The main focus in these applications should be on the *fairness* [emphasis added] of the intended trial without the missing evidence, and not on whose fault

---

[43] *Murphy v DPP* [1989] ILRM 71.
[44] *Mitchell v DPP* [2000] 2 ILRM 396.
[45] *Braddish v DPP* [2002] 1 ILRM 151 at 157.
[46] *Dunne v DPP* [2002] IESC 27.

it is that the evidence is missing, and what the degree of that fault may be. The latter factors, however, are not always irrelevant.[47]

McGuinness J agreed with Hardiman J as follows:

> Where a court would be asked to prohibit a trial on the grounds that there was an alleged failure to seek out evidence, it would have to be shown that any such evidence would be clearly relevant, that there was at least a strong possibility that the evidence was available, and that it would in reality have a bearing on the guilt or innocence of the accused person. It would also be necessary to demonstrate that its absence created a real risk of an unfair trial.[48]

[7.35] Fennelly J, in a strong dissenting judgment, took the view that the State's evidence had not been challenged by the applicant, who bore the burden of proof with regard to the authority's possession of the video evidence. In *Dunne v DPP*[49] Fennelly J pointed out that, unlike *Braddish*,[50] here it had not been established that the video evidence had actually been in the possession of the gardaí and refused the order of prohibition. In *Swaine v DPP*,[51] it was held that the prosecution's duty not to hold back material evidence helpful to a defendant may vary with the seriousness of the offence.

Belief evidence

[7.36] The Oireachtas has given belief evidence evidential status in s 3(2) of the Offences Against the State (Amendment) Act 1972, which provides as follows:

> Where an officer of the Garda Síochána, not below the rank of Chief Superintendent, in giving evidence in proceedings relating to an offence under the said section 21, states that he believes that the accused was at a material time a member of an unlawful organization, the statement shall be evidence that he was then such a member.

That section expressly says that the Chief Superintendent's belief 'shall be evidence'.

[7.37] In *People (DPP) v Mulligan*[52] Keane CJ commented that:

> the legislature has provided that that [the belief of the Chief Superintendent] is to be evidence and ... the weight to be given to that evidence then was entirely a matter for the court of trial ... It may well be said, and indeed has been said, that the legislature has significantly altered the normal law of evidence and altered it

---

[47] *Dunne v DPP* [2002] IESC 27 at 27.

[48] *Dunne v DPP* [2002] IESC 27 at 3.

[49] *Dunne v DPP* [2002] IESC 27, Fennelly J.

[50] *Braddish v DPP* [2002] 1 ILRM 151.

[51] *Swaine v DPP* [2002] IESC 30.

[52] *People (DPP) v Mulligan* (17 May 2004, unreported).

unambiguously and unequivocally in favour of the prosecution and against the defence in a case of this nature.

This section was extensively considered by the Supreme Court in *DPP v Kelly*[53] where Fennelly J stated:

> That type of evidence is, in itself, a novelty. Under the normal rules of evidence, only expert witnesses are permitted to give evidence of opinion or belief and even then not on simple questions of fact. The Chief Superintendent may, no doubt, be regarded as an expert in his allotted field. That, however, is not the real problem. The real problem is that, where privilege is claimed, as it inevitably is, the defendant does not know the basis of that belief. He does not know the names of the informants or the substance of the allegations of membership. Without any knowledge of these matters, the accused is necessarily powerless to challenge them. Informants may be mistaken, misinformed, inaccurate or, in the worst case, malicious. None of this can be tested. [54]

[7.38] Significantly, Fennelly J noted a striking analogy between the procedure of the Dutch court in *Kostovski v Netherlands*[55] and the procedure here. That case concerned anonymous witnesses and the European Court of Human Rights considered the accused did not have an adequate opportunity to challenge and question them and, although acknowledging the importance of the fight against organized crime, found a violation of art 6 of the European Convention of Human Rights. However, Fennelly J noted that the court 'modified its stance in *Doorson*' but quotes from a dissent by Ryssdal and de Meyer JJ, warning that it is not permissible to resolve such problems by departing from fundamental procedure. Ultimately, Fennelly J reasoned that there is an inescapable obligation on the courts to guarantee the overall fairness of a trial, of which the right to cross-examine one's accuser is an essential element.

> While there may be derogations for overriding reasons of public interest from normal procedural rights of the defence, these must not go beyond what is strictly necessary and must, in no circumstances, to use the language of Lord Bingham, 'imperil the overall fairness of the trial'.[56]

Fennelly J found in the circumstance that there was not any overall fairness but he warned 'the matter might be quite different in a case where the evidence of the Chief Superintendent was the sole plank in the prosecution case, where the privilege had been successfully claimed and the accused had given evidence denying the charge'.[57]

---

[53] *DPP v Kelly* [2006] IESC 20.
[54] *DPP v Kelly* [2006] IESC 20 at 16–17/27.
[55] Fennelly J in *DPP v Kelly* [2006] 1 ESC 20 p 26/27.
[56] Fennelly J in *DPP v Kelly* [2006] 1 ESC 20
[57] *Kostovski v Netherlands* [1989] 12 EHRR at 27.

[7.39] The Criminal Justice Act 2007, s 7 provides that, in bail applications, evidence of a Chief Superintendent where (s)he says they believe refusal is necessary to prevent the commission of serious offences is admissible evidence and that refusal is necessary for that purpose.

Further statutory exceptions that might also be seen to provide exceptions to the rule are:

 (i) Proceeds of Crime Act 1996, s 8 provides that where a garda states he believes property to be the proceeds of crime, that is evidence of same;

 (ii) Domestic Violence Act 1996, s 3(4)(b) provides that where an applicant for a barring order states a belief (s)he has a legal or beneficial interest in property the subject of the barring order, which equals or rivals that of the respondent, that is evidence of same; and

 (iii) Competition Act 2002, s 9 provides in relation to proceedings under the Act, that the court can admit the opinion evidence of a person having the requisite qualifications or experience.

Intoxication

[7.40] An area where a good deal of controversy has arisen, both as to the question of the admissibility of the evidence of a non-expert witness on the issue, and as to the impact of such testimony if admitted on the ultimate issue at trial, is that of evidence as to the existence, degree and effect of intoxication. Specifically in the context of charges of driving while intoxicated and the inability to drive while intoxicated, the admissibility of garda evidence (which is treated as non-expert testimony for the purpose of the rule) as to drunkenness and capability to drive has arisen. This was facilitated by the original charge under the Road Traffic Act 1961, where the standard was adjudged in terms of incapacity as opposed to intoxication concentration. Incapacity was acknowledged to vary with the person (*AG v Ryan*[58]), and thus many difficulties resulted in the adjudication of same. In 1989 Pierse noted convictions were up to 65 per cent greater since the introduction of scientific tests in the area.[59] However, the incapacity standard may still well be utilised in the event of a refusal to give a sample and is of considerable jurisprudential worth in terms of differing views expressed as to the value of opinion evidence.

---

[58] *AG v Ryan* [1975] IR 367.

[59] Pierse, *Road Traffic Law in the Republic of Ireland* (Tottel Publishing, 1989), p.182. CSO statistics for 2205 drink driving offences show the number of arrests as 11,646; the number of convictions as 4,140, representing a conviction rate of 36%. (National Crime Council – www.crimecouncil.gov.ie/statistics-cri-crime-tables.html-7/10/2009).

[7.41] The definitive position under Irish law as to the admissibility of non-expert opinion evidence on drunkenness and incapacity to drive, within the context of a charge of intoxicated driving under s 49 of the 1961 Act (using the said 'incapacity test', ie whether the defendant was under the influence of an intoxicant to such an extent as to be incapable of having proper control of the vehicle), is set out in *AG (Ruddy) v Kenny*.[60] The prosecution here tendered the evidence of a garda witness, to the effect that, in his opinion, the defendant 'was drunk and incapable of driving the vehicle'.

[7.42] In the High Court, Davitt P stated:

> Drunkenness, unfortunately, is a condition which is not so exceptional or so much outside the experience of the ordinary individual, that it should require an expert to diagnose it. In my opinion a Garda witness may give evidence of his opinion as to whether a person is drunk or not.

In relation to the second question – whether a non-expert may express his opinion as to whether a defendant is drunk to such an extent as to be incapable of exercising proper control over a mechanically propelled vehicle – Davitt P continued:

> It seems to me that if it is admissible for an ordinary witness to express his opinion as to whether a defendant is drunk or not, it should be admissible for him to express an opinion as to how drunk he was.

[7.43] On appeal to the Supreme Court, the majority endorsed Davitt P's position that non-expert opinion evidence was admissible on both issues. In terms of both determination of the ultimate issue at trial (incapacity due to intoxication) and the subjectivity involved in the criteria, the decision is assailable. In this regard, Kingsmill Moore J's dissent in the Supreme Court in *AG(Ruddy) v Kenny*[61] is noteworthy:

> It is a longstanding rule of our law of evidence that, with certain exceptions, a witness may not express an opinion as to a fact in issue. Ideally in the theory of our law, a witness may testify only to the existence of fact which he has observed with one or more of his own five senses. It is for the tribunal of fact – judge or jury as the case may be – to draw inferences of fact, form opinions and come to conclusions. The witness, as far as possible, puts the judge and jury in the position of having been present at the place and time when the fact deposed occurred and having been able to make the observations. The witness may be lying, his powers of observation may be deficient, his ability to express clearly what he observed may be inadequate, his memory may be faulty. These are inescapable hazards. But it is possible to avoid the further hazards of prejudice,

---

[60] *AG (Ruddy) v Kenny* (1960) 94 ILTR 185.
[61] *AG (Ruddy) v Kenny* (1960) 94 ILTR 185 *per* Kingsmill Moore J at p 189.

faulty reasoning and inadequate knowledge which would be introduced if a witness were allowed to have his opinion and the tribunal of fact were allowed to act upon it.

[7.44] In addition to placing the issue in the context of the role of a witness (testimonial) and that of the arbiter of fact (determinative) in the legal process, Kingsmill Moore J reminds us of the vagaries of the term concerned. He pointed out that admitting evidence of opinion that a person was drunk is grounded on the vagueness of that term, which can incorporate anything from 'stone cold sober' to 'dead drunk'. All is dependent on what that particular witness understands as drunkenness. Kingsmill Moore J similarly objected to the admission of a further expression of opinion as to whether the defendant was incapable of driving a motor vehicle. Opinion evidence by a non-expert, he regarded as being 'either otiose or dangerous', particularly when the expression of opinion is as to the exact question at issue. He concluded:

> I am of the opinion that the interests of justice can be adequately served by getting a witness to describe the appearance, movements, demeanour, actions and words of a person whose condition is in question and leaving it to the District Justice to draw his own conclusions.

[7.45] Other jurisdictions have grappled with these same issues in a similar context and it is interesting to consider and contrast their views. The English courts considered the question in *R v Davies*.[62] In relation to the same dual issue considered in *Kenny*, Parker LJ held that opinion evidence as to whether the defendant was drunk was admissible and opinion evidence as to the defendant's capability to drive inadmissible.

[7.46] In *Sherrard v Jacob*,[63] the Northern Ireland Court of Appeal held opinion evidence as to the issue of drunkenness admissible. On the issue of capability to drive, Curran and McVeigh JJ held opinion evidence on the issue inadmissible while McDermott LCJ would have deemed opinion evidence on both issues admissible. His dissenting judgment is again interesting for a perspective on the matter which takes issue with the artificiality of so restricting opinion evidence – a logic perhaps not dissimilar to that favoured by the Irish courts in *Kenny*. McDermott LCJ stated:

> I can find no good reason for allowing the non-expert witness to give his opinion of the driver's observable condition, and then denying him the right to state an opinion on the consequences of that observed opinion, as far as driving is concerned.

---

[62] *R v Davies* [1962] 3 All ER 97.
[63] *Sherrard v Jacob* [1975] NI 151.

The logic of this 'all or nothing' approach is persuasive, but could just as easily be used to argue the contrary position, ie, that favoured by Kingsmill Moore J – non-admissibility on both issues.

[7.47] Howsoever that might be, the position is now a well-established one that the opinion of a non-expert is admissible on both these issues and, given that proof of intoxication by reference to a certificate of alcohol concentration in such cases has now superceded opinion evidence, is not likely to be reviewed. However, the question of a non-expert's opinion has arisen as seen in *DPP v Richard Kenny*,[64] where a doctor (albeit an expert, although not perhaps on this issue) was tendered to give evidence as to the accused's observable condition. The accused was arrested under s 49(6) of the Road Traffic Act 1961. On arrival at the garda station he consented to a sample of blood being taken by a designated registered medical practitioner. No analysis was ever made of that sample. Subsequently, he was charged with the offence of being intoxicated to such an extent as to be incapable of having proper control of his vehicle, contrary to s 49(1)(4)(a) of the Road Traffic Act 1961, as amended.

[7.48] At the hearing the issue centred on whether the medical practitioner concerned could give evidence as to his observation of the accused, and his opinion as to his fitness to drive. The case stated concerned the same issue, namely whether a right to privacy existed such as that he should have been cautioned as to the tendering of such evidence. It was submitted that, notwithstanding his lawful arrest, the accused was entitled to his privacy in the sense that persons, including the doctor, could not be brought into his company for the purpose of observing his behaviour. Barron J noted that in *Sullivan v Robinson*[65] Davitt P dealt with the need to caution suspects in circumstances akin to the present case, and felt these similar to situations of confession or admission in so far as the same principles apply. *Per* Barron J:

> That ... suggests that the evidence of the condition of an accused should not be given by a doctor called on behalf of the gardaí unless such accused had consented to be examined or tested. There is not however anything in the passage which suggests that evidence cannot be given as to the condition of the accused by those who were lawfully required to deal with him or has otherwise observed him lawfully.

[7.49] Here the accused had consented to a sample of his blood being taken by the doctor. Barron J felt it was perfectly permissible for the doctor to give evidence of his observation of the accused incidental to the taking of that sample. Many of the authorities cited on behalf of the applicant dealt with cases

---

[64] *DPP v Kenny* (8 March 1990, unreported), HC, Barron J.
[65] *Sullivan v Robinson* [1954] IR 161.

where evidence was obtained while the accused was in unlawful detention. These cases he felt had no bearing on the present case. The two questions raised were thus answered as follows:

(1)   The accused does have a right to privacy while in custody.

(2)   This right of privacy is not breached by observation of the accused by persons who are lawfully required to deal with him while in custody. Whether it would be breached by observation of the accused by persons in any other category and if so in what circumstances, does not arise for decision.

Although perhaps in the broader context of opinion evidence, those opinions of experts may prove in future to be more controversial than non-experts, issue can still arise (as in the case of drunkenness and capability to drive) as to the admissibility of such testimony.

[7.50] The mandatory nature of garda opinion in the context of road traffic offences arose in *DPP v Lynch*.[66] Here the respondent was prosecuted under s 13 of the Road Traffic (Amendment) Act 1978 for failure to permit a designated medical practitioner to take a specimen of his blood or providing for same a specimen of urine. The respondent was acquitted and a case stated to the High Court. The facts were that Garda Fitzgerald, on 10 October 1989, stopped a motor vehicle driven by the respondent, formed an opinion that the latter was incapable of driving, arrested him and brought him to the Bridewell. The respondent was later introduced to a registered medical practitioner, and was requested to permit the doctor to take from him a sample of his blood or provide him with a sample of urine, but refused.

[7.51] Counsel for the respondent submitted that the charge should be dismissed for want of evidence validating the arrest, to the effect that the garda, when making the arrest, had formed the opinion that the respondent was committing or had committed an offence under the Road Traffic Acts. The appellant, conceding that no positive evidence to this effect had been given, and that such was a necessary link in the chain of proof to lead to a conviction, submitted there was a clear inference that the garda had formed the necessary opinion. The appellant relied on the Supreme Court decision of *DPP v O'Connor*[67] in particular. However, the circumstances in that case were of a very extreme nature, involving the driving of a bus in a very dangerous manner etc. That judgment should not be read, according to O'Hanlon J:

---

[66]   *DPP v Lynch* (7 November 1990, unreported), HC, O'Hanlon J.
[67]   *DPP v O'Connor* [1985] ILRM 333.

[as] a statement that in every case where a Garda informs a person who is being arrested that he is being arrested under the provisions of s 49(6) of the Road Traffic Act 1961 (as amended by the Road Traffic (Amendment) Act 1978) there is a necessary inference to be drawn he has concurrently formed the opinion that the person who is placed under arrest is committing or has committed an offence under s 49.

The rule in *Hollington v Hewthorn*

[7.52] Before considering further the implications of greater reliance on expert testimony amidst increasing concern as to its probity, mention should be made of the existence of a particular rule in the context of the Irish law on opinion evidence which has been statutorily reformed in our neighbouring jurisdictions of Northern Ireland and England. The rule is that laid down in the case of *Hollington v Hewthorn*.[68] It provides that a judicial finding is inadmissible as evidence of the facts found in relation to different proceedings. For example, if D runs his car up on a footpath and hits someone and is subsequently charged and convicted of careless driving, the rule provides that in a subsequent civil action for personal injuries, arising out of that same incident, the plaintiff will not be able to introduce evidence of such conviction as proof of the defendant's negligence. This is because that finding is regarded as judicial opinion on the matter. It is otherwise, of course, if the defendant in the initial charge pleaded guilty. In that event, evidence of his plea (analogous to a confession) would be admitted. It is evidence of the judicial finding on the facts that is excluded by the rule. Of course, in practice, the rule may well be more honoured in the breach than the observance and has been removed in other jurisdictions where it fell into disrepute. In any event, it is mitigated in effect because of the practical factors dictating the plaintiff's keeping a 'watching brief' on the prior criminal action which, if successful, will indicate the relative ease with which the lower civil standard of proof will be met if the criminal standard has already been attained. In England the rule in *Hollington v Hewthorn* was overruled by the Civil Evidence Act 1968, ss 11–13 in regard to civil cases, with the Police and Evidence Act 1984, ss 74 and 75 making similar provision for criminal cases. In *Kelly v Ireland*,[69] O'Hanlon J in the High Court left open the question of whether *Hollington v Hewthorn* was good law in Ireland.

[7.53] In *People (DPP) v Ward*,[70] an application had been made on behalf of the defence to introduce evidence in the course of the appeal consisting of the

---

[68] *Hollington v Hewthorn* [1943] 1 KB 587.
[69] *Kelly v Ireland* [1986] ILRM 318 at 327.
[70] *People (DPP) v Ward* (22 March 2002), CCA, Murphy J.

transcripts of the hearings of the trials of *Meehan*[71] and *Gilligan*[72] in the Special Criminal Court. With regard to the question of their admissibility, Murphy J[73] commented:

> It is difficult to see any circumstances in which a finding made in a subsequent case in any court, criminal or civil, as to the character or integrity of any witness or party could be made evidence on the appeal. However there are extreme cases in which facts established in later cases may so undermine the basis on which an earlier case had been decided that it would be appropriate to have regard to the later case on an appeal in the former.

[7.54] The Court referred to the English Court of Criminal appeal decision *R v Williams; R v Smith*[74] (where it had emerged that police who had carried out the investigation had fabricated evidence) as illustrative of the range of matters in which evidence given in a later trial might be admissible on appeal from an earlier one. To avoid any possible injustice, the court in *Ward* had permitted the applicant to extract material from transcripts in the two subsequent trials relating to specified topics which might have had the capacity to undermine the substance of a fair trial.

Expert evidence: personal injuries actions

[7.55] There is a long-established practice in personal injury actions of examination of a plaintiff by a medical specialist on behalf of the defence, traditionally in the presence of the plaintiff's expert. The practice of joint examination gave way, however, to examination of injured plaintiffs on their own by defence specialists. This led to a situation where complications, not readily discernible from particulars furnished to the defence (which right has emerged on a joint examination) would arise at trial. Section 45 of the Courts and Court Officers Act 1995 attempted to address that difficulty in so far as it provided that notwithstanding any rule of privilege pertaining to legal advice, attaching to such documents any such report from an expert intended to be called to give evidence of a medical opinion in relation to an issue in the case could be ordered to be disclosed by the court.

[7.56] The objective was to shorten the length of personal injury trials and to reduce costs. Under the Rules of the Superior Courts (No 6) (Disclosure of Reports and Statements) 1998,[75] new rules introduced in October 1998 further

---

[71] *People(DPP) v Brian Meehan* (29 July 1999, unreported), SCC.

[72] *People (DPP) v Gilligan* (22 March 2002, unreported), SCC.

[73] *People (DPP) v Ward* (22 March 2002), CCA at 19–20/20.

[74] *R v Williams; R v Smith* [1995] 1 Cr App R 74.

[75] (SI 391/1998). Although the Rules came into force on 14 October 1998, they apply to proceedings begun on or after 1 September 1997.

clarified the situation to ensure that actions covered included any claim for charges for personal injuries, however caused, and reports included a report from any expert including doctors, engineers, scientists etc. The rules require both parties to disclose all reports and statements of experts whom they intend to call as witnesses. The Supreme Court in *Payne v Shovlin*[76] held this to mean that all reports, including preliminary expert reports not adduced at trials must be disclosed. Kearns J considered that as the 1998 rules introduced an exception to the general privilege attaching to communications made in contemplation of litigation, that latter being, itself an exception to the rule that all information should be available to a court, should itself be strictly interpreted.

Expert opinion: controversy

[7.57] Throughout the law of evidence are found examples of judicial scepticism with regard to the probity of certain types of evidence, either because of the intrinsic nature of the evidence or the manner in which it was obtained. For this reason, rules have been developed to mark judicial wariness in the admissibility, for example, of confession evidence and consequently the requirement of voluntariness was developed. By contrast, forensic evidence, particularly, was regarded as being of that species of expert testimony which was objective, rational, scientific, immutable and reliable.

[7.58] Hence the judiciary, with what may appear to have been unseemly haste, rushed to rely on same, and defence counsel, faced with a species of knowledge of which they did not even have the rudiments to begin querying, accepted it at face value and threw in the metaphorical towel. This was a particularly insidious development given the absence of independent forensic laboratory testing facilities in this country. Gradually, however, question marks began to appear over the actual probity of the glass shards found in the accused's clothing, or the carpet fibres on his shoes. Although they did match those of the house in which the crime was perpetrated, the apparent potency weakened when it was discovered that such materials enter this country in very large quantities, and their distribution is such that carpet fibres in Ballymun are similar to those in Killorglin, as the glass strands in Galway are to those in Meath.

[7.59] Difficulty also pertains as to the safeguarding of procedure observance in the obtaining of forensic results. Witness the controversy as to the concentration of test material used, and the ultimate probity of its results, in the light of scientific developments in the '*Birmingham Six*' case. The use of the Griess test on the defendants to give a positive result was interpreted by the Home Office scientists (Dr Skuse in particular) to give a 99% certainty that the men had been

---

[76] *Payne v Shovlin* [2006] IESC 5.

in recent contact with high explosives. In fact, the Griess test was subsequently discovered to react positively with nitrocellulose, an everyday substance also found on veneers and present on the railway seats and playing cards with which the men had been in contact. Quite apart, then, from difficulties with regard to the adherence to procedure in the carrying out of the test in that case, a changing scientific consensus as to its merit or probative worth was evident. This, in relation to what the trial judge termed 'the clearest and most overwhelming evidence I have ever heard'.

[7.60] Difficulties in challenging confession evidence have recently been ameliorated by the development of techniques enabling linguistic analysis of words allegedly spoken by defendants (the Morten test of linguistic analysis used in the '*Armagh Four*' case) and electrostatic document analysis, or ESDA, (used to challenge the contemporaneity of police notes in the '*Birmingham Six*'[77] case). All such developments raise concerns surrounding the implications of forensic or expert testimony for legal proceedings, particularly severe in criminal jury adjudication.[78]

DNA evidence

[7.61] The difficulty is, of course, a cultural one: a clash between the scientific world accustomed to 'black holes' and 'scientific revolutions'[79] and the legal one where such qualified certainties are not sufficient. A manifestation of this clash, and the difficulties lawyers must face in coming to terms with same, is evident from the controversy with regard to DNA (genetic fingerprint) evidence, its probity and the obtaining of same.

[7.62] Moreover, the context in which this concern had developed highlights the difficulties of funding the expertise for mounting such challenges (particularly important for the defence). Indeed the extent to which the Irish legislature facilitated the obtaining of genetic fingerprinting evidence and its subsequent admissibility in criminal trials – without adequate procedural safeguards or defence access to independent forensics, and in the light of growing scientific unease as to its probity – is worrying. Lawyers and legislators alike must become aware that science is no more immutable than human nature; human fallibility has an input at the procedural level of the application of 'the test' and the test itself may be less probative empirically than originally mooted.

---

[77] See further Jackson, *One Word against Another: the Effect of ESDA Evidence* (1991) Vol 7 Ir Crim LJ 18; Woffinden, *Miscarriages of Justice* (Hodder and Stoughton, 1989).

[78] See further 'Spinal Trap For Courts' (1992) *The Sunday Tribune*, 2 February at p 4.

[79] Kuhn, The *Structure of Scientific Revolutions* (2nd edn, University of Chicago Press, 1970).

[7.63] DNA provides a perfect example of this clash of legal and scientific culture. Based on the discovery that we each have a genetic fingerprint which is individual and so identifiable to us, DNA fingerprint evidence was initially tendered in immigration claims based on blood relationships and in paternity suits. (See, for example, *JPD v MG*,[80] where a wife sought an order pursuant to s 38 of the Status of Children Act 1987 to the effect that both children and husband and wife should submit to DNA tests. The context was one where the plaintiff husband was seeking sole custody of the children, the defendant wife alleging they were not in fact his.) Gradually it found its way into criminal trials, offering particular potential in the context of sexual offences, where traces of blood or semen could link one person to a particular incident.

[7.64] One of the first criminal trials in the United Kingdom to illustrate the potential of this evidence, both in terms of exoneration and implication, was that of *R v Pitchfork*,[81] where Pitchfork was both discovered and convicted of murder, rape and indecent assault on the basis of his DNA fingerprints, and a 17-year-old youth, initially arrested and charged for the offence, was exonerated. Yet, quiescent in that case was an indication of the potential for a miscarriage of justice inherent in this type of forensic testimony. Pitchfork had initially evaded capture on the basis of the substitution of a sample from a friend for his own. This fact served as an early indicator of the importance of procedure and effective monitoring of the manner in which samples are obtained and tested. These difficulties may be compounded, of course, where in a criminal case (unlike an immigration or paternity case) there may only be a very small sample available, which may be damaged or have deteriorated to some degree.

[7.65] All of these variable considerations and facts which impact upon this type of evidence came to light in the American context where leading scientists first warned of the dangers inherent in an unqualified acceptance by the legal world of the products of science. The result is an interesting insight into a cultural clash, which results when two particular fields of knowledge, having different perspectives, attempt to fashion an alliance which is not cognisant of the implications of an unquestioning acceptance of the premises of the other. The history of this clash between scientific discovery and legal adjudication is valuable for the insight it gives into the potential for injustice should law follow too readily at the heels of 'cutting edge' science.

---

[80] *JPD v MG* [1991] ILRM 212.
[81] *R v Pitchfork* (1998) *The Guardian*, 23 January.

[7.66] In the June 1989 issue of the journal *Nature*, Dr Eric S Lander, in an article entitled 'DNA Fingerprinting on Trial',[82] described the pitfalls in the forensic use of the technique of DNA fingerprinting. Central to the difficulty was that DNA, like most other evidence, requires interpretation. 'Interpretation' of data is inevitably influenced by a difference in perspective between legal and scientific investigation. The journal's editor commented that:

> Both pretend to discover truth, science by continually narrowing the range of allowable dispute, the law by its supposition that the judicial process can conjure truth from whatever data are available. Courts are not content with declaration that defendants are, say, 60% guilty, nor should they be ...

[7.67] Dr Lander pointed out that DNA fingerprint evidence, since first introduced in a trial in Florida in 1988, had been used in more than 80 criminal trials in the United States. Trial judges, he suggested:

> ... have raced to admit DNA fingerprinting as evidence on the grounds that the methods are 'generally accepted in the scientific community', citing the application of RFLP's in DNA diagnostics and accepting claims that false positives are virtually impossible.

Dr Lander took issue with the courts' enthusiasm:

> With due respect, the courts have been too hasty. Although DNA fingerprinting clearly offers tremendous potential as a forensic tool, the rush has obscured two critical points: first, DNA fingerprinting is far more technically demanding than DNA diagnostics; and second, the scientific community has not yet agreed on standards that ensure the reliability of the evidence.

[7.68] Dr Lander pointed out that DNA fingerprinting results were being introduced into US criminal courts without adequate safeguards: 'Not only are mixing experiments and internal controls often omitted, but some laboratories use no objective standards whatsoever for declaring a match'. Lander's rather disturbing conclusion, then, is that the scientific community has failed to attain rigorous standards to which courts, attorneys and forensic testing laboratories can look for guidance – with the result that some of the conclusions presented to the courts are quite unreliable. This danger was graphically illustrated by reference to one particular murder trial in New York.

The Castro case

[7.69] On 5 February 1987, Vilma Ponce and her two-year-old daughter were stabbed to death in their Bronx apartment. The police, acting on a tip-off, interviewed Jose Castro, a local handyman. A small bloodstain on Castro's watch was sent for analysis. It is here that the difficulties arose. Dr Lander discusses the procedure used by the laboratory concerned (Lifecodes), and takes

---

[82] Lander, *DNA Fingerprinting on Trial* (1989) 339, *Nature* 501–505.

issue with it, in so far as it was not sufficiently cognisant of the importance of procedure and the dangerous implications of not adequately monitoring comparison in this context. Lifecodes issued a report to the District Attorney stating that the DNA patterns on the watch and of the mother matched, and reporting the frequency of the pattern to be about 1 in 100,000,000 in the Hispanic population. The report indicated no difficulties or ambiguities, yet according to Dr Lander, there was several. For example, with regard to comparison of DNA bands found on the watch and in the mother, Dr Lander commented that:

> The tendency to use lane-to-lane comparison to distinguish between bands and artifacts is perfectly natural; such comparison can be quite helpful in certain experiments. However, in my opinion, it is inappropriate in DNA fingerprinting analysis of unknown samples – as one runs the risk of discounting precisely those differences that would exonerate an innocent defendant. Forensic laboratories should be required to use objective criteria for identifying the bands in each lane, and to use experiments to rule out proposed artifacts.

[7.70] According to Dr Lander, when a result is reported to have an error rate of 1 in 100,000,000, it seems essential that the underlying data are not left as a matter of subjective opinion. Under the objective matching rule in this case, the bands were poor matches – yet a match was declared. Dr Lander concludes that there had been a significant misunderstanding about the matching rule Lifecodes had been using. In any event, he feels visual matching is inappropriate in DNA fingerprinting, in as much as:

(1)   many alleles have very similar sizes;

(2)   the accuracy of the measurement process is reported to be known; and

(3)   without an objective definition of a match, there is no meaningful way to determine the probability that a declared match might have arisen by chance.

[7.71] Further difficulties arose with regard to the control of DNA in that case, of which no precise record had been kept. Moreover, the small quantity of DNA on the watch was clearly degraded, and as nearly 90% of alleles in the Hispanic population lie above 10.25 kb, one could not be sure whether the sample was a homozygous for a 10.25 kb, as contended, or a heterozygote with a higher band undetected due to degradation.

[7.72] Other difficulties also included the fact that whatever matching rule is used to declare a forensic match, should also be used for counting the matches occurring in the population database; yet, in fact, Lifecodes did not use the same matching rule. In addition, to justify applying the classic formulas of population genetics in the *Castro* case, the Hispanic population must be in the

HardyWeinberg equilibrium. In fact, it is not.[83] In terms of Dr Lander's analysis of the procedure used by the laboratory for the DNA matching process, the *Castro* case itself is significant in terms of the manner of discovery of the inadequacies of the process.

[7.73] In the *Castro* case, the prosecution witness, whose testimony was intended to provide the court with a primer on DNA analysis, became concerned about the evidence tendered and organised a joint scientific meeting of experts from either side to review that evidence. The result was a statement by the experts to the effect that 'the DNA data in the case are not scientifically reliable enough to support the assertion that the samples ... do or do not match'. The prosecution nevertheless persisted with the case, in the course of which, former prosecution witnesses now testified for the defence.

[7.74] Although ultimately a vindication of expert credibility or ethics in this context, the case may be seen to illustrate the inability of lawyers alone to raise a doubt sufficient to pierce the veil of scientific immutability. Lawyers, without scientific knowledge and co-operation, have difficulty contending with such testimony. Dr Lander instances a death penalty case where a Lifecodes scientist testified to the effect that the process was a very simple one 'Either it matches or it doesn't. It's like if you walk into the parking lot and see two Fords parked next to each other.'[84] The statement is patently misleading, as DNA discrepancies are not necessarily visible to the eye, but lawyers must themselves become aware, and make the court aware, of that fact. Some degree of tenacity may well be called for, as in the case of *New York v Neysmith*.[85] The accused hired Lifecodes to compare his blood with the allegedly incriminating semen samples, and challenged their initial reaction that the blood may not have been his own, which led to their second contention that a further sample had a different source, and to the third submission, which resulted in their admission that an error had occurred. Neysmith had almost lost his liberty as a result of the error.

[7.75] Significantly, DNA evidence has been most recently invoked in the United States in aid of indigent defendants who are on death row in an attempt to prove their innocence. This is as a result of the Innocence Project run by Barry Scheck and Peter Neufeld at the Benjamin N Cardozo Law School, New York,

---

[83] Lander, *DNA Fingerprinting on Trial* (1989) 339, *Nature*, p 504. The classic test for *HardyWeinberg* equilibrium is based on the principle that the rate of homozygosity in a population containing distinct subgroups will be higher than would be expected under the assumption of random mating. This is not without considerable significance in the context of the Irish population.

[84] *State v Caldwell* (No. 88-9-2938) (Sup Ct, Cobb County, Ga) (1989) *per* Lander, 'DNA Fingerprinting on Trial', 339 NATURE 501 (1989), p 505.

[85] (1987) Lander, p 505.

which reportedly has exonerated 131 prisoners serving long sentences following DNA testing.[86]

[7.76] In an early article on the issue in the British context, Andrew Hall[87] expressed concern that, although not per se posing a threat to civil liberties, 'the uniqueness of the procedure ... may hold unique dangers in the absence of a critical approach by both lawyers and forensic scientists'. Hall elucidated the fear that the process should become 'a black box into which the scientific evidence is placed at one end and the verdict in a criminal case is produced at the other'. Hall rightly pointed out that it is the very complexity of the science involved in DNA analysis that may pose difficulties. Lawyers and juries may well not understand it and become overwhelmed by it. The evidence is unlike fingerprint evidence, in so far as accuracy depends on extremely precise measurement of the distance DNA fragments have travelled in the gel and, as seen, minute discrepancies between DNA fingerprint bands, not necessarily visible to the eye, may wholly undermine positive identification. In *Doheny*[88] Phillips LJ, emphasised in an important judgment on DNA evidence, that the expert witness should not express a view on the probability of the defendant's guilt, given the DNA match. That is for the jury to decide.

[7.77] One further difficulty is posed by the current access absence of laboratories in Ireland providing alternative testing facilities. The requisite control may therefore be more apparent than real. The dangers of inadequate testing or regulation of procedure will not be revealed if evident, and a failure to provide adequate safeguards will increase the risk of the conviction of, or failure to exonerate, the innocent and perhaps aid the acquittal of the guilty.[89]

[7.78] In *People (DPP) v Howe*,[90] Butler J directed an acquittal because the DNA evidence was considered unreliable as the forensic scientist had no qualification in statistics and so could not determine the probability of the DNA

---

[86] *Law Society Gazette*, Vol 100 No 01 at p 13, 'Morton's Musings'. See also http://www.innocenceproject.org.

[87] *Andrew Hall 'DNA fingerprinting-black box or black hole?'* (1990) 140 NLJ 203.

[88] *Doheny* [1997] 1 Cr App R 396, CA.

[89] See further comments of Hall, p 204, namely: 'Another unique feature of the technique is the virtual monopoly over testing procedures. The *Jeffreys* testing system is subject to patent, and so far as the writer is able to discover, only the police scientific laboratories and Cellmark Diagnostics, a private company, are able to apply the procedure in the United Kingdom ... since the same procedures are used by the police forensic laboratories and by Cellmark, if laboratory techniques are less than perfect, or if the underlying science is flawed, there may simply be a replication of the same inaccurate result. Where a scientific process is unregulated and the procedure is essentially a 'trade secret' what protection is there in this vitally important area?'

[90] *People (DPP) v Howe* (2003) *The Irish Times*, 15 October, CCC, Butler J.

belonging to another. Furthermore, the prosecution had not disproved that the accused had a brother with similar DNA.

[7.79] In *People(DPP) v Allen*,[91] the evidence was admitted, but the Court of Criminal Appeal gave a strong warning:

> Expert evidence comparing DNA profiles is a comparatively recent scientific technique and indeed it would appear that it is still being perfected ... One of the primary dangers ... is that ... a jury could jump to the conclusion that it is infallible. That, of course, is not so in the case of DNA evidence, at least in the present state of knowledge.[92]

[7.80] These issues need to be addressed by the Irish legislature. Unfortunately, in the haste to provide adequate powers for the gardaí to obtain samples to use in the detection and prosecution of crime, the Irish legislature would seem to have lost sight of the context – both forensic and legal. Despite advances in forensic science and DNA testing in particular, the point should not be lost that there is a different culture in operation in both these contexts, and as the *Castro* case still demonstrates, usurpation of the one by the other diminishes both.

[7.81] The Law Reform Commission's Consultation Paper on Expert Evidence states, in relation to DNA evidence, that:

> [i]n recent years, the use of DNA evidence in trials, particularly in criminal trials by the prosecution, has burgeoned. However, although the public at large is now tentatively acquainted with the principles underlying the use of such evidence, most of this knowledge has been imparted through the media, television and film, and thus the public perception is such evidence may be inaccurate. As a result, expert evidence continues to be necessary in any case involving DNA evidence to explain to the jury the complex principles of DNA technology and evidence.[93]

Criminal Justice (Forensic Evidence) Act 1990

[7.82] Since the introduction of the Criminal Justice (Forensic Evidence) Act 1990, it has been apparent that the Irish legislature and public favour the implementation of provisions securing the facility for use of genetic fingerprinting information in the criminal process. The 1990 Act, as passed, provides that the powers conferred on An Garda Síochána to obtain such information are without prejudice to any other powers exercisable by them. Such other powers would include all relevant garda common law and statutory powers. Particularly noteworthy, perhaps, are those related to 'ordinary' fingerprinting, and those found under the Status of Children Act 1987. Recent

---

91 *People (DPP) v Allen* [2003] 4 IR 295.
92 *People (DPP) v Allen* [2003] 4 IR 295 at 299 *per* McCracken J.
93 LRC CP 52–2008, at para 2.25, p 43.

provision has been in the context of an arrest under s 4 of the Criminal Justice Act 1984, in relation to which, regulations provide that fingerprints, palm prints or photographs shall not be taken of, or swabs or samples taken from, a person in custody except with his written consent.[94]

[7.83] In the context of arrests that don't come under the Criminal Justice Act 1984, provision is made by the Regulations as to the Measuring and Photographing of Prisoners 1955.[95] These permit an untried person to have fingerprints taken if he has been informed of his right to object, but does not do so. Without his consent, he may nevertheless be fingerprinted with the Minister's authority or upon approval of an application of a garda (not below the rank of Inspector) to a Justice of the District Court or, in Dublin, by a Commissioner or Deputy Commissioner.

[7.84] Authority in relation to those detained under s 30 of the Offences Against the State Act 1939 is provided by s 7(1) of the Criminal Law (Jurisdiction) Act 1976, which allows fingerprinting and explosives tests (hair and skin swabs also) to be carried out. Relevant in this context is the Status of Children Act 1987, Part VII, which makes provision for the use of blood tests as evidence in questions of parentage arising in civil proceedings. Section 37 of the 1987 Act defines 'blood tests' as any test carried out with the object of ascertaining inheritable characteristics. According to the explanatory memorandum, this includes such tests as serological analysis, enzyme analysis, tissue typing and DNA profiling.

[7.85] Under s 38 of the 1987 Act, a court, either of its own motion or on an application by any party to the proceedings, can give a direction for the use of blood tests for the purpose of assisting the court to determine parentage. Section 39 of that Act provides that a blood sample should not be taken from that person, except with his consent. However, the court may draw such inferences, if any, from the failure to consent, as appear proper in the circumstances (s 38(1)). Interestingly, s 43 provides for penalties for personation of blood tests.

[7.86] In accordance with the regime under the 1990 Act, it is that period consequent to arrest that is most significant. This is because the benchmark as to when an individual can become the subject of such a test is under s 2 of the Act when that person is 'in custody' under s 30 of the Offences Against the State Act 1939 or s 4 of the Criminal Justice Act 1984. Presumably that means any time during the period following the arrest, right up to appearance in court. Difficulties inherent in the concept of 'custody' arise: the position of an

---

[94] Criminal Justice Act 1984 (Treatment of Persons in Custody in Garda Síochána Stations) Regulations 1987 (S1 119/1987, reg18).

[95] Regulations as to the Measuring and Photographing of Prisoners (S1 114/1955).

individual 'helping the police with their inquiries' (presumably, if voluntary not in custody, if in *People (DPP) v O'Loughlin's*[96] situation a valid subject for the test) an individual deemed not to be voluntarily helping the police with their inquiries, a garda witness declared that he would have arrested the accused if he had attempted to leave); that of an individual unlawfully arrested (whether 'cured' or not, *People v Walsh*[97] allowed for the concept of 'curing' of an unlawful period of arrest – where individual has not been told of the reason for same) and that of an individual held longer than the permitted period (*People v Madden*[98] where failure to observe strictly the temporal limitations of the s 30 detention provisions in a situation where the accused commenced making a confession statement shortly before the expiry of same and was detained further to facilitate its completion, led to the court constituting same a breach of rights).

[7.87] Presumably, all of the jurisprudence to date on that issue, exercised in the context of other forms of evidence (eg testimony or real evidence (*People (DPP) v Kenny*)),[99] should apply with at least as much vigour here. Counter arguments based on the immutability or reliability of DNA data could not be sustained in light of *Kenny*.

[7.88] Samples that can be taken under the 1990 Act are divided in terms of those that require consent on the part of the person concerned and those which do not. Section 4(b) of the 1990 Act provided that the appropriate consent must be given in writing in relation to the following samples:

  (i)   blood;

  (ii)   pubic hair;

  (iii) urine;

  (iv)   saliva;

  (v)   a swab from a body orifice or a genital region; and

  (vi)   a dental impression.

The other samples allowed, which were provided for by the Act – namely, hair other than pubic hair, a nail, any material found under a nail, a footprint or similar impression of any part of the person's body other than a part of his hand or mouth – did not require consent.

[7.89] There has been some change to this area in so far as the Criminal Justice Act 2006 provides in s 14 an amendment to the 1990 Act which substitutes ss 4–8A for ss 4–8. The effect of these changes is that mouth swabs and saliva may

---

[96] *People (DPP) v O'Loughlin* [1975] IR 85.

[97] *People v Walsh* [1980] IR 294.

[98] *People v Madden* [1977] IR 336.

[99] *People (DPP) v Kenny* [1990] ILRM 569.

now be taken *without* the consent previously required under the 1990 Act. Section 8A clarifies that where a sample of hair other than pubic hair is taken, it may be done by plucking and should contain sufficient root for forensic testing.

[7.90] This method of distinguishing between those samples – the taking of which does or does not require consent – merits criticism on two grounds. Firstly, the exhaustive listing of all samples to be taken under the auspices of the 1990 Act is questionable, in terms of the ongoing development of this science to facilitate testing of less obvious material for a DNA profile. DNA profiling, therefore, might be feasible under other garda powers which the Act does not prejudice, but would then be without even these limited safeguards foreseen by the Act.

[7.91] Secondly, the list method is a non-principled basis for distinction, and in similar fashion to the categorical approach of the English Act ('intimate' and 'non-intimate'), facilitates all too readily a modification of that number requiring consent which is what happened under the Criminal Justice Act 2006.[100]

[7.92] There is a requirement under the 1990 Act that the garda officer with the requisite authorisation (who cannot be below the rank of Superintendent (s 2(5)(a) of the 1990 Act) has 'reasonable grounds' for suspecting the involvement of the person from whom the sample is to be taken. Whether – given that the individual is already 'in custody' in relation to that crime – these would ever be found to be absent is questionable, and unlike the analogous prerequisite in warrant procedures for entry onto private property, there is no provision for an outside (judicial) review of same. In general, as seen, warrant procedures require the swearing of information before an independent third party – usually someone with judicial standing.

A further requirement is that there must be a belief that the sample will tend to confirm or disprove the involvement of the person (s 2(5)(b) of the 1990 Act). Since this does not require conclusiveness from the test result, the aim of the section is not clear.

[7.93] Provision is also made under s 2(b) of the 1990 Act for informing the individual of the nature of the offence, the authorisation that has been given and

---

[100] Sections 62–63 of the Police and Criminal Evidence Act 1984 permit the taking of 'intimate' and 'non-intimate' samples. Section 65 defines an 'intimate' sample as: 'a sample of blood, semen or any other tissue, fluid, urine, saliva or pubic hair, or a swab taken from a person's body orifice'. A 'non-intimate' sample means: '(a) a sample of hair other than pubic hair; (b) a sample taken from a nail or under a nail; (c) a swab taken from any part of a person's body other than a body orifice; (d) a footprint or similar impression of any part of a person's body other than a part of his hand'.

the fact that the results may be given in evidence. Although the provision does include a caution of sorts, it is as remiss as the equivalent English provision in failing to provide a requirement relating to legal advice or prior judicial authorisation (s 62(2) of the Police and Criminal Evidence Act 1984). Section 2(8) of the 1990 Act requires that certain samples be taken by a medical practitioner: blood, pubic hair, swabs from body orifices or genital regions.

[7.94] In the event of refusal of consent by an individual to the provision of a sample where consent is required, the 1990 Act provides at s 3 that such inferences 'as appear proper' may be drawn from such refusal by the court, and although such refusal may not in itself lead to a conviction of an offence, it can amount to evidence corroborative of any evidence in relation to which the refusal is material.

[7.95] Once the sample has been taken and the matter analysed and the result recorded, a major issue arises as to the use of that information – apart from its presentation in court in relation to the given charge. Section 4 of the 1990 Act provides for the destruction of samples and records (in this regard it is more comprehensive than its English counterpart, s 64 of the Police and Criminal Evidence Act 1984) in the case of acquittals, non-prosecutions or non-continuance of charges against an accused. A clawback provision allows for the Director of Public Prosecutions to make application that there is 'good reason' why such records or samples should not be destroyed, and so gain an order for their retention (s 4(5) of the 1990 Act).

[7.96] No guidelines have been issued in relation to how this power might be exercised. As well as raising broader issues as to the maintenance of State DNA data banks, spectres of area and regional testing in the aftermath of a crime, and compulsory testing of citizens – on a more basic level of concern, this raises the issue of what is being stored in the cases of those individuals who have been convicted or when there constitutes a 'good' reason to maintain data.

[7.97] A cursory glance at the 1990 Act's provisions, then, indicates its shortcomings. Issues are not only inadequately provided for – they have not been addressed. Yet the implications for the pre-trial procedure of our criminal law are considerable. Perhaps undue haste on the part of our legislators to introduce these provisions leaves now, at the next stage of the process, lawyers with the task of challenging the result. However, as seen, it requires fiscal and temporal resources beyond those of the average defence lawyer to take issue with same. Moreover, it demands a degree of tenacity, as the clients (particularly if recidivists) may be indigent, and all too anxious to accept the offer of a guilty plea in the face of apparently conclusive evidence.

[7.98] The scientific and legal communities have both expressed concern about the safeguards, procedures and adequacy of testing facilities. Issues of adequate resources, both scientific and financial, to deal with the introduction of forensic evidence into the criminal justice system have to be addressed before such garda powers should be invoked. If the legal system is to maintain any credibility in this area – in terms of guarantees of 'due process' to those individuals caught within it or trial in accordance with presumptions of innocence and adequate redress, – all concentration of effort from a legislative point of view should not be at the level of garda powers to obtain substances (with a fair degree of encroachment on individual rights), which is often of no particular use unless admissible. Courts and lawyers, with the aid of the scientific community, must stringently guard against the too readily admissible of the evidence obtained, unless adequately and rigorously tested in accordance with scientific consensus and procedure. Defence counsel must have a real opportunity to test same.

[7.99] If such provision is not made prior to the availability and enforcement of those powers, the criminal justice system will have been reduced to the imprimatur of the police station regime, and criminal justice moved correspondingly back. To this extent, the 'DNA controversy' may foreshadow a lot of things to come and constitute, in microcosm, the true forensic battlefield for further criminal trials. Quite apart from challenging the dynamics of science itself, Irish lawyers will find that in the most mundane and uncontroversial occasions, they must grapple with the increasingly present 'expert'.

[7.100] Difficulties remain in relation to DNA, as enumerated by Redmayne.[101] Doubts about the significance of matching a DNA profile can arise at the stage of the procedures used by the lab to prepare the DNA profile and declare a match (samples may be confused or mislabelled or, as in *R v Deen*,[102] there may be a dispute regarding the number of bands matching); in the statistical techniques used to determine a match probability (racial groups may have a very low rate of genetic variation); and in the combination of match probability with prior odds (the jury may have earlier information, for example that an eyewitness said it was a Greek person – this would be different from proving he just came from the same city of 3 million). Of course there is an additional difficulty where it is likely the accused and the perpetrator come from the same population subgroup.

[7.101] The *Auld Report* in England has made recommendations including one that the various expert witness organisations should concentrate their work in

---

[101] Redmayne, 'Doubts and Burdens: DNA Evidence, Probability and the Courts' [1995] Crim LR 464.

[102] *R v Deen* (1994) The Times, 10 January.

one body that will set standards for forensic scientists. *Auld* also recommends that experts' overriding duty should be to the court, courts should have the power to control the admissibility of expert evidence and to authorise expenditure on experts' fees in publicly defended cases, experts should meet before the trial and identify the extent to which they agree and disagree, and courts should have the power to order experts to meet to discuss areas of disagreement and to prepare a joint report thereon. However, courts are not to be empowered to appoint or select experts.[103]

[7.102] One area where 'expertise' has recently proliferated is that of historic sex abuse cases. In such instances, in order to explain the element of delay in a manner which complies with the recognition of an exception to expeditious trial in such cases, expert evidence is tendered as to the normal reaction of someone subjected to such abuse. The same experts have been tendered in very many cases and questions have been raised by the courts as to their 'expertise', the reliability (and recognition) of the science involved in certain cases and their methodology. Criticism of the expert witness testimony is a feature of these cases, with Hardiman J in *JO'C v DPP*[104] finding the nature of the examination by the psychologist to have been 'gravely inadequate'.[105] Expert witnesses in both the presentation of evidence and recognition of their area of research or expertise, have met with sharply differing judicial views of their testimony (see, for example, the contrasting views of McGuinness and Denham JJ in *PC v DPP*[106]). In *NC v DPP*,[107] the actual unavailability of the hypnotist under whose ministrations the complainant had revived her memory of events forming the basis of the complaint (which also triggered the other complaints made by her sister), where the trial would have taken place 40 years and 10 months after the first alleged assault, led Hardiman J, in granting the application to restrain prosecution, to point out that there was therefore no effective test or control of the mechanism of alleged recovery, rendering this a situation 'fraught with the risk of unfairness'. This view is supported by that of a working party of the Royal College of Psychiatrists in the UK which in reviewing this topic concluded:

> Evidence does not support the view that mcmory enhancement techniques actually enhance memory. There is evidence to support the view that these are powerful and dangerous methods of persuasion.[108]

---

[103] Lord Justice Auld, *Review of the Criminal Courts of England and Wales* TSO (2001).

[104] *JO'C v DPP* [2000] 3 IR 478.

[105] *JO'C v DPP* [2000] 3 IR 478 at 527.

[106] *PC v DPP* [1999] 2 IR 25.

[107] *NC v DPP* [2001] IESC 54 at p 18, Hardiman J.

[108] See further Brandon et al, 'Recovered memories of childhood sexual abuse' (1998) 172 *British Journal of Psychiatrists* 296.

Practical pointers in relation to the examination of the expert witness

Examination-in-chief

[7.103] In establishing the 'expertise' of a tendered witness, the onus of proof is on counsel calling the witness to establish his status on the basis of qualification or day-to-day experience in the area. A witness should be encouraged not to be shy or unforthcoming in the elucidation of same. In this regard, see for example, the decision of O'Hanlon J in *DPP v O'Donoghue*.[109] This case constituted an appeal by way of a case stated against the decision of District Justice Windle to dismiss a charge brought against the respondent for failure to permit a designated registered medical practitioner to take from him a specimen of his blood (or provide a specimen of urine for same), contrary to s 13(3) of the Road Traffic (Amendment) Act 1978. The evidence had shown that the doctor had been introduced by the sergeant in charge as 'the designated registered medical practitioner', that the doctor had been asked in the District Court the rhetorical question, 'I think you are a registered medical practitioner?' to which he replied 'I am'. The next question was: 'Were you designated by the gardaí on the night in question?' to which he replied, 'I was'. The District Justice took the view that this failed to elicit confirmation of a necessary fact for the purposes of the prosecution, ie that the doctor was at the time he attended the station a registered medical practitioner. All that had been established was that he was introduced as such by the sergeant, and that on the day the matter came before the District Court he confirmed that as of that time he was a registered medical practitioner.

[7.104] O'Hanlon J noted that *Martin v Quinn*[110] involved confirmation by the Supreme Court that it was necessary to prove that the person for whom the defendant had failed to provide a specimen of his urine was a registered medical practitioner. The Supreme Court also held that the testimony of that person that he was such a practitioner at the relevant time was *prima facie* evidence of that fact and, unless rebutted, would support a conviction. O'Hanlon J commented that this latter finding constituted an acceptance of some relaxation of the application of the 'best evidence' rule, which would otherwise give rise to the intolerable burden of having to produce formal proof of qualifications held by professional witnesses on every occasion when they were called on to give evidence. An appropriate form of *prima facie* evidence must still be furnished, however, and O'Hanlon J did not consider that the prosecution could ask for the rule of evidence to be further relaxed when it could be satisfied by the simple expedient of the registered medical practitioner testifying as to his status as

---

[109] *DPP v O'Donoghue* (15 February 1979, unreported), HC.
[110] *Martin v Quinn* [1980] IR 244.

same 'at the material time'. As the necessary formal evidence was not given in this case, the appeal was dismissed.

Cross-examination

[7.105] There are three basic options with regard to the manner in which an expert witness can be cross-examined:

(i) putting questions to the expert that place a different interpretation on the facts upon which the expert has based his opinion and eliciting, if possible, answers which show that the different interpretation of the facts – an interpretation which is favourable to the cross-examiner's case – is reasonable;

(ii) challenging the expert witness's opinion by confronting him with authoritative works, or even his own writings, which cast doubt on the correctness of his opinion; and

(iii) establishing that the expert witness formed his opinion without taking into consideration facts that have either been established, or which the cross-examiner hopes to establish and which modify, or should modify, the expert's opinion.

In such manner, and by reference to the most appropriate and suitable tactic on the occasion, the lawyer can vindicate his client's interests and participate in the process of maintaining the province of legal adjudication.

Reform

[7.106] The *Law Reform Commission's Consultation Paper on Expert Evidence* noted that examples of the types of expert opinion appearing in Irish courts[111] are in patent case, foreign law, custom and practice of a trade or profession, technical or scientific terminology and the meaning of foreign words (interpretation). The Commission also noted that, '[n]owadays, in reaching a conclusion, the expert is permitted to rely on prior studies, statistics and research, academic literature and works of reference in their field of expertise. This has been termed "non-specific hearsay".'[112]

[7.107] This issue was considered in *People DPP v Boyce*[113] where the appellant argued that the expert had relied on statistical information in scientific literature and not on his own knowledge and this should not have been allowed. The court held that:

---

[111] Law Reform Commission, Consultation Paper on Expert Evidence (LRC CP 52–2008) at pp 42–49.

[112] Law Reform Commission, Consultation Paper on Expert Evidence (LRC CP 52–2008) at p 54.

[113] *People (DPP) v Boyce* [2005] IECCA 143.

[i]n a long established exception to the hearsay rule an expert can ground or fortify his or her opinion by referring to works of authority, learned articles, recognized reference norms and other similar material as comprising part of the general body of knowledge falling within the field of expertise of the expert in question.

[7.108] The ability of an expert to rely on second-hand information, eg the statements or narration of events by a patient, in order to form his expert opinion is permissible. This can occur in cases of sexual abuse and delay where the psychiatrist is called to explain the reasons for the delay. It has been held that the expert can believe the complainant and use that information in their opinion, although the statements are not admissible as proof of their truth but as the basis upon which the expert formed their opinion.[114] In *DW v DPP*[115] McGuinness J held in the context of evidence of delay in cases of child sex abuse:

All such evidence is open to challenge in cross-examination. It must, however, be borne in mind that it is not the task of the expert witness to assess the credibility of the complainant or the guilt or innocence of the applicant. The truth or otherwise of the complaints is to be tested at the trial.

[7.109] In nullity cases in Ireland a similar issue arose in the context of the admissibility of psychiatric evidence. In *F v L (Orse F)*[116] Barron J held that he could not accept such evidence as true and in *RT v VP*[117] Lardner J held that evidence based on an individual the expert had never met or examined was hearsay.

[7.110] In *JWH (Orse W) v GW* and *DK v TH (Orse TK)*,[118] however, evidence was admitted from psychiatrists concerning the mental state of the respondents, even though the respondents had not been examined by the experts, O'Higgins CJ feeling that the matter should go to weight and not admissibility.

[7.111] In *Southern Health Board v C*,[119] in proceedings to impose a fit person order, a father objected to a videotape of an interview with his child and a social worker which formed the basis of an allegation of sexual abuse. O'Flaherty J took the view that the videotape was not hearsay evidence as it did not constitute independent evidence of the child but a material part of the expert testimony of the social worker.

---

[114] See *Phillion v The Queen* [1978] 1 SCR 18 at 24 referred to in Law Reform Commission, *Consultation Paper on Expert Evidence* (LRC CP 52–2008) at p 57.

[115] *DW v DPP* [2003] IESC 54.

[116] *F v L (Orse F)* [1990] 1 IR 348.

[117] *RT v VP* [1990] 1 IR 545.

[118] *JWH (Orse W) v GW* and *DK v TH (Orse TK)* (25 February 1998, unreported), HC – both cases heard on same day.

[119] *Southern Health Board v C* [1996] 1 IR 219.

Junk science

[7.112] An important dimension to the Law Reform Commission report is related to junk science, which is the term used to refer to the abuse of science and scientific terminology in the court room by importing irrelevant or inaccurate evidence to advance a party's arguments. The Commission pointed out that in Ireland, unlike other jurisdictions, 'there is no admissibility test which requires the party to demonstrate that the expert evidence they purport to adduce can be considered as being founded on a sufficiently reliable basis.'[120] One could, of course, argue that there is such a rule and it is provided by the threshold of relevance. Indeed, this is evident from the decision in *NC v DPP*[121] where the Supreme Court rejected a prosecution in circumstances where hypnosis was used to recover memory. Difficulties were caused here by the absence of the therapist from the trial and uncertainty regarding dates etc, but nonetheless the case illustrates, as the Commission noted, 'that the Irish courts will require a high level of proof of the reliability of any novel form of expertise, even if no formal reliability test has been enunciated.'[122]

[7.113] The Commission noted that in the US most states follow *Daubert*,[123] which requires the evidence to be empirically validated rather than generally accepted, marking a greater degree of scrutiny on the part of courts in the US. In England the courts have demonstrated a willingness to accept unconventional evidence.[124]

The Commission, in any event, made the provisional recommendation that a judicial guidance note be introduced outlining the factors that can be taken into account by the trial judge when assessing whether the expert evidence in question meets the requisite reliability threshold.[125]

---

[120] Law Reform Commission, Consultation Paper on Expert Evidence (LRC CP 52 – 2008) at para 2.301, p 102.

[121] *NC v DPP* [2001] IESC 54.

[122] (LRC CP 52 – 2008) at para 2.301, p 103.

[123] *Daubert v Merrell Dow Pharmaceuticals* 509 US 579.

[124] For example, facial mapping (*R v Stockwell* [1993] 97 Cr App 260) and ear print evidence (*R v Kempster* [2003] EWCA Crim 3555).

[125] (LRC CP 52 – 2008) at para 2.390, p 125.

Chapter 8

Privilege

All animals are equal but some animals are more equal than others.

Orwell, *Animal Farm*

Introduction

[8.01] The area of the law of evidence relating to privilege is divided into that which is called private privilege and that which has been called, in turn, Crown privilege, state privilege and, more recently, public privilege. State or public privilege, having had its origins in a very limited attachment to matters of state security or defence (the design of submarines or warships or the like), has been broadened to take account of instances of confidentiality which should not become public because of the greater usefulness of the relationship involved to the public. In a sense, what results is a balancing act by the courts, taking into account the damage that would be done to the relationship involved, and the public good, against that of the good that would be done in terms of the administration of justice, should the information be revealed. Private privilege has a much more absolute, if limited, effect.

[8.02] Private privilege attaches to certain relationships which have been specifically fostered by the courts where a witness can choose on the basis of that relationship to refuse to reveal certain information. That this category of privilege is limited is not surprising, for the recognition of private privilege attaching to these relationships inevitably cuts down on the amount of relevant information before a court of law, which correspondingly reduces that court's ability to engage in the effective administration of justice. Although there may well come a day when state or public privilege will subsume the area of private privilege, those who are party to a private privilege will jealously guard the independence it gives in terms of non-scrutiny by the court of the reasonableness of the decision to raise that private privilege.

Private privilege

[8.03] Privilege relates to an instance when one is not obliged to answer particular questions or produce particular documents. It is important to distinguish between privilege in this context and competence. In relation to competence, the incapacity of the witness is complete, and prevents that particular witness from testifying at all. Private privilege, on the other hand, may well be waived by its possessor. When a witness raises a privilege in a criminal trial, he/she is relying on a legal right to withhold certain information which would otherwise be relevant and admissible. The state is obviously reluctant to grant such privileges, as they exclude relevant and probative evidence which might enable justice to be done between the parties to the litigation. However, private privilege has been held to attach or to arise in the situations outlined in the following paragraph. This means that individuals in these situations may choose to raise a privilege and so refuse to answer particular questions or produce particular documents. Equally, however, they may well decide to waive the particular privilege. In either event, it is existent.

[8.04] Privilege arises in the following situations:

> *(1) Lawyer/client privilege or legal professional privilege*
>
> If the witness is a lawyer, this privilege allows the lawyer as a witness to refuse to disclose communications made to him by his client without the client's consent; if the witness is a client, this privilege allows the client to refuse to disclose communications made to him by his lawyer.
>
> *(2) 'Without prejudice' communications*
>
> In civil proceedings, disclosing 'without prejudice' communications made to a witness without the consent of the parties to the communication is a breach of privilege.
>
> *(3) Marital privilege*
>
> This relates to the disclosure of communications made to a spouse by the other spouse during the marriage.
>
> *(4) Privilege against self-incrimination*
>
> This is a privilege which allows a witness to refuse to answer incriminating questions in criminal and civil cases.

Legal professional privilege

[8.05] The rationale or reasoning behind the existence of legal professional privilege is that of encouraging the client to put all facts before the lawyer, not just the ones which favour his position. Yet this is undeniably another obstacle to the truth, and further proof that the law is not a scientific investigation for the discovery of truth. Indeed, Bentham[1] objected to the privilege, on the ground that if a man was guilty, there should be nothing to betray, and that abolition of the privilege would lead to tighter professional standards amongst lawyers as it

---

[1]   Bentham, *A Rationale of Judicial Evidence* (1827) Book IX, Pt IV, c 5.

would remove any power to hide an accused's guilt. Yet in modern conditions, skilful cross-examination may be used to mitigate any possible harm such privilege might cause, and it is arguably necessary for the successful perusal of a lawyer/client relationship.

[8.06] This privilege was recognised in *Wheeler v Le Marchant*,[2] where Jessel MR stated that the protection was of a very limited nature, and restricted to the obtaining of the assistance of lawyers, as regards the conduct of litigation or the right to property. It has never gone beyond the obtaining of legal advice and assistance, and all things reasonably necessary in the shape of communication to the legal advisers are protected from production or discovery in order that that legal advice may be obtained safely and sufficiently.

[8.07] There are two basic aspects to legal professional privilege:

    (i)   lawyer/client communications; and

    (ii)   communications with third parties.

These two categories are examined in turn.

Lawyer/client communications

[8.08] Communications between a lawyer and client may not be given in evidence without the consent of the client. In order to attract this legal professional privilege, however, the communication must occur in the course of a professional legal relationship. Thus, a conversation with a lawyer in the course of a social event, or in relation to non-professional business, would not be covered by the privilege. The authority which suggests that the legal professional privilege in this instance belongs to the client is the decision in *Minter v Priest*,[3] where it was held that the client can waive or not waive the privilege as he sees fit.

[8.09] It has similarly been held that the privilege here does not extend to third parties. In the case of *Schneider v Leigh*,[4] which involved an action for personal injuries, a claim of privilege was made by Dr Leigh in relation to a medical report which he had compiled on the plaintiff's injuries. In the context of the personal injury action, the defendant company would have had legal professional privilege with regard to that letter. However, the action involved here was one where the plaintiff alleged that he was defamed in the communication sent by Dr Leigh to that company. The plaintiff therefore sued Dr Leigh, and the issue arose as to whether Dr Leigh could claim that legal

---

[2]   *Wheeler v Le Marchant* (1881) 17 Ch D 675.
[3]   *Minter v Priest* [1930] AC 588.
[4]   *Schneider v Leigh* [1955] 2 All ER 173.

professional privilege. The court held that no legal professional privilege attached to Dr Leigh here. (Although under the substantive law of defamation, it might have been possible for Dr Leigh to have taken refuge in the defence of qualified privilege, ie that of a person making a statement with a genuine reason for so doing. Another possible defence might have been that of justification.)

[8.10] Legal professional privilege attaches only to confidential communications. It is not applied, therefore, to a letter which is written, for example, on a client's instruction. Such an instance arose in the decision of *Bord na gCon v Murphy*.[5] In this case Bord na gCon wrote to Murphy accusing him of being in breach of the Greyhound Industry Act 1958. Subsequently, Murphy was convicted of offences under that Act, and he appealed. On appeal, Bord na gCon wished to put in evidence against Murphy a letter which related to the offence, and which was written by Murphy's solicitor in reply to the Bord's initial communication to Murphy. The High Court refused to allow that document to go in because Murphy had not given permission to it being tendered in evidence. The Supreme Court held, however, that correspondence between Murphy's solicitor and Bord na gCon was inadmissible in evidence because it constituted hearsay, and not because of the privilege. The court did say that the correspondence and the statement were not confidential, and therefore would not in any event be inadmissible on grounds of legal professional privilege.

[8.11] In *R v Crown Court ex p Baines & Baines*,[6] it was held *inter alia* that conveyancing documents are not privileged, as they do not come within the meaning of the giving of advice, consisting as they do of records of the financing of a house purchase.

[8.12] One qualification on the ambit of legal professional privilege in relation to solicitor and client is that it does not extend to communications made in furtherance of a criminal offence. These are excluded from the rubric of the privilege, as had been held in a line of authority, including the decision in *R v Cox & Railton*.[7] The communication must be shown to be preparatory to a crime and not merely be a warning. In *Butler v Board of Trade*,[8] an unsolicited letter from a lawyer to a client advising him that certain conduct would be likely to lead to his being prosecuted was held to constitute a mere warning and so not to come under the decision in *Cox & Railton*. In the Irish context, the court in *People (AG) v Coleman*[9] held that the document in question was an attempt to

---

5   *Bord na gCon v Murphy* [1970] IR 301.
6   *R v Crown Court ex p Baines & Baines* [1987] 3 All ER 1025.
7   *R v Cox & Railton* (1884) 14 QBD 153.
8   *Butler v Board of Trade* [1970] 3 All ER 593.
9   *People (AG) v Coleman* [1945] IR 237.

procure the subornation of witnesses and, therefore, even if it had reached the solicitor in question as intended, it would not be a privileged communication since it contemplated and suggested the commission of a crime.

[8.13] The question of the ambit of the privilege in terms of various types of communications on different issues that pass between lawyers and clients arose in *Smurfit Paribas Bank Ltd v CAB Export Finance Ltd.*[10] The issue here was whether the defendant's claim to legal professional privilege in respect of communications passing between it and its solicitors was carried in law. The facts concerned a dispute between the plaintiff and defendant, with regard to the defendant's floating charge. Following an order for discovery, the defendant claimed privilege in relation to correspondence between it and the solicitor then acting for it in relation to the charge. The documents in question did not request or contain legal advice about the transaction, but held reference to instructions regarding the drafting of documentation necessary to the transaction. In the High Court these documents were deemed not privileged (Costello J) on the grounds that they did not request or contain legal advice and contained no information that could be regarded as confidential. Reliance was placed on *Smith-Bird v Blower*,[11] in which a letter written to the solicitors by the defendant, in answer to an inquiry as to whether he had agreed to sell the property in question, was deemed not privileged. In the Supreme Court, Finlay CJ[12] identified the relevant policy issue as being:

> ... the requirement of the superior interest of the common good in the proper conduct of litigation which justified the immunity of communications from discovery insofar as they were made for the purpose of litigation as being the desirability in that goal of the correct and efficient trial of actions by the courts.

[8.14] Finlay CJ referred to *Minter v Priest*,[13] which gives support to the notion that the extent of the privilege is outside that of actual or contemplated litigation. He commented that some cases appear to support a contention that it is sufficient if legal assistance, other than advice, only were sought. However, Finlay CJ noted that the ultimate decision as to the existence of a privilege, lies with the courts.[14] Finlay CJ further noted that:

> The existence of a privilege or exemption from disclosure for communications made between a person and his lawyer clearly constitutes a potential restriction and diminution of the full disclosure both prior to and during the course of legal proceedings which in the interests of the common good is desirable for the

---

[10] *Smurfit Paribas Bank Ltd v CAB Export Finance Ltd* [1990] ILRM 588.
[11] *Smith-Bird v Blower* [1939] 2 All ER 406.
[12] *Smurfit Paribas Bank Ltd v CAB Export Finance Ltd* [1990] ILRM 588 at 593.
[13] *Minter v Priest* [1930] AC 588.
[14] As *per Murphy v Dublin Corporation* [1972] IR 215.

purpose of ascertaining the truth and rendering justice. Such privilege should, therefore, in my view, only be granted by the courts in instances which have been identified as securing an objective which in the public interest in the proper conduct of the administration of justice can be said to outweigh the disadvantage arising from the restriction of disclosure of all the facts.[15]

[8.15] Hence, where a communication is made to a lawyer for the purpose of obtaining from such a lawyer legal advice, whether at the initiation of the client or the lawyer, Finlay CJ was satisfied that it should in general be privileged, or exempt from disclosure, except with the consent of the client. Similar considerations, he found, do not apply to communications made to a lawyer for the purpose of obtaining his legal assistance, other than advice. He continued:

> There are many tasks carried out by a lawyer for his client, and properly within the legal sphere, other than the giving of advice, which could not be said to contain any real relationship with the area of potential litigation. For such communications there does not appear to me to be any sufficient public interest or feature of the common good to be secured or protected which could justify an exemption from disclosure.

[8.16] Finlay CJ thus affirmed the trial judge's decision. McCarthy J's judgment is to the same effect:

> In the instant case, the fundamental issue arises from the contrasting demands – candour by the client to his solicitor and the public interest in the true resolution of litigation. In my view communication of fact leading to the drafting of legal documents and requests for the preparation of such, albeit made to a solicitor unless and until the same results in the provision of legal advice, is not privileged from disclosure.[16]

The decision in *Smurfit* was followed in *Miley v Flood,*[17] which extracted the principle that a communication only attracts privilege if it seeks or contains legal advice and that the communication of any other information is not privileged. Therefore, it was held that the identity of a client is not privileged, as it is a 'mere collateral fact'.

[8.17] In *Buckley v Incorporated Law Society,*[18] correspondence between the complainants and the respondent society regarding the alleged misconduct of a solicitor was held not to be privileged because the complainants were not consulting the Law Society as a legal adviser.

---

[15] *Smurfit Paribas Bank Ltd v CAB Export Finance Ltd* [1990] ILRM 588 at 594.
[16] *Smurfit Paribas Bank Ltd v CAB Export Finance Ltd* [1990] ILRM 588 at 597, McCarthy J.
[17] *Miley v Flood* [2001] ILRM 489.
[18] *Buckley v Incorporated Law Society* [1994] 2 IR 44.

[8.18] In *Buckley v Bough*[19] the plaintiff was claiming damages from the defendant for medical negligence. After an order for discovery, the defendant claimed legal professional privilege over a number of documents. It was challenged as the documents concerned a hearing of the Fitness to Practice Committee under the Medical Practitioners Act 1978. Morris J held that the documentation consisting of correspondence between the defendant's solicitors was not communicating legal advice to the defendant so as to attract legal privilege. Should there have been any privilege attaching on the basis of the patient-medical practitioner relationship, it was, in any event, being waived by the patient.

[8.19] If the issue of privilege is involved in a criminal trial when the accused is trying to exculpate himself, the courts will probably not allow legal professional privilege to attach in relation to exculpatory evidence. This is because the importance of the relationship which has led to the recognition of a privilege, in this instance, could not override the importance of not convicting an innocent person.

[8.20] In *R v Barton*,[20] the defendant worked in a solicitor's office. He was charged with fraudulent conversion in the course of his employment with that firm of solicitors. A solicitor who was a partner in the firm said that certain documents could not be produced at trial because they were privileged. The accused wanted them produced in an effort to exculpate himself. Caulfield J stated that working on the rules of natural justice, no privilege could attach here. He commented 'the law will not allow a solicitor or anyone else to screen from the jury information which if disclosed might enable a man to establish his innocence'. (In that instance the judge relied on the rules of natural justice, in particular the *audi alterem partem* rule, yet in Ireland, one could arguably rely on the even stronger rule of constitutional justice.)

[8.21] In *R v Ataou*,[21] the accused's solicitor discovered during the trial that he was in possession of a statement by a former client, now testifying against the accused, which was inconsistent with that testimony and favourable to the accused. The court gave permission for use of the statement in cross-examination, but surprisingly criticised the solicitor. Arguably again, the basis for admissibility in Ireland would be greater, and that criticism less. In *Ataou*, the Court of Appeal emphasised that, in the joint trial situation, where the privilege belongs to one of the defendants, and the information, if revealed, would exonerate him and cause harm to the other party, the trial judge must

---

[19] *Buckley v Bough* (2 July 2001, unreported), HC, Morris P.
[20] *R v Barton* [1972] 2 All ER 1192.
[21] *R v Ataou* [1988] 2 All ER 321.

balance the conflicting interests of the defendants. The defendant seeking to introduce the privileged information must show, on the balance of probabilities, that his legitimate interest in seeking to breach the privilege outweighs the co-defendant's in its maintenance.

Communications with third parties

[8.22] The second aspect to the legal professional privilege rule relates to communication between clients and third parties or between legal advisers and third parties which are made for the purpose of pending or contemplated litigation. 'Pending litigation' refers to a situation when some legal proceeding has been issued in relation to the issue, for example, where parties have either issued civil bills or plenary summons in the High Court. 'Contemplated litigation' is a rather more difficult concept: it is clear that there has to be a definite proposal of litigation, not a mere anticipation of it.

[8.23] Earlier Irish case law includes the decision in *Kerry County Council v Liverpool Salvage Association*[22] where, because no litigation was then in contemplation, the claim of privilege failed, and *Rushbrooke v O'Sullivan,*[23] where documents prepared with a view to ascertaining whether litigation should be initiated at some future time (but not with a view to actual or threatened litigation) were not privileged.

[8.24] In the case of *Alfred Crompton Amusement Machines v Commissioners of Customs & Excise,*[24] documents were received in relation to same. However, these documents concerned the market value of a number of one-armed bandit machines. It was held therefore that they were not entitled to legal professional privilege as their only purpose was to permit the assessment of purchase tax, and not to assist in litigation.

Dominant purpose

[8.25] A similar incident occurred in the decision of the House of Lords in *Waugh v British Railways Board.*[25] The facts of this case were that the plaintiff's husband, who was employed by the defendant Board, received injuries in a collision between locomotives and died. The practice of the Board when such an accident occurred was that on the day of the accident a brief report was made to a railway inspectorate. Soon after, a joint internal report (joint inquiry report) was prepared, including statements of witnesses, and that was also sent to the

---

[22] *Kerry County Council v Liverpool Salvage Association* (1903) 38 ILTR 7.
[23] *Rushbrooke v O'Sullivan* [1926] IR 500.
[24] *Alfred Crompton Amusement Machines v Commissioners of Customs & Excise* [1973] 2 All ER 1169.
[25] *Waugh v British Railways Board* [1980] AC 521.

inspectorate. The inspectorate then made a report for the Department of Environment. The heading of the joint inquiry report said that it had to be sent to the Board's solicitor so it could advise the Board. The question arose as to whether the joint inquiry report was then privileged. Lord Wilberforce commented as follows: 'unless the purpose of submission to the legal advisor in view of litigation is at least the dominant purpose for which the relevant document was prepared the reasons which require privilege to be extended to it can not apply.' Yet that is not to go so far as to require litigation to be the sole purpose of the communication.

[8.26] In a similar vein, Lord Edmond Davies reasoned as follows. He would deny a claim to privilege when the litigation was merely one of several purposes of equal or similar importance intended to be served by the material sought to be withheld from disclosure, and *a fortiori* where it was merely a minor purpose. However, similarly, he would not go so far as to require litigation to be the sole purpose of the document:

> But in so much as the only basis of the claim to privilege in such cases as the present one is that the material in question was brought into existence for use in legal proceedings, it is surely right to insist that, before the claim is conceded or upheld, such a purpose must be shown to have played a paramount part.

[8.27] This 'dominant' purpose as to the test of privilege from disclosure in such circumstances has been endorsed in Ireland in *Silver Hill Duckling Ltd v Minister for Agriculture*[26] and in *Davis v St Michael's House.*[27] In *Silver Hill Duckling Ltd v Minister for Agriculture,*[28] the defendants were claiming damages for loss of a flock of ducks who had to be destroyed following an influenza outbreak. The defendant claimed privilege on the ground that certain documents had come into being in contemplation of and for the purpose of advising the Minister in relation to the plaintiff's claim. O'Hanlon J was of the view that as it was apparent that the disparity between the two parties in terms of the amount of compensation to be claimed would have to be resolved by litigation – litigation could be regarded as apprehended and the documentation privileged.

[8.28] In *PJ Carrigan Ltd v Norwich Union Fire Society Ltd,*[29] the defendants, on being notified by the plaintiffs of a claim in relation to a fire, commissioned a report from loss adjusters, as they viewed the claim with suspicion. O'Hanlon J took the view that they were contemplating, even at that stage, the possibility of

---

[26] *Silver Hill Duckling Ltd v Minister for Agriculture* [1987] IR 289.
[27] *Davis v St Michael's House* (25 November 1993, unreported), HC, Lynch J.
[28] *Silver Hill Duckling Ltd v Minister for Agriculture* [1987] IR 289.
[29] *PJ Carrigan Ltd v Norwich Union Fire Society Ltd* [1987] IR 618.

repudiating liability under the policy, and so the report had been obtained in apprehension of litigation. The purpose is determined objectively. In a Court of Appeal decision in *Guinness Peat Properties v Fitzroy*,[30] it was held that a letter written by a firm of architects to their professional indemnity insurers, notifying the insurers of a possible claim against the architects, was privileged because the dominant purpose of the letter was to enable the insurers to obtain legal advice or to conduct litigation which was then in prospect. Accordingly, the architects were granted an injunction prohibiting the plaintiffs, to whom the letter had inadvertently been disclosed, from using the letter in an action against the architects. The Court of Appeal took an objective view of the evidence as a whole, ie looking at the reality of the situation, in terms of the reason why the letter was brought into existence – being that of the insurers' interest in seeing that such claims were defended. In those circumstances it was felt the letter owed its genus to the dominant purpose that it should be used for the purpose of obtaining legal advice and any ensuing litigation. *Per* Lord Slade:

> ... I accept that the dominant purpose of the letter was to be viewed objectively on the evidence, particularly by reference to the intention of the Insurers who produced its genesis ... I accept that so viewed, the dominant purpose was to produce a letter of notification which would be used in order to obtain legal advice or to conduct or aid in the conduct of litigation which was at the time of its production in reasonable prospect.[31]

[8.29] Consideration of the purpose of a communication in the context of legal professional privilege and its attachment occurred in the Irish case of *Bula Ltd v Crowley*.[32] As often occurs, the challenge to the claim of privilege was in the context of affidavits of discovery, in this case submitted by Ulster Investment Bank Ltd and Allied Irish Investment Bank Ltd. The plaintiff's challenge to one group arose solely from the use of the word 'purposes' as distinct from 'purpose'. The plaintiff alleged that the privilege extended only to those documents which came into existence for the purpose of obtaining legal advice. They asserted that once documents are created for two different purposes, one of which would attract privilege and the other not, then it must be asserted, and if necessary established, that the dominant purpose was the one attracting privilege before such a claim can succeed. (*Silver Hill Duckling Ltd v Minister for Agriculture*[33] and *Tromso Sparebank v Beirne*[34] relied on.) *Per* Murphy J:

> ... it seems to me that the principle is material only where it appears that a document or documents came into existence for a duality of reasons one of which

---

[30] *Guinness Peat Properties v Fitzroy* [1987] 2 All ER 716.
[31] *New Law Journal*, 15 May 1987 at p 453.
[32] *Bula Ltd v Crowley* [1990] ILRM 756.
[33] *Silver Hill Duckling Ltd v Minister for Agriculture* [1987] ILRM 516.
[34] *Tromso Sparebank v Beirne* [1989] ILRM 257.

would attract the privilege and the other not. In the present case ... in effect the defendant has sworn that *all* the purposes for which the documents in question were brought into existence were privileged and accordingly it would be neither necessary nor appropriate to assert that there was a particular dominant purpose.

[8.30] A second attack was made on certain categories of alleged privilege on the basis that communications between the banks with each other or with any of the other defendants are not privileged as such and would only be privileged on the same basis as communications with a third party, ie only if they were made at the express or implied suggestion of the legal advisers to one or other of the parties for the purpose of obtaining legal advice and for the purpose of litigation existing or in contemplation of the time.[35] *Per* Murphy J:

> Of and insofar as the communications consist of legal advice there can be no doubt whatever but that they are privileged in the hands of the client on whose behalf they are obtained. Equally well it seems to me that the same advice is privileged in the hands of a third party who shares a common interest in the litigation with the client whether or not the third party is joined in the proceedings.[36]

[8.31] The privilege attaches to 'communications'. Communications in this sense are those which are communicated orally or in writing. Thus, to postulate a hypothetical situation, should a woman stab her husband, and go to her solicitor, a statement such as 'I stabbed him', would constitute a communication which would be privileged. However, should that woman be carrying a knife dripping with blood, the solicitor may well be asked about her demeanour and no privilege attaches to the instance of the blood and the knife, as these are not communications but information available to anyone.

[8.32] The privilege may also be lost by waiver and a party may well choose to waive a privilege in relation to particular evidence. However, a party cannot be over selective in terms of waiver. A party cannot tender only part of a document, as this may result in disclosure of parts merely favourable to that party. The whole of the document must lose its privilege.[37]

[8.33] The privilege arises even where someone mistakenly believes a person to be a lawyer, whether that mistake is innocent or the result of deceit.[38]

---

[35] *Hamilton v Nott* (1873) LR 16.
[36] See *Buttes Gas & Oil Co v Hammer* [1981] QB 223.
[37] *Great Atlantic Insurance Co v Home Insurance Co* [1981] 2 All ER 485.
[38] *Fauerheerd v London General Omnibus Co Ltd* [1918] 2 KB 1565.

Loss of the privilege

[8.34] The qualification on the doctrine of legal professional privilege, and one that is somewhat questionable in its roots, yet presents an undeniable instance when the privilege may be lost, relates to instances when third parties may gain access to information which is prima facie privileged.

[8.35] In the case of *R v Tompkins*,[39] the appellant was charged *inter alia* with handling goods which included a stereo identified by a Mr Evans as having special characteristics – to wit, a loose button. The appellant denied that a button had ever been loose on the stereo, and was then confronted with a note which he had written to his counsel saying that he had glued the button back on with air-fix glue. Prosecuting counsel had found the said note on the floor of the courtroom. In the absence of the jury, the document was ruled inadmissible. However, counsel for the prosecution asked questions based on its contents, ie had the appellant glued the button back on. He said he had. An appeal was launched on the basis of the use of the information obtained in breach of an alleged privilege between counsel and client, this being contrary to natural justice. Lord Ormrod noted that the argument of how the document came into the possession of the prosecution had not been pursued. He then commented:

> Privilege in this context relates only to the production of a document; it does not determine its admissibility in evidence. The note, though clearly privileged from production was admissible in evidence once it was in the possession of the prosecution.

He referred to *Butler v Board of Trade*,[40] where this point was made – ie once the privileged document is in the hands of the party who wishes to use it (and who is not party to the privilege), the question of privilege disappears and the question becomes one of admissibility and it is admissible even though it was obtained in breach of confidence. This line of authority goes back, it was alleged, to the decision in *Calcraft v Guest*.[41]

Mistaken disclosure

[8.36] The general principle in relation to mistakenly disclosed documents is said to have been laid down by the case of *Re Briamore Manufacturing Ltd (in liq)*,[42] where in proceedings to set aside an alleged fraudulent preference, the liquidator's solicitor made a mistake in his list of documents for discovery, including documents for which privilege could have been claimed, and which

---

[39] *R v Tompkins* (1977) 67 Cr App Rep 18B.
[40] *Butler v Board of Trade* [1971] Ch 680.
[41] *Calcraft v Guest* [1898] 1 QB 759.
[42] *Re Briamore Manufacturing Ltd (in liq)* [1986] 3 All ER 132.

should have been included in the list of documents which he objected to produce. The respondent's solicitor was shown copies of the privileged documents, read them and made notes of their contents and a photocopy of at least one of them. Although the liquidator's solicitor informed the respondent the following day, the respondent's solicitor nevertheless made a formal request for copies of the privileged documents. The Registrar refused to order delivery of copies of the privileged documents. The respondent appealed. It was held that it was too late for the liquidator to correct the mistake in the list and, consequently, the respondent was entitled to the copies sought. The appeal would therefore be allowed on production of the documents ordered.

[8.37] In a subsequent decision of *English and American Insurance Co Ltd v Herbert Smith & Co*,[43] it was held in a situation where a bundle of papers given by counsel to his clerk for return to his instructing solicitors were mistakenly delivered to counsel's chambers for the first defendant, that the plaintiffs were entitled to their order that the defendants deliver up the papers concerned, and that they be restrained from using them until after judgment in the action. The court recognised the obvious difficulties in reconciling decisions in this area, some concentrating on the right of the client to maintain his entitlement to confidentiality and enforcement against anybody holding privileged documents, others upholding the rule that evidence which is relevant should be admitted, however obtained. The position, the court decided, was dependent on whether proceedings are taken before the document is tendered in evidence or not. On the face of it, that decision was conclusive in that particular case. There was no dispute that the documents were legally professionally privileged and there was no dispute that Messrs Herbert Smith had obtained information from them. In those circumstances, the relief should be granted. However, certain arguments were put by counsel which should be mentioned. Firstly, that the present case was one where receipt of the confidential information by Messrs Herbert Smith was entirely innocent. The court was not, however, satisfied that the receipt of the information was so entirely innocent. The second argument was that application of the *Calcraft v Guest* principle – namely that if when you get to trial you still have a document and you tender it, evidence of that document is admissible, notwithstanding that it may have been improperly obtained – would result in the information being used in this instance. The court, however, felt bound by the previous decisions of *Ashburton v Pape*[44] and *Goddard v Nationwide Building Society*,[45] in so far as relief should be granted to the

---

[43] *English and American Insurance Co Ltd v Herbert Smith* [1988] FSR 232.
[44] *Ashburton v Pape* [1913] 2 Ch 469.
[45] *Goddard v Nationwide Building Society* [1987] QB 670.

plaintiff. It is interesting to note that following on this conclusion the court commented:

> I confess that this is a result which gives me some satisfaction. Legal professional privilege is an important safeguard of a man's legal rights. It is the basis on which he and his advisers are free to speak as to matters in issue in litigation and otherwise without fear that it will subsequently be used against him. In my judgment it is most undesirable if the security which is the basis of that freedom is to be prejudiced by mischances which are of everyday occurrence leading to documents which have escaped being used by the other side.[46]

[8.38] A similar vindication of legal professional privilege is found in the decision of Hoffman J in *Chandler v Church*.[47] In this particular case, discovery of documents which were *prima facie* protected by legal professional privilege was sought on the grounds that privilege did not attach to a communication between a client and his legal adviser which was intended to facilitate the commission of a crime or fraud. It was held, however, that the fact the defendant might be using his solicitors to put forward a bogus defence, did not outweigh the fact that the plaintiffs were seeking, for the purpose of making good their charge of fraud, disclosure of what the defendant had told his solicitors to enable them to defend him against that charge, and accordingly discovery was refused. It is interesting to note the comments of Hoffman J:

> This submission seems to me to raise a point of considerable importance. It suggests that if the plaintiffs can induce prima facie evidence that the defendant is mounting a bogus defence, with or without the assistance of manufactured documents, he can penetrate professional privilege and require production of the opposing solicitor's notes, letters, instruction to counsel and so forth. I find this a startling proposition. All the cases which have been cited to me concerned the disclosure of legal advice taken in connection with a particular transaction which was alleged in subsequent civil or criminal proceedings to have been criminal or fraudulent. None involved an allegation of fraud in the conduct of the proceedings themselves.

[8.39] Finally in *Guinness Peat Properties v Fitzroy*,[48] it was further noted by the Court of Appeal that the relevant principles in relation to loss of legal privilege in such circumstances were as follows:

> (1) Where solicitors for one party to litigation have on discovery mistakenly included a document for which they could properly have claimed privilege in a

---

46 *English and American Insurance Co Ltd v Herbert Smith & Co* [1988] FSR 232 *per* Sir Nicholas Brown Wilkinson VC at 239.
47 *Chandler v Church* [1987] 137 NLJ 451.
48 *Guinness Peat Properties Ltd v Fitzroy Robinson Partnership* [1987] 2 WLR 1027 *per* Slade J 1045.

list of documents without claiming privilege, the court will ordinarily permit them to amend the list ... at any time before inspection of the document has taken place.

(2) However, once in such circumstances the other party has inspected the document in pursuance of the rights conferred on him ... the general rule is that it is too late for a party who seeks to claim privilege to attempt to correct the mistake by applying for injunctive relief. Subject to what is said in (3)(b) below the *Briamore*[49] decision is good law.

(3) If, however, in such a last-mentioned case the other party or his solicitor either:

(a)   has procured inspection of the relevant document by fraud, or

(b)   on inspection realises that he has been permitted to see the document only by reason of an obvious mistake,

the court has the power to intervene for the protection of the mistaken party by the grant of an injunction in exercise of the equitable jurisdiction illustrated by the *Ashburton, Goddard & Herbert Smith*[50] cases. Further in my view it should ordinarily intervene in such circumstances unless the case is one where the injunction can properly be refused on the general principles affecting the grant of a discretionary remedy, for example on the ground of inordinate delay ...

[8.40] The Irish courts have considered loss of the privilege by disclosure in the context of *Bula Ltd v Crowley*,[51] where the plaintiffs contended *inter alia* that as legal advice is disseminated within (and *a priori* without) the corporate structure of a litigant, the claim to privilege may be lost. Murphy J expressed the opinion that there was no doubt this was the case where the dissemination involved the disclosure of the advice to the public or a significant part of it. Where a litigant abandons confidentiality, he can hardly claim privilege. However, more difficult questions arise where the legal advice remains confidential, but records are made or documents created, which contain some reference expressly or by implication to such advice. Murphy J referred to Style and Hollander,[52] who suggest that, '[a] document which merely passes on legal advice within the firm or company is privileged. If the communication goes further, privilege will be lost.' This would mean that if, for example, the minutes of a board meeting simply summarise the solicitor's advice, it is privileged. But if the board discusses the same, any minutes of their discussion are not privileged. Murphy J did not agree with this approach:

---

[49]   *Re Briamore Manufacturing Ltd (in liq)* [1986] 3 All ER 132.

[50]   *Ashburton v Pape* [1913] 2 Ch 469; *Goddard v Nationwide Building Society* [1987] QB 670 and *English and American Insurance Co Ltd v Herbert Smith & Co* [1988] FSR 232.

[51]   *Bula Ltd v Crowley* (19 December, 1989) HC, Murphy J; [1990] ILRM 756 (SC).

[52]   *Style and Hollander on Documentary Evidence* (4th edn, Sweet & Maxwell, 1993), p 103.

... I find it difficult to see how one could maintain that precise boundary. The essence of legal professional privilege is that a client should not have to disclose the legal advice which he has received. This purpose could be disclosed by a company being forced to disclose minutes of a meeting resolving to take a particular action having regard to but without disclosing the express contents of a legal opinion. For example to advert to the existence of counsel's opinion and to resolve to lodge the full amount of the plaintiff's claim would surely be as revealing as disclosing the contents of the opinion itself. It seems to me that in the present case the documents ... are expressly concerned with and would of necessity disclose to a material extent confidential legal advice given to one or other of the two defendants in pursuit of their common interest. In my view the claim to privilege should be upheld.

[8.41] The vigour of the judicial defence of this heading of privilege is evident. The *Calcraft v Guest* exception to legal professional privilege does seem, however, somewhat unjust. As Heydon points out, it arose in an age (*Tomkins*), where eavesdropping and interception of communications was difficult, rare and unfavoured. Yet now there are more efficient mechanical methods of eavesdropping, not so easily guarded against, therefore it would not be enough for a client to take reasonable precautions. If a client knew of this exception, it might result in a reluctance to speak and thus undermine the rationale of the existence of the privilege.

[8.42] In this regard it is interesting to note the English courts' reluctance to admit such evidence where there has been fraud in the obtaining of information. Rather more important in the context of the Irish courts, is their very different perspective on admissibility. The English courts traditionally have admitted evidence which is relevant no matter how it had been obtained.[53] Indeed this principle is relied on specifically in the *Tomkins* decision. Yet the Irish courts do not start from such a principle, and will refuse to admit evidence because of the manner in which it was obtained when they see fit. The issue arises of how this would affect their treatment of this third exception to the rule on legal professional privilege.

[8.43] In *Breathnach v Ireland (No 3)*[54] a claim of legal professional privilege had been made concerning garda files connected with the investigation of the offence with which the plaintiff had been charged, as well as a report to the DPP for his decision as to whether to initiate a prosecution against the plaintiff. It was submitted that the documents were privileged on the ground *inter alia* that they had come into being in contemplation of litigation. The High Court held that the principle of public policy which protected from discovery communications

---

53 *Kuruma, Son of Kaniu v R* [1955] AC 197.
54 *Breathnach v Ireland (No 3)* [1993] 2 IR 458.

between lawyer and client made in contemplation of litigation, had no application to documents submitted by an investigating officer to the notice party (DPP) for the purpose of obtaining his decision as to whether or not a prosecution should be instituted.

[8.44] Legal professional privilege, according to Keane J:[55]

> ... enables a client to maintain the confidentiality of two types of communication:
>
> (1)   communications between him and his lawyer made for the purpose of obtaining and giving legal advice; and
>
> (2)   communications between him or his lawyer and third parties (such as potential witnesses and experts) the dominant purpose of which was preparation for contemplated or pending litigation.
>
> With regard to communications in the first category, it has recently been held by the Supreme Court in *Smurfit Paribas Bank Ltd v AAB Export Finance Ltd* [1990] 1 IR 469 that the privilege does not extend to communications made to a lawyer for the purpose of obtaining legal assistance other than advice ...
>
> As has also been frequently pointed out, the privilege is that of the client and may only be waived by him. The position of the Director of Public Prosecutions is, of course, somewhat different: he does not stand in the relationship of 'client' to any other lawyer. He is in a sense both lawyer and client, since he formulates the legal opinion on which the institution or non-institution of a prosecution is based and he then becomes one of the parties to the subsequent litigation. However, be that as it may, the public policy which protects from discovery communications in the first category undoubtedly applies equally to communications between the Director of Public Prosecutions and professional officers in his department, solicitors and counsel as to prosecutions by him which are in being or contemplated ...
>
> It was obvious, however, ... that the great bulk of them [the documents] consist of the garda files assembled for the purpose of the investigation of the crime which gave rise to the original criminal proceedings and the report by the investigating gardaí which was forwarded to the Director of Public Prosecutions so that a decision could be taken by him as to whether a prosecution should be initiated against the plaintiff and other persons ... [T]he documents in question in this case could not be equated to the documents which come within the second heading of legal professional privilege, ie communications between a client or his lawyer and third parties the dominant purpose of which is preparation for contemplated or pending litigation.

---

[55]   *Breathnach v Ireland (No 3)* [1993] 2 IR 458 at 472–474.

[8.45] In *Cecily Cunningham v President of the Circuit Court and DPP*[56] the applicant who was charged with seven offences contrary to s 23 of the Offences Against the Person Act 1861 sought judicial review on grounds of delay. Affidavits sworn on behalf of the DPP referred to correspondence giving rise to complications in the cases. The High Court refused discovery of such correspondence and the applicant appealed to the Supreme Court. The DPP argued that such correspondence should not be discovered as it related to the core function of deciding whether or not to prosecute. It was held that the DPP can claim privilege on any document but must list every document whether he was willing to disclose it or not.

Is legal professional privilege merely a rule of evidence?

[8.46] It is sometimes suggested that legal professional privilege is more than just a rule of evidence. Kelly J in *Miley v Flood*[57] states '[l]egal professional privilege is more than a mere rule of evidence. It is a fundamental condition on which the administration of justice as a whole rests.' In that case, Kelly J reiterated his quotation from Lord Taylor of Gosforth in *R v Derby Magistrates Court; Ex p B*,[58] previously quoted by Kelly J in *Duncan v Governor of Mountjoy Prison*,[59] namely:

> The principle which runs through all these cases, and the many other cases which were cited, is that a man must be able to consult his lawyer in confidence, since otherwise he might hold back half the truth. The client must be sure that what he tells his lawyer in confidence will never be revealed without his consent. Legal professional privilege is thus much more than an ordinary rule of evidence, limited in its application to the particular facts of a particular case. It is the fundamental condition on which the administration of justice as a whole rests.

[8.47] Other jurisdictions, such as Canada, have taken a similar view. In *Solosky v Canada*,[60] the Supreme Court of Canada described the right to communicate with a lawyer as a fundamental civil and legal right, while in *Descoteaux v Mierzwinksi*,[61] the Supreme Court of Canada took the view that the right to legal confidentiality had developed from a rule of evidence into a substantive right. In *Esso Australia Resources Ltd v Sir Daryl Dawson*,[62] the Federal Court of Australia said '[i]n the case of legal professional privilege, secrecy is defended on the basis that it would promote the administration of justice.'

---

[56] *Cecily Cunningham v President of the Circuit Court and DPP* [2006] 3 IR 541.
[57] *Miley v Flood* [2001] 2 IR 51 at 65.
[58] *R v Derby Magistrates Court; ex p B* [1996] 1 AC 487 at 507.
[59] *Duncan v Governor of Mountjoy Prison* [1997] 1 IR 558.
[60] *Solosky v Canada* (1980) 105 DLR (3d) 745 at 760.
[61] *Descoteaux v Mierzwinksi* [1982] 1 SCR 860.
[62] *Esso Australia Resources Ltd v Sir Daryl Dawson* [1999] FCA 363 at para 26.

[8.48] In a similar vein, one could see the commentary in *Hanahoe v Hussey HC*[63] *per* Kinlen J:

> It is essential in our society that lawyers of the highest ability should be available to provide a full and proper defence to persons accused of criminal offences. Unfortunately, public opinion does not always accept that principle and sometimes lawyers are identified with their clients which clearly violates principle 18 of the United Nations basic principles on the role of lawyers. It is a fundamental right in a democratic society that an accused person be fully appraised of all charges made against them and that they have the choice of legal representation. This right is embodied in article 6 of the European Convention on Human Rights. It would undermine our society if that were not so. The courts must protect these standards. Sometimes criminal lawyers are wrongly accused of colluding with their clients and sharing in the profits of crime. These are very serious allegations and should not be accepted until there is proof to establish them. The vast majority of criminal lawyers provide wonderful work to secure liberty and to protect our democratic institutions. Sometimes a lawyer might be regarded, because of his success, as an enemy of the State. They are in fact a bulwark to protect justice and the people and are essential in any real democracy.

'Without prejudice' statements

[8.49] The purpose or the rationale of the privilege attaching to 'without prejudice' statements or communications, is that of reduction of litigation by the encouragement of settlements. If a party makes an offer to settle a matter which is about to be litigated, such might be considered an admission of liability if it could be entered in evidence. However, the rule is that any offer made 'without prejudice' cannot be entered in evidence without the consent of the maker and receiver. This is obviously necessary if any settlement is to be entered into, prior to a court hearing, and any negotiation is to be pursued.

[8.50] Should agreement be reached between the parties to the litigation, as a result of the 'without prejudice' negotiation, the privilege ceases to apply, for the parties' rights have been changed. The 'without prejudice' communication can then be looked at to determine if agreement has in fact been reached, and to determine the terms of that agreement. This is important should a dispute arise as to same.[64] Although the use of 'without prejudice' is a *prima facie* indication that the communication is in furtherance of a settlement, those words contain no magic properties and are not conclusive. This was held in *O'Flanagan v Ray-Ger Ltd*.[65] It also will not be allowed as a cloak for illegality or impropriety as

---

[63] *Hanahoe v Hussey HC* [1998] 3 IR 69 at 106–107.
[64] *Tomlin v Standard Telephones and Cables Ltd* [1969] 3 All ER 201.
[65] *O'Flanagan v Ray-Ger Ltd* [1983] IEHC 83, Costello J.

held in *Greenwood v Fitts*,[66] where the defendant told the plaintiff he would perjure himself and/or leave the jurisdiction if they succeeded.

[8.51] A decision of the House of Lords in *Rush & Tomkins Ltd v Greater London Council*,[67] however, enters a *caveat* to this principle. The situation was one where proceedings between the plaintiffs and the first-named defendant had been settled by the payment of £1.2m by the first-named defendant, which included a sum representing an assessment of the value of the second defendant's claim. The plaintiffs then discontinued their action against the first defendant. The second-named defendant applied for discovery of the 'without prejudice' correspondence which had passed between the plaintiffs and the first defendant leading up to the settlement in order to ascertain the value which had been placed on their claim by the plaintiffs and the first defendant.

[8.52] It was held by the House of Lords, however, that the 'without prejudice' correspondence entered into with the object of affecting the compromise of an action, remained privileged after the compromise had been reached and, accordingly, the correspondence was inadmissible in any subsequent litigation connected with the same subject matter, whether between the same or different parties and, furthermore, was also protected from subsequent discovery by other parties to the same litigation.

[8.53] While the discovery by the other parties to the same litigation might be generally comprehensible, the suggestion that the correspondence remains privileged even as between the same parties, deserves some consideration. Perhaps this refers only to a situation where subsequent litigation is other than that connected with the actual terms of the agreement of the settlement itself? Support for this is to be found in the judgment of Lord Griffiths,[68] where he stated: 'Thus the "without prejudice" material will be admissible if the issue is whether or not the negotiations resulted in an agreed settlement ...' Further, the policy behind the decision is made clear in the final paragraph of Griffith LJ's judgment, where he commented:

> I have come to the conclusion that the wiser course is to protect 'without prejudice' communications between parties to litigation from production to other parties in the same litigation. In multi-party litigation it is not an infrequent experience that one party takes up an unreasonably intransigent attitude that makes it extremely difficult to settle with him. In such circumstances it would, I think, place a serious pressure on negotiations between other parties if they knew that everything that passed between them would ultimately have to be revealed to

---

[66] *Greenwood v Fitts* (1961) 29 DLR 260.
[67] *Rush & Tomkins Ltd v Greater London Council* [1988] 3 All ER 737.
[68] *Rush & Tomkins Ltd v Greater London Council* [1988] 3 All ER 737 at 740.

the one obdurate litigant. What would in fact happen would be that nothing would be put on paper, but this is in itself a recipe for disaster in difficult negotiations which are far better spelt out with precision in writing.[69]

[8.54] In *South Shropshire District Council v Amos*,[70] the Court of Appeal held that the fact that a document is headed 'without prejudice' does not conclusively or automatically render it privileged. If a claim for such privilege is challenged, the court will look at the document to determine its nature. However, all documents which form part of negotiations between parties are *prima facie* privileged if marked 'without prejudice', even if the document merely initiates negotiations, and even if the document does not itself contain an offer.

[8.55] In *Ryan v Connolly & Connolly*[71] the facts concerned the circumstances in which a defendant should not be permitted to rely on a defence under the Statute of Limitations 1957. The plaintiff had been involved in a collision with a car (he was driving a motorbike) on 26 April 1995. He sustained injuries and his motorbike was damaged. On 23 May 1995 his solicitors wrote to the first and second defendants stating that they were at fault and he was claiming damages. Her insurers wrote on 11 July 1995 to the plaintiff's solicitors, a letter headed 'without prejudice'. All letters – with one exception – from the insurers were similarly headed. Following a medical report received by the insurers from their doctor on the client, several letters were issued to the solicitors requesting whether they were in a position to discuss settlement. The last of these, on 2 July 1998, was after the limitation period of three years had expired. Two issues arose in the High Court, the first of which was whether, since virtually all letters from the insurance company were headed 'without prejudice', it was privileged and could not be taken into account by the court. Keane CJ noted the rationale of the privilege as follows:[72]

> It is clear that this rule has evolved because it is in the public interest that parties should be encouraged, so far as possible, to settle their disputes without resort to litigation …This is how the rule was explained in *Cutts v Head* [1984] 1 Ch 290, and it is clear from that and other authorities that the presence of the heading 'without prejudice' 'does not automatically render the document privileged. In any case where the privilege is claimed but challenged, the court is entitled to look at the document in order to determine whether it is of such a nature as to attract privilege.

> The rule, however, although firmly based on considerations of public policy, should not be applied in so inflexible a manner as to produce injustice. Thus

---

[69] *Rush & Tomkins Ltd v Greater London Council* [1988] 3 All ER 737 at 742.
[70] *South Shropshire District Council v Amos* [1987] 1 All ER 340.
[71] *Ryan v Connolly & Connolly* [2001] 1 IR 627.
[72] *Ryan v Connolly & Connolly* [2001] 1 IR 627 at 631.

where a party invites the court to look at 'without prejudice' correspondence, not for the purpose of holding his opponent to admissions made in the course of negotiations, but simply to demonstrate why a particular course had been taken, the public policy considerations may not be relevant. It would be unthinkable that the attachment of the 'without prejudice' label to a letter which expressly and unequivocally stated that no point under the Statute of Limitations would be taken if the initiation of proceedings was deferred pending negotiations, would oblige a court to decide, if the issue arose, that no action of the defendant had induced the plaintiff to refrain from issuing proceedings.

[8.56] Hence the court here was entitled to look at the correspondence, although it did not avail the plaintiff, as Keane CJ could find nothing therein to indicate that they were treating the case as one in which any defence on liability was being abandoned or that they would not raise the Statute of Limitations.[73] Although this judgment may appear to take a narrow view of the privilege, that is probably a factor of the particular facts of the case. The rationale of the privilege in achieving and promoting settlements will probably ensure its future is more aligned with the approach taken by the English Court of Appeal in *Unilever plc v Proctor & Gamble*[74] where Walker LJ stated the privilege has a wide and compelling effect, pointing out that '[o]ne party's advocate should not be able to subject the other party to speculative cross-examination on matters disclosed or discussed in without prejudice negotiations simply because those matters do not amount to admissions.'

Marital privilege

[8.57] The privilege of husband and wife is not to disclose any communications made by the other spouse during the marriage. The privilege originated in the Evidence (Amendment) Act 1853, which provided that all communications between spouses should be privileged. Section 3 provided that:

> no husband shall be compellable to disclose any communication made to him by his wife during the marriage, and no wife shall be compellable to disclose any communication made to her by her husband during the marriage.

This section had no application to criminal proceedings, as when it was passed, neither the accused nor the spouse of an accused was ever competent to give evidence in such proceedings. Part V of the Criminal Evidence Act 1992 rendered spouses competent in criminal proceedings as prosecution witnesses, and compellable in a limited number of circumstances. Section 26 of 1992 Act, however, provides that 'nothing in this Part shall affect any right of a spouse or former spouse in respect of marital privacy.'

---

73 *Ryan v Connolly & Connolly* [2001] 1 IR 627 at 634.
74 *Unilever plc v Proctor & Gamble* [2001] 1 All ER 783 at 793.

The privilege against self-incrimination

[8.58] This privilege protects everyone from having to answer, in a court of law, any question or produce any document or any article if, in the opinion of the judge, it would be liable to expose him to a criminal charge. No one is bound to answer any questions which would, in the opinion of the trial judge, have a tendency to expose that witness to any criminal charge, penalty or forfeiture which the judge regards as reasonably likely to be preferred or sued for. This so-called privilege against self-incrimination is based on the rationale that it is repellent for someone to be compelled to give answers exposing him or her to the risk of criminal punishment. In *R v Minahane*[75] it was held that one could not rely on the privilege if the answer were going to incriminate strangers. This decision would have implied that spouses were already covered by the privilege, yet this would not be constitutional in light of Henchy J's dicta in *DPP (Walsh) v Kenneally*.[76] However, the Law Reform Commission[77] considered that this privilege should be extended to cover answers tending to incriminate the spouse of a witness. This they proposed in substitution for the existing marital privilege, and is, in that regard, perhaps less obnoxious than the notion of the unity of spouses which grounded the original extension of the privilege against self-incrimination.

[8.59] The question of reasonable foreseeability of the charge or the reality of the witness's fear of incrimination must be addressed. In the decision of *State (Magee) v O'Rourke*,[78] Ó Dálaigh CJ considered that before a person could raise the point that he might be incriminated under foreign law if he were to answer certain questions or produce certain documents, there would have to be a reasonable possibility that the individual in question would be sent to the foreign country in question. In the case of *R v Boyes*,[79] the witness concerned invoked the privilege in a situation where that witness had already been given a pardon under the Great Seal. This protected that witness from prosecution for the offence before the courts, but he asserted the privilege on the basis that it did not prevent his impeachment by the House of Commons. Yet this latter proceeding was so unlikely an event that the Court of Queen's Bench denied him his right to the privilege. The court commented:

---

[75] *R v Minahane* (1921) 16 Cr App Rep 38.
[76] *DPP (Walsh) v Kenneally* [1985] ILRM.
[77] Law Reform Commission, *Report on Competence and Compellability of Spouses as Witnesses* (LRC 13 –1985), p 73.
[78] *State (Magee) v O'Rourke* [1971] IR 205.
[79] *R v Boyes* (1861) 1 B & S 311.

We think that a merely remote and naked possibility, out of the ordinary course of the law and such as no reasonable man would be affected by, should not be suffered to obstruct the administration of justice.

[8.60] In a similar vein is the nineteenth century case of the *King of Two Sicilies v Willcox*,[80] where it was held that the privilege did not extend to answers that would incriminate a witness under foreign law. This was followed in the decision of *R v Alterton*.[81] However, in the decision of *US v McRae*,[82] the United States government filed a writ in London seeking an account of money which the plaintiff had paid to the defendant during the Civil War. The defendant alleged that he was liable to forfeiture of property under United States law if he answered certain questions. It was clear from the pleadings that proceedings had already started in the United States so the court allowed such privilege to be claimed.

[8.61] The category of penalties in respect of which such privilege may be claimed was widened by our accession to the European Communities. Note the decision in *RTZ Corporation v Westinghouse Electric Corporation*,[83] where the penalties imposed for breach of terms of the EC Treaty and of Council Regulations were held to qualify.

[8.62] The privilege against self-incrimination applies not only to directly incriminating answers, but to answers tending indirectly to incriminate the witness. Yet the commentary of Megarry VC in the Court of Appeal in the case of *British Steel Corporation v Granada TV*[84] to the effect that the privilege was not as broad as to allow a witness to determine its ambit, is worth consideration: 'To answer this question might lead to a train of enquiry which if pursued might lead to some evidence which if adduced, might tend to incriminate me'. The court need not accept such a witness's view of potential incrimination and can override it.

[8.63] Some mention should be made in this context of inroads into the privilege against self-incrimination, or the so-called right to silence on the part of an accused in the context of forensic evidence. As has been seen elsewhere, ss 18 and 19 of the Criminal Justice Act 1984 impinge somewhat on the privilege against self-incrimination, to the extent that failure to account for possession of something, or presence in a particular place, on the part of an accused may lead to an inference being made by the court which may amount to corroboration of

---

[80] *King of Two Sicilies v Willcox* (1851)1 Sim NS 301.
[81] *R v Alterton* [1912] 2 KB 251.
[82] *US v McRae* (1868) IR 3 Cr App 79.
[83] *RTZ Corporation v Westinghouse Electric Corporation* [1978] AC 547.
[84] *British Steel Corporation v Granada TV* [1981] AC 1096.

any evidence against the accused. In a similar vein, provision under the Criminal Justice (Forensic Evidence) Act 1990, to the effect that the refusal of an accused to consent to the taking of certain samples for the purposes of DNA testing can lead to such an inference, is also of note in the context of incursion on such a traditional right.

[8.64] Despite the fact that there still exists a privilege against self-incrimination, the extent to which it has been affected by changes in the rules in relation to the right to silence undoubtedly has had an impact. There are now more situations, again increased by Criminal Justice Act 2006, where inferences can be drawn from silence.

[8.65] In *Curtin v Dáil Éireann*[85] an issue arose relating to the privilege against self-incrimination. The Supreme Court held here that the use of a power conferred on an Oireachtas committee to direct any person to send to the committee any documents in his possession did not give rise to considerations of self-incrimination and that there was a distinction between a requirement that a person give a statement or give evidence that might tend to incriminate him, and a requirement that a person produce for inspection – whether by An Garda Síochána or another organ of the state – a physical article including a document. The court specifically endorsed the ECt HR decision of *Saunders v UK*[86] where that court distinguished between respecting the will of a person to stay silent and the use in criminal proceedings of material which may be obtained through compulsory powers and which have an existence independent of the will of the suspect, eg documents, urine samples etc.[87] It also endorsed the decision of *Schmerber v California*[88] where the US Supreme Court distinguished between the right of an accused not to be compelled to testify against himself and the withdrawal of blood and use of its analysis.

Sacerdotal privilege

[8.66] An additional category has been created by the Irish courts in attaching a recognised private privilege to the relationship between priest and parishioner. The origins of this particular privilege, which does not have counterparts in other common law jurisdictions, are located in a decision of Gavan Duffy J in the High Court in the case of *Cook v Carroll*.[89] The facts of the case involved a plaintiff's action against the alleged seducer of her daughter, now pregnant. The

---

[85]   *Curtin v Dáil Éireann* [2006] 2 IR 556.
[86]   *Saunders v UK* [1997] 23 EHRR 313.
[87]   *Curtin v Dáil Éireann* [2006] 2 IR 556 at 634 *per* Murray J.
[88]   *Schmerber v California* (1966) 384 US 757.
[89]   *Cook v Carroll* [1945] IR 515.

parish priest who had interviewed the parties, refused to give evidence as a witness. The question of whether he was therefore guilty of contempt of court was reserved for judgment. Gavan Duffy J adopted Wigmore's 'general principles of privileged communications'[90] to the effect that four fundamental conditions are necessary to establish a privilege against disclosure of communications between persons standing in a given relation:

(1)　the communications must originate in a confidence that they will not be disclosed;

(2)　this element of confidentiality must be essential to the full and satisfactory maintenance of the relation;

(3)　the relation must be one which in the opinion of the community ought to be sedulously fostered; and

(4)　the injury which would ensue to the relation by the disclosure of the communication must be greater than the benefit thereby gained for the correct disposal of litigation.

It was held by Gavan Duffy J that in the present case these four conditions were satisfied, and so a privilege existed.

[8.67] This somewhat surprising recognition of a privilege attaching to communications with a priest, was followed by a decision which to some degree cut down on the potential ambit of the privilege in *Cook v Carroll*. This restriction on the potential of *Cook v Carroll* is perhaps not surprising, in light of both the potential damage to the courts' ability to receive all relevant evidence, which would ensue should the same four principles be applied to other confidential relationships, and the particular reasoning of Gavan Duffy J in the *Cook v Carroll* decision. Gavan Duffy J, prior to the recognition of the privilege, commented as follows:

> In a State where 9 out of every 10 citizens were Catholic and on a matter closely touching the religious outlook of the people, it would be intolerable that the common law, as expounded after the reformation in a Protestant land, should be taken to bind a nation which persistently repudiated the Reformation as heresy. When as a measure of necessary convenience we allow the common law generally to continue in force, we meant to include all the common law in harmony with the national spirit; we never contemplated the maintenance of any construction of the common law affected by the sectarian background. The Oireachtas is free today to determine how far our courts are to recognise the sacerdotal privilege but I am not concerned with that aspect of the matter. I am concerned with the juristic system of evidence surviving to us from an alien

---

90　Wigmore, *Treatise on the Anglo-American System of Evidence in Trials at Common Law* (3rd edn, Boston: Little, Brown, 1940), para 2285.

policy, and it is unthinkable that we should have imposed on ourselves in this matter the regrettable preconceptions of English judges as having here the binding force of law, when merely re-echoed by pre-treaty judges in Ireland.

[8.68] In the subsequent decision of *Forristal v Forristal & O'Connor*,[91] the facts concerned a letter written by one party to the parish priest of another party, that letter being defamatory of the latter. The priest showed the letter to the defamed party, and allowed him to borrow it for legal advice. In subsequent proceedings the priest claimed privilege of a sacerdotal nature in regard to the letter. Deale J distinguished *Cook v Carroll* on the facts, holding that one of the parties was not a parishioner of the priest in this instance and the communication itself was of dubious confidentiality. Furthermore, the manner of communication (ie a letter through the post) imported a risk that the letter might miscarry and the priest had parted with the letter to the plaintiff's solicitor. Finally, an additional risk was taken by the first defendant by choosing to write on paper. No sacerdotal privilege thus attached to the letter in question.

[8.69] In this regard it can be seen that despite the adoption of Wigmore's principles, the Irish courts have not taken the opportunity to attach private privilege to certain confidential relationships satisfying those criteria. As previously pointed out, this is perhaps preferable in terms of the administration of justice, and although it leaves the anomaly of the recognition of such a privilege in certain circumstances with regard to a Catholic priest, perhaps the mode or route of reform should be the abolition of such a privilege rather than its extension to other analogous personages. In this regard it is interesting to note that the Criminal Law Revision Committee[92] in England considered attaching a privilege to certain analogous relationships – ie that of doctor/patient or psychiatrist/patient and that of a minister of religion and parishioner – yet ultimately concluded that such was not desirable. In relation to the arguments for conferring a privilege for communication to a minister for religion, the committee felt the interests of religion, morality and society generally would dictate that a person who is willing to confide in a minister about his wrong-doing should be encouraged to do so in the confidence that there is no danger the minister will be compelled to reveal that confidence in legal proceedings. With regard to the argument that it is in accordance with the wishes of church leaders that such would be the position, the great majority of the Committee,[93] while fully sympathising with the arguments, were opposed to recommending the conferment of a privilege in respect of these communications. Their main

---

[91] *Forristal v Forristal & O'Connor* (1966) 100 ILTR 182.
[92] Criminal Law Revision Committee, *Eleventh Report: Evidence (General)* Cmnd 4991 (1972).
[93] Criminal Law Revision Committee, *Eleventh Report: Evidence (General)* Cmnd 4991 (1972), paras 273–274.

reason for so doing was that there should be no restriction on the right of a party to criminal proceedings to compel a witness to give any information in his possession which is relevant to the charge, unless there is a compelling reason in policy for the restriction and the arguments for the proposal are not strong enough for this purpose. Additionally the comment was made that:

> ... it might occasionally happen that one of two accused persons had confessed to a minister that he alone, and not his co-accused, committed the offence. Even if any minister of religion felt able to stand by and let a possible innocent person be convicted while a minister was in a position to exculpate him by giving evidence, we should not wish to recommend legislation which would allow this.

[8.70] In the context of medical practitioners, the Eleventh Report considered a strong proposal from the British Medical Association as to the conferment of such a privilege, particularly to doctors practising in psychiatry, yet again they rejected this contention. They commented as follows:

> The argument for this is that the public interest requires that a person should seek medical advice when this is necessary and should be able to speak freely to his doctor even about something embarrassing or discreditable without the danger that the doctor might have to give evidence about this in court. But we think that even if any privilege were given it would be wrong to go as far as this. To do so might exclude information which is important in the interests of justice to have before the court.

> For example it would be a scandal if a criminal who had been injured when blowing a safe or committing a robbery could prevent the doctor who had attended him from revealing what the criminal told him about how he came by his injury. There would be a strong case for giving a narrower privilege according to which a person who had told a doctor practising psychiatry in confidence about an offence ... could object to the doctors giving evidence about this.

[8.71] However, in the end, the Committee decided by a large majority that for reasons similar to those in relation to ministers of religion in particular, the unlikelihood that any difficulty would arise in practice meant they should not recommend that any privilege should be conferred in relation to medical practitioners.

Marriage counsellors

[8.72] An addendum to this particular debate as to the recognition of sacerdotal privilege concerns the position of marriage counsellors, and in particular situations where marriage counsellors are in fact priests. In a decision in the High Court in *ER v JR*,[94] Carroll J considered the question of whether a privilege

---

[94] *ER v JR* [1981] ILRM 125.

should attach to a situation where a marriage counsellor who was a priest counselled a married couple. Carroll J took the decision in *Cook v Carroll* into account, together with the English case of *Pais v Pais*.[95] In considering Wigmore's four principles, as enunciated in *Cook v Carroll*, Carroll J found that the four conditions did indeed apply to the situation of a priest as a marriage counsellor. She stated that the Article with regard to the special position of the Catholic Church in the Constitution was neither relevant nor essential to this fact. The fact that the marriage counsellor was a priest, did, however, add weight to the relationship. She would include here a minister of religion as well as a priest. She felt that advice given by a minister of religion has an added dimension not present between lay people. Although commenting that courts should be slow to admit new categories of privilege, Carroll J felt that the guarantee of confidentiality was important in building up confidence between a marriage counsellor and the spouses. She considered whether the privilege should attach to all communications, or some communications, and determined that it either existed in relation to all communications or not at all. She noted that in the English case of *Pais*, the privilege had been held to attach to communications made by spouses to a marriage counsellor, and to be that not of the counsellor but of both spouses. In a similar vein, Carroll J determined here that the privilege was that of the spouses, not the priests. She would reserve the question of whether the privilege can arise where the marriage counsellor is not a priest or a minister of religion. Carroll J's judgment differs from that in *Pais v Pais* in so far as, in that case, the privilege attaching to the marriage counselling situation seemed to be an extension of the marital privilege, rather than having any particular religious dimension. Even though in that specific case the marriage guidance counsellor was also a priest, it was emphasised by the English court that there was no authority for a privilege attaching to the priest himself. What is not clear is the source of Carroll J's privilege, in so far as there seems to be a reliance on the fact that the marriage counsellor was a priest, in so far as the general issue of marriage guidance counselling and the attachment of a privilege thereto because of the married relationship of the spouses, is not addressed. This is in contrast to the English case, where the privilege attaching to the communications is specifically said to be that of the spouses and accordingly can be said to be part of, or an extension of, the marital privilege itself. Certainly the English authorities make it quite clear that the significant or determinative factor is not the individual's identity as a priest. What precisely is the distinguishing factor in the Irish case is perhaps not so clear, particularly since Carroll J reserves the question of whether the privilege would attach to a non-religious counsellor.

---

[95] *Pais v Pais* [1970] WLR 830.

[8.73] Section 7 of the Judicial Separation and Family Law Reform Act 1989 made provision for the adjournment of proceedings to assist reconciliation or agreements on separation, provided that for such purposes, any oral or written communication between either spouse and any third party (whether or not made in the presence of the other spouse) and any record of such communication caused to be made by such third party, should not be admissible as evidence in any court (s 7(7)). This is now amended by the Family Law (Divorce) Act 1996, which provides for the non-admissibility of evidence of communication relating to reconciliation or separation by the insertion of s 7(A) as follows:

> 7A. – An oral or written communication between either of the spouses concerned and a third party for the purpose of seeking assistance to effect a reconciliation or to reach agreement between them on some or all of the terms of a separation (whether or not made in the presence or with the knowledge of the other spouse), and any record of such a communication, made or caused to be made by either of the spouses concerned or such third party, shall not be admissible as evidence in any court.

[8.74] A commentary on this somewhat controversial area is offered by the courts in *Johnston v Church of Scientology Mission of Dublin Ltd.*[96] The plaintiff here was suing the defendants for damages for conspiracy, misrepresentation, breach of constitutional rights, libel and the return of moneys paid by her to the first defendant. An order for discovery was made against the defendants, who claimed sacerdotal privilege in respect of certain counselling notes. The notes arose from spiritual practices of 'auditing' and 'training' conducted on a one-to-one basis. The High Court refused to recognise the claim of privilege here, while making the point that it could be waived by the person being counselled, and ordered discovery. The Supreme Court allowed the defendants' appeal in relation to documents held in the United Kingdom, however, on the basis that documents to be discovered must be in the possession, custody or power of a party. Here they were not.

[8.75] In the High Court Geoghegan J pointed out that *ER v JR* in one sense extended the principle in *Cook v Carroll* in that it went beyond the relationship between parish priest and parishioner, but on the other hand repudiated the idea that the priest counsellor could himself have a privilege he would have to waive.[97] Geoghegan J offered the opinion that the seal of the confessional may be protected even against waiver by the penitent. However, he rejected here the analogy between the practices involved and the seal of the confession:

---

[96] *Johnston v Church of Scientology Mission of Dublin Ltd* [2001] 1 IR 682.
[97] *Johnston v Church of Scientology Mission of Dublin Ltd* [2001] 1 IR 682 at 685.

I think that the absolute unwaivable privilege which probably does attach in Irish common law to the priest penitent relationship in the confessional is *sui generis* and is not capable of development in the manner suggested.[98]

[8.76] With regard to the privilege which may arise in relation to a priest or minister as counsellor, this can always be waived by the person being counselled. Geoghegan J commented further:

> Furthermore, although Carroll J left the question open, I would be inclined to think that in modern times when all kinds of secular counselling is available, and in particular marriage counselling, there may well be a privilege which the courts would uphold in some circumstances, but it would always be capable of waiver unilaterally by the persons being counselled.[99]

Here the plaintiff waived any privilege and so no claim of sacerdotal privilege was upheld.

Journalistic privilege

[8.77] The issue of whether journalists can claim a privilege with regard to their informants or sources has also been raised in the Irish context. In the case of *Re Kevin O'Kelly*,[100] O'Kelly, a journalist, was called as a prosecution witness in proceedings in the Court of Criminal Appeal. O'Kelly refused to answer a particular question, claiming journalistic privilege with regard to sources. The case was referred to the Supreme Court, where Walsh J commented that:

> ... journalists or reporters are not any more constitutionally or legally immune than other citizens from disclosing information received in confidence. The fact that a communication was made under terms of expressed confidence or implied confidence does not create a privilege against disclosure.

[8.78] The Supreme Court, however, substituted a fine of £250 for the three-month sentence imposed by the Special Criminal Court. The non-existence of a particular privilege attaching to journalists was confirmed by English authorities in *AG v Mulholland*[101] and *British Steel Corporation v Granada TV Ltd.*[102] In England, however, the situation has been altered by legislation, in so far as s 10 of the Contempt of Court Act 1981 now gives journalists privileges in relation to their sources unless some other overriding public interest requires them to reveal same. There are four such specified public interest headings.

---

[98] *Johnston v Church of Scientology Mission of Dublin Ltd* [2001] 1 IR 682 at 686.
[99] *Johnston v Church of Scientology Mission of Dublin Ltd* [2001] 1 IR 682 at 686.
[100] *Re Kevin O'Kelly* (1974) 108 ILTR 97.
[101] *AG v Mulholland* [1963] 2 QB 477.
[102] *British Steel Corporation v Granada TV Ltd* [1981] 1 All ER 417.

[8.79] The Law Reform Commission, in a Consultation paper and subsequent Report on *Contempt of Court*,[103] included proposals with regard to journalistic privilege. In essence, these are to the effect that the law relating to a journalist's obligation to give evidence, and when doing so to answer questions, should not be changed. The Law Reform Commission did not perceive the Court of Criminal Appeal in *Re O'Kelly* as foreclosing the possibility of legislation providing for such a privilege, on the grounds that it is the judiciary alone whose function it is to prescribe what is to constitute evidence (they refer, for instance, to s 16 of the Central Bank Act 1989).

[8.80] The question then resolves itself, according to the Commission, into one concerning possible leeway given to the Oireachtas in prescribing cases where a witness is not obliged to disclose a source:

> We consider that the Constitution permits a legislative exclusion of this nature, provided it serves a rational goal which can be justified or defended on the basis of factors to which the Constitution attaches importance, and which does not infringe against the requirements of natural justice.[104]

Looking at *Cook v Carroll's* statement of Wigmore's fourfold text, the Commission does not regard the present law as inhibiting the publication of material which should in the public interest be published.

[8.81] In regard to journalistic ethics the Commission quoted *Re Buchanan*[105]:

> Every truly democratic system of government rests upon the rule of law, and no system is truly democratic if it does not. If the law of the land is to rule, it follows of necessity, that the courts that administer the law must not be impeded in the performance of the function by any who give their allegiance however sincerely, to the private codes of minorities, however admissible codes may, for other purposes be.

The Commission stated that it does not wish to minimise the desirability or moral worth of journalistic codes, but it is equally manifest that the claim to follow the prescriptions of a journalistic trade union – or disinterested professional or vocational norms – should in no sense give to a journalist the right to override constitutional or statutory principles as to the admissibility of evidence.

[8.82] The drawbacks to the recognition of journalistic privilege it enumerated as follows:

---

[103] Law Reform Commission, Consultation paper *Contempt of Court* (July 1991). Law Reform Commission Report on *Contempt of Court* (LRC 47–1994)

[104] Law Reform Commission, Consultation paper *Contempt of Court* (July 1991) at p 245.

[105] *Re Buchanan* [1964–1965] NSWR 1379 at 1380.

(1)   An unscrupulous journalist might publish exaggerated or imagined information or allegations.

(2)   An unscrupulous informant could whisper exaggerated/false information in a journalist's ear without fear of discovery, eg Anglo-Irish relations in Northern Ireland would become open to manipulation.

(3)   Arguments in favour of privilege based on the public's 'right to know' are self-defeating since allegations cannot be adequately investigated because the source of information is withheld – asserting the public's right to know on one hand; denying it on the other.

[8.83] Finally, the Commission commented:

> Moreover as we have already noted, while *O'Kelly's* case is authority for the proposition that journalists enjoy no privilege as such to withhold the sources of their information, this is not to say that the court will never have regard to the confidentiality of the communication. The tests in *Cook v Carroll* were formulated by Gavan-Duffy J in the context of confidences to a spiritual advisor, but that, is not to say that they could not be applied in other contexts. If all the requirements there laid down were established, a court might not consider it proper to order a journalist to disclose his source, even though the evidence was relevant and admissible.[106]

[8.84] In their subsequent Report the Commission remained of the view that "... it would be unacceptable for a court to be deprived of evidence which might be necessary to do justice between the parties in a particular case. In such circumstances, the paramount interest of the public in the administration of justice must, in our opinion, take precedence over the public interest in freedom of information."[107]

The minority of the Commission however did favour legislation similar to the English s 10 Contempt of Court Act 1981 providing for limited situations in which a witness should not be obliged to disclose a source, while the majority was satisfied '... that the broad powers available to the court under the Constitution, as decided in *O'Kelly* should not and cannot be limited or restricted in any way.'[108]

The non recognition of the existence of a separate heading of privilege attaching to journalists once again relegates the issue to that of judicial discretion operative in the developing field of public privilege.

---

[106] Law Reform Commission, Consultation paper *Contempt of Court* (July 1991) at p 247.
[107] Law Reform Commission Report on Contempt of Court (LRC 47–1994), para 4.28.
[108] (LRC 47–1994), para 4.39.

[8.85] The most recent consideration of the claim of journalistic privilege is in the Supreme Court decision *In the Matter of an Application pursuant to section 4 of the Tribunal of Inquiry (Evidence) (Amendment) Act 1997 as amended by section 3 of the Tribunal of Inquiry (Evidence) (Amendment) Act 2004.*[109] This case concerned the wish of the Mahon Planning Tribunal to investigate a leak of confidential information to the Irish Times and the counterveiling claim of confidentiality of journalistic sources by Mr Keena public affairs correspondent of the Irish Times and Ms Kennedy editor. The Irish Times had published the contents of a letter it received anonymously regarding the investigation by the Tribunal of certain payments made by Bertie Ahern when he was Minister for Finance in 1993. The article quoted from the contents of the letter which formed part of the confidential investigations of the Tribunal. The Tribunal ordered production of the documents and Ms Kennedy said they had been destroyed. She and Mr Keena refused to answer any questions which in their view would give assistance identifying the source of the anonymous communication. The Tribunal sought orders from the High Court to compel Ms Kennedy and Mr Keena to comply with the Tribunals orders. The High Court delivered judgment on 23 October 2007 requiring the appellants to attend the Tribunal and answer all questions regarding the source and whereabouts of document. In so doing the High Court balanced the rights of the Tribunal to enforce confidentiality against the entitlement of the appellants as journalists under art 10 of the ECHR. In doing so they remarked on the destruction of the documents as 'an outstanding and flagrant disregard of the rule of law' pointing out that in so doing the journalists had 'cast themselves as the adjudicators of the proper balance to be struck between the rights and interests of all concerned'.[110] The High Court had therefore held that the defendants privilege against disclosure of sources was overwhelmingly outweighed by the pressing social need to preserve public confidence in the Tribunal.[111]

[8.86] The Supreme Court noted that the principal focus of the appellants' submission on appeal was a critique of that balance struck by the High Court between the rights of the Tribunal and the appellants. Invoking the ECHR the appellants submitted that "…in the case law of the European Court of Human Rights…the balance has almost always been struck by that court in favour of protection of journalist's sources. Extraordinarily strong counterveiling

---

[109] *In the Matter of an Application pursuant to section 4 of the Tribunal of Inquiry (Evidence) (Amendment) Act 1997 as amended by section 3 of the Tribunal of Inquiry (Evidence) (Amendment) Act 2004* [2009] IESC 64.

[110] *In the Matter of an Application pursuant to section 4 of the Tribunal of Inquiry (Evidence) (Amendment) Act 1997 as amended by section 3 of the Tribunal of Inquiry (Evidence) (Amendment) Act 2004* [2009] IESC 64, para 23 *per* Murray CJ.

[111] [2009] IESC 64, para 28 (Murray CJ).

circumstances are required before a journalist can be obliged to disclose sources."[112]

The appellants argued that the High Court had been led into error by its extremely critical views regarding the destruction of the documents and had taken the erroneous view that for this reason the journalists privilege against disclosure had almost no weight.[113] The Supreme Court determined that the appeal turned entirely on the balance struck by the High Court between the power of the Tribunal to investigate and the right of the appellants to refuse to disclose any information about their sources.[114] The Supreme Court noted the judgments of the European Court of Human Rights which "emphasise not merely the fundamental right to freedom of expression but, in the case of the press, its indispensable contribution to the functioning of a democratic society."[115]

[8.87] The Supreme Court stated that that Court:

> ...constantly emphasises the value of a free press as one of the essential foundations of a democratic society, that the press generates and promotes political debate, informs the public in time of elections, scrutinises the behaviour of governments and public officials and, for these reasons, that persons in public life must expect to be subjected to disclosure about their financial and other affairs, to criticism and to less favourable treatment than those in private life. Generally, therefore, restrictions on freedom of expression must be justified by "*an overriding requirement in the public interest*".[116]

The Supreme Court refers to the ECHR decisions in *Fressoz and Roire* and *Goodwin v United Kingdom*[117] both of which upheld the claim of privilege with regard to journalistic sources and found violations of art 10. Chief Justice Murray in the Supreme Court goes on to point out that the resolution of these issues lies properly in the courts and not solely with the journalists:

> At this point I raise the question as to whether it can truly be said to be in accord with the interests of a democratic society based on the rule of law that journalists, as a unique class, have the right to decide for themselves to withhold information from any and every public institution or court regardless of the existence of a compelling need, for example, for the production of evidence of the commission of a serious crime. ...Who would decide whether the journalist's source had to be

---

[112] [2009] IESC 64, para 31.

[113] [2009] IESC 64, para 32.

[114] [2009] IESC 64, para 40.

[115] [2009] IESC 64, para 47.

[116] [2009] IESC 64, para 49.

[117] *Fressoz & Roire v France* (1999) 31 EHRR 28; *Goodwin v United Kingdom* (1996) EHRR 123.

protected? There can be only one answer. In the event of conflict, whether in a civil or criminal context, the courts must adjudicate and decide, while allowing all due respect to the principle of journalistic privilege. No citizen has the right to claim immunity from the processes of the law.[118]

The Supreme Court finds that the High Court focus on the issue of the opprobrium attaching to the journalist actions in destroying the document to be misguided causing it to adopt an erroneous approach to the balancing exercise.

> "Once the High Court had devalued the journalistic privilege so severely, the balance was clearly not properly struck."[119]

The Tribunal's application was therefore dismissed.

[8.88] This decision makes it quite clear however that although on this occasion the journalist's privilege was upheld it is firmly within the discretion of the courts to make that adjudication in each case based on a balancing of the interests involved and not within the call of the individual journalist. Hence in the aftermath of this case it is clearer than ever that there is no head of private privilege attaching to journalists and that it is firmly in realm of public privilege that any such claim may lie.

Police privilege

[8.89] Formerly, if one asked a police officer in the witness box the source of his information, he would claim a privilege and have such claim accepted on the basis that communications between police and their informants were privileged.[120] (This was followed in *State (Quinn) v Ryan*).[121]

[8.90] In the case of *State (Hanley) v Holley*,[122] it was considered whether the basis on which this privilege could be claimed should be varied. In essence, police privilege should be treated in a manner akin to a state privilege as per the decision in *Murphy v Dublin Corporation*,[123] ie that a claim of privilege as the general classification to be applied to police communications could not be sustained, so that each privilege should be claimed by the police on individual occasions and be examined by the court when that arises. This approach was confirmed by Keane J and can be said to have relegated police/informant

---

[118] *In the Matter of an Application pursuant to section 4 of the Tribunal of Inquiry (Evidence) (Amendment) Act 1997 as amended by section 3 of the Tribunal of Inquiry (Evidence) (Amendment) Act 2004* [2009] IESC 64, para 61 (Murray CJ).

[119] [2009] IESC 64, para 69 *per* Murray CJ at para 69.

[120] *People (AG) v Simpson* [1955] IR 105.

[121] *State (Quinn) v Ryan* [1965] IR 70.

[122] *State (Hanley) v Holley* (24 June 1983, unreported), HC.

[123] *Murphy v Dublin Corporation* [1972] IR 215.

communications within that heading of public or state privilege where they possibly more suitably belong.

[8.91] With regard to national security, the decision of Barrington J in *State (Comerford) v Governor of Mountjoy Prison*[124] is worth considering. Barrington J allowed a prison governor to claim privilege in relation to information with regard to the threatened kidnap of the prison warder and a breakout from a prison. A privilege was therefore recognised as to a source on the part of a prison governor. Again, this should perhaps be seen as an aspect of public privilege rather than that of private – not one which attaches to a particular relationship either because of the nature of the relationship, or the class of communications involved, but because of an adjudication of the court on the basis of a balancing of the interests involved.

[8.92] In the context of the revelation of the identity of informers and protection of the accused, it is interesting to note the Court of Appeal decision in *R v Agar*,[125] where the court found that the trial judge had paid too much attention to the prohibition on asking a witness to reveal the identity of police informers and too little attention to the interests of the accused who was being tried for possession of drugs with intent to supply.

[8.93] Counsel for the accused here had, in fact, confidentially been informed that X, whom the accused alleged had set him up, was a police informer. The judge ruled in chambers that counsel could not cross-examine the police about X's role or reveal the matter to the client. The Court of Appeal quashed the conviction and criticised such practice of going behind the accused's back. *Per* Lord Mustill:

> There was a strong ... overwhelming public interest in keeping secret the source of information, but ... there was an even stronger public interest in allowing a defendant to put forward a tenable case in the best light.[126]

[8.94] Because these adjudications on the balancing of public interests will inevitably arise in such areas, it is much better to categorise these as cases of public interest immunity, amenable in such manner to judicial discretion or control. Such reclassification, as *per* Keane J in *Holley*,[127] should commend itself to Irish law and continue.

[8.95] Arguments tending to crystallise police privilege or informer privilege have emerged in the context of the increased prevalence of statutory provision

---

[124] *State (Comerford) v Governor of Mountjoy Prison* [1981] ILRM 86.

[125] *R v Agar* [1990] 2 All ER 442.

[126] *R v Agar* [1990] 2 All ER 442 at 448.

[127] *State (Hanley) v Holley* (24 June 1983, unreported), HC.

facilitating garda belief evidence, which tends to be based on asserted police informer sources that then cannot be revealed. The original such provision is s 3(2) of the Offences Against the State (Amendment) Act 1972:

> Where an officer of the Garda Síochána, not below the rank of Chief Superintendent, in giving evidence in proceedings relating to an offence under [s 21 of the Offences Against the State Act 1939], states that he believes that the accused was at the material time a member of an unlawful organisation, the statement shall be evidence that he was then such a member.

There have been a number of decisions concerning that provision and other occasions when the garda witness has asserted a privilege with regard to source on the grounds that to reveal the source would be a danger to life or the safety of the state.

[8.96] In *DPP v Special Criminal Court*[128] Paul Ward sought disclosure of a number of statements taken by Gardaí in the context of his trial for the murder of Veronica Guerin. Assistant Commissioner Hickey gave evidence that those who provided information about organized crime faced a death sentence if their co-operation became known. The Supreme Court held that it was for the trial court to decide what should be disclosed and it could examine the statements in question to see if they could help the defence case. This has become an increasing issue of concern in the context of cases where the belief of a guard of a certain rank would form the basis of a criminal conviction, for example in relation to membership of a private organisation.

[8.97] In *DPP v Kelly*,[129] Kelly had been convicted in the Special Criminal Court of membership of an unlawful organization contrary to s 21 of the Offences Against the State Act 1939, as amended by s 2 of the Criminal Law Act 1976. He appealed and the following question was sent to the Supreme Court: does the limitation on the ability of the accused to cross-examine as to the basis for the evidence render the trial unfair under Art 38? In other words, if a person is charged with membership of the IRA and the evidence against them is the Chief Superintendent's belief that they are such a member and the Chief Superintendent, when asked for the source of his knowledge, claims privilege, is that inability to cross-examine to be considered unfair? The Supreme Court held here that the trial court does not fail to guarantee a fair trial by accepting a claim of privilege based on informer information and not permitting cross-examination of the Chief Superintendent as to the sources for that belief.

[8.98] The key here is the trial court and trial judge is involved in making that assessment. The Chief Superintendent does not simply assert informer privilege

---

128 *DPP v Special Criminal Court* [1999] 1 IR 60.
129 *DPP v Kelly* [2006] 3 IR 20.

and that is the end of it; the trial judge has to be happy that there is a justifiable case being made. That makes it clear that informer privilege is not an extra head of private privilege but more properly viewed as an aspect of public privilege. This is because the judge is still centrally involved in weighing up the real threat relative to the loss to the other side in terms of this information being held back.

Informer privilege then, although referred to as though it is a separate heading of private privilege, is in fact part of public or state privilege. It is not one of those very limited and jealously guarded headings of private privilege, such as lawyer/client privilege, which has existed for many years.

[8.99] *DPP v Kelly* was itself approved in *DPP v Binead*.[130] In *Binead* the individuals concerned had been convicted of being members of an illegal organisation – the IRA – contrary to s 21 of the Offences Against the State Act 1939, as amended by s 2 of the Criminal Law Act 1976. Chief Superintendent Kelly had given evidence of his belief that the applicants were, prior to the date of their arrest and independently of the events relating to their arrest, members of an illegal organisation. Counsel for the defendants argued in relation to same that, as there was no opportunity to investigate whether or not there was any reasonable basis for the belief, their rights under Art 38 of the Constitution were breached and an imbalance in the trial contrary to 'equality of arms' as required by art 6 of the ECHR was created. The Court of Criminal Appeal held that where belief evidence under s 3(2) of the Act of 1976 was admitted, and there was a claim of privilege in respect of the underlying facts, material or sources which led to the belief, the trial was not unfair in circumstances where the court ruled that it would not convict without supportive or corroborative evidence of that belief.

[8.100] The Court of Criminal Appeal considered the arguments but decided that the restrictions on the ability to cross-examine the garda witness did not constitute a failure to grant a fair trial. In doing so they followed the Supreme Court decision in *Kelly* but they also adopted specifically Fennelly J's consideration of the art 6 argument made here. In particular, it is interesting to note Fennelly J's reference to *Doorson v Netherlands*[131] where he says the European Court modified the earlier stance it took in *Kostovski v Netherlands*[132] where they had found a violation of art 6 by reason of the absence of the right to cross-examine anonymous witnesses. In *Doorson* the court held that although art 6 does not expressly require the interest of witnesses and victims to be taken into consideration, the life liberty or security of a person may be at stake and states should organize their criminal proceedings so that those interests –

---

[130] *DPP v Binead* [2007]1 IR 374.
[131] *Doorson v Netherlands* (1996) 22 EHRR 330.
[132] *Kostovski v Netherlands* (1990) 12 EHRR 434.

protected by other provisions of the Convention – are not imperilled. Fennelly J in *Kelly* stated:[133]

> In subsequent years the European court had adhered to the principle that the fair administration of justice holds an important position in a democratic society and that the measures restricting the rights of the defence should be restricted to what is strictly necessary ... Recognition of the legitimate public interest in protecting police sources of information or the safety of informers or witnesses has led to the acceptance of the possible justification of the withholding of relevant information from disclosure to the defence.

[8.101] In *DPP v Donoghue*[134] the Court of Criminal Appeal (Macken J) considered again the argument of an art 6 breach. The court here found no breach of Art 38 following *Kelly*. In relation to art 6 the court held the entitlement to the disclosure of relevant evidence is not an absolute right and in criminal proceedings there may be competing interests, such as national security or the need to protect witnesses at risk of reprisal, which must be weighed against the rights of the accused. The garda witness here had relied on the fundamental guarantee to life assured by art 2 of the ECHR as the basis upon which to claim privilege in respect of the names of his sources.

[8.102] The *Report of the Special Rapporteur on Child Protection*[135] reiterated the recommendation of the Law Reform Commission in its *1990 Report on Child Sexual Abuse* in relation to informer immunity and privilege in the context of child abuse.[136] The Rapporteur was of the view that there was a need to extend the category of persons/bodies who currently enjoy this immunity.[137] The Report notes that the Protection of Persons Reporting Child Abuse Act 1998 protects a person from civil prosecution in respect of communication of concerns over abuse if (s)he discloses such information and in doing so acts reasonably and in good faith when forming the opinion and communicating it. The Report notes that this is not a privilege but immunity and only applies to information communicated to designated persons (Gardaí and certain employees of the HSE):[138]

> The Law Reform Commission has called for a higher level of protection to be afforded to informants, a recommendation which is reiterated in this report. While certain persons already have immunity from prosecution in reporting

---

[133] *DPP v Kelly* [2006] 3 IR 20 at para 73.
[134] *DPP v Donoghue* [2008] 2 ICLMD 20 CCA.
[135] Shannon, Report of the Special Rapporteur on Child Protection (November 2007).
[136] Law Reform Commission, Report on Child Sexual Abuse (LRC 32 – 1990), p11.
[137] Shannon, *Report of the Special Rapporteur on Child Protection* (November 2007), p xix.
[138] Shannon, *Report of the Special Rapporteur on Child Protection* (November 2007) at para 5.3.4.

suspected cases of child abuse, a more coherent and comprehensive regime should be put in place by statute. There is a need to extend the category of persons/bodies that enjoy immunity from suit in respect of communications concerning child abuse. In addition to those already protected by the 1998 Act others involved in the care of children should be included eg employees of certain child agencies, school counsellors and others in similar positions. In addition the legislation should be amended so as to deem the actual communication to be privileged. It is noted that the extension of the categories of privilege in Ireland is a relatively rare phenomenon due to the prevailing philosophy of the balance lying in favour of the court having all available information before it so as to make an informed decision. With this in mind it is recommended ... such privilege should be decided on a case-by-case basis.

Although this makes it clear that this privilege should, if introduced, be under the head of public privilege with discretion falling to the court, the recommendation is an interesting one, adding to the 'head' of informer privilege as well as continuing to manifest the phenomenon of reform at the harsher end of the criminal justice system, which involves those alleged to be child abusers.

Private privilege: conclusion

[8.103] In conclusion, it can be said that the instances of private privilege remain limited, and the courts have shown some reluctance to extend same. Exceptions have been seen in the case of marriage guidance counsellors, and/or priests, and their relationships with clients. Whether this is a desirable development or not is questionable. Particularly in terms of the overriding public interest in the administration of justice, it is not desirable that there should be an increased incidence of automatic exclusion of relevant evidence from perusal by the courts of trial. To this extent, the recognition of private privilege has far more implications for the interest of the administration of justice than analogous developments in the public sphere of a balancing approach to instances of confidential communications. Perhaps, moreover, it is in that latter realm that confidential relationships should be dealt with, where the courts have an opportunity to adjudge the importance of the relationship concerned, the gravity of the particular incident involved and the quality and import of the communication for litigation, before making a decision. Private privilege leaves that decision to the witness and so is much more powerful, more potentially detrimental to the administration of justice and more valuable to the relationship.

[8.104] Hence, it is perhaps appropriate that private privilege would be confined to certain situations where there has been perceived to be a need for total frank disclosure without danger of discovery. Legal professional privilege is an instance of this. Marital privilege, it is suggested, should be abolished as it particularises a relationship which again could be dealt with more effectively elsewhere, and in many situations does not require an automatic attachment of privilege. Similarly journalistic privilege, and priest/parishioner privilege, should be dealt with under the auspices of public privilege, as could doctor/ patient relationships. Also, the privilege against self-incrimination, which has proven to be something of a misnomer, should merit re-examination, particularly in light of recent incursions on such privilege on the part of witnesses and/or the accused, which have not been considered in that light. Finally, perhaps a legislative formatting of the basis for the privileges and their exceptional loss should be provided for in legislation.

Public privilege

[8.105]

> So when can we quit passing laws and raising taxes? When can we say of our political system, 'stick a fork in it, it's done'? When will our officers, officials and magistrates realise their jobs are finished and return, like Cincinnatus to the plough or, as it were to the law practice or the car dealership? The mystery of government is not how Washington works but how to make it stop.
>
> O'Rourke, *Parliament of Whores* (Picador, 1991), p 14.

As was seen in the context of private privilege, certain matters, otherwise relevant, may be excluded and evidence regarding them held inadmissible on the ground that they are privileged. Privilege may arise by reason of public policy, or from the circumstances of the matter itself. When the privilege arises by reason of public policy, it is usually termed state or public privilege.

[8.106] One of the initial issues that arises in this area, is as to the use of the term 'privilege' in this context. At one time, this area was referred to as 'Crown privilege', which gradually became 'state privilege' and then 'public interest' immunity. The reasons for debate or change in the nomenclature are perhaps best given expression by Lord Simon in *Duncan v Cammell Laird & Co Ltd*:[139]

> privilege, in relation to discovery, is for the protection of the litigant and could be waived by him, but the rule that the interest of the State must not be put in jeopardy by producing documents which would injure it is a principle to be observed in administering justice, quite unconnected with the interests or claims of the particular parties in litigation, and indeed is a rule on which the judge should if necessary, insist, even though no objection is taken at all.

[8.107] In a similar vein is the comment by Lord Simon in *Rogers v Secretary of State for the Home Department*[140] to the effect that privilege is properly

---

[139] *Duncan v Cammell Laird & Co Ltd* [1942] AC 624 at 641.

applicable only to a claim that could be waived. This was reasserted by Lord Fraser in *Air Canada v Secretary of State for Trade (No 2)*:[141] 'public interest immunity is not a privilege which may be waived by the Crown or by any party.' With regard to the waiver of public interest privilege, it is notable that although in England the view is taken that because it involves adjudication of where the public interest lies, waiver has no application here,[142] two decisions of the Irish Supreme Court indicate a different approach.

[8.108] In *McDonald v RTÉ*[143] the plaintiff had brought libel proceedings against RTÉ, which he alleged had accused him of membership of the IRA and involvement in the murder of a Co Louth farmer in 1991. The defendant had subpoenaed several gardaí who consulted with the defendant and its legal advisers at its request. The trial was adjourned and the plaintiff sought discovery from the defendant of all documents grounding its defence of justification. Privilege was claimed over two files, on grounds of public interest. This, the plaintiff argued, had been waived because the defendant had had sight, and possibly temporary possession, of those files. McGuinness J (with whom the other members of the court agreed) held that such did not amount to waiver, but did not expressly hold it was possible to so waiver public interest privilege. Fennelly J reserved his position.

[8.109] The doubt remaining was resolved by *Hannigan v DPP.*[144] Here the applicant sought inspection of a letter between the DPP and gardaí as to the prosecution of the applicant in the District Court. The respondent claimed public interest privilege, which the applicant alleged had been waived by the disclosure of a confidential portion of the letter on an affidavit filed by the respondent. Hardiman J approved of the position in Matthew and Malek on *Discovery*:[145]

> [t]he general rule is that where privileged material is deployed in court in an interlocutory application, privilege in that and any associated materials is waived.

The decision in *Hannigan* would support the view that when the contents of a document have been disclosed, any subsequent claim of waiver will be ineffective.

[8.110] A second distinction between this area of the law and that of private privilege is that which arises in the context of criminal proceedings, namely, the

---

[140] *Rogers v Secretary of State for the Home Department* [1973] AC 388.

[141] *Air Canada v Secretary of State for Trade (No 2)* [1983] 2 AC 394 at 436.

[142] *Rogers v Secretary of State for the Home Department* [1973] AC 388 at 407; *Air Canada v Secretary of State for Trade* [1983] 2 AC 394 at 436.

[143] *McDonald v RTÉ* [2001] 1 IR 355.

[144] *Hannigan v DPP* [2001] 1 IR 378.

[145] Matthew and Malek, *Discovery* (Sweet & Maxwell, 1992), para 9.15.

onus on the court to give overriding force to the interest of the accused in establishing his innocence. If the evidence establishes this, it will be disclosed regardless of the disadvantage of disclosure. Hence, this 'privilege' is a rare occurrence in criminal trials as it is liable to be overridden in the interest of protecting the innocent from conviction.

[8.111] This category of evidence is now wider than was originally thought. Lord Hailsham gave expression to this in *D v National Society for Prevention of Cruelty to Children*:[146] 'The categories of public interest are not closed and must alter from time to time whether by restriction or extension as social conditions and social legislation develop.' It is most useful, perhaps, to sketch the origins of the immunity, and hence indicate its current parameters and the manner of the courts' application of its rubric.

Origins of public privilege

[8.112] One of the early English cases in this area that illustrates the principle and the occasion of its application is *Duncan v Cammell Laird & Co Ltd*.[147] The defendants, in a claim for damages for negligence in relation to the construction of a submarine, were told by the Board of Admiralty to object to the production of documents in their possession in their capacity as government contractors. The structure of the submarines was felt to be a matter that affected national security and ought to be kept secret, particularly when the country was at war. The claim to privilege was thus upheld, and the decision is one which illustrates clearly a situation where disclosure of particular information contained in a document would have threatened state interest.

[8.113] A claim may also be based, however, not on the particular information contained in the document sought to be discovered, but in the fact that that document belongs to a class of documents which ought to be thus privileged. A recognition of this basis for the claim of public privilege or immunity is found in the statement of Lord Salmon in *Rogers v Secretary of State for the Home Department*[148] that there are:

> classes of documents and information which for years have been recognised by the law as entitled in the public interest to be immune from disclosure. In such cases the affidavit or certificate of the Minister is hardly necessary.

Lord Salmon instanced Cabinet minutes as an example of such documents. Lord Reid recognised the existence of such classes of documents in *Conway v Rimmer*,[149] yet queried the basis for same:

---

[146] *D v National Society for Prevention of Cruelty to Children* [1978] AC 171.
[147] *Duncan v Cammell Laird & Co Ltd* [1942] AC 624.
[148] *Rogers v Secretary of State for the Home Department* [1973] AC 388.

I do not doubt that there are certain classes of documents which ought not to be revealed whatever their content may be ... But I do not think that many people would give as the reason that premature disclosure would prevent candour in the Cabinet. To my mind the most important reason is that such disclosure would create an ill-informed or captious public or political criticism.

[8.114] This issue of inspection by the court of the claim was earlier discussed in *Conway v Rimmer*[150] in the context of disclosure of confidential character reports on a probationary police constable in an action brought by him against a former superintendent claiming damages for malicious prosecution. The House of Lords, in this case, inspected the documents in question and ordered their production. The House identified the process as one of weighing on balance two public interests: that of the nation, or the public service, in non-disclosure and that of justice in the production of the documents. If the minister asserts that to disclose the *contents* of the document should or might do the nation or public service a grave injury, the court will be slow to question that. Unless there is an error of judgement or law on the part of the minister, or a lack of good faith, the court should not even go as far as to inspect the document. In 'class' cases, however, the minister's certificate is more likely to be open to challenge.

Irish case law on public privilege

[8.115] The case law in Ireland indicates that the Irish courts have diverged also from the principle of *Duncan v Camell Laird*, refusing blanket claims of state privilege. In *AG v Simpson*,[151] Davitt P in the High Court stated with regard to a claim of state privilege:

> To be a proper claim of privilege ... must be made in pursuance of public policy and based upon the ground that disclosure would be detrimental to the public interest ... the court will not allow [the claim of privilege] unless satisfied that the head of the department of State concerned ... has in fact considered the communication in question, and has in fact formed the opinion that its disclosure would be detrimental to the public interest.

[8.116] In the subsequent decision in *Murphy v Dublin Corporation and Minister for Local Government*,[152] this matter was given further consideration. The facts involved an inspector's report in relation to a compulsory purchase order, which the plaintiff, Murphy, wished to see. In the High Court, Kenny J dismissed Murphy's application and endorsed the House of Lords' decisions of *Glasgow Corporation v Central Land Board*[153] and *Conway v Rimmer*,[154] which

---

[149] *Conway v Rimmer* [1968] AC 910.
[150] *Conway v Rimmer* [1968] AC 910.
[151] *AG v Simpson* [1959] IR 105.
[152] *Murphy v Dublin Corporation and Minister for Local Government* [1972] IR 215.
[153] *Glasgow Corporation v Central Land Board* (1956) SC 1.

laid down that a court should normally endorse a minister's decision unless: (a) it was shown not to have been arrived at in good faith; (b) it is unreasonable; or (c) it is based on a misunderstanding. This principle was subject to two general rules:

(1)   certain classes of documents ought not to be produced at any time; and

(2)   documents which either in the minister's view should not in the public interest be published, or belong to a class which as a matter of policy he thinks should not be published, ought to be withheld.

[8.117] The Supreme Court disagreed with Kenny J, thereby establishing a departure from the traditional position of the law in this area of presupposing the validity of the ministerial claim. Walsh J in the Supreme Court held that there:

> ... can be no documents which may be withheld from production simply because they belong to a particular class of documents ... once the court is satisfied that the document is relevant the burden of satisfying the court that a particular document ought not to be produced lies upon the party or the person, who makes such a claim ... It may well be that it would be rare or infrequent for a court after its own examination, to arrive at a different conclusion from that expressed by the Minister, but that is far removed from accepting without question the judgment of the Minister ... The principles of *Duncan v Cammell Laird & Co Ltd* were based on considerations which are inconsistent with the supremacy of the judicial power under the Constitution in the administration of justice. Those principles were first formulated when such constitutional supremacy did not exist; they do not now prevail.

[8.118] It is interesting to note the rationale for this decision and departure from previous subservience to ministerial claims of privilege in this area: that of the judicial mandate to administer justice and its distinct and superior nature to that of the ministerial function (that of the government with which this privilege is allied) under the Constitution.

[8.119] Further consideration of the position under Irish law in relation to claims of public privilege or public immunity was given in the decision of *Geraghty v Minister for Local Government.*[155] The plaintiff here appealed to the Minister for Local Government against a decision of the planning authority refusing her planning permission. The minister again refused permission, which led to the plaintiff going to the High Court, claiming a declaration that the plaintiff's determination was *ultra vires* the Local Government (Planning and Development) Act 1963 and void. In making discovery of documents, the defendant objected to the production of:

---

[154] *Conway v Rimmer* [1968] AC 910.
[155] *Geraghty v Minister for Local Government* [1975] IR 300.

documents covering normal departmental procedure in dealing with an appeal including arrangements for the oral hearing, departmental minutes between officers of the Minister regarding the appeal, correspondence between the Department and Chief State Solicitor's office regarding the action.

The ground for such objection was that discovery of documents of that class would be contrary to public policy and detrimental to the public interest.

[8.120] Kenny J, having examined the 22 documents in question, held that:

(i) the defendant should produce 19 documents; and

(ii) the documents from the legal adviser to the minister attracted legal professional privilege and should not be produced.

[8.121] The Supreme Court, affirming the High Court order except in relation to one document, held *inter alia*:

(i) that the party objecting to the production of documents must justify his objection in respect of each individual document and not in respect of the class to which the documents are alleged to belong; and

(ii) it is the duty of the High Court to examine each of the documents.

Hence, at an earlier stage than the English courts, the Irish judiciary are seen to have mitigated the effect of a ministerial claim of privilege under this head, and asserted their right and duty to examine the documentation in question.

[8.122] It is worthwhile to recall in this regard the decision of Keane J in *State (Hanley) v Holley*,[156] which concerned an unsuccessful claim of privilege in relation to police informants. Keane J varied the basis on which such was claimed, ie not as a general classification of privilege attaching to police communications, but in a manner similar to state privilege, as delineated in *Murphy v Dublin Corporation*, leading to each claim of privilege being examined by the court when it occurs.

[8.123] The general principles to be applied in this area by the Irish courts are regarded then as having been laid down in *Murphy v Dublin Corporation* and *Geraghty v The Minister for Local Government*. These were subsequently identified and applied in *Folens v The Minister for Education*[157] by Costello J who pointed out the relevant principles as summarised by Walsh J in the *Murphy's* case:

> Where documents come into existence in the course of carrying out of the executive powers of the State, their production may be adverse to the public interest in one sphere of Government in particular circumstances. On the other

---

[156] *State (Hanley) v Holley* [1984] ILRM 149.

[157] *Folens v Minister for Education* [1981] ILRM 21.

hand, their non-production may be adverse to the public interest in the administration of justice. As such documents may be anywhere in the range from the trivial to the vitally important, somebody or some authority must decide which course is calculated to do the least injury to the public interest, namely, the production of the document or the possibility of the denial of right in the administration of justice. It is self-evident that this is a matter which falls into the sphere of the judicial power for determination.

[8.124] Indeed, that passage, which neatly summarises the position under Irish law, was again quoted and applied to the facts of the case by Murphy J in *Incorporated Law Society of Ireland v Minister for Justice*.[158] The plaintiffs here, in pursuance of their action against the defendants brought an application seeking an order allowing them to inspect certain documents in possession of the defendants. The defendants pleaded state privilege for the documents. In support of such claim was an affidavit that included the following statement, revelatory of the rationale of the claim:

> I object to producing these documents on the grounds that confidential communications of this nature made between public servants should be protected from disclosure in the interests of the efficient and proper running of the Public Service. I submit that the disclosure ... would tend to hinder the free communication necessary for the proper running of the Public Service.

[8.125] Murphy J, in accordance with Walsh J's enunciated principles, however, saw it as the function of the court:

> ... to determine first whether the production of the documents referred to would be detrimental to the efficiency of the public service and secondly, whether such prejudice outweighs the interest of the plaintiffs in their claim to have justice administered by the court.

In accordance with precedent, and with the consent of the parties, Murphy J had read the documentation in question. He expressed the view that the possibility that documentation might be open to inspection at a later date in pursuance of discovery could inhibit the transmission and recording of advices within the public service. In addition, the present case concerned correspondence between individual ministers of government, necessarily of a sensitive and important nature. However, even bearing that consideration in mind, Murphy J commented that he was satisfied that there was, 'nothing in the documentation for which this particular claim of privilege is made which has any special potential for damage in the proper administration of the public service.' In fact, given the level of expertise displayed in these documents, Murphy J opined it might, rather, enhance same.

---

[158] *Incorporated Law Society of Ireland v Minister for Justice* [1987] ILRM 42 at 43.

[8.126] Murphy J felt that in many such applications it would be difficult to evaluate the benefits which would flow to a plaintiff from disclosure. However, in this case, he did feel that to deny the plaintiff's access:

> would be to impose some measure of injustice on them and in my view that injustice is almost necessarily greater than the potential damage to the public service which I regard as minimal in the present case.

The comments of Murphy J are interesting in two respects: with regard to, first, the sensitive nature of ministerial communications and, second, the difficulty of determining the value of disclosure to the party seeking it. Here Murphy J felt it could not be assessed until the case was at hearing.

[8.127] English case law in this area has been somewhat controversial. The first of these decisions worthy of note is that of *Secretary of State for Defence v Guardian Newspapers Ltd.*[159] The document in question was a secret memorandum from the Ministry of Defence concerning the handling of publicity in relation to the installation of nuclear weapons at an RAF base. The original had gone to the Prime Minister and six copies to senior members of government and the Cabinet Secretary. A photocopy was leaked to the defendants and published. The Crown requested a photostat so that it could attempt to identify the informant from the markings on the documents. The defendant refused, relying on s 10 of the Contempt of Court Act 1981 to the effect that a person is not required to disclose information in a publication for which they are responsible, unless it established to the satisfaction of the court that disclosure is necessary in the interests of justice or national security or for the prevention of crime. The trial judge held the Crown was entitled to discovery of the document, as s 10 did not prevent the enforcement of proprietary rights.

[8.128] The defendants appealed to the Court of Appeal and further to the House of Lords. The House of Lords noted that the prohibition in s 10 of the 1981 Act against the court making an order to disclose was of general application, subject only to four exceptions in that section: interests of natural justice, national security, prevention of disorder or crime. The onus of proof is on the party seeking the order, here, the Crown. The evidence presented was sufficient to discharge the onus of showing disclosure was necessary in the interests of national security. The risk to national security lay not in the publication of the particular document but in the possibility that whoever leaked it might in future leak other classified documents, the disclosure of which would have much more serious consequences for national security.

---

[159] *Secretary of State for Defence v Guardian Newspapers Ltd* [1984] 3 All ER 601.

[8.129] The rationale of the prohibition in s 10 of the 1981 Act, according to Lord Diplock, was that it encouraged the purveyors of information, the publishers, decide what information to publish and they were not confined to that which is in the public interest (*cf* Lord Denning in the Court of Appeal). In the absence of the prohibition, sources would dry up.

[8.130] In *D v NSPCC*,[160] the NSPCC had received a complaint about the treatment of a 14-month-old girl, as a result of which an inspector called at the parents' home. The mother in question brought an action against the Society for damages for personal injuries alleged to have resulted from the Society's negligence. The Society receives and investigates complaints from the public under express pledges of confidentiality. It applied for an order that there be no discovery of any documents which revealed, or might reveal, the identity of the complainant. The Society grounded its application in the proper performance of its duties which required that the absolute confidentiality of information be preserved as, if such sources were revealed, they would dry up, and such would be contrary to the public interest.

[8.131] In the House of Lords, Lord Diplock stated that the private promise of confidentiality must yield to the general public interest that in the administration of justice, truth will out, unless by reason of the character of the information or the relationship of the recipient of information to the informant, a more important public interest is served, by protecting the information or the identity of the informant from disclosure in a court of law. The public interest that the NSPCC relied upon, was analogous to that protected by the well-established rule that the identity of police informers may not be disclosed in a civil action.[161] In relation to police informers, the balance was on the side of non-disclosure, except where upon the trial of a defendant for a criminal offence disclosure of the identity of the informer could help to establish the defendant's innocence. Lord Diplock noted that information given to a Gaming Board had been protected from disclosure in *R v Lewes Justices ex p SS Home Dept.*[162] It was held there that the justification for such protection was analogous to that of police informers. However, the court had not accepted the Board's proposition that wherever a party to legal proceedings claims that there is a public interest to be served by withholding documents or information from disclosure in those proceedings, it is the duty of the court to weigh that interest against the countervailing public interest in the administration of justice in the particular case and to refuse disclosure if the balance tilts that way.

---

[160] *D v National Society for Prevention of Cruelty to Children* [1978] AC 171.
[161] *Marks v Beyfus* (1890) 25 QBD 494.
[162] *R v Lewes Justices ex p SS Home Dept* [1973] AC 388.

[8.132] In the instant case, Lord Diplock noted that the Court of Appeal had rejected the Society's claim on the basis that Crown privilege was only available where the public interest involved was the effective functioning of departments or other organs of central government. Lord Diplock saw no reason for so confining it. In *Conway v Rimmer*, the public interest to be protected was the effective functioning of a county police force. Here, he noted, it was the effective functioning of an organisation authorised under an Act of Parliament to bring legal proceedings for the welfare of children. The House also noted that there had already been recognition of immunity in relation to the child care investigation records of local authorities in wardship cases. Hence the Law Lords recognised that a public interest was to be protected and deserved recognition in the circumstances. They thus abandoned the restrictive traditional view of the privilege as espoused in the Court of Appeal, but did not go so far as to accept confidentiality, per se, as the basis of such privilege. Indeed, that confidentiality is not a bar to adducing evidence in court was also emphasised in *X Ltd v Morgan-Grampian Ltd.*[163]

[8.133] While in *D's* case there is a ready analogy with other informer-type situations, sufficient to ground the privilege, there is also evident in the decision the emergence of a general doctrine of public interest. This was subsequently further developed in a series of decisions including *Science Research Council v Nasse*,[164] *Neilson v Laugharne*[165] and *Hehir v Metropolitan Police Commissioner.*[166]

[8.134] An Irish case concerning an adjudication as to the importance of the recognition of the privilege here, as against the effective pursuance of an action by the plaintiff, is *Gormley v Ireland.*[167] This case concerned the issue as to whether a claim of executive privilege in relation to a number of documents should be allowed, in so far as the interest of the state based on that claim outweighed the right of the individual litigant to have access to the documents in accordance with the exercise of his constitutional right to assert his legal rights in an appropriate fashion before the courts.

[8.135] The claim related to the plaintiff's right to an appropriate salary in his employment by An Post, having regard to a period of internment spent under the Offences Against the State Amendment Act 1940. The defendants denied virtually all of the facts on which this claim was based. Hence, the documents in

---

[163] *X Ltd v Morgan-Grampian Ltd* [1990] 2 All ER 1 at 15.
[164] *Science Research Council v Nasse* [1980] AC 1028.
[165] *Neilson v Laugharne* [1981] 1 All ER 829.
[166] *Hehir v Metropolitan Police Commissioner* [1982] 2 All ER 235.
[167] *Gormley v Ireland* (7 March 1991, unreported), HC, Murphy J.

the possession of the defendants were undoubtedly relevant to the issue. Objection was taken to their production, however, on grounds of national security. Despite the involvement of the Offences Against the State Act, such a claim was not sustained. However, Murphy J recognised that they were unquestionably confidential, sensitive documents, recording, for the greater part, submissions and advices by senior civil servants to ministers and indeed to the government. It was in the public interest that communications of this nature should be made on the basis that they would not be disclosed in legal proceedings, unless the court is satisfied that the public interest in this regard is outweighed.

[8.136] Of the documents in question, those relating to the detention and subsequent alleged refusal of the plaintiff to give an undertaking with regard to membership of a proscribed organisation were ordered to be disclosed. Other documentation, which comprised largely of correspondence with the gardaí, was highly confidential material, disclosure of which might be significantly detrimental to the public interest. While the said documents might be of some value to the plaintiff, they were not fundamental to his case. They were thus not ordered to be disclosed. Finally, the court stressed the function of discovery as being solely for the proper processing of litigation. Hence, copies were to be made by the solicitor only for counsel briefed, and not to be inspected by other persons.

Tromso Sparebank v Beirne (No 2)

[8.137] The High Court decision in *Tromso Sparebank v Beirne (No 2)*,[168] which deals with the issue of legal professional privilege, may indicate in its approach a discontent with the ambit of private privilege which hampers adjudicative scrutiny of evidence without the alleviation of judicial control. That case concerned proceedings for damages instituted by the plaintiff – a Norwegian savings bank – arising out of the dishonour of two promissory notes for almost £12m. The Northern Bank Ltd, one of the defendants, sought discovery of a number of documents, including copy documents in relation to which the plaintiff had claimed legal professional privilege. Costello J first considered the claim in relation to copies of documents which were not in themselves privileged but were obtained for the purpose of obtaining legal advice. In support of the claim of privilege was the statement in the *White Book (the Supreme Court Practice)*[169] to the effect that original or copy documents obtained or that were prepared by a party for the purpose of obtaining a solicitor's advice in view of pending or anticipated proceedings, are privileged.

---

[168] *Tromso Sparebank v Beirne (No 2)* [1989] ILRM 257.
[169] *The Supreme Court Practice (White Book)* (Sweet and Maxwell, 1988) para 24-5-10.

This statement was based on *The Palermo*[170] and *Watson v Cammell Laird & Co Ltd.*[171]

[8.138] However, in support of the defendant's submission that this should not be followed as being too wide, was a statement by Denning MR in *Buttes Gas & Oil Co v Hammer (No 3)*[172] *that,* 'if the original is not privileged, neither is a copy made by the solicitor privileged'. Despite an express disapproval of that statement by the court in *R v Board of Inland Revenue ex p Codibert,*[173] Costello J concluded as follows:

> I see no reason why legal professional privilege should apply to the copy documents with which this case is concerned. Legal professional privilege exists so that a litigant can have redress to his legal advisers in circumstances which enable him to have complete confidence that the communications made to him and from him will be kept secret ... I cannot see that the protection of the interests of a litigant requires the privilege to be extended to copies of documents which came into existence prior to the contemplation of litigation, documents which are themselves not privileged and which the other side could probably inspect as a result of a third party discovery order and which they could have produced at the trial pursuant to a *subpoena duces tecum.* The rules of court are designed to further the rules of justice and they should be construed by the court so that they assist in the achievement of this end. If inspection of the documents cannot conceivably injure the interests of one party and may well assist the other to ascertain the true facts of the case prior to trial I do not think that the court should put a gloss on the rules which would prevent this result ...[174]

[8.139] Costello J later acknowledged the privilege to attach to letters between the legal advisers of the plaintiff bank, both to one another and to the bank itself, and did not find favour with the suggestion that the privilege had been waived because the plaintiff bank had alleged in its pleadings that it was the holder of the notes in good faith and that, as this was now an issue in the proceedings, the steps taken, including the legal advice taken when obtaining the notes, became relevant and the privilege was waived. Costello J acknowledged in so doing that 'it is important ... to maintain the principle of legal professional privilege'.

[8.140] However, that statement and particular vindication of the privilege is at odds with the earlier circumspection in light of the need to 'further the rules of justice'. The latter is surely more relevant to the sphere of public interest immunity than to the realm of private privilege, where in the context of the

---

170 *The Palermo* (1883) 9 PD 6.
171 *Watson v Cammell Laird & Co Ltd* [1959] 2 All ER 757.
172 *Buttes Gas & Oil Co v Hammer (No 3)* [1981] QB 223.
173 *R v Board of Inland Revenue ex p Codibert* [1988] 3 WLR 522.
174 *Tromso Sparebank v Beirne & Ors (No 2)* [1989] ILRM 257 at 261–262.

limited instances where it applies its invocation at the behest of the parties to the relation is paramount. Costello J seemed to respect this with regard to the waiver of the privilege in the context of the second set of documents considered, yet his construction of the law in relation to copy documents moves an interpretation at odds, not only with previous determinations, but perspectives on the area. The decision, moreover, would also seem somewhat at odds with that of Murphy J subsequently in *Bula v Crowley*.[175]

[8.141] Costello J's decision may be indicative of a broader desire on the part of the judiciary to extend the rubric of judicial discretion to the private privilege area as part of a corresponding development and enhancement of the public interest immunity sphere. Together with possible greater cohesiveness and fewer anomalies with regard to particularisation of certain relationships (marital, legal, professional etc), this would have the merit, from a judicial perspective, of an enhanced mandate to secure the administration of justice and its reconciliation with competing public interests.

[8.142] That this mandate to balance competing public interests is secured, and founded on judicial sovereignty in the administration of justice, was emphasised in the context of recent challenges to the basic philosophy inherent in *Murphy* and *Geraghty*, namely, that under Irish law the concept of Crown privilege or public interest immunity is subservient to judicial, and not ministerial, discretion.

Bula Ltd v Tara Mines

[8.143] In *Bula Ltd (in receivership) v Tara Mines Ltd, Minister for Energy & Others*,[176] judgment arose out of an affidavit of discovery made on behalf of the Minister for Energy. Some 60 documents were confidential and sensitive to a greater or lesser degree, and in relation to which the minister was entitled to claim executive privilege. Other documents were furnished to the court for the purpose of determining whether the interest of the minister, and the public through him, in maintaining the confidentiality of these communications, was greater than the need of the plaintiffs and the right of the public generally, to ensure that inspection was made of all documentation which would be necessary for the proper exercise of the constitutional right to have access to the courts set up under the Constitution. *Per* Murphy J:

> Virtually all of the documents inspected by me concern advice given at the highest level by senior civil servants to Government Ministers and submissions by Ministers to Cabinet based on such advices. In some cases the documentation

---

175 *Bula v Crowley* (25 July 1991, unreported), HC.
176 *Bula Ltd v Tara Mines Ltd (No 4)* [1991] 1 IR 217.

contains what might be described as a very frank analysis of the conduct and character of persons engaged in various pursuits. It may appear also that there was not unanimity between all advisers on all topics. Again it is almost inescapable that advices of this nature should contain some reference direct or indirect to views expressed by the Attorney General. It was my anxiety to ascertain how far factors of that nature created a particular concern for the Minister.

[8.144] Reliance was placed in part on the desirability of not inhibiting civil servants in giving candid advice to the Executive by ordering disclosure in this case. However, Murphy J pointed out that since *Geraghty*,[177] all administrators must now be conscious that no absolute privilege attaches to documents containing advice to Ministers, so that any caution or ill effects induced by that consideration had already occurred. What the hearing did bring to light, *per* Murphy J, however, is that the minister's concern that the form in which certain cabinet documents are cast should not be disclosed.

[8.145] Murphy J found the said form to be similar to that of documents prepared by internal advisers of a substantial company for presentation to its board of directors. Some of the information, *per* Murphy J, was 'essentially private, confidential, commercial advice'. Some contained reference to legal advice in relation to which the minister could rely on legal, as opposed to executive, privilege. Some documents had no bearing on issues in the present case and should not be disclosed. Murphy J concluded that:

> In the circumstances it seems to me that the correct balance between the interest of the public in securing an effective public service and the proper administration of justice is to be found by permitting the inspection of all the documents submitted to the court but subject to sealing up or pasting over by any appropriate means so much of the documents as consist or disclose the following:
>
> (1) Legal advice obtained by the Minister from the Attorney General or any other legal adviser.
>
> (2) A review of the conduct or affairs of their parties (particularly those engaged in the mining industry) wholly unrelated to any issue arising in the present proceedings.
>
> (3) The form in which submissions are made to the Government as distinct from the contents of such submissions. In my view it would be appropriate to provide the title of the submission and the date thereof and to obliterate the remainder of the formal submission and the queries raised thereon.

---

[177] *Geraghty* [1975] IR 306.

Ambiorix Ltd v Minister for Environment

[8.146] *Ambiorix Ltd v Minister for Environment*[178] was a Supreme Court decision in a similar vein. The grounds of appeal were against the order of the trial judge granting discovery of documents, including memoranda from government and Cabinet documents, and included the contention that the Supreme Court should reconsider the decision and the principles laid down in *Murphy v Dublin Corporation.*[179]

[8.147] Specifically, it was submitted that a class or category of documents, consisting of documents emanating at a level not below that of assistant secretary and for the ultimate consideration of government ministers, should be absolutely exempt from production and should not be examined by a judge before privilege was granted to them unless the judge was dissatisfied with the accuracy of the description of the document.

[8.148] There was no contention, as the Chief Justice noted in this case, that the documents were not relevant to the issues arising on the plaintiff's action. The Chief Justice stated that the flaw in the appellant's submission here was that it ignored the constitutional origin of the *Murphy* decision. The principles set out in that case by Walsh J were as follows:[180]

(1) Under the Constitution the administration of justice is committed solely to the judiciary in the exercise of their powers in the courts set up under the Constitution.

(2) Power to compel the production of evidence (which, of course, includes a power to compel the production of documents) is an inherent part of that judicial power and is part of the ultimate safeguard of justice in the State.

(3) Where a conflict arises during the exercise of the judicial power between the aspect of public interest involved in the production of evidence and the aspect of public interest involved in the confidentiality or exemption from production of documents pertaining to the exercise of the executive powers of the State, it is the judicial power which will decide which public interest shall prevail.

(4) The duty of the judicial power to make that decision does not mean that there is any priority or preference for the production of evidence over other public interests, such as the security of the State or the efficient discharge of the functions of the executive organ of the Government.

(5) It is for the judicial power to choose the evidence upon which it might act in any individual case in order to reach that decision.

---

[178] *Ambiorix Ltd v Minister for Environment* [1992] 1 IR 277.
[179] *Murphy v Dublin Corporation* [1972] IR 215.
[180] *Ambiorix Ltd v Minister for Environment* [1992] 1 IR 277 at 284–285 *per* Finlay CJ.

[8.149] The Chief Justice then went on to say that these principles led to certain practical conclusions applicable to a claim of privilege by the Executive of the nature here arising:

(a)   The Executive cannot prevent the judicial power from examining documents which are relevant to an issue in a civil trial for the purpose of deciding whether they must be produced.

(b)   There is no obligation on the judicial power to examine any particular document before deciding that it is exempt from production, and it can and will in many instances uphold a claim of privilege in respect of a document merely on the basis of a description of its nature and contents which it (the judicial power) accepts.

(c)   There cannot, accordingly, be a generally applicable class or category of documents exempted from production by reason of the rank in the Public Service of the person creating them, or of the position of the individual or body intended to use them.

The Chief Justice added, however, that he preferred to leave further consideration of the issue of the safety of the state until it arose for decision in a case.

[8.150] With regard to the issue of a privilege attaching to communications between third parties and government departments, taking the form of submissions to such departments by citizens, originating in the belief they would be treated in confidence, the court noted there was no public interest in keeping such communications immune from production. The Chief Justice did point out, however, that a party obtaining documents by discovery was prohibited from making use of such, other than for the purpose of the action, otherwise a contempt of court would be perpetrated.

[8.151] McCarthy J's view is perhaps the most significant in locating the *Murphy* decision firmly in judicial sovereignty in the administration of justice, discovery of documents being part of the constitutional guarantee of fair procedures.

Breathnach v Ireland (No 3)

[8.152] As a result of these decisions, the courts engaged in an exercise of balancing the public interest in the administration of justice (which obviously requires as much information as possible to be available to the court) and the public interest put forward in favour of non-disclosure. A case which illustrates this process is the decision in *Breathnach v Ireland (No 3)*.[181] In *Breathnach*, in addition to reliance on legal professional privilege to prevent disclosure, the

---

[181] *Breathnach v Ireland (No 3)* [1993] 2 IR 458.

DPP felt that communications made by gardaí to the DPP were in circumstances where they believed they would be confidential, and that it was necessary to maintain the confidentiality of such communications in order to ensure full disclosure by the gardaí (of their suspicions, opinions etc), hence it was in the public interest not to disclose such documents.

[8.153] Keane J emphasised that any claim of privilege by reference to a document belonging to a class of documents had been emphatically rejected by *Murphy, Ambiorix* and his own decision in *DPP (Hanley) v Holly*.[182] The process which he was to engage in was described thus by Keane J:[183]

> [T]he court, as I understand the law, is required to balance the public interest in the proper administration of justice against the public interest reflected in the grounds put forward for non-disclosure in the present case. The public interest in the prevention and prosecution of crime must be put in the scales on the one side. It is only where the first public interest outweighs the second public interest that an inspection should be undertaken or disclosure ordered. In considering the first public interest, it is necessary to determine to what extent, if any, the relevant documents may advance the plaintiff's case or damage the defendant's case or fairly lead to an enquiry which may have either of those consequences. In the case of the second public interest, the various factors set out by Mr Liddy must be given due weight. Again, as has been pointed out in the earlier decisions, there may be documents the very nature of which is such that inspection is not necessary to determine on which side the scales come down. Thus, information supplied in confidence to the gardaí should not in general be disclosed, or at least not in cases like the present where the innocence of an accused person is not in issue, and authorities to that effect, notably *Marks v Beyfus* (1890) 25 QBD 494, remain unaffected by the more recent decisions, as was made clear by Costello J in *Director of Consumer Affairs v Sugar Distributors Ltd* [1991] 1 IR 225. Again, there may be material the disclosure of which would be of assistance to criminals by revealing methods of detection or combating crime, a consideration of particular importance today when criminal activity tends to be highly organised and professional. There may be cases involving the security of the State, where even disclosure of the existence of the document should not be allowed. None of these factors – and there may, of course, well be others which have not occurred to me – which would remove the necessity of even inspecting the documents is present in this case.

[8.154] With regard to the specific question of the garda files and whether they attracted privilege here on the grounds of public interest, Keane J concluded:[184]

---

[182] *DPP (Hanley) v Holly* [1984] ILRM 149.
[183] *Breathnach v Ireland (No 3)* [1993] 2 IR 458 at 469.
[184] *Breathnach v Ireland (No 3)* [1993] 2 IR 458 at 472–474.

It is obvious that in every case where the commission of a crime, whether trivial or serious, is suspected, documentary material will be assembled by the gardaí irrespective of whether a prosecution is ever initiated. The fact that the documents in question may, as in the present case, be submitted by the investigating gardaí to the Director of Public Prosecutions in order to obtain his decision as to whether a prosecution should be instituted could not possibly give that material the same status as, to take an obvious example, a medical report obtained by a plaintiff in a personal injuries action solely for the purpose of his claim. If privilege exists in relation to such documents, it can only be because of the other factors referred to by Mr. Liddy, of which undoubtedly the most important is the desirability of freedom of communication between the gardaí and the Director of Public Prosecutions may subsequently be disclosed in court proceedings is clearly a matter which has to be taken into consideration in determining whether the public interest in the particular case requires its production.

In civil proceedings, the desirability of preserving confidentiality in the case of communications between members of the executive has been significantly eroded as a factor proper to be taken into account by the courts: see in particular the speech of Lord Keith in *Burmah Oil Co Ltd v The Bank of England* [1980] AC 1090 and the observations of McCarthy J in *Ambiorix v Minister for the Environment* [1992] 1 IR 277. However, different considerations would appear to apply to communications between the gardaí and the Director of Public Prosecutions, where the public interest in the prevention and prosecution of crime must be given due weight. It would be clearly unacceptable if in every case where a person was acquitted of a criminal charge, he could, by instituting proceedings for wrongful arrest or malicious prosecution, embark on a fishing expedition through all the files of the gardaí relating to the case. The circumstances of the particular case must determine, in the light of the constitutional principles to which I have referred, whether an inspection should be undertaken by the court and whether, as a result of that inspection, production of any of the documents should be ordered.

The plaintiff's claim includes one for damages for malicious prosecution. If he is to succeed in his claim, he will have to establish as a matter of probability that one or more of the defendants played a part in the institution of the criminal proceedings and, in so doing, acted maliciously and without reasonable and probable cause. It has already been held by the Court of Criminal Appeal that the primary facts found by the Special Criminal Court could only have led to the inference that the interrogation of the plaintiff which culminated in the making of incriminating statements by him did not comply with fair procedures and to the further inference that the statements could not be regarded as voluntary. The factors referred to by the court in reaching that conclusion were, principally, the place and time at which the enquiry was conducted and the unexplained failure to comply with the plaintiff's request that a solicitor be present during the interrogation. I appreciate that, unlike some of the other evidential issues, no question of res judicata arises in relation to those findings. However, in exercising my discretion as to whether particular documents should be produced, I do not think I can disregard the evidential context, as indicated by those findings, in which the issues arising in the present proceedings will ultimately fall to be determined. The material furnished by such of the gardaí as were concerned in the interrogation to the Director of Public Prosecutions might well furnish evidence which would be of significance in establishing a want of reasonable or probable cause for the prosecution. This, of course, is in no sense to pre-judge that issue, which will have to be resolved at the trial of the action. It seems to me that the public interest in the administration of justice outweighs the desirability in general of preserving the confidentiality of such documents.

Irish case law on tribunals

[8.155] In *Goodman International v Hamilton*,[185] members of the Oireachtas joined as notice parties had made serious allegations against the applicants before the respondent, the sole member of a tribunal inquiry into the beef processing industry. They refused to disclose the identities of those persons who had supplied them with the information on which the allegations were made. They argued in the High Court that the relationship between a member of the public and a member of the Oireachtas, in such a situation, was a relationship within the preconditions of *Cook v Carroll*. The court found it unnecessary to decide this point, but approved of the dictum of Lord Edmond-Davies in *D v NSPCC* that where a communication was made in the context of a confidential relationship, such that disclosure of the communication would be in breach of some ethical or social value involving the public interest, the court had a discretion to uphold a refusal to give evidence in relation to the communication, provided it was clearly demonstrated that the public interest would be better served by excluding such evidence. The court was also of the view that the extension of the categories giving rise to a private privilege would be contrary to *Murphy*, *Geraghty* and *Ambiorix*, and emphasised that the exclusion of admissible and relevant evidence was contrary to the public interest in the administration of justice. On the facts, the High Court felt the discretion of the tribunal would be exercised in favour of non-disclosure.

[8.156] *Goodman International v Hamilton*[186] is significant for two reasons: it indicated that the days of extending the heads of private privilege were over (that would be contrary to the whole ethos of *Murphy* etc.), and it emphasized that keeping any admissible and relevant evidence from the courts is contrary to the public interest in the administration of justice. Given the proliferation in Irish life of tribunals, as we adhere to a preference for dealing with issues via

---

[185] *Goodman International v Hamilton* [1993] 3 IR 320.
[186] *Goodman International v Hamilton* [1993] 3 IR 320.

tribunals proceedings[187] rather than through the courts, it is unsurprising that a number of tribunals have led to the question being raised on judicial review proceedings as to whether individuals can withhold information from tribunal proceedings or the tribunal itself can refuse to reveal information.

[8.157] *Howlin v Mr Justice Morris*[188] arose in the context of the Morris Tribunal,[189] which was concerned with allegations of police corruption in Donegal. Deputy Howlin, a member of Dáil Éireann had received certain information regarding the garda investigation that indicated it was compromised. The question arose as to whether he could be forced to reveal his sources. The respondent requested the applicant to make all documents relating to information received by him available. The applicant claimed they were privileged under Art 15.10 of the Constitution, which confers a power on the Oireachtas to protect the papers of its members. The respondent made an order for discovery of the documents and the respondent sought *certiorari* on the basis of an absolute privilege under Art 15.10 or a privilege at common law. The High Court quashed the order for discovery and an appeal went to the Supreme Court. It was held that the only kind of privilege Deputy Howlin could plead was that of so called common law privilege, which was not privilege in the strict sense but was a question of public interest immunity. The respondent had carried out the balancing exercise in relation to public interest immunity and the view that he took on it was unassailable. Hence the Supreme Court agreed with his view that discovery should be ordered here of Deputy Howlin's information. The court also noted that the 'innocence at stake' exception to privilege applied to an investigation into corruption as well as to a criminal trial – the allegations here suggested that people had been 'framed' and convicted of criminal offences and so presented in an acute form the innocence at stake situation.

[8.158] In *O'Callaghan v Mr Justice Mahon*[190] a witness at the Mahon tribunal (Tom Gilmartin) had made serious allegations about a businessman, Owen O'Callaghan. Prior to Gilmartin giving evidence, the applicant was given a statement of the evidence he proposed to give, from which parts had been redacted. When Gilmartin gave evidence in public session he raised a number of serious allegations not contained in the disclosed statement. O'Callaghan sought discovery of all documents recording prior oral and written statements by Gilmartin so as to cross-examine on inconsistencies. The respondents ruled that

---

[187] Tribunals are established under the Tribunals of Inquiry (Evidence) Act 1921 and are entitled to fashion their own procedure to ensure the efficient execution of their work.
[188] *Brendan Howlin v Mr Justice Morris* [2006] 2 IR 321.
[189] The Tribunal of Inquiry into Complaints Concerning Some Gardaí in the Donegal Division set up pursuant to resolutions of Dáil Éireann and Seanad Éireann on 28 March 2002.
[190] *O'Callaghan v Mr Justice Mahon* [2006] 2 IR 32.

he was not entitled to disclosure of these prior statements as the information had been given confidentially to the tribunal, although they would disclose statements revealing glaring contradictions. O'Callaghan sought disclosure and a declaration that refusing to disclose all such statements amounted to a breach of fair procedure. The respondents said that the tribunal had adopted a policy of confidentiality regarding communications by potential witnesses during its preliminary examination, as to do otherwise would have a detrimental effect on the work of the tribunal. It argued that its decision was within its discretion as master of its own procedures, although it accepted on the authority of *Flood v Lawlor*[191] that this is subject to the constitutional rights of persons appearing before it.

[8.159] The High Court granted the relief sought and the respondents appealed to the Supreme Court. The Supreme Court dismissed the appeal but ordered the matter back to the High Court for further disclosure as to the extent of disclosure that was necessary. Their view was that confidentiality did not arise automatically when a person made grave allegations to a tribunal. As Hardiman J put it:

> In my view, the tribunal cannot by the unilateral adoption of a 'policy' on its own part confer the quality of confidentiality, absolute unless the tribunal itself waives it, on any material. To permit the tribunal to do this would, in my view, be to allow it in effect to legislate for the deprivation of a party before it of rights to which he is entitled.[192]

However, the Supreme Court held the respondents owed an obligation to those who gave information in the preliminary investigative stage to keep such information confidential unless and until it was required by someone impugned to vindicate his right to a good name.

[8.160] There are some very significant statements issuing from the Supreme Court with importance for delineating the boundaries of discretion for future tribunal proceedings. It is interesting to note that Hardiman J in his judgment in the Supreme Court makes reference to his earlier judgment in *P'OC v DPP*[193] regarding difficulties in prosecution for offences said to have taken place many years in the past, in order to underscore the importance of availability of information which may reveal discrepancies:

> While the proceedings before the tribunal are obviously not a criminal trial, they are proceedings to which the notion of due process is relevant. This is especially so where, as in relation to the applicant, grave allegations are made without

---

[191] *Flood v Lawlor* [2000] IESC 76.
[192] *O'Callaghan v Mr Justice Mahon* [2006] 2 IR 32 at p.76, para 107, *per* Hardiman J.
[193] *P'OC v DPP* [2000] 3 IR 119.

notice in circumstances where the credibility of the person making them is a serious issue ... In my view it is a matter of common justice and indeed common sense, that a witness who makes a grave allegation against another may be contradicted out of his own mouth where that is possible. If a right to do this were not assured, cross examination would be gravely hampered and even subverted. It is a statement of the obvious to say that the credibility of a particular statement made by a particular person is reduced or destroyed of he has made a contradictory statement on a previous occasion, unless that can be explained in some way. Conversely, consistency enhances the credibility of a statement.

These propositions have been recognized for centuries in the common law. This is demonstrated by the elaborate provision in the law of evidence allowing the proof, in certain circumstances, of both previous inconsistent statements by a witness under cross examination on the one hand and proof of previous consistent statements in certain circumstances on the other.[194]

[8.161] Hardiman J went on to consider European Court of Human Rights jurisprudence regarding 'equality of arms' and referred to *Rowe & Davis v UK*,[195] which held that the UK practices re disclosure constituted a violation of art 1. Hardiman J was of the opinion that:

... the hearing of very grave allegations before a tribunal of inquiry which not merely sits in public but whose proceedings are in practice accorded enormous publicity, attracts for persons whose reputations are impugned procedural rights analogous to (though often varying in detail from) those of a defendant in a criminal trial. These are the rights enunciated in *In re Haughey* [1971] IR 217.[196]

Hardiman J identified those inquiries that do not seek to fix individuals with responsibility for grave wrongdoing and have large volumes of uncontradicted evidence before them, saying that no court would interfere lightly with their legitimate procedural discretions. He emphasised, however, that:

...this tribunal is at another extreme and features:-

very grave allegations some of which, if true, would constitute breaches of the criminal law;

clear and obvious attacks on the good name of the applicant which is constitutionally protected;

the personal credibility of the notice party as a vital factor;

little or nothing in the way of a paper trail or corroboration;

immediate and extensive media coverage of un-notified allegations.

---

[194] *O'Callaghan v Mr Justice Mahon* [2006] 2 IR 32 at pp 57–58 *per* Hardiman J.
[195] *Rowe & Davis v UK* (2000) 30 EHRR 1.
[196] *O'Callaghan v Mr Justice Mahon* [2006] 2 IR 32 at p 61, para 56.

> These features ... seem to me to require all the rights enunciated in *In re Haughey* ... and a very full scope for their exercise on the part of a person impugned. But the discretion of a tribunal or similar body may be very much greater in a less extreme situation and I do not wish anything said in this context to undermine that discretion.[197]

[8.162] Ultimately the finding that no legal quality of confidentiality attaches to an allegation made to the tribunal, directly or indirectly, once the subject matter of the allegation becomes the subject of a 'full public inquiry' is sufficient to dispose of the issue in the case, but Hardiman J made an interesting comment about that full public inquiry. He noted the tribunal was in its eighth year and its dealings with Gilmartin had been over a period of seven years, (though not continuously) and all of these dealings with the exception of days in March 2004 had been in private. The tribunal was charged to conduct a full public inquiry. The preliminary investigation was to establish if there was sufficient evidence to warrant proceeding to full public inquiry. The tribunal here had also used the private inquiries to gather information. That had not been challenged in these proceedings but Hardiman J commented:[198]

> I am deeply concerned that, if the information gathered in the private phase is to be shrouded in permanent secrecy there is a grave danger of a shift in the very nature of the tribunal itself. This procedure would alter the tribunal from being a public inquiry with a private, limited, preliminary phase to one in which a good deal of the real business would be done in private ... There would be a danger, perhaps, if these procedures became general, that a tribunal might itself become invested in the evidence of a particular witness to the point where it became insensitive as to contradictions in his or her evidence.

Geoghegan J (with whom Fennelly J agreed) expressed the view that a wide latitude is given to tribunals to fashion their own procedures and the courts should not lightly interfere and, although agreeing with Hardiman J, gave a slightly narrower basis for his view, preferring to base his decision on *Re Haughey* than 'consider to what extent the numerous cases and statutes relating to the law of evidence for the purposes of the courts must necessarily be applied to every cross examination in a tribunal.'[199]

[8.163] *Howlin* and *O'Callaghan* both demonstrate the limitations of discretion of tribunals in that there is a balancing of the interests of securing the information in the interest of the public and the desire of the tribunal to have access to as much information as possible, and how damaging it would be for the person concerned if the information were not revealed. Ironically,

---

[197] *O'Callaghan v Mr Justice Mahon* [2006] 2 IR 32 at p 62, para 58–59.
[198] *O'Callaghan v Mr Justice Mahon* [2006] 2 IR 32 at pp 78–79, para 117.
[199] *O'Callaghan v Mr Justice Mahon* [2006] 2 IR 32 at 82, para 125 *per* Geoghegan J.

confidentiality can be claimed both as a basis for not revealing information to the tribunal, as in *Howlin*, and also for the tribunal itself refusing to make evidence available, as in *O'Callaghan.*

[8.164] In *DPP v Special Criminal Court; Paul Ward*[200] all but 40 statements made by 20 persons had been made available to the defendant's legal advisers on his trial in the Special Criminal Court for murder. A prosecution witness swore that if the confidential information in relation to organised crime was to become known, they would face a death sentence and it would be impossible to investigate organised crime. The Special Criminal Court felt an injustice might be done if Ward's legal advisers were not allowed to see the statements, so if he was willing to waive his personal rights of inspection, and being informed of their contents, they could be produced to his lawyers. On appeal, the High Court (Carney J) held that the Special Criminal Court had altered the relationship between lawyer and client and felt the court itself should inspect the documents. The appeal to the Supreme Court was dismissed, but that court commented that the prosecution task was not just to secure a conviction, but to be 'ministers of justice' in disclosing any evidence that might help the defence. The informer's privilege, they held, was of ancient origin (*Marks v Beyfus*;[201] *People v Reddan*;[202] *Skeffington v Rooney*[203] followed) and was subject only to the 'innocence at stake' exception.

[8.165] In *Johnston v Church of Scientology*,[204] the defendants argued that such a degree of confidentiality attached to the counselling notes that the court must weigh up the public interest in the preservation of such confidentiality against the normal public interest in the disclosure of all relevant evidence, and must in all the circumstances come down in favour of preservation of the confidentiality. Geoghegan J in the High Court disagreed:

> ...I reject also the argument that there is a greater public interest in upholding the confidentiality than the public interest in relevant evidence being produced in court for the purposes of the administration of justice.[205]

[8.166] In *People v Nevin,*[206] the appellant in pursuing an appeal from her murder conviction, sought disclosure from the DPP of certain documents relating to a document drawn up by the anti-racketeering unit of the gardaí in

---

[200] *DPP v Special Criminal Court; Paul Ward* [1999] 1 IR 60.
[201] *Marks v Beyfus* (1890) 25 QBD 494.
[202] *People v Reddan* [1995] 3 IR 560.
[203] *Skeffington v Rooney* [1997] 1 IR 22.
[204] *Johnston v Church of Scientology* [2001] 1 IR 682.
[205] *Johnston v Church of Scientology* [2001] 1 IR 682 at 687.
[206] *People v Nevin* (13 December 2001, unreported), CCA, Geoghegan J.

which Jack White's Inn was listed as a public house with possible IRA connections. Several weeks after the conviction, the Chief State Solicitor had informed the appellant's solicitor of this document. The significance of it was that the appellant had in her evidence suggested that her late husband was a member of the IRA. The DPP claimed privilege either on the grounds of legal professional privilege (gardaí seeking legal advice) or that the list was furnished in confidence and disclosure would reveal the methodology of gardaí in investigating any potential for disturbance of the public peace. The court was satisfied the claim of legal professional privilege was well founded but also the claim of public privilege:

> ... [T]he court would hold that the claim of confidentiality by the Director should be upheld because in the act of balancing the interests of the Director as set out in the affidavit of Deputy Commissioner Conroy on the one hand in non-disclosure and the interests of justice and fair procedures for the appellant on the other the court is quite satisfied that the arguments for non-disclosure outweigh the arguments for disclosure.[207]

[8.167] Whether or not public privilege ultimately develops to subsume that relating to the heads of private privilege, its future is secure, having been intimately identified with judicial sovereignty and the separation of powers. Undoubtedly, in this jurisdiction at least, it will lead to an enhancement of the role of judicial discretion and scrutiny in an area the territory of which is gradually being carved out.

[8.168] The overall tension that pervades the area of privilege generally is that between the importance of the relationship and what is being safeguarded therein, relative to the cost that there is in terms of withholding relevant information from the courts in the interests of the administration of justice. There is an acknowledgement that both are in the public interest.

[8.169] The interface between traditional constructions of justice and fairness and of what that might comprise in Irish constitutional and Strasbourg human rights terms is emerging as a very real issue in the context of public privilege claims, where the ability of the judiciary to (re)cast the interests involved in terms which define public interest as well as identify minimum content of fair procedure may well be most significant and have an influence well beyond that area of law. It is striking that once again the margins – for example, here of tribunal proceedings and the clash of rights and interests – provide the context for judicial construction of what is minimum and fair in procedure. It is also ironic that in doing so the judiciary may very well be making the case for their own prevalence and centrality to how we do justice.

---

[207] *People v Nevin* (13 December 2001, unreported), CCA at 7.

Chapter 9

The Rule Against Hearsay

> He had taken my story, with all its – what was it Haslet said? – with all its frills and fancy bits, and pared it down to stark essentials. It was an account of my crime I hardly recognised, and yet I believed it. He had made a murderer of me. I would have signed it there and then, but I had nothing to write with. I even searched my clothing for something sharp, a pin or something, with which to stick myself, and scrawl my signature in blood. But what matter, it did not require my endorsement. Reverently I folded the page in four and placed it under the mattress at the end where my head would be. Then I undressed and lay down naked in the shadows and folded my hands on my breast, like a marble knight on a tomb, and closed my eyes. I was no longer myself. I can't explain it, but it's true. I was no longer myself.

Banville, *The Book of Evidence*

Introduction

[9.01] Cross describes the rule against hearsay as follows: 'a statement other than one made by a person while giving oral evidence in the proceedings is inadmissible as evidence of any fact stated'.[1] The rule operates, therefore, to potentially exclude informal oral remarks, formal written statements, sworn testimony in previous proceedings, as well as gestures, signs, photographs etc. The reason behind this exclusionary rule affecting otherwise relevant and probative evidence, is that if the maker of the statement does not testify, he is not available for cross-examination (*per* Wigmore: 'the greatest legal engine ever invented for the discovery of truth'[2]), nor can his demeanour be observed or credibility tested. Moreover, it is desirable that the best evidence be available to the court and that the danger of inaccuracy through repetition be avoided.

[9.02] Hence the rule is located in the faith in the power of cross-examination, distrust of the jury's ability to evaluate hearsay and a fear that, if allowed, the courts would be swamped with hearsay evidence. The rule is one that has developed with the format of the modern trial and is deeply wedded to our process of legal investigation. Correspondingly, it is difficult to overcome, however apparently archaic or undesirable at times, without legislative

---

[1] *Cross on Evidence* (6th edn, Butterworths, 1985), p 454.
[2] Wigmore, *A Treatise on the Anglo American System of Evidence in Trials at Common Law* (3rd edn, Boston: Little Brown & Co, 1940) Vol 5 (Chadbourne revision).

intervention (see the House of Lords decision in *Myers v DPP*[3]). The definitive statement of the hearsay rule and its ambit and effect in Irish law is to be found in the judgment of Kingsmill Moore J in *Cullen v Clarke*:[4]

> ... there is no general rule of evidence to the effect that a witness may not testify as to the words spoken by a person who is not produced as a witness. There is a general rule, subject to many exceptions, that evidence of the speaking of such words is inadmissible to prove the truth of the facts which they assert ... This is the rule known as the rule against hearsay. If the fact that the words were spoken rather than their truth is what it is sought to prove, a statement is admissible.

[9.03] The rule against hearsay, like other rules of evidence, does not automatically apply to administrative tribunals. However, if the circumstances are such that admission of such evidence would result in a breach of natural/constitutional justice, adherence with same would seem to be required.[5]

[9.04] The disadvantages of the rule against hearsay are obvious: the exclusion of evidence of a dead, unavailable or unidentifiable person; the extra cost involved in proving relevant facts; and the exclusion of evidence otherwise thought to be reliable, which may indeed prevent an accused from exonerating himself. There are, however, exceptions to the rule, which in the nature of things – and particularly in the context of the law of evidence – are more important than the rule itself. These exceptions have been carved out by the courts over the years and would now seem to be static. They originate from the fact that the categories concerned involved particularly reliable types of evidence, or are centred on the unavailability of better evidence.

[9.05] The facts in *DPP v Myers*[6] are instructive as they demonstrate the extent to which evidence can be excluded by such a rule. Essentially this decision excluded manufacturers' records of car engine numbers as inadmissible hearsay. Myers and others had been involved in a scheme whereby they bought crashed cars (with log books) and then stole and sold on similar matching cars using the crashed cars' log books and claiming the cars were the reconstituted crashed cars. The prosecution had to establish that the log books belonged to the original crashed cars, not the stolen similar vehicles which they were selling on, and they could only do this by reference to the manufacturers' records. The said records standing alone (as they could not, for example, be proved by those who had compiled them in the course of their duty or use them to 'refresh their memories' as the latter could not be identified) constituted hearsay evidence and

---

[3] *Myers v DPP* [1965] AC 1001.
[4] *Cullen v Clarke* [1963] IR 368 at 378.
[5] *Kiely v Minister for Social Welfare* [1971] IR 21.
[6] *Myers v DPP* [1965] AC 100.

so were inadmissible. The Crown argued, however, that another exception needed to be carved out to the rule in order to allow these records. The House of Lords refused to carve out such an exception to the hearsay rule. (The Criminal Evidence Act 1965 in England was passed to reverse the effect of that decision.) In *Myers,* the House of Lords emphasised that further exceptions to the hearsay rule on the basis that evidence was particularly reliable, or the best available, would not now be justified. In Ireland it seems likely the position is similar.

[9.06] Griffiths[7] has commented that the decision in *Myers* is one of particular judicial cowardice. He stated that the case illustrates the absurdity of the continuance in effect of a rule now archaic and out of tune with modern social conditions in its refusal to the courts of the facility or ability to rely on 'business records' (which would be regarded as eminently receivable in the business world on important everyday affairs) simply because of the inability to point to the particular worker who compiled the ledger in question, which was of value in identifying stolen cars.

[9.07] In *People (DPP) v Byrne,*[8] facts similar to that in *Myers* arose in the Irish context. The applicant, a car dealer, had been convicted of handling a motor car knowing or believing it to be stolen. Evidence was given by a number of witnesses relating to the importation of the stolen vehicle: from an employee of National Vehicle Deliveries Ltd who produced a form with his signature relating to the examination and recording of its chassis and engine number at Rosslare; the lorry driver who signed for its delivery to the motor dealership; an employee who inspected the vehicle and signed a form containing its chassis number; an officer of the Revenue, as to the results of his examination of the registered vehicle and the mismatch between identification numbers; and an officer of the Motor Taxation Office who produced original documents relating to the reconstructed vehicle. On appeal, it was alleged the trial judge erred in admitting evidence that was inadmissible under *Myers*. To come within the remit of the Criminal Evidence Act 1992, it was argued, that evidence would have to have been given by persons who compiled the documents, and a certificate pursuant to s 6 of that Act to that effect had not been produced.

[9.08] The Court of Criminal Appeal held that the prosecution was not obliged to produce a certificate under s 6 of the 1992 Act to render the evidence admissible. Each witness had identified a document (s)he had personally filled in or signed. As the situation was distinct from *Myers* (where such employees who had so compiled the documentation could not have been identified), the Criminal Evidence Act did not have to be invoked. In essence, the court held

---

[7]   Griffiths, *Politics of the Judiciary* (Glasgow, Fontana Press, 1977).
[8]   *People (DPP) v Byrne* (7 June 2000, unreported), CCA.

these individuals were themselves testifying as to knowledge which they had, and hence it was not hearsay. By referring to the documents, they were simply 'refreshing their memories', as is often allowed, for example, to gardaí in consulting their notebooks.[9]

In *Meehan*,[10] *Myers* was distinguished in the context of mobile phone records of phone calls, as it was held that unlike *Myers* the telephone records were compiled by machine without any human intervention. Direct evidence had been given about names, number assignment and the use thereof. The court in *Meehan* felt that 'given further that the generation of all other information was solely by the computer, ie mechanically without personal interference or input, the records were, in the view of this court, clearly admissible.'[11]

The distinction between original evidence and hearsay evidence

[9.09] In *Subramaniam v DPP*[12] the accused was charged with the unlawful possession of ammunition. The defence put forward was that one of the accused, having been captured by terrorists, had acted under duress. The question arose as to the admissibility of conversations between the accused and the terrorists for the purpose of establishing the defence. At trial the judge adjudged the statements to constitute hearsay and so be inadmissible. On appeal to the Privy Council it was held that a statement constitutes hearsay and is inadmissible when the object of the evidence is to establish the truth of what is contained in the statement. It is not hearsay and is admissible when it is proposed to establish by the evidence, not the truth of the statement, but the fact that it was made. Here, statements made by terrorists to the appellant, whether true or not, if they had been believed by the appellant, might reasonably have induced in him a fear of instant death if he did not obey.

Implied assertions

[9.10] The issue has arisen as to whether the rule against hearsay applies not only to express assertions and conduct intended to be assertive (eg nods and gestures), but also to statements or conduct not intended to be assertive, but which rest on an assumption of fact believed by the maker of the statement or actor, which can be inferred by the court.

---

[9] See *Northern Banking Company v Carpenter* [1931] IR 268; *Lord Talbot de Malahide v Cusack* (1864) 17 ICLR 213.
[10] *People (DPP) v Meehan* [2006] 3 IR 468.
[11] *People (DPP) v Meehan* [2006] 3 IR 468 at 482, *per* Kearns J.
[12] *Subramaniam v DPP* [1956] 1 WLR 965 PC.

There is a certain amount of difficulty with the case law on this issue, as it is not always apparent if the statement is being admitted because it does not constitute hearsay, or by virtue of an exception to the hearsay rule.

[9.11] In *Lloyd v Powell Duffryn Steam Coal Co Ltd*,[13] the issue arose as to whether a child was the son of a man who had been killed in the course of his employment with the respondents. There was evidence to the effect that the deceased, knowing the child's mother to be pregnant, promised to marry her, and had told a friend and his landlady that he was going to marry her because of the pregnancy. The Court of Appeal determined the statement to be a declaration against interest and therefore admissible in evidence under an exception to the hearsay rule. The House of Lords, on the other hand, deemed the statement to be admissible, but not as an exception to the hearsay rule, rather because the state of mind of the deceased and his intentions with regard to the child were relevant in their own right. The testimony of the witness was as to the act, ie to the deceased speaking these words, and it was the speaking of the words which was the matter being put in evidence and which possessed evidential value. Thus, the statement was admissible, not constituting hearsay.

[9.12] In *Teper v R*[14] the accused had been convicted of arson, and evidence of a policeman was tendered to the effect that some 26 minutes after the fire had started and about a furlong away, he had heard a woman say, 'Your place is burning and you are going away', and noticed a car with a man in it who resembled the accused. The Privy Council deemed the evidence inadmissible, not falling within an exception to the hearsay rule, being without the ambit of the doctrine *of res gestae*. (Heydon[15] comments in relation to this decision that the evidence could have been excluded on the basis that it did not constitute hearsay, as the innuendo in the statement was not clear and could be irrelevant as to who caused the fire.)

[9.13] Another relevant decision in the area is that of *Ratten v R*,[16] where the facts concerned a shooting of the accused's wife with a gun, which he alleged to have been accidental. Evidence was tendered to the effect that around the time of the shooting, a telephonist received a call from the accused's house and heard a woman's voice, evidently hysterical, say, 'Get me the police, please'. The Privy Council determined this did not constitute hearsay. Yet, even if it was considered to be hearsay, it would come within the ambit of the exception constituted by the doctrine of *res gestae*. Lord Wilberforce reasoned that:

---

[13] *Lloyd v Powell Duffryn Steam Coal Co Ltd* [1914] AC 733.
[14] *Teper v R* [1952] 2 All ER 447.
[15] Heydon, *Cases and Materials on Evidence* (2nd edn, Butterworths, 1984), p 318.
[16] *Ratten v R* [1971] 3 All ER 801.

The mere fact that evidence of a witness includes evidence as to words spoken by another person who is not called is no objection to its admissibility. Words spoken are facts just as much as any other action by a human being. If the speaking of the words is a relevant fact, a witness may give evidence that they were spoken. A question of hearsay only arises when words spoken are relied on "testimonially", ie as establishing some fact narrated by the words.

Lord Wilberforce's reasoning was to the effect that the words were only facts showing the woman was in a state of fear. (Heydon commented that the evidence was relied on, not only because signs of fear were present, but also because they were justified and sincere.)

[9.14] Uncertainty as to how implied assertions are to be treated by the rule against hearsay: whether the rule against hearsay applies and those statements that are admitted have been rendered admissible by virtue of an exception thereto, or whether the rule does not apply at all to implied assertions was resolved by the House of Lords in *R v Kearley*[17] taking the view that implied assertions were covered by the hearsay rule and so held evidence that people called at the defendant's home asking for drugs was not admissible as evidence that the defendant was a drug dealer. Despite criticism of this stance[18] it is nonetheless evident that to hold that implied assertions do not amount to hearsay is to distinguish between express and implied assertions. Yet the dangers of inaccurate memory, observation etc, are just as strong in relation to both, and the safeguard of cross-examination is absent. More recently the common law rule in England has been abrogated by statute.[19]

Exceptions to the rule against hearsay

[9.15] There are, of course, exceptions to the hearsay rule, which are often more important than the rule itself.

Admissions

[9.16] One party to an action may give evidence of a statement by or on behalf of the other party, which is adverse to the latter's case. This can occur in both civil and criminal cases. In criminal cases, where the admission is made by the accused, it is called a confession and particular considerations applied. If the statement is not made to a 'person in authority' in a criminal case, it is termed an admission, as it is in all civil cases.

---

[17] *R v Kearley* [1992] 2 AC 228.
[18] Tapper, 'Hearsay and Implied Assertions' (1992) 108 LQR 524.
[19] Section 115 of the Criminal Justice Act 2003 defines hearsay statements as those in which there was an intention to cause another person to believe in the truth of the matter.

Confessions

[9.17] One of the more controversial exceptions to the hearsay rule is that concerning confession statements. Confession statements have been controversial, not least because confessions tend to be contested by the individual who is the subject of the charge and denies making such a statement. Some such denials have been subsequently vindicated as many alleged miscarriages of justice would have involved convictions based on confession evidence. Confessions of their nature emerge from that very tense, coercive environment that is the pre-trial period of detention. For these reasons, and in light of miscarriages of justice, particularly in neighbouring jurisdictions, cautionary elements have become attached to the tendering of such statements. The Irish legislature's response was the Criminal Procedure Act 1993.[20] Section 10 of that Act introduced a requirement that there be corroboration of confession evidence:

> Where at a trial of a person on indictment evidence is given of a confession made by that person and that evidence is not corroborated, the judge shall advise the jury to have due regard to the absence of corroboration.

[9.18] In *People v O'Neill*[21] a charge of armed robbery of a post office on Bandon Road, Cork had been proffered against the applicant. The only evidence tendered consisted of a number of verbal statements that he was alleged to have made. The issue that arose on appeal was the adequacy of the trial judge's direction to the jury on the matter of corroboration and whether there could be corroboration here where the only evidence was of hairs found in a balaclava but no sufficient proof had been given that it was the accused's hair. The trial judge directed the jury as to the meaning of corroboration in accordance with *Baskerville*.[22] The Court of Criminal Appeal said that the direction was adequate but that the evidence of the hair could not amount to corroboration *per Baskerville* because there was not sufficient proof that the hair was the hair of the applicant. Therefore the probative value of the hair was so slight, it was not capable of corroborating the statements made by the applicant. Nonetheless even though the forensic evidence was only slightly supportive, the court felt statements were sufficient for the jury to convict:

> Looking at the entire of the trial there was not only strong but compelling evidence to admit the statements. There was access to a solicitor, the admissions were not in the form of abject admissions, there was an assault on the gardaí.

---

[20] For a full account of the background to this legislation and the aforementioned miscarriages, see Hardiman J's judgment in CCA in *People v Connolly* [2003] IR 1.

[21] *People v O'Neill* (28 January 2002, unreported), CCA.

[22] *R v Baskerville* [1916] 2 KB 658.

Even though the forensic evidence as to hair samples was only slightly supportive of the guilt of the applicant the evidence of the statements was strong enough for a jury to convict and the court therefore refuses the application for leave to appeal conviction. [23]

This case makes it clear that the corroboration requirement is a weaker corroboration requirement as the jury here could convict in what was effectively the absence of corroboration in the *Baskerville* sense.

[9.19] In *People v Connolly*,[24] however, there was a successful appeal on the basis of the failure of a trial judge to give an adequate corroboration warning. The only evidence against the accused here was a signed inculpatory statement allegedly made while in custody. The trial judge here, it was argued, had given an insufficient warning to the jury as to the need for corroboration. Hardiman J, delivering the judgment of the Court of Criminal Appeal, stated that it was impossible for the jury to have due regard as to the absence of corroboration in accordance with s 10 unless the term was properly explained to them:

> [I]t is not unduly burdensome, in my view, to require that corroboration be explained. It is also necessary I think, briefly and meaningfully, to explain why it is natural to look for corroboration in serious cases and equally why, in some cases, even the most diligent search will be unavailing.[25]

This case is further significant in that in this context, and with an account of the miscarriages of justice in these cases in Ireland and other jurisdictions including reference to then Martin Committee Report[26] which had noted Canadian material consisting of a study conducted by Professor Alan Grant on audio visual recording of interviews in Ontario indicating Canadian defence lawyers were of the view that such recording was more accurate than police note taking.[27] Hardiman J[28] gave a warning in relation to confession evidence and its general receptivity in the Irish courts:

> It is clear from the history of legal and legislative concern with uncorroborated confessions over a period of nearly two decades that legislators and judges alike have emphasised the importance of the audio-visual recording of interviews. This is routine in most first world common law countries. Its failure to become routine, or even remotely to approach that status in this country, nearly twenty

---

[23] *People v O'Neill* (28 January 2002, unreported), CCA, p 5/5 Fennelly J; Carroll & Barr JJ.

[24] *People v Connolly* [2003] 2 IR 1.

[25] *People v Connolly* [2003] 2 IR 1 at 16, *per* Hardiman J.

[26] *Report of Committee to Enquire into Certain Aspects of Criminal Procedure* (Chairman Judge Frank Martin) Government of Ireland, March 1990.

[27] *Report of Committee to Enquire into Certain Aspects of Criminal Procedure*, p 36 referred to by Hardiman J in *People v Connolly* [2003] 2 IR 1 at 10.

[28] *People v Connolly* [2003] 2 IR 1 at 17–18, *per* Hardiman J.

years after statutory provision for it was first made, has ceased to be a mere oddity and is closely approaching the status of an anomaly. It also has the consequence that, in a very high percentage of criminal trials, there is a hard fought issue ('the trial within a trial') as to the admissibility of statements which are often the whole or a large part of the prosecution case. Twelve years ago the Martin Committee reported that this situation had virtually ceased in Ontario because of audio-visual recording. The courts have been very patient, perhaps excessively patient, with delays in this regard. The time cannot be remote when we will hear a submission that, absent extraordinary circumstances (by which we do not mean that a particular garda station has no audio-visual machinery or that the audio-visual room was being painted), it is unacceptable to tender in evidence a statement which has not been so recorded.

[9.20] Although one of the more controversial exceptions to the hearsay rule is that concerning confession statements, in relation to the format of a confession, it is noteworthy that a confession statement does not have to take any particular form: it can be oral or in writing, signed or unsigned. These factors and their presence or absence does not affect the admissibility of the confession, but simply its weight or probative value. Moreover, the confession does not have to be in the exact words used by the accused. In *AG v McCabe*,[29] Kennedy CJ stated:

> However desirable to have the *ipsissima verba of* a deponent it is not the law that the statement of an accused person must as a matter of law be rejected if it is not in his *ipsissima verba*.

[9.21] The Criminal Justice Act 2007 makes provision with regard to the admissibility of recordings of confessions as follows:

57 Admission in evidence of recording of questioning of accused by Garda Síochána

(1) A court may admit in evidence at the trial of a person in respect of an offence—

    (a) a recording by electronic or similar means, or

    (b) a transcript of such a recording,

or both of the questioning of the person by a member of the Garda Síochána at a Garda Síochána station or elsewhere in connection with the investigation of the offence.

(2) Any statement made by the person concerned that is recorded in a recording which is admitted in evidence under subsection (1) may be admissible in evidence at the trial concerned notwithstanding the fact that—

---

[29] *AG v McCabe* [1927] IR 129.

(a) it was not taken down in writing at the time it was made, or

(b) that statement is not in writing and signed by the person who made it,

or both.

(3) This section shall not affect the admissibility in evidence at the trial of a person in respect of an offence of any statement that is recorded in writing made by the person during questioning by a member of the Garda Síochána at a Garda Síochána station or elsewhere in connection with the investigation of the offence (whether or not that statement is signed by the person) and irrespective of whether the making of that statement is recorded by electronic or similar means.

[9.22] The question has arisen as to whether a distinction should be made in this context between inculpatory and exculpatory statements, in terms of the rules relating to the admissibility of confessions. In *Piche v R*,[30] the Supreme Court of Canada rejected the contention that the rules only applied to inculpatory statements, as did the court in *Commissioners of Customs and Excise v Harz*.[31]

Voluntariness

[9.23] A mandatory requirement in relation to confessions is that they must be voluntary. Voluntariness is a prerequisite to the admissibility of any confession. The traditional definition of 'voluntariness' is that of Lord Sumner in *Ibrahim v R*:[32]

> a voluntary statement in the sense that it has not been obtained ... either by fear of prejudice or hope of advantage exercised or held out by a person in authority and the onus is on the prosecution tendering that statement to show that it is voluntary in that sense.

This formula was adopted by Kennedy CJ in *AG v McCabe*.[33]

[9.24] The definition of voluntariness thus expressed contains three elements: that of a 'threat' or 'inducement' and the concept of a 'person in authority'. Each of these elements has been subjected to a measure of interpretation and application by the courts, which varies in accordance with the perceived rationale or function of the rule, put forward as including:

–   the reliability principle,

–   the protection principle,

–   the principle against self-incrimination, and

–   the deterrence principle.

---

[30] *Piche v R* (1970) 11 DLR.
[31] *Commissioners of Customs and Excise v Harz* [1967] 1 AC 760.
[32] *Ibrahim v R* [1914] AC 599 at 609, PC.
[33] *AG v McCabe* [1927] IR 129.

Early decisions such as *R v Warickshall*,[34] and the development of the doctrine of confirmation by subsequent fact, support the reliability principle as the appropriate rationale for this requirement, yet more recent decisions (as will become evident) seem to take a somewhat broader approach.

Historical development

[9.25] Traditionally judges were sceptical of confession evidence for a variety of reasons, including that of the criminal context in which they were being tendered: ie the prisoners came, in the main, from the poorer classes and were not aware of their rights (including the right to silence); criminal punishments were savage (with the death penalty frequently being imposed); little possibility of appeal existed; the accused was incompetent as a witness; and financial difficulties were faced by the accused person in both securing legal representation and the presence of witnesses, in the absence of a legal aid system (see Hailsham LJ in *DPP v Ping Lin*[35]). Moreover, there was a general distrust of the police, given expression by the sentiments of Cave J in *R v Thompson*:[36]

> ... I always suspect these confessions which are supposed to be the offspring of penitence and remorse, and which nevertheless are repudiated by the prisoner at the trial. It is remarkable that it is of very rare occurrence for evidence of a confession to be given when the proof of the prisoner's guilt is otherwise clear and satisfactory; but when it is not clear and satisfactory, the prisoner is not infrequently alleged to have been seized with the desire ... to supplement it with a confession: a desire which vanishes as soon as he appears in a court of justice.

[9.26] Moreover, current psychological support seems to underline the need for scepticism in this area, in so far as even in the absence of any improper behaviour on the part of police officers, persons detained and subjected to questioning experience a heightened sense of suggestibility, which may render them likely to confess to crimes which they have not committed.[37] In *Miranda v Arizona*[38] the United States Supreme Court referred to this as the inherently coercive nature of interrogation.

[9.27] Yet judicial opinion has not always been so trenchantly suspicious of confession evidence. At one stage in the nineteenth century, it was felt that the definition of what constituted an inducement was too broad. Baron Parke, in response to an attempt in *R v Baldry*[39] to exclude a confession on the basis that

---

[34] *R v Warickshall* (1783) 1 Leach 263.
[35] *DPP v Ping Lin* [1976] AC 574.
[36] *R v Thompson* (1893) 2 QB 12 at 18.
[37] Driver, 'Confessions and the Social Psychology of Coercion' (1968) 82 Harv LR 42.
[38] *Miranda v Arizona* (1966) 384 US 436.
[39] *R v Baldry* (1852) 2 Den 430.

the constable had warned the prisoner that he need not say anything and that if he did it could be used in evidence against him, commented: 'The rule has been extended too far and justice and common sense have too frequently been sacrificed at the shrine of mercy.' Erie J, in a similar vein, remarked:

> I am of the opinion that when a confession is well proved it is the best evidence that can be produced; and that unless it be clear that there was either a threat or a promise to induce it, it ought not to be excluded.

[9.28] The question of whether the 'tide of liberalism' should be halted today, given the changed nature of our criminal justice system, has also been more recently raised as *per* Lord Reid in *Commissioners of Customs and Excise v Harz*:[40]

> ... many of the so-called inducements have been so vague that no reasonable man would have been influenced by them, but one must remember that not all accused are reasonable men and women: they may be very ignorant and terrified by the predicament in which they find themselves. So it may have been right to err on the safe side.

Inducement

[9.29] In *R v Smith*,[41] a sergeant major's statement to troops on parade, in the aftermath of a theft, to the effect that none of them would come off parade until he discovered the truth about what happened, was held to constitute an inducement. In *R v Richards*,[42] the Court of Appeal deemed that the statement of a police officer to the appellant (who had lied about his movements) – 'I think it would be better if you made a statement and told me exactly what happened' – amounted to an inducement. In *R v Baldry*, the phrase, 'You had better tell the truth', amounted to an inducement; in *R v Thompson*[43] the phrase, 'It will be the right thing to make a clear breast of it', constituted an inducement. In *AG v Cleary*,[44] the threat to take the accused to the doctor, in the context where such a medical examination would reveal if the woman had recently given birth, was held to amount to a threat for the purposes of the rule.

[9.30] An inducement obviously covers physical threats and non-physical threats (eg non-secret trial), but must not be so remote as to have no effect on the accused. The use of tricks or mistakes is not covered, and does not affect admissibility. Some older English cases indicate spiritual threats will not suffice, which seems illogical.

---

40   *Commissioners of Customs and Excise v Harz* [1967] 1 AC 760.
41   *R v Smith* [1959] 2 QB 35.
42   *R v Richards* [1967] 1 All ER 829.
43   *R v Thompson* (1892) 2 QB 12.
44   *AG v Cleary* (1938) 72 ILTR 84.

[9.31] If there is a series of confession statements involved, an inducement in relation to an earlier, or initial confession, may not be effective in relation to a later one: for example, because of lapse of time (in *R v Smith*, a nine-hour interval). An inducement need not relate to the prosecution in order to be effective. The House of Lords rejected such an argument in *Commissioners of Customs and Excise v Harz*.[45]

Irish case law on confession evidence

[9.32] On examination of the Irish case law in relation to the admissibility of confession evidence, it is interesting to consider the extent to which exclusion is simply a matter of: (a) the application of the voluntariness requirement (as traditionally defined, or more recently adorned with the notion of 'oppression'), or (b) an expression of a distaste for the concept of arrest for the purpose of investigation through the medium of interrogation, or (c) an aspect of the additional concept of illegally obtained evidence (particularly evidence obtained in a deliberate and conscious breach of constitutional rights), now obviously relevant to the realm of confession evidence as well as to that of 'other' types of 'real' evidence. Connected with the particular basis of the exclusion, is the preferred rationale for same.

[9.33] In *People (AG) v Flynn*,[46] Flynn had been convicted of five counts of unlawful carnal knowledge of his niece. As a result of a garda interview with the niece, he had been brought to the garda station for questioning. After two hours, the interviewing garda went for lunch, and the applicant was locked in a cell. Sergeant Mulligan brought a meal to the applicant and a conversation ensued, in the course of which the applicant spoke of his relations with women in England and with his niece – claiming that he had practised 'coitus interruptus' with all of them. As a result, the sergeant advised the applicant it would be 'just as well' for him to 'tell the truth'. When the interviewing garda returned at 2:00 pm, the sergeant told him the applicant was prepared to make a statement, which he did and duly signed. The trial judge admitted the statement, and one of the grounds of appeal to the Court of Appeal centred on whether the statement should have been admitted. Davitt P's reasoning is instructive:

> It seems to us that all the circumstantial evidence favours the view that there must have been some inducement used by Sergeant Mulligan to persuade the applicant to agree to make a statement and that it is more than likely that it was to the effect that it would be better for him to do so.

> Having regard to the probability and to the undoubted fact that the purpose of arresting the applicant and bringing him to the station was to get a statement from

---

[45] *Commissioners of Customs and Excise v Harz* [1967] 1 AC 760.
[46] *People (AG) v Flynn* [1963] IR 255.

him; that though interviewed for nearly two hours in the morning he persisted in denying all his niece's allegations; that he was kept nearly seven hours in custody, and that he was released only when he had made a statement admitting nearly all her allegations, we consider that notwithstanding the evidence of the garda in question, it is impossible to be sure that the statement was voluntarily made.

[9.34] *DPP v Pringle McCann & O'Shea*[47] is a decision illustrating a certain lack of judicial consistency on the question of what constitutes an inducement or threat sufficient to eliminate voluntariness, together with indicating a greater judicial tolerance of lengthy interrogations. Pringle had been convicted of capital murder, which occurred in the course of a bank robbery. The Court of Appeal stated that although forensic and other evidence had been adduced by the state, Pringle would not have been convicted but for the fact that the court of trial construed certain words spoken after arrest by the accused as an admission of guilt, and held also that those words were admissible in evidence.

[9.35] Pringle had been arrested under s 30 of the Offences Against the State Act 1939, and interviewed on numerous occasions and at considerable length. In the course of one of the last of the interviews, the court of trial found, as a fact, that the accused, speaking to the members of An Garda Síochána who were interviewing him said: 'I know that you know I was involved but on the advice of my solicitor I am saying nothing and you will have to prove it all the way.' The court of trial found the words to be admissible and thus constituted an admission of guilt. An appeal was heard, *inter alia*, against that finding. O'Higgins CJ, delivering the judgment of the Court of Criminal Appeal, felt it appropriate to consider the interpretation of the words in the context in which they were spoken.

[9.36] O'Higgins CJ pointed out that during the 43 hours prior to these words being spoken, Pringle had been interviewed for lengthy periods by the gardaí. They had informed him of the evidence against him. He had spoken to his solicitor for approximately two hours following his arrest at 3 pm on 19 July 1980, and on four subsequent occasions prior to making the admission. His solicitor advised him to say nothing in answer to the questions he was asked, and throughout his interviews, when asked to comment on the evidence, he said nothing. He maintained this attitude up to 9:30 am on 21 July. During the said period of questioning (over the weekend) Pringle's girlfriend was also brought to the station and questioned, as was a friend of Pringle's.

[9.37] It is interesting to note the court's use of this context to interpret the statement as an admission of guilt. It is also interesting to note that Pringle's continuing silence, despite lengthy questioning by police – coupled with

---

[47] *DPP v Pringle, McCann & O'Shea* (22 May 1981, unreported), CCA *per* O'Higgins CJ.

consultation with his solicitor and advice to stay silent – which were matters mitigating against the voluntariness of the statement made by the accused in the earlier case of *People (AG) v Flynn* and in the later Supreme Court decision in *Hoey,* here militate in favour of its admission. *Per* O'Higgins CJ, delivering the judgment of the Court of Criminal Appeal:[48]

> The Court has no doubt that when viewed in the context in which they were spoken the words used by the accused were an admission by him that he was involved in the raid and the killing of the Gardaí about which he was being questioned and in respect of which the Gardaí had given him detailed evidence which they had persistently claimed implicated him in those crimes. It is to be noted that the accused did not acknowledge that the Gardaí had a suspicion that he was involved in those crimes – such an acknowledgment would not have implied an admission by him of his guilt in the crimes. Nor was he acknowledging that the Gardaí had a belief in his guilt – again, a statement by him that his interrogators believed in his guilt would not convey any admission on his part that their belief was a correct one. What he in fact said amounted to an admission of his appreciation that those who were accusing him of the crimes of murder and armed robbery knew that he had committed them, and this admission was accompanied by a statement that on the advice of his solicitor he was going to say nothing and an observation that the Gardaí were going to have to prove the case themselves.

> It is to be noted that the acknowledgment which he made of the knowledge of the Gardaí was not qualified in any way. It can only be regarded as an admission by him of his involvement in the crimes they were investigating. The Court has not lost sight of the submission made on the accused's behalf that there was no evidence of the intonation in the accused's voice when he spoke the words. But it is of the opinion that such evidence is not necessary to establish beyond a reasonable doubt their meaning and the absence of such evidence had not in any way weakened the prosecution's case.

[9.38] With regard to the further submission that, first, Pringle's questioning was so oppressive and so undermined the will of the accused as to result in the alleged admission not being a voluntary one, second, that the admission had been procured by improper inducements and threats which equally vitiated it as admissible evidence, and third, that the court should hold that the questioning failed to reach the standard of basic fairness which should have been applied during the period of his custody and so the words should not be admitted in evidence, the court is equally facilitatory, in terms of its admission.

---

[48] *DPP v Pringle, McCann & O'Shea* (22 May 1981, unreported), CCA *per* O'Higgins CJ, at p 23/54.

[9.39] O'Higgins CJ felt there was no evidence to suggest an irregularity in the custody of the accused or breach of his common law or constitutional rights, and so would only consider the claim of inadmissibility based on oppressive questioning and threats and improper inducements. O'Higgins CJ noted that the Supreme Court in *DPP v Breathnach*[49] had adopted the description of oppressive questioning given by McDermott LJ in an address to the Bentham Club and adopted by the Court of Appeal in England in *R v Prager*:[50]

> Questioning which by its nature, duration or other attendant circumstances (including the factor of custody) excites hopes (such as the hope of release) or fears or so affects the mind of the subject that his will crumbles and he speaks when otherwise he would have stayed silent.

The court further approved the statement of Sachs J in *R v Priestly*:[51]

> if ... to my mind this word in the context of the principles under consideration imports something which tends to sap and has sapped the free will which must exist before a confession is voluntary.

[9.40] In applying those principles to this case, O'Higgins CJ noted the accused was interviewed over lengthy periods, but it was not continuous and he had five consultations with his solicitor – two in the afternoon and evening of 19 July, two on the morning and evening of 20 July and one in early hours of 21 July. The court stated:

> The length of the duration of the interviewing of the accused combined with the shortness of the duration of the sleep he obtained do not in themselves establish the validity of the submission now being considered.

He says it is obvious, as the court of trial pointed out, that:

> what may be oppressive as regards a child, an invalid, or an old man or somebody inexperienced in the ways of the world may turn out not to be oppressive when one finds that the accused person is of tough character and an experienced man of the world.[52]

The court continued:

> And so when a court is considering an allegation such as has been made in this case the physical mental and emotional characteristics of the person whose will it is said was undermined must be considered ... It is to be noted that in this case the accused was a man of 42 years of age, in good health, who for some years prior to his arrest had been a fisherman in the Galway area. He was apparently an

---

49 *DPP v Breathnach* (16 February 1981, unreported), SC.
50 *R v Prager* (1972) 56 Cr App Rep 151.
51 *R v Priestly* (1965) 50 Cr App Rep 183.
52 *DPP v Pringle, McCann & O'Shea* (22 May 1981, unreported), CCA *per* O'Higgins CJ, at pp 37–38/54.

experienced man of the world not unused to conditions of physical hardship. It was clearly open to the court of trial to hold that the will of such a man would not have been so undermined by the interview he had experienced and by lack of sleep that he spoke the inculpatory words when otherwise he would have remained silent ...

The accused had had the benefit of five visits from his solicitor prior to the time interviewing recommenced on the morning of July 21, the last having taken place just before he went to bed in the early hours of Monday morning. He was advised by his solicitor that he was entitled to remain silent and that he was not required to answer questions. Those visits and the advice he obtained must have strengthened his resolve and assisted in counteracting any weakness of will which the conditions of his custody and the questioning by the Gardaí may have produced.[53]

Finally, the court pointed out, in relation to an allegation that the incriminating words were spoken as a result of inducements and threats having been made, that:

> ... although such threats and inducements may have been a motive which brought the accused to admit his involvement in the crimes ... they cannot be regarded as having been oppressive in the sense of having so undermined the will of the accused that he spoke when otherwise he would have remained silent.[54]

[9.41] Exactly what is meant by this is unclear, unless it is merely to emphasise the distinct and separate effect of 'oppression' and threat or inducement with regard to admissibility. Any threat which may have ensued from the interviewing of Pringle's girlfriend the court of trial found to be ineffective in so far as its effect was dissipated by subsequent events, including a visit with his solicitor. He had not given this explanation at the 'trial within the trial' or 'voir dire' (hearing before the Special Criminal Court to determine admissibility of the confession). Moreover, the words of the statement were inconsistent with such a desire to shield a friend. On any possible construction of the events and despite the lengthy interrogation and acknowledgment of possible inducements or threats (if not oppression), the statement went in.

[9.42] An interesting contrast with *Flynn* and *Pringle* is provided by the decision of the Supreme Court in *DPP v Hoey*,[55] which contains some evidence of the notion that the purpose of an arrest should not be that of interrogation and, if it

---

[53] *DPP v Pringle, McCann & O'Shea* (22 May 1981, unreported), CCA *per* O'Higgins CJ, at p 38/54.

[54] *DPP v Pringle, McCann & O'Shea* (22 May 1981, unreported), CCA *per* O'Higgins CJ, at p 42/54.

[55] *DPP v Hoey* (16 December 1987, unreported), SC, McCarthy, Walsh, Henchy JJ.

is, the result is an inadmissible confession. This is coupled with a modern interpretation of the voluntariness formula.

[9.43] In that case, as a result of a search carried out under a warrant on 11 August, the gardaí discovered a gun and quantity of ammunition in the premises where Hoey resided. Hoey fled. On 4 November, Hoey presented himself at a garda station with his solicitor, and was interviewed for a period of three hours up until 9:30 pm (in the course of which Hoey spoke to his solicitor at 9:25 pm). At 10:30 pm, until 11:00 pm, the interview resumed, and Hoey made a statement, constituting the only evidence against him. Up until that point, the accused had refused to say anything. His confession occurred in response to a statement to him by a detective to the effect, 'it must be someone in the house. Will I have to get members to go up to your family and see if anyone will take responsibility?' The appellant then admitted responsibility, stating 'I am taking responsibility but I am not involving any other person'. At trial, the Special Criminal Court had admitted the statement, on the basis that the detective's statement had been the occasion, but not the cause, of the admission. The Court of Criminal Appeal had determined that it was open to the Special Criminal Court to accept the detective's evidence that it was not intended as a threat, but to draw the appellant's attention to what would happen if he did not take responsibility.

[9.44] The approaches of the three Supreme Court judges on appeal are interesting. McCarthy J felt it to be immaterial what the detective believed. It may well be, he reasoned, that the statement was a correct summary of the facts, yet that is not the point – nor is the purpose of the statement, 'the purpose can hardly have been other than to get the accused to make an admission'. The test, *per* McCarthy J, is whether or not in the circumstances in which the statement was made, following on and occasioned by the observation of the detective, it can be free from any reasonable doubt that it was voluntary. He concluded it cannot.

What is interesting about McCarthy J's judgment is the extent to which it reveals an echo of the earlier cases (including *Flynn*), indicating dissatisfaction with the police practice of using arrest and questioning in the aftermath of same, for the purpose of investigation.

[9.45] Walsh J's judgment, on the other hand, would seem more indicative of a faithful application of the voluntariness test – albeit involving an assessment of the inducement in the particular context (ie conscious of the 'natural concern' of Hoey for his family). Walsh J concluded:

> ... the effect of the words irrespective of what they were intended to mean was that they were calculated to convey that the appellant's family would be left

undisturbed and free from further interrogation by the Gardaí, if the appellant admitted responsibility.

That amounted to an improper inducement, rendering the confession inadmissible.

[9.46] A concern for the apparently 'oppressive' nature of questioning is evident from the judgment of Henchy J, where again emphasising the insignificance attached to the motive of the detective, he referred to the question having 'vitiated the free will' of the appellant, his free will having been 'overborne', and his resolution to remain silent having been broken. Amongst each of the members of the Supreme Court, it is evident that despite agreement on the issue of the fact that *mala fides* is not necessary on the part of the 'person in authority' for the purposes of the rule and the ultimate conclusion that the confession in this instant is inadmissible, there is no consensus but rather divergence with regard to support for any one rationale of the rule (McCarthy J, police misconduct or the deterrence principle; Walsh J, voluntariness/reliability or the trustworthiness rationale; and Henchy J, oppression – the privilege against incrimination or the protectionist principle). Furthermore, in *DPP v Healy*[56] there is an implicit recognition of the 'inherently coercive nature of interrogation' by Finlay CJ:

> The undoubted right of reasonable access to a solicitor enjoyed by a person who is in detention must be interpreted as being directed towards the vital function of ensuring that such person is aware of his rights and has the independent advice which would be appropriate in order to permit him to reach a truly free decision as to his attitude to interrogation to the making of any statement, be it exculpatory or inculpatory. The availability of advice from a lawyer must, in my view, be seen as a contribution at least towards some measure of equality in the position of the detained person and his interrogators.

[9.47] This issue was further addressed in the subsequent Supreme Court decision of *People (DPP) v Kenny*,[57] where Finlay CJ, delivering the majority judgment, commented that in their judgments in *Healy*, both he and McCarthy J adopted what he termed 'the absolute protection test for evidence obtained by reason of a breach of a detained person's constitutional right of access to a lawyer.' Preference for that principle leads to interesting repercussions for the interpretation of the *O'Brien* formula and, in particular, the meaning of deliberate and conscious breach – fraught with obvious importance and relevance for persons subjected to questioning in garda custody.

---

[56] *DPP v Healy* [1990] ILRM 313.
[57] *People (DPP) v Kenny* [1990] ILRM 569.

'Person in authority'

[9.48] In *Deokinian v R*,[58] the accused confessed to a trusted friend while in police custody. The trusted friend had promised to help him recover money he was alleged to have stolen. The argument was put forward that someone regarded as being 'close to the police' (as here), constituted a 'person in authority' for the purpose of the rule. The Privy Council rejected same on the basis that here, the individual was rather a trusted friend. Yet some scepticism with regard to the requirement of 'person in authority' was evident (Viscount Dilhorne):

> The fact that an inducement is made by a 'person in authority' may make it more likely to operate on the accused's mind and lead him to confess. If the ground on which confessions induced by promises held out by persons in authority are held to be inadmissible is that they may not be true, then it may be that there is a similar risk that in some circumstances the confession may not be true if induced by a promise held out by a person not in authority, for instance, if such a person offers a bribe in return for a confession.

In this context, it is noteworthy that the Criminal Law Revision Committee in England recommended the abolition of the 'person in authority' requirement.[59]

[9.49] Various categories of persons have been held to satisfy this requirement for the purposes of the rule: a high-ranking officer (sergeant) has been held to be a person in authority with respect to soldiers (*R v Smith*[60]), and a headmistress vis-à-vis schoolgirls (*R v McLintock*).[61] In *Deokinian,* the implication was that if someone is known by the accused to be close to the police, that person could be considered a person in authority.

[9.50] In *DPP v Ping Lin*,[62] the House of Lords took into account the fact that a superintendent's remark, alleged to affect the admissibility of an accused's confession, was made subsequent to, and did not precede, the accused's admission. The House of Lords did state that no intention of inducing a confession was necessary, and that it was not necessary to show any improper conduct by the person in authority to render the confession inadmissible.

[9.51] It has also been held that, although the inducement was made by someone not in authority, if it was made in the presence of a person in authority, the position is the same as if that person had himself held out the inducement, unless

---

[58] *Deokinian v R* [1961] 1 AC 20.
[59] Criminal Law Revision Committee, *Eleventh Report: Evidence (General)* Cmnd 4991 (1972).
[60] *R v Smith* [1959] 2 QB 35.
[61] *R v McLintock* [1962] Grim LR 549.
[62] *DPP v Ping Lin* [1976] AC 574.

he indicated dissent from it (*R v Cleary*[63]). In *People v Murphy*,[64] a garda enlisted the help of a citizen, whose remark to the accused, 'Go with the garda, it's for your own good', when followed by a statement from the accused, was treated as that of a person in authority for the purpose of the rule. It has also been held that the confession rule applies if the inducement takes the form of a suggestion from an accused to police.[65]

[9.52] In the Canadian case of *Rothman v The Queen*,[66] the Supreme Court of Canada held that the test of whether someone is a 'person in authority' in relation to the accused is a subjective one. What is important, therefore, is whether or not the accused thinks that person is, for example, a police officer. In this case, therefore, the court admitted statements made by the accused to a police officer in disguise, who was put into the same cell as the accused and whom the accused thought of as a fellow prisoner. With one 'fell swoop', therefore, the Supreme Court preserved and protected the operation of police undercover officers. Again, this decision seems out of line with a trustworthiness rationale. Yet if one takes as true the premise that the threat in order to effect the credibility of the confession must emanate from someone in authority, it is logical to regard the person in question subjectively, from the point of view of the accused, to determine whether or not he is a person in authority, and to regard the effect of the threat objectively if emanating from a person in authority (eg a police officer), yet subjectively if emanating from a person not in authority in relation to the accused.

[9.53] In *People (DPP) v McCann*,[67] McCann had been convicted of the murder of his wife and their foster child who died in a fire at their home. The accused had been arrested under s 30 of the Offences Against the State Act 1939, on suspicion of having committed an offence under s 2 of the Explosive Substances Act 1883, a scheduled offence for the purpose of the Offences Against the State Act 1939. He was brought to Tallaght garda station at 2:07 pm, where he was questioned, but he denied any involvement and refused to answer questions about the explosion. He was visited by his solicitor at 3:34 pm, and for the rest of that day maintained that, on the advice of his solicitor, he had nothing to say. The following day he was interviewed extensively and remained generally silent.

[9.54] On the morning of 6 November 1992 he had met with his two brothers and told them he and his wife had a suicide pact. They asked him to repeat that

---

[63] *R v Cleary* (1963) 48 Cr App Rep 116.
[64] *People v Murphy* [1947] IR 236.
[65] *R v Zaveckas* [1970] 1 All ER 413.
[66] *Rothman v The Queen* (1981) 121 DLR (3d) 578.
[67] *People (DPP) v McCann* [1998] 4 IR 397.

to the gardaí, which he did. At 12 o'clock, midday, one of his brothers came into the interview room and said the applicant wanted to make a statement. The applicant told one of the gardaí he wanted him to ask the questions. His brothers and his solicitor were present. In the course of that interview he admitted starting the fire. At 1:22 pm the member in charge entered the interview room and told the applicant he was released under the provisions of s 30. Nevertheless the applicant returned a couple of minutes later and the interview continued at 1:29 pm with the same parties present.

[9.55] The applicant appealed on the grounds, *inter alia*, that the trial judge erred in law in holding the inculpatory statements admissible, having regard to:

(a)   breach of the Judges' Rules;

(b)   the oppressive circumstances of the applicant's detention; and

(c)   the finding that his brothers were not persons in authority vis-à-vis the applicant having regard to the inducements they made to him while in detention in Tallaght garda station.

[9.56] O'Flaherty J, delivering the judgment of the Court of Criminal Appeal, noted[68] that the applicant was visited by two solicitors at different times during his detention (five visits in all from 'these very experienced solicitors'), was visited by two doctors, given access to tablets he was taking for stress since the fire, and had an opportunity to sleep and eat. There was no suggestion the Custody Regulations 1987 were breached in any material way.

[9.57] The breach of the Judges' Rules alleged was forbidding the questioning of a suspect. However, the suspect here had asked the detective to lead with questions, these were not then for the purpose of cross-examination but to maintain direction and coherence as *per* the trial judge. With regard to inducements, O'Flaherty J reasoned[69]:

> It is not suggested that any threats were offered to the applicant and the judge found that there were no inducements. It is true that the gardaí persistently asked the applicant to tell the truth and indicated that they held a certain view of his guilt. As regards the situation of his brothers, Bernard and Michael, the applicant never made the case that Michael attempted to influence him in any way and as regards Bernard, once again, the most he did was to urge him to tell the truth and, on occasion, to protect the reputation of their family.

[9.58] O'Flaherty J[70] reiterated Walsh J's view in *Shaw*, that a desire to interrogate cannot justify an arrest under s 30. The trial judge had said a s 30

---

68   *People (DPP) v McCann* [1998] 4 IR 397 at 409.
69   *People (DPP) v McCann* [1998] 4 IR 397 at 409.
70   *People (DPP) v McCann* [1998] 4 IR 397 at 410.

detention was not intended to be a 'genteel encounter'. O'Flaherty J expressed the view that:

> [I]t is clear that the very word 'interrogation' means more than some form of gentle questioning and, provided there are no threats or inducements or oppressive circumstances, then the gardaí are always entitled to persist with their questioning of a suspect.

The trial judge had also laid emphasis on the fact that the applicant had a successful background in business and sport, was highly intelligent ('probably functioning at a higher level than his interrogators'[71]) and was highly manipulative. With regard to what constitutes an inducement, O'Flaherty J adopted the following test:[72]

> ... (a) were the words used by the person or persons in authority, objectively viewed, capable of amounting to a threat or promise? (b) Did the accused subjectively understand them as such? (c) Was his confession in fact the result of the threat or promise?

[9.59] Applying that to the case before him, noting that the trial judge had found no such inducement, O'Flaherty J continued:

> It is true that on occasions, in making the admissions he did, the suspect was tearful, distressed and shaking but these symptoms are consistent with the reaction of a person who was recollecting the dreadful deeds that had been done. Further, an argument was advanced before the learned trial judge, and repeated before us, that an unprecedented amount of access had been given to the suspect as regards the visits by his brother. One or other or both brothers had visited him on the three days he was in custody. The Court rejects this submission as quite extraordinary, as did the trial judge.

[9.60] The trial judge had held that the decision in *Hoey* did not extend:

> ... to the pressure emanating from an accused's family, stemming from embarrassment over its dirty linen being washed in public or the consequences for a family member (this was their mother) with a weak heart.[73]

The trial judge had concluded the brothers were not 'persons in authority'. According to Flaherty J, the question of whether the brothers could be said to be persons in authority 'has always been held to mean someone engaged in the arrest, detention, examination or prosecution of the accused or someone acting on behalf of the prosecution.'[74] Hence this ground was also unsuccessful.

---

[71] *People (DPP) v McCann* [1998] 4 IR 397 at 410.
[72] *People (DPP) v McCann* [1998] 4 IR 397 at 411.
[73] *People (DPP) v McCann* [1998] 4 IR 397 at 411.
[74] *People (DPP) v McCann* [1998] 4 IR 397 at 412.

[9.61] *McCann's* case provides an interesting contrast with *Hoey* and is more reminiscent of *Pringle* in its approach to the characteristics of the individual vis-à-vis assessment of 'oppressive circumstances' and its dismissal of pressure, such as visits from family or girlfriend in light of access to solicitors etc. It is also somewhat prescient of the decision of the Special Criminal Court in *Ward*, where he was referred to as an experienced s 30 detainee, yet not in so far as the family or girlfriend visits were viewed therein.

[9.62] Access to a lawyer is also something that can be seen to be used to mitigate other potentially exclusionary factors. This is questionable given the lawyer's partial role in terms of limited access and not continuous presence during interrogation. The limitations placed on legal access are illustrated in *Lavery v Member in Charge Carrickmacross Garda Station,*[75] where this was considered in the context of an extended detention under ss 30(4) and (4)(A) of the Offences Against the State Act 1939,[76] the latter having been in response to the Omagh bombing, and the allegations put to the accused relating to his having stolen a vehicle subsequently used to plant the bomb in Omagh. In a judgment delivered by O'Flaherty J, the Supreme Court held: 'The solicitor is not entitled to be present at the interviews'.[77] *Lavery v Member in Charge Carrickmacross Garda Station*[78] put the death knell on the notion that you would have a constant presence or access to a solicitor in the pre-trial process. It is likely that appeals will go to Strasbourg connected to similar issues.

[9.63] There was also an ongoing concern on the part of the judiciary that, while on one hand they were safeguarding rights or monitoring what happens during the pre-trial period, at the same time the legislature was increasing the powers of detention available to police. Under s 30 of the Offences Against the State Act 1939 you could be arrested and questioned for 24 hours, then a further 24. For many years the gardaí used that provision whenever they needed to in respect of all crime but were always nervous when using it outside subversive activities related to Northern Ireland. For that reason there was gradual lobbying to get powers of detention for 'ordinary' crime and that was the origin of s 4 of the Criminal Justice Act 1984. This introduced a six-hour power of detention after arrest for questioning in relation to most criminal offences, which period could be extended by a further 6 hours. That power of detention was seen at the time as so significant that it could not become operational in law until two things happened:

---

[75] *Lavery v Member in Charge Carrickmacross Garda Station* [1999] 2 IR 390 (SC).
[76] As inserted by the Offences Against the State (Amendment) Act 1998, s 10.
[77] *Lavery v Member in Charge Carrickmacross Garda Station* [1999] 2 IR 390 at 396.
[78] *Lavery v Member in Charge Carrickmacross Garda Station* [1999] 2 IR 390.

1. a garda complaints board was established; and

2. regulations were introduced with regard to the treatment of people in garda custody.

[9.64] The latter took the form of The Criminal Justice Act 1984 (Treatment of Persons in Custody in Garda Síochána Stations) Regulations 1987 (SI 119/ 1987). This introduced a number of requirements: a custody record must now be kept by a member in charge for the purposes of recording. There were new rules about who should be present, how many people and how long the sessions should be etc. The significance of these regulations was that they supplemented what had existed up until then as governing the pre-trial process, ie the Judges' Rules, a series of administrative directions about how to treat people after arrest. The Judges' Rules were fairly minimal in terms of what they directed. What is significant, however, and a characteristic shared by both the judge's rules and the regulations is that neither is mandatory in effect if there is a breach. If there is a failure to follow the judge's rules or if there is a failure to comply with the regulations pertaining to custody introduced under the 1984 Act, it is quite clear the just as the judge's rules themselves were never regarded as mandatory in effect, in relation to the 1984 Act any breach of the custody regulations will not be mandatory in effect and will not lead to the automatic exclusion of a confession."

[9.65] There has been a plethora of case law which involved breaches of regulations which have not on every occasion been successful because the rules are discretionary in effect and not mandatory.

The third element which has come into play more recently, in terms of the monitoring of pre-trial process, is the introduction of audio-visual taping of interrogation sessions. Given the extended regime of detention subsequent to arrest, this is even more significant (see earlier paras **2.91–2.92**).

[9.66] The Offences Against the State Act 1939, s 30 made provision for detention for a period of 24hrs + 24hrs. Section 4 of the Criminal Justice Act 1984 introduced detention for 6hrs + 6hrs in the context of all crime. In 2006 the Criminal Justice Act of 2006, s 9 added another 12hrs to that latter provision, so it became detention for 6hrs + 6hrs + 12hrs = 24hrs. The Criminal Justice (Drug Trafficking) Act 1996 s 2 then allowed 7 days' detention, which would previously have been thought extraordinary. That period is broken up and there must be a review after 48 hours by a District Court judge to check whether there is sufficient evidence to allow arrest to continue. Judicial review in that sense is built into the Act and had to be because of the ECHR requirements and, specifically, the decision of *Brogan v United Kingdom*,[79] which ruled that you could not have detention of that length without review. Nonetheless the

---

[79] *Brogan v United Kingdom* (1989) 11 EHRR 117.

landscape of detention is now immeasurably altered. The Criminal Justice Act 2007 provided that 7 day detention would also apply in the context of certain serious offences not just drug trafficking;[80] while the Criminal Justice (Amendment) Act 2009 extended the ambit of 7 day detention even further by applying it to the organised crime offences under the 2007 Act. Part 4 of the Criminal Justice (Amendment) Act 2009 added a further possible 24 hours to a section 30 detention (subject to judicial authorisation). There have also under the 2009 Act been considerable changes to the procedure applicable in seeking judicial approval of such extensions of detention. (See paras **2.91–2.92**).

[9.67] In *C v DPP*,[81] admissibility of the accused's statements was challenged on the grounds that at the time when they were made, the accused had had one hour's sleep in a period of 30 hours and had, in the early hours of the morning at the party, consumed a significant quantity of alcohol. Counsel for the accused argued that there was an onus on the state to show beyond reasonable doubt that a statement was voluntary, and that there was no physical or psychological pressure placed on the accused, or excessive questioning. This was not, it was argued, overcome here. It was also contended that the trial judge had a discretion to exclude statements if the manner in which they were obtained fell below acceptable standards of fairness, which it was contended they did in this case because of the accused's lack of sleep and amount of drink he had consumed. Refusing leave to appeal, the Court of Criminal Appeal held that the trial judge found, as a matter of fact, that the accused was in a perfectly coherent condition at all times and seemed perfectly normal to the doctor, and that that finding should not be disturbed. The emphasis laid on the doctor's opinion here, however, is questionable in light of the fact that the doctor was there primarily to take samples and did not carry out a full medical examination.

Constitutional dimension

[9.68] Relevant also, in the context of the admissibility of confession statements, is the issue of constitutional rights. The pre-trial period, which covers that entire period between the first encounter with the police, right up until the individual faces a court of law, is one fraught with potential for the abuse of rights. Many of these rights have a constitutional dimension, and indeed the courts have recognised that a necessary corollary of the vindication of the accused's rights in

---

[80] Section 50 of the Criminal Justice Act 2007 provides that 7 day detention provisions are extended to murder involving use of a firearm or explosive; murder to which s 3 of the Criminal Justice Act 1990 applies; an offence under s 15 of the Non-Fatal Offences Against the Person Act involving use of a firearm.

[81] *C v DPP* (31 July 2001, unreported), CCA.

the course of the trial itself is the recognition of such rights in the pre-trial period, without which the accused would be greatly disadvantaged at trial.

[9.69] Underlying all of this are issues related to powers of arrest, detention, interrogation etc. In so far as they are related to the issue of the admissibility of confession evidence (which by its nature will have been obtained in the course of the pre-trial period), these will now be addressed.

[9.70] Article 40.4.1° of the Constitution enunciates the general principle that 'No citizen shall be deprived of his personal liberty, save in accordance with law.' Traditionally, the legitimate deprivation of liberty was solely achieved through arrest. In *Dunne v Clinton*,[82] Hanna J declared:

> In law there can be no half-way house between liberty of the suspect, unfettered by restraint, and an arrest. If a person under suspicion, voluntarily agrees to go to a police station to be questioned, his liberty is not interfered with, as he can change his mind at any time. If, having been examined, he is asked and voluntarily agrees to remain, he is still a free subject and can leave at any time. But a practice has grown up of 'detention' as distinct from arrest. It is, in effect, keeping a suspect in custody – without making any definite charge against him and with the intimation in some form of words or gesture, that he is under restraint and will not be allowed to leave. As, in my opinion, there could be no such thing as notional liberty, this so-called detention amounts to arrest and the suspect has in law been arrested and in custody, during the period of his detention.

The extent to which the above statement continues to represent the law must be questioned in light of developments such as the power of detention consequent on arrest, introduced into the 'normal' criminal justice process by s 4 of the Criminal Justice Act 1984.

[9.71] Along with such modifications have come additional safeguards applying to the pre-trial detention period. Prior to consideration thereof, however, it is useful to note the extent to which common law and constitutional rights have been both recognised and vindicated by the courts in the pre-trial period. The right to know the reason for the arrest, and the charge against one, was recognised in England in *Christie v Leachinsky*[83] and adopted in Ireland in *Re O'Laighleis*.[84] In the latter case, however, the appellant did not satisfy the court that he did not know why he was being arrested. It was held, moreover, that such would not have rendered his detention unlawful. In *People v Walsh*,[85] O'Higgins

---

[82]   *Dunne v Clinton* [1930] IR 366.

[83]   *Christie v Leachinsky* [1947] AC 573.

[84]   *Re Ó Laighleis* [1960] IR 93.

[85]   *People v Walsh* [1980] IR 294.

CJ held that the failure to inform the appellant at the moment of arrest of the reason for same (ostensibly because of the large number of people present in the public house where the arrest took place), did not affect the legality of his subsequent detention. The appellant had not asked the reason for the arrest and, shortly thereafter, had been informed of same at the station.

[9.72] In *DPP v McCormack*,[86] the defendant was charged under s 49(2) of the Road Traffic Act 1961, as inserted by s 10 of the Road Traffic Act 1994. The garda had informed the defendant that she was of the opinion that he had consumed intoxicating liquor, that she required he provide a breath specimen, and of the penalty for non-compliance. The breath specimen proved positive and she arrested him. The District Court judge found as a fact that the garda did not inform the defendant that he was being arrested under s 49(8) of the Road Traffic Act 1961, nor pursuant to any statutory provision, nor in layman's language or otherwise that he was being arrested relating to the consumption of intoxicants, nor that he was being arrested. On a case stated to the High Court, McGuinness J held that, provided an arrested person knew why he had been arrested, the arrest was valid, and this might be communicated to him without the use of technical or precise language, or even implied to him if the circumstances were such he must know of the general nature of the offence for which he was being arrested.

[9.73] The recognition of the right to counsel had been established in the context of a criminal trial in *State (Healy) v Donoghue*[87] (and a consequent right to be informed of same – see Griffin J in the Supreme Court). In the pre-trial period, some doubt lingered as to the constitutional right to counsel and the corresponding right to be informed of such a right.

[9.74] The Supreme Court decision in *DPP v Healy*,[88] however, quelled such doubts, and placed said right on a sound constitutional footing. The right, moreover, can be exercised on the accused's behalf by relatives or friends and once a solicitor has arrived at the station, the accused has a right of access to him. The argument that the police refused or delayed immediate access by the solicitor, taking the view that it was 'bad manners' to interrupt the interrogation, was not accepted as sufficient.

[9.75] The decision is interesting from a number of perspectives, not least for the purpose of arrest itself. Reliance had been placed by the prosecution on the fact that the probable consequence of permitting the interview to be interrupted by

---

[86] *DPP v McCormack* [1999] 4 IR 158.
[87] *State (Healy) v Donoghue* [1976] IR 325.
[88] *DPP v Healy* [1990] ILRM 313.

the arrival of a solicitor would be that the accused would change his mind and stop making an incriminating statement.

[9.76] The appellant, on the contrary, contended that the prosecution's reason for postponing access on the basis of permitting the statement to be made without interruption, was unreasonable, having regard to the fact that it violated one of the major objectives of the right of access to a solicitor, namely, that of securing for the detainee information and advice with regard to his rights – in particular, the right of avoiding self-incrimination. Significantly, this view was endorsed by members of the court *per* Finlay CJ (Walsh and Hedermann JJ concurring):

> The undoubted right of reasonable access to a solicitor enjoyed by a person who is in detention must be interpreted as being directed towards the vital function of ensuring that such person is aware of his rights and has the independent advice which would be appropriate in order to permit him to reach a truly free decision as to his attitude to interrogation or to the making of any statement, be it exculpatory or inculpatory.

Griffin J stated:

> The main, if not the sole, purpose of the right of access to a legal adviser is to enable the detained person to obtain advice as to his rights, and in particular advice as to whether, in the circumstances, it would be in his best interests to make a statement or to refuse to make one.

The court, as a whole, perceived the right of access to a solicitor as a constitutional right – part of the fundamental requirement of fair procedure which must be adhered to throughout the pre-trial period. It did not, however, address the issue of whether there was a right to be informed of such right.

[9.77] The right to be brought before a court within a reasonable period of time was a logical consequence of the traditional function of arrest itself. In relation to arrests on foot of a warrant, such a right originated from s 15 of the Criminal Justice Act 1951. In relation to arrests made without a warrant, the right has its origins in common law. The issue arose as to what constituted a 'reasonable time'. In *Dunne v Clinton*,[89] it was stated:

> no hard and fast rule can be laid down to cover every case. It must depend on many circumstances such as time, the place of the arrest, and the number of the accused, whether a Peace Commissioner is easily available and such other matters as may be relevant.

[9.78] In *Doherty v Liddane*,[90] in an action for damages for false imprisonment, 26 hours was held to be excessive: a court is always available within 24 hours. In

---

[89] *Dunne v Clinton* [1930] IR 366.
[90] *Doherty v Liddane* [1940] Ir Jur Rep 58.

People v Shaw,[91] Costello J adopted the approach of the English courts in *John Lewis and Co Ltd v Timms*:[92]

> The question throughout shall be: has the arrester brought the arrested person to a place where his alleged offence can be dealt with as speedily as is reasonably possible? All the circumstances of the case must be taken into consideration in deciding whether this requirement is complied with. A direct route and rapid progress are no doubt matters for consideration, but they are not the only matters. Those who arrest must be persuaded of the guilt of the accused, they cannot bolster up their assurances or the strength of their case by seeking further evidence and detaining the arrested man in the meantime or taking him to some spot where they may or may not find further evidence. Whether there is evidence that the steps taken were unreasonable or the delay too great is a matter for the judge.

[9.79] A delay in bringing a person to trial was alleged in *State (O'Connell) v Fawsitt*[93] and *State (Brennan) v District Justice Conlon*.[94] In the former case, the principles to be applied were set out by the Chief Justice:

> A person charged with an indictable offence and whose chances of a fair trial have been prejudiced by excessive delay should not be put to the risk of being arraigned and pleading before the jury.[95]

That principle was relied upon by the applicants in *Hannigan v District Justice Clifford* and *O'Flynn v District Justice Clifford*,[96] who argued that to charge them in respect of offences alleged to have been committed 18 months previously, was to subject them to such delay as to seriously prejudice their right to a fair trial. The applicants had been arrested on 3 September 1986 under s 30 of the Offences Against the State Act 1939, released without charge and subsequently charged on 8 February 1988 in relation to offences alleged to have been committed on 7 August 1986.

[9.80] Walsh J in the Supreme Court, approved of the statement of principle in the earlier decisions, but distinguished those cases from the present application in so far as in the former cases the alleged delay was one in bringing a person to trial after he had been charged. Walsh J acknowledged that:

> ... excessive delay may prejudice the chance of a fair trial for a variety of reasons such as a disappearance or death of witnesses, failure of human memory and many other causes.

---

[91] *People v Shaw* [1982] IR 1.

[92] *John Lewis and Co Ltd v Timms* [1952] AC 676, *per* Porter LJ.

[93] *State (O'Connell) v Fawsitt* [1986] IR 362.

[94] *State (Brennan) v District Justice Conlon* [1986] ILRM 635.

[95] [1986] ILRM 635 at 652.

[96] *Hannigan v District Justice Clifford and O'Flynn v District Justice Clifford* [1990] ILRM 65.

The essential difference here, however, *per* Walsh J, was that there was no suggestion of any delay between the bringing of charges and the progress to trial:

> What is in issue ... is what is claimed to be the unfair delay between the initial arrests under s 30 of the Offences Against the State Act 1939, and the bringing of the charges in February 1988.

Walsh J stated that while:

> it is quite clear that once a charge has been brought then the matter must be prosecuted without undue delay or otherwise that might prejudice a fair trial.

> However with regard to the interval between the forming of suspicion and a decision to charge everything depends upon the circumstances of the case.

[9.81] While these circumstances may indicate that the charges were not laid until an inexcusable delay had occurred, and so an accused could be hampered for similar reasons to those given in *State (O'Connell) v Fawsitt*, there was *per* Walsh J:

> ... no evidence in the present case that any circumstances existed to indicate that the prosecuting authorities were in a position to institute their prosecution before they did so or that the delay which occurred between the commission of the offences and the bringing of the charges against persons who were already suspected persons for 18 months was such as could lead to the conclusion that a right to a fair trial had been prejudiced.

[9.82] It would seem that although the same principles apply, therefore, to a delay in charging an accused as those relating to being brought to trial, the presumption that delay will prejudice the accused in the latter context is much stronger than in the former where a case will have to be made on the circumstances.

Development and change of the arrest process

[9.83] In this context, it is useful to comment briefly on the changing nature of the function of arrest, and the extent of the requirement to bring an arrested person before a court within a reasonable period of time.

[9.84] The reason why this is of such importance in the context of hearsay, and in particular confession evidence, is because it is the rules in relation to arrest and detention which, in governing the pre-trial interrogation process, impact upon the admissibility of confession evidence. Although the manner in which the statements were obtained is only one factor pertaining to admissibility (the other factor here being voluntariness), it is a very significant one. Given that many cases still focus on the admissibility of confessions (eg *Ward*) and that powers of detention have been the subject of considerable augmentation by the legislature (eg Criminal Justice (Drug Trafficking) Act 1996), it might be expected that future case law will focus on exactly these pre-trial considerations in relation to confessions, in much the same way as the laws on search and seizure have become encrusted with constitutional argument.

[9.85] The advent of a practice of 'helping the gardaí with their inquiries' and the practice of interrogation consequent on arrest, grew up in the aftermath of the use of s 30 of the Offences Against the State Act 1939, which provided the gardaí with a power to detain persons for an initial period of 24 hours, followed by a further potential period of 24 hours.

[9.86] Police interrogation skills were thus 'honed' (on the basis *per* Stephens that it is far easier to sit in the shade rubbing hot pepper into some poor devil's eyes, than search about under the hot sun looking for clues[97]). Extension of detention periods under s 30 of the 1939 Act are grounded on the suspicion of the officer that the detainee has committed a scheduled offence. This suspicion has to be expressly proved at the subsequent trial of the accused, to legitimate his detention. It cannot be inferred either from the signing of the formal direction or by hearsay evidence of a verbal direction. Thus in *People (DPP) v Byrne*,[98] where the Chief Superintendent concerned had died and could therefore not testify as to his state of mind at the time of the extension, at trial an incriminating statement made by the accused during that extended period was deemed inadmissible. Walsh J stated that:

> ... the production of the document in question could not be offered as proof of what was the state of mind of Chief Superintendent Joy when he directed an extension of the period of arrest. Apart from the hearsay nature of the evidence, it made it impossible for any examination or cross-examination to be made of the actual state of mind of the Chief Superintendent which is necessary proof of fact in the case.

[9.87] Hence Walsh J held that as it was well-established that a person who is under arrest, but whose arrest is not in accordance with law, is being held in violation of his constitutional right to liberty, and any evidence obtained during that period is inadmissible, and a confession made during the extended period of detention, should be excluded.

[9.88] There followed a demand for police powers of detention for the purposes of interrogation in relation to 'ordinary' or 'non-subversive' crime. The police were then using s 30 of the 1939 Act in relation to 'ordinary' offences, but this was felt to be a practice of doubtful validity (unnecessarily so, as witness the

---

[97] Stephens, *A Digest of the Law of Evidence* (12th edn, London: Macmillan and Co, 1936).
[98] *People (DPP) v Byrne* [1989] ILRM 613.

subsequent Supreme Court decision in *DPP v Quilligan*,[99] where the Supreme Court sanctioned the use of s 30 in relation to both 'subversive' and 'non-subversive' crime).

[9.89] The Criminal Justice Act 1984, s 4 thus made provision for a period of detention of an initial six hours, followed by a further potential six-hour period following an arrest, in relation to offences carrying at least a five-year period of imprisonment. Such a power did not come into force until the introduction, however, of a series of regulations regarding the treatment of persons in garda custody and a Garda Complaints Tribunal. Section 9 of the Criminal Justice Act 2006 amended s 4 of the Criminal Justice Act 1984 to provide for a possible additional twelve hours on the approval of chief superintendent.

Provisions regarding the treatment of persons in custody

The Judges' Rules

[9.90] Traditional safeguards regarding the treatment of persons in garda custody following an arrest were provided by the 'Judges' Rules'. The Judges' Rules were, in essence, a series of administrative directions, originally handed down by the judiciary in England in *R v Voisin*,[100] but since updated. The rules, as they apply here, are set out by Walsh J in *People (AG) v Cummins*.[101]

[9.91] It is important to remember that these rules are purely discretionary in effect, and breach of them does not automatically lead to the exclusion of evidence. They are as follows:

(1) When a police officer is investigating a crime there is no objection to his putting questions to persons from whom he thinks useful information may be obtained.

(2) When a police officer has made up his mind to charge someone with a crime, that person should be cautioned before further questioning.

(3) Persons 'in custody' should not be questioned without the usual caution being administered.

(4) If the prisoner wishes to volunteer a statement, the usual caution should be administered, ending with the words 'be given in evidence'.

(5) The caution administered to a formally charged prisoner should be 'do you wish to say anything in answer to the charge? You are not obliged to say anything unless you wish to do so, but whatever you say will be taken down in writing; and may be given in evidence'.

---

[99] *DPP v Quilligan* [1987] ILRM 606.
[100] *R v Voisin* [1918] 1 KB 531.
[101] *People (AG) v Cummins* [1972] IR 312.

(6)   The absence of a caution before a statement does not automatically exclude that statement, but a caution should be given as soon as possible.

(7)   If a voluntary statement has been made by the prisoner, further questioning should only be as to the details of same.

(8)   In the case of two or more persons charged, the statements of one should be shown to the other, yet should not be meant to invite a reply.

(9)   A statement should, if possible, to taken down in writing and signed.

[9.92] It should also be noted that in *Travers v Ryan*,[102] Finlay P stated that:

> in relation to a person under 14 years of age it is most desirable in the interests of justice that, unless there are practical impossibilities, if they are suspected of crime they should not be questioned except in the presence of a parent or some person 'of an adult kind' in the position of guardian.

By implication, these same principles should apply to extensions under s 30 of the Offences Against the State Act 1939.

[9.93] In essence, the weakness of the Judges' Rules is that they are not mandatory in effect, merely granting to the trial judge a discretion as to whether to exclude evidence obtained by reason of their breach or not.

The Custody Regulations 1987

[9.94] The Criminal Justice Act 1984 (Treatment of Persons in Custody in Garda Síochána Stations) Regulations 1987[103] introduced under the Criminal Justice Act 1984, are of similar effect to the Judges' Rules. Section 7(3) of the 1984 Act provides:

> A failure on the part of any member of the Garda Síochána to observe any provision of the regulations shall not of itself render that person liable to any criminal or civil proceedings or of itself reflect the lawfulness of the custody of the detained person, or the admissibility in evidence of any statement made by him.

The main thrust of the Custody Regulations is to provide for a monitoring of the accused's treatment in custody by means of a 'custody record' kept by a designed officer in charge; regulated sessions of interrogation; and provision for rest periods etc.

[9.95] In *DPP v Spratt*,[104] O'Hanlon J interpreted s 7(3) of the 1984 Act as follows:

---

[102] *Travers v Ryan* [1985] ILRM 163.
[103] SI 119/1987.
[104] *DPP v Spratt* [1995] 1 IR 585.

The phrase 'of itself' is obviously an important one in the construction of the statutory provisions, and I interpret the sub-section as meaning that non-observance of the Regulations is not to bring about automatically the exclusion from evidence of all that was done and said while the accused person was in custody. It appears to be left to the court of trial to adjudicate in every case as to the impact the non-compliance with the regulations should have on the case for the prosecution.

[9.96] In *DPP v Devlin*,[105] Budd J held that, in addition to adjudicating on whether there had been a breach of the Custody Regulations, the trial judge must assert what impact that had on the case for the prosecution. This was applied in *DPP v Cullen*,[106] where the respondent had been charged with drink driving, which was dismissed by the District Justice on the basis of breaches of the Custody Regulations whereby the respondent had not been handed a notice of his rights while in custody, and had not had his rights read to him or explained to him. Ó Caoimh J concluded the District Justice had erred in not having gone on to consider the effect of these breaches on the prosecution case. He indeed expressed a doubt whether, given that it was mandatory for a suspect to give a sample, any failure regarding the Custody Regulations would have a causative link to the evidence justifying its exclusion.

[9.97] With regard to monitoring the pre-trial period, the *Martin Committee Report*,[107] included recommendations of electronic/video recording of interrogation sessions in the garda station. Section 27 of the 1984 Act made provision for the introduction of same. The effectiveness of such presupposes the absence of an increase in the number of confessions obtained on the way to the station.

[9.98] In *People (DPP) v O'Connell*,[108] the appellant had been questioned in excess of the four-hour period authorised by the Custody Regulations. He had been told he was not obliged to continue but he had declined rests. The Court of Criminal Appeal held that the regulations (reg 12(4)) did not allow waiver by an arrested person (this was confirmed in *People (DPP) v Reddan & Hannon*[109]). In *O'Connell* other breaches of the regulations, including failure to make entries in the custody record, failure to contact the appellant's solicitor and the fact that the appellant had no sleep, all contributed to the Court of Criminal Appeal's

---

[105] *DPP v Devlin* [1998] IEHC 138, Budd J.
[106] *DPP v Cullen* [2001] IEHC 21, Ó Caoimh J.
[107] *Report of the Committee to Enquire into Certain Aspects of Criminal Procedure* (1990) (Chairman Judge Frank Martin).
[108] *People (DPP) v O'Connell* [1995] 1 IR 244.
[109] *People (DPP) v Reddan & Hannon* [1995] 3 IR 560.

decision that the inculpatory statement made by the appellant should not have been admitted.

[9.99] In *DPP v Spratt*[110] it was held that where a breach of the Custody Regulations has occurred, it should be determined whether the accused has been thereby prejudiced and whether any information might not have been obtained, save for the breach. With regard to the relationship between the Judges' Rules and the Custody Regulations, Keane J in *People (DPP) v Darcy*,[111] emphasised that a suspect is entitled to the protection of both.

[9.100] One controversial aspect of the rules is their provision to do with the undesirability of questioning an accused with regard to the charge on foot of which he is arrested. This is, indeed, indicative of the perspective of some of the function of the arrest (ie not as a means of garnering information), but indicative of the culmination of the investigative process. As we have seen, provision for after-arrest detention has to some extent weakened that proposition; yet even prior to that, the police had developed a practice of arresting persons on what was known as a 'holding charge' – ie, a more minor charge than the original offence – and then questioning the accused with regard to that, usually significantly more important, offence.

[9.101] In *DPP v Quilligan*,[112] the Supreme Court addressed that issue, and effectively sanctioned the use of such holding charges (such as the malicious damage arrest in that case, where the accused were then questioned about a murder) as long as there was 'some reality' to the more minor charge – even if it was both submerged in time and overshadowed in importance, by the graver offence.

[9.102] The approach was further endorsed by the decision of the Court of Criminal Appeal in *People (DPP) v Howley*,[113] where the court considered an application for leave to appeal against a murder conviction which related to the trial judge's admission of a statement of an incriminatory nature. The applicant had been arrested under s 30 of the Offences Against the State Act 1939 on suspicion of having committed a scheduled offence (maiming cattle). He was interrogated with regard to the disappearance of the deceased. A further detention period was sanctioned, in the course of which, he made a statement admitting the murder.

---

[110] *DPP v Spratt* [1995] 2 ILRM 117.
[111] *People (DPP) v Darcy* (29 July 1997, unreported), HC.
[112] *DPP v Quilligan* [1987] ILRM 606.
[113] *People (DPP) v Howley* [1989] ILRM 629 (affirmed by the Supreme Court), [1988] IECCA 2.

[9.103] The applicant contended that to render the statement admissible, the prosecution must establish that the primary or predominant motive for the arrest was the necessity to investigate the maiming of cattle – which they had failed to do. The trial judge had ruled solely on the basis that the arrest was lawful, hence the statement was admissible, also noting, however, that the offence was a real offence.

[9.104] Finlay CJ referred in *Howley* to *People (DPP) v Walsh*,[114] where a similar issue arose and Walsh J commented:

> The fact that there was a great disproportion between the nature of the offence in question and that the greater concentration of police effort was on the investigation into the more serious of them, namely the murder charge, is not in itself sufficient to establish as a reasonable probability that the arrest in respect of malicious damage charge was simply a colourable device to hold the accused in custody for an ulterior purpose on an alleged offence in which the Guards had no interest.

[9.105] Finlay CJ also referred to *Quilligan*,[115] which again supports the view that once there was a bona fide suspicion, the fact that the importance of the offence was very slight in relation to the offence of murder being investigated was not significant. Finlay CJ, therefore, rejected the predominant motive test and saw the test as being that:

> the court must ascertain whether the arrest under s 30 is a genuine bona fide arrest carried out on a suspicion actually held of complicity by the applicant in a real schedule offence. If it is, then the arrest is and remains lawful and statements made which otherwise cannot be objected to on grounds of fairness or the form of questioning with regard to any matter must be admissible in evidence. If on the other hand, the arrest is made a device to secure the detention of a person who is not really under a bona fide suspicion with regard to the commission of a real scheduled offence but whom the Gardaí wish to interview with regard to murder which is not a scheduled offence then the position is different.

[9.106] McCarthy J in *People (DPP) v Healy*,[116] in commenting with regard to the function and/or purpose of the s 30 power of detention after arrest, endorsed what Walsh J stated in *Quilligan's* case:

> The object of the powers given by section 30 is not to permit the arrest of people simply for the purpose of subjecting them to questioning. Rather is it for the purpose of investigating the commission or suspected commission of a crime by the person already arrested and to enable that investigation to be carried on without the possibility of obstruction or other interference which might occur if

---

[114] *People v Walsh* (25 July 1986) SC.
[115] *DPP v Quilligan* [1987] ILRM 606.
[116] *DPP v Healy* [1990] ILRM 313 *per* Walsh J.

the suspected person were not under arrest. Section 30 is part of the statute law of the state permanently in force and it does not permit of any departure from normal police procedure save as to the obligation to bring the arrested person before a court as soon as reasonably possible.[117]

[9.107] Again in *Hannigan v Clifford*,[118] Walsh J in the Supreme Court commented that *Quilligan* had laid down the principles governing s 30 arrests: 'persons cannot be arrested under that section simply for the purpose of enabling evidence to be gathered'. Despite a suggestion by Griffin J in *People v Shaw* that the *O'Brien ratio* (see paras **4.50–4.52** on search and seizure; illegally obtained evidence) was confined to instances of real evidence, and did not apply to the question of the admissibility of confession evidence, it seems to now be generally accepted (see the comment of O'Higgins CJ in *People v Lynch*) that the said formula is also applicable to confession statements. Hence, a statement may well be voluntary and yet not admissible.

[9.108] In *People v Shaw*,[119] Shaw's constitutional right to liberty was held to be superseded by the constitutional right to life of the victim. Hence, although there was a deliberate and conscious breach of constitutional rights, there were extraordinary excusing circumstances for that breach. Interesting in that decision are two contrasting views as to the function of arrest. *Per* Walsh J:

> No person may be arrested (with or without warrant) for the purpose of interrogation or the securing of evidence from that person. If there exists a practice of arresting persons for the purpose of 'assisting the police with their enquiries' it is unlawful. In such circumstances the phrase is no more than a euphemism for false imprisonment.

Per Griffin J:

> I do not think it is correct to state without qualification that no person may be arrested with or without a warrant for the purpose of interrogation, or securing evidence from that person.

Griffin J stated further with regard to the hierarchy of rights:

> Although the right to personal liberty is one of the fundamental rights, if a balance is to be struck between one person's right to personal liberty, for some hours or even days and another person's right to protection against danger to his life, then in any civilised society in my view, the latter right must prevail in circumstances such as those which confronted Superintendent Reynolds.

---

[117] *DPP v Quilligan* [1987] ILRM 606 at 624.
[118] *Hannigan v Clifford* [1990] ILRM 65.
[119] *People v Shaw* [1982] IR 1.

[9.109] In *People v Lynch*,[120] there was a conflict of evidence with regard to whether the appellant had remained voluntarily in the police station.[121] Due to a failure to resolve same by the jury, the confession was ultimately excluded on the basis that the accused had been subjected to 22 hours of interrogation where, *per* O'Higgins CJ:

> ... so obstructive and dominating a feature of this interrogation was its length, that such should not have been ignored or overlooked. The fact that the appellant was subjected for almost 22 hours to sustained questioning, never had the opportunity of communicating with his family and friends and never being permitted to rest or sleep until he made an admission of guilt, all amount to such circumstances of harassment and oppression as to make it unjust and unfair to admit in evidence anything he said.

[9.110] O'Higgins CJ felt that the trial judge 'in exercising his discretion ignored the features of oppression, harassment and fatigue which should have caused the statements, even if prima facie voluntary, to be excluded'. It is also interesting to note O'Higgins CJ's rejection of Griffin J's suggestion as to a restriction of the *O'Brien* ratio to real evidence:

> Once the Constitution has been violated for the purpose of securing a confession on that ground alone, the fruits of the violation must be excluded from evidence. Nor can it be said that the matter can safely be left to a decision on the fairness or the voluntary nature of a statement. If such confessions were ever admitted in evidence, because it was voluntary or because it was fairly taken or for any other reason, then the courts would, in the words of Warren CJ, 'be made party to lawless invasions of the constitutional rights of citizens by permitting unhindered governmental use of the fruits of such invasions'.

The basis on which the statement was excluded in *Lynch* is uncertain. It was not on the basis of the unlawful deprivation of liberty and consequent breach of constitutional rights adhering thereto (due to a factual discrepancy, remaining unresolved), nor it would seem on the basis of the voluntary nature of the statement (despite reference to 'oppression') but rather on the basis of fairness. Is this a forerunner of the *Healy* decision's reference to a constitutional right to fairness of procedure in the pre-trial process perhaps, which will now operate to subsume the hitherto group of miscellaneous rights in that period?

If the latter proposition is correct, the implication is that the 'Judges' Rules' in Ireland have not been alone in having amended or augmented the 'voluntariness' requirement, in so far as a reference to oppression is included.

---

[120] *People v Lynch* [1982] IR 64.
[121] Cf, the later case of *People (DPP) v Conroy* returned said determination to the realm of judicial activity: *People (DPP) v Conroy* [1986] IR 460.

[9.111] Some expansion of the *Ibrahim*[122] formula did occur in the United Kingdom, when 'oppression' was introduced as part of the principles in the introduction to the Judges' Rules in 1964. This concept was subsequently defined in *R v Priestly*[123] as importing something:

> ... which tends to sap, and has sapped that freewill which must exist before a confession is voluntary – whether or not there is oppression in an individual case depends upon many elements. They included such things as the length of time of any individual period of questioning, the length of time intervening between periods of questioning, whether the accused person has been given proper refreshment or not, and the characteristics of the person who makes the statement. What may be oppressive as regards a child, an individual or an old man or somebody inexperienced in the ways of this world may turn out not to be oppressive when one finds that the accused is of a tough character and an experienced man of the world.

This was followed in *R v Praeger*[124] and adopted by the Irish Court of Criminal Appeal in *People (DPP) v McNally* and *People (DPP) v Breathnach*, where it would seem that the lack of oppression was regarded as part of the compliance with the voluntariness requirement.

[9.112] In Canada, the concept of oppression is seen not as a separate concept but one of the factors taken into account in determining whether the accused gave his statement voluntarily within the *Ibrahim* formula. In *Horwath v Queen*[125] a 17-year-old youth, unintentionally but without his consent, was put into a light hypnotic state and made inculpatory statements. The trial judge had described the accused's mental condition at the end of the interview as being one of complete emotional disintegration. The Supreme Court held, in restoring the trial judge's verdict, that the voluntariness test in *Ibrahim* was not exhaustive in relation to the circumstances where a statement was involuntary and therefore inadmissible. Here the statement was not voluntary, because of the way it was induced. In *Ward v Queen*[126] it was held, in the case of an accused giving statements to police after a serious car accident, when the accused was visibly in a state of shock, that the:

> ... examination of whether there was any type of advantage or fear of prejudice inducing the statement is simply an investigation of whether the statement was freely and voluntarily made in considering the mental condition of the accused to

---

[122] *Ibrahim v R* [1914] AC 599.
[123] *R v Priestly* (1965) 51 Cr App Rep 1.
[124] *R v Praeger* [1972] 1 All ER 1114.
[125] *Horwath v Queen* [1979] 3 WCB 181.
[126] *Ward v Her Majesty, the Queen* [1979] 2 SCR 30.

determine whether or not the statement represented the operating mind of the accused.

Hence, it would appear that the Canadian courts have developed a somewhat wider notion of voluntariness.

[9.113] In *R v Flynn and Leonard*,[127] Lord Lowry CJ invoked the notion of 'oppressive circumstances' to infringe the voluntariness requirement in the context of confessions emanating from the Hollywood Interrogation Centre, a place described by the court as amounting to a virtual 'confession factory', ie physically constructed in such a manner as to encourage or indeed compel a detained person to make a confession of guilt.

[9.114] The voluntariness requirement, it cannot be over-emphasised, is a peremptory requirement – a pre-condition to admission, but not solely a determination of admissibility. Other factors, as seen hitherto, can then operate to influence a trial judge to exercise his discretion to refuse to admit same. A trial judge does not, however, as emphasised by Walsh J in *People (AG) v Cummins*,[128] have any discretion to admit a confession which is not voluntary. Whether matters affecting the pre-trial process, therefore, are classified as part of that pre-emptory voluntariness requirement, or the rather more vulnerable 'constitutional right to fairness' in that process, is not without significance.

Detention under the Criminal Justice (Drug Trafficking) Act 1996

[9.115] Section 2(1) of the Criminal Justice (Drug Trafficking) Act 1996 provides that where a member of An Garda Síochána arrests without warrant a person he suspects with reasonable cause of having committed a drug trafficking offence, that person may be detained for up to a maximum of seven days. Initially they can be held for six hours on the authorisation of the 'member in charge', which period can be extended up to 18 hours by a Chief Superintendent and subsequently by a further 24 hours by a Chief Superintendent. Any further detention may then be authorised by a District Court judge who may grant an extension of 72 hours, at which time a Chief Superintendent can apply to the District Court judge for a further 48 hours. Such extensions will only be authorised where the person granting the extension is satisfied further detention is necessary for 'the proper investigation of the offence concerned and that the investigation is being conducted diligently and expeditiously'.[129]

[9.116] The judicial intervention here is to comply with the European Court of Human Rights determination in *Brogan v United Kingdom*.[130] In *DPP v Early,*

---

[127] *R v Flynn and Leonard* (24 May 1972, unreported) Belfast City Commission.
[128] *People (AG) v Cummins* [1972] IR 312.
[129] Criminal Justice (Drug Trafficking) Act 1996, s 2(2)(g)(i).
[130] *Brogan v United Kingdom* (1989) 11 EHRR 117.

O'Riordan, Kelly & Maguire,[131] several individuals were arrested under s 2 of the Criminal Justice (Drug Trafficking) Act 1996, but their extension was sanctioned by a District Court judge not so authorised under the legislation, and so they were released. They were re-arrested but successfully challenged the arrest on the basis that they could only be re-arrested under s 4 of the Criminal Justice (Drug Trafficking) Act 1996, under which new information is required before parties can be rearrested. These proceedings arose by way of judicial review. McGuinness J identified the safeguard in s 4 as being one against repeated detention by the gardaí on the same offence without any new information having come to light. She went on to reason:

> However this is different from the situation which can arise where a person has been released from detention under ... section 2 of the 1996 Act and at a later stage a decision is made by the Director of Public Prosecutions or by the gardaí to charge that person with an actual offence ... It is essential to distinguish carefully and clearly between arrest for the purposes of detention for investigation and arrest for the purposes of charging the alleged offender, of bringing him or her before the Court and of initiating the procedures ... which eventually will lead to his or her trial.

This approach reveals the extent to which the arrest process has changed and offers a dual approach to arrest which sanctions and mainstreams that of interrogation.

Confrontation between the police and the citizen

[9.117] Given the desire to vindicate the individual's rights, yet accommodate police investigations, it is interesting to view the judicial perspectives on the status of the inquiry. In *McCarrick v Leavy*,[132] Davitt P in the High Court stated that it was never intended by the Judges' Rules that a police officer should caution every person of whom he proposed to ask a question. In the Supreme Court in that case, Walsh J commented:

> A failure to comply with the provisions of the Judges' Rules gives a discretion to the trial judge to refuse to admit the evidence in question, but the exercise of that discretion is not governed by whether or not the statement is voluntary. A statement obtained in breach of the provisions of the Judges' Rules is admissible provided it is a voluntary one. But the fact that it is a voluntary one does not take away the trial judge's discretion to refuse to admit the evidence if it has been obtained in violation of the Judges' Rules ...

---

[131] *DPP v District Justices Early, O'Riordan Kelly & Maguire* [1998] 3 IR 158.
[132] *McCarrick v Leavy* [1964] IR 225.

[9.118] In *People v O'Loughlin*,[133] it was held that a suspect could be said to be 'in custody' from the moment the garda had made up his mind to charge him. On the facts, it was held that from the time the gardaí realised that the accused's initial oral explanation had not been substantiated by their enquiries, the accused had been detained deliberately in unlawful custody in contravention of his constitutional rights, and his written statement, made during such unlawful detention, should not have been admitted.

[9.119] One of the difficulties arising, particularly in relation to those detained consequent on arrest, is in respect of the status of the questioning of those persons thus detained. In *People v Madden*,[134] the Court of Criminal Appeal held that the obligation of the suspect arrested under s 30 to account for movements under s 52 of the Offences Against the State Act 1939, did not prohibit further questioning of that person by the gardaí. This was confirmed in *People v Kelly*[135] by Finlay P, who commented:

> So to hold would be to create a uniquely anomalous position whereby a person arrested at common law under suspicion of having committed an ordinary offence could be questioned by the Garda Síochána, and provided due procedures and fair treatment were afforded to him, any answers he gave to such questions would be admissible in evidence against him, whereas a person arrested under s 30 – a statute specifically enacted to deal with more serious crimes tending to undermine the stability of the state could not be so questioned.

[9.120] Arrest, as previously noted, was traditionally a process indicative of the end of the state's investigative process. However, change had occurred as a result of the evolution of powers of detention consequent on arrest – originally invoked under s 30 of the Offences Against the State Act 1939. The judiciary, in conjunction with this development, had become watchful of any overspill from this original 'extraordinary' realm, into the 'ordinary' criminal justice system. Judgments such as that of the Supreme Court in *People v Lynch*[136] effectively abolished the police tactic of 'inviting someone into the police station to help them with their inquiries'. Note the comment of the then Garda Commissioner McLaughlin:[137]

> ... for a while we surmounted this problem of being unable to detain a suspect by inviting him to come voluntarily to the Garda Station to be interviewed. For many years, suspects who had in this fashion come voluntarily to Garda Stations were

---

[133] *People v O'Loughlin* [1979] IR 85.
[134] *People v Madden* [1977] IR 336.
[135] *People v Kelly* [1983] ILRM 271.
[136] *People v Lynch* [1981] ILRM 389.
[137] McLaughlin, 'Legal Constraints in Criminal Investigation' (1981) Vol XVI Part 2 Ir Jur (ns) 217.

interviewed unless they expressed a desire to leave the station. This procedure was acceptable and statements made during these interviews were treated as admissible in court provided of course that they were otherwise voluntary and taken in accordance with the Judges' Rules.

[9.121] The comment of Walsh J in *Lynch*, where the accused was held without any lawful arrest for 22 hours and questioned, was to the effect that:

> If a person is asked to come to a Garda Station and he goes voluntarily, he has been asked to come for some particular purpose, to give assistance in the investigation of a crime or some other purpose. When he is subjected to interrogation of a nature which would suggest he may well be a suspect in the case or questioned or interrogated in circumstances which reasonably would give rise to that inference, he should be informed that he is free to leave at any time unless and until he is arrested.'[138]

[9.122] In *DPP v Kelly*,[139] the appeal of the accused against his conviction, obtained solely on the basis of a number of written statements and one comprehensive written statement made while in police custody, was based on the fact that while under a s 30 arrest, Kelly was moved in the course of his detention to a number of garda stations in succession. The point of law of public importance certified by the Court of Criminal Appeal to the Supreme Court, was whether a person arrested under s 30 and detained in a particular garda station and then transferred to another garda station ceased, by reason of that transfer, to be in lawful custody.

[9.123] The Supreme Court held that as long as the duration of the detention was within a permitted period, the plurality of places or removals did not contravene the section. The Chief Justice commented:

> ... if in any case, the removal of a person detained under section 30, from one Garda Station or other place to another was *mala fides* or was done for the purposes either of harassment or isolating him from assistance or access to that which he could properly be entitled, then that fact itself would clearly render his detention unlawful.

[9.124] Significant here also is the decision of *Trimbole v Governor of Mountjoy*,[140] where Egan J stated that:

> ... the only rational explanation for the section 30 arrest on 25 October 1984, was to ensure that the applicant would be available for arrest and detention when Part II of the 1965 Act would apply to the Commonwealth of Australia. There was a

---

138 This was followed in *People v Coffey* (6 March 1981, unreported) and *DPP v Herron* (27 October 1981, unreported).

139 *DPP v Kelly* [1983] ILRM 271.

140 *Trimbole v Governor of Mountjoy* [1985] ILRM 465.

gross misuse of s 30 [of the 1939 Act], which amounted to a conscious and deliberate violation of constitutional rights. There were no extraordinary excusing circumstances.

[9.125] An important determination, in the context of a breach of the accused's constitutional rights, is as to the actual status of the accused's detention. This led to some difficulty in *Lynch*, in so far as there had not been a determination at trial on the facts, as to whether the accused was in fact free to leave the garda station, and so was there voluntarily. The Supreme Court in *Lynch*, moreover, suggested such determination – as to whether there had been an illegal detention – should be made by the jury. According to O'Higgins CJ:

> In my view, the jury, either by a specific question, or by an appropriate direction ought to have been asked to decide, as a question of fact, material to the defence, whether the appellant's evidence that he had been held against his wishes was or was not true.

[9.126] Subsequently, in *People (DPP) v Conroy*,[141] the Supreme Court declined to follow that view. *Per* Henchy J:

> ... a jury informed of the circumstances and contents of inadmissible evidence would be unfit to try the issue of guilt or innocence since it would lack the characteristic of impartiality and the alternative of having separate juries determine the two issues would be inconsistent with the unitary and unbroken trial with a jury guaranteed by the Constitution.

Such matters were for determination by the trial judge in the absence of the jury.

[9.127] To the extent that the pre-trial process is now encrusted with procedure, one may find a parallel movement (echoing the earlier change in the focus from trial (procedural) to pre-trial) from police station (pre-trial and procedural) to 'on the street' confrontation. The 'status' of the individual (hallmark of procedural monitoring) may then merit increasing attention in that context.

[9.128] The decision in *People v Ward*[142] gives an interesting insight into the approach of the gardaí to interrogation and judicial attitudes to that pre-trial process behaviour. The beginning of the court's judgment gives the context in which it was decided:

> On 26 June 1996 Ms Veronica Guerin, a distinguished brave journalist who specialised in the investigation of crime, was brutally murdered when riddled with bullets as she sat in her car waiting for traffic lights to change at the Naas Road, Boot Road junction, Clondalkin, Dublin.

---

[141] *People (DPP) v Conroy* [1986] IR 460.
[142] *People v Ward* (27 November 1998), SCC, Barr J.

The case against Ward comprised verbal admissions allegedly made by him in custody under s 30 of the Offences Against the State Act 1939 (the first three of the four pillars of the case against him, according to the state) and the testimony of Charles Bowden, an accomplice. Given the centrality of the admissions to the state's case, the following comment made by the Special Criminal Court is revelatory:

> The accused is an experienced Section 30 detainee having been arrested on that basis on earlier occasions and he stated in evidence that he was well aware of the importance in his own interest of adopting a policy of total silence in the course of interrogation and he alleged that he did so.

[9.129] In the course of his detention, Ward's girlfriend, Vanessa Meehan, and his mother, Elizabeth Ward, 74 years of age, were taken to visit him. Neither of these visits was requested by Ward. In relation to this treatment, which is reminiscent of that meted to Pringle (an aforementioned miscarriage of justice case)[143] when his girlfriend was also brought in while he was in custody, the Special Criminal Court commented:

> The police were under severe pressure to bring charges in relation to that crime. The coincidence that the accused's capitulation after more than 14 hours of silence during interrogations had occurred immediately after a visit by Ms Meehan is a remarkable volte face which gives rise to unease and raises a series of pertinent questions ... In reality was the visit a deliberate ploy devised by the police to soften up the accused and cause him to incriminate himself as to the murder?

Describing the history of the accused's interrogation as 'very remarkable indeed', the court concluded with regard to the visit by Ward's mother:

> The court is satisfied beyond all reasonable doubt that the visit from Mrs Ward was a deliberate ploy devised and orchestrated by the police in a final effort to prevail on the accused to disclose what he had done with the gun ... The court is satisfied that the visit was not arranged for any humanitarian purpose but was a cynical ploy which it was hoped might break down the accused ...[144]

[9.130] The court's conclusion with regard to the alleged admissions and their admissibility is fairly damning:

> Both meetings amounted to a conscious and deliberate disregard of the accused's basic constitutional right to fair procedures and treatment while in custody. They constituted deliberate gross violations of the fundamental obligation which the interrogators and their superiors had of conducting their dealings with the accused in accordance with the principles of basic fairness and justice ... In all

---

[143] *DPP v Pringle McCann & O'Shea* (22 May 1981, unreported), CCA.
[144] *People (DPP) v Ward* (27 November 1998), SCC Barr J at p 13/39.

the circumstances the court is satisfied that in the interests of justice and fairness all admissions allegedly made by the accused during the period of his detention at Lucan garda station must be ruled inadmissible.

The Court also has some element of doubt about whether the alleged verbal admissions were in fact made by the accused or where, as he contends, he made no admissions at all during the entire period of his detention.[145]

Of course, in declaring the admissions inadmissible, there remains quiescent in this non-jury court the artificiality of the court members, being triers of fact, ignoring them.

[9.131] The remaining leg of the prosecution case was the testimony of the accomplice Charles Bowden, alleged by the defence to be similar to that of the supergrass-type witness in Northern Ireland, in that he struck a deal with the state and was part of its new Witness Protection Programme. The court did not accept the argument that Bowden was a supergrass, requiring special caution, but declared itself to be 'deeply mindful of the fundamental principle of criminal law that it is unsafe to act upon the evidence of an accomplice which is not corroborated in some material particular implicating the accused.' In relation to Bowden, the court commented:[146]

The Court accepts without any doubt that Charles Bowden is a self-serving, deeply avaricious and potentially vicious criminal. On his own admission he is a liar and the court readily accepts that he would lie without hesitation and regardless of the consequences for others if he perceived it to be in his own interest to do so. The Court fully appreciates that assessment of his evidence must be made with great caution and with the foregoing firmly in mind.

Having so classified the witness, the Special Criminal Court then convicted Ward on the sole basis of Bowden's testimony.

[9.132] Ward's conviction was, of course, subsequently overturned by the Court of Criminal Appeal, largely on the basis of the lack of credibility of the witness who required corroboration. It is worth remembering here, also, that confessions attract a corroboration warning by virtue of s 10 of the Criminal Procedure Act 1993.

[9.133] The comments made with regard to audio-visual recording and judicial supervision of the pre-trial process on appeal in *People v Connelly*[147] were further endorsed in *DPP v Diver*.[148] In that case the defendant had been

---

[145] *People (DPP) v Ward* (27 November 1998), SCC Barr J at p 14/39.
[146] *People (DPP) v Ward* (27 November 1998), SCC Barr J at p 22/39.
[147] *People v Connolly* [2003] 2 IR 1.
[148] *DPP v Diver* [2005] IESC 57.

convicted of the murder of his wife. The Court of Criminal Appeal had certified a point of law of exceptional public importance to the Supreme Court as to whether, having regard to the nature of the breaches of the custody regulations in this case, the learned trial judge correctly exercised his discretion in ruling in favour of admissibility of each of the statements made by the applicant while in detention under s 4 of the Criminal Justice Act 1984.

[9.134] The interviews of the accused had not been audio visually recorded and the record in writing by various gardaí was grossly deficient. The trial judge had found multiple breaches of the 1987 Regulations for the Treatment of Persons in Custody and a failure to record any part of an entire interview during which it was conceded the defendant had consistently denied involvement in the crime. All of the gardaí involved, Hardiman J noted, 'are well known in the area of criminal investigation and all are competent, knowledgeable and experienced.'[149] Hardiman J found the breaches of regulations not to be trivial or inconsequential but 'on the contrary, grave, obvious and deliberate'.[150] He pointed out that, while written records of what an accused says in custody provide a more reliable record than unaided recollection, '[a]udio visual recording is ... infinitely superior.'[151]

[9.135] Hardiman J then gave a lengthy comment on garda powers to detain:[152]

> The garda power to detain persons and question them, with no one else present, is a statutory power of huge significance. Its exercise gives rise to the commitment of enormous amounts of court time and has given rise in the past to miscarriages of justice. Where there has been a breach of the regulations due to a failure to record *'so far as practicable'* an interview with an accused, the task of the trial judge is to determine whether ... the failure ... has prejudiced the fairness of the trial ... The issue is ... whether the fairness of the trial of the accused would be prejudiced by the admission of statements made by him or her in respect of which the regulations were not followed.[153]

He continued:

> I wish to reiterate that the gardaí are not entitled to exercise editorial control over what is said. Nor are they entitled to cherry pick what is to be recorded. It is utterly unacceptable to omit denials. It is important to provide sufficient context to allow for an evaluation of what is said especially where, as here, the defendant was allegedly making ambiguous or inconclusive verbal statements, and manifesting symptoms of distress. All this is trite, because it has been said so

---

[149] *DPP v Diver* [2005] IESC 57 at 6/23, *per* Hardiman J.

[150] *DPP v Diver* [2005] IESC 57 at 10/23, *per* Hardiman J.

[151] *DPP v Diver* [2005] IESC 57 at 10/23, *per* Hardiman J.

[152] *DPP v Diver* [2005] IESC 57 at 11/23, *per* Hardiman J.

[153] *DPP v Diver* [2005] IESC 57 at 10–11/23, *per* Hardiman J.

often and it is said so often because gardaí have regularly avoided audio visual recording, made selective notes, and breached the clear and simple regulations for the treatment of persons in custody, apparently believing that such breaches will attract nothing worse than a judicial rebuke.[154]

Hardiman J pointed out that for at least three decades, the courts have urged compliance with such rules and deplored their breach. He refers to his judgment in *Connelly* and points out that it has been stated publicly that recording takes place in 96% of garda interviews yet, he said, this is not the frequency represented in those cases that reach the appeal courts. On the issue of the alleged omissions, he found in favour of the accused and pointed out that were this the only evidence against the accused the conviction would be quashed because of such breach. Despite additional evidence, the conviction was quashed and a re-trial directed.

[9.136] *DPP v Murphy*[155] involved a situation where the accused was convicted of conspiracy to cause an explosion likely to endanger life. The context was the Omagh bombing in Northern Ireland on 15 August 1998. He appealed *inter alia* on the ground that the Special Criminal Court wrongly admitted evidence of interview notes and alleged utterances by the accused. The Special Criminal Court had also failed to grant a direction to acquit when there was evidence before the court that police witnesses had altered notes of written interview and lied under oath. The accused had been arrested under s 30 Offences Against the State Act 1939.

[9.137] Counsel for the accused had urged the Court of Criminal Appeal to follow the approach of courts in Northern Ireland and England, which quash convictions where notes of interviews were altered. In the Court of Criminal Appeal, Kearns J pointed out, however, that 'there is no automatic rule as to the effect of police officers found to be lying in the witness box'.[156] He stated further that:

> [The Court of Criminal Appeal] do not consider that the court of trial brought to the issue of the possible contamination of evidence or to the evaluation of the surviving garda evidence that degree of extra critical analysis which was surely warranted …[157]

For that reason the Court of Criminal Appeal in *Murphy* felt compelled to set the conviction aside as unsafe.

---

[154] *DPP v Diver* [2005] IESC 57 at 11/23, *per* Hardiman J.

[155] *DPP v Murphy* [2005] IECCA 1, judgment delivered by Kearns J.

[156] *DPP v Murphy* [2005] IECCA 1 at 14/30 *per* Kearns J.

[157] *DPP v Murphy* [2005] IECCA 1 at 16/30 *per* Kearns J.

[9.138] *People (DPP) v Kelly*[158] provides an interesting example of where the courts invoke basic fairness in relation to the pre-trial process and find it to be infringed in particular when the extended powers under the Offences Against the State Act 1998 are invoked. The accused here had been arrested under s 30 in relation to possession of explosives but his detention was extended by a Chief Superintendent on 1 July 2003 and a challenge was made in relation to interviews thereafter where the focus of interviewing changed to the subject of his membership of the IRA, and in particular to being interviewed in circumstances where s 2 Offences Against the State (Amendment) Act 1998 would be invoked. The defence challenged the fairness of the interviews on a number of grounds, including that the interviews on 2 July had not been video recorded, and the Special Criminal Court (O'Donovan J delivering the judgment) referred to Hardiman J's judgment in *DPP v Connelly*.[159] They also held that basic fairness required that he be reminded of his right to consult a solicitor. The courts also agreed that the interviews on 2 July seemed more a mechanism for invoking s 2 than eliciting information, which they said offended the principle of fair procedures in *State (Healy) v Donoghue*.[160] The extent to which the principle of basic fairness to the accused is invoked to ground the decision here and the review of garda behaviour in the pre-trial process and (mis)use of garda power is significant. The court also made reference to the ECHR jurisprudence, in particular art 5(c) and the necessity to justify an arrest under s 30 with reasonable and bona fide suspicion, as the court noted had been held in *DPP v Quilligan*[161] (where there had been reference to the concept of a holding charge and the necessity of reality to the reason for the arrest). The linkage with the ECHR, focus on basic fairness as constitutional requirement and references to previous decisions eliciting this is reminiscent of *McGrail* and offers the rules relating to admissibility stronger grounds which they may well need in relation to ever-extending police powers.

[9.139] There are a number of other decisions of this hue that deserve some mention. *McCormack v Judge Circuit Court and DPP*[162] is a High Court decision in which judgment was given by Charleton J. The applicant here had been charged in relation to a bag-snatching incident in Dublin as he had been seen on the street 15 minutes before the incident and his clothing matched the description given of the assailant. He sought to restrain the respondents from trying him on the basis that gardaí, on arresting him, failed to properly conduct

---

[158] *People (DPP) v Kelly* (26 November 2004), SCC reported (2004) *The Irish Times*, 14 January.
[159] *DPP v Connelly* [2003] 2 IR 1.
[160] *State (Healy) v Donoghue* [1976] IR 325.
[161] *DPP v Quilligan* [1986] IR 495.
[162] *McCormack v Judge Circuit Court and DPP* [2008] 1 ILRM 49, [2007] IEHC 23.

the interviews with him (which were video recorded) and that his right to fair trial had been undermined by their failure to preserve all the CCTV footage in the area. The specifics of the first issue related to the alleged chaotic nature of the interview and the failure of the gardaí to give him an adequate opportunity to make his case. Charleton J, in relation to the latter, noted that:

> [t]here is a growing practice ... of persons arrested for crime to use the opportunity of being questioned in Garda custody to deny the offence. Sometimes the statements made will be entirely self serving but may, nonetheless, subject to the discretion of the trial judge as to the admissibility of confession evidence, be presented as part of the prosecution case.[163]

This discretion, he suggests, is a matter connected with the admissibility of exculpatory statements and the rule against self-corroboration.

[9.140] Charleton J pointed out that it is the duty of the gardaí in investigating crime to act reasonably and it is not the purpose of a police interview to enable the accused to make a case on video so that it can be played to the jury. The accused, after all, has the option of cross-examining witnesses or calling or giving evidence himself for that purpose. Charleton J commented on the videoing of interviews and implications for police practice as follows, which illustrates perhaps the outer limits of judicial tolerance:

> Since the time when members of police forces were required, pursuant to the *Judges' Rules*, to attempt to write down an accused's persons answer to an accusation, it has always been complained that this was done through a filter of 'garda prose' or that what was said is not accurately reflected in the written document; people, in general, speak about seven times faster than they write. Now that tape recordings of interviews are available it has to be expected that interviews recorded on video will be either chaotic, laconic or otherwise reflect the real circumstances of conversation between people who may be under pressure of accusation, of work or of life. That is what these videos, in fact, reflect. I do not regard the language used, with the occasional profanity, as being beyond the norm that one would hear in this city at any time of the day or night. I do not think that saying that '*any solicitor will advise a client to remain silent*' degrades anyone. Nor do I regard the interview as being unstructured. In fact it occurs to me that the gardaí were doing a good job of attempting to keep the accused to the point in his answers and of dealing with the material which it was necessary for them to deal with in the course of the interview. So, there was no opportunity lost to the accused supposing he wished to avail of it, and supposing he was entitled to it, and there was no abuse of his rights. Of course, the written note gets only some of what was said. The relevant rule requiring a written note is soon to be changed and, in any event, it was never the law that absolutely everything had to be written down by gardaí conducting an interview.[164]

---

[163] *McCormack v Judge Circuit Court and DPP* [2008] 1 ILRM 49, [2007] IEHC 23 at para 4.
[164] *McCormack v Judge Circuit Court and DPP* [2008] 1 ILRM 49, [2007] IEHC 23 at para 10.

[9.141] Finally, the court made the point that it did not have any jurisdiction to decide questions of admissibility in advance by way of judicial review:

> Trial judges['s] ... function is to apply the rules of evidence and to exercise judicial discretion in accordance with the relevant balance which the law requires in particular instances.

Charleton J saw this case as a classic one requiring rulings by the trial judge:

> It seems to me that there is no case to be made, on the evidence before me, that there is any garda misconduct, or any lost opportunity or any failure to act fairly. These principles, in any event, are not isolated principles which stand alone as if the purpose of a criminal trial was to examine garda conduct and not to try the accused. The purpose of a criminal trial is to test whether the prosecution have sufficient admissible evidence to discharge the burden of proof to the requisite standard. Any argument that might be made as to unfairness, or lost opportunity, must be placed squarely within the existing common law principles as to rules of evidence where, I might add, they can only impact on any question as to admissibility of evidence in the rare cases where an appropriate discretion is vested in a trial judge; and there only in circumstances where the trial judge is bound to take these vague notions into account. The only relevant example is the limited discretion to exclude unfairly obtained evidence.[165]

With regard to prohibiting a criminal trial, the power of prohibition according to Charleton J should be exercised with great caution, his reference to cases such as *Z v DPP*,[166] indicating how unlikely an event he thinks this might be.

[9.142] In *People v Casey*[167] the applicants had been charged with murder and convicted. An issue raised on appeal was as to the admissibility of three cautioned statements made by the second applicant in the garda station. It was held dismissing the appeal that, although there were technical breaches of the Judges' Rules and Custody Regulations, the substance of his rights were preserved. The second applicant was under 17 years of age at the time of questioning and so was accompanied by his care worker who was employed by the Mid-Western Heath Board. The alleged breaches of the Judges' Rules and Custody Regulations concerned the absence of the care worker at the applicant's request for 15 minutes and the failure to contemporaneously record any exchange during same as well as the failure to record any exchange in the period after he made his second statement and before he made his third. The court referred to and followed *People (DPP) v Darcy*[168] where there had been a breach of the Custody Regulations requirement that not more than two gardaí

---

[165] *McCormack v Judge Circuit Court & DPP* [2008] 1 ILRM 49 at 54.

[166] *Z v DPP* [1994] 2 IR 476.

[167] *People v Casey* [2004] IECCA 49, McGuinness J.

[168] *People (DPP) v Darcy* (29 July 1997, unreported).

participate in the interviewing at any one time. Keane J, delivering the judgment of the court, held the substance of the applicant's rights was preserved. McGuinness J in *Casey* said this case was analogous to *Darcy* in that '[t]here were technical breaches of the Judges' Rules and of the Regulations but the substance of the applicant's rights was preserved.'[169] This demonstrates the large discretion quiescent in such cases, but the guidance of 'fairness' as seen in *Kelly*[170] may become even more significant in future cases influencing how the judiciary use that discretion in the context of a harsher police powers regime.

It is certainly significant that the changes with regard to the extension of detention periods brought about by the Criminal Justice (Amendment) Act 2009, involve a lowering of the garda rank required for authorisation of extension (from Chief Superintendent to Superintendent); a facility for the reception of hearsay evidence from a garda seeking an extension, as well as provision that the application for extension of detention can be heard otherwise than in public and in the absence of the suspect and his/her legal representatives. This would seem to make the case for close judicial scrutiny of these extraordinary powers at a later stage if necessary. Of course the latter begs the question as to whether there is a later stage – if not the infringement on the individual's rights will not have recourse to that remedy.

The doctrine of *res gestae*

[9.143] Under the doctrine of *res gestae* evidence that is relevant to the 'transaction' and arising contemporaneously with it may be admissible. The doctrine has been rather more critically described by Lord Tomlin in *Holmes v Newman*,[171] as 'a phrase adopted to provide a respectable legal cloak for a variety of cases to which no formulae of precision can be applied'. Some idea of the more modern rationale behind this exception to the hearsay rule is to be gleaned from Lord Wilberforce's statement in *Ratten v R*:[172] 'it must be for the judge by preliminary ruling to satisfy himself that the statement was so clearly made in circumstances of spontaneity and involvement in the event, that the possibility of concoction can be disregarded'. The traditional view was that statements coming within this exception formed part of the event. Hence, the requirement of contemporaneity between the statement and the fact in issue was viewed quite strictly, and any difference in location between the event and the utterance, was significant.

---

[169] *People v Casey* [2004] IECCA 49 at 13/16 *per* McGuinness J.
[170] *People (DPP) v Kelly* (26 November 2004), SCC reported (2004) *The Irish Times*, 14 January.
[171] *Holmes v Newman* [1931] 2 Ch 112.
[172] *Ratten v R* [1972] AC 378 at 389.

[9.144] A classic illustration of the original, very strict, interpretation of the requirement of contemporaneity is to be found in *R v Beddingfield*.[173] Here the deceased's throat had just been cut, and she walked out of the room where the accused was, and said, 'Oh dear Aunt, see what Beddingfield has done to me'. The statement was excluded, because it was made after the act was completed. The present position is quite different, as seen from the rationale as expanded in modern terms in *Ratten*:[174]

> The possibility of concoction, or fabrication, where it exists, is on the other hand an entirely valid reason for exclusion, and is probably the real test which judges in fact apply. In their Lordships' opinion this should be recognised and applied directly as the relevant test: the test should be not the uncertain one whether the making of the statement was in some sense part of the event or transaction. This may often be difficult to establish such external matters as the time which elapses between the events and the speaking of the words (or vice versa), and differences in location being relevant factors but not, taken by themselves, decisive criteria. As regards statements made after the event it must be for the judge, by preliminary ruling, to satisfy himself that the statement was so clearly made in circumstances of spontaneity or involvement in the event that the possibility of concoction can be disregarded. Conversely, if he considers that the statement was made by way of narrative of a detached prior event so that the speaker was so disengaged from it as to be able to construct or adapt his account, he should exclude it. And the same must in principle be true of statements made before the event. The test should be not the uncertain one whether the making of the statement should be regarded as part of the event or transaction. This may often be difficult to show. But if the drama, leading up to the climax has commenced and assumed such intensity and pressure that the utterance can safely be regarded as a true reflection of what was unrolling or actually happening, it ought to be received. The expression *res gestae* may conveniently sum up these criteria, but the reality of them must always be kept in mind: it is this that lies behind the best reasoned of the judges' rulings.

[9.145] Lord Wilberforce looked at various authorities and concluded:[175]

> ... there is ample support for the principle that hearsay evidence may be admitted of the statement provided it is made in such conditions (always being those of approximate but not exact contemporaneity) of involvement or pressure as to exclude the possibility of concoction or distortion to the advantage of the maker or the disadvantage of the accused.

On the facts, Lord Wilberforce opined that since around the time the accused's wife was shot (allegedly accidentally) the local exchange received a telephone

---

[173] *R v Beddingfield* (1879) 14 Cox CC 341.
[174] *Ratten v R* [1972] AC 378 at 389 *per* Lord Wilberforce.
[175] *Ratten v R* [1972] AC 378 at 390.

call from the accused's house, where a female voice called hysterically, 'Get the Police', had that been considered hearsay evidence, it was still admissible under the doctrine of '*res gestae*'.

[9.146] Lord Wilberforce felt that there was ample evidence of a close and intimate connection between the statement ascribed to the deceased and the shooting which occurred very shortly afterwards:

> The way in which the statement came to be made (in a call for the police) and the tone of the voice used showed intrinsically that the statement was being forced from the deceased by an overwhelming pressure of contemporary event. It carried its own stamp of spontaneity and thus was endorsed by the proved time sequence and the proved proximity of the deceased to the appellant with his gun.[176]

[9.147] Cross[177] attempted to divide the admissibility of *res gestae* evidence into four categories:

(1) *Statements accompanying and explaining relevant acts.* In *R v Edwards*[178] the wife of the accused handed a knife to a neighbour saying she would feel safer if it was out of the way. It was held that the statement was admissible as evidence to prove that previous threats had been made by the accused to his wife. The vital prerequisites were satisfied: the statement was contemporaneous with the act in question, the statement was made in relation to the act and it was made by the person performing the act. In *People (DPP) v Bishop*[179] a challenge was made to evidence relied on by the prosecution, which consisted of documentation and other material found inside a Peugeot car belonging to the occupier of the house outside which it was parked. The gardaí had a search warrant for the house but the state's case did not rely on the warrant but on the owner's consent with regard to the car. Part of the evidence was the evidence of words actually spoken by the owner and, as the owner did not give evidence, it was argued it was hearsay and should not have been admitted. It was held that the words were merely accompanying the actions of handing over the keys and so did not contravene the hearsay rule.

(2) *Spontaneous statements in relation to an event in issue.* In *Davies v Fortior*[180] the statement of the deceased emitted on falling into an acid

---

[176] *Ratten v R* [1972] AC 378 at 391.
[177] *Cross on Evidence* (6th edn, Butterworths 1985), p 580.
[178] *R v Edwards* (1872) 12 Cox CC 230.
[179] *People (DPP) v Bishop* [2005] IECCA 2, Geoghegan J.
[180] *Davies v Fortior* [1952] 1 All ER 1355.

bath ('I shouldn't have done it') was admitted in a subsequent civil action in relation to the accident.

(3)   *Statements in relation to the maker's contemporaneous state of mind or emotion.* In *R v Vincent, Frost & Edwards*,[181] at a public meeting where it was alleged that general alarm had been caused, statements were admitted to show fear. Authorities conflict as to whether the doing of an act can be inferred from a statement of intention to do it: in *R v Wainright*[182] the statement of a murdered girl that she was going to D's place was deemed admissible to show her state of mind and intention, but not admissible as evidence that she had indeed gone to D's place, whereas in *R v Buckley*[183] in the context of the murder of a police officer who had expressed an intention to go to D's house, the statement was admitted as evidence in relation to the issue of whether he did in fact go there.

(4)   *Statements of physical sensation.* This is admissible as evidence of the speaker's contemporaneous sensation, but not as to its possible cause: *R v Nicholas.*[184] *According to* Chief Baron Pollack in that case one can say in evidence that one has indeed got a wound, but not how one got it.

[9.148] A House of Lords decision on the issue of *res gestae* is that of *R v Andrews.*[185] The facts concerned the appellant and another man who knocked on the door to the victim's flat, and when the victim opened it, stabbed him in the stomach and robbed the flat. The victim was discovered minutes later and the police arrived quite soon after. The victim was seriously wounded and told the police he had been attacked by two men. He gave the name of the appellant and the name and address of the other man. He then became unconscious, was brought to hospital and died two months later. The appellant was tried for murder, and the Crown sought to admit the victim's statement. The accused appealed on the basis that the statement should not have been admitted on the basis of the doctrine of *res gestae*. The House of Lords confirmed the approach to the doctrine of *res gestae* elucidated in *Ratten* and subsequently applied in *R v Blastland*,[186] *R v Nye & Loan*,[187] *R v Boyle*[188] and *R v O Shea*.[189] Hence, the

---

181   *R v Vincent, Frost & Edwards* (1840) 9 C & P 275.

182   *R v Wainright* (1875) 13 Cox CC 171.

183   *R v Buckley* (1873) 13 Cox CC 293.

184   *R v Nicholas* (1846) 2 Car & Kir 246.

185   *R v Andrews* [1987] 1 All ER 513.

186   *R v Blastland* [1985] 2 All ER 1095.

187   *R v Nye & Loan* (1978) 66 Cr App Rep 252.

188   *R v Boyle* (6 March 1986, unreported) UKHL.

189   *R v O Shea* (27 July 1986, unreported) UKHL.

defence counsel's argument that hearsay must form part of the criminal act for which the accused is being tried, as *per Beddingfield*, contending that *Ratten* essentially involved an extension of exceptions to the hearsay rule, was therefore invalid.

[9.149] Lord Ackner stated he did not accept that Lord Wilberforce's principles involved an extension to this exception and felt that, in accordance with same, *R v Beddingfield* would not be so decided today. Indeed, he felt there could hardly be a case where the words uttered carried more clearly the mark of spontaneity and intense involvement. The trial judge, therefore, *per* Lord Ackner, must ask the following questions:

(1)   Can the possibility of concoction or distortion be disregarded?

(2)   Looking at the circumstances in which the statement was made, was the utterance an instinctive reaction, with no possibility of concoction?

(3)   Were there circumstances of spontaneity? Was the mind of the declarant still dominated by the event?

(4)   If there are special features in the case (apart from the time factor) the judge must be satisfied that the circumstances were such that, having regard to the special feature of malice, there was no possibility of concoction or distortion to the advantage of the accused.

(5)   Is there a possibility of error? Given the fallibility of human recollection, this must affect the weight of the evidence, for example, if there were special features, as here, where the deceased had drink taken, the trial judge must decide if he can exclude the possibility of error.

Declarations against proprietary/pecuniary interests

[9.150] In *Lalor v Lalor*,[190] the facts of the case were such that Delaney (since deceased) had purchased certain leaseholds and reassigned them to trustees for his sister Maria. After her death, her husband attempted to upset the trust on the grounds that he was the beneficial owner. He relied on a conversation he had with Delaney, which was alleged to have been contrary to the latter's proprietary interest. *Per* Fitzgibbon J:

> I am of the opinion that the interest against which the statement appears to be made, must, in order to supply that sanction which, after the death of the party, is accepted as a substitute for an oath, be an interest existing at the time of making the statement.

---

[190] *Lalor v Lalor* (1879) 4 LR 678.

[9.151] *Flood v Russell*[191] concerned a statement by a wife (now deceased) to the effect that her husband, who pre-deceased her, had made a will giving her a life interest in certain real estate. It was admitted as being a declaration against pecuniary or proprietary interest for the reason that had there been no will, her share in the intestacy would have been considerably more than the life estate.

Declarations by deceased persons in the course of duty

[9.152] In *Harris v Lambert HC*,[192] entries by a deceased solicitor in his diary were sought to be put in evidence. They were objected to on the grounds of their not having been made in the performance of his duty to this client, but for purposes of recording and later claiming costs. It was held that there was sufficient authority for the proposition that notes can be received if made in discharge of a duty by a solicitor with a view to an ultimate duty to do a specific thing.

Declarations as to pedigree matters

[9.153] This exception is normally confined to questions strictly of descent of relationship. In *Palmer v Palmer*,[193] 'A' devised lands to his son for life and then to his son's sons in order of seniority and in succession. The third of 'B's' sons, in an action to gain possession of the lands, was permitted to prove the death of his two elder brothers by means of family repute under this exception.

Declarations as to public rights

[9.154] In *Giant's Causeway Co Ltd v AG*[194] the original ordinance survey map made in 1832 by an officer of engineers and produced from the custody of the Ordinance Department was held admissible in a matter involving questions of public interest. In this case the latter interest was that of a right-of-way.

Post-testamentary declarations by testators as to the contents of their wills

[9.155] In *the Goods of George Ball*,[195] on the death of the testator, his will was seen to be a copy, bearing a statement by him that he had substituted the copy for the original. It was held that declarations made by a testator both before and after the execution of his will are, in the event of its loss, admissible as secondary evidence of its contents.

---

[191] *Flood v Russell* (1891) 29 LR Ir 91.
[192] *Harris v Lambert HC* [1932] IR 504.
[193] *Palmer v Palmer* (1886–7) 18 LR Ir 192.
[194] *Giant's Causeway Co Ltd v AG* (1905) 5 Ir Jur Rep 381.
[195] *In the Goods of George Ball* (1890) 25 LR Ir 556.

Dying declarations of the deceased on a charge of homicide

[9.156] An oral or written declaration of a deceased person is admissible evidence of the cause of his death at a trial for his murder or manslaughter, provided he was under a settled, hopeless expectation of death when the statement was made, and provided he would have been a competent witness if called to give evidence at that time. The underlying rationale of this rule is the presumption that a person is unlikely to die with a 'lie on his lips'. It is a purely Christian ethic at basis, which assumes the sanction of imminent death to be equivalent to that of the oath. The important elements governing this exception are that the deceased is aware of the danger of *imminent* (though not necessarily immediate) death. Evidence which might be preferred indicating this awareness would include that of anointment. In *Crown v Mooney*,[196] the declaration was held inadmissible as the deceased had not been told expressly that she was dying, though the doctor had told her she was dangerously ill and the clergyman warned her to prepare for death.

[9.157] The form of the declaration was considered in *R v Fitzpatrick*,[197] where Palles CB stated that he was quite prepared to decide, either upon principle or upon authority, if it be held that a dying declaration was inadmissible only because it was cast in narrative form, although it had been given in answer to questions put. But in the second place, he was also of the opinion that the portion of the written document which was relied upon by the prisoner as vitiating the whole declaration, was not part of the dying declaration at all, nor within the rule which treated such dying declarations as being an exceptional class of evidence. He had always regarded it as a settled rule of practice that the fact that a declaration was based on answers to questions went to the weight, but never to the admissibility, of the evidence.

[9.158] Of great importance is the limitation of admissibility to cases of homicide. Hence in *Smith v Cavan County Council*,[198] on a claim for compensation which was a quasi-criminal matter, a dying declaration was held not admissible, as the rule applied only to cases of homicide. Of course, should the witness recover, however miraculously, a charge of homicide will evidently not lie, and on whatever the relevant charge, the witness can, if necessary, be called to testify.

---

[196] *Crown v Mooney* (1851) 5 Cox CC 318.
[197] *R v Fitzpatrick* (1912) 46 ILTR 173.
[198] *Smith v Cavan County Council* (1927) 58 ILTR 107.

Special provisions – exceptions to the Hearsay Rule

[9.159] Exceptional provisions which have developed allowing for the introduction of hearsay evidence in certain proceedings are as follows:

Admission of documentary evidence

[9.160] The Criminal Evidence Act 1992 made major changes to the operation of the rule against hearsay, in so far as it concerns documentary evidence and its admissibility in criminal proceedings. Part II of the 1992 Act provides that information contained in a document shall be admissible as evidence of any fact therein of which direct oral evidence would be admissible, if the information was compiled 'in the ordinary course of business' (not restricted to commercial enterprises, s 1) and supplied by a person who had, or may reasonably be supposed to have had, personal knowledge of the matters dealt with (s 5). Evidence of admissibility (s 6) must be provided by means of a certificate signed by a person who occupies a position in relation to the management of the business in the course of which the information was compiled and notice given of such documentary evidence under s 7. Section 8(1) further provides that such evidence shall not be admitted if the court is of the opinion that, in 'the interests of justice', such should not be admitted.

[9.161] In *Company Sergeant Berigan*,[199] a complaint was made that documents were admitted without proof that they were originals, emerging from proper custody, identified by those responsible for their creation. In response, the prosecution relied upon s 5 of the Criminal Evidence Act 1992, which provides that information contained in a document is admissible in criminal proceedings as evidence of any fact therein of which direct oral evidence would have been admissible if the information was compiled in the ordinary course of business and supplied by a person who had, or may reasonably be supposed to have had, personal knowledge of the matter. The court rejected the argument that s 5 addressed the difficulty raised by the applicant. The prosecution evidence only identified the documents; there was no evidence that they were compiled in the ordinary course of business or the information supplied by a person who had, or might reasonably be supposed to have, knowledge of the matters in the documents.

[9.162] Section 8(2) of the 1992 Act provides that, in so considering, the court should have regard to all the circumstances, including whether the information is reliable (s 8(2)(9)) and authentic (s 8(2)(b)), and that its admission or exclusion will result in unfairness to the accused (s 8(2)(c)). The last, perhaps, is the most

---

[199] *Company Sergeant Berigan* (1 November 2001), Courts Martial Appeal Court, *Annual Review of Irish Law 2001*, p 304.

interesting circumstance and will require a judicial assessment of the extent to which the rationale of the hearsay rule (itself not confined exclusively to trustworthiness as seen) is rooted in a belief that orality, cross-examination and confrontation are elements or prerequisites to 'fairness' to the accused.

[9.163] Section 8(3) of the 1992 Act provides that in estimating the weight to be attached to information, regard shall be had to the circumstances from which any inference can reasonably be drawn as to its accuracy or otherwise. Evidence as to the credibility of the supplier of information is admissible by virtue of s 9.

Copies of documents

[9.164] Section 30 of the 1992 Act provides that copies of a document may be produced in evidence (whether or not the original is in existence) and authenticated in such manner as the court may approve and it is immaterial how many removes there are between copy and original or how (including facsimile) the copy was produced. 'Document' here includes film, sound recording and video recording.

[9.165] The extent to which videos or computer-generated information can be interfered with will undoubtedly become a factor here, as will the question of how it can be safeguarded or secured against such interference so as to be admissible.

[9.166] The Criminal Evidence Act 1992 provides in Part 2 that information that is compiled in the 'ordinary course of business' can be admitted in criminal proceedings.

PART II ADMISSIBILITY OF DOCUMENTARY EVIDENCE

4. Definition (Part II)

In this Part "business" includes any trade, profession or other occupation carried on, for reward or otherwise, either within or outside the State and includes also the performance of functions by or on behalf of—

    (a) any person or body remunerated or financed wholly or partly out of moneys provided by the Oireachtas,

    (b) any institution of the European Communities,

    (c) any national or local authority in a jurisdiction outside the State, or

    (d) any international organisation.

5. Admissibility of documentary evidence

(1) Subject to this Part, information contained in a document shall be admissible in any criminal proceedings as evidence of any fact therein of which direct oral evidence would be admissible if the information—

    (a) was compiled in the ordinary course of a business,

(b) was supplied by a person (whether or not he so compiled it and is identifiable) who had, or may reasonably be supposed to have had, personal knowledge of the matters dealt with, and

(c) in the case of information in non-legible form that has been reproduced in permanent legible form, was reproduced in the course of the normal operation of the reproduction system concerned.

(2) Subsection (1) shall apply whether the information was supplied directly or indirectly but, if it was supplied indirectly, only if each person (whether or not he is identifiable) through whom it was supplied received it in the ordinary course of a business.

(3) Subsection (1) shall not apply to—

(a) information that is privileged from disclosure in criminal proceedings,

(b) information supplied by a person who would not be compellable to give evidence at the instance of the party wishing to give the information in evidence by virtue of this section, or

(c) subject to subsection (4), information compiled for the purposes or in contemplation of any—

(i) is a member of it and controls the composition of its board of directors; or

(i) criminal investigation,

(ii) investigation or inquiry carried out pursuant to or under any enactment,

(iii) civil or criminal proceedings, or

(iv) proceedings of a disciplinary nature.

(4) Subsection (3) (c) shall not apply where—

(a) (i) the information contained in the document was compiled in the presence of a judge of the District Court and supplied on oath by a person in respect of whom an offence was alleged to have been committed and who is ordinarily resident outside the State,

(ii) either section 14 (which deals with the taking of a deposition in the presence of such a judge and the accused) of the Criminal Procedure Act, 1967, could not be invoked or it was not practicable to do so, and

(iii) the person in respect of whom the offence was alleged to have been committed either has died or is outside the State and it is not reasonably practicable to secure his attendance at the criminal proceedings concerned, or

(b) the document containing the information is—

    (i) a map, plan, drawing or photograph (including any explanatory material in or accompanying the document concerned),

    (ii) a record of a direction given by a member of the Garda Síochána pursuant to any enactment,

    (iii) a record of the receipt, handling, transmission, examination or analysis of any thing by any person acting on behalf of any party to the proceedings, or

    (iv) a record by a registered medical practitioner of an examination of a living or dead person.

(5) Without prejudice to subsection (1)—

    (a) where a document purports to be a birth certificate issued in pursuance of the Births and Deaths Registration Acts, 1863 to 1987, and

    (b) a person is named therein as father or mother of the person to whose birth the certificate relates, the document shall be admissible in any criminal proceedings as evidence of the relationship indicated therein.

(6) Where information is admissible in evidence by virtue of this section but is expressed in terms that are not intelligible to the average person without explanation, an explanation of the information shall also be admissible in evidence if either—

    (a) it is given orally by a person who is competent to do so, or

    (b) it is contained in a document and the document purports to be signed by such a person.

6. Evidence of admissibility

(1) In relation to information contained in a document which a party to criminal proceedings wishes to give in evidence by virtue of section 5, a certificate—

    (a) stating that the information was compiled in the ordinary course of a specified business,

    (b) stating that the information is not of a kind mentioned in paragraph (a) or (b) of section 5 (3),

    (c) either stating that the information was not compiled for the purposes or in contemplation of any investigation, inquiry or proceedings referred to in section 5 (3) (c) or, as the case may be, specifying which of the provisions of section 5(4) applies in relation to the document containing the information,

    (d) stating that the information was supplied, either directly or, as the case may be, indirectly through an intermediary or intermediaries (who, or each of whom, received it in the ordinary course of a specified business), by a person who had, or may reasonably be supposed to have had, personal knowledge of the matters dealt with in the information and, where the intermediary, intermediaries or person can be identified, specifying them,

(e) in case the information is information in non-legible form that has been reproduced in permanent legible form, stating that the reproduction was effected in the course of the normal operation of a specified system,

(f) where appropriate, stating that the person who supplied the information cannot reasonably be expected to have any, or any adequate, recollection of the matters dealt with in the information, having regard to the time that has elapsed since he supplied it or to any other specified circumstances,

(g) unless the date on which the information was compiled is already shown on the document, specifying the date (or, if that date is not known, the approximate date) on which it was compiled,

(h) stating any other matter that is relevant to the admissibility in evidence of the information and is required by rules of court to be certified for the purposes of this subsection,

and purporting to be signed by a person who occupies a position in relation to the management of the business in the course of which the information was compiled or who is otherwise in a position to give the certificate shall be evidence of any matter stated or specified therein.

(2) For the purposes of subsection (1) it shall be sufficient for a matter to be stated or specified to the best of the knowledge and belief of the person stating or specifying it.

(3) Notwithstanding that a certificate may have been given pursuant to subsection (1), the court—

(a) shall, where a notice has been served pursuant to section 7(2) objecting to the admissibility in evidence of the whole or any specified part of the information concerned, and

(b) may, in any other case,

require oral evidence to be given of any matter stated or specified in the certificate.

(4) If any person in a certificate given in evidence in any proceedings by virtue of subsection (1) makes a statement material in those proceedings which he knows to be false or does not believe to be true, he shall be guilty of an offence and shall be liable—

(a) on summary conviction, to a fine not exceeding £500 or imprisonment for a term not exceeding 6 months or both, or

(b) on conviction on indictment, to a fine or imprisonment for a term not exceeding 2 years or both.

7. Notice of documentary evidence

(1) Information in a document shall not, without the leave of the court, be admissible in evidence by virtue of section 5 at a trial unless—

(a) a copy of the document and, where appropriate, of a certificate pursuant to section 6 (1) has been served on the accused pursuant to section 6(1) of the Criminal Procedure Act, 1967, or

(b) not later than 21 days before the commencement of the trial, a notice of intention so to give the information in evidence, together with a copy of the document and, where appropriate, of the certificate, is served by or on behalf of the party proposing to give it in evidence on each of the other parties to the proceedings.

(2) A party to the proceedings on whom a notice has been served pursuant to subsection (1) shall not, without the leave of the court, object to the admissibility in evidence of the whole or any specified part of the information concerned unless, not later than 7 days before the commencement of the trial, a notice objecting to its admissibility is served by or on behalf of that party on each of the other parties to the proceedings.

(3) A document required by this section to be served on any person may, subject to subsection (4), be served—

(a) by delivering it to him or to his solicitor,

(b) by addressing it to him and leaving it at his usual or last known residence or place of business or by addressing it to his solicitor and leaving it at the solicitor's office,

(c) by sending it by registered post to him at his usual or last known residence or place of business or to his solicitor at the solicitor's office, or

(d) in the case of a body corporate, by delivering it to the secretary or clerk of the body at its registered or principal office or sending it by registered post to the secretary or clerk of that body at that office.

(4) A document required by this section to be served on an accused shall be served personally on him if he is not represented by a solicitor.

8. Admission and weight of documentary evidence

(1) In any criminal proceedings information or any part thereof that is admissible in evidence by virtue of section 5 shall not be admitted if the court is of opinion that in the interests of justice the information or that part ought not to be admitted.

(2) In considering whether in the interests of justice all or any part of such information ought not to be admitted in evidence the court shall have regard to all the circumstances, including—

(a) whether or not, having regard to the contents and source of the information and the circumstances in which it was compiled, it is a reasonable inference that the information is reliable,

(b) whether or not, having regard to the nature and source of the document containing the information and to any other circumstances that appear to the court to be relevant, it is a reasonable inference that the document is authentic, and

(c) any risk, having regard in particular to whether it is likely to be possible to controvert the information where the person who supplied it does not attend to give oral evidence in the proceedings, that its admission or exclusion will result in unfairness to the accused or, if there is more than one, to any of them.

(3) In estimating the weight, if any, to be attached to information given in evidence by virtue of this Part, regard shall be had to all the circumstances from which any inference can reasonably be drawn as to its accuracy or otherwise.

9. Evidence as to credibility of supplier of information

Where information is given in evidence by virtue of this Part—

(a) any evidence which, if the person who originally supplied the information had been called as a witness, would have been admissible as relevant to his credibility as a witness shall be admissible for that purpose,

(b) evidence may, with the leave of the court, be given of any matter which, if that person had been called as a witness, could have been put to him in cross-examination as relevant to his credibility as a witness but of which evidence could not have been adduced by the cross-examining party, and

(c) evidence tending to prove that that person, whether before or after supplying the information, made (whether orally or not) a statement which is inconsistent with it shall, if not already admissible by virtue of section 5, be admissible for the purpose of showing that he has contradicted himself.

10. Amendment of Criminal Procedure Act, 1967

The Criminal Procedure Act, 1967, is hereby amended—

(a) by the substitution, for paragraphs (d) and (e) of section 6 (1) of that Act (which provides for the service of documents on an accused), of the following paragraphs:

"(d) a statement of the evidence that is to be given by each of them,

(e) a copy of any document containing information which it is proposed to give in evidence by virtue of Part II of the Criminal Evidence Act, 1992,

(f) where appropriate, a copy of a certificate pursuant to section 6(1) of that Act, and

(g) a list of exhibits (if any).", and

(b) by the substitution, for section 11 of that Act (which provides for service of additional documents on an accused after he has been sent forward for trial), of the following section:

11. Additional documents

(1) Where the accused has been sent forward for trial the Director of Public Prosecutions shall cause to be served on him a list of any further witnesses whom he proposes to call at the trial, with a statement of the evidence that is to be given by each of them, a list of any further exhibits, a statement of any further evidence that is to be given by any witness whose name appears on the list of witnesses already supplied, any notice of intention to give information contained in a document in evidence pursuant to section 7(1)(b) of the Criminal Evidence Act, 1992, together with a copy of the document and any certificate pursuant to section 6(1) of that Act, and copies of any statement recorded under section 7 and any deposition taken under that section or under section 14.

(2) Copies of the documents shall also be furnished to the trial court.".

12. Evidence of resolution of Dáil or Seanad

In any criminal proceedings evidence of the passing of a resolution by either House of the Oireachtas, whether before or after the commencement of this section, may be given by the production of a copy of the Journal of the proceedings of that House relating to the resolution and purporting to have been published by the Stationery Office.

Wardship proceedings

[9.167] *Eastern Health Board v MK & MK*[200] involved the applicant seeking to make the three children of the respondent parents wards of court. The evidence of a speech therapist and a senior social worker was tendered as to what was said to them by the children and a video of the children was produced. The allegation was that one of the children had been sexually abused by his father. Without this evidence, no order could be made. The matter went to the Supreme Court on the question of whether this hearsay evidence should be admitted. The Supreme Court held that wardship jurisdiction differed from the norm and that the nature of that jurisdiction, which involved holding the welfare of the child paramount, justified a departure from the normal rules of evidence. They accepted, however, that the allegations were being received in the context of the welfare of the

---

[200] *Eastern Health Board v MK & MK* [1999] 2 IR 99.

children in terms of assessing the risk to the children, and that it did not follow that the hearsay evidence was automatically capable of proving the truth of its contents. (The decision in *Southern Health Board v CH*[201] was approved.) This was a particularly distinctive case involving an eight-year old, emotionally disturbed boy with below-average intelligence and speech difficulties. The trial judge's determination had been that it would be damaging to bring him to court to give evidence about his father. Moreover, such proceedings were on the civil side of the house, where the implementation of evidence rules is always more lenient than in a criminal court.

Bail proceedings

[9.168] The Bail Act 1997 extended the pre-existing grounds on which bail could be refused and made provision that bail can be refused if the gardaí and courts think further crimes will be committed. Under the Act, there is provision for hearsay evidence to be admitted to support such apprehension. However in *DPP v McGinley*[202] Keane CJ, on a bail application, refused to admit hearsay evidence tendered by the gardaí with regard to threats that had been made to the victim's family. It was held by Supreme Court that the defendant was entitled to have evidence given on oath and tested by cross-examination. Section 7 of the Criminal Justice Act 2007 provides that the opinion evidence of a Chief Superintendent that refusal of bail is necessary to prevent commission of serious offences is admissible.

Civil proceedings – children

[9.169] The Children Act 1997 makes provision for the admissibility in civil proceedings of evidence given by children through television link or video or some other intermediary. It also provides for the admissibility of hearsay evidence. The relevant provisions are:

Children Act 1997

[9.170] Section 23 of the 1997 Act states:

> (1) Subject to subsection (2), a statement made by a child shall be admissible as evidence of any fact therein of which direct oral evidence would be admissible in any proceeding to which this Part applies, notwithstanding any rule of law relating to hearsay, where the court considers that—
>
> > (a) the child is unable to give evidence by reason of age, or
> >
> > (b) the giving of oral evidence by the child, either in person or under section 21, would not be in the interest of the welfare of the child.

---

[201] *Southern Health Board v CH* [1996] 1 IR 219.
[202] *DPP v McGinley* [1998] 2 IR 408.

(2) (a) Any statement referred to in subsection (1) or any part thereof shall not be admitted in evidence if the court is of the opinion that, in the interests of justice, the statement or that part of the statement ought not to be so admitted.

(b) In considering whether the statement or any part of the statement ought to be admitted, the court shall have regard to all the circumstances, including any risk that the admission will result in unfairness to any of the parties to the proceedings.

(3) A party proposing to adduce evidence admissible in proceedings to which this Part applies by virtue of subsection (1), shall give to the other party or parties to the proceedings—

(a) such notice, if any, of that fact, and

(b) such particulars of or relating to the evidence,

as is reasonable and practicable in the circumstances for the purpose of enabling such party or parties to deal with any matter arising from its being hearsay.

(4) Subsection (3) shall not apply where the parties concerned agree that it should not apply.

[9.171] With regard to the weight of such evidence, s 24 of the 1997 Act makes the following provision:

(1) In estimating the weight, if any, to be attached to any statement admitted in evidence pursuant to section 23, regard shall be had to all the circumstances from which any inference can reasonably be drawn as to its accuracy or otherwise.

(2) Regard may be had, in particular, as to whether—

(a) the original statement was made contemporaneously with the occurrence or existence of the matters stated,

(b) the evidence involves multiple hearsay,

(c) any person involved has any motive to conceal or misrepresent matters,

(d) the original statement was an edited account or was made in collaboration with another for a particular purpose, and

(e) the circumstances in which the evidence is adduced as hearsay are such as to suggest an attempt to prevent proper evaluation of its weight.

[9.172] Further provision is also made with regard to credibility. Section 25 provides:

Where information is given in a statement admitted in evidence pursuant to section 23—

(a) any evidence which, if the child who originally supplied the information had been called as a witness, would have been admissible as relevant to his or her credibility as a witness shall be admissible for that purpose,

(b) evidence may, with the leave of the court, be given of any matter which, if that child had been called as a witness, could have been put to him or her in cross-examination as relevant to his or her credibility as a witness but of which evidence could not have been adduced by the cross-examining party, and

(c) evidence tending to prove that the child, whether before or after supplying the information, made (whether orally or not) a statement which is inconsistent with it shall, if not already admissible, be admissible for the purpose of showing that the witness has contradicted himself or herself.

Reluctant witnesses

[9.173] Changes with regard to admissibility of hearsay evidence were introduced by the Criminal Justice Act 2006 in the context of reluctant witnesses who have made a statement prior to the trial but refuse to testify, deny making the statement or give evidence materially inconsistent with the earlier statement. Part 3 of the Criminal Justice Act 2006 provides for the admissibility of certain witness statements:

15. Definitions (Part 3)

In this Part—

"audiorecording" includes a recording, on any medium, from which sound may by any means be produced, and cognate words shall be construed accordingly;

"proceedings" includes proceedings under section 4E (application by accused for dismissal of charge) of the Act of 1967 where oral evidence (within the meaning of subsection (5) of that section) is given;

"statement" means a statement the making of which is duly proved and includes—

(a) any representation of fact, whether in words or otherwise,

(b) a statement which has been videorecorded or audiorecorded, and

(c) part of a statement;

"statutory declaration" includes a statutory declaration made under section 17 or 18;

"videorecording" includes a recording, on any medium, from which a moving image may by any means be produced, together with the accompanying soundrecording, and cognate words shall be construed accordingly.

16. Admissibility of certain witness statements

(1) Where a person has been sent forward for trial for an arrestable offence, a statement relevant to the proceedings made by a witness (in this section referred to as "the statement") may, with the leave of the court, be admitted in accordance with this section as evidence of any fact mentioned in it if the witness, although available for cross-examination—

    (a) refuses to give evidence,

    (b) denies making the statement, or

    (c) gives evidence which is materially inconsistent with it.

(2) The statement may be so admitted if—

    (a) the witness confirms, or it is proved, that he or she made it,

    (b) the court is satisfied—

        (i)   that direct oral evidence of the fact concerned would be admissible in the proceedings,

        (ii) that it was made voluntarily, and

        (iii) that it is reliable, and

    (c) either—

        (i)   the statement was given on oath or affirmation or contains a statutory declaration by the witness to the effect that the statement is true to the best of his or her knowledge or belief, or

        (ii) the court is otherwise satisfied that when the statement was made the witness understood the requirement to tell the truth.

(3) In deciding whether the statement is reliable the court shall have regard to—

    (a) whether it was given on oath or affirmation or was videorecorded, or

    (b) if paragraph (a) does not apply in relation to the statement, whether by reason of the circumstances in which it was made, there is other sufficient evidence in support of its reliability, and shall also have regard to—

        (i)   any explanation by the witness for refusing to give evidence or for giving evidence which is inconsistent with the statement, or

        (ii) where the witness denies making the statement, any evidence given in relation to the denial.

(4) The statement shall not be admitted in evidence under this section if the court is of opinion—

    (a) having had regard to all the circumstances, including any risk that its admission would be unfair to the accused or, if there are more than one accused, to any of them, that in the interests of justice it ought not to be so admitted, or

(b) that its admission is unnecessary, having regard to other evidence given in the proceedings.

(5) In estimating the weight, if any, to be attached to the statement regard shall be had to all the circumstances from which any inference can reasonably be drawn as to its accuracy or otherwise.

(6) This section is without prejudice to sections 3 to 6 of the Criminal Procedure Act 1865 and section 21 (proof by written statement) of the Act of 1984.

17. Witness statements made to members of Garda Síochána

(1) A person who makes a statement to a member of the Garda Síochána during the investigation of an arrestable offence (not being a person who is at that time suspected by any such member of having committed it) may make a statutory declaration that the statement is true to the best of the person's knowledge and belief.

(2) For the purposes of section 1(1)(d) of the Statutory Declarations Act 1938 a member of the Garda Síochána may take and receive a statutory declaration made under subsection (1).

(3) Instead of taking and receiving such a statutory declaration the member may take the person's statement on oath or affirmation and for that purpose may administer the oath or affirmation to him or her.

18. Other witness statements

(1) In this section—

"competent person" means a person employed by a public authority and includes an immigration officer who is deemed to have been appointed as such an officer under section 3 of the Immigration Act 2004;

"public authority" means—

(a) a Minister of the Government,

(b) the Commissioners of Public Works in Ireland,

(c) a local authority within the meaning of the Local Government Act 2001,

(d) the Health Service Executive,

(e) a harbour authority within the meaning of the Harbours Act 1946,

(f) a board or other body (not being a company) established by or under statute,

(g) a company in which all the shares are held by, or on behalf of, or by directors appointed by, a Minister of the Government, or

(h) a company in which all the shares are held by a board or other body referred to in paragraph (f), or by a company referred to in paragraph (g).

(2) A person who makes a statement to a competent person in the course of the performance of the competent person's official duties may make a statutory declaration that the statement is true to the best of the person's knowledge and belief.

(3) For the purposes of section 1(1)(d) of the Statutory Declarations Act 1938 a competent person may take and receive a statutory declaration made under subsection (2).

19. Regulations concerning certain witness statements which are recorded

(1) The Minister may, in relation to any statements of witnesses that may be videorecorded or audiorecorded by members of the Garda Síochána while investigating offences, make provision in regulations for—

    (a) the manner in which any such recordings are to be made and preserved, and

    (b) the period for which they are to be retained.

(2) Any failure by a member of the Garda Síochána to comply with a provision of the regulations shall not of itself—

    (a) render the member liable to civil or criminal proceedings, or

    (b) without prejudice to the power of a court to exclude evidence at its discretion, render inadmissible in evidence anything said during the recording concerned.

20. Amendment of section 4E of Act of 1967

Section 4E (application by accused for dismissal of charge) of the Act of 1967 is amended in subsection (5)(b)—

    (a) by the substitution of "section 4F, or" for "section 4F." in subparagraph (ii), and

    (b) by the addition of the following subparagraph:

> "(iii) any other videorecording, or an audiorecording, which may be admitted by the trial court as evidence of any fact stated in it.".

[9.174] Section16(4) provides the usual exclusionary power or discretion to the court to exercise on the basis of fairness to the accused and the undefined 'interests of justice'. Section 16(4) states:

The statement shall not be admitted in evidence under this section if the court is of opinion—

    (a) having regard to all the circumstances, including any risk that its admission would be unfair to the accused, or if there are more than one accused, to any of them, that in the interests of justice it ought not to be admitted.

Proceeds of crime and Criminal Assets Bureau

[9.175] Under the Proceeds of Crime Act 1996, s 8 allows hearsay evidence of a member of the Criminal Assets Bureau as to the possession of property and its connection with the proceeds of crime. This can play a pivotal role in relation to the making of an order under s 3 of the 1996 Act. McGuinness J suggested in *Gilligan*[203] that a court should be slow to make orders under s 3 in the absence of other corroborating evidence. Moriarty J in *M v D*[204] shared that circumspection.

Offences against the State

[9.176] Under the Offences Against the State (Amendment) Act 1998, which was enacted in the aftermath of the Omagh bombing, ss 2–5 concern changes in the rules of evidence. While, in the main, these relate to inference provisions, s 4 admits what would otherwise be inadmissible hearsay in so far as its provisions allow for inferences to be drawn with regard to membership, from any statement or conduct by a person accused of membership of an unlawful organisation, which statement or conduct implies or leads to a reasonable inference that he was at the material time a member.

Organised crime

[9.177] The most recent provision is found in the Criminal Justice (Amendment) Act 2009 with regard to providing a facility for a garda seeking extension of detention to give hearsay evidence.

Section 21(1)(f)(4BC)(a) provides that in an application for such extension:

> ... it shall not be necessary for a member of the Garda Síochána, other than the officer making the application, to give oral evidence for the purposes of the application and the latter officer may testify in relation to any matter within the knowledge of another member of the Garda Siochana that is relevant to the application notwithstanding that it is not within the personal knowledge of the officer.

Reform

[9.178] The Law Reform Commission, in its *Report on the Rule Against Hearsay*,[205] stated that the disadvantages of the hearsay rule are mitigated in practice as the courts freely allow hearsay evidence of probative value when tendered by the defence. In civil cases parties similarly agree to waive the rule, or the trial judge may discourage a pressing argument from counsel on the issue. While, strictly speaking, there is no judicial discretion to excuse or allow breaches of the hearsay rule, should the latter occur, even in a criminal case, no

---

[203] *Gilligan v CAB* [1998] 3 IR 185.

[204] *M v D* [1998] 3 IR 175.

[205] Law Reform Commission, *Rule Against Hearsay Working Paper* (LRC 9-1980), p 11.

miscarriage of justice can be adjudged to have occurred, in accordance with s 5(1)(a) of the Courts of Justice Act 1928.

[9.179] However, such a solution is undesirable in not providing sufficient certainty for the parties to know where they stand in advance of the case and to facilitate a prediction of the outcome with some degree of accuracy. The Criminal Evidence Act 1992 did make some considerable provision for the admissibility of hearsay evidence in certain circumstances. These relate primarily to the admissibility of certain documentary evidence in criminal proceedings. Outside of such specific exceptional provisions, the strength of the rule prevails. For example, in *DPP v Det Sgt Kelly v McGinley*,[206] Keane J, on a bail application, refused to admit hearsay evidence tendered by the gardaí with regard to threats to the victim's family. Objection to its admissibility was upheld on the basis of natural justice.

[9.180] The Balance in the Criminal Law Review Group, when established on 2 November 2006, had as part of its terms of reference 'modifying the rule in relation to hearsay evidence.' With regard to the rule against hearsay, the Review Group noted that the fundamental principle of the rule is sound. It identifies its rationale as follows:

> The fundamental reason for the rule is that if out of court statements made by persons who were not required to attend to give evidence were freely admissible in evidence, the path would be clear for those who wished to invent and fabricate evidence. This would be especially true in criminal cases. If the rule were to be generally relaxed, it would for example be possible for an accused to tender evidence of alleged admissions to the crime made by third parties who were not before the court for cross examination.[207]

[9.181] The Balance in the Criminal Law Review Group also noted *Kiely v Minister for Social Welfare*[208] where the importance of allowing a person affected by evidence the opportunity to test its veracity by cross-examination was considered essential to fair procedure. They noted that the rule can at times operate in a highly technical fashion and saw merit in codifying it. There are limitations, however, to what can be achieved because of constitutional concerns:

> Allowing hearsay evidence by consent does not require any change in the law as it is permissible at present. However certain fundamental principles are clear in respect of allowing hearsay without the consent of the accused. Any significant

---

[206] *DPP v Det Sgt Kelly v McGinley* (20 May 1998, unreported), SC.
[207] *Balance in the Criminal Law Review Group Final Report* (Dept of Justice, Equality and Law Reform, 15 March 2007), p 228.
[208] *Kiely v Minister for Social Welfare* [1977] IR 267.

easing of the position regarding hearsay evidence would be much more than a procedural issue, and would cause significant problems in a jury-based system. The right to cross examine is a fundamental constitutional right: see *In re Haughey*[209] and *Maguire v Ardagh*.[210] Allowing hearsay in criminal cases deprives the defendant of that right in practice or at least has the potential to undermine that right. Therefore there would need to be very considerable caution in allowing much greater hearsay evidence.[211]

The Balance in the Criminal Law Review Group concluded that the rule against hearsay should not be generally relaxed and doubted whether Ireland could go the route of the UK where Part 11 of the Criminal Justice Act 2003 makes all hearsay evidence admissible subject to an 'interests of justice' test.[212] They stated:

> There is not the same principled objection to hearsay in merely quasi-criminal matters, such as bail or confiscation of assets, but to allow widespread hearsay in the criminal trial itself would pose a major threat to fundamental principles.[213]

Further exceptional provisions – incremental reform

[9.182] Hence it can be seen that specific incursions on the rule against hearsay are being made with regard to exceptional provisions for particular cases. This is a phenomenon which has been seen to be common to many areas of evidentiary law reform. It shares the difficulty with other such moves of a failure to consider the implications for the underlying principle of such change. This incremental mechanism of change, with the particular context in question invoked as justification, risks avoidance of acknowledgement that any real impact on principle occurs, when in fact it does. The 'old chestnut' of the rule against hearsay has proven no more impervious to this phenomenon than other so-called 'obstructionist' rules of evidence.

---

[209] *In re Haughey* [1971] IR 217.

[210] *Maguire v Ardagh* [2002] 1 IR 385.

[211] *Balance in the Criminal Law Review Group Final Report* (Dept of Justice, Equality and Law Reform, 15 March 2007), p 230.

[212] Criminal Justice Act 2003, s 114.

[213] *Balance in the Criminal Law Review Group Final Report* (Dept of Justice, Equality and Law Reform, 15 March 2007), p 231.

Chapter 10

Similar Fact Evidence

How can we know the dancer from the dance?

Yeats, 'Among School Children'

Introduction

[10.01] In general the three principles governing the admissibility of similar fact evidence can be stated as follows:

(i)   evidence of past bad behaviour, if offered as evidence that a particular act was done, must be relevant;

(ii)   even if relevant, evidence of past bad behaviour is inadmissible if its only relevance is to show that the actor has a bad disposition;

(iii) even if (i) and (ii) are satisfied, such evidence is inadmissible or can be excluded if its prejudicial effect outweighs its probative value.

[10.02] Lord Herschell enunciated the basic exclusionary premise with regard to evidence as to the accused's past misconduct in the nineteenth-century landmark decision of *Makin v Attorney General for New South Wales*:[1]

> It is undoubtedly not competent for the prosecution to adduce evidence tending to show that the accused has been guilty of criminal acts other than those covered by the indictment, for the purpose of leading to the conclusion that the accused is a person likely from his criminal conduct or character to have committed the offence for which he is being tried.

That is the general rule. However, the exception to that basic principle, which is largely what concerns us in this chapter, was formulated by Lord Herschell as follows:

> On the other hand the mere fact that the evidence adduced tends to show that commission of other crimes does not render it inadmissible if it be relevant to an issue before the jury, and it may be so relevant if it bears upon the question whether the acts alleged to constitute the crime charged in the indictment were designed or accidental or to rebut a defence which would otherwise be open to the accused.

---

[1]   *Makin v Attorney General for New South Wales* [1894] AC 57 at 65.

[10.03] The rationale for the general reluctance of the courts to admit or allow the production by the prosecution of so-called 'similar fact evidence' as evidence going to prove the commission of an offence before the court is based on fears as to its unduly prejudicial nature. Largely, the fear is that a jury will 'give a dog a bad name and hang him'. It is felt, moreover, that such evidence gives rise to too many collateral issues, and may well lead to differential law enforcement by encouraging the police to look for suspects with records.

[10.04] Generally speaking, similar fact evidence is tendered by the prosecution against the accused. It may also, however, in a rape case, consist of the introduction of evidence by the defence of prior occasions of sexual intercourse between the accused and the complainant, as proof of consent on the occasion in question.[2] Conduct in respect of which the accused was acquitted cannot normally be relied upon as similar fact evidence.[3]

[10.05] In the case of *R v Z*,[4] the defendant was charged with rape. He had been tried for rape on four previous occasions and convicted once. The Crown wanted to call all four previous complainants to give evidence of his conduct towards them, in order to negate his defence of consent. The trial judge ruled that the evidence of the three complainants in respect of which the defendant had been acquitted was inadmissible. The Court of Appeal dismissed an appeal and it came before House of Lords. The House of Lords allowed the appeal and overruled the decision of *G v Coltart*.[5] They looked at the principle of double jeopardy, which prevented a defendant being prosecuted for an offence on the same, or substantially the same, facts as the previous prosecution, but held that relevant evidence was not inadmissible merely because it showed or tended to show that the defendant had in fact been guilty of a previous offence of which he had been acquitted. The House of Lords took the view that the evidence of the three previous complainants was not adduced to show that he was guilty on those occasions, but rather to show by similar facts his guilt of the offence for which he was being tried.

[10.06] Lord Hutton reasoned in the *Z* case as follows:[6]

> In the present case the defendant is not placed in double jeopardy because the facts giving rise to the present prosecution are different to the facts which gave rise to the earlier prosecutions. The evidence of the earlier complainants is

---

2   *R v Riley* (1887) 18 QBD 481.
3   *Kemp v R* (1951) 83 CLR 341; *G v Coltart* [1967] 1 QB 432; and cf *R v Miles* (1943) 44 SR WSW 198.
4   *R v Z* [2000] 2 AC 483.
5   *G v Coltart* [1967] 1 QB 432.
6   *R v Z* [2000] 2 AC 483 at 506.

accepted to be relevant and to come within the ambit of the similar fact rule and I am of opinion therefore that it is not inadmissible because it shows the defendant was, in fact, guilty of the offences of rape of which he had earlier been acquitted.

Therefore, the House of Lords under the previous law (now changed since the Criminal Justice Act 2003) was happy to have acquittals admitted as similar fact evidence.

[10.07] In the Irish case of *DO v DPP*,[7] the Supreme Court addressed the issue of the admissibility of acquittals. It did so, however, from a slightly different perspective – one of revisiting a conviction on the basis of such evidence. The facts here concerned a teacher who had been convicted of a number of offences of sexual assault and rape in relation to a boy, D. Part of the evidence led against him (as similar fact evidence) was that of two other boys, B and M, who made allegations of sexual assault, but not rape, against the teacher. Subsequent to his conviction on the counts relating to D, the applicant had been tried in relation to the offences comprising the acts of which B and M had given evidence leading to the his conviction. He was tried and acquitted by a jury in respect of the counts in relation to B and M. The defendant appealed against his conviction and part of his appeal involved a question of exceptional public importance, which was identified by the Court of Criminal Appeal and sent for consideration to the Supreme Court, namely: 'Is a conviction rendered unsafe and unsatisfactory where it is procured in part by similar fact evidence of extraneous offences in respect of which the convicted person is subsequently tried and acquitted?' State counsel argued that at the time of the trial, the similar fact evidence was properly admissible in law, although she did offer the view that the DPP in practice would not seek to rely on similar fact evidence that had itself been the subject of a trial leading to an acquittal, while not committing however to any view as to the admissibility in law of such evidence. The Supreme Court considered the issue and concluded, as stated by Hardiman J on the issue, that:

> the fact that the acquittals on the counts representing the similar fact evidence took place *after* the convictions on the counts in respect of which the same material was used as similar fact evidence does not prevent this Court or the Court of Criminal Appeal from taking the acquittals into account when considering if the convictions are unsafe or unsatisfactory.

[10.08] The issue of whether evidence is sufficiently similar to be admitted if dissimilarities emerge when it is given at trial arose in *DPP v D O'S*.[8] Four counts of sexual assault and three counts of rape perpetrated between September

---

[7]   *DO v DPP* [2006] IESC 12.
[8]   *DPP v D O'S* [2004] IECCA 12, McGuinness J.

1997 and February 1998 against DC, then eleven, were proferred against the applicant, then a remedial teacher in Cork area. He was convicted and appealed *inter alia* on the basis that the trial judge erred in admitting the evidence of PB and JM, two other young witnesses who had been pupils at the school and attended the remedial classes given by the applicant. The applicant drew attention to the inconsistencies between their evidence and that of the complainant.

[10.09] Endorsing the approach of the trial judge, which had been to follow the judgment of Barron J in *DPP v BK*,[9] the court here concluded that 'there were indeed strong similarities in the location, the timing and the manner in which the three witnesses alleged that the applicant committed the particular offence of rubbing his penis against their backs while correcting their work in the remedial classroom.'[10] While accepting that dissimilarities of detail had emerged in the course of their evidence, the court did not regard these as significant and concluded that 'the evidence falls on the right side of the clear line of division between similar fact evidence and system evidence …[and] the learned trial judge was correct in both admitting the evidence of PB and JM and in refusing to discharge the jury subsequent to their evidence.'[11]

[10.10] While it used to be thought that similar fact evidence could only be admitted to show *mens rea* and not *actus reus*, that perception was ended by the decision in *R v Ball*,[12] where such evidence was introduced to establish that acts of incestuous intercourse between the accused brother and sister took place. It is also noteworthy that the prosecution cannot credit an accused with elaborate defences in order to facilitate the introduction of such evidence (*Thompson v R*[13]). Rather, the defence that similar fact evidence is introduced to rebut in such a situation must have been raised in substance. The prosecution may, however, rebut defences reasonably likely to be run by the accused (*Harris v DPP*[14]).

Rationale for admission

[10.11] Should similar fact evidence be admitted, the courts are said to do so on the basis of the unlikelihood of coincidence. To take the facts of *R v Ball*[15] as

---

[9] *DPP v BK* [2000] IR 199.
[10] *DPP v D O'S* [2004] IECCA 12 at 29.
[11] *DPP v D O'S* [2004] IECCA 12 at 30.
[12] *R v Ball* [1911] AC 47.
[13] *Thompson v R* [1918] AC 221.
[14] *Harris v DPP* [1952] AC 694.
[15] *R v Ball* [1911] AC 47.

illustrative of this reasoning, is effectively to ask: 'Wouldn't it be odd if a brother and sister, who had committed incest frequently in the past, now lived together as man and wife, sleeping in the same bed, without committing incest?' The dangers of this type of reasoning were given clear expression by Lord Hewart CJ in *R v Bailey*[16]:

> It is so easy to derive from a series of unsatisfactory accusations, if there are enough of them, an accusation which at least ... appears satisfactory ... It is so easy to collect from a mass of ingredients, not one of which is sufficient, a totality which will appear to contain what is missing.

[10.12] In order to minimise the dangers in this context, courts have looked for a high degree of similarity between the evidence proferred and the incidents now before the courts. *Heydon* explains this approach as follows: 'Similarity narrows the gap between proving the accused was a wrongdoer in general and proving he did this particular wrong.'[17]

[10.13] Because of the difficulties surrounding the establishment or indeed the explanation of when similar fact evidence is admissible, a 'categorical' approach has found some favour in terms of designating the occasions of admission. In large part, the basis for this categorical approach can be found in Lord Herschell's statement in *Makin v Attorney General for New South Wales*,[18] which was subsequently interpreted and used by the court as a definitive framework or formula for admission, rather than being representative of a general approach.

[10.14] Since the 'categories' have had such an important influence on the development of the law in this area, and the treatment of this type of evidence by the court, it is worthwhile delineating each together with some of the case law and the manner in which they have been applied. Initially these categories were regarded as closed (*R v Bond*[19]), but Viscount Simon, in *Harris v DPP*,[20] gave expression to the notion that they were not closed and operated rather as touchstones of admissibility.

---

[16] *R v Bailey* [1924] All ER 466.
[17] Heydon, *Evidence: Cases and Materials* (2nd edn, London, Butterworths, 1984), at 262.
[18] *Makin v Attorney General for New South Wales* [1894] AC 57 at 65.
[19] *R v Bond* [1906] 2 KB 389.
[20] *Harris v DPP* [1952] AC 694.

The categories

(1) Admissibility of evidence of conduct on other occasions which is of particular relevance in spite of its tendency to show bad disposition

[10.15] *R v Smith*[21] is illustrative of this 'category' of admissibility of evidence of past bad behaviour. Smith was charged with murdering his wife in her bath by drowning her. Two other former wives of Smith had been drowned in the same manner. Each had made a will in Smith's favour. On each occasion, he had bought a suitable bath, placed it in a room which could not be locked from the inside and taken each of the wives the doctor with the suggestion that she suffered from epileptic fits. Each drowning allegedly occurred because of the onset of such a fit while bathing.

[10.16] In *R v Armstrong*,[22] evidence of subsequent behaviour on the part of the accused was introduced to similar effect. The defendant here was charged with the murder of his wife by arsenic poisoning. The defence alleged she had committed suicide. The accused, when found to be in possession of arsenic, claimed it was purchased for the purpose of killing weeds. Evidence to the effect that Armstrong had attempted to poison a man with arsenic eight months after his wife's death was admitted because it suggested the accused was lying when he said he had purchased poison for an innocent purpose.

(2) Admissibility of evidence which forms part of the same transaction to such an extent that the acts are so inextricably bound up that it is impossible to differentiate between them

[10.17] The facts of the decision in *R v Ellis*[23] illustrate the situations covered by this category. The prisoner here was charged with stealing six marked coins. Evidence was presented to the effect that marked coins had been placed in the till and the prosecutrix's son had watched the prisoner withdraw these with money obtained for customers. On his arrest, the accused was found to be in possession of both marked and unmarked coins, amounting in total to the amount missing from the till. Evidence tendered to show he had stolen the unmarked coins was admitted because it went to show the history of the till from the time when the marked money was put into it, up to the time when the money was found in the possession of the prisoner.

[10.18] *O'Leary v R*[24] is another decision illustrating the ambit of this category. Employees of a timber camp had engaged in a drunken orgy over a period of

---

[21] *R v Smith* [1914–15] All ER 262 (CA).
[22] *R v Armstrong* [1922] 2 KB 555.
[23] *R v Ellis* (1826) 6 B & C 145.
[24] *O'Leary v R* (1946) 73 CLR 566.

several hours. The following morning, one of their number was found near to death, having been beaten on the head with a bottle, had petrol poured over him and been set alight. The High Court of Australia held that evidence of violent assaults by the accused on other employees, including the deceased, during the orgy, all of which involved brutal blows to the head, was admissible. Dixon J commented:

> Without evidence of what, during that time, was done by those men who took any significant part in the matter and especially evidence of the behaviour of the prisoner, the transaction of which the alleged murder formed an integral part could not be truly understood and isolated from it could only be presented as an unreal and not very intelligible event.

The third and fourth categories are perhaps more conveniently dealt with together.

(3) Admissibility of evidence to show system or (4) to rebut a defence.

[10.19] The first of these two categories perhaps best fits the overall appellation of this type of evidence, as evidence where a very high degree of similarity in the *modus operandi is* required – so-called 'hallmark' cases.

[10.20] The decision in *Makin*[25] is itself illustrative of the type of situation contemplated. *Makin*, sometimes referred to colourfully, if crudely, as the 'babyfarmers' case, involved a husband and wife accused of murdering a baby, which they had taken in return for a small sum of money from its natural parent. The baby's body was found buried in the Makin's backyard. The accused disclaimed all connection with the mother of the baby and denied all knowledge of the body. Evidence was introduced to the effect that other babies' bodies (which the Makins also denied knowledge of) had been found in the backyards of other houses occupied by the accused, and admitted on the basis that it was 'strikingly similar' and to rebut the accused's suggestion of coincidence and the possible defence that the child's death was accidental.

[10.21] *R v Straffen*[26] is another case in point. The accused here was charged with strangling a young girl. The death had occurred on an occasion when the accused had escaped from Broadmoor (an institution for the criminally insane), where he was incarcerated after being found unfit to plead to charges of having killed two small girls. The accused had commented to the police, 'I did not kill her', at a time when neither the police nor the newspapers had made reference to the death of a girl. Evidence was admitted here of the two previous murders of young girls committed by Straffen, in order to identify him as the perpetrator in

---

[25] *Makin v Attorney General for New South Wales* [1894] AC 57 at 65
[26] *R v Straffen* [1952] 2 QB 911.

this case. The grounds of admission were: first, that each of the victims was a young girl; second, each of the young girls was killed by manual strangulation; third, no attempt was made at sexual interference nor was there any apparent motive for the crime. Further, there was no evidence of a struggle, and no attempt made to conceal the body.

The extent to which these factors may not be perceived as sufficient to warrant admissibility of the evidence of past bad behaviour, is surely now questionable.

[10.22] The case of *People v Dempsey*,[27] provides a less controversial Irish example of the admissibility of evidence of past bad behaviour to rebut the defendant's claim of 'chaste courtship' in a situation where he was charged with unlawful carnal knowledge of a girl between fifteen and seventeen years of age. The past behaviour in this case consisted of evidence of earlier occasions of sexual activity between the defendant and the girl in question.

[10.23] Part of the controversy in these cases can be related to the claim of similarity or indeed relevance, which can be controversial and a product not so much of fact, as the inherent attitudes and prejudices of the trial judge. Here, as so often before perceived in the rules of evidence, can be seen the influence of the politics or tenor of the times.

[10.24] *R v Thompson*[28] is a classic case in point, and although now of dubious precedent value, given its subsequent perception by the courts, serves well to illustrate the dangers of the type of reasoning the admissibility of past behaviour on the part of the accused can spawn. In *Thompson*, evidence was admitted to rebut a defence of mistaken identity and to prove the unlikelihood of the identified man having the accused's disposition, as proven by past acts.

[10.25] The facts were that the accused was charged with involvement in acts of gross indecency with two boys on 16 March. A second appointment had been made for 18 March, on which occasion the accused was arrested by the police. The police searched the accused's house and found photographs of naked boys and powder-puffs. These latter were admitted in evidence against the accused. Lord Sumner's reasoning is renowned for the comment which has survived to overshadow the remaining reasoning in that case:[29]

> The evidence tends to attach to the accused a peculiarity which, though not purely physical, I think may be recognised as properly bearing that name. Experience tends to show that these offences against nature connote an inversion of normal characteristics which, while demanding punishment as offending

---

[27] *People v Dempsey* [1961] IR 288.
[28] *R v Thompson* [1918] AC 221.
[29] *R v Thompson* [1918] AC 221 at 235.

against social morality, also partake of the nature of an abnormal physical property. A thief, a cheat, a coiner, or a housebreaker is only a particular specimen of the genus rogue, and, though no doubt each tends to keep to his own line of business, they all alike possess the by no means extraordinary mental characteristic that they propose somehow to get their living dishonestly. So common a characteristic is not a recognisable mark of the individual. Persons, however, who commit the offences now under consideration seek the habitual gratification of a particular perverted lust, which not only takes them out of the class of ordinary men gone wrong, but *stamps them with the hallmark of a specialised and extraordinary class as much as if they carried on their bodies some physical peculiarity.*

[10.26] The dictum in *Thompson* was subsequently applied in *R v Sims*[30] and in *R v Hall*.[31] In essence the logic applied here in these cases was that once a homosexual offence was alleged against an accused, evidence that he had a homosexual propensity was automatically admissible in evidence. It is a logic which had little to commend it, and was subjected to much criticism. In *Boardman v DPP*[32] the question of law as to whether homosexual offences did indeed form a separate category for the purposes of the admissibility of similar fact evidence, was considered by the House of Lords. The House of Lords rejected this contention. In the words of Lord Hailsham: 'There is not a separate category of homosexual cases. The rules of logic and common sense must be the same for all trials where similar fact or other analogous evidence is sought to be introduced.'

[10.27] *DPP v Boardman* is of greater importance as will be seen, however, in terms of forging a new approach to the issue of similar fact evidence, which by this stage was exhibiting the confines, limitations and anomalies of the strict categorical approach. In *DPP v Boardman* the facts concerned charges of attempted buggery against the defendant headmaster with S, a pupil, and of inciting H, another pupil, to commit buggery. The trial judge in that case held H's evidence admissible on the count regarding S, and vice versa. The House of Lords approved the admissibility of the evidence, deeming the evidence of both pupils to have been strikingly similar in time and methods of advance. The court criticised *Thompson*, and emphasised the necessity of showing striking similarity and not just suggesting same on grounds of coincidence. To this extent, *Thompson* is of doubtful authority.

---

[30]   *R v Sims* [1946] 1 KB 53.
[31]   *R v Hall* [1952] 1 KB 302.
[32]   *Boardman v DPP* [1975] AC 421.

(5) Admissibility of similar fact evidence to rebut the defence that the acts performed were totally innocent, and involved no guilty intent

[10.28] This category is exemplified by the facts of *R v Bond*,[33] which involved a doctor who was charged with using instruments with an intent to procure an abortion. The defence put forward was that of using the same for *bona fide* medical purposes. Evidence was admitted that the doctor had told the woman in question that he had 'put dozens of girls right', alongside the testimony that he had performed an abortion on her also.

[10.29] In summary, then, the categorical approach aside, the essence of the principles or prerequisites for admissibility here are:

(i) the evidence must be relevant;

(ii) the evidence must be relevant by way of an argument relying at some stage upon an inference drawn from the disposition of the accused; and

(iii) the evidence must be discreditable to the accused in some way.

[10.30] In relation to the third point, which has not been addressed hitherto, it is quite clear that the concept of discredit here extends further than merely the commission of crimes. In *R v Barrington*,[34] the prosecution sought to bolster the evidence of three young complainants of acts of indecency perpetrated by an accused with evidence from three other girls. The girls' evidence implied that the accused had gone through the same preliminary technique – recruiting them ostensibly for babysitting – and had used similar inducements, including pornographic magazines. Notwithstanding the fact that it was not alleged that any acts of indecency or criminal conduct occurred, the evidence was admitted.

The distinct nature of sexual cases

[10.31] The 'special category' view of certain cases propounded in *Thompson*[35] makes a reappearance, even in the aftermath of *Boardman*,[36] and requires further consideration. Lord Sumner's observations were interpreted to the effect that if they involved homosexual behaviour, or were committed against children, sexual offences were so distinctive as to justify the admission of evidence that would not otherwise go in under the rule.

---

[33] *R v Bond* [1906] 2 KB 389.

[34] *R v Barrington* [1981] 1 All ER 1132.

[35] *Thompson v R* [1918] AC 221.

[36] *Boardman v DPP* [1975] AC 421.

[10.32] In *King*,[37] the accused was charged with gross indecency, attempted buggery and assault. In cross-examination he was asked, 'Are you a homosexual?', to which he answered, 'yes'. This was deemed admissible where he denied committing the acts. The Court of Appeal saw the evidence as coming plainly within the principle laid down in *Thompson*.

[10.33] In *Sims*,[38] the charges against the accused were those of sodomy and gross indecency with four different men on different occasions. The refusal of an application to try these separately was upheld on the basis that they were relevant and probative in relation to each other. The Court of Appeal was of the view that sodomy was a crime in a special category and hence 'the repetition of the acts is itself a special feature connecting the accused with the crime'.[39] The court would also have applied this logic to offences against children.

[10.34] In *Boardman*, however, the House of Lords had expressed the view that homosexual cases were not to be placed in a special category. Lord Hailsham explained the distinction as follows:

> In a sex case ... whilst a repeated homosexual act by itself might be quite insufficient to admit the evidence as confirmatory of identity or design, the fact that it was alleged to have been performed wearing the ceremonial head-dress of a Red Indian chief or other eccentric garb might well in appropriate circumstances suffice.[40]

[10.35] In *Novak*,[41] the accused had met boys in places of amusement, offering them money to play gambling machines, and then shelter at his house. He then committed acts of buggery and attempted buggery whilst sharing a bed with them. Bridge LJ expressed the view that this was not committing offences in a strikingly similar manner:

> If a man is going to commit buggery with a boy he picks up, it must surely be a commonplace feature of such an encounter that he will take the boy home with him and commit the offence in bed.[42]

Bridge J saw the picking up at amusement arcades as a similarity in the surrounding circumstances, and not a similarity as required in the commission of the crime:

> It is a similarity in the surrounding circumstances and is not, in our judgment, sufficiently proximate to the commission of the crime itself to lead to the

---

[37] *R v King* [1967] 2 QB 388.
[38] *R v Sims* [1946] 1 KB 531.
[39] *R v Sims* [1946] 1 KB 531 at 540.
[40] *Boardman v DPP* [1975] AC 421 at 454.
[41] *R v Novak* (1976) 65 Cr App R 107.
[42] *R v Novak* (1976) 65 Cr App R 107 at 112.

conclusion that the repetition of this feature would make the boys' stories inexplicable on the basis of coincidence.[43]

[10.36] In *Johannsen*,[44] by contrast, on similar facts, the court found striking similarity:

> The prosecution's case was that between May and December 1975 he made a practice of accosting boys in amusement arcades and similar places, offering them money or a meal or treating them to a game, taking them to his accommodation or on to the beach, and there committing the offences charged ... We have no hesitation in deciding there were striking similarities ...[45]

Hence it can be seen that there was some uneven application of the law post *Boardman*.

[10.37] The House of Lords, in *DPP v P*,[46] attempted to resolve these divergences. The facts were that the accused was convicted of the offences of rape and incest against his two daughters. The issue before the House was whether or not the evidence of one daughter was properly admitted against the accused in relation to the other. Both daughters gave evidence of a prolonged course of domination by the accused of the whole family, and there was evidence the accused had contributed to the costs of abortions for both. The House of Lords held that the probative force of the evidence is what is required, which is not restricted to 'striking similarity'. The fact that there was no more similarity beyond that of the 'stock in trade' of child abuse, appearing in the majority of cases, did not mean that it was inadmissible.

[10.38] There is a difficulty here regarding the prejudicial nature of such evidence, surely, relative to the limited field within which the accused could lie, and the likely easy satisfaction thereby of 'similarity'. If this is somehow evident in *P*, it is even more so in *H*. The facts of *R v H*[47] involved charges against the accused of sexual offences against his adopted daughter and his stepdaughter. The girls had both confided in the accused's wife three years after the commission of the alleged offences, having discussed the matter first between themselves. The adopted daughter had brought the allegations to the attention of her mother at the prompting of her boyfriend. He had moved into the family home shortly after the accused's arrest. The defence alleged the young woman was using the story as an excuse to reject the boyfriend's advances, and that the two young women might have colluded. The question was whether this

---

[43] *R v Novak* (1976) 65 Cr App R 107 at 112.

[44] *Johannsen* (1977) 65 Cr App R 101.

[45] *Johannsen* (1977) 65 Cr App R 101 at 103.

[46] *DPP v P* [1991] 2 AC 447.

[47] *R v H* [1995] 2 All ER 865.

risk of contamination was a question of admissibility for the trial judge, or a matter of weight for the jury. The House of Lords decided that, save in exceptional cases, the matter was one of weight for the determination of the jury. Doran and Jackson – noting[48] that the laws of evidence have already gone a considerable way to ease the task of prosecution in such cases (corroboration requirements, video link etc and *R v P*[49] making it more feasible to prosecute cases on the basis of more than one witness) – commented:

> At some point, however, the question must arise as to whether the course of change has moved too far in one direction and whether the protection of the accused's interests have been sacrificed to an unacceptable degree in the interest of securing convictions in this highly sensitive class of case.[50]

Instead of showing concern with regard to usurpation of the jury's fact-finding domain, the House of Lords, they argue, 'should perhaps also have turned its mind to the judicial responsibility to ensure that the accused receives a fair trial.[51]

[10.39] The Law Commission in the UK[52] considered whether sexual offences should constitute a separate category and in its paper in 1996 gave the view that, if anything, the arguments for exclusion would be stronger in the case of sexual offences because it is more prejudicial, but they did not support the concept that it should have its own category.

Relevance in other cases

[10.40] Outside the sphere of sexual cases, the relevance test has been applied more consistently. In *Mansfield*,[53] the accused was charged with three counts of arson. The fires occurred within three weeks in a hotel where the accused lived, and in two hotels where he worked as kitchen porter. In each case, he had opportunity, lied to police on questioning and his wastepaper bin was found at the third. Each fire was held admissible in relation to the other.

---

[48] Dolan and Jackson, 'Cross-admissibility of Similar Fact' [1995] 2 All ER, Annual Review, Evidence 224.

[49] *R v P* [1991] 3 All ER 337.

[50] Dolan and Jackson, 'Cross-admissibility of Similar Fact' [1995] 2 All ER, Annual Review Evidence 266 at 230.

[51] Dolan and Jackson, 'Cross-admissibility of Similar Fact' [1995] 2 All ER, Annual Review Evidence 244 at 230.

[52] Law Commission, 'Evidence in Criminal Proceedings: Previous Misconduct of a Defendant' (CP No 141 London Stationery Office, 1996).

[53] *R v Mansfield* [1978] 1 WLR 1102.

[10.41] In *Rance*,[54] charges of corruptly procuring payment to a local councillor were levied against a building company director. R claimed he had been deceived into signing a false certificate describing the councillor as a sub-contractor. Evidence was admitted of similar payments by false certificates to other councillors.

[10.42] With regard to the possibility of evidence being introduced prior to a particular defence (eg innocent association) actually being raised by the defence, *Harris v DPP*[55] takes the view that the prosecution are not required to wait until the accused has actually raised the specific defence. Some cases in the past have suggested that a complete denial by the accused might mean that evidence of a succession of such incidents (which might well be relevant to innocent association) would not go in (*Chando*r,[56] *Flack*[57]). The House of Lords in *Boardman* did not agree, as in both the accused is saying the accuser is lying.

Burden and standard of proof

[10.43] The prosecution should establish evidence of the extraneous acts beyond reasonable doubt. If there has not been a conviction, this means the acts must be proven as if the accused were charged with them. The full criminal standard applies.[58]

Irish case law

[10.44] While the Irish courts have not forged an identifiable or original jurisprudence in this area, they have generally followed – at least tacitly – the traditional English position with regard to the admissibility of this type of evidence. In general, therefore, an exclusionary approach is adopted unless some reason (not necessarily, but usually, those of the categories of inclusion) persuades the court otherwise.

[10.45] In the case of *AG v McCabe*,[59] the facts of which concerned the deaths of six people as a result of a house being set on fire, the accused was charged with the murder of one of their number. The Court of Criminal Appeal held that the evidence of the other deaths had been correctly introduced at trial.

---

[54] *Rance* (1975) 62 Cr App R 118.
[55] *Harris v DPP* [1952] AC 694.
[56] *R v Chandor* [1959] 1 QB 545.
[57] *R v Flack* [1969] 2 All ER 784.
[58] *McGranaghan* [1995] 1 Cr App R 559.
[59] *AG v McCabe* [1927] IR 129.

[10.46] In *AG v Joyce and Walsh*,[60] the Court of Criminal Appeal held that evidence that on an earlier occasion the accused had put guano into the deceased's milk, was correctly introduced to prove a state of mind and motive on the part of the accused.

[10.47] In a similar vein, the decision of *AG v Fleming*[61] followed *Joyce*, and in the context of an accused charged with the murder of his wife, introduced evidence that he had previously attempted to poison his wife. Both occasions were alleged to be related to his promise to marry a young girl, who on the second occasion was pregnant with his child. The earlier attempt, according to the court, illustrated the tenor of the relationship between the accused and his wife and his malice toward her.

[10.48] In the decision of *People (AG) v Kirwan*,[62] the Court of Criminal Appeal held that evidence that the accused had previously been in prison was admissible, as was a charge of the accused having murdered his brother, as it came under the rule in *Makin's* case and was relevant to an issue before the jury.

[10.49] The decision of the Court of Criminal Appeal in *People v Wallace*[63] illustrates the later approach of the Irish courts to such evidence. The facts of the case were as follows. Three brothers were convicted of the larceny of leather jackets and two suits at Thurles, Co Tipperary, on 26 February 1981 and of an attempt to steal clothing at the same premises on 10 March 1981. Two of the brothers appealed the convictions.

[10.50] On the first occasion, 26 February 1981, the facts established were that two men entered the men's outfitters in question and proceeded to the back of the shop where the suits and jackets were kept, one of them carrying a cardboard box covered with cellotape, which he held against his chest. A third man came into the shop, looking for a white shirt with a peaked collar. When the first two men had left the shop, and the third declared himself not satisfied and departed, a quantity of leather jackets and two suits were found to be missing, although there had been no sales. On 19 March 1981, when the owner and his wife were present in the shop, two men again entered carrying a cardboard box in similar manner to the earlier occasion. A third man entered asking for a shirt with a peaked collar. The owner remained with the first two. After a while they left, followed by the third. None had purchased anything.

[60] *AG v Joyce and Walsh* [1929] IR 526.
[61] *AG v Fleming* [1934] IR 166.
[62] *People (AG) v Kirwan* [1943] IR 279.
[63] *People v Wallace* (1983) 2 Frewen 125, McWilliam J.

[10.51] On appeal it was argued, *inter alia*, that there should have been separate trials. McWilliam J referred to the decision in *Harris v DPP*,[64] where, when there were eight counts of larceny at a market during three successive months – each similarly carried out, but on the first seven occasions there being no further evidence to associate the accused specifically with the thefts – the trial judge ruled there was no good reason for ordering a separate trial on the eighth count, since the charges formed part of a series of offences of the same or a similar character. The House of Lords held that the trial judge had properly exercised his discretion. The House of Lords there also approved of Lord Herschell's general statement of principle in *Makin*.[65]

[10.52] On the point of appeal, the Court of Criminal Appeal held in *Wallace* that evidence given of the first incident was relevant on the second count, to show that such a box could be used for the purpose alleged in the second count. Another submission made in *Wallace* was that the trial judge, in his charge to the jury, did not direct their attention to the evidence relevant to the identification of the accused on the first count, although he did warn the jury about the dangers when dealing with evidence of visual identification.

[10.53] In *Harris*,[66] Viscount Simon had indicated what is necessary in a charge to the jury in a case like this. The trial judge had not warned the jury that the evidence called in support of the earlier counts did not in itself provide confirmation of the charge. Hence, the jury may have been swayed, however illogically, in reaching its verdict on the eighth count by the earlier evidence. Viscount Simon reasoned, therefore, that they should have been warned of this danger.

[10.54] In the *Wallace* case, however, McWilliam J concluded that the trial judge had dealt very fully with the dangers of visual identification. However, he had not specifically referred to the evidence which related to the visual identification of the accused in relation to the first count. The trial judge treated the evidence as cumulative, as in *Harris*.[67] Hence, the verdict on the first count *per* MacWilliam J should be reversed.

[10.55] Regarding the second count, McWilliam J concluded that evidence in relation to the first offence was relevant in order to establish that a box of that sort could be used for the purpose of stealing clothes. The box was prepared and held in such a way as to give the impression that it was closed, whereas it was actually half open so that articles could be put into it without disturbing the

---

[64] *Harris v DPP* [1952] All ER 1044.
[65] *Makin v Attorney General for New South Wales* [1894] AC 57 at 65.
[66] *Harris v DPP* [1952] All ER 1044.
[67] *Per* McWilliam J in *People v Wallace* (1983) 2 Frewen 125 at 128.

apparent fastening. Hence, the evidence thus designated 'similar fact evidence', or evidence of past misconduct on the part of the accused, was deemed admissible in those circumstances.

[10.56] The Irish courts, for their part, have clung somewhat to the categorical approach. However, a preference for a 'balancing' of the probative worth and prejudicial value of the evidence (whether it be relevant via propensity or not) is apparent in the judgment of Black J in *People (AG) v Kirwan*,[68] and could be used to develop an independent jurisprudence in the area. Black J placed the rationale for exclusion firmly in the danger to the guarantee of a fair trial to the accused. (This danger was formerly located in the thought-process of a juror, who was not trained to act judicially: *DPP v MacMahon*).[69]

[10.57] *Kirwan*[70] involved the admissibility of 'similar fact evidence' which revealed that the accused had been in prison for four years before his arrest for his brother's murder. The evidence was as follows. Firstly, the murder victim in question had been dismembered with professional skill: there was evidence tendered that the accused had learned the trade of butcher while in prison. Secondly, the prosecution claimed the accused, in order to avoid detection, had drugged a fellow lodger: there was evidence here that he had luminal tablets in his possession and was, according to the prison doctor's testimony, acquainted with this drug since prison. Finally, there was evidence that after the death, the accused had a large amount of money in his possession – unusual in so far as when he had recently left prison he had only a small sum of money. The majority of the Supreme Court admitted the evidence as highly relevant. Black J, entering a reservation, could not see the relevance of revealing that the first witness was a prison warden or that the second was a prison doctor. In relation to the third factor, however, he felt on the whole it was necessary to reveal the evidence. The approach of Black J was novel, in so far as it indicated an overall balancing approach in favour of the accused, which would operate to exclude such evidence where it was not sufficiently probative to warrant its admission and consequent prejudicial effect.

[10.58] In *People v BK*,[71] the applicant was convicted on several counts of attempted buggery and indecent assault against various young males. He appealed on the basis that each of the counts – in so far as they related to a different boy – should have been tried separately. The Court of Criminal Appeal held that the test as to whether the counts should be heard together was whether

---

[68] *People (AG) v Kirwan* [1943] IR 279.
[69] *DPP v MacMahon* [1984] ILRM 461.
[70] *People (AG) v Kirwan* [1943] IR 279.
[71] *People v BK* [2000] 2 IR 199.

the evidence of each would be admissible on the other. To be so admissible, the probative value of such evidence must outweigh its prejudicial effect. The facts and judgment of the court merit attention in so far as they constitute a relatively recent statement by the Irish courts of their approach in this area.

[10.59] Barron J, giving the judgment of the court, noted that count number eight charged attempted buggery on a date unknown between 1 April 1982 and 30 September 1989 with JMD, a male person, and count nine charged attempted buggery on a date unknown between 1 April 1985 and 30 September 1988 with JH, a male person. Count number one was indecent assault against WMD, a male person, on a date unknown between 1 January 1983 and 31 December 1987, and count number two was buggery on a date unknown between those same dates with WMD.

[10.60] The defendant had been convicted on counts eight and nine. The relevant ground of appeal was that each of the counts, so far as they related to a different boy, should have been tried separately. Counsel submitted that to allow the counts relating to the different boys to be tried together would in effect provide corroboration, where there was none in law. The prosecution argued there was a sufficient similarity between the offences in that they were all alleged to have been committed against young boys in the applicant's care in Trudder House, a residential home for traveller children run by the Eastern Health Board. Holding that the real test as to whether the counts should be heard together was whether the evidence in respect of each would be admissible on each of the other counts, Barron J commented:

> For such evidence to be so admissible, it would be necessary for the probative value of such evidence to outweigh its prejudicial effect. In practice, this test is applied where there is a similarity between the facts relating to the several counts. On the one hand, there is system evidence which is so admissible; and, on the other hand, there is similar fact evidence, which is inadmissible. In the latter case, the reason is that, just because a person may have acted in a particular way on one occasion does not mean that such person acted in the same way on some other occasion. System evidence on the other hand is admissible because the manner in which a particular act has been done on one occasion suggests that it was also done on another occasion by the same person with the same intent.[72]

[10.61] The distinction between system and similar fact (although Barron J commented that the latter is sometimes used to refer to the former) was made by applying a test 'to ensure that the effect of the natural prejudice which will arise from similarity of allegation is overborne by the probative effect of the evidence.'[73]

---

[72] *People v BK* [2000] 2 IR 199 at 203.
[73] *People v BK* [2000] 2 IR 199 at 203.

[10.62] Barron J referred to the decision of *AG v Duffy*,[74] where the accused was charged with four separate counts of indecent assault and gross indecency against four different male persons on four different occasions. All counts were heard together. A retrial was ordered on the basis that to try the four offences together was to supply corroboration for each of them, when in law there was no such corroboration:

> Human nature, however, is too strong to have allowed the jury to disregard the cumulative effect of evidence given at the same trial in respect of four distinct offences of almost precisely the same character.[75]

[10.63] Barron J then reviewed the decisions in *Sims, Boardman* etc. He noted that the decision in *Boardman* seemed to have been regarded as a decision that similar fact evidence was admissible only when there was a striking resemblance between the evidence relating to the several counts. Whether this was necessary was further considered in *P*, where Lord MacKay of Clashfern stated that the essential feature of evidence which was to be admitted was that 'its probative force in support of the allegation that an accused person committed a crime is sufficiently great to make it just to admit the evidence, notwithstanding that it is prejudicial to the accused in tending to show that he was guilty of another crime.'[76]

[10.64] Barron J further interpreted MacKay LJ's judgment as follows:

> Where the identity of the perpetrator is unknown some special feature is necessary before evidence is admissible to establish that it was the same perpetrator in each case. Where, however, the alleged perpetrator in each case is known, it is not necessary to have that special feature because the issue is no longer was it done by the same person, but was an offence committed on each occasion.
>
> In the former type of case, the issue of admissibility relates to establishing that not only was a crime committed on each occasion, but committed by the same person. In the latter type of case, of which the present is one, the issue of admissibility relates not to whether the same crime has been committed, but to whether offences were committed at all, or, if so, as here, as to their nature.[77]

[10.65] Barron J pointed out that Budd J considered these cases in *B v DPP*[78] and stated with regard to the reason for admitting evidence of multiple accusations:

---

[74] *AG v Duffy* [1931] IR 144.

[75] *AG v Duffy* [1931] IR 144 at 149, Kennedy CJ.

[76] MacKay in *DPP v P* [1991] 2 AC 447 at 460.

[77] Per Barron J in *People v BK* [2000] 2 IR 199 at 209–210.

[78] *B v DPP* [1997] 3 IR 140.

It seems that the underlying principle is that the probative value of multiple accusations may depend on part of their similarity, but also on the unlikelihood that the same person would find himself falsely accused on various occasions by different and independent individuals. The making of multiple accusations is a coincidence in itself, which has to be taken into account in deciding admissibility.[79]

[10.66] According to Barron J, a number of principles emerge from these cases:

(1) The rules of evidence should not be allowed to offend common-sense

(2) So, where the probative value of the evidence outweighs its prejudicial effect, it may be admitted.

(3) The categories of cases in which the evidence which can be so admitted, is not closed.

(4) Such evidence is admitted in two main types of cases:–

(a) to establish that the same person committed each offence because of the particular feature common to each; or

(b) where the charges are against one person only, to establish that offences were committed.

In the latter case the evidence is admissible because:-

(a) there is the inherent improbability of several persons making up exactly similar stories;

(b) it shows a practice which would rebut accident, innocent explanation or denial. [80]

[10.67] In *BK*, the court was of opinion that the joinder of counts one and two with eight and nine was incorrect because the evidence went no further than saying that because the applicant was charged with offences against one boy, he was more likely to have committed the offences alleged against the other boys.

[10.68] The court did find a connection between counts one and two and eight and nine, in so far as they were alleged to have been committed by a carer in Trudder House against inmates of that institution, but concluded that the facts in each case showed a different picture: counts one and two were alleged to have been committed in a dormitory at night, whereas the other two were alleged to have been committed in a caravan to which the applicant and other boys had gone to spend the night. The accused's conduct in relation to one and two was open, whereas in the other two furtive. Barron J concluded:

---

[79] *Per* Budd J in *B v DPP* [1997] 3 IR 140 at 157.
[80] *Per* Barron J in *People v BK* [2000] 2 IR 199 at 210–211.

The evidence in relation to counts number 8 and 9 ... does show the necessary nexus to allow the evidence on the one to be admitted in relation to the other and *vice versa*. They are alleged to have been committed in unusual but identical circumstances, on a visit to the caravan; while the two were sleeping in a double bed; in the same furtive manner; and by broadly similar actions. There were also differences. But overall the similarities were sufficient to make it a jury question as to whether the offence alleged on each count had been committed.[81]

The court held that the inclusion of counts one and two, however (even though the jury disagreed on those counts), created unfair prejudice, resulting in an unsatisfactory trial.

[10.69] *People v Selliah Ramachchandran*[82] was a case involving a charge of harassment under s 10 of the Non-Fatal Offences Against the Person Act 1997. The applicant had been convicted and sentenced to three years as well as restrained with regard to communicating etc, with the complainant and her family. The facts related to a history of correspondence and events involving the applicant, some of which pre-dated the Act. The prosecution sought to defend the latter on the basis that it was necessary to paint in the background of this particular case. However, the Court of Criminal Appeal held that 'in the circumstances of this case, the opening of this entire correspondence had tended to prejudice the applicant rather than to introduce anything of probative value.'[83]

Judicial discretion/reform

[10.70] In *DPP v D O'S*,[84] as seen earlier (paras **10.08–10.09**), the accused had been tried before the Central Criminal Court on charges of sexual assault, rape etc. which related to the abuse of one DC who had been a pupil at a school in the Cork area, the events alleged to have happened between September 1997 and February 1998. The accused was a remedial teacher and appealed against conviction and sentence on the basis that the evidence of PB and JM should not have been admitted at all. Given the court's endorsement of *BK*, and the approach taken therein to similar fact evidence it is worth examining the reasoning with regard to why this evidence was deemed to satisfy that standard and have been properly admitted at trial. McGuinness J reasoned as follows:

... the applicant, through his counsel, drew attention to the various inconsistencies and dissimilarities between the evidence of the complainant and that of PB and JM. He pointed out that the evidence of DC was that the applicant abused him furtively, having isolated him in a locked room with no other boys

---

[81] *Per* Barron J in *People v BK* [2000] 2 IR 199 at 210–211.

[82] *People v Selliah Ramachchandran* [2000] 2 IR 307.

[83] *People v Selliah Ramachchandran* [2000] 2 IR 307 at 311, *per* Barrington J.

[84] *DPP v D O'S* [2004] IECCA 12, McGuinness J.

being present. The evidence of PB disclosed alleged criminal conduct which was engaged in openly in the presence of other boys both during morning and lunchtime classes. Moreover, the complainant maintained he had attended the lunchtime classes on his own so that PB could not have been there whereas PB gave evidence of being present. Furthermore, the complainant had given evidence that the applicant's penis could not have touched the lower part of his back because of the plywood back on the chair, whereas PB said he could feel the applicant's penis on his back about halfway up. The evidence of the three boys was also contradictory in regard to the attitude assumed by the applicant – whether he was standing, kneeling or genuflecting. The evidence of JM also complained of alleged wrongdoing which was openly engaged in the presence of other boys.[85]

[10.71] McGuinness J looked at Barron J's judgment in *BK* and noted the distinction he drew between 'similar fact evidence' and 'system evidence'. For such evidence to be admissible he reasoned the probative value had to outweigh the prejudicial effect:

> System evidence ... is admissible because the manner in which a particular act is being done on one occasion suggests that it was also done on another occasion by the same person and with the same intent. [86]

McGuinness J. considers the trial judge's direction and ruling in the case before her on appeal which had held that this evidence was indeed admissible.

[10.72] The trial judge's ruling with regard to the evidence is quoted by McGuinness J as follows:[87]

> Insofar as sexual assault is concerned, the evidence of these two young men bears a striking resemblance in respect of one aspect of DC's complaints to the manner in which he describes the accused's behaviour towards him. And the very striking resemblance between what they say and the evidence which DC gave, as I say, in respect of one aspect of the complaints which he makes against Mr O'S. To that extent Mr Sammon submits that that evidence is of probative value in this case and I have no doubt that that is so. But Mr Sammon goes further and he says it is of high probative quality and so much so that its probative value outweighs its admitted prejudicial effects insofar as the accused is concerned. And essentially what he is saying is that the interest of justice demand that the jury have available to them this evidence, otherwise they will not be getting anything like the full picture. Now, I accept that there are various laws which limit evidence which a jury may hear and to that extent a jury may in certain cases be asked to try a case in blinkers. And perhaps it was inappropriate for him to use that phrase in the context of this application. However, it does

---

[85] *DPP v D O'S* [2004] IECCA 12 at 21 *per* McGuinness J.
[86] Barron J in BK at p 203 quoted by *DPP v D O'S* [2004] IECCA 12 at 23, *per* McGuinness J.
[87] *DPP v D O'S* [2004] IECCA 12 at 27 *per* McGuinness J.

seem to me, and I accept the application of Mr Sammon, that this evidence is of a high probative value and I think it would be wrong and contrary to the interests of justice to allow this case to proceed in the absence of that evidence ... Accordingly, I will direct that PB and JM may be called to give evidence in accordance with the statements which are included in the book of evidence which has been served on the accused.

[10.73] The trial judge had admitted evidence on the basis that the probative value outweighed prejudicial effect – the question whether that was a correct assessment by the trial judge was reviewed on appeal by McGuinness J[88] as follows:

The question before this court is whether the learned trial judge rightly exercised his discretion in admitting the evidence of these two witnesses. The learned trial judge clearly identified the test which he had to apply. This test has been well established in the earlier law and approved by this court in the *Director of Public Prosecutions v BK*. The learned trial judge held that there were 'striking similarities' between the evidence of PB and JW and that of DC. In the view of this court, there were indeed strong similarities in the location, the timing and the manner in which the three witnesses alleged that the applicant committed the particular offence of rubbing his penis against their backs while correcting their work in the remedial classroom. In the course of the actual evidence, a number of dissimilarities of detail emerged, for example, in respect of timing, with regard to the presence or absence of other persons, with regard to the exact position taken by the applicant while correcting their work. Such dissimilarities are not entirely surprising. The court is considering the evidence of three young boys who at the time of the alleged offences were in or about eleven years of age, still attending primary school. They were giving evidence at a trial which took place some three years later. Even in the case of adult witnesses, the recall of matters of detail may be difficult after a lapse of three years. If, indeed, the evidence of the three witnesses concurred exactly in every detail, it might well have given rise to a suspicion that they had conspired to concoct their evidence or at least had contaminated their evidence by discussing it in advance between themselves.

The type of assault described by PB and JM was unusual as well as similar in nature to that described by DC and this would add to the probative value of the evidence of the other two boys in the context of the evidence of the complainant. In the view of this court, the evidence of PB and JM with its unusual and similar features, was indeed what was described by Barron J in the *BK* case as 'system evidence'. As Barron said it is admissible 'because the manner in which a particular act has been done on one occasion suggests that it was also done on another occasion by the same person and with the same intent.'

---

[88] *DPP v D O'S* [2004] IECCA 12 at 29 *per* McGuinness J.

[10.74] Hence McGuinness J concluded that the trial judge was right to allow the boys' evidence. It is interesting to reflect on the dissimilarities, and query with hindsight and the benefit of many cases in this area, whether the location, timing and manner were strikingly similar. One is reminded of the criticisms of Lord Sumner's judgment in *Thompson*[89] and comments in subsequent amusement arcade cases such as *Novak*[90] from Lord Bridge querying whether the similarity in approach there was really leading to a necessary conclusion of inexplicability on basis of coincidence.

[10.75] It is important to recall the general discretion a judge has to exclude or limit the admissibility of evidence in this, as in the context of any type of evidence and to exclude evidence of extraneous acts or disposition regarding to the risk of prejudice involved.

Other jurisdictions

[10.76] The High Court of Australia had to consider this area of the law in *Pfennig v R (No 2)*.[91] The facts in this case concerned the murder of a young boy after his abduction for sexual purposes. The abduction was in a white van, his bicycle being taken also and subsequently left in a place suggesting accidental death. The accused was charged with the murder, and it was proposed to adduce in evidence his conviction following a plea of guilty for the abduction of a young boy in a white van for sexual purposes, while leaving his bicycle in a way to suggest accidental death, all of which had occurred a year later. The victim on that occasion had escaped. There was also evidence the accused had told his wife after arrest for the second crime, that he had been contemplating such a crime for a year. On the day before the murder, he had attempted to induce two other young boys to enter his van, and questioned a man about a nude bathing spot which was where the bicycle was found. He had also admitted talking to the deceased boy on the day of the murder. As Tapper notes,[92] however, without the evidence of the commission of the other crime (which was much stronger) the accused would not have been convicted, as he was. His conviction was appealed to the High Court, and it is there that some interesting insight was given to this area, particularly in the judgment of McHugh J, which, though agreeing with all the others, was, as Tapper says,[93] 'challengingly different' in approach. McHugh J was 'scathing about the idea of balancing two such incommensurable factors as "probative force" and "prejudicial effect". He preferred instead to

---

[89] *Thompson v R* [1918] AC 221.
[90] *R v Novak* (1976) 65 Cr App R 107.
[91] *Pfennig v R (No 2)* [1995] 69 ALJR 147.
[92] Tapper, 'Dissimilar Views of Similar Facts' (1995) Vol III LQR 381 at 382.
[93] Tapper, 'Dissimilar Views of Similar Facts' (1995) Vol III LQR 381 at 383.

consider the requirements of a fair trial, and how far the trial would be fair if the propensity evidence were to be admitted … In each case according to McHugh J the nature of the risk of unfairness requires to be analysed.'[94]

[10.77] It is helpful to recite the dangers or objections to similar fact evidence identified by McHugh J which might profitably be used to guide the courts in cases where the admissibility of such evidence arises:

1.   That it creates undue suspicion against the accused and undermines the presumption of innocence.

2.   That tribunals of fact, particularly juries, tend to assume too readily that behavioural patterns are constant and that past behaviour is an accurate guide to contemporary conduct; common assumptions about improbabilities of sequences are often wrong and when the accused is associated with a sequence of events such as deaths/injuries, a jury may too readily assume the association to not be innocent.

3.   Other misconduct may cause the jury to be biased against the accused (give a dog a bad name and hang him).

4.   Trials would be rendered more lengthy and expensive; police might be encouraged to pursue those with criminal records at the expense of traditional investigation; and rehabilitation might be undermined if the accused's record could be used against him.

[10.78] Very often arguments sustaining change in rules of evidence can be made on a once-off basis. In that light, it is interesting to note that the Violence Against Women Act 1994 amended the Federal Rules of Evidence in the United States by making prior sexual assaults by alleged rapists admissible in trials of rape or sexual assault.[95] Yet, are these not precisely the cases where a jury, on learning of the accused's previous behaviour, will readily assume he has done so again regardless of the strength of the state's case? There is also, of course, the question as to whether we have, or should have, diminishing confidence in the reliability of such previous convictions.

[10.79] It is also argued that to conceal the record is to deceive the jury. Yet if the decision to allow the convictions in is to affect the jury's scrutiny of the evidence against the accused in this instance, and allow them to engage in 'forbidden' reasoning, perhaps that limited deception is justifiable. Once again, the issue is one of fairness and principle here.

---

[94]   Tapper, 'Dissimilar Views of Similar Facts' (1995) Vol III LQR 381 at 384.

[95]   See critical article by Baker, 'Once a Rapist? Motivational Evidence and Relevancy in Rape Law' (1997) 110 Harv LR 563.

[10.80] If one goes back to the underlying premise or rationale of the rule, it is far easier to explain or refashion the structure. To further bolster the validity of this approach, it is interesting to note the recognition of the fundamental issues involved here by representatives of the judicial and academic sides of the debate.

[10.81] See the comment of Lord Hailsham in *Boardman*:

> When there is nothing to connect the accused with a particular crime except bad character or similar crimes committed in the past, the probative value of the evidence is nil and the evidence is rejected on that ground. When there is some evidence connecting the accused with the crime, in the eyes of most people, guilt of similar offences in the past might well be considered to have probative value ... Nonetheless, in the absence of a statutory provision to the contrary, the evidence is to be excluded under the first rule in *Makin* because its prejudicial effect may be more powerful than its probative effect, and thus endanger a fair trial because it tends to undermine the integrity of the presumption of innocence and the burden of proof. In other words, it is a rule of English law which has its root in policy, and by which, in Lord du Parcq's phrase, logicians would not be bound.[96]

[10.82] In like vein, Zuckerman has commented:

> It has been recognised for a long time that the risk attendant on evidence of previous crime, or other morally repugnant conduct, is not so much over estimation of its own probative weight as the distortion of the entire process of adjudication. Similar fact evidence threatens the two central principles or our criminal justice. The first is that in any criminal trial the accused stands to be tried, acquitted or convicted, only in respect of the offence with which he is charged. The second is that conviction must take place only if the jury are persuaded of the accused's guilt beyond all reasonable doubt.[97]

The Irish judiciary should take the opportunity presented of forging a novel approach to the admissibility of similar fact evidence. To do otherwise may not prove true to our constitutional or jurisprudential rights, and we risk further floundering in the academic quagmire which is the admissibility evidence of the accused's past misconduct in a criminal trial.

[10.83] In *DPP v DO*[98] in the Supreme Court, Hardiman J, in particular, addressed what he called a narrower issue: assuming that the similar fact evidence was rightly admitted, whether the use then made of that evidence by the DPP and the conduct of the prosecution generally, corresponded to the

---

[96] *Boardman v DPP* [1974] 3 All ER 887 at 904.
[97] Zuckerman, 'Similar Fact Evidence – The Unobservable Rule' (1987) 103 LQR 187.
[98] *DPP v DO* [2006] IESC 12.

purpose for which such evidence may lawfully be admitted and the requirement of fairness generally. We have seen previously cases where Hardiman J looked at the conduct of the cross-examination. In considering same and the use of similar fact evidence, he came to the following conclusion:[99]

> I have no doubt that this cross-examination is all of a piece and was all designed to lead up to the allegations expressly made in the last three pages: that the defendant 'fitted the bill' and 'had the profile' of a 'vicious sexual abuser'. To express this in terms of the language of the cases on misconduct evidence, it expressly constituted allegations that the defendant should be seen as a result of criminal conduct (in relation to the boys) and character (being unmarried, not pursuing relationships with women anymore, refraining from sexual intercourse as a matter of religious principle and, later, because of declining interest, and being involved in boy scouts, rather than going somewhere where he might find female company), had a disposition to commit the offences of the sort charged. This is precisely the use of the evidence relating to previous misconduct or character which has been regarded as inadmissible for centuries.

[10.84] Hardiman J obviously approved of the distinction between character and disposition evidence and regarded the latter as inadmissible – in other words avoiding the reasoning that because he is that type of person, he committed the offence. That seems eminently sensible and harks back to the origins of the rule– something lost in the UK now where that distinction has been abandoned. With regard to the very lengthy cross-examination in this case, Hardiman J noted that state counsel justified large parts of it by saying that they arose naturally out of the plaintiff's assertion of heterosexuality. Hardiman J characterised the questioning as an attempt to establish a disposition and stated:[100]

> I cannot agree that an assertion that the plaintiff is a bachelor of heterosexual orientation 'opens the door to cross examination along the lines that he is, by disposition, a paedophile. Statements as to marital status are routinely made by witnesses, even in traffic accident cases. Moreover the cross examination was not directed at suggesting that the appellant was homosexual or bisexual: indeed the cross examination elicited quite deliberately that the appellant had no full sexual experience with either sex. The cross-examination was directed at painting a picture of him as a pervert and a paedophile and at very little else.

Later on he comments:

> In my view the similar fact evidence and the evidence of character was used in cross examination of the complainant deliberately and almost exclusively to establish his disposition. It was done in language which was to use counsel's own term, extravagant; in the words of the Court of Criminal Appeal the cross examination was not particularly attractive in tone. I feel this is an

---

[99] *DPP v DO* [2006] IESC 12 at 14 *per* Hardiman J.
[100] *DPP v DO* [2006] IESC 12 at 16 *per* Hardiman J.

understatement and at various aspects of the appellant's life, not themselves of any probative value, were used to portray him as one who 'fitted the bill' of a paedophile. This is in clear breach of the very long established rule of law summed up in the first paragraph quoted above ... Lord Herschell. It was also unjustified by anything said in the course of the defence case.[101]

[10.85] This judgment is a useful reminder of the basis of admission, which is not one involving logic assumed that because this person is in general like this, he committed this offence. That is not the relevance needed here and perhaps the overemphasis on balancing probative with prejudicial effect obscures the need to first establish relevance – the 'Indian headdress' element as *per* Lord Hailsham in *Boardman*.[102] That may be the legacy of *BK*. The use to which the evidence was put and the extent of cross-examination of the individual meant that the argument that you are not supposed to make was made in this case. It was not the argument, as Barron J said, that suggested it was also done on another occasion, linking the person with a particular act, it was, rather, alleging that he is this kind of person and because he is this kind of person he could commit this kind of offence.

Elsewhere in the judgment[103] Hardiman J refers to such reasoning as an 'attempt to appeal, in a court of law, to pure impressionistic prejudice.'

[10.86] One added difficulty is trying to discover what juries do with past records if they get them and how influential they are. There is very little empirical evidence, and very few studies in this area. One such study which does exist is that conducted by Sally Lloyd Bostock.[104] She notes that this evidence is excluded in the first place is because it is unduly prejudicial, and can lead to stereotypical thinking with regard to criminality. Significantly, her finding is that certain types of records or offences are much more influential than others. In other words, it is the type of offence that is most significant for these purposes. The absence of previous dissimilar convictions is not significant, but the presence of dissimilar and yet repugnant offences (like a sexual offence) is hugely prejudicial and this is regardless of what the issue before the court currently is. That should indicate that caution is needed, particularly regarding the potentially powerful effect of a prior record of offences that a jury might view as particularly abhorrent. If the offence being tried is an equally reprehensible one, given that being charged with these offences is prejudicial in the first place, any subsequent reference to a prior abhorrent offence will multiply that prejudice manifold and arguably prevent fair trial of the accused.

---

[101] *DPP v DO* [2006] IESC 12 at 17 *per* Hardiman J.

[102] *Boardman v DPP* [1975] AC 421 at 454 *per* Lord Hailsham – see para **10.34**.

[103] *DPP v DO* [2006] IESC 12 at 14.

[104] Lloyd Bostock, 'The effect on juries of hearing about the defendant's previous criminal record: a simulation study' [2000] Crim LR 734.

Chapter 11

Cross-Examination of the Accused

> Someone must have been telling lies about Joseph K, for without having done anything wrong he was arrested one fine morning.
>
> Kafka, *The Trial*

Introduction

[11.01] In criminal cases if the accused gives evidence, he may not be cross-examined about his other offences, previous convictions or bad character, unless evidence of the previous offences or convictions about which he is asked would have been admissible in-chief, or unless he has thrown his 'shield' away by putting his character in issue, by casting imputations on the character of the prosecutor, or by giving evidence against another person charged in the same proceedings.

[11.02] The Criminal Justice (Evidence) Act 1924 (the equivalent of the Criminal Evidence Act 1898 in England) ensured the competence of an accused at a criminal trial. In order to ensure, however, that the accused was not unduly disadvantaged compared to other witnesses, by virtue of the fact that he could be questioned about his record or past behaviour, and in order to ensure that the prosecution was not stymied by the use of the privilege against self-incrimination by the accused, a compromise position was reached in the Act. The position is one that modifies the privilege against self-incrimination in relation to an accused, while giving the accused what is termed a 'shield' in relation to his past record. The relevant and important provisions for the law of evidence in this regard are ss 1(e) and 1(f) of the 1924 Act. These provisions provide as follows:

1(e)   A person charged and being a witness in pursuance of this Act may be asked any question in cross-examination notwithstanding that it will tend to incriminate him as to the offence charged.

1(f)   When giving evidence an accused person shall not be asked and if asked shall not be required to answer, any question tending to show that he has committed or been convicted of or been charged with any offence other than that wherewith he is then charged, or is of bad character, unless:

(i) the proof that he has committed or been convicted of such other offences is admissible evidence to show that he is guilty of the offence wherewith he is then charged; or

(ii) he has personally or by his advocate asked questions of the witnesses for the prosecution with a view to establishing his own good character or has given evidence of his own good character, or the nature or conduct of the defence is such as to involve imputations on the character of the prosecutor or the witnesses for the prosecution; or

(iii) he has given evidence against any other person charged with the same offence.

[11.03] Section 1(f) of the 1924 Act was enacted when the accused's competence to testify at trial had been assured. It was seen as unfair if an accused were placed in the same position as an ordinary witness, as he could be questioned about past convictions and the jury might understand these as going to his guilt, instead of credibility. However, total protection would leave the accused witness free to smear other witnesses, and thus render him in a better position than that of an ordinary witness. Section 1(f), therefore, is a compromise.

[11.04] An initial question to be addressed in the context of an examination of these provisions, is that of the relationship between s 1(e) and s 1(f) of the 1924 Act. This very question was discussed by the House of Lords in *Jones v DPP.*[1] The facts of the case concerned an accused who was charged with the murder of a girl guide. The accused set up a false alibi before the trial, alleging that he had spent the night in question with a prostitute and that his wife had been angry because of his late return. This account was strikingly similar to testimony given by the accused at an earlier trial when he had been convicted of the rape of a girl guide. The prosecution got leave to cross-examine the accused to show similarities in the account and that they were so close as to render the defence incredible.

[11.05] The manner of cross-examination must have created the impression in the jury that the accused had shortly before this murder committed or been charged with some other offence reported in a Sunday newspaper. The accused, in the examination-in-chief, had himself admitted being in trouble with the police before, and a similar admission was contained in a statement of the accused to the police, which was put forward by the accused's counsel. An appeal by the accused against the admission of his record was rejected by the Court of Criminal Appeal and the House of Lords on the grounds that the cross-examination did not tend to show the accused's bad record or character, because

---

[1]   *Jones v DPP* [1962] AC 635.

'tending to show' meant to reveal to the jury for the first time, rather than tending to prove.

[11.06] The House of Lords presented two views of the issue and two perspectives on the relationship of s 1(e) and s 1(f). The majority position was taken by Lords Reid, Simons and Morris. The majority view of s 1(e) was a narrow one in that it allowed questions directly incriminating the accused with regard to the offence charged. With regard to their interpretation of s 1(f), their construction of the phrase 'tend to show' was to the effect that 'tends to show' meant 'tends to suggest to the jury'. The crucial point as far as the law is concerned, was whether these questions were to be considered in isolation or in light of what had gone before in the trial. Lord Reid commented:[2]

> ... I do not think that the questions ought to be considered in isolation. If the test is the effect the questions would be likely to have on the minds of the jury that necessarily implies that one must have regard to what the jury had already heard. If the jury already knew that the accused had been charged with an offence, a question inferring that he had been charged would add nothing and it would be absurd to prohibit it. If the obvious purpose of this proviso is to protect the accused from possible prejudice, as I think it is, then show must mean reveal because it is only a revelation of something new which could cause such prejudice.

[11.07] The position taken by Lords Devlin and Denning was somewhat different. With regard to their construction of s 1(f) of the 1924 Act, Lord Denning commented that the questions tended to show that Jones had been charged with an offence, even though he himself had brought out the fact that he had been previously charged in a court of law with another offence. Lord Denning commented as follows:[3]

> It is one thing to confess to having been in trouble before. It is quite another to have it emphasised against you with devastating detail. Before these questions were asked by the Crown all the jury knew was that at some unspecified time in the near or distant past, this man had been in trouble with the police. After the questions were asked, the jury knew in addition, that he had been very recently in trouble for an offence on a Friday night which was of so sensational a character that it featured in a newspaper on the following Sunday ... and that he had been charged in a court of law with that very offence. It seems to me that questions which tend to reveal an offence, thus particularised, are directly within the prohibition in s 1(f) and are not rendered admissible by his own vague disclosure of some other offence.

---

2   *Jones v DPP* [1962] AC 635 at 663–664.
3   *Jones v DPP* [1962] AC 635 at 667.

[11.08] Thus the conclusions of Lords Devlin and Denning were that the questions were prohibited by the proviso in s 1(f) of the 1924 Act, and the prosecution had not given evidence in order to lay a foundation for its admissibility within the exception in s 1(f). Had the question rested solely on s 1(f), the question would have been deemed to be inadmissible. However, the minority construed s 1(e) of the 1924 Act in such a manner that the questions were seen to be admissible under that proviso. Moreover, the minority felt that this gave a clearer guide to the prosecution on the basis that the criteria of relevance under s 1(e) in terms of incriminating the accused was a better guide than that put forward by the majority in relation to s 1(f). Lord Devlin stated that:

> The difficulty and danger inherent in the approach adopted (by the majority) is that it sets no clear limits to the extent of the cross-examination ... Relevance affords a clear guide as to what the limit should be; revelation does not ... I do not think that some vague rule which enables the prosecution to ask what it likes so long as it does not make out the accused's character to be substantially worse than he himself had suggested would be at all a safe guide.[4]

In summary, therefore, both the majority and minority agreed that the questions were admissible. However, the majority's view was one of a narrow s 1(e) (pro-accused) and a broad s 1(f) (anti-accused). The minority view was one of a broad s 1(e) (anti-accused) and a narrow s 1(f) (pro-accused).

[11.09] With regard to the interpretation of the prohibition in s 1(f) of the 1924 Act, and in particular the use of words other than 'convicted of' an offence, the question arises as to the admissibility of, for example, previous acquittals on the part of the accused.

[11.10] In the case of *Maxwell v DPP*,[5] the accused was charged with manslaughter alleged to have occurred in the course of procuring an abortion. He gave evidence of his own good character, and was asked in cross-examination about a previous acquittal on the same charge. Viscount Sankey commented that for questions to be permissible under s 1(f)(ii) of the 1924 Act, they must be relevant to the issue of the accused's own good character and, if not, they could not be admissible. He felt that it seemed clear that the mere fact of a charge could not, in general, be evidence of bad character or be regarded otherwise than as a misfortune:[6]

> The mere fact that a man has been charged with an offence is no proof that he committed the offence. Such a fact is therefore irrelevant; it neither goes to show

---

4   *Jones v DPP* [1962] 1 AC 635 at 713.
5   *Maxwell v DPP* [1935] AC 309.
6   *Maxwell v DPP* [1935] AC 309 at 320.

that the prisoner did the act for which he is actually being tried nor does it go to his credibility as a witness.

It does not result from this conclusion that the word 'charged' in proviso (f) is otiose; it is clearly not so as regards the prohibition; and when the exceptions come into play there may still be cases in which a prisoner may be asked about a charge as a step in crossexamination leading to a question whether he was convicted on the charge, or in order to elicit some evidence as to statements made or evidence given by the prisoner in the course of the trial on a charge which failed, which tend to throw doubt on the evidence which he is actually giving, though cases of this last class must be rare. In general ... no question should be asked under proviso (f) unless it helps to elucidate the particular issue which the jury is investigating or goes to credibility.

Loss of the shield: section 1(f)

[11.11] The first exception to the prohibition in s 1(f) of the 1924 Act relates to a situation where it is permissible to cross-examine the accused about evidence which has already been admitted in-chief. This situation is largely referred to as the 'similar fact evidence' scenario (see **Chapter 10**). Section 1(f)(i) provides that: 'The proof that he has committed or been convicted of such other offences is admissible evidence to show that he is guilty of the offence wherewith he is then charged.' This, the admissibility of similar fact evidence, is dealt with in Chapter 10 and so will not be considered further here. Suffice it to say that if such evidence of previous conduct is admissible in-chief by the prosecution, then obviously the accused can be cross-examined with regard to same.

[11.12] Section 1(f)(ii) of the 1924 Act provides that where an accused has:

... personally or by his advocate asked questions of the witnesses for the prosecution with a view to establishing his own good character or has given evidence of his own good character, or the nature or conduct of the defence is such as to involve imputations on the character of the prosecutor or the witnesses for the prosecution; or

This first part of this second exception to the protection in s 1(f) of the 1924 Act deals with situations where the accused has asserted his own good character. Character, according to the decision in *Selvey v DPP*,[7] means reputation and disposition. It has been held that, to attack the character of a person who is not a prosecution witness is not to assert one's own good character (*R v Lee*[8]). Nor does the exception apply if the defence witness, unasked, praises the defendant's character. The question has arisen in the past of the divisibility of character evidence, but the modern position is taken to be that the accused's character is

---

[7]   *Selvey v DPP* [1970] AC 304.
[8]   *R v Lee* [1976] 1 All ER 570.

indivisible. This means that the accused's entire record is admissible, whether it suggests defective credibility, or not.[9]

[11.13] In *Douglas*,[10] it was held that the accused put his character in issue when he was cross-examined with a view to showing that he had not drunk alcohol for several years, which had the effect of contrasting him with a co-accused who had been drunk at the time of the relevant accident.

[11.14] A fairly recent Irish case which is helpful in relation to admissibility of an accused's good character is *People (DPP) v Ferris*.[11] Ferris was accused of indecent assault and he sought leave to appeal on grounds that the trial judge had incorrectly allowed evidence as to his character to be introduced by the prosecution. The alleged offences (indecent assault on a male person contrary to s 62 of the Offences Against the Person Act 1861) had been committed over a period of about nine years against a four-year old until he was 13. Ferris was a friend of the parents of the complainant and had frequently visited their home. The alleged offences had occurred when Ferris took the complainant for drives in the Dublin area. Ferris gave evidence and completely denied the charges. Issues arose during appeal because Ferris's defence decided to call as witnesses two aunts of the complainant. They were called to explain a family dispute concerning attendance at a funeral. The first aunt had two children, a boy and a girl, and she was asked about contact between Ferris and her children. She confirmed Ferris had met them, had taken them out and there was no complaint on her part regarding same. The other aunt had two girls. Again she confirmed that he been in their company alone and she had no complaints. The second aunt had also expressed the opinion that the allegations against Ferris were untrue.

[11.15] Arising from that, counsel for the prosecution asked the trial judge to recall the applicant to cross-examine him and he relied on s 1(f) (ii) of the Criminal Justice (Evidence) Act 1924 to the effect that the defence had given evidence of the applicant's good character and had lost his shield. The defence argued that character was not at issue, and the aunts were there to explain a family dispute. The trial judge ruled that the defence had given evidence for the purposes of proving his character and the judge allowed the introduction of evidence of pornographic videos and literature found when Ferris's home was searched. The appeal was on the basis that that evidence should not have been admitted. It was powerful evidence once admitted and unsurprisingly the result had been a conviction.

---

[9] *Stirland v DPP* [1944] AC 315.
[10] *R v Douglas* (1989) 89 Crim App R 264.
[11] *People (DPP) v Ferris* [2008] 1 IR 1, CCA, Fennelly J.

[11.16] In considering the appeal, an interesting judgment was delivered by Fennelly J:[12]

> The common law has acted on one fundamental principle of proof since early modern times and since the abandonment of the primitive methods of proof of Saxon times. This rule has operated for centuries and is that the only evidence which is admissible at a criminal trial, whether for or against the guilt of the accused, is evidence which is relevant. This means evidence which tends to prove or disprove whether the accused committed the act with which he is charged. Evidence of character is, in general, not admissible. It was said that evidence of good character first came to be allowed for the defence only in capital cases on the humane principle of acting in *favorem vitae*. In that sense it was an anomaly. It was a distraction from the true nature of the inquiry. The judges were strict about it. They realised it was dangerous to try a man on the basis of his reputation, because it ran the risk that injustice would be done. This Court has maintained these principles and has been vigilant to ensure that the character of the accused be not put in issue unless the relevant statutory provisions are strictly met (eg *The People (Director of Public Prosecutions v McGrail* [1990] 2 IR 38).
>
> It is important to recall that, prior to the reforms of the law, in England in 1898 and here by the Act of 1924 that, subject to limited statutory exceptions, the accused as a matter of general principle was not allowed to give evidence in his own defence. Thus where evidence of good character came, exceptionally, to be given it had to be given by other witnesses. The Act of 1924 contained only provisions concerning the competency of the accused or his or her spouse to give evidence in criminal cases. It remedied the glaring injustice of depriving the accused to swear to his own innocence. All the provisions of the Act deal with this change or its procedural consequences ... Paragraph (f) [of section 1] is the provision said to be relevant to this case. The accused, who chooses to give evidence, abandons his shield against evidence of bad character in any of the situations mentioned in sub-paragraphs i), ii) or iii). The situation said to be relevant to the present case is that which occurred when the accused 'has given evidence of his good character'. But, assuming the evidence of the aunts to speak to the character of the accused, it was not the accused who gave it. It is true that the situation envisaged earlier in the sub-paragraphs, engages the responsibility of the advocate of the accused in the event he seeks to establish his good character through cross-examination of prosecution witnesses. However, there is no provision for the case where the defence calls character witnesses other than the accused. The reason is clear. There was no need for such a provision. The reforms effected by the Act of 1924 did not require any provision for the case where the defence called character witnesses other than the accused. The rights of the prosecution to call rebutting character evidence was already covered by the common law.

---

[12] *People (DPP) v Ferris* [2008] 1 IR 1 at p 7.

In the present case, however, the prosecution did not seek to rely on those common law provisions by calling rebutting evidence. It chose, instead, to introduce the damning matter by cross-examination of the accused. That was directly prohibited by s 1(f), unless one of the provisos applied. In fact, as already stated, none of the exceptions applied. Specifically, the accused had given no evidence of his own good character. ..The Court is, therefore, of the view that the learned trial judge was in error in deciding that the evidence given by the aunts came within one of the statutory exceptions and in permitting the applicant to be cross-examined on the subject of his character or previous behaviour. Since he had no power to permit the evidence to be given in this form, the issue of his discretion does not arise.

It is, therefore, not strictly necessary to consider the position at common law. However, it appears doubtful whether the nature of the evidence elicited by the cross examination would have been admissible even in the form of evidence in rebuttal.

According to the decision in *Ferris*, therefore, one can only cross-examine the accused on his record where the accused himself gives or initiates a discussion of evidence of own good character.

[11.17] A similarly restrained approach with regard to loss of the shield – here in the context of evidence put forward by the accused himself – is found in *DPP v DO*[13] (see para **10.07** re similar fact evidence). The facts here were that the applicant was a primary school teacher convicted of a number of offences of sexual assault and rape in relation to a boy, D. He was convicted of one count of rape and sentenced to 10 years, but subsequent to the conviction he appealed and a certain number of issues were considered on appeal, one of which related to the manner of his cross-examination at trial. Cross-examination had been lengthy, with 473 questions being asked. Cross-examination essentially was justified by counsel for the state in so far as the state claimed the accused had referred to his involvement in the Scouting movement, had said he was unmarried and that he was of a 'heterosexual orientation'. They were relied upon as opening the door and justifying cross-examination, which it was alleged on appeal, amounted to asserting that he had the disposition to commit offences in question. It was held that the statement of the accused that he was heterosexual did not justify questioning involving inferences from his involvement with the Boy Scouts.

[11.18] The judgment of Hardiman J first endorsed the importance of cross-examination:[14]

---

13 *DPP v DO* [2006] IESC 12.
14 *DPP v DO* [2006] IESC 12 at 9.

In proceedings such as the present, where everything that makes life worth living may be at stake, it is to be expected that cross-examination on both sides will be hard, detailed, challenging and bruising. It is equally clear that much discretion must be left to the cross-examiner ... No topic can be taboo, so long as it passes the criteria of having some proper use in the cross-examiner's task.

With these things fully in mind, I have to say that I have never heard or read a cross-examination like the one featured in this case. The appellant, the defendant in a criminal trial, was an unmarried man, a schoolteacher, and a person who has held high office in a scouting organisation. On this basis a remarkable series of questions was put to him culminating in the last three pages of the cross-examination with suggestions that he 'fitted the bill' of the type of person that '[the complainant] contends that you are, a vicious sex abuser...' It was then put to him that he did so 'in terms of profile': the first aspect of this profile put by counsel was 'this interest in scouting and boy scouts'. It was then put to him that:

> '...The profile you have is the profile that one expects to find of a person who had a deviant interest or a perverted interest in terms of suffering from paedophilia' and that he had violated [the complainant].

It will be observed that this is plainly, openly, and in so many words, cross-examination as to the defendant's disposition to commit offences of this sort on the basis of his criminal conduct (the similar fact evidence) and criminal character.

[11.19] The State's case was that because he said he was unmarried, heterosexual and involved in scouting, he was asserting his own character and they therefore proceeded to extensively cross-examine him about his general character. Thereby they established what they could not have done otherwise, asserting that he would have engaged in such activity in the past. Hardiman J went into some detail in terms of the cross-examination, pointing out *inter alia* that when the defendant said he was unmarried and, at his current age, was unlikely to marry, counsel responded there's always Lisdoonvarna. Counsel commented at another stage that he didn't seem to have very many erections. Counsel referred to previous relationships, and to the defendant's assertion of his religious principles in relation to sexual activities, and counsel put to him the question that there were people, although they subscribe to certain codes, be they religious or ethical, who break them. He was asked had he ever had sexual intercourse with a female person. A similar question followed about a male person. A little later counsel asked, what he did with his sexual urges. It is documented by Hardiman J in this manner just how extraordinary the extent to which the very extensive questioning was devoted to establishing that he was exactly the sort of person likely to be attracted to children.

[11.20] This case is a particularly clear example of what was not regarded as permitted by an assertion of good character, what is not allowed in cross-examination. As Hardiman J concluded:[15]

> I have no doubt that this cross-examination is all of a piece and was all designed to lead up to the allegations expressly made ... that the defendant 'fitted the bill' and 'had the profile' of a 'vicious sexual abuser'. To express this in terms of the language of the cases on misconduct evidence, it expressly constituted allegations that the defendant should be seen, as a result of criminal conduct (in relation to boys) and character (being unmarried, not pursuing relationships with women anymore, refraining from sexual intercourse as a matter of religious principle and, later, because of some declining interest, and being involved in boy scouts, rather than going to some place where he might find female company), had a disposition to commit offences of the sort charged.

> That is precisely the use of evidence relating to previous misconduct or character which has been regarded as inadmissible for centuries.

[11.21] That is a very useful reminder of the first principles lying behind the rule and in like manner to *McGrail*[16] shows a welcome predisposition on the part of the Irish judiciary to ground decisions in fairness and give effect to rules such as exclusion of similar fact evidence even where elliptically offered as here in the context of cross-examination. Cynically, there is an opportunity for the prosecution, if they *know* they could never make the case on similar fact, as it is missing perhaps that distinctive 'hallmark' feature or quality, to have a second stab if the accused asserts good character.

[11.22] Even in situations where the accused drops or loses the shield, there is the overarching discretion that resides with the trial judge, to weigh up prejudicial effect and probative value. There is a concern particularly if there is a similarity between offence and past record that the jury will engage in forbidden reasoning. There is also operative here a distrust of the prosecution which may resort to other tactics when it cannot get something in under similar fact evidence.

[11.23] The second limb of s 1(f)(ii) of the 1924 Act provides as follows: 'or the nature or conduct of the defence is such as to involve imputations on the character of the prosecutor or the witness for the prosecution.'

It is useful to look at some of the earlier Irish decisions as to the interpretation of the provisions under the 1924 Act.

---

[15] *DO v DPP* [2006] IESC 12 at 10–11.
[16] *DPP v McGrail* [1990] 2 IR 38.

[11.24] In *Attorney General v O'Shea*[17] the accused was convicted of murder. Evidence was given against him by a Civic Guard who hid under the bed in the accused's house and testified to incriminating conversations between the accused and his sister with regard to the disposal of the clothing used in the crime. It was alleged that the garda was subjected to such rigorous and searching cross-examination as to result in the loss of the shield by the accused because of imputations cast on the character of prosecution witnesses. This argument was rejected. *Per* Kennedy CJ:

> ... testing of the truth and accuracy of their testimony by legitimate cross-examination, however severe, is not ... conduct of the defence as to involve imputations ... within s 1(f)(ii).

[11.25] In *People (AG) v Coleman*,[18] the appellant was convicted of performing a criminal abortion on Judith Bolton (the principal prosecution witness). She had married Mr Mifsud (responsible for the pregnancy) who also testified against Coleman. Cross-examination of both Mifsud and Bolton involved the following imputations:

(1)   that Mr Mifsud had performed the illegal operation of Miss Bolton;

(2)   they conspired to charge Coleman with a crime they knew he was innocent of;

(3)   prior to her marriage, Mrs Mifsud had used contraceptives, contrary to Church teaching; and

(4)   they married with the objective of defeating justice.

The trial judge allowed cross-examination and it was upheld on appeal.

[11.26] In *People (AG) v Bond*[19] the trial judge did not give adequate direction as to the fact that evidence as to previous convictions is admitted only in relation to credit and not as to guilt. A retrial was ordered.

[11.27] In *Selvey v DPP*,[20] the facts concerned an accused charged with buggery of a young man. The prosecution evidence was to the effect that the claimant had been sexually interfered with and indecent photographs were found in the accused's room. The accused denied the charge and said that the photographs had been planted, and alleged the complainant had told him he was prepared to go on the bed; he had already done so for £1 and would do so again. The trial judge asked if he were suggesting to the jury that the complainant be disbelieved because he was 'that sort of young man'. To this, the accused answered yes,

---

[17]   *Attorney General v O'Shea* [1931] IR 713.
[18]   *People (AG) v Coleman* [1945] IR 237.
[19]   *People (AG) v Bond* [1966] IR 214.
[20]   *Selvey v DPP* [1970] AC 304.

which led to cross-examination on the accused's prior homosexual offences, but not on his convictions for dishonesty. The accused appealed and the House of Lords considered the issue and reasoned as follows. The House felt that the words of the statute should be given their ordinary meaning. This implied that when imputations are cast on the character of prosecution witnesses to show their unreliability as witnesses independently of evidence given by them, and also when such imputations are necessary to establish the accused's defence, the section permits cross-examination of the accused on his record. In essence, this interpretation confirmed the earlier approach taken by the Court of Criminal Appeal in *R v Hudson*,[21] where Lord Alverstone CJ stated:

> ... the words ... must receive their ordinary and natural interpretation and it is not legitimate to qualify them by inserting the words 'unnecessary' or 'unjustifiably' or 'for purposes other than that of developing the defence' or other similar words.

[11.28] In substance, this means that any attack by the accused on prosecution witnesses, even if that is an essential part of and a prerequisite to the running of the accused's defence, will result in the loss of the protection of the shield given by s 1(1) of the 1924 Act.

[11.29] There are, however, three qualifications on this interpretation. First, there is the rape situation, where an allegation of consent on the part of the complainant will not amount to an imputation, despite a suggestion that the complainant was a dangerous liar and possibly promiscuous (*R v Turner*).[22]

[11.30] The second exceptional situation is that which relates to a denial of allegations. In *R v Rouse*,[23] the accused said, in relation to a chief prosecution witness, 'he is a liar'. It was held, however, that that was merely a plea of 'not guilty' put in forcible language, and did not amount to an imputation within the meaning of the section. Thus, an accused can plead not guilty and deny facts alleged by the prosecution without fear of the loss of the shield.

[11.31] Furthermore, to suggest the reason for the prosecution witness's lie, does not amount to an imputation unless that reason itself suggests bad character. For example, it has been held that to suggest that the witness lied because he wished the accused no longer to have contact with his wife, is not an imputation as to a bad marriage and is not a sign of bad character (*R v Manley*[24]). The more elaborate the attack, the more likely it is to constitute an imputation. Examples of what have been deemed to be imputations are that someone is a

---

21 *R v Hudson* [1912] 2 KB 464.
22 *R v Turner* [1944] KB 463.
23 *R v Rouse* [1904] 1 KB 185.
24 *R v Manley* (1962) 126 JP 316.

homosexual, as in *Bishop*,[25] or where reference was made to a customs officer asking the accused's mother to 'have a word with him', as in *Courtney*.[26]

[11.32] The third qualification on this so-called *Hudson* doctrine relates to the words 'the nature or conduct of the defence'. This exception covers remarks incidental to the defence in question. Examples would include spontaneous remarks or answers given in cross-examination as a result of the prosecution counsel's attempt to trap the accused. Irrelevant remarks would also be covered.

[11.33] Even as thus qualified by the above three exceptions, the doctrine laid down in *Hudson* makes the position difficult for the accused, where he attempts to do any more in a defence contradicting the prosecution than merely explain away those facts that the prosecution allege.

[11.34] Much of the controversy with regard to *Hudson* has been resolved in the Irish context by the Irish Court of Criminal Appeal, in the case of *DPP v McGrail*.[27] The defence allegations in this case had been to the effect that the prosecution witnesses had fabricated evidence of verbal admissions. The facts concerned the entry of detectives to a flat in a house in Dublin, on foot of a search warrant. The accused dropped the keys to the flat and attempted to leave through a window. He was apprehended and the prosecution alleged that, while on the floor, he was asked by the detectives whether there were guns in the flat, to which he replied that there were. A subsequent search found firearms, ammunition, masks, balaclavas etc. The accused made a number of verbal statements after caution, which were taken down in writing, but which he did not sign. The defence alleged that the accused did not make any verbal admissions, did not point out any hiding place for the guns and that the gardaí were trying to convict him by inventing verbal statements. Counsel for the prosecution at trial applied for leave to cross-examine the accused as to his own character on grounds that the nature of the defence involved imputations on the character and credibility of garda witnesses.

[11.35] Leave to cross-examine was granted under s 1(f)(ii) of the 1924 Act and the accused in his direct evidence stated he had previous convictions which related to cars. On appeal, Hederman J, delivering the judgment of the court, stated that the trial judge erred in principle in ruling that the case made by the defence put the character of the prosecution witnesses in question. He said that every criminal trial involved an imputation as to the character of somebody. If the defence stated that witnesses for the prosecution were not to be believed in their evidence, that was an imputation as to their character. This was inevitable if

---

[25] *Bishop* [1975] QB 274.
[26] *Courtney* [1995] CrimLR 63.
[27] *DPP v McGrail* [1990] 2 IR 38.

an accused person was not to be seriously hampered in his defence. A ruling otherwise would have the effect of inhibiting the conduct of the defence, in that an accused person who had a criminal record might be intimidated into abandoning an effort to put the truth of the evidence of a prosecution witness in issue, lest his own character outside the facts of the trial was then put in issue.

In this particular instance, the case against the accused was based on confessions which he denied making to the police. The inescapable inference was that the police were lying.

[11.36] It would be intolerable, according to Hederman J if an accused was confined to suggesting a mistake or other innocent explanation to avoid any risk of subjecting his own character to cross-examination. It would be otherwise if the defence case was that this was the usual practice of the police in respect of any person they prosecuted.

[11.37] It is worth quoting at length from Hederman J's judgment:[28]

> Every criminal trial involves an imputation as to the character of somebody. The mere fact than an accused is accused of a criminal offence and that evidence is offered to support that view is, in effect, an imputation against the character of the accused. If the accused, either by giving evidence or through his counsel's cross-examination of witnesses for the prosecutions, suggests to them that they are not to be believed, that is also an imputation as to their character, in as much as it is suggested to them that they are telling an untruth, if that is the way the matter is put to them. The defence may even require, in its effort to rebut the prosecution's case, to suggest to the witness and to the court, that in fact the real author of the crime, if it has been proved to have been committed, is not the accused but one or other, perhaps, of the witnesses for the prosecution. Such a course of conduct is inevitable if an accused person is not to be seriously hampered in the conduct of his defence. Any ruling otherwise would have the effect of inhibiting the conduct of the defence in that an accused person, who may have a criminal record, may be intimidated into abandoning an effort to put in issue the truth of the evidence of a prosecution witness lest his own character outside the facts of the trial be put in issue ...

> Similarly, when the case against an accused is based on confessions alleged to have been made by him, and he denies that he made any such statements to the police, the inescapable inference is of course that the police are not telling the truth. But that again is a matter which is not independent of the facts of case. It would be different if it had been suggested to the policeman that this was their usual practice in respect of any persons they prosecuted for the purposes of discrediting their testimony in the case at hearing. It would be quite an intolerable situation if an accused person, in the context of the defence in cross-examining prosecution witnesses the veracity of whose evidence he was challenging, should

---

[28] *DPP v McGrail* [1990] 2 IR 38 at 48–50.

be required to confine himself to suggesting a mistake or other innocent explanation to avoid the risk of having his own character put in issue.

The provisions of the Criminal Justice (Evidence) Act 1924 prohibit putting in evidence the bad character of the accused unless 'the nature or conduct of the defence is such as to involve imputations on the character of the prosecutor or witnesses to the prosecution'. The question is what construction is to be put on the words 'imputation on the character of the prosecutor or witnesses to the prosecution'. In the view of the court this must be construed as applying only to imputations made on the character of the prosecutor or his witnesses independent of the facts of the particular case, as, for example, where it is suggested the witnesses are of such general ill-repute that they are persons not to be believed. To put to a prosecution witness that he fabricated the evidence he is giving, or that he or other witnesses for the prosecution combined together to fabricate evidence for the particular trial in question, may be necessary to enable the accused to establish his defence, if in fact his defence is that he made no such statement to one or more of the prosecution witnesses. It seems immaterial whether the allegation of untruthfulness is made directly to a witness or witnesses or in the necessary inference on the question put. If the accused gives evidence and if, for example, he denies the facts of the offence alleged against him, and it is put to him that he is not telling the truth, is that to be taken as an attack by the prosecution on his character? The court thinks not. A distinction must be drawn between questions and suggestions which are reasonably necessary to establish either the prosecution case or the defence case, even if they do involve suggesting a falsehood on the part of the witness of one or the other side, on the one hand, and on the other hand, an imputation of bad character introduced by either side relating to matters unconnected with the proofs of the instant case.

Hederman J concluded that:

> A procedure which inhibits the accused from challenging the veracity of the evidence against him at the risk of having his own previous character put in evidence is not a fair procedure.[29]

[11.38] This is a very strong defence of the right of an accused to put forward their side of the story. Hederman J read into the words of s 1(f)(ii) a qualification. He very clearly, on the basis of fair procedure, departed from *Hudson* and gives the accused the right to make an attack on prosecution witnesses if it is necessary to the defence – not a generalised attack that would lead to loss of the shield, but, if it is necessary, to challenge the veracity of evidence by prosecution witnesses.

[11.39] The view of the Court of Criminal Appeal was to the effect that s 1(f)(ii) of the 1924 Act must be construed as applying only to imputations made on the

---

[29] *DPP v McGrail* [1990] 2 IR 38 at 51.

character of the prosecutor or his witnesses, independent of the facts of the particular case. A distinction should be drawn between questions or suggestions which are reasonably necessary to establish either the prosecution case or the defence case, even if it does involve suggesting a falsehood on the part of a witness. It is otherwise when an imputation of bad character is introduced relating to matters unconnected with the proofs of the material case. Even in the latter case, the trial judge had discretion to refuse leave to cross-examine about previous convictions or bad character because of the danger of unfairness to an accused person who has previous convictions. Hederman J concluded by saying that the principles of fair procedure must apply. A procedure which inhibited the accused from challenging the veracity of the evidence against him, at the risk of having his own previous character put in evidence, was not fair procedure. Recent English decisions to the effect that any challenge to the veracity of the evidence of the prosecution was sufficient to open the way for a cross-examination of the accused as to his character, should not then be followed.

[11.40] This is an interesting departure on the part of the Irish courts from the rigours of the *Hudson* doctrine, and is to be welcomed in so far as the result of the application of that doctrine was once seen to unduly prejudice certain accused persons, ie those with criminal records. Moreover, yet again the Irish courts are locating their justification for amending the rules in the requirements of fair procedure, seen to underlie so very many of the rules of evidence in Irish law.

[11.41] Section 1(f)(iii) of the 1924 Act provides for the admissibility of an accused's record, where 'he has given evidence against any other person charged with the same offence'.

[11.42] In the case of *Murdoch v Taylor*,[30] the facts concerned the joint trial of Murdoch (with a criminal record) and Lynch (no criminal record) for receiving stolen goods. Lynch gave evidence implicating Murdoch. Murdoch gave evidence in cross-examination alleging that Lynch alone had control and possession of the box containing the stolen goods. He was then cross-examined on his record. The Court of Criminal Appeal and the House of Lords dismissed Murdoch's appeal, which had alleged, *inter alia*, that s 1(f)(iii) of the 1924 Act only applied to evidence given in examination-in-chief and with hostile intent, and that the trial judge had discretion as to whether to allow said cross-examination on record or not.

[11.43] Lord Donovan, in relation to the first argument, commented that the effect upon the jury was the same, whether the evidence was given on

---

[30] *Murdoch v Taylor* [1965] AC 574.

examination-in-chief or cross-examination. In relation to the second point, he felt that it was the effect of the evidence on the minds of the jury which mattered, not the state of mind of the person who gave it. He felt that one had to look at the evidence in context, and that if the effect of the evidence upon the mind of the jury was to be taken as the test, it cannot be right to regard it in isolation in order to decide if it is evidence against the co-accused. If parliament had meant by s 1(f)(iii) to refer to evidence which was by itself conclusive against the co-accused, it would have been easy for them to say so, he reasoned. Murdoch's evidence was clearly to that effect. In relation to the exercise of a discretion on the part of the trial judge, the court felt that the trial judge had no discretion to prevent a co-accused from cross-examining under s 1(f)(iii). ('So far as the prosecution is concerned the matter should be one for the judge's discretion ... where the coaccused seeks to exercise the right different considerations apply this right can not be fettered in any way.'[31]) This approach was confirmed by the Privy Council in the case of *Liu Meilin v R*.[32]

[11.44] In *Varley*,[33] the Court of Appeal added guidance for trial judges to help determine whether an accused is entitled to cross-examine another on his character. The two accused here were jointly charged with robbery. One admitted he and the other had participated in the robbery but claimed he had acted under duress from his co-accused. The co-accused, in turn, gave evidence he had taken no part in the robbery and that evidence given that he had was untrue. The latter was cross-examined on his record, on the basis that he had given evidence against the other. The Court of Appeal laid down the following guidelines:

(1)   If it is established that a person jointly charged has given evidence against the co-defendant that defendant has a right to cross-examine the other as to previous convictions and the trial judge has no discretion to refuse an application.

(2)   Such evidence may be given during chief or during cross-examination.

(3)   It has to be objectively decided whether the evidence either supports the prosecution case in a material respect or undermines the defence of the co-accused. A hostile intent is irrelevant.

(4)   If consideration has to be given to the undermining of the other's defence care must be taken to see that the evidence clearly undermines the defence. Inconvenience to or inconsistency with the other's defence is not of itself sufficient.

---

[31]   *Murdock v Taylor* [1965] AC 574 at 593.
[32]   *Liu Meilin v R* [1989] 1 All ER 359.
[33]   *Varley* [1982] 2 All ER 519.

(5) Mere denial of participation in a joint venture is not of itself sufficient to rank as evidence against the co-defendant. For the proviso to apply, such denial must lead to the conclusion that if the witness did not participate then it must have been the other who did.

(6) Where the one defendant asserts or in due course would assert one view of the joint venture which is directly contradicted by the other, such contradiction may be evidence against the co-defendant.[34]

Hence, if the witness's evidence has the effect of supporting the prosecution case against the co-accused and so undermines the co-accused's case more than it does that of the prosecution, cross-examination is allowed.

[11.45] *R v Kirkpatrick*[35] is an example of an instance when it was accepted that the accused's defence did not have such an effect on the co-accused's case so as to allow cross-examination as to record. Here, the accused gave evidence that he was asleep during the offence. The co-accused's case, by contrast, was that he had intervened to prevent the commission of the offence. It was held the former had not given evidence against the latter, as he had not supported the prosecution case against him.

The distinction may be difficult to perceive in practice, as undoubtedly such would affect the credibility of that accused, which would have undermined his defence, hence strengthening the case against him.

[11.46] An example of a case where character evidence was introduced without justification in an Irish court – as revealed on appeal – demonstrates how academic refined distinctions as to the meanings of the exceptions to s 1(f) might be in reality. The context, moreover, is the non-jury Special Criminal Court where the artificiality of judges instructing themselves on rules of evidence applies, although one might argue this was a situation where they should have been advantaged in being aware of the law and the general rule as to inadmissibility of past bad behaviour. In *People (DPP) v Murphy*,[36] Murphy was convicted of conspiracy to cause explosion and was sentenced to 14 years. This case arose out of the 1998 Omagh bombing. The context was thus a highly charged one, the bombing having led to the deaths of 29 people, with 300 injured. The evidence against Murphy comprised, in part at least, mobile phone tracking etc, which has become more common, and there are a number grounds of appeal in relation to that. He lodged 40 grounds of appeal in all. The accused alleged that the court breached his entitlement to the presumption of innocence by having evidence of previous convictions admitted in evidence.

---

[34] *Varley* [1982] 2 All ER 519 at 522.

[35] *R v Kirkpatrick* [1998] CrimLR 63.

[36] *People (DPP) v Murphy* [2005] IECCA 1, Kearns J.

[11.47] The general rule, of course, is that previous convictions are not admissible unless the situation comes under similar fact evidence or the accused drops the shield under the exceptions to s 1(f). Here the court of trial had had regard to the accused's previous convictions although it was not a similar fact evidence case and he had not given evidence or put his character in issue. Why did the previous convictions go in? No case had been made to the admissibility of previous convictions. The Court of Criminal Appeal noted that at the outset of the case there was a lengthy hearing regarding the legality of his arrest and detention. During the course of that hearing, which was solely for the purposes of examining the basis for the arrest of Murphy, hearsay evidence was given about Murphy's previous convictions and the suspicion of the arresting officer that Murphy had been involved in certain organisations.

[11.48] That was one possible source of this material. When the court on appeal also looked at the transcript of the trial, they noticed that the accused's counsel when cross-examining one of the guards, made reference to the fact that Murphy had been convicted in 1976. Again, that was not formal evidence: it was simply a question put to the guard by counsel. The Court of Criminal Appeal pointed out:

> At no stage did the prosecution attempt to lead formal evidence of previous convictions, nor did the court of trial indicate it intended relying on same or afford the defence any opportunity of making submissions as to the admissibility or otherwise of such material prior to delivering judgment.[37]

The Court continued:[38]

> To have regard to previous convictions in respect of which no admissible evidence was tendered and where no grounds for doing so were established, can only be seen as a significant erosion of the presumption of innocence, whether couched in terms which go to corroboration or in terms which suggest that previous convictions are probative in some way of the guilt of an accused person in relation to a specific offence. While this was not a jury trial where the risk of prejudice would be glaringly obvious, it is impossible to avoid the conclusion that the previous convictions and bad character of the accused (as so found by the court) formed a significant element in the court's decision to convict. We remain of this view, even though the court at a later point in its judgment indicated it was satisfied to convict on the basis of the admissions of the accused alone.

> There is a consistent line of authority of long standing to the effect the conviction is unsafe where evidence of previous convictions has been improperly introduced
> …

---

[37] *People (DPP) v Murphy* [2005] IECCA 1 at 19.
[38] *People (DPP) v Murphy* [2005] IECCA 1 at 19–20, Kearns J.

> This court is driven to the inescapable conclusion the court of trial fell into error in relying upon either the material contained in the *voir dire*, or in counsel's questions to admit as probative evidence which was manifestly inadmissible.

Hence, for this reason, the court felt the conviction of the accused was unsafe and unsatisfactory.

[11.49] This is yet another interesting example of the effectiveness of the rules of evidence being based on the assumption of a division of function between judge and jury. It is also an interesting vindication of the rules not admitting evidence of previous convictions. On a particular level, the case is a stark reminder of how powerful this evidence is and how it can find its way in where it operates to usually prejudicial effect. On a general level, it also raises questions of the ability of the Special Criminal Court to operate effectively.

Credibility/guilt distinction: judicial discretion with regard to divisibility of character

[11.50] In *R v Watts*,[39] the appellant was of low intelligence and had two previous convictions for sexual offences against children. A young married woman had been indecently assaulted near his home by a man answering his description. He made plain admissions to the police and was charged accordingly. The accused presented an alibi defence at trial and claimed the police had fabricated evidence against him. He was then cross-examined under s 1(f)(ii) of the 1924 Act and convicted. He appealed on the basis that the trial judge had wrongly exercised his discretion by allowing cross-examination with regard to previous convictions.

[11.51] In the Court of Appeal, judgment was delivered by Lord Lane CJ who felt that the nature and conduct of the defence was plainly such here as to involve imputations on the character of two police officers within s 1(f)(ii) of the 1924 Act. He noted that there was also no doubt, but that the only relevance of the previous convictions admitted by virtue of that subsection, was as to the credibility of the prisoner, and the jury must not be asked to infer guilt from such convictions. He commented that 'this in many cases requires the jury to perform difficult feats of intellectual acrobatics. In the view of this court the present case is a good example'.

[11.52] Lord Lane CJ continued:

> In any event it seems to us that where the exercise of discretion is concerned, which is the problem here, each case is a case on its own and has to be considered on its own particular facts.

---

[39] *R v Watts* [1983] 3 All ER 101.

The jury in the present case was charged with deciding the guilt or innocence of a man against whom an allegation of indecent assault on a woman was made. They were told that he had previous convictions for indecent assaults of a more serious kind on young girls. They were warned that such evidence was not to be taken as making it more likely that he was guilty of the offence charged, which it seems it plainly did, but only as affecting his credibility, which it almost certainly did not. The prejudice which the appellant must have suffered in the eyes of the jury when it was disclosed that he had previous convictions for offences against young children could hardly have been greater. The probative value of the convictions on the sole issue on which they were admissible, was at best, slight. The previous offences did not involve dishonesty. Nor were they so similar to the offence which the jury were trying that they could have been admitted as evidence of similar facts on the issue of identity. In short, their prejudicial effect far outweighed their probative value. We would not have allowed this particular man to have been cross-examined about these particular convictions in these particular circumstances.

[11.53] It is interesting to contrast the decision in *Watts* with a later retraction by Lord Lane CJ in *R v Powell*.[40] *Per* Lord Lane CJ:

A defendant with previous convictions for similar offences may indeed have a very great incentive to make false allegations against prosecution witnesses for fear of greater punishment on conviction. It does however require careful direction from the judge to the effect that the previous convictions should not be taken as indications that the accused has committed the offence.

The fact that the defendant's convictions are not for offences of dishonesty, in fact that they are for offences bearing a close resemblance to the offences charged, are matters for the judge to take into consideration when exercising his discretion, but they certainly do not oblige the judge to disallow the proposed cross-examination.

[11.54] The most fundamental question is what part of an accused's record is admissible, since it goes only to credibility here and not guilt. The danger to be avoided here is that of the 'forbidden reasoning', where jurors take what seems to be very little about creditworthiness (say a conviction for rape) and use it as evidence of predisposition (on a charge of a sexual offence).

[11.55] A related danger is the use by the prosecution of 'previous offences' to demonstrate bad character, when such evidence should not have been introduced as similar fact evidence. In *Barsoum*,[41] questioning, which was held to have gone too far, was as to the accused's previous similar convictions, how his defences had been disbelieved therein and as to the details of the offences.

---

[40] *R v Powell* [1988] 1 All ER 193.
[41] *Barsoum* [1994] CrimLR 194.

[11.56] In *McLeod*,[42] the Court of Appeal offered the following guidance:

(a) The mere fact that the previous offences are similar to that charged, or suggest that the accused has the propensity to commit an offence such as that charged does not prevent the prosecution from cross-examining about them, even though their true relevance is confined to the accused's credibility.

(b) Nonetheless, unless it is contended that the previous offences would anyway be admissible on the issue of guilt (for example as similar fact evidence) there should be no cross-examination prolonged or extensive enough to divert the jury from the real issue in the case, which is whether or not the accused committed the offence charged.

(c) The fact that the accused had previously offered a similar defence, which a previous jury has rejected, for example a false alibi or the alleged 'planting' of evidence, may be a proper subject for cross-examination, because it may reflect on the accused's credibility.

(d) The judge retains a discretion to restrain cross-examination which tends to show particularly bad character, and should take into account both the degree of prejudice likely to be caused to the accused, and the gravity of the attack made on the prosecution in deciding how to exercise his discretion.

[11.57] There are a lot of factors at play in the context of the accused as witness. One is connected to trust in the jury. A great deal of concern has been expressed over the years in several jurisdictions about whether juries could be trusted with past record evidence. To date, the law in this jurisdiction and the traditional common law did not trust the jury and approached this type of evidence on the basis that it was excluded, and only in rare circumstances could it came back in.

Reform

[11.58] The urge for reform characterizing discussion of this issue has come to fruition in England under the Criminal Justice Act of 2003. Debate had started with the Eleventh Report of the *Criminal Law Revision Committee* in 1972, and been followed through by a number of reports,[43] culminating ultimately in the Auld Report in 2001, which reviewed reform of the rules of evidence in this area, amongst other things. The theme of trusting magistrates and juries was most prevalent in these discussions and the change in approach is from 'is there a reason to include it?' to 'is there a reason to exclude it?'

---

[42] *McLeod* [1994] 1 WLR 1500.

[43] For example, Royal Commission on Criminal Justice 1993, Law Commission 1994, Law Commission Consultation Paper 1996 and the 2001 Labour Party manifesto.

[11.59] The Auld Report itself gave rise in time to a White Paper, 'Justice for All', in July 2002 and that became the Criminal Justice Act of 2003. Part 11 of that Act deals with evidence and Chapter 1 of that Part deals with evidence of bad character.

Section 98 defines evidence of a person's 'bad character' as:

> evidence of, or a disposition towards, misconduct on his part, other than evidence which—
>
> (a) has to do with the alleged facts of the offence charged or
>
> (b) evidence of misconduct in connection with the investigation or prosecution of that offence.

[11.60] Section 99 of the Criminal Justice Act 2003 abolishes the common law rules for admissibility of this type of evidence. Having abolished these common law rules, the Act then enumerates in s 101 what are referred to as 'gateways' (seven situations) via which a defendant's bad character becomes admissible. There were a number of problems with this. The Criminal Justice Act 2003 was brought into force in December 2004, yet the judiciary had not been given training in relation to the changes. Hence the Court of Appeal then had to deal with a number of appeals and took the approach of collecting them into batches so that experienced judges could give guidance to the courts below in regard to what was a major sea-change in the law. Whereas the courts for years had excluded this type of evidence, here it was to be introduced overnight. The relevant sections are ss 98–108.

[11.61] Section 101 sets out the seven gateways when a defendant's bad character is admissible. These are, under s 101(1), if:

(a) all parties to the proceedings agree to the evidence being admissible;

(b) the evidence is adduced by the defendant himself or is given in answer to a question asked by him in cross-examination and intended to elicit it;

(c) it is important exculpatory evidence;

(d) it is relevant to an important matter in issue between the defendant and the prosecution;

(e) it has substantial probative value in relation to an important matter in issue between the defendant and a co-defendant;

(f) it is evidence to correct a false impression given by the defendant; or

(g) the defendant has made an attack on another person's character.

Ground (d) would seem very broad and one might wonder how *Ferris or DO*[44] would have fared under (b). A limited amount of discretion is retained, however, in relation to grounds (d) or (g) in that if it appears to the court that the admission of evidence would have an adverse effect on the fairness of the proceedings, the court ought not to admit it (s 101(3)). A number of cases have commented on these changes, giving guidance as to their implementation.

[11.62] In *R v Hanson*[45] the standard directions to be given by a judge in relation to admissible evidence of bad character adduced by a co-accused are set out:

> The starting point should be for Judges and practitioners to bear in mind that Parliament's purpose in the legislation ... was to assist in the evidence based conviction of the guilty, without putting those who are not guilty at risk of conviction by prejudice.[46]

> ... in any case in which evidence of bad character is admitted to show propensity, whether to establish offences or to be untruthful the judge in summing up should warn the jury clearly against placing undue reliance on previous convictions. Evidence of bad character cannot be used simply to bolster a weak case, or to prejudice the minds of a jury against a defendant ... [P]ropensity is only one relevant factor and they must assess its significance in the light of all the other evidence in the case.[47]

[11.63] In *R v Renda*[48] the Court of Appeal indicated the limited extent to which it would interfere with the trial judge's decision by stating that 'the trial judge's "feel" for the case is usually the critical ingredient of the decision at first instance which this court lacks. Context therefore is vital'.[49] The appellant, the Crown alleged, had sought to convey the impression that he was a man of good character. Here an issue arose as to the concept of misconduct in a situation where the Crown sought to ask questions about a prior incident of violence where the accused was found unfit to plead. Misconduct under s 112(1) is defined as including reprehensible behaviour, other than the conviction for offences. The Crown had argued, and the trial judge agreed, that this constituted misconduct within the Act. On appeal, that was upheld, the Court of Appeal stating:

> We agree that the appellant was not 'convicted' of a criminal offence. We also accept that as a matter of ordinary language, the word 'reprehensible' carries with it some element of culpability or blameworthiness. What however we are

---

[44] *People (DPP) v Ferris* [2008] 1 IR 1; *DPP v DO* [2006] IESC 12.

[45] *R v Hanson* [2005] EWCA Crim 824.

[46] *R v Hanson* [2005] EWCA Crim 824, para 3.

[47] *R v Hanson* [2005] EWCA Crim 824, para 18.

[48] *R v Renda* [2005] EWCA Crim 2826.

[49] *R v Renda* [2005] EWCA Crim 2826, para 3.

unable to accept is the mere fact that the appellant was found unfit to plead some 18 months after an apparent incident of gratuitous violence has occurred, of itself, connotes that at the time of the offence his mental acuity was so altered as to extinguish any element of culpability when the table leg was used in such a violent fashion. On the face of it, this was reprehensible behaviour, and there was no evidence ... to suggest otherwise.[50]

Later on they point out that the trial judge explained that its relevance in this particular case was confined to helping the jury decide whether the appellant had tried to present himself as a 'rather better man' than he actually was, and whether he was in truth, as the jury might consider he was seeking to convey, deserving of sympathy.[51]

[11.64] A similar clarification of s 101(1)(f) was given in *R v Weit*[52] where the court pointed out that a simple denial of the offence alleged cannot be treated as a false impression given by the defendant. This was not the situation here however where, '[t]he appellant put himself forward as a man who not only had no previous convictions but also enjoyed a good reputation as a priest.'[53]

[11.65] Finally, in *Robinson v R*,[54] Hooper J commented on the need to avoid unduly perplexing the jury, pointing out that, 'the judge must also consider the necessity to give directions which will not needlessly perplex juries. If juries are needlessly perplexed then the defendants in their care will not receive a fair trial.'[55]

[11.66] Suggestions as to reform in Ireland began with former Minister for Justice, Michael McDowell, when he was establishing the Balance in Criminal Law Review Group, pointing to the rules of evidence relating to character evidence. The Group's report was delivered on 15 March 2007. One issue they looked at was the admissibility of bad character of the accused. They identified that the reason for the rules as they are is that it is generally considered that the admission of bad character evidence will have a disproportionately prejudicial effect on the jury.[56] This they acknowledged was supported by such limited empirical evidence that existed, such as Sally Lloyd Bostock's study.[57]

---

[50] *R v Renda* [2005] EWCA Crim 2826 at para 24.
[51] *R v Renda* [2005] EWCA Crim 2826 at para 25.
[52] *R v Weit* [2005] EWCA Crim 2866.
[53] *R v Weit* [2005] EWCA Crim 2866 at para 43.
[54] *Robinson v R* [2005] EWCA Crim 3233.
[55] *Robinson v R* [2005] EWCA Crim 3233 at para 81.
[56] Balance in the Criminal Law Review Group, Final Report (Dept of Justice, 15 March 2007) at p 100.
[57] Lloyd Bostock, 'The Effect on Juries of Hearing about the Defendant's Previous Criminal Record: A Simulation Study' [2000] CrimLR 734.

[11.67] They went on to consider the reforms that they might suggest in relation to the rules as they currently are. Ultimately, the Review Group did not feel they could recommend any general relaxation of the law in this area. They did, however, recommend some changes to the 1924 Act and these related to permitting an accused to be cross-examined as to bad character where he makes an imputation on the character of the deceased or an incapacitated victim. They also considered that such evidence should be admissible where a defence witness (and not simply the defendant) gives evidence as to the accused's good character.[58] Furthermore, they considered the prosecution should be entitled to adduce evidence of the accused's bad character where the accused does not give evidence.[59]

[11.68] The Group also looked at the issue of a situation where the accused does not directly lead evidence of good character but nonetheless 'impliedly' asserts this by other evidence or even appearance, trying to achieve the same effect indirectly by evidence suggesting he's a respectable person. They point to the UK Eleventh Report on Evidence, which gave an example of a case that occurred in London in the early 1970s.[60] An accused with a long criminal record was charged with conspiracy to rob. He went into the witness box wearing a dark suit and looking as though he were a respectable businessman. When his counsel asked when and where he had met his co-accused, he replied 'about 18 months ago at my golf club. I was looking for a game and the Secretary introduced us.' This was put forward as an example of giving a false impression. This has now been addressed in the UK by s 105 of the Criminal Justice Act 2003. The Review Group felt that a modest reform of s 1(f) of the 1924 Act to deal with this should be effected. They suggested the UK provisions could be a starting pointing to introducing that particular change here.

[11.69] The Review Group felt particularly strongly about the issue of attacking the character of a deceased, for example, in a homicide case.[61] They pointed out that if an accused makes an imputation on a deceased's character, there is no comeback. There had been a lot of submissions from victims' groups on this issue that seemed persuasive. The Review Group's recommendation here was "in a case where injured party has died or become incapacitated such that he or she unable to give evidence, where the defence attacks the character of the injured

---

58   *Cf People (DPP) v Ferris* [2008] 1 IR 1.
59   Balance in the Criminal Law Review Group, Final Report (Dept of Justice, 15 March 2007), p 101.
60   Balance in the Criminal Law Review Group, Final Report (Dept of Justice, 15 March 2007), p 110.
61   Balance in the Criminal Law Review Group, Final Report (Dept of Justice, 15 March 2007), p 117.

party, the shield would be dropped and the accused would be liable to cross-examination as to his/her character without leave of the court. This would involve the amendment of s 1(f)(ii) of the Criminal Justice Evidence Act 1924 to allow a further category of case in which cross-examination is permitted (ie by adding reference to the injured party including a deceased or incapacitated injured party)".[62]

Although, a proposal for such an amendment was contained in Head 25(2) of the Scheme of Criminal Procedure Bill 2009 published by the Department of Justice, it was not subsequently contained in the Criminal Procedure Bill 2009 as initiated in the Seanad in June 2009.

[11.70] One recurrent issue that is central to any reform process is how real is the risk in admitting character evidence. Spencer[63] has written extensively on evidence of bad character and identified what he regards as the real risk that exists in admitting the defendant's bad character although, interestingly, he is not against the changes made to the law by the UK Act:

> What is the real risk with admitting evidence of the defendant's bad character? I believe that the real danger is not so much that the tribunal of fact will be unduly prejudiced by it; instead, it is the risk that it will be used to tip the scales in a case in which the rest of evidence is weak or non-existent. A gruesome illustration of this problem is the famous case of Oscar Slater,[64] who was wrongly convicted and sentenced to death for the murder of a Miss Gilchrist in Glasgow in 1908, was reprieved and, after 19 years digging granite in a prison quarry in Peterhead, was released and compensated out of public funds when his conviction was eventually quashed in 1928. At his trial, the prosecutor made much of his general bad character, as a man who lived on the edge of the law, changing wives, surnames and addresses regularly, and existing on the proceeds of gambling and (it seems) of prostitution. In his direction to the jury, the judge famously said: "He has maintained himself by the ruin of men and the ruin of women, living for years past in a way that many blackguards scorned lived. A man of that kind has not the presumption of innocence in his favour which is a form in the case of every man, but a reality in the case of the ordinary man."[65] This case is often cited by those who argue that admitting evidence of a defendant's bad character is always unfair and dangerous. But it seems that the real problem in that affair was that the bad character evidence was admitted, and made much of, to supplement a case in which the rest of the evidence was completely worthless. The only evidence linking Oscar Slater, either directly or indirectly, with the victim of the offence were several 'fleeting glance' identifications, all of them highly suspect.

---

62 Balance in the Criminal Law Review Group, Final Report, p 144.

63 Spencer, *Evidence of Bad Character* (Hart, 2006), p 13.

64 *Slater v HM Advocate* [1928] JC 94.

65 [1928] JC 94 at 96

As one English commentator, Sir Herbert Stephen, put it, Slater was convicted and sentenced to death on evidence that no English judge would have allowed to go to a jury, and on which 'no bench of magistrates in England would have ordered the destruction of a terrier which was alleged to have bitten somebody'.

[11.71] On the other hand, there are views such as that of Colin Tapper[66] on the changes introduced in this area by the Criminal Justice Act 2003. He considers there still is a risk of prejudice inherent in leaving such evidence in. He reminds us that re-using convictions where someone has done their time, bringing them back in again, could distort the whole system of criminal justice:

> Unfortunately the position remains that the balance of research and even anecdote recounted by the Law Commission suggests that the danger of prejudice is extremely high. Nor should the degree to which such further use of convictions in respect of which the defendant has served his sentence might discredit, and distort, the fairness of the whole system of criminal justice be too lightly dismissed.[67]

His conclusion is that the Criminal Justice Act 2003 provisions constitute 'an illiberal reaction to the problems the old law presented … [A]nomalies and vagueness have been exacerbated rather than eliminated.'[68] He also points out – which is a fair point – that the 2003 Act reliance on discretion epitomised in s 101(3) (adverse effect on fairness) is no substitute for rules.[69] Tapper concludes the provisions represent a missed opportunity.

Conclusion

[11.72] Lord Lane CJ's judgment in *Watts*[70] with regard to the exercise of judicial discretion in relation to the non-admissibility of an accused's record, when its probative value in terms of credibility is slight, and its prejudicial effect in the eyes of the jury is great, is compulsive in terms of its logic.

[11.73] While the issue is arguably of less importance now in Ireland, given the judgment in *McGrail*,[71] which eases the burden placed on the judiciary to ameliorate the harshness of the *Hudson*[72] doctrine by the use of judicial

---

66 Tapper, 'The Criminal Justice Act 2003: Evidence of Bad Character' [2004] CrimLR 533.
67 Tapper, 'The Criminal Justice Act 2003: Evidence of Bad Character' [2004] Crim LR 533 at 549.
68 Tapper, 'The Criminal Justice Act 2003: Evidence of Bad Character' [2004] Crim LR 533 at 554.
69 Tapper, 'The Criminal Justice Act 2003: Evidence of Bad Character' [2004] Crim LR 533 at 555.
70 *R v Watts* [1983] 3 All ER 101.
71 *People (DPP) v McGrail* [1990] 2 IR 38.
72 *R v Hudson* [1912] 2 KB 464.

discretion to disallow cross-examination on record, it is still an important one in terms of the difficulty of directing the jury as to the relevance of the record lying only to the credibility of the accused. The fundamental issue is raised by Lord Lane CJ in *Watts*, namely, the ability of the jury to engage in the 'intellectual gymnastics' necessitated by the section, or the justification or validity of requiring same. Is such a record of 'character' (undivided) ever relevant to credibility? Can a jury ever be expected to draw such distinctions? And in the light of *McGrail* in the Irish context, can such admission, introduction and direction ever ensure fundamental fairness to an accused?

[11.74] It is in this light that the issues of character, credibility, divisibility of record and judicial discretion need to be considered in the Irish context of reform.

Index

All references are to *paragraph* numbers.

Accomplices
corroboration, and, 6.24–6.52

Accused persons
competence, and, 11.02
cross-examination, and
conclusions, 11.72–11.74
credibility/guilt distinction, 11.50–11.69
introduction, 11.01–11.10
judicial discretion as to divisibility of character, 11.50–11.71
legislative basis of rule, 11.02
loss of the 'shield', 11.11–11.49
privilege against self-incrimination, 11.02
similar fact evidence, 11.11
prosecution witnesses, and, 5.45

Administrative tribunals
hearsay, and, 9.03

Admissibility of evidence
documents
copies of documents, 9.164–9.165
generally, 9.160–9.163
statutory provisions, 9.166
generally, 3.09–3.11
illegally obtained evidence, and, 4.01

Admissions
hearsay evidence, and, 9.16

Adversarial system
illegally obtained evidence, and, 4.05

Arrest
confessions, and, 9.83–9.89
generally, 2.34–2.40

Arrestable offences
search warrants, and, 4.26–4.27

Autrefois acquit
competence and compellability, and, 5.45

Bad character
cross-examination of accused, and, 11.01

Bail
generally, 2.71–2.85
hearsay evidence, and, 9.168

Belief evidence
expert witnesses, and, 7.36–7.39

Blood samples
expert evidence, and, 7.88–7.102

Burden of proof
evidential burden, 3.24–3.26
generally, 3.20–3.21
legal burden, 3.20
persons bearing burden, 3.27–3.28
probative burden, 3.20
res ipsa loquitur, 3.29–3.35
reverse burden
Criminal Justice Act 2007, and, 3.69–3.75
generally, 3.47–3.68
human rights issues, 3.75–3.76
rule in *Woolmington v DPP*
exceptions, 3.43–3.88
generally, 3.36–3.42
insanity, 3.43
peculiar knowledge principle, 3.78–3.88
reverse burden, 3.47–3.77
statutory provisions, 3.44–3.46
shifting, 3.22–3.23
similar fact evidence, and, 10.43
types, 3.20

Calling of witnesses
competence and compellability, and, 5.10–5.11

Causation
search warrants, and, 4.91

Character
cross-examination of accused, and, 11.01

Children
competence and compellability, and
generally, 5.16–5.28
reforms, 5.29–5.33
hearsay evidence, and, 9.170–9.175

Common knowledge rule
expert witnesses, and, 7.28
Competence and compellability of witnesses
accused as prosecution witness, 5.45
calling of witnesses, 5.10–5.11
children's evidence
generally, 5.16–5.28
reforms, 5.29–5.33
Criminal Justice Act 2006, and, 5.36–5.40
cross-examination, 5.03–5.07
defendant's spouse as witness, 5.41–5.44
diplomats as prosecution witness, 5.46
elicitation of testimony
generally, 5.12–5.13
process, 5.02–5.08
examination-in-chief, 5.02
hostile witnesses, 5.09
inappropriate questions on cross-examination, 5.35
introduction, 5.01
mental disability, 5.15
oaths, 5.12–5.13
physical disability, 5.14
process of elicitation of testimony
cross-examination, 5.03–5.07
examination-in-chief, 5.02
re-examination, 5.08
re-examination, 5.08
reforms
accused as prosecution witness, 5.45
children's evidence, 5.29–5.33
Criminal Justice Act 2006, 5.36–5.40
defendant's spouse as witness, 5.41–5.44
diplomats as prosecution witness, 5.46
inappropriate questions on cross-examination, 5.35
other witnesses, 5.34
vulnerable witnesses, 5.34
Confessions
arrest process changes, 9.83–9.89
constitutional dimension, 9.68–9.82
corroboration, and, 6.88–6.90

generally, 9.17–9.22
historical development, 9.25–9.28
inducement, 9.29–9.31
Irish case law, 9.32–9.47
'person in authority', 9.48–9.67
voluntariness, 9.23–9.24
Confrontation
hearsay, and, 9.117–9.142
Contempt of court
journalistic privilege, and, 8.79
sacerdotal privilege, and, 8.66
Convictions
proof, as, 7.52–7.54
Corroboration
accomplices, 6.24–6.52
children's evidence, 6.121–6.126
confession evidence, 6.88–6.90
discretion to give warning
children's evidence, 6.121–6.126
sexual offences, 6.117–6.120
doctrine of recent complaint, 6.10–6.18
fair trial jurisprudence, 6.171–6.179
fairness, 6.127–6.129
generally, 6.01–6.09
historic sex abuse cases, 6.130–6.135
're-claiming' 6.136–6.170
required as matter of law, 6.19–6.22
required as matter of practice, 6.23–6.90
role of popular culture, and, 1.02
sexual offences
discretion to give warning, 6.117–6.120
fairness, 6.127–6.129
historic sex abuse cases, 6.130–6.135
visual identification
introduction, 6.91
rationale, 6.92
requirement, 6.93–6.116
Witness Protection Programme, 6.53–6.87
Credibility
cross-examination of accused, and, 11.50–11.69
Criminal Assets Bureau
search warrants, and, 4.30–4.31

Criminal Justice Act 2006
competence and compellability, and,
5.36–5.40
Criminal justice system
arrest, 2.34–2.40
bail, 2.71–2.85
constitutional constraints, 2.09–2.15
decision-making, 2.51–2.95
drug trafficking
detention, 2.65
generally, 2.61–2.70
intimidation of witnesses, 2.70
proceeds of crime, 2.68–2.69
search warrants, 2.66–2.67
ECtHR constructing rights in context
generally, 2.117–2.119
jurisprudence, 2.120–2.123
extension of exceptional provision,
2.86–2.95
extraordinary arrest, 2.41–2.50
future perspectives and new rights,
2.96–2.106
general concept, 2.01–2.08
Irish National Crime Forum, 2.05–2.08
judicial concept of 'fair' procedure,
2.16–2.31
non-jury courts, 2.13–2.14
normalisation, 2.32–2.33
proceeds of crime, 2.61–2.70
right to silence, 2.107–2.116
special courts, 2.10
state of emergency, 2.11
terrorism, 2.56–2.60
victims, 2.02
Criminal Records Bureau
s 8 PCA 1996 orders, 9.175
Cross-examination
accused, and
conclusions, 11.72–11.74
credibility/guilt distinction, 11.50–
11.69
introduction, 11.01–11.10
judicial discretion as to divisibility of
character, 11.50–11.71
legislative basis of rule, 11.02
loss of the 'shield', 11.11–11.49

privilege against self-incrimination,
11.02
similar fact evidence, 11.11
competence and compellability, and
Criminal Justice Act 2006, 5.36–5.40
generally, 5.03–5.07
inappropriate questions, 5.35
credibility and guilt, 11.50–11.69
divisibility of character, 11.50–11.71
expert witnesses, and, 7.105
inappropriate questions, 5.35
privilege against self-incrimination,
11.02
right to silence, and, 2.107
similar fact evidence, 11.11
Crown privilege
And see **Public privilege**
generally, 8.01
Defendant's spouse
competence and compellability, and,
5.41–5.44
Dental impressions
expert evidence, and, 7.88–7.102
**Detention under drug trafficking
legislation**
generally, 2.65
hearsay evidence, and, 9.115–9.116
Diplomats
competence and compellability, and,
5.46
Direct evidence
generally, 3.03
Disability
competence and compellability, and,
5.14–5.15
Discretion to give warning
corroboration, and
children's evidence, 6.121–6.126
sexual offences, 6.117–6.120
DNA evidence
Castro case, 7.69–7.81
Criminal Justice (Forensic Evidence) Act
1990, 7.82–7.102
generally, 7.61–7.68
Doctrine of recent complaint
corroboration, and, 6.10–6.18

Documentary evidence
generally, 3.05
hearsay evidence, and
copies of documents, 9.164–9.165
generally, 9.160–9.163
statutory provisions, 9.166
Dominant purpose
legal professional privilege, and, 8.25–8.33
Drug trafficking
detention, and
generally, 2.65
hearsay evidence, 9.115–9.116
generally, 2.61–2.70
intimidation of witnesses, 2.70
proceeds of crime, 2.68–2.69
search warrants, 2.66–2.67
Dying declarations
res gestae, and, 9.156–9.158
ECtHR constructing rights in context
generally, 2.117–2.119
jurisprudence, 2.120–2.123
Entry for purpose of arrest
search warrants, and, 4.28–4.29
Evidence
basic concepts, 3.01
burden of proof
evidential burden, 3.24–3.26
generally, 3.20–3.21
legal burden, 3.20
persons bearing burden, 3.27–3.28
probative burden, 3.20
res ipsa loquitur, 3.29–3.35
reverse burden, 3.47–3.77
rule in *Woolmington v DPP*, 3.36–3.46
shifting, 3.22–3.23
types, 3.20
categories
direct evidence, 3.03
documentary evidence, 3.05
real evidence, 3.04
determination of ultimate issue, 3.14–3.19
functions of judge and jury, 3.06

peculiar knowledge principle, 3.78–3.88
receivability
discretion to exclude relevant evidence, 3.12–3.13
generally, 3.07–3.08
relevance/admissibility distinction, 3.09–3.11
reverse burden
Criminal Justice Act 2007, and, 3.69–3.75
generally, 3.47–3.68
human rights issues, 3.75–3.76
standard of proof
generally, 3.89–3.96
tribunal proceedings, 3.97–3.117
terminology, 3.02
Woolmington v DPP rule
exceptions, 3.43–3.46
generally, 3.36–3.42
insanity, 3.43
peculiar knowledge principle, 3.78–3.88
reverse burden, 3.47–3.77
Evidential burden
burden of proof, and, 3.24–3.26
Evidentiary fact
categorisation of evidence, and, 3.02
receivability of evidence, and, 3.07
Examination-in-chief
competence and compellability, and, 5.02
expert witnesses, and, 7.103–7.104
Expert witnesses
belief evidence, 7.36–7.39
common knowledge rule, 7.28
cross-examination, 7.105
defence access to evidence, 7.32–7.35
evidence of fact, 7.29–7.31
examination-in-chief, 7.103–7.104
introduction, 7.03
'junk science', 7.112–7.113
preservation of evidence, 7.32–7.35
qualification, 7.04–7.27

Expert witnesses (contd)
reform, 7.106–7.111
rule in *Hollington v Hewthorn*, 7.52–7.56
ultimate issue, and
common knowledge rule, 7.28
generally, 7.17–7.19
intoxication, 7.40
fairness, and, 6.129
Extraordinary arrest
generally, 2.41–2.50
Fact evidence
And see **Opinion evidence**
generally, 7.29–7.31
Fact relevant to the issue
categorisation of evidence, and, 3.02
receivability of evidence, and, 3.07
Facts in issue
categorisation of evidence, and, 3.02
receivability of evidence, and, 3.07
Factum probandum
categorisation of evidence, and, 3.02
receivability of evidence, and, 3.07
Factum probans
categorisation of evidence, and, 3.02
receivability of evidence, and, 3.07
Fair trial jurisprudence
corroboration, and, 6.171–6.179
'Fair' procedure
generally, 2.16–2.31
Fairness
corroboration, and, 6.127–6.129
'Fight theory'
illegally obtained evidence, and, 4.05
'Genetic fingerprint' evidence
Castro case, 7.69–7.81
Criminal Justice (Forensic Evidence) Act 1990, 7.82–7.102
generally, 7.61–7.68
Geneva Convention
competence and compellability, and, 5.46
'Golden thread'
burden of proof, and, 3.36–3.46

Hearsay
admissibility of documentary evidence
copies of documents, 9.164–9.165
generally, 9.160–9.163
statutory provisions, 9.166
admissions, 9.16
bail proceedings, 9.168
civil proceedings
Children Act 1997, 9.170–9.172
introduction, 9.169
confessions
arrest process changes, 9.83–9.89
constitutional dimension, 9.68–9.82
generally, 9.17–9.22
historical development, 9.25–9.28
inducement, 9.29–9.31
Irish case law, 9.32–9.47
'person in authority', 9.48–9.67
voluntariness, 9.23–9.24
Criminal Records Bureau
s 8 PCA 1996 orders, 9.175
detention under drug trafficking legislation, 9.115–9.116
disadvantages, 9.04
distinction between original evidence and hearsay evidence, 9.09
documentary evidence
copies of documents, 9.164–9.165
generally, 9.160–9.163
statutory provisions, 9.166
exceptions
admissions, 9.16
confessions, 9.17–9.89
confrontation between police and citizen, 9.117–9.143
detention under drug trafficking legislation, 9.115–9.116
generally, 9.04–9.05
introduction, 9.15
treatment of persons in custody, 9.90–9.114
implied assertions, 9.10–9.14
introduction, 9.01–9.08
meaning, 9.01
Hearsay (contd)

offences against the state, 9.176–9.177
proceeds of crime
  s 8 PCA 1996 orders, 9.175
res gestae
  categories, 9.147
  declarations against proprietary/
  pecuniary interests, 9.150–9.151
  declarations as to pedigree matters,
  9.153
  declarations as to public rights, 9.154
  declarations by deceased persons in
  course of duty, 9.152
  dying declarations of deceased on
  charge of homicide, 9.156–9.158
  generally, 9.143–9.149
  post-testamentary declarations by
  testators as to contents of their wills,
  9.155
treatment of persons in custody
  Custody Regulations 1987, 9.94–
  9.114
  Judges' Rules, 9.90–9.93
  special provisions, 9.09–9.16
  wardship proceedings, 9.167
Historic sex abuse cases
  corroboration, and, 6.130–6.135
Hollington v Hewthorn, **rule in**
  generally, 7.52–7.54
  personal injuries actions, 7.55–7.56
Hostile witnesses
  competence and compellability, and,
  5.09
Human rights
  corroboration, and, 6.171–6.179
  reverse burden, and, 3.75–3.76
Identification evidence
  introduction, 6.91
  rationale, 6.92
  requirement, 6.93–6.116
Illegally obtained evidence
  causation, 4.91
  English courts' approach, 4.46–4.47
  'fruit of the poisoned tree', 4.92
  historical perspective, 4.08–4.13
  introduction, 4.01–4.07

Irish courts' approach, 4.50–4.90
judicial approach
  causation, 4.91
  conclusion, 4.93–4.109
  English courts, 4.46–4.47
  'fruit of the poisoned tree', 4.92
  introduction, 4.45
  Irish courts, 4.50–4.90
  US courts, 4.48–4.49
search and seizure, 4.14–4.18
search warrants
  arrestable offences, and, 4.26–4.27
  Criminal Assets Bureau, for, 4.30–
  4.31
  entry for purpose of arrest, and, 4.28–
  4.29
  generally, 4.19–4.23
  issue, 4.26–4.44
  judicial approach, 4.45–4.109
  proceeds of crime, and, 4.30–4.31
  purposes of drug trafficking, for,
  4.32–4.34
  purposes of surveillance, for, 4.35–
  4.44
  recent changes. 4.24–4.25
  US courts' approach, 4.48–4.49
Implied assertions
  hearsay evidence, and, 9.10–9.14
**Inappropriate questions on cross-
examination**
  competence and compellability, and,
  5.35
Inducement
  confessions, and, 9.29–9.31
Innocent until proven guilty
  illegally obtained evidence, and, 4.06
Insanity
  rule in *Woolmington v DPP*, and, 3.43–
  3.46
Interrogation
  confessions, and, 9.25–9.26
Intimate samples
  generally, 7.82–7.102
Intimidation of witnesses
  drug trafficking, and, 2.70

Intoxication
  determination of ultimate issue, and, 3.15
  opinion evidence, and, 7.40–7.51
Irish National Crime Forum
  generally, 2.05–2.08
Journalistic privilege
  conclusion, 8.104
  generally, 8.77–8.88
Judges
  functions, 3.06
Judges' Rules
  treatment of persons in custody, and, 9.90–9.93
'Junk science'
  expert witnesses, and, 7.112–7.113
Juries
  directions as to corroboration, and
    children's evidence, 6.121–6.126
    sexual offences, 6.117–6.120
  functions, 3.06
  general role, 1.07–1.10
Lawyer/client communications
  legal professional privilege, and, 8.08–8.21
Legal burden
  burden of proof, and, 3.20
Legal professional privilege
  conclusion, 8.103–8.104
  dominant purpose, 8.25–8.33
  generally, 8.05–8.06
  introduction, 8.04
  lawyer/client communications, 8.08–8.21
  loss of, 8.45–8.35
  mistaken disclosure, 8.36–8.45
  rule of evidence, as, 8.46–8.48
  third party communications, 8.22–8.24
Live television links
  vulnerable witnesses, and, 5.27–5.28
Marital privilege
  conclusion, 8.104
  generally, 8.57
  introduction, 8.04
Marriage counsellors
  privilege, and, 8.72–8.76

Mental disability
  competence and compellability, and, 5.15
Mistaken disclosure
  legal professional privilege, and, 8.36–8.45
Nolle prosequi
  competence and compellability, and, 5.45
Non-expert witnesses
  opinion evidence, and, 7.02
Non-intimate samples
  generally, 7.82–7.102
Non-jury courts
  generally, 2.13–2.14
Oaths
  competence and compellability, and, 5.12–5.13
Offences against the state
  res gestae, and, 9.176–9.177
Opinion evidence
  conviction as proof, 7.52–7.54
  DNA evidence
    Castro case, 7.69–7.81
    Criminal Justice (Forensic Evidence) Act 1990, 7.82–7.102
    generally, 7.61–7.68
  expert witnesses
    belief evidence, 7.36–7.39
    common knowledge rule, 7.28
    cross-examination, 7.105
    defence access to evidence, 7.32–7.35
    evidence of fact, 7.29–7.31
    examination-in-chief, 7.103–7.104
    introduction, 7.03
    'junk science', 7.112–7.113
    preservation of evidence, 7.32–7.35
    qualification, 7.04–7.27
    reform, 7.106–7.111
    rule in *Hollington v Hewthorn*, 7.52–7.56
  intoxication, 7.40–7.51
  introduction, 7.01–7.02
  non-expert witnesses, 7.02
Opinion evidence (contd)
  rule in *Hollington v Hewthorn*

generally, 7.52–7.54
personal injuries actions, 7.55–7.56
ultimate issue, and
common knowledge rule, 7.28
generally, 7.17–7.19
intoxication, 7.40
fairness, and, 6.129
Ordinary course of business
hearsay, and, 9.166
Organised crime, 9.177
Orifice swabs
expert evidence, and, 7.88–7.102
Past behaviour
similar fact evidence, and, 10.01
Peculiar knowledge principle
generally, 3.78–3.88
Pecuniary interests
res gestae, and, 9.150–9.151
Pedigree
res gestae, and, 9.153
Personal injuries actions
role of expert evidence, and, 7.55–7.56
Physical disability
competence and compellability, and,
5.14
Police
general role, 1.11
privilege, 8.89–8.102
Post-testamentary declarations
res gestae, and, 9.155
Preservation of evidence
expert witnesses, and, 7.32–7.35
Previous convictions
cross-examination of accused, and,
11.01
Principal fact
categorisation of evidence, and, 3.02
receivability of evidence, and, 3.07
Principle against self-incrimination
See also **Privilege against self-**
incrimination
confessions, and, 9.24
Private privilege
conclusion, 8.103–8.104
generally, 8.03
introduction, 8.01–8.02

legal professional privilege
dominant purpose, 8.25–8.33
generally, 8.05–8.06
lawyer/client communications, 8.08–
8.21
loss of, 8.45–8.35
mistaken disclosure, 8.36–8.45
rule of evidence, as, 8.46–8.48
third party communications, 8.22–
8.24
marital privilege, 8.57
privilege against self-incrimination,
8.58–8.65
types, 8.04
'without prejudice' statements, 8.49–
8.56
Privilege
Crown privilege, 8.01
introduction, 8.01–8.02
journalistic privilege
conclusion, 8.104
generally, 8.77–8.88
legal professional privilege
conclusion, 8.103–8.104
dominant purpose, 8.25–8.33
generally, 8.05–8.06
lawyer/client communications, 8.08–
8.21
loss of, 8.45–8.35
mistaken disclosure, 8.36–8.45
rule of evidence, as, 8.46–8.48
third party communications, 8.22–
8.24
marital privilege
conclusion, 8.104
generally, 8.57
marriage counsellors, 8.72–8.76
police privilege, 8.89–8.102
private privilege
conclusion, 8.103–8.104
generally, 8.03
introduction, 8.01–8.02
legal professional privilege, 8.05–8.48

Privilege (contd)
marital privilege, 8.57

privilege against self-incrimination, 8.58–8.65

types, 8.04

'without prejudice' statements, 8.49–8.56

privilege against self-incrimination, 8.58–8.65

public privilege

generally, 8.105–8.111

introduction, 8.01

Irish case law, 8.115–8.

origins, 8.112–8.114

sacerdotal privilege, 8.66–8.71

state privilege, 8.01

types, 8.01

'without prejudice' statements, 8.49–8.56

Privilege against self-incrimination

cross-examination of accused, and, 11.02

generally, 8.58–8.65

introduction, 8.04

Probative burden

burden of proof, and, 3.20

Proceeds of crime

drug trafficking, and, 2.68–2.69

generally, 2.61–2.70

hearsay evidence, and

s 8 PCA 1996 orders, 9.180

search warrants, and, 4.30–4.31

Proprietary interests

res gestae, and, 9.150–9.151

Protection principle

confessions, and, 9.24

Public hair samples

expert evidence, and, 7.88–7.102

Public privilege

generally, 8.105–8.111

introduction, 8.01

Irish case law

Ambiorix Ltd v Minister for Environment, 8.146–8.151

Breathnach v Ireland (No 3), 8.152–8.154

Bula Ltd v Tara Mines, 8.143–8.145

generally, 8.115–8.136

tribunals, on, 8.155–8.169

Tromso Sparebank v Beirne (No 2), 8.137–8.142

origins, 8.112–8.114

Public rights

res gestae, and, 9.154

Real evidence

generally, 3.04

Receivability of evidence

categorisation of evidence, and, 3.07–3.08

Recent complaint doctrine

corroboration, and, 6.10–6.18

Recovery of proceeds of crime

search warrants, and, 4.30–4.31

Re-examination

competence and compellability, and, 5.08

Relevance of evidence

discretion to exclude, 3.12–3.13

generally, 3.09–3.11

similar fact evidence, and, 10.40–10.42

Reliability principle

confessions, and, 9.24

Res gestae

categories, 9.147

contemporaneity, and, 9.143–9.144

declarations against proprietary/pecuniary interests, 9.150–9.151

declarations as to pedigree matters, 9.153

declarations as to public rights, 9.154

declarations by deceased persons in course of duty, 9.152

dying declarations of deceased on charge of homicide, 9.156–9.158

generally, 9.143–9.149

physical sensation statements, 9.147

post-testamentary declarations by testators as to contents of their wills, 9.155

Res gestae (contd)

spontaneous statements, 9.147

state of mind of accused, 9.147

statements accompanying and explaining acts, 9.147

Res ipsa loquitur
burden of proof, and, 3.29–3.35

Reverse burden
Criminal Justice Act 2007, and, 3.69–3.75
generally, 3.47–3.68
human rights issues, 3.75–3.76

Right of fair trial
corroboration, and, 6.171–6.179

Right to silence
confessions, and, 9.25
generally, 2.107–2.116
reverse burden, and, 3.47–3.68

Rule against hearsay
admissibility of documentary evidence
copies of documents, 9.164–9.165
generally, 9.160–9.163
statutory provisions, 9.166
admissions, 9.16
bail proceedings, 9.168
civil proceedings
Children Act 1997, 9.170–9.172
introduction, 9.169
confessions
arrest process changes, 9.83–9.89
constitutional dimension, 9.68–9.82
generally, 9.17–9.22
historical development, 9.25–9.28
inducement, 9.29–9.31
Irish case law, 9.32–9.47
'person in authority', 9.48–9.67
voluntariness, 9.23–9.24
Criminal Records Bureau
s 8 PCA 1996 orders, 9.175
detention under drug trafficking
legislation, 9.115–9.116
disadvantages, 9.04
distinction between original evidence
and hearsay evidence, 9.09
documentary evidence
copies of documents, 9.164–9.165
generally, 9.160–9.163
statutory provisions, 9.166
exceptions

admissions, 9.16
confessions, 9.17–9.89
confrontation between police and
citizen, 9.117–9.142
detention under drug trafficking
legislation, 9.130–9.131
generally, 9.04–9.05
introduction, 9.15
treatment of persons in custody, 9.90–9.114
implied assertions, 9.10–9.14
introduction, 9.01–9.08
meaning, 9.01
offences against the state, 9.176–9.177
proceeds of crime
s 8 PCA 1996 orders, 9.175
res gestae
categories, 9.147
declarations against proprietary/
pecuniary interests, 9.150–9.151
declarations as to pedigree matters, 9.153
declarations as to public rights, 9.154
declarations by deceased persons in
course of duty, 9.152
dying declarations of deceased on
charge of homicide, 9.156–9.177
generally, 9.143–9.149
post-testamentary declarations by
testators as to contents of their wills, 9.155
treatment of persons in custody
Custody Regulations 1987, 9.94–9.114
Judges' Rules, 9.90–9.93
special provisions, 9.159–9.178
wardship proceedings, 9.167

Rule in *Hollington v Hewthorn*
generally, 7.52–7.54
personal injuries actions, 7.55–7.56

Rule in *Woolmington v DPP*
exceptions
insanity, 3.43
peculiar knowledge principle, 3.78–3.88
reverse burden, 3.47–3.77

statutory provisions, 3.44–3.46
general rule, 3.36–3.42
insanity, and, 3.43
peculiar knowledge principle, and, 3.78–3.88
reverse burden, and
    Criminal Justice Act 2007, and, 3.69–3.75
    generally, 3.47–3.68
    human rights issues, 3.75–3.76
statutory provisions, and, 3.44–3.46

Rules of evidence
adjudicative process, 1.04
adjincative process, 1.05
changuing social needs, 1.27–1.32
legal professional privilege, and, 8.46–8.48
role of jury, 1.07–1.10
role of media, 1.18–1.26
role of police, 1.11
role of popular culture, 1.01–1.04
trial, 1.05–1.06

Sacerdotal privilege
generally, 8.66–8.71

Saliva samples
expert evidence, and, 7.88–7.102

Samples
generally, 7.88–7.102

Search and seizure
generally, 4.14–4.18

Search warrants
arrestable offences, and, 4.26–4.27
causation, 4.91
Criminal Assets Bureau, for, 4.30–4.31
drug trafficking, and, 4.32–4.34
English courts' approach, 4.46–4.47
entry for purpose of arrest, and, 4.28–4.29
'fruit of the poisoned tree', 4.92
generally, 4.19–4.23
introduction, 4.02
Irish courts' approach, 4.50–4.90
issue
    arrestable offences, for, 4.26–4.27

Criminal Assets Bureau, for, 4.30–4.31
entry for purpose of arrest, for, 4.28–4.29
purposes of drug trafficking, for, 4.32–4.34
purposes of surveillance, for, 4.35–4.44
recovery of proceeds of crime, for, 4.30–4.31
judicial approach
    causation, 4.91
    conclusion, 4.93–4.109
    English courts, 4.46–4.47
    'fruit of the poisoned tree', 4.92
    introduction, 4.45
    Irish courts, 4.50–4.90
    US courts, 4.48–4.49
proceeds of crime, and, 4.30–4.31
purposes of drug trafficking, for, 4.32–4.34
purposes of surveillance, for, 4.35–4.44
recent changes. 4.24–4.25
recovery of proceeds of crime, for, 4.30–4.31
surveillance purposes, for, 4.35–4.44
US courts' approach, 4.48–4.49

Self-incrimination
See also **Privilege against self-incrimination**
confessions, and, 9.24

Sex abuse cases
corroboration, and, 6.130–6.135

Sexual offences
corroboration, and
    discretion to give warning, 6.117–6.120
    fairness, 6.127–6.129
    historic sex abuse cases, 6.130–6.135
fairness, 6.127–6.129
Sexual offences (contd)
jury directions, 6.117–6.120
role of popular culture, and, 1.02
sex abuse cases, 6.130–6.135
similar fact evidence, and

generally, 10.31–10.39
introduction, 10.04–10.08
warnings, 6.117–6.120
Silence, right to
confessions, and, 9.25
generally, 2.107–2.116
reverse burden, and, 3.47–3.68
Similar fact evidence
bad behaviour, and, 10.01
burden of proof, 10.43
categories, 10.13–10.30
conduct on other occasions which is of
particular relevance in spite of its
tendency to show bad disposition, of,
10.15–10.16
forms part of same transaction to such
extent that acts are so inextricably bound
up that it is impossible to differentiate
between them, which, 10.17–10.18
introduction, 10.01–10.10
Irish case law, 10.44–10.69
judicial discretion, 10.70–10.75
other jurisdictions, in, 10.76–10.86
rationale for admission, 10.11–10.14
rebut defence, to, 10.19–10.27
rebut defence that acts performed were
totally innocent, to, 10.28–10.30
relevance in other cases, 10.40–10.42
sexual offences
generally, 10.31–10.39
introduction, 10.04–10.08
show system, to, 10.19–10.27
standard of proof, 10.43
Special courts
generally, 2.10
Spontaneous statements
res gestae, and, 9.147
Spouses
competence and compellability, and,
5.41–5.44
Standard of proof
generally, 3.89–3.96
similar fact evidence, and, 10.43
tribunal proceedings, 3.97–3.117
State of emergency

generally, 2.11
State privilege
And see **Public privilege**
generally, 8.01
Surveillance
search warrants, and, 4.35–4.44
Terrorism
generally, 2.56–2.60
Third party communications
legal professional privilege, and, 8.22–
8.24
Treatment of persons in custody
Custody Regulations 1987, 9.94–9.114
Judges' Rules, 9.90–9.93
Tribunal proceedings
standard of proof, and, 3.97–3.117
Ultimate issue
expert evidence, and
common knowledge rule, 7.28
generally, 7.17–7.19
intoxication, 7.40
fairness, and, 6.129
generally, 3.14–3.19
**UN Convention on the Rights of the
Child**
competence and compellability, and,
5.29
Unlawfully obtained evidence
causation, 4.91
English courts' approach, 4.46–4.47
'fruit of the poisoned tree', 4.92
historical perspective, 4.08–4.13
introduction, 4.01–4.07
Irish courts' approach, 4.50–4.90
judicial approach
causation, 4.91
conclusion, 4.93–4.109
English courts, 4.46–4.47
'fruit of the poisoned tree', 4.92
introduction, 4.45
Unlawfully obtained evidence (contd)
Irish courts, 4.50–4.90
US courts, 4.48–4.49
search and seizure, 4.14–4.18
search warrants

arrestable offences, and, 4.26–4.27
Criminal Assets Bureau, for, 4.30–4.31
entry for purpose of arrest, and, 4.28–4.29
generally, 4.19–4.23
issue, 4.26–4.44
judicial approach, 4.45–4.109
proceeds of crime, and, 4.30–4.31
purposes of drug trafficking, for, 4.32–4.34
purposes of surveillance, for, 4.35–4.44
recent changes. 4.24–4.25
US courts' approach, 4.48–4.49

Urine samples
expert evidence, and, 7.88–7.102

Victims
generally, 2.02
search warrants, and, 4.32–4.34

Visual identification
introduction, 6.91
rationale, 6.92
requirement, 6.93–6.116

Voluntariness
confessions, and, 9.23–9.24

Vulnerable witnesses
competence and compellability, and, 5.34

Wardship proceedings
hearsay evidence, and, 9.11

Warnings
corroboration, and
children's evidence, 6.121–6.126
sexual offences, 6.117–6.120

Will contents
res gestae, and, 9.155

'Without prejudice' communications
generally, 8.49–8.56
introduction, 8.04

Witness Protection Programme
corroboration, and, 6.53–6.87

Witnesses
accomplices, 6.24–6.52
accused as prosecution witness, 5.45
calling of witnesses, 5.10–5.11
children's evidence
generally, 5.16–5.28
reforms, 5.29–5.33
competence and compellability
children's evidence, 5.16–5.28
introduction, 5.01–5.13
mental disability, 5.15
physical disability, 5.14
reforms, 5.29–5.46
confessions, 6.88–6.90
corroboration
accomplices, 6.24–6.52
confession evidence, 6.88–6.90
discretion to give warning, 6.117–6.126
doctrine of recent complaint, 6.10–6.18
fair trial jurisprudence, 6.171–6.179
fairness, 6.127–6.129
generally, 6.01–6.09
historic sex abuse cases, 6.130–6.135
're-claiming' 6.136–6.170
required as matter of law, 6.19–6.22
required as matter of practice, 6.23–6.90
visual identification, 6.91–6.116
Witness Protection Programme, 6.53–6.87
cross-examination, 5.03–5.07
defendant's spouse as witness, 5.41–5.44
diplomats as prosecution witness, 5.46
doctrine of recent complaint, 6.10–6.18
elicitation of testimony
generally, 5.12–5.13
process, 5.02–5.08
examination-in-chief, 5.02
hostile witnesses, 5.09

Witnesses (contd)
  inappropriate questions on cross-
    examination, 5.35
  mental disability, 5.15
  oaths, 5.12–5.13
  physical disability, 5.14
  process of elicitation of testimony
    cross-examination, 5.03–5.07
    examination-in-chief, 5.02
    re-examination, 5.08
  re-examination, 5.08
  visual identification
    introduction, 6.91
    rationale, 6.92
    requirement, 6.93–6.116
  vulnerable witnesses, 5.34
  Witness Protection Programme, 6.53–
  6.87

***Woolmington v DPP* rule**
  exceptions
    insanity, 3.43
    peculiar knowledge principle, 3.78–
    3.88
    reverse burden, 3.47–3.77
    statutory provisions, 3.44–3.46
  general rule, 3.36–3.42
  insanity, and, 3.43
  peculiar knowledge principle, and, 3.78–
  3.88
  reverse burden, and
    Criminal Justice Act 2007, and, 3.69–
    3.75
    generally, 3.47–3.68
    human rights issues, 3.75–3.76
  statutory provisions, and, 3.44–3.46